THE FAMILY IDIOT

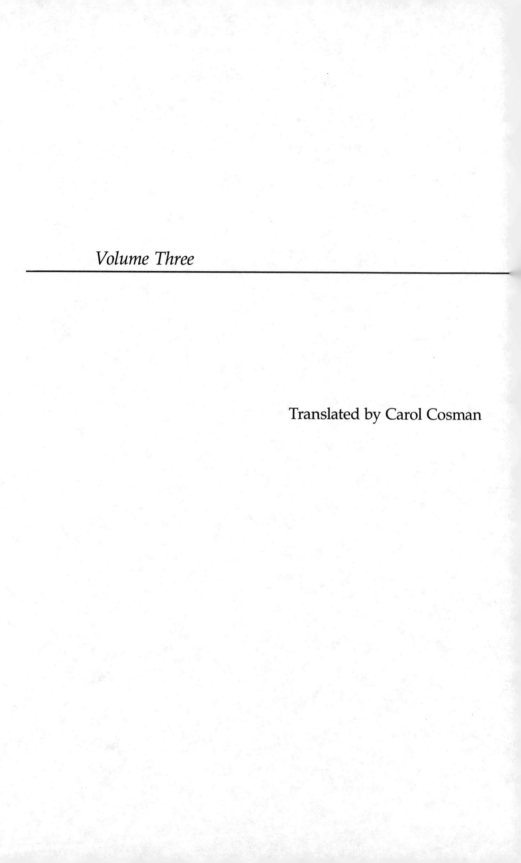

Volume Three

Translated by Carol Cosman

Jean-Paul Sartre

THE FAMILY IDIOT

Gustave Flaubert

1821–1857

The University of Chicago Press • Chicago and London

Originally published in Paris as part two, books two and three, of *L'Idiot de la famille: Gustave Flaubert de 1821 à 1857,* © Editions Gallimard, 1971.

The University of Chicago Press, Chicago 60637
The University of Chicago Press, Ltd., London

© 1989 by The University of Chicago
All rights reserved. Published 1989
Printed in the United States of America
98 97 96 95 94 93 92 91 90 89 5 4 3 2 1

Library of Congress Cataloging in Publication Data

Sartre, Jean Paul, 1905–80
  The family idiot.

  Translation of: L'Idiot de la famille.
  1. Flaubert, Gustave, 1821–1880. 2. Novelists,
French—19th century—Biography. I. Title.
PQ2247.S313   843'.8[B]   81-1694
ISBN 0-226-73509-5 (v. 1)   AACR2
      0-226-73510-9 (v. 2)
      0-226-73516-8 (v. 3)

An earlier version of pages 162 and 168–76 of this volume appeared in *Ploughshares* 12, nos. 1 and 2 (1986): 71–88, © 1986 by The University of Chicago.

CONTENTS

TRANSLATOR'S NOTE

I would like to give special thanks to Charles A. Krance for his help in preparing this volume for publication.

CAROL COSMAN

Personalization (continued)

BOOK TWO
School Years

From Legend to Role: The "Garçon"*

At the beginning of November 1851, Gustave writes to Louise: "We were a pleaid of young madcaps who lived in a strange world, believe me. We alternated between madness and suicide. There were some who actually killed themselves, others who died in their beds, one who strangled himself with his tie, several who ruined themselves with debauchery out of sheer boredom—it was beautiful!" Shortly afterward he revisited his school, not without a certain poignant melancholy: the changes made in the old pile of stones prevented him from recapturing certain memories, and the current schoolboys looked rather stupid. Where had the time gone . . .? etc. Much later, in the *Préface aux Dernières Chansons*, completed on 20 June 1870, he takes up this theme again and develops it:

> I am ignorant of the dreams of schoolboys today. But ours were superb examples of extravagance. The last flowerings of Romanticism which, compressed in the provincial setting, made strange boilings in our brains. One was not simply a troubador, insurrectionary and exotic—one was above all an artist . . . one ruined one's eyes reading novels in the dormitory. One carried a dagger in one's pocket like Antony. One did more: out of disgust with existence, Bar—— shot himself in the head with a pistol; And—— hanged himself with his tie. We merited little praise, certainly, but what hatred of all platitudes! What yearning for grandeur! What respect for the masters!

Yet these confidences regarding his school life between the age of fifteen and seventeen have quite another ring to them when Flaubert

---

*"De la geste au rôle: Le Garçon." In what follows, Sartre plays on the different meanings of the term *la geste*—deed, exploit, legend, epic performance, even behavior. It is impossible to render this term by a single English equivalent in all contexts.—Trans.

serves them up to us *still warm,* and when he is still shut up in his "box." He writes quite vehemently in *La Dernière Heure* in January 1837:

> I very early felt a profound disgust with men from the moment I came into contact with them. From the age of twelve I was sent to school. There I saw a model of the world, its vices in miniature, its sources of ridicule, its little coteries, its petty cruelty; I saw the triumph of strength, mysterious emblem of the power of God; I saw faults that would later become vices, vices that would later be crimes, and children who would be men.

In *Mémoires d'un fou,* written eighteen months later, he returns to the horror and contempt his schoolmates inspired in him, which extends this time to all the teaching staff as well:

> I was at school from the time I was ten, and I rapidly developed a profound aversion to people. That society of children is as cruel to its victims as the other small society, that of men. The same injustices of the crowd, the same tyranny of prejudice and strength, the same egotism . . . I was thwarted in all my inclinations: in class for my ideas, at recess for my penchant for solitary unsociability . . . So I lived there alone and bored, plagued by my teachers and jeered at by my peers.

For this "noble and elevated soul," thwarted in his inclinations, tormented by teachers, by fellow students, it was the mob; it was the stupid, jeering crowd that pushed Marguerite to suicide:

> I can still see myself sitting on the class bench, absorbed in my dreams of the future, thinking the most sublime things the imagination of a child can invent, while the teacher mocks my Latin verses and my schoolmates look at me, sneering! The imbeciles! *They,* laugh at *me! They,* so weak, so common, such pea-brains; *I,* whose mind was drowning in the limits of creation, who was lost in all the worlds of poetry, who felt greater than all of them, who received infinite pleasures and had celestial ecstasies with every intimate revelation of my soul. I, who felt great like the world.[1]

The contradiction between these two series of testimonies is surely astonishing. Since the first spares no one, Gustave's disgust would seem to be universal; not a single allusion to the "pleiad of young madcaps." I would even say it is arranged for the purpose of denying

---

1. *Mémoires d'un fou.*

that possibility: *all* of them are imbeciles, *all* of them are cruel—he feels *greater than any of them.* Only a loner would seem capable of such impotent rage; if he had been part of a band of young extravagants, there would be more arrogance than meanness in his scorn. In the second series, on the other hand, his benevolence, with time, becomes universal; the *Préface* contrasts two generations: the schoolboys of 1830 were all romantics; those of 1870—what are they?[2] In general, the two judgments, both universal, seem strictly incompatible. All vulgar and cruel, all extravagant and generous—Gustave does not even seem to consider that a choice must be made.

Clearly, he lives his own temporalization as a process of degradation, which necessarily implies in him a tendency to idealize the past. He himself repeatedly observes that he does not enjoy what he possesses and bitterly regrets what he has lost. It is true: he underestimates the present and overestimates it once it has passed. But he does not turn from absolute black to absolute white. Besides, even if he systematically prefers *what has happened,* it would seem that in this particular case his change of heart would be much more comprehensible if it were the other way around. Whatever the adolescent's reticence might have been, if his comrades did indeed "alternate," like him, between madness and suicide, it is not credible that he should have condemned them without appeal *while they were despairing together.* The adult, on the contrary, knows that in certain "souls" nobility is not authentic. A letter of 15 December 1851 informs us that the man with the dagger who took himself for Antony was none other than Ernest.[3] This did not prevent him from becoming "dutiful": "As a magistrate he is reactionary; as a husband he will be cuckolded and . . . [will spend] his life between his female, his children, and the turpitude of his profession."[4] As for Alfred, "who ruined himself with debauchery simply to escape boredom," Gustave now knows that his friend's nonchalant conformism—which presented itself as a simple rejection of what Cocteau called the "conformism of anticonformism"—depended in fact on the solid prejudices of his class. Might we not be surprised that Gustave ignores his disappointments and distributes laurels unreservedly? We could understand the ado-

2. We shall see later that Gustave detested these newcomers; to his mind they were positivists and republicans who had no more dreams.
3. "He too was an artist, he carried a dagger and dreamed dramatic plans." *Correspondance* 2:270.
4. Ibid.

lescent praising his friends, the man judging them more subtly; but we find the opposite: in his youthful writings there is no trace of that elite of which, thirty years later, he felt honored to have been a part.

Between the two sets of testimonies, one might be inclined, despite everything, to lean in favor of the earlier—if only for the raging passion spontaneously expressed there—if it were not partially contradicted by the facts. No, Gustave was not the butt of his masters. Nor was he the scapegoat of his classmates. In October 1831, or in the first days of 1832, he entered the *Collège royal* in the fourth year. In September he had the first honorable mention of excellence. In the seventh year he met Gourgaud-Dugazon, who became his professor of literature, and Chéruel, who taught him history. The two men held him in high esteem. Gourgaud, touched by Romanticism, encouraged him to write: on 14 August 1835, a month after the end of the school year, Gustave, speaking to Ernest about his literary works (he had just finished *Frédégonde*, a drama that was lost), adds in the same paragraph: "Gourgaud gives me narratives to compose." These were stylistic exercises proposed to a budding writer and not "holiday homework." We know of two—*Matéo Falcone* and *L'Anneau du prieur*. Gourgaud must have appreciated them since Flaubert kept them. When the young teacher was appointed to Versailles, his former student continued to correspond with him. At the age of twenty, consumed by self-doubt, Gustave retained enough confidence to ask Gourgaud for encouragement. We know, moreover, of the influence of Cheruel, a student of Michelet's who introduced Gustave to, or developed his taste for, history and directed him to numerous readings—Barante, no doubt, and certainly Augustin Thierry, from whom the boy borrowed the subject of his *Frédégonde*. He confided in Chéruel as much as he did in Gourgaud since he showed him his historical essays—in 1837, for example, the plan for his essay *La Lutte du sacerdoce et de l'Empire*. The friendship between Flaubert and Gourgaud-Dugazon does not seem to have survived the crisis of 1844, but one is inclined, reading the boy's letters, to hold the elder responsible for the slackening of ties.[5] On the other hand, although Chéruel also left Rouen, for a chair at the Sorbonne, we know from a letter of 1858 to Mlle de Chantepie that his student from Normandy continued to visit him. There is no doubt that during his years at school Gustave encountered pedants and idiots among the teaching staff—this is the

5. "Your letters are awaited for trimesters and semesters," Gustave writes to him in 1842 in a warm letter.

rule. But there was hardly room for complaint since—and this is the exception—he had the luck to have known as an adolescent two teachers whom he could continue to love and respect when he reached adulthood. Jean Bruneau is correct when he says that the year 1835–36 was "essential in Flaubert's literary evolution." It was no less so in his "sentimental education": men showed confidence in him. Nevertheless, this is what he writes three years later in the *Mémoires*:

> My taste and sensibility were therefore warped, as my teachers said, and among so many beings with such base inclinations[6] my independence of mind caused me to be considered the most depraved of all; I was pulled down to the lowest rung by my very superiority. They barely conceded I had imagination, meaning, according to them, an exultation of the brain akin to madness.[7]

What ingratitude. Two men have singled him out, supported him, and while he still benefits from their solicitude he pillories the teaching staff without exception. This would suffice to prove the partiality of his testimony.[8]

The administration itself was rigid and meddlesome; we shall see further on that, beginning in 1831, it entered into open conflict with the students following certain political incidents. But Gustave had the right to special consideration: Achille-Cléophas, the best mind in Normandy, was a highly respected member of the Academic Council. J. Félix reports, plausibly, that a copy of the little manuscript journal that Flaubert and Chevalier edited together (an issue of *Art et Progrès* which we no longer possess) may have fallen into the hands of the headmaster. Having picked up malicious allusions to certain teachers, he would have been inclined to dismiss the guilty parties, and the intervention of the chief surgeon may have convinced him to give up any plan to take even the most minimal sanctions against them.[9] Even if the story is not true, it circulated around 1880 among his former

6. These were simply his schoolmates.

7. *Mémoires d'un fou.*

8. A single false note in this story which, as we shall see, is not without importance: in July 1835 Gustave did not figure in the list of honors. It was only in the eighth term that he won the prize for history. There is nothing unusual about this: the encouragements of Chéruel and Gourgaud bore fruit only at the end of a whole year. But Flaubert at this period might have been much more grateful to them if they had accorded him honorific distinctions at the outset—we shall see why in this very chapter.

9. J. Félix, *Gustave Flaubert* (Rouen: Ed. Schneider). Published shortly after Flaubert's death and no doubt prompted by it, this work is useful on one point only: through the Flaubert legend that it retells, it permits us to reconstruct the attitude of the Normandy bourgeoisie toward the doctor's younger son.

schoolmates and probably among those who entered the *collège* after he had left which would indicate that they regarded him as one of the privileged.

Moreover, a letter of 12 July 1835 gives us proof that Gustave, far from being a martyr to pedants and study masters, knew how to defend himself and, when necessary, to attack: "I have had a dispute with Gerbal, my honorable study master, and I told him that if he continued to annoy me, I was going to give him a good thrashing and a bloody jaw, literary expression." And Jean Bruneau informs us that this Gerbal—or Girbal—named master of studies at Rouen on 18 April 1834 (he was twenty-eight years old), was dismissed in 1835 "without reference, discharged by the headmaster,"[10] either at the end of classes in July or in the first trimester of the next school year. If we put these two facts together, we cannot doubt that the threats Gustave made publicly figured among the motives for dismissal. Gerbal had lost all authority—if he ever had any—and must have tried to recover himself with misplaced severity; the student uproar must have increased during the study hour, and the altercation reported by Flaubert was no doubt only one episode in the war of nerves the students waged against him. Whether this study master in distress did or did not make an unjust remark to Gustave, the boy knew very well whom he was dealing with, and when he threatens to rough him up, he is certainly conscious of the admiring approbation of his comrades. We see, in the light of this incident, that he sometimes took the side of the executioners. As for the administration, far from dismissing the scandalous child who had threatened *coram populi* a representative of the school authority, it boots out the study master and keeps the favored son without even punishing him.

Flaubert and his fellow students, then, shared *at the very least* the solidarity of combatants. This solidarity survived as long as he lived with them, and we shall see that he would get himself dismissed from school for having taken part in a *collective* act of insubordination. Under these conditions, how can we lend credence to the accusations he brings to bear in the *Mémoires?* This handsome adolescent, a strapping loudmouth, son of a respected professional man, always ready to take part in any disorder, demoralizing father Eudes's boarders who took courses at the *collège*—are we to believe that he was a scapegoat? Impossible. Childhood is conformist out of anguish; in school,

10. A note found and cited by J. Bruneau.

the scapegoats are sacrificial lambs: through laughter, through insults, practical jokes and beatings, such kids are symbolically executed in order to annihilate in their persons all forms of the *abnormal*. Whom do these anxious adolescents choose as their victims? An outsider, the son of a foreigner or beggar, whose appearance or accent is always a reminder of his origin, a stutterer, an invalid, a *minus habens* whose mental difficulties frighten them, a deformed or ill-favored student whose ugliness repells them. A Flaubert, *never*. It is true that Gustave, too, has his "anomaly," which he experiences as a defect and of which he became more acutely conscious at school; but this invisible defect of being exists for him, not for them.

In any case, the pleiad of young madcaps *does exist*, and if not its undisputed leader, he often becomes its instigator: he is the one who organizes the procession of skeletons, he is the one who incites them to play that broad, hundred-act comedy whose main character is called "the Garçon." Dumesnil is wrong in writing that "Gustave scarcely formed any ties at school." To the names cited by his hagiographer—Alfred Nion, Germain des Hogues, Charles d'Arcet, Frédéric Baudry—we would have to add *at least* those of Hamard and Pagnerre. Maxime du Camp made Flaubert's acquaintance at the home of a former schoolmate, Ernest Le Marié, who introduced him, not without admiration, under the name of "Vieux Seigneur." And these are only the *friends* who would maintain more or less close relations with Gustave into his maturity—with the exception of Germain des Hogues, who died in 1843 but was certainly loved.[11] Gustave would visit Nion until his death; his ties with Baudry would slacken only in 1879. As for Pagnerre, he is still mentioned in the winter of 1863–64— Gustave is expecting him for lunch: "He is one of the creators of the Garçon; that constitutes a freemasonry never to be forgotten." If we take as generally true the commonplace that "life separates" schoolboys who were once close friends, we must regard the author of *Mémoires d'un fou* as exceptionally privileged from this point of view as well. There is no doubt that in the years around 1835 the good knights of the pleiad were surrounded by devoted and enthusiastic hangers-on. This was enough to transform a constellation into a galaxy.

We must still explain the contradiction between the two series of

11. G. des Hogues was buried in Nice. In April 1845, from Marseille, Gustave writes to Alfred that he will go to see their friend's grave; he finally gives up the idea because "it would have seemed funny."

9

testimonies. Two passages—both from *Mémoires d'un fou*—will come to our aid:

> I would spend whole hours with my head in my hands, looking at the floor of my study or at a spider spinning its web on our master's chair; and when I would wake up staring, they would laugh at me, the laziest of them all—I, who never had one positive idea, who showed no penchant for any profession, who would be useless in this world where everyone must go ahead and take his piece of the pie, and who would never be anything but a good-for-nothing, at best a clown, an animal tamer, or a maker of books.

> I had a satirical and independent temper, and my mordant and cynical irony spared neither the caprice of one nor the despotism of all.

Is this really the *same man*—the dreamy destroyer, the good-for-nothing, consumed by the infinite, whose dazes were the delight of his classmates—and the cynic with a quick tongue ready to disparage the laughers? Gustave could not have sketched these very different portraits of himself within a few days of each other without being conscious, if only implicitly, of the ambiguity of his persona, in other words, of the ambivalence of his feelings toward his classmates. Or, to put it another way, the two series of testimonies, although separated in time, both have their origin in the double relationship the young boy experienced with his fellow students. It was not in retrospect that negative was transformed into positive; it was *at school* that he continually swung from one sign to the other, at times tormented and at times tormentor. In his writings he condemns his schoolmates without reservation and without recourse; not a shred of hope: it was *them* and *him*. In daily life he was far from such intransigence. He had *his* group. Although he doesn't breathe a word about them in the *Mémoires*, in *La Dernière Heure*, or in *Novembre*, he took pride in *prodding into action* those comrades who were suffused, as he was, with the *mal du siècle*, and who would *act out* everywhere—on the playground, in class, in the streets, even in church—the dry despair of being bourgeois. His youthful works, in which the discourse of despair becomes a nocturnal monologue, are neither more nor less true than the clownish and sinister comedy he is pleased to begin again with his troop each day, from dawn to dark, which cannot be played without passwords or symbols, in short, without "freemasonry." Let us beware of concluding that he does not live what he writes and does not write what he lives. If he plays a double game, it is because reality is double. No doubt there is a certain amount of bad faith, of insincerity, in the grand couplets of the *Mémoires*, but these would not even be conceivable if they were not inspired by a deeply felt unease. In fact, he lives both aspects of his school life; yet there are reasons—*which we must discover*—why he is silent about the one *on the level of writing*, and why a more or less explicit option makes him choose *to fix* the other *in writing*. At the age of thirty it is the other way around: the objective ambiguity remains; he still feels that horror of school, so bitterly experienced, since he evokes it so vividly in the first paragraphs of *Madame Bovary*. It is all there: the absurd pomp of the administration, the pedantry of the masters, the sneers of the students whose idiotic, apelike agility serves only to prove their baseness in the face of the immense, dreamy stupidity of Charbovary, the child who as a man will have the singular glory of dying for love. But other intentions—without contradicting his vow of misanthropy—will choose to highlight the positive aspect of his dead youth. What is involved, then, is not a radical transmutation but an intentional change of perspective of the sort that makes us see either five or six cubes in certain designs, depending on whether we see the shaded or the light areas as the background. What we must explain here is the instability itself, which from 1832 until 1839 causes him constantly to move back and forth from one view to the other. We shall understand it better if we consider that the young Flaubert, entering the *collège* in Rouen, at once finds a "collective" characterized by a *structure* and a community defined by a singular *history*.

A. Structure

Gustave, by his own admission, saw the "society of children" as prefiguring the society of men: the same injustice of the crowd, the same tyranny of prejudice and force, the same egotism. Are we to believe that the scholarly community is the model of every possible society? Hasn't he, without knowing it, moved from one type of society to *one* other? He says he was "thwarted" in his "penchant for solitary unsociability." Was he then so unsociable before 1832? He sometimes escaped, of course, took refuge in stupors in order to extricate himself from the pressures of his surroundings. But can we call him solitary—the boy who until the age of ten didn't leave Caroline's side, who called Ernest "his friend for life" or "till death," who liked to spend long hours at Alfred and Laure's house, who amused himself in the company of the Vasse children and others, sons and daughters of his

11

parents' friends? Moreover, the first contact with his schoolmates could not have been so bad, since he wrote to Ernest, 3 April 1832: "When you come, Amédée, Edmond, Madame Chevalier, mama, 2 servants and perhaps some students will come to see us act." *Perhaps some students:* his aversion for his comrades was not immediate. He had ties to certain of them; he invited them to the famous performance at Easter 1832 which marked the peak and the end of his dramatic career. They may not have come, they may have laughed at him, but it was neither their absence nor their offensive remarks that determined Gustave's general relations with his fellow students. Before going to school, and even in his first year as a boarder, the boy was not unsociable; he *became* unsociable after leaving the society of the family. With his earliest friends, those he met at their fathers' homes or his own, he had the intersubjective relations of feudalism. The families had mutual ties, these children knew each other through their parents; the bond of vassal to lord, spilling beyond the family network, structured the entire little society. When the kids romped under the maternal eye (interchangeable mothers, unvarying eye, the same in all of them, charged with the same vigilance and the same authority of paternal origin), they were all vavasors surveyed by the great vassals, delegates from the council of lords. Relations that were falsified but overprotected by the parents, who were omnipresent even in their absence—the children anticipated them when they wrote to each other, felt compelled to add a line now and then in which the fathers greet the fathers through the sons' pens. To cite only one example, we shall not find a single letter from the years 1831–33 that does not contain allusions to the relationship between the Flauberts and the Chevaliers: "Heartfelt greetings to your dear family from me" (31 December 1830). "Your dear father is always the same . . ." (4 February). "I beg you to give me news of your dear aunt as well as of your fine family . . ." [12] (11 February). "Your dear papa is a little better, the remedy papa gave him made him more comfortable and we hope that he will soon be cured" (15 January 1832). "My father and mother and I offer our respects to your dear parents" (23 August 1832), etc. In becoming friends, Ernest and Gustave merely *perpetuated* the courtly relations between their lords; they felt encouraged in them, their ties were *sacred*.

This is not all. In that interfamilial hierarchy, Gustave was convinced that his family held first place: he shared with Achille and

12. *Sic.*

Caroline the certainty that a Flaubert was *wellborn*. It is true that through their mother they preserved distant links with the Normandy gentry, but to their mind these links had only symbolic value: their blue blood guaranteed—neither more nor less than their Canadian ancestors' "Indian blood"—the aristocracy of fact which was transmitted by Achille-Cléophas to his progeny. There is a *Flaubert honor*, a collective and instituted pride, that each of the children must uphold wherever he goes. To measure the extent to which Gustave was heir to this pride, we have only to read the letters he writes in 1857 to his brother Achille at the time of his trial:

> Information on the influential position my father and you had and have in Rouen are all to the good; they thought they were attacking a poor nobody, and when they first saw that I had means, they began to open their eyes. They should know at the Ministry of the Interior that in Rouen we are what is called *a family*, meaning that we have deep roots in the country, and that by attacking me, especially for immorality, many people will be offended. Try using your skill to have it said that there will be a certain danger in attacking me, in attacking us, because of the coming elections.[13]

Two days later, the same thing:

> The only really influential thing will be Father's name and the fear that a condemnation will prejudice the people of Rouen in the future elections . . . In short, the prefect, Monsieur Leroy, and Monsieur Franck-Carré must write directly to the director of the Sureté Générale telling them what influence we have and how much this would outrage the morality of the region. This is purely a political affair . . . What will stop it is making them see the *political inconvenience* of the thing.[14]

With what fatuousness he writes on 30 January: "Maître Sénard's speech was splended . . . He began by talking about Father, then you, and finally me . . . 'Ah! You are attacking the second son of Monsieur Flaubert! . . . No one, Monsieur l'avocat général, and not even you, can give him lessons in morality.'"[15] This last passage is all the more piquant as Gustave, we shall see later, had deliberately written a *demoralizing* work. But who would dare attack the morality of Monsieur Flaubert's son? Attacked *as an individual*, Gustave's first reaction is to defend himself as *son of the family*, as a member of a familial commu-

13. *Correspondance* 4:141, 3 January 1857.
14. *Correspondance* 4:143.
15. Ibid., pp. 158–59.

nity. "We are a family!" Nothing in common with those animal colonies that congregate around the couple who engendered them; for Flaubert, a "family" is characterized by the inheritance of responsibilities and virtues, which is why he even takes pride in the fact that Achille-Cléophas's office should have come to Achille rather than falling into strange hands. The Messieurs de Flaubert have this in common with the nobility of the sword, that they give inexhaustibly of their person. The inhabitants of Rouen are obligated to them; the proof: a bumbling functionary need merely attack the younger son of the philosophical practitioner and he will lose the government elections. Hence that wonderful line, "this would outrage the morality of the region." Do we see the people of Rouen, enraged by this insult, staying away from the polls or voting for the opposition candidate? In 1857 Achille-Cléophas had been dead for ten years; his eldest son was far from his caliber, and his clientele was well aware of it, while his younger son buried himself in the country with an old woman and a child; relations between the two brothers were not the best, and the elder preferred to pay visits to his mother and younger brother on Sundays rather than invite them to his home, especially to his exclusive dinners. Be that as it may, dominated even in solitude by his high and noble lineage, the scandalous writer—whom Rouen would not adopt before his death—could calmly write: "There could be some danger in attacking me." He immediately adds, it is true, "in attacking *us* . . ." But this is politeness or calculated flattery; the "attacking me" says it all, since Gustave was convinced from his earliest years that every Flaubert child, whatever his place and circumstance, was the qualified representative of the entire family.

This was how the little boy imagined his future as a schoolboy even before entering the *collège*. He was not beginning his studies in complete ignorance: the royal *collège* of Rouen was an integral part of the Flaubert saga—Achille had excelled there until 1830. For a very young child, things have the impenetrable density of what has always been there: a hundred-year-old forest, animals who were there when he was born, a monument, they are all part of the same thing; the world presented, transmitted, given by his parents seems to him *instituted* rather than natural. Better, institution seems to be nature and nature institution. As far back as Gustave can remember, his older brother has been a *collégien*; it is his instituted nature. On weekdays, Achille is absent. On holidays he shows up in uniform, he has the right to talk to his heart's content; he recounts his life, his successes, and the philosophical practitioner's eyes brighten. Gustave knows from hearsay the curriculum, the gardens, the classrooms, the long corridors of the school; he has heard them talking about the great collective ceremonies, which scare him a little: going to bed in the dormitories, waking up to the bells, group meals in the refectory. There are the actors as well—he can already call them by name: the masters, who are judged worthy of respect, friendly, or despicable according to criteria that elude him; the fellow students, good boys of an inferior species, certainly not all stupid, who get out of breath in their vain attempts to catch up with the agile Achille. Before the Fall, Gustave did not view his brother's laurels with a jaundiced eye. He could not conceive that they were the reward of assiduous effort; rather he imagined them to be an *honor* conferred upon the Flaubert son from the first day. His older brother had the right to praise and prizes—by blood. What is more, the adults did not refrain from announcing to the younger child that he would gather the same laurels when his turn came. Thus, as a developing society sees its future image in a more advanced one, Gustave seized upon the present Achille as his own future. An instituted future: he would be that same schoolboy who spoke in such a reasonable way, he would at once be given the same honor, he would dress in the same uniform, and in every subject, every year, he would garner all the prizes. First place would come to him by right because it was the only thing worthy of a Flaubert: it awaited him, he knew in advance the words the masters would use to assure him of their admiration.

Doctor Flaubert must at times have tried to make him understand that he would not triumph without effort; he would have insisted on the moral aspect of the enterprise: it was Gustave's *duty* to show himself worthy of an exceptional father and brother. Until he was eight years old, the little boy viewed his mission calmly: good blood cannot lie. From birth he held a power which—he willingly admitted—contained the obligation to vanquish but also the right and the means. What was involved was merely a ritual: represented by their children, the respectable fathers of Rouen would come to bow before the chief surgeon, who had begun his third childhood in Gustave's person.

After the Fall, this calm certainty thickened, darkened, was suffused with anguish, but the misunderstanding remained. Relegated to the lowest rung of the family, Gustave thought it would kill him. But the hierarchy established among the Flauberts concerns only them; the lowest member of the Hôtel-Dieu is still first in the town. In other words, a Flaubert idiot is still good enough to make a stir at the *collège* and sweep away all the prizes. However, something has changed: he was earlier in the father's good graces, but no longer is. In order to restore this original relationship, would it be enough to excel in everything from the fourth year to the sixth? No; bent beneath those trophies, what would he have proved? That he is a Flaubert goes without saying, but not the greatest of the future Flauberts, the only one worthy of the eponymous hero. When the little boy begins his studies, Achille has been out of school ten years, but the old place still echoes with his name. What can Gustave do that his older brother has not already done? He will equal him, that's all. And so the perspective changes: he will not be able to defeat the usurper and regain paternal favor on this ground; it's simply a matter of *not losing*. And when he has shown himself a worthy successor in every way to Achille-Cléophas and Achille, the paterfamilias's judgment will still not be challenged: as he cannot help winning, these triumphs—which he owes to his blood—cannot compensate for his past faults. All the little adept of this gloomy pietism can hope for is an act of perfectly gratuitous generosity by which his lord will decide to reinstate him in Paradise. Thus for the Roundheads, all men are lost, but God in His infinite love will perform that veritable miracle of according salvation to a few of these Hell-bound victims. Religious consciousness consists, then, of knowing oneself to be damned in all justice and of never despairing of divine charity: no action can procure salvation, but some acts can discourage God from offering it to us. We know what deadly boredom characterizes the thread of these lives. It is that same boredom which Gustave expects to encounter at school. A single command: not to contravene the law. One certainty: he will not contravene. And another: he runs no risk of losing but has nothing to gain. Eight years, eight new terms, each one similar to the one before, everything foreseen, everything lived over again, and every July the same gathering of tired laurels begins again, always the same. At most, a viper may sometimes lurk beneath these dull leaves: and what if the younger boy's performance in school should confirm that he is by nature inferior to Achille? First in all things, he will *in any case* have only feudal relations with his fellow students: in class they will be his unfortunate rivals; in play, his vassals. Therefore, they don't count. But what if the school year were to turn out badly? In that case, Gustave would risk remaining at the head of the class with a lower average than Achille had obtained in the same year; the paternal judgment would be confirmed and maintained forever. This infuriating thought pricks him and vanishes; we cannot say it torments

16

him, but it is enough to conceal from him the true nature of scholarly competition.

Few children have been farther from understanding the reality of bourgeois education and less adapted to the social demand that conditions it. Bound to Achille's past by his own Fall, aspiring to shape the present in the image of the past, he enters school haunted. Committing the disastrous blunder of taking his classmates for a simple plural mediation between himself and his brother, he approaches the competitive "little society" that incorporates him as if it were a hierarchically structured community and prepares eight years of hell for himself. What the "society of children" does offer the little vassal is not the image of society in general—this does not exist, nor does man—but quite simply that of French society under Louis-Philippe, or rather of triumphant bourgeois society at the stage of primitive accumulation.

> *"Anyone who puts a grade on a paper is an asshole."*
> —On the walls of May

Gustave enters unsuspiciously into the serial circularity of a heated competition produced and established by the real competitive system that intends it as an "introduction to bourgeois life'" This means that the little vassal will be made to swallow his blue-blooded pride by a certain practico-inert "collective". Apparently, he is asked to reproduce the taught "material" or to make something of it through what is called *his* work. It is all very personal, it seems: "Do you know *your* lesson? Conjugate *your* Latin verbs for me!" In fact, nothing is his. Nor is it anyone's. In this circular system, an ungraspable centrifugal force determines the value of each student, not only—nor especially—in relation to his own work but in relation to that of others. He is judged not by what *he* does, understands, and knows but rather by what the others understand, know, and do or have not done, known, or understood. Not in relation to the real knowledge of the time but deliberately in relation to the meager information and uncultivated intelligence of the companions tossed him by chance. To value each one in relation to all the others makes him other than himself, compels him *as other* to condition all the others. In order to initiate them into the society of adults, children are pushed willy-nilly into the abstractly fabricated universe of pure otherness.

The Jesuits started it; it was they, of course, who built the *col-*

17

lège at Rouen—we know that they wanted to win over a resentful bourgeoisie from the Jansenists and Protestants. The victors of July replaced them and made "humanism" an instrument of dehumanization. Since man—meaning bourgeois man—defined himself under Louis-Philippe as competitor, the "humanities" had to be structured competitively. To begin with, the principle of egalitarianism was introduced into teaching. It was the systematic dismantling of the last bastions of feudalism; the sons of the ruling class all had the same opportunities at the outset. It was the end of the gracious gift, of homage and blood ties; in this way the bourgeoisie thought to crush in embryo any compliance with tyranny. The new gentlemen wanted to do business in peace; they did not want their children falling into the hands of the "Warlords" at a time when the citizen-king aspired to deserve the epithet "Napoleon of Peace." Since this liquidation was not followed by any reevaluation of human relations, schoolboys would be saved from feudal ideology only at the price of a "reification" imposed by the system. Two types of relations were admitted among them: if they took the same courses, competition; in all other cases, simple coexistence. Individuals would no longer assert themselves in the name of mysterious powers passed on to them by their families—this was undeniable progress. On the other hand, the new class system was still worse than the hierarchy of the Old Regime, since *real* property was reflected in the competitive order of the *collège*. In the former, as in the latter, nothing was offered and nothing was received. The new class system substituted exchange value for use value, transforming property into merchandise: payment effaced the mark of human effort and that of the former owner; a *thing* was all that remained. There is the same relation between the schoolboy and his product: the bond of interiority that unites this young worker with his work is broken by paying him for it with a *grade*. In fact, the number set down on an essay is equivalent, all things being equal, to the price of a piece of merchandise. And just as the merchant or manufacturer is threatened in his property—which has become his objective reality or his "interest"—by other reified property owners, so the student is *endangered* in the quantified object that has ceased to be his product in order to become his objective reality. His class ranking becomes his *interest* to the extent that the scholarly system is intentionally structured in the image of competitive society. In the France of 1830, where practically no monopolies existed and the economy remained protected by high customs duties, competition revealed to the bourgeois his true underpinnings: it was a selective system based on scarcity, and its result, if not its purpose, was the concentration of goods. The iron laws of bourgeois economics necessarily have the effect of facilitating necessary liquidations—social, judicial, and even physical[16]—that is, of suppressing superfluous candidates. In this indirect but pitiless form of the "struggle for life," every man in the ruling classes is a millionaire in hope but equally a potential bankrupt. The Rouen manufacturer who makes an effort to lower his costs feels his interest threatened *everywhere*, never directly or in a standoff with his rivals but, to the contrary, by a seriality that may depreciate it without ever attacking it, by the machines—to take up a previously cited example—that his competitors, unbeknownst to him, have imported from England.

In the closed circle of the "little scholarly society," his son experiences the same tension to the degree that scholarly competition serves the purpose of eliminating the greatest number of candidates possible before "starting out in life." He is threatened directly (constituted character, illnesses, personal relations with the teacher) and, even more, indirectly, as he has been thrust into a collective where the forces and events that can raise or lower his grade and instantly change his class ranking are in great part outside his field of action and frequently manifest themselves as unforeseeable accidents, at least in relation to him.[17] In this sense, in a competitive field, accident and the luck of others are an integral part of my own objective reality, which I must cling to, though I lack the means to preserve it intact.

Obviously, scholastic competition is not fatal—at least in principle—and for many children it assumes a ludic aspect, for apparently money has been replaced with dry beans. The school years, however, will not end without some memorable shipwrecks: adolescents are withdrawn from school under the pretext that they could not "keep up." What class doesn't have its dropouts, victims of a system so fashioned that it had decided their fate in advance and awaited them *in order to eliminate them?* The *collège* works a triple *Verdinglichung:* it identifies the schoolboy with his *quantified* product; it substitutes for

---

16. The suicide of bankrupts is a frequent theme in the literature of the nineteenth century. Not without reason.

17. Can he prevent a newcomer entering the school during the year, someone better taught and more competent, from stealing his ranking and with that his grade (the tendency of teachers being, in general, only rarely to exceed a certain *maximum* quota which they have fixed in advance, so if the new boy holding first place is graded 15/20, the former first has a good chance of falling to 14)? Or a schoolmate, until now more mediocre, from suddenly waking up, catching up with him, and overtaking him? Or a new teacher from disconcerting him with his teaching methods? Etc.

human relations of interiority the inert relations between things in order to dispose of those who cannot adapt themselves to the law of exteriority. Teaching petrifies the content of granted knowledge in such a way that, having itself become a thing, it is homogeneous with the *interest* of the competitors and allows them to be evaluated according to the quantity of their accumulated knowledge. However, the selectionist intention did not appear clearly at this period, either to parents or to children; indeed, in 1830, not all the families that sent their sons to secondary establishments were rich—far from it.[18] And Bouilhet, for example, who was without a fortune, combined a real taste for learning with the determination to rise to the upper levels of society. Nonetheless, rare as the students were whose fathers paid the electoral tax, the majority of these sons of the professional class lived in comfort and could even count on their parents' leaving them property. In other words, the future professionals were recruited among the sons of professionals, that is, from the highest stratum of the middle classes. It would take more than half a century and the promotion of the petite bourgeoisie—which began with the Third Republic and radicalism—for the state apparatus, faced with an increase in both volume and number of candidates for culture, to think of implementing the arrangement devised in the eighteenth century and to transform—in conformity with the will of the founding fathers— virtual eliminatory measures into a real process of elimination. The criminal absurdity of the system became manifest to schoolboys themselves only in those last years, following the steadily climbing percentage of children educated at the secondary level.[19] Between 1830 and 1880, selection operated elsewhere and otherwise: the viscosity of class was such that very few families among the unprivileged would have taken it into their heads to send their children to the establishments of the bourgeois university. A first sorting was accomplished, then, on the level of primary instruction: rural France—from 1830 to 1850, in any case—knew how to pray but not how to read.

As a consequence, the young gentlemen from the sixth to the final year were authorized to feel "at home." The competitions, for the most part, had scarcely any practical significance—the students knew

18. It will be noted that Charles Bovary is rather poor and enters the *collège* because his mother has ambition. And he will feel displaced there.

19. The baccalaureate at first seemed to be a simple rite of passage allowing the sons of the bourgeoisie to accede to the direct exercise of the powers of their class. But from the beginning of the twentieth century it has tended increasingly to take on the character of a competition, which allows the unmasking of its selective nature.

they were taken care of in advance. In the meantime, they had to "do their humanities." After seven or eight years of studies, these young people would sit for the baccalaureate, a simple review of acquired knowledge. The certainty that indulgent teachers would accord the title of bachelor to all candidates who reached the mean level, and would "fish out" a good number of those who did not, contributed to give the jousts of the school year a sufficiently academic character. These adolescents were hardly excited at the prospect of being awarded a certificate of membership in the bourgeoisie at the end of their secondary studies, since they knew were bourgeois by birth.

Of course, all competition creates antagonisms; by giving these secondary students conflicting interests, the artificially instituted competition between them tended to make each one the others' enemy. Even if the children did not yet feel the gravity of scholarly confrontations and the reality hidden by the system, for the boy who—through vanity, ambition, paternal demands—held onto his place in the ranks, his comrades, whoever they were, represented a permanent danger. But this objective and abstract structure, which defined them by discord, was tempered by concrete allegiances: the same milieu, the same age, the same teachers. They fought *among themselves,* of course, more or less zealously, but above all they were united in the battle they waged against *the others*—parents, teachers, and, in a sense, previous generations. And so this inevitable conflict remained schematic or masked; we shall soon see that between 1830 and 1848 it could be masked no longer. Each one of the boys was dual: for himself and for everyone; history brought together these adolescents who were structured by the system as rival and incommunicable solitudes. They defined themselves as the agents and victims of a serial circularity; at the same time they became integrated into tacitly sworn (or simply fused) groups, in which everyone came to see everyone else not as *the other* but as the same. *Terror-fraternity:* this collectivity, one of the most imperious that exists, is permanently terrorist and often terrorized by the secret societies it conceals in its midst, but in its very ambivalence the relation that unites its members is direct, basically ethical, and humane. In this first half of the nineteenth century, the accent is on the group—living, legislating, acting—rather than on the serial combination of solitudes atomized by competition. Nevertheless, the former does not suppress the latter. And this sheds some light on the dual judgment Gustave brings to bear on his comrades: the jeering fools and the madcaps with their extravagant feats are the same, depending on whether they are viewed in the light of the terror-fraternity or

21

the competitive treadmill. And not for an instant does any one of them cease objectively to be the others' rival and their brother: no common violence will prevent the man with the dagger from being ranked twelfth in Latin verse composition, *ahead* of his neighbor on the right, the pirate, *behind* his neighbor on the left, the lady-killer. Yet these adolescents spontaneously used two value systems without ever—in contrast to Gustave—mistaking or confusing them. No vicious circle for these schoolboys: in Latin composition, on the basis of bourgeois egalitarianism, they concurred that the best man should win, or rather they considered, with indifference, that the man who won was the best. Among themselves, on the schoolyard gravel, in the refectory, in the dormitory, in the street, the group imposed its values, produced its leaders, instituted them, then liquidated them one after the other in the name of that absolute norm, integration. It would never have occurred *to them* to disqualify the power of their current chief by remembering his position in the latest class ranking, *or* to deplore the fact that the blind schoolmasters did not consider one's prestige when they corrected one's compositions, *or* to submit to some pipsqueak who was ranked first, *or* to challenge someone's scholarly success on the pretext that he was not capable of defending himself with his fists. They moved from one world to the other with a simple roll of the drum. As we shall see, for a moment they took it into their heads to use the formidable power of the group to dissolve the imposed seriality. Without much success: afterward, they played the politics of dual membership grudgingly, in order to avoid the worst—in other words, they managed.

Gustave will not manage, for the simple reason that he too uses both systems, but *in reverse*. From the *instituted* "little society" of competition he demands confirmation of Flaubert primacy. His indefinable *"quality"*—something evidently rather close to the charismatic power that the sworn group recognizes in its leaders—is something he aspires to affirm *in competition;* he demands that the numerical ranking restore the feudal hierarchy. The error is significant: Achille-Cléophas is not *first* in his family in the sense that the schoolteachers and the headmaster use this term—he could not be called *primus inter pares;* he was a *prince* (*princeps*), and this means that he reigned in virtue of the *"mana"* he possessed. Ranking and hierarchy are two conflicting ordinations. In a hierarchy, all are protected, the humble as well as the superior; there is no question of atomizing or excluding, only of integrating. Liberal society, on the other hand, no sooner proclaims the equality of all its members than it seeks to rank them in order of decreasing quantity, with the intention of excluding the least endowed. This is the source of the young schoolboy's unease: Gustave exhausts himself trying to decipher a coded text by means of a code suited to other messages. However, in the course of these eight years of endless eliminations, the system grabs him and subjects him, like his schoolmates, to *Verdinglichung*. Disappointed, bewildered, he looks around at his comrades and for the first time discovers in them the effects of competitive atomization and reification, which he mistakes for their character traits. We must examine this in detail.

When the doors of the *collège* close behind him, the child is anxious—he would speak in the *Mémoires* about his night fears—but not yet miserable: he is the son of a good family who has come to be consecrated; full of superiority, he sits at his writing desk in the midst of inferiors. Indeed, in the beginning it seems that fortune smiled upon him the better to hobble him. In the fifth term, during the school year 1832–33,[20] he was first five times and received the first honorable mention of excellence. And then, beginning the following year, everything falls apart, he does *poor work*. The first years are the most painful to his pride: sixth, seventh: not once is his name mentioned, at least in the *Journal de Rouen,* most of the prize lists being lost. Bruneau ventures to remark that he could have "garnered ample honorable mentions"—the papers were capricious at this period, sometimes listing all the awards, sometimes only mentioning the prizes. This is formally true but contradicted by Gustave's own testimony: he claims in the *Mémoires* that he was "mocked by the masters, pulled down to the lowest rung." Even if he is exaggerating, that judgment is relevant only to the years 1833–34 and 1834–35. Beginning in the eighth term, Gustave could not seriously claim to be last in the class. It was the sixth that was decisive: he was bewildered, rage and spite overwhelmed him, his pride was wounded, he literally did not know where he was or what he was doing. After the seventh term, however, the interest shown in him by Chéruel and Gourgaud put an end to his unbearable confusion. Not immediately, but little by little: in the ninth term he received two prizes, in history and natural history; in the tenth, the same two. In his Rhetoric year, second prize in history, second honorable mention in French. In other subjects he seems to have been able to stay, at least beginning in 1835, in the highest group, hardly falling below tenth place (there were twenty-five stu-

---

20. No trace of Gustave's presence at the school remains from the preceding year, that is, from the fourth term, when he was between nine and ten years old.

dents in the class). Nonetheless, the wounds remained. And the rancor; his disgust in the end becomes insurmountable since—as I will demonstrate—he is secretly aiming to be taken out of the school. We know that he will succeed in the first trimester of the school year 1839–40, having obtained first place in philosophy composition, the ultimate compensation. He prepared for the baccalaureate at home and passed it in the required time, without honorable mention though not without effort.[21]

How should we judge these results? If it were anyone but Gustave, I would say they were quite good. The dunce and the prodigy are both monsters, two victims of the family institution and of institutionalized education: if a child had to adapt—and he did then—to a competitive and selective system, it was hoped that he might remain in the average in all things. Alas, Gustave is *already* a monster. Flaubert honor commands him to excel and at the same time throws him unarmed into the competitive arena. His misfortune is to be *wellborn* without being so: the *quality* that comes from lineage has nothing in common with talents, and "blood" speaks only when it is spilled on the battlefield. But the blood of the Flauberts should have spoken first on the benches of the *collège*, for it was there that Achille-Cléophas, distinguished by the First Consul, had received his titles of nobility. The innate virtues Gustave claimed to inherit from his father were strength of mind, penetration, a broad view of things, rigor, and efficacy—everything that, in fact, had been denied him at an early age; these had to be in evidence at each test or he would fail. Or, rather, these qualities would have to manifest themselves on their own when he needed them. Here is the child caught up in the toils of competition without even comprehending its nature; Flaubert *honor* compels him to risk dishonor every day in a dubious combat in which he tries futilely to demonstrate what seemed to him acquired in advance and consequently above all demonstration. The a priori suddenly becomes an a posteriori, a "far off" objective that can only be reached through a lengthy enterprise. On-the-spot transformation:

21. "I was decreed a bachelor, received my degree on Monday morning . . . Arrived back at the house, N—was there for lunch. I threw myself on a bed and slept, a bath in the evening, several days of rest." *Souvenirs,* p. 81. The anguish, the overwork of the previous days is evident. Furthermore, we shall see that Doctor Flaubert, even before the exam, was worried: his son needed a change of air, of place, of ideas; hence the famous journey—the Pyrenees, Marseille, Corsica—that Gustave made with Doctor Cloquet.

one must prove, prove again, keep proving; one must become what one believed one was; the child appears to himself on the horizon of a merciless struggle, a cruel game in which he doesn't know the rules. From this point of view, in the light of Flaubert pride and its requirements, the results of his efforts whenever he imagines them seem *humiliating and pitiful*. Tormented by shame and envy, his anger does not abate. "A nervous irritation . . . made me sick and distracted, like a bull sick from being stung by insects." An excellent comparison: the bull stung by horseflies doesn't see, doesn't understand what is happening to him; it is the same with Gustave, suffering from a new and incomprehensible alienation, for competitive serialization makes him indirectly dependent on others.

This said, one wonders why the younger of the Flaubert sons, having begun so well, begins to stumble at the first test. After all, couldn't the young writer, at this time showing a precocity that astonished everyone, have succeeded as well as Achille? If he put so much passion into claiming first place, why didn't he obtain it? Was he less intelligent than his brother? He believed this, as we shall see, without quite daring to admit it to himself, so wrenching was the idea. But so what? Stupidity is the most common thing in the world, everyone is stupid, each in his own way;[22] it is a fact of oppression generally. Gustave was neither more nor less gifted than his fellow students; his scholastic failure—or at least what he took for it—rests on causes of three complementary kinds.

1. The first, which I am not going to stress, is his constitutional passivity. It facilitates mnemonic acquisitions (raw perceptions, montages) but is hardly conducive to mental operations, particularly in the exact disciplines where one starts with a *practical decision* (negation or affirmation) in order to reach another decision of the same sort by way of rigorous reasoning. This voluntarist commitment must be maintained until the end; it is not simply a matter of passing from one step to the next. One must continue to affirm or deny what one has advanced in the first place along with the consequences derived from that proposition. In this domain, theory is practice since it organizes the field of possibilities as a function of the demonstration in progress: the most abstract reasoning is necessarily an experiment. Conversely, practice is theory to the extent that it takes as its aim the

---

22. This is precisely what Gustave will seek to demonstrate in the unfinished second part of *Bouvard et Pécuchet*.

accumulation of information. No depth[23] in these systematic analyses, merely a question of treating the external object *in exteriority;* to think, says Brunschvicg, is to measure. Gustave's thought is never conceptual; it does not *measure*—it hesitates, gropes, never denies or affirms, passionately attaching itself to an idea, then detaching itself and remaining in doubt. His ruminations are crossed by flashes that abruptly reveal a seamless totality and are then immediately extinguished, leaving him blind, incapable of *analyzing* his intuition or of expressing it through an articulated discourse. Not that he is incapable of *intellection:* when the "master" is at the blackboard and speaks while tracing signs, Gustave understands quite well what he is being taught; he enters into the reasons advanced, he grasps their logical connections and necessity—on this point his intelligence largely equals his brother's. But this is because the teacher's affirmative power has worked its way into him, because *another* affirms and denies in his stead and in his head, because intellection is sustained by the principal of authority. No sooner does he find himself alone again—especially if he must resolve a problem on his own—than his borrowed certainties evaporate, he repeats to himself without conviction the reasonings he has heard the evening before; not that he refuses his consent—he is simply not prepared to give it. Lacking such preparedness, he is incapable of repeating the intellectual act, properly speaking: the evidence vanishes; it is replaced by doubt—certainly not methodical doubt, which requires volition, or even the doubt of the skeptic, which must be a *parti pris,* but rather a confused distrust.

For these reasons, and for others that we shall examine later, nothing is more alien to Gustave than the spirit of analysis he so often claims for himself; he lacks the means to dissect an object along its finest lines and similarly lacks the means to recompose it. On the contrary, what characterizes his thought is *depth,* in other words, syncretism. This mode of predialectic knowledge—through the vague perception of totalities, encompassing contradictions, circularities—is closer to *comprehension* than to the act of judging; it is valuable to the extent that its object is itself syncretistic, that is, has bearing on *lived experience.* And we shall see later that Emma's feelings—despite Sainte-Beuve's couplet on the emergence of surgery in literature—are never *analyzed;* Gustave reveals them, irreducible wholes that succeed one

23. I do not mean, of course, that analytic thought is *superficial,* which would make no sense. But simply that notions of depth and superficiality have no currency in this domain. The concept must be clear and distinct and apply precisely to its object, nothing more.

another in an order highly alien to voluntarism but with an apparent contingency that masks a "vital" necessity. These mental dispositions allow him to write a masterpiece and to transform the object as well as the methods of fiction; such a turn of mind is hardly propitious for studying mathematics or the natural sciences, nor is it to much more advantage in the study of logical or grammatical analysis, in Latin and Greek composition, or even in translation. By examining the "scenarios" for *Madame Bovary* we shall see that Gustave, thank God, never knew how to "make an outline"; hence the "composition" of this work is an unexpected marvel. But this also explains why the poor boy was never dazzling in French *composition*: in seven years, one honorable mention; that year, once again, the prize went to Bouilhet, who was more methodical. It is striking that Gourgaud should have taken an interest in Gustave as a teller of stories; beneath the student's mediocre products this teacher could distinguish the promise of the future writer, but he had no wish to give the writer scholarly rewards that the student did not deserve. It was only fair: at the time when Gustave was writing *L'Anneau du Prieur,* the essays he turned in were banal and rather worthless, to judge from those we have. It is to the harsh but scrupulous honesty of Gourgaud-Dugazon that Gustave alludes when he writes in all bitterness: "They barely conceded that I had imagination, meaning, according to them, an exultation . . . akin to madness." In short, Gourgaud and Chéruel paid attention *outside the competitive system* to the monster, the "madman," whose very anomaly prevented him from meeting their demands *within the system.*

2. The crisis of identification grew. In the gloomy dungeon of the Hôtel-Dieu, the child found himself compelled to act out his objective-being, which belonged to others. At least he knew they saw that being in his singularity; their very demands were singular, even in the paternal curse there was a kind of cruel solicitude, a meticulous concern to inflict on the child exquisite torments conceived for him alone. He knew why and for whom he was working. Making progress did not interest him in itself, its purpose was to draw a smile from his Lord; thus, the labor was not distinguished from the cult and had meaning only in this unique and sacred little world.

At school he no longer understood anything. The sacred was abolished, stripping words of their cultural meaning: "application," "effort," "progress," "merit"—these words, now devoid of all connection to love, to homage, designated measurable quantities. Not only did he no longer know why or for whom he should work, the very meaning of work escaped him. How could he, who thought of his father's teaching as the fierce, sweet relationship of a sadistic hero with a masochistic martyr, bring himself to be judged by a relatively unknown person before a bunch of unknowns? The ego to which his teachers addressed themselves, and which they demanded he make the agent of a universal practice, no longer had anything in common with the cursed little boy for whom all practice was loving and individual. Within the family his anomaly was censured—and hence recognized. The teacher seemed to be unaware of it, or in any event it was not taken into account: when he turned toward Gustave, he addressed himself only to the abstract universality of the Kantian "I think" that lay inside the child. Hence Gustave's confusion: he feels affected by this formal *I* that is evoked in him; he cannot deny its existence, yet he does not recognize himself in it. It is certainly Gustave, since it is the universal subject, and it is not Gustave, since that unity of all practices, that vehicle of categories, does not take account of his constitutional passivity, and since this new role, designating him as absolute *agent*, is repugnant to his passivity. But what can he oppose to it in his innermost thoughts? At first, Others constitute authority: as they see him, so he believes he is. And then, the little monster, sickly and princely, is also a role: this character never stops haunting him, but it has no consistency, rather like the persistent, vague memory of a dream. Just as the abstract egalitarianism of teaching imposes on all students, in spite of themselves, the feeling of being *essentially* interchangeable, so this feeling is the starting place for becoming *primus inter pares*. Gustave resists more than the others but cannot prevent himself from internalizing this objective interchangeability:

> I never liked a regulated life, fixed hours, an existence run by the clock in which thought must stop with the bell, in which everything is predigested for centuries and for generations. This regularity may no doubt suit the majority, but for the poor child who thrives . . . on dreams . . . it is suffocating to thrust him into our atmosphere of materialism and good sense for which he feels horror and disgust.[24]

If we want to understand this repugnance, we must recall that Gustave's life within the family was highly regulated: Doctor Flaubert, overwhelmed with duties, divided between the medical school, the hospital, and his clientele, was forced to employ his time very strictly.[25]

24. *Mémoires d'un fou*, chapter 5.
25. At seven o'clock in the morning, rounds; after that the students were summoned, there were operations, then free consultations at the hospital. Lunch, visits to

Gustave never complained about it, and later at Croisset, as his niece bears witness, he established—neither out of necessity nor out of habit—a schedule that varied only with the seasons. So it wasn't having time for fantasy and caprice that he missed at school. Quite the contrary, he always enjoyed living in the cyclical milieu of repetition—even if the overprotection of which he was the object gave his occupations and the maternal attentions a subjugating regularity at the Hôtel-Dieu. And he revered that superior, unique discipline that compelled him to take his medicine at the same time each day, to lunch everyday at noon; the structured temporality of the Flauberts— eternal return of the seasons and ceremonies in constantly reaffirmed feudality—constituted him heir, vassal, and future lord in his own eyes. And now he is suddenly projected into the time of the "majority." This purely quantitative designation clearly marks his bitterness and his contempt; his comrades constitute a *numerous group:* all identical in *quality,* they figure in the scholastic whole as *unities.* Our imaginary aristocrat finds it unbearable to be constrained to live within the physical and bourgeois duration of clocks, an infinitely divisible continuum which, starting with its own universality, designates him as universal atom. At the Hôtel-Dieu, certainly, time was precious only for Achille-Cléophas; the little boy himself had enough to spare and was unaware that the chief surgeon measured his by the clock; Gustave had no need to measure that loose, boring, and comfortable duration that was himself. At school, when temporality is quantified, he is disoriented; not only does he deny the administration the right to measure his dreams by the same yardstick used to measure his schoolmates' labors and foolish games; he also does not understand how they can assign to everyone—thus to him as well, as universal subject—the same amount of time to complete an imposed task (two hours for a history composition, four for a French composition). We shall see him later at Croisset mulling things over at his desk, tracing two words, crossing them out, dreaming again, recopying them, adding a third word, dropping his pen, getting up, going to look at the Seine, throwing himself onto his couch, lying there prostrate with his eyes closed, yawning, going back to his desk, crossing out the three words he had written, and so on. Certain critics have deduced from this that he was greatly exaggerating when he spoke of his

---

the paying clientele; at four o'clock, return to the Hôtel-Dieu, follow-up rounds, examinations of entering patients and emergencies. Before going to bed, he went through the rooms checking on patients just out of surgery.

"forced labor." A hasty conclusion: he did *his* work at *his* rhythm; we have no grounds for doubting that he was *living* in a kind of prison. But, as the popular expression has it, he *took his time*. This long, slow, vegetative and quasi-vegetal duration—which will be the temporal structure of *Madame Bovary*—served to replace the rapid movement of action. It allowed his passive constitution to be penetrated by problems, saturated with them. Unable to analyze them, he wrote them down by means of a patient erosion or, after a certain incubation period, found a solution for them not through a willed and clearly self-conscious synthesis but through an obscure, organic parturition. He did not labor, he was *in labor*—this is the temporality of passive activity. We can easily imagine that the dreamy child had brought his own time to school with him; only the bells prevented him from *taking* it. This hindered him profoundly; by interposing the practical time of "I think" as one of the givens of his duration, the school authorities substituted for his own time the spatial-temporal continuum of mechanism, which could only produce in him a tremendous, disordered agitation—with the inevitable result that he turned in botched and incomplete essays. "*I'm* the laziest of all," he says, with that mixture of shame and swagger we have come to know quite well. The laziest, no: laziness does not exist. Gustave works badly because school time and his internal temporalization are at odds, and because he can neither completely relinquish his own time nor definitely settle into the other. He does his work badly because he no longer recognizes himself: when he sees his schoolmates in class, during study time, calmly settled into temporal universality, it seems to him that he—Prince Flaubert—is but a universal *manqué*, and that his originality becomes the ridiculous and weighty burden that prevents him from rising to the purity of "I think." In the competitive circularity, the only bond between man and man that Gustave recognizes, homage, seams to be an impossible principle. But unable to attribute this to the system (who would have done, at his age and in his time?), the little boy takes on responsibility for it himself (perhaps he is not a Flaubert?) or puts it on others (they are robots). As we have seen, in the beginning he was not so unsociable; he was made unsociable when, though he couldn't understand why, his relations with his comrades were revealed to him as at once *reified* and the prototype of all human relations (the feudal bond being suddenly cast into the imaginary). He made this discovery, of course, through the continually repeated humiliation of not being first in the class and through the savage *envy* he felt for those ahead of him.

Yet who can name a society more feudal than the society of children? Indeed, there is none. Providing we look at them *outside of class.* Tall, handsome, and a loudmouth, Gustave could have imposed himself at will—as he did a little later, when all was lost. The unfortunate thing is that he looked for hierarchy *during class hours* in the very places where it was banished *a principio.* Disappointed, he defined his comrades not as they were but as competition made them: these were indifferent beings who seemed to him in their very banality inexplicably superior—those who succeeded, at least—to the poor monster burdened with singularities who was thrown into their midst. At recess, the competitive universe crumbled—for everyone except the poor lacerated child, who dwelled on his humiliations and could no longer get his bearings. In the schoolmates who approached him to ask him to join their games, what could he see but identical and pluralized "I thinks"? Thus his unsociability is here merely the internalization of an atomizing egalitarianism that does not allow individuals stripped of their concrete existence any rapport but relations of exteriority. On the one hand, he feels contempt for them on principle; although a culpable obstinacy prevents them from recognizing it, they are nonetheless rustics, born into the peasantry: their families do not visit the Flaubert home. On the other hand, persisting in his rancor, he defines them even in the schoolyard—the place of cliques, gangs, or simple coexistence—by the competitive circularity which makes every competitor, simply by *being-there,* a potential rival, a marginal thief who, without giving him so much as a glance, without the slightest concern for him, can devalorize him by taking his place. In each of them Gustave approaches the universalized, interchangeable self stripped of its singularity and yet, on the whole, fallen, contemptible, and threatening: a pure "I think" inimical to itself. Indifferent, atomized, they *signify* him *"uomo qualunque,"* whereby they treat him as an equal; superior without displaying the least mark of their superiority, they show him that he dishonors the Flauberts. Inferior, they throw him back on his empty and painful pride at being a false aristocrat by their arrogant claim to be his peers. And as they are all that at once, though at three different levels, Gustave has only one recourse: to escape them and himself. "I would withdraw with a book of verse." [26]

3. Beginning in the eighth term, he harbored the hidden intention of losing. In fact, the solicitude of Chéruel and Gourgaud allowed him

26. *Mémoires d'un fou.*

31

to get a grip on himself: he escaped from the anonymity of serial circularity by finding himself once more the singular object of lordly generosity. His case is not unique—we know a thousand examples of students bewildered by the system who have been given courage by a *special* smile from the teacher and have then set to work *for him:* the feudalization of the competition allows them to tolerate the purely bourgeois rivalry. I know some who needed no more than this to leap up to the rank that Gustave sought in vain. For him, many difficulties were smoothed over: a better rapport with the masters, with his classmates,[27] competition tamed. Why didn't he take advantage of the occasion to "climb up the ladder"? There is progress, certainly, and his name figures among the honorable mentions. But if he really wanted to triumph, couldn't he have done better? Constitutional passivity is not an insurmountable obstacle: it is not a total and pathological lack of pragmatism but a passive activity; it contains a principle of inertia, a gentle force that inclines to quietism; but obstinacy instead of will can surmount it on a provisional basis, especially at school, where the student is supported, buttressed by collective habits, by the activism of teachers. The *passive agent* remains an agent in that he surpasses his present state through projects and modifies what he is through his intentional connection with what he will be. This minimum of transcendence allows the teacher to slip inside the pupil and *desire in his place,* if only the pupil will lend himself to it or at least not resist. Gustave resisted, no doubt about it. That "laziness" he boasts of and deplores is no longer, beginning in the eighth term, simply a lack of adaptation—it implies secret consent. Why? Because it is *too late.* By which we understand, too late *for him.* Others have "caught up" in the tenth term, in the eleventh, or even *in extremis.* But they had no guarantee at the outset. For the younger son of the Flauberts, there is one: disgraced by his father, he aspires to win this idiotic lottery not *for the sake of winning* but *in order not to lose,* not to aggravate his case. They expect him, he thinks, to emulate his brother; if so, he has already lost, it's all over; he has already proved that he will never equal Achille, stumbling from the outset when the other performed like a champion. The child feels moved by a secret malice: I will not become a bad copy of my older brother.

Achille, indeed, had the glorious privilege of carrying his identification with the father to an extreme. He was the first Flaubert to study at the Rouen *collège*. Achille-Cléophas willingly spoke to him of his

27. It was in the eighth term that he edited and distributed *Art et Progrès*.

own adolescence, of laurels won in the distant capital at the time when Bonaparte was not yet Napoleon: these archetypal events stimulated the ardor of the firstborn but did not hamper him. *Elsewhere, in other times,* the paterfamilias had accomplished these miracles so that Achille, in Rouen under the Bourbons, could accomplish his own. Everything was new for the lucky child invested by his father with the duty of consolidating the family glory by achieving the conquest of Normandy. *He invented what he repeated*—this was enough to give him breathing space. Product of the chief surgeon, he had consequently only one passion: to reproduce his progenitor by producing himself. If he was first in natural history, and if he learned from his father that *he* in his time in the same year had the same place with a better grade, Achille was quite content, having once and for all admitted the paterfamilias's superiority: the Creator made the Creature in his image, compelling him to resemble his maker to the best of his ability but not to equal him.

Gustave invents nothing: day after day he replays his brother's school days, in the same places, on the same benches, with at least some of the same teachers. This is a deliberate trap. The paterfamilias has said to his cursed younger son: go on, duplicate my career beginning at the *collège,* and perhaps I shall forgive you. The child hastened to obey, the trap closed on him: it was Achille's career he had to duplicate. Bewildered by his first failures, the younger son understood this much at least: by striving to reproduce his father, he would merely produce himself as a lesser Achille; this would only underscore the Usurper's inferior traits and make manifest his own relative-being. What is he doing but reliving, one by one, minutes already lived? Fresh and vibrant as they were nine years ago, they are reborn somewhat faded: "Gustave, remember your brother," say the oldest teachers. "He did this composition. On the same subject. I gave him an 18. Try to get at least a 14!" A commendable but sadistic form of encouragement. This school, which Achille saw, ran about, lived in, which restores the rhythm of that past life by the ringing of its bells and by the permanence of its scholarly programs, imposed tasks, and activities, is none other than Achille himself transformed into categorical imperatives; conversely, Achille is the *collège* fetishized. Through the tall figure of his older brother, fully present in the inertia of the buildings, Gustave's own temporalization—without ceasing to be the silent spring of existence—seems to him the means chosen by a glorious past to reactivate itself without glory: it makes him heir to an enemy force.

What can he do? Common sense proposes an alternative: let him break the bank or resign himself to his fate. We have already understood that he can do neither. Break the bank—what does that mean? That a "noble despair" should come to his aid? The lost years cannot be effaced, as we have just seen, merely by equaling his brother in those to come; Gustave must simply break all the family records and demonstrate his genius where Achille was merely exceptional. Only then will he have played his hand: by a stroke of lightning, the younger son will have reproduced his own father, leaving his older brother standing there, dazed.

This solution, I'm afraid, was never contemplated. Certainly, genius—to use this dated word so painfully dear to Gustave—is an excessively demanding condition. If the unloved child had had the temerity to demand more of himself and of reality, his scores would have been improved.[28] But what could he do against the double limit imposed on him from without? First of all, genius invents; frequently it discovers the problem by beginning with its solution. So it has no currency at school. The teachers have learned the questions and answers at the same time; they teach them in their turn; for every problem articulated they expect a solution, only one, the *right* one, which the schoolboy will fish for in the authoritative course, where it has been given in advance more or less explicitly. If Gustave accepts the system, he will enclose himself in a *finite* circle of dispensed, acquired knowledge to be reproduced, and by that very circumstance will limit himself to hopping around its circumference. Second, the only way of surpassing his older brother, the family heir supported by a fortunate father, would be, as Gustave knows, to revive the abrupt mutation by which the paterfamilias moved from one social class to another. This exhausting enterprise, by which a veterinarian's son tore himself from his native milieu, is something neither of his offspring can imagine repeating, simply because its very success prevents it from being started over again. Here we have the other objective limit: Gustave can never turn himself into a poor peasant and conquer the culture of the rich with his fists. It is therefore quite true that he has been confined within Achille and that it is, a priori, impossible for him to leave his prison. His positive qualities, his skills, his intelligence, his application (when he can apply himself) do not strictly belong to him:

28. This audacity was not something he lacked, as we shall see, but he exercised it in another sphere, that of totalized unreality.

these qualities, objectively required by learning and, in a way, impersonal, are eminently those of his brother—Achille; and he alone is marked by them because he has pushed them to the limit. Less developed in the younger brother, they seem like the collective attributes of the House of Flaubert. What strictly belongs to Gustave is, on the contrary, negative. The fogs, the distractions, the bewilderments, the stupor, the waking dream—in short, imagination, "exultation . . . akin to madness, according to them." He must therefore make a rending choice: to be a "remake" of Achille or, if he wants *to be himself,* to begin with a shipwreck, to renounce all scholarly success, to become *the* dunce.

We surmise that he did not make a choice; he was horrified by the first alternative and terrified by the second: he would have had to find the strength, in himself and by himself alone, to oppose the dictates of Flaubert pride and thus to become an object of universal scorn. Therefore he persists in his efforts, but his repugnance at letting himself be defined in relation to Achille, in his relative-being, silently undermines those efforts, deprives them of some of their efficacy. He works half-heartedly, his limbs grow heavy, his fingers can barely support his pen; he has just begun to concentrate on his task when an image comes to him, he tries to grasp it, and suddenly it flits away. Nataurally, Gustave *does not pursue* these stalling actions, they pursue him. Anonymous, unperceived, they do not prevent obedience or even the gestures of zeal; the child does not grasp them *in himself,* they are reflected to him by the object: schoolbooks confront him with a quasi-human resistance, sentences decompose into words without warning, and words in turn, even the most familiar, all at once dazzle him, appear impenetrably strange. The result: even in subjects where he might excel he achieves only semisuccess, or rather semifailure. As insidious and veiled as they are, however, and although they derive their efficacy strictly from their clandestine nature, these behaviors are no less intentionally structured, by which we should understand that they have a meaning. A meaning which, on the still elementary level of industrious behavior, endlessly reveals and conceals itself but is to be found again, explicitly unconstrained, on the more complex level of superstructures.[29] It is striking, for example, that in chapter 5

29. Keeping things in perspective, and without forgetting that education and culture are superstructural determinations—taking a society in its generality—it seems evident to me that one must consider the behaviors involved in apprenticeship in the closed setting of the Napoleonic secondary school, especially when these were taught

of the *Mémoires*, just as he is complaining of being "cast down to the lowest rung by [his] very superiority," he describes the poems of Byron that he "would read on the side" *in opposition* to teachers, schoolmates, and his father, in these terms: "This colossal poetry makes you dizzy and makes you fall into the bottomless pit of infinity." The dizziness of the fall is what torments Gustave. In order to quietly escape the curse that condemns him to being only a mediocre copy, he simply dreams of letting himself slip into nonbeing, as if on this level his body had understood what his heart dared not admit: that he would distinguish himself from his older brother in direct proportion to the quantity of nothingness he could incorporate. Here again he has recourse to the technique of gliding; since the paterfamilias has proclaimed him a "relative being" and defined him by his inferiority, the young boy goes beyond this statutory inferiority by falling into the blind night to the point of no return, where his incapacity will put him *beneath all comparison;* then, perhaps, he will rise again by means of a different, still unforeseen authority. This *intention of losing his standing* will be inscribed in him—that is, in his body—all the more slowly as it must first escape everyone's notice; and then, as we well know, Gustave is incapable of revolt, which is what it would be if he were suddenly to drop to the lowest place. No; on the contrary, it is a question of rather too sustained an act of *consent,* a resignation all the more dubious since, as we have seen, his pride is incapable of resignation. Gradually, day after day, the intention will become dizzying—we shall see its role in the crisis of 1844. But it is important to note that it was already at work during his school years. At that moment, the only possible way of grasping this behavior— intentionally structured but necessarily stifled—was in the realm of metaphysical poetry *and* on the level of generalization and ethical rationalization, as if he were trying to conceal from himself its purely idiosyncratic meaning by presenting it in the form of a paradox, a sys-

---

on the basis of competitive circularity, to be the infrastructural determinations of the young apprentice. In this way he learns his bourgeois-being (his family relations have already revealed it to him but in an ambiguous and masked form, as we have just seen in the case of Gustave, who, having gone from the Hôtel-Dieu to boarding school, falls from feudalism into the bourgeoisie, while the Flaubert family, despite certain semi-paternalistic characteristics, straddles the line that separates the middle classes from the high bourgeoisie). What will be called the superstructure in this closed field will be, for example, the schoolboys' ideology, a collection of myths which are conditioned by the competitive mode of assimilating knowledge, by this knowledge itself, and by the implicit and "spontaneous" refusal to assume the legacy of their work, to become the narrow products of their products. We shall return to this.

tem of negative values. *Ivre et Mort* in effect contains a eulogy of Hughes and Rymbault, the "two best drinkers in the region"; Gustave sings their praises and declares their reputation superior to that of artists and great leaders. And he adds, not without arrogance: "Like all great men called to this earth who are misunderstood, they too were misunderstood by the upper classes, who understand only the passions that debase but not those that degrade." The passions that debase: passions for gold, sex, honors. The passions that degrade: systematic drunkenness, intentional destruction of the human faculties, deliberate repetition and radicalization of the first Fall. The point is *to fall*, dead drunk, beneath the human condition, lower than beasts. This "sublime," mad insistence on falling ever lower into the ignoble cannot be understood *ideologically* except as the practical implementation of a black morality whose first principle is that man is odious and whose first consequence is that he must be destroyed everywhere, but first in oneself. This is only normal for a misanthrope who began by hating himself. It is less clear to him at the moment that this theory, which makes self-destruction the only morally acceptable activity, is really based on the blind, mad desire to escape all corroding comparison, and that man, the measure of all things, the marvel of civilization that he claims to destroy in himself, is simply his brother.

Here he is, then—like father, like son, noblesse oblige—always and everywhere obliged to affirm Flaubert *quality;* aristocracy in him is no more than a categorical imperative, and at the same time he cannot prevent himself from feeling that a subterranean intention to lose makes him an accomplice in his "insufficiency," whereas a few years earlier he believed he was its innocent victim. A bad conscience is added to his unhappiness: the theory of systematic self-destruction is still only an abstract justification for that guilt which he still finds scarcely comprehensible. What disturbs him is that the moment he affirms its primacy, he senses that he is rejecting it. Let us understand that we are dealing not with resignation or modesty but with rage. Pride is the sole source of these two contradictory postulations: it is worthier to risk infinite loss—which he will attempt alone—than to expose himself as a botched Flaubert. It would be better for him to be a wild child, raised by beasts and captured by hunters, without human knowledge, without the use of an articulated language, than to be an intellectual with a pea brain; in the depths of nothingness he might find a superior aristocracy—in any case, greatness lies in taking the plunge. That utterly divided pride, which pushes him simultaneously to seek the first place among men and the last among beasts, is paralyzed in its contradiction and finds neither the strength to raise Gustave up to the heights nor the supreme audacity[30] to let him fall to the depths.

> "The fools! *They,* laugh at *me!"*
> *Mémoires d'un fou*

Now we can return to the question posed at the outset but not yet answered: how did Flaubert actually experience his relations with his schoolmates? If we recall that Gustave wrote his first works, up to and including *Smarh,* when he was still at school, and that he has presented the society of children as prefiguring adult society, we shall be able to verify the adolescent's explicit testimony on his school years by comparing it to those of his youthful works that aim to describe relations among men. To the extent that the little boy does not draw his characters from Romantic convention or from his constituted misanthropy, these men are at first no more than thirteen years old, and in the end hardly more than sixteen.

Gustave has no fewer than three negative and contradictory conceptions of his connection to the members of the competitive community. From the first, these conceptions coexist, although only one of them is explicit; they will develop rapidly, without their declared opposition putting an end to their coexistence. We might say that they are passional stances and that their contradiction is not *lived* by Gustave, who vacillates continuously from one to the other. He looks at his comrades in different ways, depending on whether he takes them for inessential characters in the battle against Achille; for unfortunates—victims and accomplices of a system that drags them round in an infernal circle; or for all-powerful, cruel usurpers who have stolen his rightful title. They are peasants, he is a prince; they are poor devils, brutalized and desiccated by forced integration, whereas he is unintegrated, saved by the vastness of his soul at the price of mortal destitution; they are wild beasts, he is their prey. As we shall see, he holds three images of man and human life.

I shall pass quickly over the first: it was forged before 1832, and the years at school changed it only by making it more extreme. It is not

---

30. He will have this somber temerity once, as we shall see, in the blackest and longest night of his life, in that extraordinary moment when the freedom will be born to choose neurosis, and when the neurosis, by striking him, will become his freedom.

always *dominant* but will remain with him. In this archaic conception there is no place for serial circularity: his short stories—I shall soon return to one remarkable exception—are filled with duels or assassinations, with direct confrontations. In *Un parfum* he tells us of his plan to "bring together and *in contact* the ugly performer . . . [and] the pretty one." [31] We know that Marguerite, toward the end, wants to get her hands on her rival. A footman prevents her. In *La Peste,* no one will prevent the final confrontation, nor are we certain whether it is single combat or murder. There is no scuffle between Djalioh and Monsieur Paul; but Gustave cannot help putting "the freak of nature . . . and the marvel of civilization *in contact.*" [32] In contact: these words, which are found in *Un parfum* and in *Quid quid volueris,* are revealing: the humiliated and jealous little boy dreams of a standoff with his brother that would allow him to shriek out his hatred. In *Rêve d'enfer,* Almaroës and Satan challenge each other; what follows is a contest of strength.

The reader will have observed that all of these duellists are aristocrats *qualitatively* superior to the vulgar: Marguerite in the purity of her soul, Isabellada in the beauty of her body; Garcia and François in their princely birth; Djalioh and Satan in *anima;* Monsieur Paul and Almaroës in *animus.* The fundamental relation between lords is antagonism. Monsters and marvels face each other in a closed field, with or without witnesses. Most of the time, however, they have a public that Gustave sometimes calls the crowd, sometimes the people— awful people, imbecilic scoffers, potential lynchers: the human race, or, to put it differently, his schoolmates. When living at the Hôtel-Dieu, the little boy had no "contact" with the masses of Rouen. Where would he have learned the fear and loathing they inspire in him if not from his experience at the *collège?* "'Madwoman, madwoman!' say the people running after Marguerite!" This sentence takes on its whole meaning when we read in *Mémoires d'un fou:* "This society of children is as cruel to its victims as . . . the society of men. The same injustice of the crowd, the same tyranny of prejudice and strength, the same egotism." No doubt: Marguerite's lynchers and the fools who laugh at Flaubert *are the same.* In this archaic conception, his comrades appear as malevolent and sneering brutes, as bourgeois relying on absurd prejudices, but certainly not as competitors. These peasants are witnesses to his troubles but lack the means to forge them. He cannot

31. My italics.
32. My italics.

imagine that any one of them might take himself for the center of the world and enjoy stolen laurels on his own. They are phantoms conjured by the father's curse, and certain of them are mandated expressly to occupy first place *instead of Achille;* they are place holders, slipping between the two brothers and delaying direct confrontation, as if Gustave first had to defeat them before arriving at the fantasized standoff. We have a series of secondary trials, minor dragons that he must vanquish before measuring himself against the Usurper, simply because in his day Achille had vanquished them brilliantly. The rest of the class, the majority, form an anonymous, hostile crowd, a contemptuous chorus occupied solely in deriding the younger brother's efforts. They too are mandated: they are charged with preserving the paterfamilias's merciless laughter within the walls of the *collège.* In the stories he writes during this period, Gustave shows them—at the ball given by the Medicis, in the salons frequented by Monsieur Paul— confirming Doctor Flaubert's unjust but sovereign choice with their servile applause, reserving their offensive jibes for the poor monster he has condemned. Did they really laugh at him that much? Certainly not, as I have said above. At least—schoolboys leap at every chance to amuse themselves—no more than at anyone else. It was Gustave, made vulnerable in the extreme by "his family's sarcasms,"[33] who must have felt wounded by their innocent hilarity from the first moment he provoked it. Doctor Flaubert's irony had permanently affected him, making him laughable in his own eyes; we have seen him, from the age of eight, dreaming of being a comic actor in order to provoke at will and control in others the laughter whose permanent object he believed himself to be. What infurates him from the time he enters school is to find himself involuntarily comic, laughable in spite of himself in the midst of a crowd he judges to be hostile; once again he is bewildered, his being escapes him; once again he falls prey to others. The students and the masters share roles: the latter, by assigning homework, never lack the opportunity to mock the unfortunate younger brother; at this moment the chorus enters, scoffing; Gustave hears: "Never, no, never will you equal your brother!" Of course, nothing is real in this minor delirium except the rage and shame— what does it matter, if everything is deeply felt? It must be noted, however, that the mockery reaches him only insofar as he takes it for a perpetuation of the paternal irony; in this first moment, he is hardly concerned with what his rustic schoolmates might think of

33. *La Peste à Florence.*

40

him. A Flaubert, even when mocked, remains a Flaubert, superior by birth to the plebeian who insults him. Therefore, first by right. Even, and especially, when the facts contradict it, since the right is legitimately contested only by another right. At the moment of his first failures, he is so far from understanding the competitive system that he conceives of the *collège* in the infernal image of his family. For his part, he is the tortoise who wants to catch up with Achille; around him, behind him, above him, he hears his father's insulting laughter; the drama of the Hôtel-Dieu continues, that's all. The teachers and students have only a borrowed being; they are agents of the devil. As for his failures, he finds only one explanation: the worst is always certain; in hell (school is simply that) a right is legitimate only if it is trampled underfoot. This magical thinking would be characteristic of him until the end; until the end, Gustave would be *obsessed* with the birthright that was not granted him at the appropriate time and that he would strain to assert at every opportunity. The Goncourts were often irritated by it. Edmond comes home one day in a foul mood and notes in his journal that Flaubert is decidedly unbearable: he shouts, interrupts conversations, always wants to have the last word. If the subject is a friend, an acquaintance: "Oh, I know him better than you!" If the subject is an anecdote: "Oh, I know a better one." Oh, yes! Even at Princess Mathilde's salon, Gustave cannot bear not to be first: first as a loudmouth, first in applied psychology, first in story telling, first prize for paradox, etc. And this is the result, contrary to what Goncourt believes, not of a hypertrophied ego but, in fact, of a hypertrophied family: it is the family in him that claims the place due to a Flaubert younger son by right of blood, a place denied him for eight years at school. He knows very well that it is too late, but the impulse is stronger than he is: at Saint-Gratien, on the boulevard de Courcelles, under the malevolent gaze of his peers, he exhausts himself playing the role of "first in the class" without believing in it and without convincing anyone. He plays that first he never was, has never ceased to be, and can no longer become: in these moments, he still confuses competitive ranking with feudal hierarchy, as he did at the age of twelve.

He succeeds, nonetheless, in arriving at a somewhat clearer idea of bourgeois competition, which leads him to a second conception of human relations. *Bibliomanie*, which he wrote at the age of fourteen, seems to sum up his experience of the two preceding years. Giacomo and Baptisto never confront each other directly; they meet in the auction halls, and the stake in their struggle is the appropriation of an object—the prize, in a sense, in which each of them aspires to be objectified. The winner theoretically is neither qualitatively better or stronger but the one who spends the higher sum; in other words, the selection is quantitative. It is clear that Gustave, at the time, perfectly understood the indirect character of scholarly competition. Although he tries—by pitting only two adversaries against each other—to preserve the appearance of single combat within the serial circularity, he knows that this combat does not take place between men but between *quantities* and that these can be indefinite in number. The *auction halls* were not chosen at random; they offer an excellent image of the competitive universe:

> Giacomo [despised] Baptisto, who for some time had been sweeping away from him . . . everything that looked rare and old . . . It was always he who carried away the manuscripts; at public sales, he raised his bid and prevailed.

> Finally the moment came . . . Baptisto was in the middle, his features serene, his air calm. Giacomo first offered twenty pistoles; Baptisto kept quiet and did not look [at the book]. Even as the monk put out his hand . . . Baptisto began to say, "forty." Giacomo looked with horror at his antagonist, who was becoming increasingly impassioned as the price rose higher.
> "Fifty," he cried with all his strength.
> "Sixty," answered Baptisto.
> "One hundred."
> "Four hundred."
> "Five hundred," echoed the monk regretfully.
> . . . The sharp, broken voice of the auctioneer had already repeated "five hundred" three times, Giacomo was already grasping at happiness; a whisper escaping from someone's lips made him faint, for Baptisto . . . began to say "six hundred." The voice of the auctioneer repeated "six hundred" four times, and *no other voice answered him.*

The words I have italicized show clearly enough that the competition is overt: certainly the voice that keeps quiet is *first* poor Giacomo's. But the negative generality "no other voice" cannot be understood outside the serial circularity of a public sale where *all* those present can raise the price. In a word, the auction house is the classroom. At once the laureates of 1835, while still hypostases of Achille, begin to take on a kind of reality. The sentence that introduces Giacomo's rival into the narratives has a precision that draws our attention: "Baptisto, who for some time had been sweeping away from him . . . ," etc. *For some time:* these words cannot be related to the primal scene, nor to the Fall, nor to the great usurpation, facts that predate the story by seven years. Here the reference is to Flaubert's schoolmates who *for two years* have relentlessly been sweeping first place away from him; or, rather, it is Flaubert himself who "for some time" has perceived that they too have their own existence.

Giacomo, he tells us, "reserves . . . all his emotions for his books." He rejects friendship, love—the author would have us understand that he loves incunabula *instead of men.* Here we have the perfect collector. But one sentence in this portrait seems to resonate: "How many times *in his dreams of pride and ambition* . . . did the poor monk see the long hand of Baptisto reaching out at him." Of ambition? Thus far no one has breathed a word to us on this subject; it has been said only that Giacomo cherished books in their palpable materiality, for "their odor, their form, their title . . . the lovely word *'finis'* surrounded by two cupids." This sensuality in itself should merely lead to a calm hedonism. However, we learn without surprise that it conceals the violent desire to possess *the rarest* manuscripts, unique editions, and "to make himself a library as great as the king's." To collect things is not to break off relations with his equals but rather to establish an indirect relation to them; we cannot doubt that this monk, in his way, covets first place among men. Yet he does not dream of dominating them;[34] it is not power he claims but a *ranking number* to be assigned to him by virtue of the things he possesses. These two contrary and complementary components—the humble desire, direct and concrete, to touch, look, smell; and the arrogant ambition, abstract and indirect, to be sole proprietor of a rare object and thus deprive all other men of it, even those he does not know—are summarized and articulated in this single sentence:

> To sell everything, everything, to have that book, to have it alone, but to have it as his own; to be able to show it to all of Spain with an insulting, pitying laugh for the king, for princes, for scholars, for Baptisto, and to say: "Mine, mine, this book!" and to hold it in his two hands all his life, pressing it as he touches it,[35] smelling it as he feels it, and possessing it as he gazes at it.

34. We have seen that Gustave sometimes wishes for supreme power (Nero, Tamerlane)—out of feelings of revenge.

35. Giacomo is at the auction hall, he is allowed to touch the book that will soon be put up for sale. Meaning: he will be allowed to finger it tomorrow and forever (after the purchase) as he is doing now.

Such is Gustave; he will be like this all his life, consumed by pride—
that vulture's abstraction—and fascinated by the singularity of objects and words. Embodied by Giacomo, he covets books both for
their *qualitative* singularity and for the *quantitative* primacy their possession will give him. On the one hand, he insists on the value of
usage (meaning the sensual relation to the object), and from this
point of view his relation to the thing possessed marks its singularity.
There is no classification here; in theory, it is impossible to compare
the book such as it is *for its present or future owner* to any other book,
and equally impossible to compare that owner—inasmuch as his
practice is aimed only at revealing the singular beauty of his property—to any other possible acquirer; the relation of *this* man to *this*
thing is set in a closed circuit. On the other hand, Giacomo aspires to
be ranked above the king himself by virtue of his possession of a
greater library than the monarch's, and one composed of *rarer* books.
With *rarity* the ciruit is opened: the relation to *goods* is an indirect relation to other men, and particularly to other collectors. At once the object is revealed as *merchandise,* and Giacomo's library, only partially
complete and always future, becomes his *interest* to the extent that he
is objectified in it. It places him in danger among men insofar as any
unknown person, if rich, can do him out of a rare manuscript either
under his very nose or in Dresden, Paris, any place, without his even
knowing about it. By investing his being in his classification, he does
more than accept the competition, he solicits it. In the worst circumstances as well, since he is poor. The parabola is easy to understand:
Giacomo has the *right* to possess the most beautiful books—he alone
knows how *to treat them,* his practice exalts their beauty. Gustave has
the right to be first in the class: his intrinsic value—his *blood*, his singularity—gives a legal basis to his postulation. But the moment the
poor monk and the poor younger son try to assert their *quality*, they
are lost, for they immediately fall into the world of *quantity* and are
dragged into the infernal round of competitions where their defeat is
predictable, one lacking money and the other *means*. Held in as much
contempt by Gustave as gold itself, these means—reason, good sense,
intelligence—are in his eyes collective possessions: they circulate like
merchandise, like money; as serial objects they belong to everyone and
to no one, and have no relation to the intrinsic *quality* of the competitors. In short, the child somehow feels that his personal worth does
not help him at all in that "little society" which insists on gauging his
value as merchandise. He knows it now: *blood* does not help at all,

since it is the *cardinal* that determines the *ordinal*. Does he renounce it? Certainly not; he digs in with full knowledge, assured of his defeat. In *Bibliomanie* he returns to his old privative idea of Flaubert quality: it would no longer be his father's and brother's formidable power but the empty place left by it, the conscious and assumed *lack*, the obstinacy that knows itself to be futile. This theme—which I shall call the "inversion of quality"—does not disappear from the subsequent works where direct confrontation dominates; it merely goes underground. One even has the feeling that the boy, far from basing these competitive antagonisms on the objective structures of bourgeois society, has the misfortune of seeing them as the prototype of all human relations. *Has the misfortune:* if he had been able to see another version of himself in each of his comrades, heir like him to the institutions of liberalism, thrown into a serial circularity conceived by the state machinery expressly to introduce students to the selective competitions of adults *in the marketplace*, if he had understood that subjectivity—his own as well as that of others—was here the internalization of a structure of exteriority that defined each term by its opposition to all, he probably would have admitted that everyone lived for himself, with the means at hand, a situation that was common to all of them, and that the behavior of others, no more than his own, did not issue from that fixed essence, human nature, but rather represented every individual's effort to surpass an unsurpassable alienation. This would have disarmed his fear and his sullenness. But how could ideas of this kind possibly have occurred to an adolescent in 1835?

Yet he sometimes seems to approach a *social* vision of his adversity. I am thinking in particular of the tenth paragraph of *Agonies* (April 1838, he is sixteen years old) in which we see him comparing "man," meaning himself, to a traveler—both a "superfluous man," in Turgenev's sense, and a nomad in opposition to sedentary types, someone who distances himself from a certain place irreversibly and wants to reach another country, a town, a sanctuary: a *directed* life, adventure *infused with meaning*. And everything augures that the traveler will fail in his solitary enterprise:

> From north to south, from east to west, wherever you go you cannot take a step without tyranny, injustice, avarice, cupidity egotistically repulsing you. Everywhere, I tell you, you will find some men who will say to you: move out, you are blocking my sun; get out, you are walking on the sand that I scattered over the earth,

get out, you are walking on my property; get out, you are breathing the air that belongs to me. Oh yes! man is a traveler dying of thirst; he asks for water, he is denied it, and he dies.

Although one part of the sentence seems to refer to ownership based on work,[36] the "egotists and misers" in question are characterized by the possession of *things,* sun, air, earth, water, without any human mediation. Here, then, what is involved is "real" property as opposed to feudal *holdings* in which the object, disappearing beneath a tangle of human relationships, serves the function of mediator between men. In this apologue, the only bond between the proprietors crouched over their goods is their common refusal of any relationship. Bourgeois property reifies: these individuals, transformed by the inorganic materiality of their goods, are atoms governed by external laws. Here we have liberal atomism: the negation of each one by all and of all by each produces an archipelago of solitudes that the ruling class passes off as egalitarianism. In these unfortunates, dependent on the futile limit that circumscribes a bit of matter or on the rank number just assigned to them, Gustave unmasks above all the centripetal movement of egotism, the radically malign preference of their determination. But *whom* is he describing? Is this another example of human nature stripped bare? That is highly doubtful, for two lines later we learn that "man is a traveler." Yet we cannot say that these sedentary types have fallen outside humanity, for right at the beginning of the paragraph, speaking expressly of them, Gustave states: "Everywhere you will find some men . . ." In brief, we encounter in these few lines four sorts of "human characters." First we have "you," the readers Flaubert is addressing; and then the author himself, who by an exclamation, "Oh yes!" and a present indicative in the first person, "I tell you," points discreetly to his existence. After that we have "*some* men" who are to be found everywhere, from north to south, east to west, who are therefore legion but cannot, nevertheless—the plural is partitive by design—constitute the totality of the human race; and, finally, "man," that thirsty traveler who is neither the object of a universal concept nor anyone in particular. He is in no way defined *in exteriority* by an essence or nature but guided by a *notion,* that is, by a knowledge that integrates in itself the internal temporalization of its object and is thus actualized only by being tem-

36. But if this is the case, it will be observed that Gustave has been careful to emphasize the absurdity, the uselessness of manual labor: why scatter unproductive sand on the fertile earth?

poralized. *Man* in this text is not reducible to the sum of traits common to the representatives of our species. He is at once an archetypal event and a certain drama that unfolds in each of us. A brief adventure: journey, thirst, quest, refusal, death. It is the nature of "man" to fix upon a goal and die in the attempt, utterly abandoned, before reaching it. Gustave asserts, moveover, against individualistic atomization, that man is a *demand of man*. Whatever he may be, he claims the *gift*, he claims it in his being—which is temporality—since he has created in himself, by his original choice of becoming a traveler, that terrible emptiness, that thirst, which the gift alone can assuage. Gustave repeats here that the fundamental bond between men is that of benefactor to beneficiary. In other words, the only human society is a feudal one. It is not a given, however: confronting the adventurer who dies without having seen the Promised Land, there are only *some* dehumanized men. And it is not stretching the text excessively to attribute this dehumanization to external forces, and quite specifically to bourgeois property. These nomads, trapped by the boundaries they have drawn on the earth around themselves, which they have chosen never to cross again, have become sedentary without even noticing. For them, the drama has come to a halt in the middle of the first act, when the physical time of possessed objects became a substitute for human temporalization. Thirst has disappeared along with their human vocation; they neither ask nor give, having lost their dissatisfaction without ever being satisfied.

The traveler himself dies each day; each day one pilgrim expires, another takes his place and his role: the Passion, the Death.[37] He is recruited, and will be recruited, from among those "happy few" for whom Gustave now speaks—he is even extravagantly polite (a rare occurrence in his case), pretending that his readers are participants in this process: "wherever *you* go . . . *you* cannot take a step . . ." In our societies the human adventure still takes place, but *marginally*. All those statues of flesh, the bourgeoisie, are the products if not of their products at least of their relations to production. Enclosed in the time of reification, they are only the debasement—by bourgeois property and the institutions that preserve it—of Man on the cross, the ex-

---

37. The Christian origins of the apologue are quite obvious. The death of the traveler is certainly not equal to the Redemption. Nonetheless, he dies reaffirming the human adventure against the tyrannical concept of "human nature." Through him the tradition "man" is preserved and transmitted. In truth, this tragic character, for whom the adventure of existence constitutes reality, is very close to Pascalian man, that nonconceptualizable become-being who has a history and not an essence.

hausted traveler who asks for water and instead is heaped with gall. The struggle for life is not represented in this parable; the property owner does not give gifts but neither does he steal, too absorbed in jealously guarding his own goods to envy what others have or to desire their goods for himself. However, no one thinks of wronging the traveler: people scarcely hear his request and in all likelihood scarcely understand it; they simply let him die—that's perfectly normal, for in these human societies man does not exist. Flaubert seems to have chosen this *social* myth (I have spoken of the Christian influence, we mustn't neglect Rousseau's) quite deliberately to avoid dealing with his burning shame or, better, to be delivered from it by a change of perspective.

Indeed, these pages were written in April 1838, that is, during the Easter vacation between two school trimesters, the first rightly considered the most grueling of the year, the second seemingly irreparable because by then the chips are down and a student can reap only what he has sown. Doubtless Gustave was thinking of the school he had just left, to which he would return. These *Agonies* are the school years, forever beginning again with the eternal return of autumn; the dead man is a schoolboy, he dies in July in order to be reborn in October and set out once more on the road to his Calvary. And the dehumanized men, stubborn in their circular refusal, are certainly the schoolchildren, cleaving to their particular determinations, to their interests, that is, to their class ranking. All of them, moreover, are in danger and on the defensive; they want to guard rather than conquer, and social equilibrium results from the fact that they regard each other with mutual respect. They had set out, perhaps, on a long voyage but were stopped at the outset. Only an ill-adapted child, a lost soul who groans at every composition, fascinated by the inert and formidable power of the mechanism that crushes him, can escape reification, and that only at the price of a long-drawn-out defeat, foreseen and assumed in unhappiness. He is superior to all his competitors in his very inferiority; poorly equipped for the competition, he begins once again all the archetypically shipwrecked days of man in the face of *some* little men made robots by their very knowledge, learned techniques, and class ranking that become their interest. Illuminated by the later works, *Rêve d'enfer* here yields to us its most prosaic and perhaps its most arcane meaning: it is a "Dialogue in Hell" between a prizewinner and a dunce. They despise each other and fight with each other, but both are innocent, equally victims of the system and of the paterfamilias, who made the first a soulless calculator and the

second a soul without *means*. In *Agonies*, the adolescent is less generous to his comrades: the Iron Duke, suffering at not suffering, was not
without grandeur; he has been replaced by a legion of children, petty
owners of petty knowledge. All victims, of course, but not at all innocent—they take a certain amount of pleasure in allowing themselves
to be dehumanized. Who, then, compels them to enclose themselves
so smugly in the determination imposed on them? Confronted by
them, Satan—poor devil—holds up his head and becomes Man,
meaning the martyr of humanity.

From the time he wrote *Rêve d'enfer* until he completed *Agonies*,
then, Gustave seems to have been groping toward a compensatory vision of the world whose very desolation would be consoling: man is
perverted by society, his comrades are the miserable products of a
bourgeois order; they are monsters while Gustave himself, protected
by fortunate incapacities, becomes Man as he was, as he is *sub specie
aeternitatis*, as he might be if society did not attempt to integrate him.
His terrible destiny prevents him from bending to the rule and from
being made into a robot; his providential failures have value as signs:
they remind him that quality as such, far from *manifesting itself* in the
world of quantity, refuses to be represented in that context, even *or-
dinally*.[38] At the end of this process, the adolescent, certain of his intrinsic value, would effortlessly give up excelling in competitions
which are *on principle* devoid of meaning. He would be liberated.

But this is not the case: the younger son will never go any further;
in *Agonies* itself and in the later works he returns to the idea of "human nature," to misanthropy, to absolute pessimism. He is simply
put together in such a way that he will never resign himself to doing
mediocre schoolwork: he cannot let go. Therefore, grumbling and
cursing at teachers and fellow students, he cannot help valuing that
first place so vainly coveted, even if a surreptitiously deliberate "laziness" continually sabotages his work. In *Ivre et Mort*, finished two
months after *Agonies*, he tries to take account of his double attitude
(scholarly laurels are contemptible because I do not win them—first
prizes and honorable mentions have an absolute value because my
heart is broken when they are denied me). Here he is, constructing
with his own hands for the hundredth time the trap of anguish and

38. It is obvious that this theory, constructed to suit his cause, is almost entirely
false. Especially insofar as the relations between quantity and quality are concerned,
which are conceived here as mutually exclusive—that is, by analytic reason—when
their antinomy is in fact dialectic. In any case, Gustave tried for a time to substitute
history for nature.

horror that he is going to fall into for the hundredth time. Indeed, this story seems to be a mediation between his second conception of human relations and his third, which we shall explicate below.[39]

Single combat is again represented here as a fundamental human relationship. This direct and aristocratic confrontation (one gives one's life in order to *take* the other's) is the only feudal relationship Gustave values equally with that of the gift and homage, imagining it to be their negative.[40] Here we have evidence that the archaic conception of his first school years never really left him. Enriched by his experience of competitive structures, however, he attempts to base the fight to the death on bourgeois competition. This is the final round, the result of numerous *trials;* these relations remain indirect and common but are nonetheless indispensable, for they are what will gradually transform the two best competitors into rivals and pit them against one another in a merciless struggle where each will defend his honor as *new-made aristocrat.* In brief, the "standoff" of the two brothers is always the subject of the narrative, but instead of presenting it as the conclusion of an a priori antagonism—that is, anterior to competitive seriality—Gustave reverses the order of the terms and presents it strictly as the ultimate result of a competitive circularity in which the two adversaries have figured for many years without knowing each other, or at least without recognizing their *quality.* We might say that, this time, quality is born of quantity.

Hughes and Rymbault are two drinkers, "the most intrepid drinkers in the region." Everyone at the club "respects them and views them with admiration as illustrious and proven celebrities." Their admirers—namely the crowd of witnesses who validate their fame—*all* began as their rivals: "no defeat had tainted their fame, and when their drinking companions were stretched out on the floor, they would leave, shrugging their shoulders in pity for such poor human nature." We see that in this passage Gustave could not help emphasizing, contrary to his previous assertion, the *inborn* aristocracy of the two princes of the bottle: they are born drinkers, which immediately places them above human nature; after every victory they despise human ntaure because it constitutes the negative determination of the vanquished. This is archaic feudalism returned with a vengeance; if they were

39. This is obviously a matter of dialectic mediation, and not diachronic: the three images of man had coexisted for many years.

40. Historically it is the reverse: the "vassal-lord" bond was born of a permanent state of war (hot or cold) which pitted the possessors of horses against each other in a period when money tended to disappear.

nothing more, Hughes and Rymbault would be the useless doubles of Garcia and François.

But there is a new twist: serial circularity ensures that each of the two rivals is indirectly conditioned by the victories of the other. Without ever confronting each other, they have won all the trials and have succeeded in drinking all the others under the table. In this narrative, as at school, purely administrative considerations of ranking have conventionally defined the limits of the competition: it is a local championship, and there is nothing to suggest that Rymbault or Hughes are national, much less world-class, drinkers; these *ex aequo* are determined *in exteriority*. To which we must add that the competition is in principle *quantitative*: ranking is determined by the quantity of alcohol imbibed, in other words, accumulation. This capacity to accumulate is reckoned for each competitor by an index that marks the maximum amount of pure alcohol absorbed on the day of his best contest. A *restricting* index for all those eliminated but not for the finalists, who must beat their own records. For Hughes and Rymbault, whom no one has defeated, it is presented as a *determinatioon to surpass;* it manifests their objective being or essence to the extent that this essence is related to *what they have been.* On the other hand, insofar as it is presented as a *score to beat,* it becomes their being-in-danger-in-the-world, their interest. The two record-breakers are here reduced to two discrete quantities and the uncertain possibility of increasing them. In principle their interest is threatened by everyone, but since they have triumphed in the trials, and the administrative division artificially isolates them from more talented or more fortunate champions who may be found in other provinces, each of them becomes a mortal danger to the other. This is enough to stimulate mutual hatred: "Taciturn and gloomy, they were there [in the same club every evening] like two enemies, mutually jealous of their strengths and their renown." They are not merely miserable human beings: their "gigantic stomachs" have made them enemies *from birth,* over and beyond the wretched masses. But indirect conditioning and competition were necessary to actualize their enmity: every victory carried off by one in the absence of and perhaps unknown to the other contributed to bringing them closer to the inevitable conflict; without these *institutional* tournaments they would never have known each other, or at least they would have been limited to drinking *for pleasure.* We can discern here a new twist: *blood* demands such confrontation from the first day, but it would not have taken place without a competitive seriality which, without ever setting them against each other, compels them indirectly

51

to internalize their antagonism. In the end, they must fight; fear restrains them, hatred—induced hatred [41]—incites them:

> Pushed by vanity and fame, they addressed to each other the bloodiest and most terrible challenge: single combat in a closed field, with equal weapons, in which the vanquished would remain on the spot to proclaim the triumph of his vanquisher. It was a challenge inspired by rage, the battle would be relentless, long . . . without rest or respite; each was ready to die on the spot, and the honor and pleasure of the victory would be total. For it was a question of which of the two could drink the most.

In this combat—which he intends to be grotesque and Homeric—Gustave is going to kill his brother for the second time. He takes care, in fact, to characterize the two drinkers by their styles of life and their strategies. Rymbault has "something nervous and cunning about him; always on the defensive, he employs a clever strategy of moderation." Hughes has "bulging eyes, strength, and stupidity; [he is] full of impetuousness and anger." The former drinks like a brainy type, rationally, the way Achille worked at school; in Hughes we recognize Djalioh's stupidity but also Gustave's angry passions. And it is passion that wins: Rymbault falls down *drunk and dead*—a significant play on words: on his own, perhaps, the powerful contestant might collapse *dead drunk*. But we must confess that Hughes gives him a little help in dying:

> He drank [a last bottle] in one gulp, then raised himself up to his full height, broke the table with a kick, and threw the carafe at Rymbault's head: "Eat," he said with pride. The blood burst out and ran down their clothes like wine. Rymbault fell to the ground with horrible gasps, he was dying. "Now drink," Hughes went on . . . He put his knee on Rymbault's chest and unlocked his jaws with his hands; he forced the dying man to drink again.

Legitimate victory or murder? Impossible to determine; Gustave did not note Rymbault's collapse except by this cry from Hughes, unmotivated by any context: "You're backing out," he says to Rymbault, full of anger. Again Gustave adds that "this insult was washed away by a bottle of rum." So the reader is left in doubt, as if the impetuous younger brother had killed his older brother by a kind of deferential terror for want of the audacity—so imbued is he with his own in-

---

41. It is not provoked by *action*—mutual bad behavior—because they are alone, like atoms, and separate from each other: this hatred is simply at one with their *objective being* and grows with each of their triumphs.

feriority—to show him vanquished. He had begun, however, with the purpose of making him admit his defeat: indeed, the challenge contains a proviso that Gustave deliberately notes: "The vanquished would remain on the spot to proclaim the triumph of his vanquisher." Sadism here is pushed so far that the two men, rather than publicly admit their defeat—should it take place—are resolved, both of them, to "die on the spot." Lose life rather than lose face. It was in Hughes's interest that Rymbault should live at least a few hours to be acknowledged as vanquished *coram populi;* the winner's hatred would have been more fully satisfied had he been able to enjoy his adversary's humiliation. A cadaver can *bear witness* but not *proclaim;* by his stupid violence Hughes has doomed himself to dissatisfaction, as the end of the narrative makes clear: "He abused the cadaver again by accompanying every shovelful of earth thrown on it with an insult and a grim joke." If he had won in earnest, we can be sure that the drunk would have exchanged this suffocating, unslaked hatred for calm contempt, and that he would have "shrugged his shoulders in pity for such poor human nature." Gustave has denied himself this pleasure because at the bottom of his heart he has remained just like poor Garcia; he knows very well that his brother is unbeatable—six years of failures at his own expense have taught him that. Indeed, he is really quite unconcerned with challenging him; on days of grim violence he dreams of killing him.[42]

Is Achille really the only one at issue? Doesn't this ambiguous ending indicate that the young author, going beyond the already rehashed theme of the enemy brothers, is attempting to express in this comic frame the more recent horror that scholarly competition *itself* inspires in him? On this statement, two observations can be made. The first is that competition—which now seems to be the fundamental relation of man to his peers—*actualizes hatred,* and that, as Hegel says, through the indirect and seemingly benign conflicts of scholarly combat, every consciousness *pursues the death of every other.* In every competitor there is a potential murderer. Rare are those who will carry out the act of murder, for the simple reason that most do not go beyond the trials; this does not mean that their rancor lacks ferocity,

---

42. An identical timidity is evident in the two stories, but it becomes displaced from one story to the other. In *La Peste,* Garcia fully recognizes his inferiority; but at the moment of having him kill his brother, Gustave loses his nerve—he cannot literally recount the murder. In *Ivre et Mort,* he wants to give himself the imaginary pleasure of vanquishing and humiliating Achille; but again he loses his nerve. This time, to avoid describing the inconceivable defeat, he finds the courage to slay him quite properly.

53

only that their vanquishers are still too numerous to become the individual objects of their abhorrence. Between the finalists, on the contrary, the tension is so strong that their desire to vanquish the adversary is equal in depth to the desire to kill him. I am not the one saying this; Gustave says it himself. In his eyes Achille is no longer the issue. Nor even Rymbault or Hughes. Any individual, moreover, whether he enters a competitive circuit voluntarily or is thrown into it, is to varying degrees—according to the stakes and the upshot— seized by the sadistic desire to vanquish in order to humiliate, or he may even be struck by murderous frenzy. Is it seriality, negating feudal hierarchy and reifying human relationships, that suppresses everything in man's heart that is not hatred? Or, man being wolf to man, is it the need to hate and to inflict suffering that has set up the competitive cycle because in this system he will be fully assuaged? Gustave does not settle the question in this story; let us simply say that, for him, human relations are all determined in exteriority except one, and that these external and serial relations seem to be a projection in the quantitative world of the unique bond of interiority, reciprocal hatred; for when all is said and done, every competitor, like it or not, pursues the death of the other.

What matters to us is that in *Ivre et Mort* the young author has more or less deliberately thrown into relief the importance his fellow students assumed in his eyes. It is significant that the feudal theme of *blood*, evoked for a moment—"gigantic stomachs"—immediately gives way to that of nobility *acquired* by victories achieved *in competitions*. The finalists are ennobled as such; competitive contests reveal their *quality* even while inflaming their rage and hatred. This is a renunciation of the archaic idea of a quality that exists from the first, which the teachers are duty-bound to recognize. Naturally you must be gifted, but *for a particular competition;* a "palpable fragrance," greatness of soul, dissatisfaction, or great desire are of no use here, they confer no merit: to be "the first drinker in the region" you must have a good stomach and know the rules of the game, nothing more. Properly understood: to obtain first prize in mathematics or in Latin composition you must have the appropriate aptitude; beyond that, your heart and soul—cold and base though they may be—are of little consequence. All are commoners at the outset; aristocracy is quantitative and measured by the number of prizes garnered. This conversion can have only one meaning: Gustave's classmates exist *for themselves*, he loses face in *their* eyes—they are no longer merely usurpers; above all they *have consciousness*, they rejoice in their triumphs and in the humiliations of their vanquished comrades. The terrible proviso of the challenge the two drinkers put to each other—that the vanquished should "remain on the spot to proclaim the triumph of his vanquisher"—appears in a new light when set against a passage from the *Mémoires:* "The instructor mocked my Latin verses [and] . . . my comrades looked at me, jeering." By their sadistic and intolerable proviso—each would rather die than conform to it—Hughes and Rymbault have simply imposed on the loser, in a refinement of hatred, what Gustave was subjected to many times a week. When the instructor returns the essays, this schoolboy, mad with pride, riveted by rank to his bench, hears the praise meted out to the best. He doesn't hear his own place announced at the beginning but rather Bouilhet's, who is first, Baudry's, who is second, and so forth. Before every name a moment of hope, it's my turn, then disappointment; third: des Hogues; when at last the teacher comes to Gustave, ninth, the praise is exhausted, the reproofs begin. Gustave himself admits his inferiority; not by his voice but by his essay, criticized amidst "jeers," which becomes his reality: nonsense, false sense, countersense, solecisms, and barbarisms proclaimed in front of everyone as examples of *what not to do* are inscribed in his being—that being which he is in the eyes of others; he is defined by his failures. His vanquishers become his judges: he imagines he is seeing *them* "shrug their shoulders in scornful pity" when they hear the teacher reproach him for faults *they have not committed*—there it is, the perpetual comparison he has declared he can no longer tolerate. It happens again, ten times, twenty times every trimester; he awaits it, terrified, with just the right amount of hope to despair completely when it comes. On those days, surely, he hates the entire class—those in first place more than the others, obviously; but also those in last, for he envies their gross, carefree laziness, their stubborn indifference, their rebellious spirit, and is attracted to them by some unknown force, a heaviness of soul that frightens him.

One student among the rest deserves his abhorrence, a certain Bouilhet, Louis, who has the cheek to garner as many laurels in Gustave's class as Achille did nine years earlier in his. To this newcomer, to this "stranger from the outside," [43] everything comes easily; he triumphs while enjoying himself, even as the younger Flaubert imagines he is exerting himself for nothing: this very ease is an insult; where does he get it from since it isn't *inborn?* There are some sur-

43. He entered school in the seventh year.

geons in his family, but unknown; his father, employed in ambulance administration, became director of military hospitals under Napoleon. At the time of his death, at forty-five years of age, he had long since returned to civilian life and, in order to feed his family, had accepted the position of second steward at the château of Cany; employee, administrator, then domestic, the good man was certainly no intellectual—that much could be surmised. And yet his son gave himself the airs of the professional class; had he been born a Flaubert, the paterfamilias would have been proud of him; he would have loved a younger son like Bouilhet much more than Gustave, perhaps as much as Achille, for indeed the imposter claimed to be headed for a medical career. True, he did not excel at mathematics, but beyond that he would have been the pride of the most demanding father. In Latin he was the best; in Greek he showed such exceptional gifts that he was soon charged with a flattering task: Monsieur Jourdain [44] asked him to tutor the students who were not up to the class average, and soon he was tutoring Gustave himself. In history—which, starting in 1835, Gustave claimed as his domain—the steward's son had the cheek to distinguish himself. At least to begin with. When the younger Flaubert later achieved first place, it was with a great struggle and against adversaries of whom Louis was not the least formidable. If Louis had been a boy of only minor intellect, agile and flexible but without scope or depth, that would have been only half bad—Gustave could have caught up out of contempt. But the situation was much worse. Louis was raised by his mother, Clarisse, the widow Bouilhet, who was entrusted by the Lords of Cany with writing out compliments in verse to welcome visitors—especially when these were priests. She gave her son a taste for writing verse, and he became the official poet of his institution—on solemn occasions they had recourse to his talent. In the tenth year Bouilhet weakened a bit—he argued with Monsieur Jourdain. But that did not last long; he got himself removed from Jourdain's pension and placed in another, where, his biographer tells us, "the social level was higher." [45] This symbolic "elevation," which must have been ruinous for the poetess, had a splendid effect on the poet: the following year he won first prize in French.

If I am accused of inventing Gustave's animosity toward Louis, I will answer that it is indeed a matter of conjecture. I consider it likely

44. Louis was not a boarder at the *collège;* his mother had placed him in a private institution directed by Monsieur Jourdain.
45. Doctor André Finot, *Louis Bouilhet* (Paris, 1951; in the journal *Les Alcaloïdes*).

because it is the only satisfying solution to a small problem of literary history that the biographies mention in passing without ever bothering to resolve: Why did Flaubert and the Alter Ego—later so beloved—sit for five years in the same classes without forming any bond, even ignoring each other, when their homework and their compositions drew them both into perpetual confrontation? If I am told that they saw each other mostly during class hours, the one boarding at the school, the other at Monsieur Jourdain's, that simply introduces the element of chance and explains nothing at all. Is it so unusual for two students to be friends when one is a boarder and the other a day student? In social micro-organisms there is no such thing as chance; the group dynamic is born of internal tensions that are always *significant*, that is, *intentional*. This rule applies all the more rigorously in our case, where each of the two boys was bound to size the other up. Neither one was the kind of discreet, quiet student who goes through his years of school without drawing attention to himself. Gustave, as we shall see in this chapter, would surround himself with a loud-mouthed gang, undoubtedly from the eighth term. Bouilhet was not alone either: his reputation as poet passed from the Jourdain pension to the school, and he ruled over a small group of adolescents who wrote or wanted to write—Pascal Mulot; Dumont, a future physician; Dupont-Delporte, a future member of parliament, and others. These boys formed a small literary brotherhood to which Gustave was never admitted and probably never invited. This reciprocity of rejection is all the more striking since the two classmates had friends in common such as Germain des Hogues, also a poet, and since in certain circumstances they shared a common attitude: Bouilhet's signature figures at the bottom of an open letter to the provost which Gustave no doubt drafted and which brought about the man's dismissal. Between Gustave and Louis, then, there had never been any outburst but an indifference so marked as to be inexplicable unless it is seen as the public and disguised expression of a certain hostility.

Raised in piety by his mother and aunt, placed by them in a religiously right-thinking institution and then, at his request, in another even more so,[46] Louis, if no longer devout, remained at the very least a believing and practicing Catholic. Dissatisfied, certainly—like Gustave and the "extravagants" who surrounded him—but poor, offended at being the son of a superior domestic and at living, at least in part, if not on charity in any case on the generosity of his father's for-

---

46. "A more elevated social level" meant, at the time, "in a more Catholic milieu."

mer masters,[47] he evidenced at this time a *seriousness* that sprang from his education and from the desire to ensure his material independence as soon as possible. The deafening racket of Gustave's gang, the willed vulgarity of the "extravagants," could only annoy him, shock his sense of decorum. Good boy that he was, shy and reserved, he hadn't the slightest desire to attain "the sublime below" by cultivating the "passions that degrade"; this sort of exercise was reserved for the rich kids who wanted to make symbolic plunges without forfeiting their class status. Bouilhet, on the contrary, looked to his studies to raise him above his condition and give him access to the upper reaches of the middle classes where Flaubert was already situated by birth. A Lamartinian, when Gustave claimed to be Byronic and Rabelaisian, Louis by no means thought that scholarly success and poetic inspiration were incompatible; indeed, he saw the one as a means of assuring himself a livelihood that would allow him to give himself over to the other. Besides, he was the eldest; Clarisse had not provided him with a brother—he had two younger sisters. Hence a certain self-assurance hidden beneath his shyness and his slightly languid docility. He would change, we know, would lose his faith, would become an outspoken republican. But it is hard to see how, during his years at school, this studious and conformist pupil could have felt anything for Gustave but a moderate aversion and a good deal of mistrust. Gustave himself vacillated at this period between the "belief in nothing" and a Byronic rebellion against God. A single constant: both of these extreme attitudes led him to make mincemeat of the priests. One of his letters has already revealed this to us: in it he tells Ernest how he persecuted a "student from Eudes's place." Father Eudes was a priest and directed an institution very much like Monsieur Jourdain's. "I began by saying that I was distinguished by my hatred of priests . . . I invented . . . the grossest and most absurd obscenities about the Abbé Eudes, the poor pious boy had the most astonished look on his face." He would certainly not have dared torment Louis in this way. But surely he had aimed indirectly at Louis— Louis and the other bigots in his class—and Bouilhet for his part would scarcely have appreciated this flaunted anticlericalism.

For Gustave, this "teacher's pet" was simply a thief. When he wrote *Bibliomanie*, Bouilhet had been his classmate for two years. And we

47. Clarisse would not have been able to provide for her son's studies without the income kindly provided by the Montmorency, the lords of Cany, and by the first steward of the château.

have noted above the peculiarly precise portrait of Giacomo's rival: "Baptisto, who *for some time* had swept away from him . . . everything that seemed rare and old, Baptisto, whose renown he hated with an artist's hatred." Is this accidental? Mightn't these few words be a barely conscious allusion to the intruder who "for two years" had swept away all the honors and whom he detested *as an artist*, that is, to the second power since this usurper was doubled by a poet? Certainly Louis never stole anything from Gustave: the prizes he won would never have been awarded to Gustave in any case; if Clarisse's son had not done his last term in Rouen, the son of Achille-Cléophas would have had first honorable mention but not first prize. But the younger Flaubert did not forgive Louis for proving by his own example that one could be both a poet and first in the class, and that by direct consequence Gustave's own scholarly deficiencies did not necessarily have their source in his literary vocation. The little boy had nicely arranged things so that the immensity of his imagination was in itself a fatal gift which doomed him to the worst failures in the real and secular world: he was not lucky enough to find the appropriate metaphor, but he loved to think that "his giant's wings prevented him from walking." And here was a walking albatross. He even ran, and with stupefying velocity. Gustave is no longer a "vast bird of the seas," he is a sickly albatross. Or perhaps a sickly bird that has never flown. The good students who slog away and do not concern themselves with writing—one can despise them and disdain their victories. But such victories are given *qualitative value* when it is an artist who carries them off. How would Gustave henceforth compensate for his failures? We can gauge the intensity of his "artist's hatred" for the overly artistic Bouilhet by the depth of this new humiliation. One thing, in any case, seems certain: Gustave's fortunate rivals began to count in his eyes from the moment Louis entered the school.[48]

48. Surprisingly, these two boys, so ill disposed toward one another, were to become close friends beginning in 1846. We shall return at leisure to this friendship. Here we merely note the circumstances that made their rapprochement possible. In August 1843, Louis Bouilhet, interning at the Hôtel-Dieu *in the service of Achille-Cléophas*, was stripped of his duties and crossed off the list of students for having gone on strike with his comrades (demands: wine with dinner, the right to stay out all night when they were not on duty). Rightly or wrongly, Louis was considered the leader and was the only one of the four rebels punished by the administration (the three others, without being officially reintegrated, found work in the Saint-Yon asylum), who was expelled. This was not displeasing to Gustave, who had gotten himself expelled from school in 1840: the Lamartinian angel had rebelled, his white plumage had turned black. What must have charmed the bitter younger son was that the rebellion was made in the paterfamilias's service. If he had feared that Bouilhet would become Achille-Cléophas's fa-

At that time we see emerging in his works a third image of man and human relations. If the commoners exist in themselves and for themselves, if they are neither Achille's agents nor foolish victims of the competitive system, competition as an inhuman process disappears, in Gustave's view, and inhumanity becomes a basic trait of human na-

---

vorite disciple, he was reassured. Furthermore, the chief surgeon, had he wished to do so, could have avoided the expulsion of his student or made such punishment temporary; he did nothing of the sort, proof that he did not dote on this fellow who scrawled verses wherever he happened to be, "during a surgical operation, while helping to tie off an artery" (in the *Préface aux Dernières Chansons*). Gustave was delighted—the passive revenge of resentment—to learn that *another* was flouting his black lord, and medicine as well. Six months later, moreover, in January 1844, the unloved son of Doctor Flaubert began his solitary strike against his father, entering neurosis the way one enters a convent. Louis Bouilhet, however, gave lessons for a living: this is what came of the brilliant medical career he was counting on and which Gustave had envied in advance.

Doctor Flaubert died on 15 January, 1846. As we shall see, this had such a beneficial effect on Gustave that—by his own admission—he thought it had freed him from his neurosis. One cannot imagine better circumstances in which to reestablish contact with a former classmate who had also been the victim of the deceased's authoritarianism. Indeed, Bouilhet came to the funeral. They met again at the cemetery. In his autobiography, the Alter Ego makes this significant connection: "Death of Dr. Flaubert, my relationship with Gustave."

Gustave mentions Louis for the first time in August 1842 in a letter to the Muse. At this period they had already formed close ties. But the passage that concerns the future Alter Ego allows us to understand clearly the other reasons that led Flaubert to change his principled aversion into friendship. "He is," he says, "*a poor boy who gives lessons here for a living* and who is a poet, a *real poet* who does superb and charming things and *who will remain unknown* because he is lacking two things: bread and time" (15 August 1846; *Correspondance* 1:255). The transformation of feelings has been preceded by a change in the objective relations between the two men: Gustave *has his time to himself*, he can live without doing anything. His father had certainly given Achille the greater advantage and carried the curse of the younger son to the very end; Gustave was nonetheless an heir, he had property and could live as an aristocrat, namely, as a writer; during this time the first in the class had become a poor wretch, a beggar—he was lost. But let us not attribute to Gustave the base satisfaction of being a rich man in the presence of a humiliated prizewinner. Let us say rather that he understood the meaning of the schoolboy Bouilhet's efforts: for this poor child, to fight against poverty by deeming himself coopted from the seventh term by the professional class was to battle for poetry. What delighted Flaubert's pessimism in 1846 is that this zeal was superbly futile: Louis, first in everything but victim of Achille-Cléophas, would never be free of penury. He would not make one penny from all those accumulated prizes, hence not one hour of leisure. He was lost in advance, *like Gustave: Fatum*, relentlessly set against the only legitimate desire—to "make Art"—promised them the same future of despair. A mediocre pupil, a poor student wounded each day by the boundless superiority of fools, the younger Flaubert son opted for illness, black quietism, sequestration; in 1846 he was far from sure he had made the right choice. And here was Bouilhet, timid, unstable, a bit too nonchalant, who in school nonetheless chose voluntarism; he descended into the base arena of "the struggle for life," fought everyone, left victorious: he did *what he wanted*, quite the opposite to Gustave, *and afterward?* He would remain unknown. The

ture. Man will be *in essence* the being who seeks the death of man, and this will result in a universal confrontation which can take the form of general competition or single combat but in any event merely serves to translate the terrible aggression that characterizes our species. In 1840 Gustave had just gotten himself expelled from school—alone at

---

hermit of Croisset prophesies. With sado-masochistic: *Schadenfreude,* but without rancor or meanness: they are lost, both of them, the poor wretch who lives by giving lessons and the landowner who lives in the country busying himself with literature; neither will produce work of value. One has no time, the other has too much; they will die, and it is even excessive to say that the world will forget them for it will never have known them in the first place. Destiny clearly pursues Louis with special ferocity: this suspect feature of Gustave's prophecy would imply that he is not entirely innocent, as the general tone of his letter makes clear as well (why doesn't he write: "He is a poet, a true poet, who writes superb and charming things and who runs the risk of remaining unknown . . ."? Why begin with "He is a poor boy"? Why make himself superior to Louis in the knowledge of his final destiny, and why sum up with an epitaph a life that has not yet been lived?). The most atrocious thing, in fact, is not so much to lack talent as to have it and lack the time to use it. But Gustave's thought surely goes deeper. Indeed, this is the period when he claims to write for himself alone and asserts that he will be buried with his manuscripts; around the same time he declares that the only worthwhile success is that which one achieves in front of one's mirror. It would seem logical, in sum, that he should not pity his new friend the permanent obscurity that threatens him. Indeed, according to Gustave, poverty will prevent Louis from attaining glory because it will prevent him from writing good poetry. At first, though he will still be capable of brilliant poetry, the business of earning his bread will deprive him of leisure. Later, his material wants will deprive him of taste. After ten years of this miserable life, he will have lost even the possibility of writing. Art will have begun as a beautiful dream, then have become a torture of Tantalus, then something forbidden, then an object of indifference, and finally, toward the end of his life, a rending regret. Poverty *degrades:* this is Flaubert's secret thought, the reason for his compassion for the "poor boy."

Certainly Gustave believes he is in the same boat: as a property owner he is suffocating in leisure; he contemplates "his void," bored to death, sure of nothing except his long patience. Who, then, is to be pitied most? Gustave claims to be undecided: two armchairs in Hell, that's all. And yet this envious young man no longer envied Bouilhet (whose work was printed and performed before his); he never held it against Louis for "shooting down" the first *Saint Antoine,* when he would never forgive Maxime and consequently always sought his critical opinion. Gustave preferred being in his own shoes: that long patience, which is perhaps genius after all, he had *the means to put into practice.* And since, in spite of rhetorical prudence—"Oh, let us not slander this milk of the strong"—he believes that poverty is degrading, it is therefore up to him to prevent his friend from degrading himself. The only relationship he can have with the former prizewinner—one that goes deeper than their reciprocal literary difficulties—is that of the gift. Not the gift of money—Bouilhet does not ask him for anything, or perhaps only for a loan on occasion—but that weekly gift of comfort, of leisure, which is indispensable to creative activity, to dreaming. Every week the Alter Ego will be able to share the pleasures of Croisset, to forget the sordid realities of daily life, to steep himself in the "artist's" life; from it he will draw the courage necessary to endure the weekdays and to write, even at the end of exhausting and depressing labor, even if it should cut into his sleep. Beginning with this, as we shall see, Gustave takes charge—at least

last; the "comparison" was at an end. But he still felt his shame too keenly to forget. He scrawls a note in his journals—we shall examine it later in detail—that bears witness to his pain. The idea is simple: from Sirius's cosmic point of view, vices and virtues cancel each other out. Gustave proceeds with his demonstration by stages. Here is the first stage: "we are not shocked by two young dogs fighting, by two children hitting each other, by a spider eating a fly—we kill an insect without a second thought." Second stage: "Climb up a tower high enough . . . that people appear to be very small; once up there, if you should see one man kill another, you will scarcely be affected by it." Third stage: "A giant watches the Myrmidons." What are they doing? Naturally they are cutting each other's throats. "And how can this affect the giant"? We shall not dwell here on this lacerated soul's attempt to raise himself to the sublime point of indifference; what interests us is that human beings in this apologue have no aim other than to destroy each other. Flaubert returns to this in 1842: the hero of *Novembre*, he tells us, has known the worst moral suffering. We know nothing about this but, contrary to conventional metaphors, he does not fall over a precipice but perches on a peak; unhappiness, if great enough, endows everything that is not itself with indifference: "From the height of these summits the earth disappears, along with *everything you have torn yourself away from.*" [49] It is understood that there is no solidarity between men; the only reciprocity is antagonism. The aims of the species are common not because all are bound together in the same enterprise but because those aims set all against one and one against all—every man for himself.

As for the goods of this world, no one can acquire them without

---

in appearance. He advises, he orders, he scolds. This is what fills him with complacency. "Monseigneur" is promoted to the rank of Alter Ego, but he, Gustave, will never be his friend's alter ego. To summarize: in the system of bourgeois competition as they both experienced it at school, Bouilhet could be only Gustave's enemy; in the feudal system Gustave had constructed since childhood, only a vassal. Starting here, of course, the process reverses itself, and the false lord, as we shall see, will live secretly in dependence on his liege—as will be the case in Gustave's relations with Laporte. And then the two former classmates will discover indisputable affinities, which competitive seriality has concealed from them. But the fundamental relation that allows the younger Flaubert son to love the eldest of the Bouilhets is—beyond the egalitarianism of suitability—the difference in resources and way of life that the wealthier of the two would experience, improbably, as an excess of his vital forces, and consequently, since he uses it to give courage to the poorer, as the permanent actualization of his generosity. Gustave needed nothing less than this to soothe his wounded pride: his former vanquisher had become his "man."

49. My italics.

"tearing them away" from their former owner, or keep them without putting to death those who covet them; but sooner or later a newcomer, luckier or meaner, will tear them away in turn, kill, and flee, chased by the pack that moves in once more for the kill. Rousseau dies, followed by his Friday—noble-savage-ruined-by-society; utilitarian man, heir to his *interest*, is not slow to follow. And the origin of aggression is not even need (we realize that Gustave is speaking of bourgeois children, the only kind he knows), but rather the will to power. When two representatives of the human species encounter each other, each wants to rob, humiliate, enslave the other and then, having used him as an inert and docile object, kill him. Why? Because we are made that way: fighting cocks, bloodthirsty tigers. In these moods, the lacerated son of the Hôtel-Dieu, green with fear and rage, sees his future assassin or future victim in any classmate who approaches him. "It's him or me!" In theory. In fact, it will be *him*. Always *him*. Passive and masochistic, enclosed in his oracular pessimism, Gustave hates the other in advance, unable to prevent himself, and we know why, from seeing in him the *primacy of the Other*. For the younger Flaubert son, a schoolboy who looks at him is necessarily the aggressor. And the aggressor necessarily has the advantage: he must conquer. Gustave is mean, he knows it, he says so, but it is the meanness of the victim: he detests the world but does not believe he can change anything. Thus, for him, these permanent aggressions never end in a fair fight but in a symbolic murder where he is the victim. He is provoked, he is attacked, he is harrassed, he is not even on guard when he is thrown to the ground, stepped on, and then *eaten*. This is no metaphor but a waking nightmare that obsesses him. By rationalizing, one arrives at this: man is a cannibal. It is not hunger that drives him to eat his fellow man or some religious imperative: pride is carnivorous, it is not satisfied with vanquishing, not even with cutting the throat of the vanquished; it wants to inflict the worst pain and absolute humiliation on them—the aggressor does his victim the supreme injury of gorging on him and shitting him out. And of course this black oneirism, presented in such a form, can seem comic. But Gustave is not being rational: he is simply living in terror.

Take a look at the horrifying dreams he has at school: "My door opened, they entered: there were perhaps seven or eight of them, all had steel blades between their teeth . . . They moved together in a circle around my cradle, their teeth began clicking and it was horrible . . . They took off all my clothes and all of these were bloody; they started eating, and the bread they broke gushed blood that fell drop by drop . . . When they were no longer there, everything they had touched . . . was reddened by them. I had a taste of bitterness in my heart, and it seemed that I had eaten flesh."[50] Later we shall study the details of this dream and try to give it a general interpretation, although it has neither the freshness nor the authenticity of those dreams we remember upon waking or on the analyst's couch. Gustave reconstructed and rationalized it by linking it, there is no doubt, to a memory dating from his first years of school: so deeply had this nightmare shaken him at the time[51] that he could evoke it long afterward with relative precision, preserving, uncannily, a certain irrationality in it. The theme of castration is immediately striking, and we shall speak of it again. But for the moment we must emphasize that the theme of cannibalism is undeniably present. Here, first of all, we find "men with knives between their teeth" advancing, images of real bolsheviks according to the bourgeois myth. Suddenly their jaws are clicking, the castrating blades disappear. Blood runs everywhere, they look at the infant "with huge staring eyes without eyelids," take off his clothes, strip bare his little unbruised but bleeding body, and start eating bread, which they *break* rather than slice (the sexual symbol is clear but also the religious one: "This is my body, this is my blood"). And *the bread is bleeding:* it is the infant they are eating; the dreamer is immediately placed in the category of food; *he* is the bread and will be fed to the convivial company. The feast over, the guests "begin laughing like the death rattle of a dying man" and go away. We will have noted the association of three themes: a fixed look directed at Gustave, the bloody meal for which he is the food, and laughter. The look is *aggression*, it transforms the child into the sacramental host; after the black mass, the *dreaded* laughter echoes. When the bearded men have departed, everything is reversed: the cannibals' victim finds that he is a cannibal himself: "It seemed to me that I had eaten flesh."

In short, it is as though—whatever the other oneiric motivations— the sadistic cannibalism (I eat of man) were introduced here by the masochistic cannibalism (they eat me) and as its response. We notice that Gustave leaves the actual moment of sadism shrouded in silence. He has seen the bread bleed, and a voice whispered to him: "This is your body." But when it is his turn to eat, he is not there: he admits *being subject to the consequences* of his cannibalism and finding a taste of

50. *Mémoires d'un fou*, chapter 4.
51. "They were dreadful visions, enough to make you mad with terror." Ibid.

flesh in his mouth, but not to experiencing it directly and ordering the feast. He has nothing to do with it; he doesn't remember a thing: it *seems* to him that he has tasted his fellow man, but he does not know if this presumption is based on the horrible taste he has at the back of his throat or, in spite of everything, on an uncertain memory. A futile precaution: our dreams have no authors other than ourselves. No one—but himself—could force Gustave to fill himself with this sweetish taste, or to interpret it as he did. Temptation or revenge, his desire is *gratified*.

He betrays himself, moreover, a little later. His notes from 1840 inform us that this oneiric theme spills out beyond the consciousness of the sleeper and figures among the diurnal objects of his ruminations. He writes, in fact:[52] "The marquis de Sade forgot two things: cannibalism and wild beasts, which proves that the greatest men are still small, and above all he should have ridiculed vice as well, something he did not do, and here he is at fault." These two reproaches are not connected. But the obvious sincerity of the second[53] suffices to guarantee that of the first. No; in a mood to demolish his idols, Flaubert did not seek, in the abstract, perversions missing from the catalogue; the omission of cannibalism immediately comes to mind. Of course it involves one of his familiar fantasies, and we shall find him once again dreaming of it at the slaughterhouses in Quimper:

> At that moment I had the idea of some terrifying and enormous city, like a Babylon or Babel of cannibals, where there would be slaughterhouses for men; and I tried to retrieve something of human agony in those cut throats that howled and bled. I imagined a herd of slaves led there, ropes around their necks and knotted to irons, to feed the masters who ate them at ivory tables, wiping their lips with purple napkins. Would their bearing be more dejected, their eyes sadder, their appeals more rending?

His pity for the beasts—he professes to prefer them to men—provokes this sadistic revery. But the motivation is superficial. If he had wanted to say, in short, "And what if such a thing were done to you?" he

---

52. *Souvenirs*, pp. 72–73.
53. The systematic demoralization of humanity, according to Flaubert, must begin by a reversal of values: it will be shown that vice in its perpetually unsatisfied, gaping anxiety is superior to virtue. But in a second moment one will rise to the sublime point from which this superiority seems laughable because vices themselves are human and finite. This is what Sade did not do. Gustave condemns him because, unlike Byron and Rabelais, he did not *laugh in the face of humanity*—which the young author has sworn to do.

would have taken care to send to their deaths the powerful of this world, or herds of the well-fattened bourgeoisie. He does nothing of the kind and delights in imagining cannibalism in luxury. Ivory tables, purple napkins: it is the rich who take sensual pleasure in eating the poor.

In the note on de Sade, it will have been noticed that Gustave puts cannibalism and "wild beasts" on the same level, as if he were saying to us: if it repulses you to eat your enemy, you can always throw him to the beasts. What is really at issue is a more complex game of mirrors: man being a carnivore, it is a perverse and, for Gustave, enchanting idea to reverse the roles and have him devoured by beasts. On condition that it be done on a command that is still human but has come from on high. In his dreams, is he leaning like an emperor, over the arena where Bouilhet is being torn to pieces by tigers? In any case, the "man-animal" relationship endlessly reverses itself. Sometimes, as at the slaughterhouse, the devourer is man par excellence, the Aristocrat, and the object-to-be-devoured is sadistically debased to the condition of an edible beast; sometimes it is man who will be eaten, a great-hearted victim, throbbing and terrorized; his sacrificers are then disguised as carnivorous animals. In *Agonies*, a traveler—yet another—"walks through the great deserts of Africa." He takes a shortcut, "a path filled with serpents and wild beasts." In the middle of the path "appears . . . an enormous rock. He must . . . try to scale it." Hard work. The man "is pouring sweat, his hands grasp convulsively at every blade of grass . . . But the grass slips and he falls back discouraged." He renews his efforts many times—in vain; he curses God, he blasphemes. He girds himself one last time, he prays.

> He is climbing, he is advancing, he seems to see the smiling face
> of some angel who is calling to him, then suddenly everything
> changes . . . Ghastly vision, a serpent is going to strike him . . .
> He falls backward. What can he do now . . . He was afraid of the
> wild beasts. "And night is falling," he said, "I am ill, tigers will
> come and tear me apart." For a long time he expected someone
> to come and help him, but the tigers came, tore him apart, and
> drank his blood.

Curiously, the moral of this tale, the author tells us, concerns lovers of freedom: "And so I say to you, it is the same with you others who want to conquer freedom . . . You wait for someone to help you . . . but the tigers will come, will tear you apart and drink your blood." In fact, the poor exhausted traveler sets no other aim for himself than to reach "the nearest hut . . . which is four miles away," in order to rest, care for his wounds, and satisfy his hunger. Certainly Gustave may have wanted to symbolize his mystic quest for God, always in vain, always begun anew; he may have tried to show the change of perspective that makes him see the Prince of Darkness on the summit the moment he reaches it, and transforms the ascent into a downfall. This is all the more obvious since once again we are encountering Gustave's inner space and its absolute vertical. But beneath the explicit meaning of the parable another meaning can be divined, and the futile efforts of the traveler must remind us of those efforts made with every assignment, every composition, by our schoolboy Sisyphus. Look at it this way: in the beginning, if the poor man wants to hoist himself up to the summit of the rock that blocks his way, it is in order to reach the hut where he will find care, shelter; such is the real and immediate objective—to climb up in order to return home; to start with, Gustave seeks first place because he knows no other means of returning to paternal favor, and not for the pleasure of triumphing over his twenty-four classmates. He makes the attempt, fails, begins again—a nauseating recurrence of competitions. There is a war inside him between his increasingly desperate determination and a secret force that drags him down, making the rock smoother and the grass more slippery; his psychosomatic passivities resist Flaubert ambition, and every time the result is bewilderment, vertigo, toppling. If at first it was only a matter of reaching the hut as quickly as possible, the motive for scaling the rock is transformed to the degree that Gustave loses his strength: the return home becomes the more distant objective; another appears more immediate, more urgent—escaping the wild beasts. The modification comes only from his fatigue and from the wounds he has sustained from his repeated falls. Weakened, incapable of defending himself, he still demands rest and the safety of the inaccessible hut, but the beasts of prey—at the outset an almost negligible danger—gradually become the sole object of his concern. He divines these invisible and mortal presences, he knows they are lying in wait: delighted witnesses to his futile efforts, his classmates await his ultimate toppling. Then the great beasts will rouse themselves—first, Bouilhet; second, Baudry—and will come to sniff out their future lunch at leisure. Gustave has cleverly contrived his apologue: salvation, he confides to us at this moment, can come only from *another*. Meaning: I have lost the possibility of saving myself; I have done what I could—there was a narrow path upward, the only way out, I *was not capable* of climbing it; in this sense I *do not deserve* to be saved. If the good Samaritan were to turn up, if he were to hold out his hand to me, that would be pure generosity. But Gustave is careful to add that there is not a chance that Godot, if he exists, travels this unfrequented path. Impotent, paralyzed, guilty, the adolescent is gripped by frenzied terror beneath the glowing eyes of the nocturnal beasts, like the infant in his nightmare.

The most characteristic features of dream symbolism have been transferred to the parable unmodified: the spatial locale (Gustave is under his persecuters), the position of the body (in both cases he is lying on his back), the impotence (what can a newborn do? or a severely wounded man?), the *others'* sadistic expectation (the stares of the bearded men, the greed of the carnivores), and finally the atrocious suffering (he is eaten alive). These constants allow us to conclude that it is all the same for Gustave whether he is devoured by men or beasts, because in his nightmares—sleeping or waking—the beasts are men. His defensive sadism is induced; what comes first is the awful conviction that he is being eaten alive, and quite raw. Suddenly his comrades terrify him: tigers, leopards, lynxes, or simply wolves—what honor he does those "imbeciles so weak, so common, so pea-brained" by acknowledging their ferocity! Ferocity, indeed, will always remain an aristocratic quality in his eyes. And we shall see him as a young man, during his travels in Brittany, wax ecstatic over "the prodigious sixteenth century, an epoch of fierce convictions and frenzied loves";[54] he admires "the violent provincial rulers" who instituted "reigns of terror": "men of iron whose hearts bent no more than their swords . . . cutting their way through the crowds, raping women and looting gold."[55] Watch him describe—with such sensuous pleasure—the mores of the good old days:

> What a fine time for hatred! When you hated someone, when you
> had taken him by surprise in a treasonous meeting, but finally
> had him, held him, you could feel him dying at your leisure, hour
> by hour, minute by minute, count his death pangs, drink his tears.
> You went down to his dungeon, spoke to him, bargained over his
> punishment and then laughed at his torments, debated his ran-
> som; you lived on him, by him, by his life that was being extin-
> guished, by his gold that you took from him.[56]

54. Ed. Conard, p. 287.
55. Ibid.
56. Ibid., p. 67. The paragraph ends with these words, disturbing for Achille: "Fam-

Drinking the tears of the victim, living *by his life* as it ebbs—if this is not eating him, properly speaking, it is at the very least sucking his blood. A sadistic dream, no doubt about it, but one that is merely the internalization and defensive reversal of a pitiless cruelty that was first exercised *on Flaubert* (it didn't really exist but he truly suffered it). The process, known to psychoanalysts, consists of identifying with the aggressor. Still, it is necessary to have submitted to the aggression and to have *tasted* it. This is what happened, he thinks, at the *collège*. In this third image of human relations, born rather of terror than of an idea, he actually *ennobles* his comrades. *They* are the aristocrats, the "men of iron"; *he* is the commoner. This is a far cry from the vaunted contempt that turned his vanquishers into bourgeois sons already become bourgeois, mediocrities winning the lottery thanks to their very mediocrity. Quite far and very near: we have only to turn a page to find Gustave's arrogance once more.

In *Agonies* itself there are two travelers: one dies humiliated between the teeth of aristocrats; the other perishes, like Christ, denouncing the niggardly utilitarianism of his fellow men. Gustave oscillates between the first conception and the second without pausing long at either, for he never manages to convince himself completely of the first (he knows that neither Louis Bouilhet, nor Baudry, nor Germain des Hogues are imbeciles), and the second, which fascinates him, is nonetheless intolerable. It is difficult for him now to scorn scholarly success, which forty years earlier, at the *collège* of Sens, revealed the Flaubert *quality* in Achille-Cléophas. The adolescent is floundering in his contradictions: he never stops challenging the quantitative and competitive aspect of secondary studies; however, if the prizes one gathers at school are the signs of a mysterious election, how should he define his fortunate rivals, how should he define *himself* in relation to them? Are they in the process of affirming their nobility and of becoming the sons of their works, as was the future Doctor Flaubert? And from this perspective, is he himself entirely deprived of the quality he believed was owing to his birth? He would have to consider himself a damaged child, Achille-Cléophas's spermatic mistake: although engendered by him, Gustave would not have a drop of Flaubert blood in his veins. He would be worse than a bastard: a commoner by nature; among his classmates alone one

---

ily vengeance was being accomplished in this way, in the family, and by the house itself [*he has gone down into the underground prisons of the château of Clisson*], which constituted its power and symbolized its idea" (p. 68).

might find as many as nine petit-bourgeois more worthy than he of having such a father. Doctor Flaubert, tricked for seven years by a false resemblance, would one day be struck by his error. In this case the paternal curse never took place: the father simply turned away from a mediocrity in whom he did not recognize himself. What dreadful bitterness: Gustave lived in intimate circumstances with a genius, a noble mind; living near such a man, he learned the meaning of vassalage, and now he is forced to admit that he himself is but a commoner and must bow low to those of his rivals who have blue blood in their veins. Unless by some foul trick of the Devil he were noble in spite of everything but condemned in advance to dishonor his name: an aristocrat by his obligations but unworthy of being such by his inability to fulfill them. In either hypothesis his fellow students assume the rank of sovereign powers: either they manifest their birth by their ferocity and eat him, laughing, or—commoners but gifted—they take pleasure in crushing the failed aristocrat and make poor Gustave into a former Flaubert. At the end of this new revolution (1789), he will be—and already is—responsible for the fall of his House: lifted from the plebeian condition by an eponymous hero, it will be forced down again by merciless children as they strip the younger son of his coat of arms. In both cases the adolescent rediscovers at school and in relation to his comrades the *relative being* with which his creator had marked him within the family in relation to his older brother. In both cases Gustave's being put to death, a ritual event always begun anew, is an offering to the God of hatred and vengeance, the bloody sacrifice of a profane being by the priests of a terrible religion. At the age of sixteen, speaking of the *collège* in *La Dernière Heure*, he writes these remarkable words: "I saw there the triumph of force, mysterious emblem of the power of God." By which we should understand: when a "big boy" torments a "little boy," when a tough guy humiliates a weak one, when in scholarly competition an agile and subtle mind surpasses a great soul mired in its contradictions, when quantity triumphs over quality, this is in the order of things; Evil is sacred since God wills it. Sacred are Gustave's executioners and the tortures they inflict. What vitriol for his pride: he is compelled to recognize their superiority, not only in scholarly competitions but in the order of being, and cannot prevent himself from glimpsing through the classifications that are its "emblem" a demonic but—by *a reversal of quality*—still qualitative hierarchy in which he occupies the lowest echelon.

This pessimism is too hard on his nerves, so he quickly takes up two other explanations of his scholarly failures which are evidently more consoling. In the first, he preserves, even after his defeat, the *quality* he possessed before it; in the second, he is incomparable Man, he goes to his death with his head high, and society is at fault. However, it is to a third explanation that he continually and ever more frequently returns. Although probably the most recent—that is, the last to be made explicit, this third explanation comes from the deepest part of himself; he recognizes himself in it, and in a way it offers him more advantages than the other two and leaves him greater margin for his defensive maneuvers. If he saw in his classmates only the martyrs of a system built by their parents, he would have to absolve them; and, more generally, if man is corrupted by society in spite of himself, he ought to be acquitted. Acquit man? Man, the unique object of his resentment? The tormented child refuses; the adult will not consent to it, even at the height of his glory. For resentment, the initial project of the unloved boy, is the only way of living his situation, or rather of making it livable, since the Fall. What need has he to exonerate his persecutors when he is constanty suffering on their account? Better by far to blacken them, to darken the entire universe, to proclaim that the ethical substance of the real is radical Evil: he will suffer less, all things considered, from the disgust he endures if he is persuaded that the world is iniquity. Since Evil is the law of being, any success is a crime; in defeat, on the other hand, no matter how ignominious, one finds the Good, humiliated, crushed, but still alive; the unrealized, the unrealizable, the impossible ideal. At the extreme, failure will be all the more perfect, more total, and the Good—as infinite frustration—all the more manifest the more the humiliation of the vanquished is deserved in the order of being, the more dazzling the superiority of the vanquisher. A malign power has thrown the vanquished into the midst of the fray, entrusting him with a sublime mission but without giving him the means to accomplish it. Show that Gustave is a congenital idiot, unhappy and mean, and he is exultant: stupidity and meanness bear witness against Heaven; the sage, on the other hand, is an example of injustice, unjustly endowed with virtues of which others are deprived, most particularly little Flaubert. All the better if his classmates crush him, annihilate him, by displaying gifts he doesn't have: they will make him, in his flesh and by his misfortunes, the Grand Accuser of creation. On this level it is of little importance whether he is a nobleman unworthy of his caste or a commoner: made greater by the capabilities he lacks—they reverted to him by right since he has been denied them—he is saint and martyr in the ignoble world of the rich because he represents its *penury.*

An odd consolation, we might say. Indeed, a shipwrecked man is dying of thirst and drinks sea water. But as we know, Gustave did not invent the despair he first suffered at the age of seven and never managed to cast off; in school he merely found good use for it through a new personalizing revolution. Let them mock his Latin verses, he exaggerates his misfortune and persuades himself that he is utterly destitute; and he is the first of men precisely because an exquisite and malign premeditation has made him the very last. This strange operation—pride closing in again on injured self-esteem to deepen the wounds and lessen the pain by radicalizing it—constitutes, I would say, Gustave's preneurotic stress during his years at school. His classmates—merciless, invincible, prestigious—fought and brought him to the ground yesterday, the day before yesterday; he hasn't got a chance, their insatiable ferocity terrifies him. Here pride steps in and has only to push the shame, the terror, to an extreme: the students are wild beasts, Gustave is delivered up to them like a Christian martyr. Just as they are devouring him and enjoying his atrocious agonies, the martyr, without abandoning his own body lying in the dust, quickly slips into the skin of the distracted emperor leaning over the arena, watching with vacant eyes the last twitchings of that mutilated flesh. Thus the little boy can reassure himself that his sufferings and his death will be disqualified: shout with rage, Gustave, tear at your chest with your nails, bleed! No one is interested: your vanquishers eat you and sneer but without conviction, and Nero scarcely notices your martyrdom. Your agony, that paroxysm of being, is annulled— the Others hardly find it amusing or simply don't give a damn: "Oh yeah, it was certain ahead of time, little Flaubert isn't making the grade; oh sure, we wolf him down, but that doesn't excite us much: a pleasure so predictable, so low, so common, couldn't touch us deeply. We know all about him, that kid: suffering flesh, future loser, *nothing.*" But Gustave turns this *nothing,* the supreme mutilation—the victim is stripped of the importance he has in his own eyes—into an infinite gap: the prostrate victim bears witness before all that reality *ought not to be* since it was fatal that it should end with him. Suddenly, gasping and sacred, the executed criminal raises himself above his torturers, above Nero himself; how small they seem, these instruments of his glory. He glides upward and contemplates from above the tatters he has abandoned to them; he knows the secret of being, that "defect of nothingness." How he despises his comrades: damned like him, they will die in ignorance.

Sea water is not thirst-quenching: in order to practice the technique of arrogant humility, in order to articulate this *Cogito* of nothingness—I am nothing, therefore I am—shame must come first, and *it must persist*. Far from changing reality, his spiritual exercises would not take place if reality did not evoke and sustain them. In fact, it is when *all is lost* that he must try to live. He has grasped it now, Achille has won. Forever; Louis Bouilhet too. And all the others. They have won fairly, their capabilities are what legitimize their victories. Capabilities, for Flaubert, are positive determinations of being, powers. He has literally *nothing* to oppose to this plenitude. Two solutions: suicide or derealization. The first implies failure: *lesser-being* radicalizes itself as nonbeing. He dreams of this without adopting it. Why? Because—among other reasons—it is what his torturers want. A suicide—even as a protest—always stands as an admission. Dead, he would remain in the hands of the executioners; they could say he killed himself for having recognized that he was worth *nothing*. But this "nothing" would be, precisely, worth nothing; coming from the scornful mouths of the vanquishers, it would designate nonbeing in its inertia, the zero degree of efficacy.

In order to give *his* singular and infinite nothingness the desirable virulence, Gustave has no choice: he *must* unrealize himself or, if you will, give an imaginary fulfillment to Flaubert pride and his ambitious desires by making his real and limited failures the analogue of an absolute and metaphysical disaster. Before describing the defensive tactics he has marshaled against his aggressors, we should note that they are based on what I shall call the *Weltanschauung* of the vanquished. Upon entering into life one has nothing of one's own but an irreversible defeat; when one can only die or valorize that defeat as such, the assumed failure becomes the key to being. One must then construct an ontology, a metaphysics, an ethic from the perspective of nonbeing. The two well-known principles "In the beginning was the Word" and "In the beginning was the Act" are replaced, in this inside-out thought, by that other principle which assumes them both and simultaneously dissolves them in itself, affirming its anteriority: "In the beginning was the failure" or, put another way, "Everything has always been lost in advance." It is now fitting to examine in detail Gustave's tactics and the new spirals of his personalization.

Absenteeism

From early childhood Gustave knew how to escape the odious urgency of the real through absences which suspended the faculties of his soul. As a threatened schoolboy he takes what he has at hand: the stupors reappear and multiply; he sees to it that they come upon him at the critical moment. But, as we have seen, these evasions have acquired new structures: he had merely to internalize Christian verticality to give his intermittent disappearances that "high-low" orientation: the *high-swoon*. When the young boy is convinced that the eternal Father refuses to grant him His grace and the happiness of believing in Him, the vertical remains: "And I was atop Mount Atlas and from there I contemplated the world and its gold and its mud, and its virtue and its pride." Thirteen years old and he is perched up there, having already acquired the habit of jumping onto a peak at the least difficulty. He won't change; let us recall a line from *Novembre*, compressed by negative pride that turns sorrow into a summit: "There are as well sorrows from above, in which one is no longer anything and scorns everything." One is no longer *anything*, one scorns *everything*: the ego's swoon on the summit is accompanied, in the name of the supreme anguish that abolishes it, by an absolute contempt for being.

Here we have, *grosso modo*, the function of ecstasy: to tear Flaubert away from the real, to shield him from imminence by an absenteeism of contempt. Against whom, against what, must he defend himself? At what moment does he resort to ravishment? The previously cited passage from the *Mémoires* tells us everything: "I see myself still . . . thinking the most sublime things a child's imagination can dream of, while the teacher ridicules my Latin verses and my classmates look at me, jeering." The ecstasies take place during class when, for example, the master returns compositions and comments on them. Must we believe in accident, as Gustave has the audacity to suggest? The adolescent is dreaming, he no longer even knows where he is; laughter brings him down to earth; he is in a stupor: it's his homework, they are laughing at *him*. We shall certainly not accept this false witness. Because the entire context contradicts it; it is quite clear, in fact, that the very nature of the ecstasy discloses Gustave's bitterness and resentment. He knows beforehand that the compositions are going to be returned; he senses his position—all that's left is to suffer the *ceremony of humiliation*. It's too much—he will make his escape. Others would go over the wall and not come back. But the submissive child, incapable of rebellion, will remain present *in flesh and blood*; there is only one absence, essential though less noticeable—the absence of his soul. In other words, the absenteeist reflex is a precise and intermittent form of behavior, its source an external and definite stimulus: the need to escape class ranking and discredit it.

The procedure seems simple: disqualify the miserable, *finite* victories of man's children by putting them in contact with the infinite. The text is explicit: "They, laugh at me! . . . me, whose spirit was drowning in the limits of creation . . . I, who felt greater than them all, who received infinite pleasures . . . I, who felt as big as the world." We have yet to understand which infinite is being referred to, and by what means the adolescent transforms himself into the concrete mediation between the highly limited finitude of his comrades and that unlimited world which both contains and is unaware of them. On this point the *Mémoires* maintain a prudent silence. But a few somewhat later reflections, jotted down in his journal during the latter half of 1840, allow us to reconstruct the Flaubertian ascesis and to distinguish two infinites in him.

In the second trimester of 1840, Gustave—preparing for his baccalaureate at the Hôtel-Dieu—aspires *to believe:* he has fallen into a deep self-loathing. He has just written that he would very much like to be a mystic, adding that he has no faith and is ready to receive grace if it should please God to grant it. Some days later—some hours, perhaps—he decides that the passive abyss of his soul is not sufficiently tempting to God, and that the proverb "God helps those who help themselves" is undoubtedly true. He reflects, sits down at his desk; so great is his misery that we surprise him for the first and, to my knowledge, the last time in his life in the process of constructing something that resembles, though faintly, a line of argument—by analogy, it's true. "Infinity is the one incomprehensible thing. But who doubts it? There are, then, things beyond the scope of our intelligence and in which we believe; could there be something other than this intelligence itself that might think, something other than our reason that might be convinced?"[57] His effort stops there. But some time later, at a date impossible to pin down precisely (in any case before August 1840), he rereads this text, is irritated by it, deletes it with a red line, and, as if that were not enough, scrawls across it the final, for him unappealable, judgment—"stupid." What Gustave has just condemned is what might be called the *positive* infinite, be it personal God or Spinozist substance. This totality, sensed by the heart or

57. *Souvenirs*, p. 62.

through religious intuition, might have given him, he thinks, the feeling of having been created and mandated by a special intention; this plenitude of being might have allowed him to jump over his own limitations and lose himself in it. There is nothing to be done: if he allows himself to reason, he becomes vulnerable to scrutiny by Doctor Flaubert, who would undoubtedly have found this inelegantly handled argument stupid.

Some days or some weeks later, however, he returns to this question in a note cited above, which we must examine again because it offers the double advantage of showing us the direction of his spiritual exercises and the meaning he gives to the *negative* infinite: "We are not shocked by two young dogs fighting," [58] etc. The meaning is clear: from the cosmic point of view, or, more effectively, from the point of view of the Absolute, vices and virtues, talents and inadequacies, high or low birth, good luck and bad luck are equivalent: whether one is Doctor Flaubert, Achille, Bouilhet, or Gustave amounts to the same thing. What does seem obscure, on the other hand, is the procedure by which the young man establishes this common ground. If he had wanted merely to put the finite in contact with the infinite and dissolve all the determinations of the one in the other, two lines would have sufficed. But it is immediately apparent that he was seeking *something else*; this long *analogical* development (as B is to A, C is to B; what C is to B, D is to C, judge accordingly what X—which is to D to the nth power what D is to C—can be in relation to A, or rather what A might be in relation to X) bears no resemblance to the "thoughts" he jots down at random in his notebook and then forgets. Here Gustave proceeds slowly, by stages, as if he wanted to convince a stubborn and dull-witted interlocutor; he gives evidence of a positively Socratic patience, as if he were waiting for the other's acquiescence at each step. But in this case there is neither a Socrates nor a Phaedrus: the notebook will have no reader but its author; even Alfred had no knowledge of it. We must recognize that we are in the presence of a practical schema to facilitate Flaubert's spiritual exercises, the rudiments of certain "meditations": the stages are of no use to the "Idea," but are what should facilitate his elevation. We are dealing here with an ascesis and not a rational argument. Stage one: you regard the fighting of puppies or children with indifference; it is because you are looking down at them from above. Stage two: climb to the top of a tower—silence, below you "men are small," therefore you

58. *Souvenirs*, p. 71. Cf. above.

witness a murder undisturbed. Gustave conveys us to his tower in order to remove us from degrading daily primiscuity, from the *forced* solidarity of man with man, as well as from the enduring antagonisms that tear us apart. What calm up above! Flaubert has begun to desituate himself. In the *Mémoires* he asserted that the society of children was "cruel to its victims." He is not concerned with putting an end to this cruelty—besides, how could he, when it is part of our nature? It is enough for him not to be its object and, when it is exercised on others, not to be disturbed by it, not to *participate* in it, even inactively, through sadistic and masochistic compliance; in short, to have only, as he will say later, a "glancing acquaintance" with it. Stage three: a change of perspective; the author abandons us on our tower, we are no longer the subjects of these exercises but become—although this is left unsaid—its objects. We are simply asked to imagine a grain of sand in relation to a pyramid; we are shown a giant who impassively contemplates a pitched battle among Myrmidons. The meaning of this new stage will not escape us: there is a metamorphosis, the passage from quantity to quality. Formerly quantity alone mattered—we had simply to measure the height of the tower to determine the degree of indifference it provoked in us; neither at the summit nor at sea level did we cease to be men. Transmutation: the Myrmidons *are dwarfs,* their observer is a *giant;* size is a distinctive characteristic of both species. At the same time, of course, we are the Myrmidons. Having climbed to the highest part of the dungeon, we lean over our fellow men below and are terrified to discover a Gargantua leaning over us. Stage four: "Now you can compare Nature, God, infinite intelligence, in a word, to that man a hundred feet tall, that pyramid a hundred thousand feet high—think, by comparison, of the wretchedness of our crimes and our virtues, of our grandeur and our weakness."

Now we understand the need for these stages of the argument: what Gustave wants is not so much to show the leveling activity of the Infinite as to participate in it himself. Yet this operation is all the more difficult as he is still part of the human race, and the aspiring leveler is leveled like the others. The man-on-the-tower is only a man clinging to a platform: he profits from one of those derisory advantages which the divine eye offers precisely in order to crush it to earth in universal equivalence. The first two stages serve as preparatory exercises: Gustave's purpose is to break any attachment to the species. Between the second and third stages he sheds his skin: the giant is nothing, or nearly nothing, to infinite intelligence; he counts himself nonetheless on the side of the levelers—at least in relation to humanity, and that alone has meaning—since he is *in essence other than men,* we might say even a *superman,* who will never be cast down to the level of the anthropoids. This giant, we have understood, is Flaubert. If this should be doubted, let us refer back to the *Mémoires,* where he gives it away: "I, who felt as big as the world." Here is the aim of the ascesis: the first two steps, briskly climbed, end up as a springboard—the adolescent is preparing himself to leap beyond the species into the unknown. He wants to be the mediator between God and man, the annunciator of perfect divine indifference; this giant feels he is being eyed from above and at the same time he is leaning over an anthill and transmitting through his look the astringent power of the gaze to which he is subjected. This strange evangelist is charged with transmitting bad news: the supreme tribunal has given him a mandate to declare to the presumptuous colonizers who dispute possession of the earth, specifically to the schoolboys of Rouen, that the infinite intelligence, the infinite its unique object, has neither eyes nor ears for finite determinations. Such, then, is the exercise of absenteeism, practised with increasing ease the more frequently it is repeated; the vertical ascent must end in an abrupt mutation: Gustave is in the process of changing species. In fact, he is passing from the real to the imaginary: since this Gargantua *is not,* since Flaubert *is not* Gargantua, it is appropriate to see this process as an example of what we have called his techniques of unrealization. He can neither conceive of nor aspire to the qualitative leap except as a leap into unreality. But he is sustained by a real movement that serves as an analogue to elevation: the adolescent's imperceptible straightening up beneath the whiplash of humiliation or, still more simply, his sudden consciousness, as he stands immobile, of his great height—that is, in relation to his schoolmates. It is almost certain that Gustave was the tallest boy in his class—even Bouilhet for once ceded him first place, beaten by half a head. What persuades us that the young boy used his physical superiority in his "ravishments" is that, as we shall see, he wore himself out playing the "force of nature" and in his last years had himself called, and was pleased to call himself, *"the Giant."* So *he* is the giant who contemplates the dwarfmen, and if this imaginary Gargantua can *live* his gigantism, it is because certain structures of his organism give him the means to *feel gigantic.* We shall go no further, still lacking the tools; we must forge them, and shall do so in this chapter.

What is important here is the *negative* aspect of the infinite. Paradoxically, this total plenitude is envisaged only as *privation;* the use Flaubert makes of it is ostensibly defensive, but more secretly it is a passive aggression—the only kind a passive agent might permit himself. We now understand why, in the *Souvenirs*, just after furiously crossing out his "thought" on the infinite perceptible to the heart, Gustave once again finds "God, infinite intelligence, Nature." The real order of his meditations is the reverse of their apparent order: as we learn from *Quidquid volueris* and the *Mémoires*, the defensive techniques of elevation that refer to the *negative* infinite and will never disappear were constituted long before, during his school days at the *collège; subsequently*, in mid-1840, Gustave was uneasy with himself and tried to convert privation into plenitude. What if, at the end of the ascension, ecstasy—which as its name indicates is merely a tearing away from the self—should become *sensual pleasure?* Since the infinite is the very mainspring of my techniques, he says to himself, I must have some intuition of it: could there be something in me that thinks and is not thought? If an eye of the soul exists, it must be discovered and turned toward heaven; therefore I may be able to feel the breaking of my limitations and to communicate with the all in a peaceful, contemplative love. He would later express this fragile hope through the fount of holy water reflecting the ribs of the vaulted church: hope forever vain, conversion forever bungled. The angry line crossing out the entire paragraph is his confession *in our presence*—and the distant past of this dead life takes on for a moment, before our eyes, the appearance of a resurrected present—that he has once again missed his mark. But this failure does not concern the *negative* infinite and has no influence on the tactical use he makes of it. That is why it is permissible some time later to invoke God by fixing on paper the *moments* of his spiritual exercises. The God of love never keeps his appointments. Too bad: that deplorable absence is His problem and not the humiliated schoolboy's; the God Flaubert needs is the God of indifference, in whom man annihilates himself.

Indeed, at every stage of the ascent, the *person* evoked, observer, giant, nature, or divinity, remains perfectly anonymous: it is an unknown, an abstract power, and we are never told what it is in itself or in relation to men, but only what men are in relation to it. At every stage, all along the absolute vertical, *someone* is leaning over humanity, nothing more; the only function of these benevolent observers is to show the species crushing itself from one stage to another beneath their watching eyes and, in the final instance, annihilating itself altogether. The function of infinite intelligence is here entirely negative since it is merely required to be unaware.

The *Mémoires* offer us the results of these mental gymnastics: the moment Gustave is about to be hemmed in by the religious ceremony of humiliation and sacrificed in front of everyone by the priest of the cult, he flies up to the ceiling, a trap door opens, and the class is swallowed up. But not entirely—he has left them his hide; Flaubert, tenth in Latin verse, remains on his bench and goes down with the others in the leveling shipwreck; Gustave, the sylph, watches that student from above, sees him shrink and become indistinguishable from Pagnerre and Bouilhet. The species, abandoned to this infinite fall, becomes Liliputian, then microscopic, then nothing at all. I have reversed the movement by design: by replacing Gustave's vertical climb with the vertical fall of those around him, we obtain the same result and throw into relief the passive aggression of resentment. The method consists of *conscious* self-annihilation (he is the giant, God watches him)—I mean to remain conscious of the abolition as it is happening—in order to strike the carnivores, who still believe in their own existence, with an annihilation all the more radical as they aren't even conscious of it. Those diseased vermin sink into nonbeing without losing the foolish certainty that their wretched aims are absolutes, that it is important *in the absolute* to be Louis Bouilhet, first of the second division of the ninth term, or of Rhetoric, at the *collège* of Rouen. We can be sure that the Exterminating Angel on his perch or balcony highly appreciates the comic aspect of these zombies who set about and persist in doing each other harm, for want of knowing that they don't exist. This is clear-cut *genocide:* lacking the power to destroy it, the little misanthrope derealizes the species by transforming each of its representatives into an appearance that subsists only through misunderstanding.

Of course the *exercise*—its steps are clearly retraced in *Souvenirs*—is carefully dissembled in *Mémoires d'un fou*. Gustave claims to be ignorant of the tools of his ascesis; whether he has been pulled away from the earth or whether the doomed planet has fallen by itself into the abysses of the infinite, the fact is that he finds himself *in the air*. How? He doesn't want to know. At times the summit of Mount Atlas seems to be his natural habitat, at others a powerful arm appears to have carried him there; all means are good as long as he *undergoes* this ascension and is under no circumstances part of the genocide taking place before his very eyes. It is striking that the verbs relating to his ecstasy all reduce him to passivity. His spirit *"drowns,"* it is "lost" in all the worlds of poetry, he *receives* "infinite pleasures." Certainly a few lines earlier he tells us that he is *thinking*, but we are immediately enlightened—for him, thinking is a synonym for dreaming: "thinking the most sublime things the imagination of a child can dream of." And these products of the imagination are themselves strangers to him; they are born inside him—God knows who has impregnated him—but they are too great for his finitude. Hence we find this astonishing line: "I . . . whom a single thought of mine might reduce to ashes, were it set free." What is there to say except that the relation of this soul to its products is analogous to the relation of the profane to the sacred:[59] Gustave is an oracle, he is a Sybil, a God compels him to prophesy; he does not think, he is thought. A stranger to his dreams, he feels he is the finite but *chosen* receptacle of the pure sacred, or rather of its reflection in the imaginary. If the dream that comes to him were realized, if the Infinite were to descend in *person* into this ripple of a soul, the adolescent would burst or be burned to ashes—it is just as well that he receives only its *image*; this is enough to desituate him forever. Clearly, in order to derealize his classmates, Gustave must begin by derealizing himself as the colossal repository of the Spinozist substance.

Indeed, a passivity so pronounced ought to lead directly to fainting. In particular, the *drowning* refers us clearly to the archaic stupor as a simple deprivation of consciousness. Of course the child suggests that he drowns from excess, annihilated by the immensity of proffered treasures among which he is unable to choose. But that is scarcely convincing: one drowns without the strength, the desire, the skill to swim. Gustave doesn't make a move: he receives his revelations, but he cannot and will not fix them by an act—even by the *contemplative act*; carried off, ravished, penetrated, he has pleasure, he is pleasured, and finally the dream absorbs him. But there is no loss of consciousness: we know that he thinks about it but will never manage it, even during the night of Pont-l'Evêque; his is really a *loss of reality*. The child makes his stupor the analogue of a ravishment; he plays Ganymede, an eagle lights on him. For it is not a question merely of escaping the real—which is the underlying intention of fainting pure and simple—or even of giving himself value by a feigned ecstasy, but of taking revenge on the mockers as well. That the children of man should laugh at another child of man is simply absurd. But that they should mock a sublime dreamer whom the infinite, descended in him in the form of an imaginary determination, has raised above the human condition is sacrilege in its pure form, for the object of their laughter is inhabited

---

59. In numerous societies, he who sees the king without previous intercession must fall into ashes, struck by lightning. The metaphor of fire is therefore perfectly justified.

by the sacred: "The fools! *They,* laugh at *me! They,* who are so weak, so common, so pea-brained; *me,* whose mind was drowning at the limits of creation!" The text betrays its author; it is clear that the order of events must be reversed: the laughter comes first (or in any case the angry expectation of laughter), and Gustave chastizes his classmates by immediately playing the role of him-at-whom-no-one-has-the-right-to-laugh. Moreover, he does not initially find them "so common" or so stupid, those prestigious beasts whose bite he fears. His effort, on the contrary, aims at *constituting them as such*—he calls the Infinite to his aid in order to squash those brains which in competitive examinations seem to him larger and more profound than his own. This is not the first time someone has had recourse to the infinity of nonknowledge in order to disqualify knowledge by reproaching it for its finitude.

He has made an effort, however, to give a content to these abstract ravishments, to give a positive anchor to the negative certainty of his superiority. He has, he tells us, "infinite pleasures. . . , celestial ecstasies in the face of the intimate revelations of [his] soul." That's right: the giant discovers Flaubert *quality* in his plenitude. This is not the exterminating angel speaking: a soul reveals itself to itself and takes pleasure in itself. This would be perfect if we could believe in it, if the author himself believed in it. But how can we concede that Gustave, as we know him, as he describes himself in his works and his letters, knows *pleasure?* Later he will say of himself, "I am not made for pleasure," and it is true. Since the Fall, consumed by shame, resentment, envy, he has been in a constant rage; he writes, "Men made me corrupt and mean." [60] He is a "noble soul" whom the *collège* has wounded, parched, a soul suffocating in this little scholarly world as Almaroës does in the little sublunary world. If he has any joys, they are always poisoned by an aggravated frenzy which imperiously demands their return and their continual increase in intensity—let us recall Mazza's sexual fury, her endlessly renewed demands; it is not sensual pleasure she is after but thirst. Gustave has so little self-love: how could he possibly charm himself, how could his self-discovery crown him with ineffable delights? I am quite willing to believe that he repeated to himself with closed fists, in a state of nearly unbearable tension: "I am greater than all of them! I am a poet! I have genius! I will crush them with my glory!" And perhaps these *feigned* affirmations brought him, in the end, a shade of pleasure. But what a convulsion of the

60. In the *Mémoires,* chapter 6.

soul or, as he enjoyed saying, what "manustirpation" to obtain this imaginary gratification! Look at the rest: when Gustave writes the *Mémoires*, the school year has just ended. Yet his peevishness has not in the least abated: fools! pea-brains! If he had known during class one-hundredth of the pleasures he claims to have felt, if he had really marveled at the treasures of his soul, would he have taken offense at the laughter of the masses? Would he even have noticed it? And wouldn't the happiness of feeling "as big as the world" have compensated for those stings to his self-esteem? Better, wouldn't it have prevented him from feeling them? When a soul discovers in plenitude its incomparable *quality*, when it catches itself looking down at the human race to which it thought it belonged, it would scarcely stoop to notice the arrows shot from below by such tiny archers—*noblesse oblige*. Yet in the third chapter of the *Mémoires* he compares himself to a "bull sickened by the stings of insects." The proportion is preserved: Gustave remains a giant tormented by pygmies. But where is the contempt? Where is the indifference? Far from contemplating his torturers from above, he runs off "in the grip of a nervous irritation that makes him vehement, hot-headed," dragging along with him those insects glued to his flanks or swarming *above* his back.

Moreover, where does the content of these revelations come from? From what experience? Does he really want them to derive from experience? He takes care to tell us that he is drowning in *all* the worlds of poetry, that he feels *as big as the world*, that he has "an infinite more vast than God's, if that is possible," and that "his thought, in his delirium, flew up into realms unknown to man where there is neither world nor planets nor suns." But we must surely recognize that these obscure formulas are supposed to designate the infinite substance as a totality without parts. The young boy claims to have a rapport only with the All; a particular determination would constitute a specification of the undifferentiated, therefore limit his genius. If he must remain on his column, he must also remain on that level of abstraction where being passes unceasingly into nonbeing, and vice versa. Thus, the fog in his mind is occasionally mingled with fleeting, confused words, vague, exultant vows: "I will show that death is the world's wife . . . I will pry into the hearts of men and find nothing but pus and putrescence . . . I will tell the truth and it will be terrible . . . I will reveal that all is vanity . . . The god Fatum laughs in the face of humanity . . . the silence of infinite spaces," etc. The intimate revelations of his soul, then, pertain not to the "nature" of this monad but to his relation of interiority with the cosmic totality. In itself, moreover, this conception is quite correct: it simply describes the being-in-the-world of the human person in which the world is given as the horizon of our anchorage and not as an object of *ontic* knowledge; properly speaking, it is an immense, plural totalization and not an all. Gustave's bond to the world, envisaged as infinite but self-enclosed substance, can in truth be only a relation of exteriority. This is something he recognizes when he depicts the Infinite as knowing and taking pleasure in itself: this all-encompassing knowledge excludes the intelligence of determinations; in it, finite differences engulf each other without control and without truth. The individual, to the degree that he plays his own part, is thereby excluded from the substantial and cosmic plenitude: he defines himself negatively and exists only *in appearance;* what he takes for his being is the *all-nonbeing.* It is therefore impossible that Gustave should receive revelations on his relationship to the *positive* infinite. Unless, perhaps, he could transcend his limits and, like the finite mode in Spinoza, attain knowledge of the third kind. But it is precisely the adolescent's pessimism that makes that impossible for him: knowledge through the Infinite can be only negative for him; to dissolve himself in the All is not to rediscover absolute plenitude but to annihilate himself as a particular entity *with no compensation:* if the all thinks *itself,* it is because it has thought itself and will think itself eternally. Subject or not, this absolute has a plenary knowledge of itself at the very moment the determination attempted to play its part; nothing will be altered if the determination understands its mistake and abolishes itself. Knowledge of the third kind, for Gustave, can only be suicide. The appearance perceives that it *is not,* excuses itself—"Oh, pardon me!"—and draws the inevitable conclusion by blowing its brains out. The vexed adolescent takes the All to be the equivalent of nothing. He has said explicitly in *Novembre,* in a line cited above: "sorrows from above in which one is no longer *anything* and scorns *everything:* when they don't kill you, suicide alone delivers you from them." At the very instant when the negative infinite allows him to annihilate every individuated being, he feels an abolishing gaze pressing on him from above. This is his soul's true relationship to the absolute; these are, if you will, the kind of revelations he receives—they are unlikely to be a source of exquisite pleasure.

Certainly the ascensional movement that carries him bears a rather close resemblance to the movement of faith: it is, in any case, a transcendence. But he knows in advance that he will find nothing above him except perhaps a monstrous idol, blind and deaf, filled with itself. Indeed, the positive infinite scarcely matters to him in his furious ecstasies. Moreover, he doesn't need it; it is enough for him to regard men from the point of view of the negative infinite. Hence they are caught on the horns of a dilemma: either the absolute is not, therefore nothing is, the world dissolves into an infinite molecular pulverization, we are a nightmare of matter; or else the absolute is, therefore the universe is an all that comprehends and regulates itself, and we are nothing because the absolute does not know us. As we see, Gustave gains nothing by raising himself so high: his comrades are liquidated, true, but so is he—it is his own annihilation that awaits him at the summit. He wanted it this way, however; rather than remain a mediocre student, this Samson prefers to shake the columns of the temple and die, crushed along with the Philistines who surround him. His superiority resides in the fact that he is conscious of being nothing, while the others are nothing and are unaware of it; this superiority manifests itself by a despair that compels him *in spite of himself* to claim the existence of a God of love and to go searching for him "in those unknown realms . . . where there is neither world nor planets nor suns," when he is assured in advance that he will not meet him there. And how can we fail to recognize in the ascendant force that bears him upward his aristocratic dissatisfaction with his surroundings, with men and things, with "obsolete" nature where he feels cramped, with himself? Again we encounter the two axiological systems: ranking according to practical success and a hierarchy based on quality. No sooner is the first evoked than Flaubert hastens to replace it with the second: a directed, restrained swoon, held in check just as consciousness is about to be lost and experienced as *suffered* elevation, is evidence, in his eyes, of his personal *quality*.

Need we note here the revolution that has taken place in the child? Flaubert *quality* was at first the synthetic and positive unity of *certain* family qualities: by virtue of it, he should have been confirmed first among men. But he had to bow before unworthy youngsters. If that quality remains in spite of his failures, it must be that those failures do not put his quality in question but rather make it eminently manifest. His insufficiency of being, then, will be lived in a perpetual agony. Thus dissatisfaction—arrogant rejection of reality—does not come at first from some positive superiority the adolescent has over the human race and "decrepit" Nature because it is really internalized destitution. A destitution that initially has nothing noble or metaphysical about it and is marked by the absence of quite real capabilities that others are found to possess. The ecstasy, in effect, begins with a defeat. But this defeat—provoked by a *deserved* failure and the enraged feeling that justice is unjust—opens the way to the perception of radical evil; the schoolboy's insufficiency discloses to him the insufficiency of reality, and this totalitarian, despairing proof makes him fall into philosophical astonishment. Before his very eyes, before everyone else's. There we have it, Flaubert quality: a continual and instituted estrangement. After all, wasn't the paterfamilias a "philosophical practitioner"? Gustave goes further than Achille-Cléophas, he shows by his very defeats that human *praxis*, fundamentally tainted by *determination*, is merely a consequence of the ontological crime that was the creation. The adolescent invents his negative logic gropingly, as he goes along. See how he inverts these notions: beginning in 1835, the Devil is always situated above and swiftly carries his victims to the zenith; thus diabolic elevation is equivalent to temptation, which from a Christian view causes one to *succumb* and *fall*. To totalize is only to destroy. To be realized is to be annulled. As for *quality*, the positive pride of Doctor Flaubert and his House, it creates in Gustave an arid and desolate pride, since for him it is simply nothingness becoming conscious of itself through the incapacities of a singular person. *Nothing*, in other words, unless it is the nonbeing of being united dialectically with the being of nonbeing by a reciprocity of perspectives. The principle of this "thought" is articulated in the fifth chapter of the *Mémoires:* "cast down to the lowest rung by superiority itself." The negative—on the *social* terrain of competition—is the incontestable sign of the positive in the spiritual hierarchy.

The Failure of Absenteeism

We can easily understand that this attempt was doomed at the outset to partial failure. It was undoubtedly inspired by a Christian idea: "The last shall be first." But it is clear that the institution of the two orders cannot be achieved without the mediation of a third, which is inherent in neither. In the Gospel, it is the divine mediator who effects the reversal. This is the source of his efficacy: although this intermediary does not *really* exist, the faithful do not regard him as merely a product of their imagination, and so he cannot truly be one. The poor, the humiliated, the injured are *signified* by a constituted body, the Church, as the favored of God; they receive this signification as a constitutive trait of their *being* and internalize it as an unrealizable but absolute reality: *elsewhere*, in the eyes of an all-powerful being whose designs are mysterious, they *are* the future elect. This is not a matter of belief but a *conviction* provoked by external manipulations; the real mediator is not God but exists nonetheless: he is in the narrow sense the Church itself, in the larger sense the Christian community. A serf of the thirteenth century learns his *Christian-being* the way we learn, for example, our *French-being*. He was *created* to suffer here on earth and to enjoy eternal happiness above if he undergoes his trials with resignation. Indeed, the primary objective of religious teaching is that he must bear his condition and give up the idea of changing it; thus social injustice must seem to him a sign of divine Justice, just as Gustave's failures reveal his election to him. But in the same way that the mediation fails in Gustave's construction, so the reversal *he alone* effects can be experienced by Gustave only in the form of a *movement of the imagination;* an *average* student, he *unrealizes himself* as both last in the class and first of the elect. He will later admit it implicitly in the scenario of *La Spirale:* the hero escapes his misfortunes by quite consciously leading an imaginary life: "The greater his real suffering, the more intense are his transports into dream . . . He is shut up in an asylum, and there he knows true happiness."[61] The lower he falls, the higher he leaps into the unreal. "[This] man," says Flaubert himself, "by dint of thinking, manages to have hallucinations."[62] In other words, he deliberately cultivates the *compensatory* imagination. But while the image presents itself as a product of his mind and not *independently* as a strange apparition, he does not believe in it sufficiently for the compensation to be effective. At the extreme, however—meaning at the end of his spiritual exercises ("by dint of thinking")—his dream takes on a proper consistency, asserts itself, and convinces him: without ceasing to be unreal, its hallucinatory power allows him to disqualify reality or to inform it in such a way that it ends by signifying the contrary of what in fact it manifests: " . . . he knew all sorrows . . . and ended by triumphing over them *by virtue of the form* his dream gave him."[63] The hallucinations are therefore the recompense of ascesis. But this recompense is nothing more—at least in the eyes of men—than a delirium. At the moment of triumph, the painter in *La Spirale* is shut up in a lunatic asylum. Flaubert would write to Feydeau in 1859: "For such a long time I have pondered a novel on madness, or rather on the *way* one becomes mad."[64] In other words, the reversal by imagination lacks power ex-

61. Dumesnil, *Gustave Flaubert*, p. 451, note 1.
62. To Louise, *Correspondance* 2:76–77, 27 December 1852.
63. Dumesnil, *Gustave Flaubert*.
64. *Correspondance* 4:349.

cept to express the fundamental choice of the *imaginary attitude*, that is, no decision is made to treat reality consistently as the analogue of an unreal universe. Gustave wrote these letters *after* his "nervous illness" and considered *La Spirale* a description and explanation of it: I fell ill for having chosen the imaginary.[65] But during his years at school that option was not yet available: of course he practiced daydreaming quite frenziedly, but—as the first pages of the *Mémoires* indicate—he was restrained by the fear of going mad. He tried to compensate for the real, but not to the point of forgetting it. With the result that he *did not believe enough* in his images, hence in his superiority over his classmates. He would have had to have the courage—as he soon would— to declare: I surpass them only in imagination, that precisely is my merit and my *real* value, to have chosen to be only imaginary. He is not yet there, and his "sublime" dreams do not sufficiently defend him, as we know, against nervous irritation and bitter outbursts. He is conscious of this, writing in *Novembre*, "I uttered cries of triumph to distract myself from my solitude," which clearly means that he *played the triumphant role*. As for distracting himself, no: he is *never alone* except precisely when he unrealizes himself through imagined triumphs. But from the time of the *Mémoires*, we sense his unease: the reversal of values often seems to him a futile operation and one which ends with a humiliating tumble. Here he is after some bold flight, having returned among his classmates:

> Cradled in these vague reveries, these dreams of the future . . . transported by that adventurous thought . . . I would spend whole hours with my head in my hands, looking at the floor of my study . . . ; and when I would wake up staring, they would laugh at me, the laziest of them all—who never had one positive idea, who showed no penchant for any profession, who would be useless in this world where everyone must go ahead and take his piece of the pie, and, who would never be anything but a good-for-nothing, at best a clown, an animal tamer, or a maker of books.

After the dream of a dream, born of a refusal to communicate and a futile effort at recovering the solitude of autism, it is the nauseating return that has been felt continually at every moment of the oneiric enterprise; it is Gustave's relapse into his being-for-others, into that ungraspable, unrealizable reality that comes to him through all the

---

65. A highly lucid interpretation, as we shall see.

others. In this angry paragraph he tries once more to take an external view of himself. The revelations, the ravishments, the stunning thoughts *seen through the eyes of others* are reduced to "vague reveries." For them, the infinite absence he boasts of in his dreams is in truth only his assembled incapacities, as precise and determined as their practical capabilities: the first, indeed, present themselves *in reality* as the negation of the second. The "positive hero" of bourgeois society is defined by his efficacy: if he passes his baccalaureat, he will become a certified agent of history; his "positive ideas"—all the more clear, distinct, and useful for containing a more precise consciousness of their limits and scope—contain in themselves a conquering impulse and are merely, when all is said and done, the practical choices that put him in direct touch with the world. Against this string of pre-cut diamonds, this acute angle, Gustave can set only a vague and gentle mist, indefinite, perfectly useless. He is condemned by his passivity to being merely a "useless lout," a "good-for-nothing." Can we say that he condemns the estimate those "pea-brains" have of him? Were we to do so, we would mistake him altogether: *the others are always right*. We cannot remain insensible to the despair expressed in these few lines; of course his classmates are wrong to be right, but things being what they are, they are right all the same: Marguerite *really is* ugly, Garcia really is stupid; Gustave really is lazy, good for nothing. The ambivalence of this declaration is striking: he "gathers from the mud" those insulting names they give him—as he did a little earlier at the Hôtel-Dieu ("laughable, all right! I will be *the* comic"). Lazy, all right, useless, okay; and afterward? But that is just when he falls again: he has already uttered his cry of triumph and is not very convinced by it, so his present defiance is no longer an outlet for anything. For what he claims to assume is precisely the unacceptable: the relation to the infinite was only imaginary, his comrades always knew that; by becoming stubborn about his negative particularity as they constituted it, Gustave is conscious of playing their game. "However, they barely granted me imagination, meaning, according to them, an exultation of the brain akin to madness." According to them *and* according to him, as we have just seen. He recognizes, in his bad temper, that the relationship with the negative absolute can be answerable only to the imaginary: I have no ideas, I do not think, I never reach conclusions, *I imagine that I think*.

What if he had genius nonetheless? What if he were to become the greatest poet of his time? Well, *even so* he wouldn't convince anyone.

First of all, he would have to be able to communicate the content of his ecstasies; this cannot happen because, like underlying desires, they are "inarticulable":

> I had an infinite more vast, if that is possible, than God's, where poetry was cradled and spread its wings in a ravishment of love and ecstasy; and then it was necessary to descend from those sublime regions toward words, and how could I render in speech that harmony that rises in the heart of the poet . . . There again, the disappointment; for we touch the earth . . . By what ladder shall we descend from the infinite to the positive? By what gradations should poetry abase itself without being broken? How to shrink this giant who envelops the infinite? . . . I felt broken by my power and ashamed of my weakness, for speech is only a distant and dim echo of thought; I cursed my dearest dreams and my silent hours passed at the limit of creation; I felt something empty and insatiable devouring me.

Let us not take this admission for oratorical precaution: Gustave is speaking the truth. After the ecstasy, *it was necessary* to descend once again to words. Therefore he had a mandate for it in the ecstasy itself, and from this point of view we discover a positive intention in the ascesis: he rises up to ravishment not only to belittle his classmates but also to find a content that will make the object of a work, of a discourse that will fix its moments. But at the moment of analyzing and naming what he feels, everything escapes him: the infinite is a rebel to analysis, and then "there is no language" in which to render it. We shall see[66] that this problem is fundamental for Flaubert and that it is at the origin of his art, whose project will be to *render the unsayable indirectly.* When writing the *Mémoires,* he has not yet found an answer to the question that is tormenting him; hence his "insatiable and devouring emptiness," his "despair," his "shame." He is *afraid to write:* let poetry remain a state of the soul; losing oneself in all the worlds of poetry, so be it; drowning in the limits of creation, perfect. But what would happen if he took it into his head to *translate the silence?* If he "takes pen in hand," what will he feel when confronted by the pathetic lines he has written? A disgust with being that both solicits and rejects expression? A disgust with himself, with the mandated writer who cannot render—due to a singular impotence—what others may have rendered? Or perhaps the almost intolerable sense of having fooled himself, and of the possibility that this infinite more vast than

---

66. Cf. chapter 14 below, "From Poet to Artist."

God's has in fact no content? In this last case, it would be the discourse, sole reality, that would denounce the perfect emptiness of the ecstasy-stupor. Without any doubt he experiences these disgusts all together, with a dominant variable. He says, for example, that he is ashamed of his weakness; but this confession remains ambiguous: the weakness of human nature? Gustave's personal weakness? And why does he curse his dearest dreams, the *silent* hours spent at the limit of creation? Because they give him a false mission, a false hope? Or because they reveal themselves as reveries without content? A confidence from *Novembre* suggests that he was leaning toward the second hypothesis: "His great regret was not to be a painter; he always said he had the most beautiful pictures in his imagination. He was equally sorry not to be a musician. . . ; endless symphonies played in his head. However, he understood nothing of painting or music." A painter, thinks Flaubert, imagines pictures; a musician imagines symphonies. But I, who "admire authentic second-rate daubings and [who have] a migraine when leaving the Opera," I imagine to myself that I am a painter-imagining-a-composition, a musician-imagining-a-melody. In other words, I have neither picture nor symphony in my head: just the insatiable and devouring emptiness barely clouded by *the image of an image,* plastic or musical. This means: I am the image of a poet haunted by the image of an imaginary revelation. Moreover, it is in the order of things: since the worst is certain, a soul can escape the devil when it dreams, but when it tries to realize its dream, even in discourse, it is lost. If he has any sense, the adolescent with a passion to write will break his pen; if he is mad enough to write a book, he will be a graphomaniac and a poor stylist. Conclusion: Gustave proclaims his genius but does not believe in it.

And what would happen if, however improbably, he were to have genius? If he were to write sublime verses? The answer is given in the paragraph cited above, and it is the underlying source of his despair: even if he became the author of a masterpiece, he would not convince his classmates of his *quality:* "I . . . who would never be anything but a good-for-nothing, at best a clown, an animal tamer, or a maker of books." For him, in effect, a poem is antitruth; a novel is a discourse bearing on imaginary events and characters. Thus, *in the order of being,* the tamer of shadows or performing animals is relegated to the lowest rank; even if he is not chased away, he is nonetheless *of use* in spite of himself, and indirectly: whether he works marionettes or writes books, the products of his labor will be used by the brutal conquerors of reality for their amusement. Overworked and anxious, if they can *divert*

91

themselves for a moment with some nonsense, they might find the means, while absorbed in manifestly inconsistent lies, to think literally of nothing; through his works, Gustave the creator will be—like a woman, that tender *object*—the warrior's respite. It would of course be impossible to neglect the enraged condemnation of the philistines expressed in this bitter line: these imbeciles make imagination a means, never an end. But what? What is a superiority that is not recognized by anyone? At the time, Gustave still dreamed of glory: an adolescent, even tormented by a dark and jealous ambition, never succeeds in completely purging himself of hope. He is afraid of life but sometimes burns to enter it. So he imagines the "religious gathering" of the public, the "heaving chests," and intoxicates himself with a cannibalistic dream: he will gnaw the spectators to the bone "with words that devour like fire." This is a trap: the idle dreamer perceives too late that the "gathered" public—whom he wants to crush with his genius to compensate for the contempt of his classmates—is made up only of his classmates or their peers. Once more he has put himself in their hands. Since the entire species is rotten, if those champions of being, the children of man, persist in seeing him only as a sculptor of nonbeing and judging his works in terms of the "relaxation" they provide— which supposes a hierarchy in which Paul de Kock and Béranger rate higher than Shakespeare and Hugo—to whom shall he appeal? Such was the reading public in 1835; there was no other. The bourgeoisie have decided that Art should be good for the digestion: they go to the theater to digest and consider books the products of consumption.

Even this wouldn't matter much; but Gustave reveals to us—and he is not unaware of it himself—that he is secretly *on their side*, on the side of those opaque beings he has taken for judges. In the eighteenth chapter of the *Mémoires* he writes: "If I have experienced moments of enthusiasm, I owe them to art, and yet what vanity art is! To want to paint man in a bloc of stone or the soul in words, the feelings through sounds, and nature on a varnished canvas!" And he adds at the end of the same chapter: "Man, with his genius and his art, is but a miserable aping of something higher." We have read correctly: what irritates him about art is the unreality of its contents; to be truly a charismatic prince, above scholars and practitioners, the artist would have to *create being*. "I would like something that hadn't any need of expression or form, something pure like a perfume, strong like stone, ineffable like a song, that was at once all of these things and none of them." If art produced its own material in the way Kant's intelligible intuition makes what it conceives exist, it would be worth being an artist; but words, notes, are only delegates charged with *expressing* an absence—meaning, for Gustave, an unreality; aesthetic form, as it appears to him at this time, is a stamp imposed from the outside on a material that in itself is neither beautiful nor ugly. If beauty were to reclaim for itself some ontological dignity, it would have to produce its own material and emerge full-blown from a mind, like helmeted Minerva from the head of Jupiter; it would then be, in our conservative world where nothing is ever lost or created, an entirely new being, which would refer only to itself. Absolute, inexpressive, this being would not in any case be a means of communication between men, it would not imitate nature and would not ape creation; independent of us—and primarily of its creator—it would have, like the moon, like the sea, its own sufficiency of being and would impose itself on our sense organs as *interiority perpetuated in the exterior.* Unable to produce being *ex nihilo,* the artist will never be anything but a clown.

We shall return to this statement; the entire Flaubertian aesthetic of nonbeing is based paradoxically on the keen regret at not being able to *create* reality. I mention his disgust here only to make its motivation explicit. The ridiculous miracle-workers of art claim quite wrongly that they do better than scholars and practitioners. The latter create nothing, but by discovering natural laws they can "command nature" and change the course of things; the former change nothing, make visible nothing but mirages. To escape the terrifying and persistent intuition of his insubstantiality, the artist *plays a role,* he pretends to be that Demiurge who conceals himself or perhaps does not exist. But no sooner has he taken pen or brush in hand than he rediscovers the insufficiency of his being in the inconsistency of discourse or plastic composition, those unrealities he pulls out of his own nothingness. Is there anything more to say? Gustave dreamed of reviving in himself the positive plenitude, the sovereign intelligence and efficacy of the paterfamilias. After the Fall and the disillusionments of school, he understood that he would never manage to do this. And the choice of writing seemed to him at certain moments like an admission—it was in the cards; he took what the pioneers of being left to him: nothingness, the darkness of a directed oneirism swarming with incomplete phantoms, which revealed their transparency by dispersing at the least ray of light. Is it by reason of impotence, then, that one becomes a poet? Is art merely the humble pastime of the *minus habentes* who haven't brains enough to become "professionals"? Gustave claims to make no decision. But in the obscure passageways of his soul, *they* have decided for him: you have lost, literature is a refuge for submen

93

who are either unconscious of their subhumanity or trick themselves so as not to see it; you will know your pain since you have chosen to make yourself recognizable to those realistic kids who stand *with your father, with Achille, against you,* and who, despite your grand airs, you cannot help admitting are right.

Gustave would soon abhor machines, and particularly the railroad, all symbols of bourgeois progress; but his family so effectively conditioned him that, while secretly detesting Science, he would respect it until the end, even when in *Bouvard et Pécuchet,* terrified by his own blasphemies, he attempts to murder it. In this sense his existence is an excellent summation of those hundred years of vicissitudes in which French society would find itself constrained to absorb, willy-nilly, and digest—painfully—the methods and conclusions of experimental science. Who indeed could be better placed than the unworthy son of a celebrated practitioner to live out the contradictions that set exact knowledge against ideology, religion, and literature? But precisely for this reason Gustave was destined from his school years to lead a rearguard action which set him in conflict with himself and would not be resolved.

To compensate for his lack of scholarly success, the child Flaubert has tried to constitute himself as *daimon,* that is, as mediator between the negative infinite and the human race. But he cannot hide from himself that his ascensions are imaginary and that he is compelled, despite his great height, to *unrealize* himself as giant. This sudden insight throws into question the *value* of the unreal and would represent some kind of progress if he were fit to formulate clearly the alternatives that proceed from it and to opt for one of them: *either* limit himself to reality, submit to the judgment of his peers, accept the place his positive and practical work merits him—*or* break all his ties with being, unrealize himself totally, no longer worry about anyone's judgment, and content himself with his own *imaginary* appreciations of himself. In this last case he would have to make a rending revision, abandon his earthly ambitions, sacrifice himself to imagination out of a sincere love of nonbeing and its games. At school, he does not choose; the first option is repugnant to his pride—he was not loved enough to feel he has the right to be modest; the second option frightens him—he is not detached enough from the secular, he has revenge to take, dark passions to assuage, and he senses that this conversion would not be without catastrophe. One night, on the road to Pont-l'Evêque, freedom will pounce on him in the form of neurosis. But this passive and terrible determination requires long preparation: he will make the leap when it has become inevitable, when he has arrived at the end of suffering and is ready to "die by thought." For the moment, he would like to have it both ways, betting on the imaginary in order to make a clean sweep of reality. In fact, he loses on both accounts: being neither entirely unreal nor entirely real, in the name of existence he contests the superiorities he gives himself in imagination and finds himself once more alone and terrorized. Not only has he quite failed to "belittle" his classmates, but by escaping into the dream he has left the field to them; back at his point of departure, the traveler, broken at the foot of the rock he cannot climb, awaits the arrival of the wild beasts. Of course the wheel of torture keeps turning: before the return of the same perils, he begins his climb once more; he has lost, true, but great souls are recognized precisely in the immensity of their defeat: "My very superiority casts me down to the lowest rung." He chooses to be Sisyphus or Ixion—those two great guilt-bearers subjected to torture by repetition. And scarcely has Gustave begun his flight than he *already knows* that everything will repeat itself *as before*, and the resulting satisfaction to his amour-propre outstrips the knowledge of future humiliation. So compensatory absenteeism, without ceasing to be a defensive tactic, becomes *his* singular punishment insofar as, conscious of the tumble that will follow, he cannot—rage, terror, and misery—help using it. As we have seen, moreover, the original meaning of the stupors is bitter submission: you make life impossible for me, he says to his Lord; fine, I obey you and stop living; these bitter ecstasies are therefore above all imaginary exercises in self-destruction; they even contain a certain masochistic assent to the malice of his tormenters. Thus absenteeism symbolizes, in its spontaneous movement, an abolishment simultaneously suffered and desired. Beginning in the years 1833–35, Gustave, elaborating these semi-suicides, tried to give them all the arrogance of pride: I annihilate myself, but not alone and not altogether; you will return to the earth and will know nothing, I at least will remain formidably and lucidly conscious of my abolishment. These two aspects of his defensive strategy are presented together as inseparable: neither of them effaces the other, and Gustave lives both at once. Thus nothing will prevent the soaring eagle from feeling—not only in the future but at the very moment of his flight—like a child dying of shame. And the gloomy victories so loudly proclaimed, never felt *in reality*, never succeed in masking their odor of disguised defeats. Little Flaubert is going to lose himself and turn in the void.[67] He has tried as well to take refuge in an autistic oneirism (he is a rajah, he is Tamberlaine, he is a woman, a woman loves him with a devouring love that raises him above everyone—he is substituting an assumption for the impossible ascension), when a touch of genius assures him a provisional salvation. Tortured by the laughter of others, it is from laughter assumed, internalized, re-externalized as defensive aggression that he will demand his deliverance.

Aggressive Defense

"So I lived there alone and bored, plagued by my masters and derided by my comrades. I had a derisive and independent disposition, and my mordant and cynical irony no more spared the caprice of one than the despotism of all." Two consecutive lines; two little portraits of the same model that do not fit together: on the one side, the "noble and elevated soul," the "ardent and virgin nature" whom the materialism and cruelty of the society of children "vexes in all his tastes," the little savage "wandering alone in the long white corridors [of the] collège," unexpected victim of "beings with base impulses"; on the other, an aggressive and violent giant who attacks first, who knows how to put the scoffers in their place and to command respect. Fortunately Gustave explains to us a little further on that these two self-portraits correspond to two distinct moments in his temporalization: vexed by the contact with others, he contracted a chronic irritation that made him "impetuous and hot-headed."

First moment: the child, transplanted to an unfamiliar setting, was bewildered. If he was subjected to the mockeries of his comrades, *it was then*. In the sixth and seventh terms Gustave disturbed their conformism with his stupors. They laughed at him, they played a few tricks on him. Charles Bovary is not Gustave—although the author embodies himself several times in this character. But the future health officer's confusion when he enters school is certainly something little Flaubert experienced under the same circumstances. This identity of feelings is one justification, in the first chapter of *Madame Bovary*, for the use of the first person plural: when he recalls his first days at the collège, the author has an excessive tendency to put himself on the side of the derided; he says "we" in order to constrain himself to share solidarity with those doing the deriding and to present his char-

67. Like the narrator of the *Mémoires*, like *Smarh*.

acter *from the outside* in all his opacity. Of course, Flaubert does not find the object of laughter laughable: several young bourgeois, who are for the most part of urban origins, laugh at a little peasant, thus exorcizing his unwonted aspect. The complicity of teacher and students is evident. An unpublished passage makes this quite clear: "A new outburst [of laughter] once again caused by the unfortunate cap, which one student, in the disorder, had kicked right across the classroom to lodge in the opposite corner," is cut short by the "furious" voice of the master. "'Quiet now . . . As for you, sir, you over there, making your classmates laugh instead of conducting yourself modestly, you are going to copy the verb *"ridiculus sum"* twenty times— that will teach you to play the joker in class!'" [68] After this sudden attack, everything becomes calm once again. The master no longer concerns himself with the "poor devil"; but his classmates continue their persecution: "For the two interminable hours of his evening class, the poor *new boy*, sitting all alone on his little bench, did not raise his head, although from time to time a spitball . . . hitting him in the face made him shudder and start. He was resigned. He did not move."

If we want to understand the author's relations to this character, we must remember Gustave's attraction to idiots. Charles is not, properly speaking, an idiot, but his "slowness of mind" makes him seem like one; it is reminiscent, moreover, of that profundity possessed by fools which Gustave adores because it is *his own*. Thus we must see this first scene as a sort of negative and deliberately degraded reflection of his sublime stupors. They laugh at him, he has a stupid look with "his great staring eye," and the master, instead of punishing the laughers, inflicts an undeserved task on him as punishment every time. With this difference: Charles resigns himself; because he is deeply modest, this is his way of internalizing the derision. Gustave, mad with pride, does not resign himself. His self-esteem is wounded, the derision is internalized as resentment—it is a debt to pay off: " . . . derided by my comrades. I had a derisive disposition." The repetition, awkward as it seems, must not be attributed to negligence. "Derisive" follows "derided" because Gustave feels these words are bound together by an underlying affinity: derision is internalized peevishly as an offensive remark received in order to be externalized again as an offensive remark given. The little boy, beaten in scholastic competitions, sees the chance to vanquish his vanquishers on another ground: at recess, in the dormitory, everywhere but in the classroom, he will assert him-

---

68. *Ebauches et fragments inédits*, compiled by Gabrielle Leleu (Editions Conard), p. 9.

self; he will take the prize for peevishness, the prize for irony, the prize for blasphemy; derided in the name of conformity, conformity is what he will dismantle under the terrified eyes of his classmates. He will be malicious, mordant, offensive; his black humor, supported by his physical strength, will force them to live in a perpetual state of shock.

Let us not imagine, however, that a *decision* has been made: Gustave never decides anything. Moreover, it is no accident that the words he employs here are expressive of passivity: "*vexed* by the existence I was leading . . . [my kind of spirit] *had occasioned* in me a nervous irritation that *made* me *impetuous* and *hot-headed*, like the bull *sick* from being stung by insects." Everything is suffered. Impetuous, hot-headed—two adjectives that apply only to the *passions*—he charges at random, and at night "terrifying nightmares" ravage him. The first words of the paragraph are striking: "Although in excellent health . . ." Why does he feel the need to inform us of this? In order to make his persecutors guiltier? Undoubtedly. But when he wrote the *Mémoires* he was on the verge of illness: well before the crisis of 1844, very likely as early as 1838, he gave his father, as we shall see, cause for serious concern. Isn't he affirming his "vigors" with such bravado—as he will do again at the time of his neurosis—just to put us on the wrong track? To put *himself* on the wrong track? He is sound as a drum, this colossus: who could mistake his nervous troubles for an illness? And yet the adjective that comes spontaneously to his pen when he wants to qualify the bull is "sick." All things considered, Gustave seems to be proclaiming his health for fear of being struck down by mental illness. Besides, isn't he writing the memoirs of a *madman*? In short, he *suffers* his vehemence and his outbursts as nervous disorders: he is never their master any more than the bull is master of his fury. The *derision suffered* is externalized as *suffered aggression*—the thing happens by itself. We shall see that there are days when he is burning to slaughter the first passerby. And it must be noted that the passive character of this terrible violence that "transports" him is from the outset in danger of checking or preventing the *recurrence of laughter*. Gustave might be capable of striking out randomly at anyone, if he dared, but not of choosing his victim among those who have humiliated him, of lying in wait, watching for him silently, finding the chink in his armor and making a single, well-placed—wounding—thrust. For that, Gustave would have to master himself, to learn to channel his anger in order to transform it into active aggression, to know how to use the Flaubert heritage, the pitiless surgical gaze that makes "lies fall into fragments." Even more, he would have to *interest himself in others;* in the first place, he should not begin by keeping them at a distance. In order to hurt people one must know them, and in order to know them one must share some bond of interiority with them, find oneself in a situation where their *habitus,* their tics, their vices, their qualities compromise us in one way or another *within ourself.* We mustn't think that observation is best served by the reciprocal exteriority of the observer and the observed, and that the psychiatrist, a man of good sense, must refuse to enter into his patient's delirium in order to cure him. The exteriority of the witness merely reveals the subject's *external being,* in other words, the level of objectivity at which he is external to himself. The only way of gaining understanding is to become intimately involved, to go where the search challenges the searcher: the true psychiatrist is mad by vocation; his madness is his best tool for penetrating the madness of others. For this reason, the most formidable deriders, those who know how to make their victims bleed for a long time with a quiet but well-placed word, are found in the bosom of families: this aunt is famous for her "shrewishness," that uncle for his vitriolic comments; the old couple humiliate each other incessantly because they are both deeply bound together and *compromising* to each other.

From childhood, Flaubert declared himself a misanthrope: he kept his fellow creatures at a distance and, by means of several abstract negations, blinded himself; individuals escaped him to the extent that he chose to see only *man* in each of them and to have merely a glancing acquaintance with our species. Claiming to "survey," he neither observes nor comprehends anyone and occasionally brags about it: "I have now come round to seeing the world as a spectacle and laughing at it. What do I care about the world? I shall ask little of it, I shall let myself drift with the current of the heart and the imagination, and if someone cries out too loudly, perhaps I shall turn around, like Phocion, and say: What's all this crowing about!" [69] The incoherence of the metaphor (we know how carefully Gustave usually "follows out" his images) is quite significant: if he hasn't realized that one cannot look at the world while turning one's back on it, it is because for him, at this time, turning one's back on the world amounts to the same thing as surveying it and laughing at it; the essential thing is to escape from the real, to derealize it as spectacle by derealizing himself as spectator. He has been taught the technique by Alfred, who, enclosed

69. To Ernest, 13 September 1838, *Correspondance* 1:30.

in his arrogant indifference, has no interest in knowing men. As a good disciple, Gustave turns all his efforts to cultivating his own ignorance of them. We shall see that this incomprehension of others—so striking in his correspondence—far from hampering him in his work as a novelist will be a considerable help. He was always ignorant of the "psyche" of his friends. Alfred, Maxime, Ernest, and even Louis Bouilhet escaped him quite as much as those two lapdogs, Edmond and Jules, or Princess Mathilde. The Goncourts in particular, despite their neurotic malice or rather because of it, always knew much more about him than he knew about them. On the other hand, we shall never find wounding remarks in his letters: hateful, yes, sometimes openly so, sometimes gently dissembling; venomous, no. He is both above and below that. Above: his consciousness surveys the human race, which he totally despises; why should he have to refine, go into detail? Below: in company he is suddenly prey to a vampire—we shall see who—and too busy *filling* the stage to pay attention to anybody else.

One wonders, with some reason, how under these conditions Gustave can boast of his *irony:* isn't that attitude the very opposite of his constituted character and his aspirations? It presupposes, in effect, a slight but real detachment in relation to a concrete and singular situation. Yet Gustave is pinioned and escapes from his bonds only by taking refuge in the imaginary and in generalities. Neither in his correspondence nor in the accounts of "witnesses to his life" do we find a trace of this cheerful flippancy.[70] The Goncourts' *Journal* speaks of his licentious pleasantries, of his paradoxes; later, after Flaubert's death, Edmond will regret his "savage replies." No one thinks of crediting him with "wit." How should we understand the

---

70. It goes without saying that the irony of a pamphleteer rarely has its source in detachment alone and is accompanied by hatred or anger against a collective or an individual; Voltaire's best lines are born of wounded self-esteem. Nevertheless, irony presupposes in the "man of wit" a mode of insertion in the world which allows him, in case of danger, a certain kind of *real distancing*. It is not that he sees his adversaries as the giant sees the Myrmidons, which would deprive him of the power to *collectivize* his laughter, to communicate it to others—who would only be wounded by the universality of this pantagruelization. Quite to the contrary, such distancing allows the "man of wit" to demonstrate, in the name of certain common ends—which readers will recognize, even if they are subject to silence—the vanity, the frivolousness of the enterprises of the enemy. The ironist provokes a *loss of being* in the individual or in the thing considered, and that effect can be produced only if, taking his distance, he expresses at the same time his connivance with a certain community which will, he knows, take up the laughter on its own account. Voltaire's wit is analytic reason dismembering the privileges of the aristocracy. He makes one laugh as an *individual of a certain class.*

mordant, derisive humor he attributes to himself? The answer is in a single word that figures in the text from the *Mémoires* cited above: *cynicism*. Incapable of attacking his comrades for their particular faults, for their styles of life, their inadequacies, or their imperfections, he condemns their enterprises to their faces by demonstrating the vanity of it all with a burst of laughter. Just watch him at work. He attacks a little bigot, a pensioner at Father Eudes's. Will he try to destroy him by remarks about his stupidity or his pedantry or, if you like, his compulsion to sniff? No, because he doesn't see any of that, or isn't concerned with it. Will he try, at least, to attack him in his faith, which is perhaps somewhat vulnerable, to insinuate doubt in this smug believer? That is what someone truly evil would do, no doubt—if there were such a person. Gustave himself, highly conscious of stirring up his neighbors' interests, seeks *to scandalize*. By attacking the Church? Perhaps to begin with. But he doesn't dwell on this and he doesn't even mention such attacks in his letter. In fact, he makes the boy "sweat blood" by an orgy of obscene and *gratuitous* inventions: Father Eudes is a pederast, he sleeps with his pensioners and in particular with Gustave's unhappy neighbor; doubtless Gustave would be pleased to detail their amorous play—if this is not said, it is clearly suggested. Yet the derider knows perfectly well that his accusations do not contain a word of truth; he knows that the little believer knows it and that his comrades are not unaware of it either. And since he pretends to believe what he says, it is evident—and primarily in his own eyes—that he *is playing a role*. After all, he calmly writes to Ernest: "I was magnificent," the way one would say Kean was magnificent as Hamlet. What does Gustave want, then? To harm his neighbor by demoralizing him. And is it really demoralizing to hear calumnies that are groundless except, perhaps, for the general fact—spread by rumour—that there are some priests who are pederasts? Certainly: the pious child is terrified by these obscene imputations, even—especially—if they are notoriously false. The elaboration of his fictive frolics with Father Eudes reveals to him not his unworthiness but the reality he was unwilling to see: his spiritual guide conceals beneath his robe a member that might be animated by expert fingers or a compliant mouth. This possibility, as a consequence of the major prohibition that accompanies it, is immediately transformed if not into a positive temptation, at least into this negative one: the fear of being tempted.

The abomination, above all, is that Father Eudes can be publicly exposed. The little Catholic no doubt admired the celibacy of priests, that sacred renunciation of the flesh: he forgot their bodies because their holy chastity, by freeing them from the flesh, was itself forgotten. By deliberately slandering the mores of the good father, the little mocker is denouncing chastity itself, which is only an ineffectual lie, for the "brave genital organ" is still there. For the son of Dr. Flaubert, function creates need; if Father Eudes is not a Priapus, he still has the necessary equipment and is not prevented from dreaming of the imaginary obscenities that accompany a very real onanism. And there we have it, a fundamental principle of the Catholic church crushed. Rather cheaply, it's true—we know what a theologian would answer. But in fact it is a theological issue; a poor child sweats with fear while his neighbor blasphemes under his breath and his classmates turn around to look at him, half amused, half shocked. Hasn't Gustave in this case simply offered himself as a spectacle and, in the name of an a priori misanthropy (men are "a little more than trees, a little less than dogs," parish priests are no exception), *played the role of blasphemer?* In other words, by means of fictions recognized as such by all his listeners, he has demonstrated the universal hypocrisy and futility of a "noble" enterprise (the celibacy of priests is a sworn enterprise for every one of them) and *cynically* revealed "base" reality. It hardly matters that Father Eudes does not "bugger" his pensioners, for other priests do it in other institutions and he is tempted to do it a hundred times a day. Of that, Gustave is convinced: in *Agonies* he shows a priest running to brothels; later, without insisting on the properly carnal aspect of their desire, he would more generally denounce the *materialism* of the ministers of God; those representatives of the Ideal are absorbed in satisfying their organic needs. The shame is triple: a child believes he is defiled and that his ears are sinful; his comrades feel a vague discomfort, they laugh awkwardly, Bouilhet himself is disgusted; Ernest will read the letter meant for him without pleasure, with a certain dread. Everyone will agree that Gustave is an amusing fellow but that his cynicism sometimes spills over into baseness. This is just what the little actor wants: to embarrass, to wound the individual by attacking him, not in his idiosyncrasy but in his generality or, if you prefer, in his *human nature.* To do that, you have to *play a role:* What is his "derision," basically, in this particular case? Nothing but his desolate disbelief turning itself against others and becoming the cynical negation of faith. The unbeliever-in-spite-of-himself plays this character in public: the braggart of incredulity.

This is clearly the result of the rude remarks he tosses off to Ernest when Chevalier, a student in Paris, begins to irritate him. One day, for example, Chevalier confides to Gustave that he "is fixed in the definitive belief in a creative force, God, fatality, etc., and that granting this point will allow him to enjoy some highly agreeable moments." Nothing could be more infuriating to the young agnostic who, like Mazza, "envies and despises" believers. He answers sharply:

> I cannot imagine calling it agreeable, really. When you have seen the dagger destined to pierce your heart, the rope destined to strangle you . . . I cannot imagine what could be consoling about that. Do your best to arrive at a belief in the plan of the universe, in morality, in the duties of man, in the chastity of whores, in the integrity of ministers of state, in the goodness of man, in the happiness of life, in the veracity of all possible lies. Then you will be happy and you will be able to call yourself a believer, and three-fourths an imbecile.[71]

No doubt he was trying to wound Ernest. Yet the attack is not aimed at him as an individual but at the *act of faith* in its generality, that bigoted, philanthropic, optimistic foolishness of the sort Gustave encountered in Father Eudes's poor pensioner. It seems that Chevalier has managed this act of faith or is on his way to doing so: Gustave is going to show him the dotage that ineluctably awaits him at the end of his chosen path. We see the process: that progressive dotage, that paralysis of thought is the abstract but certain consequence of faith, whoever the believer; but because Ernest is fixed in a definitive belief, imbecility becomes his singular fate. If the option is firmly taken, the young man is lost, and it is a duty and a pleasure to let him know, disdainfully, the stages of his regression; if he is only half decided, this scornful mockery will give him a healthy jolt, like a hot cauterizing iron.

And where is Gustave in all this? *Who* is he to give such advice? The last words of the paragraph inform us: "In the meantime, remain a man of wit, skeptical and hard-drinking." Witty, skeptical, hard-drinking—this is exactly what Chevalier is not. Furthermore, Gustave uses the verb *remain* just to be polite. We should understand: *be like me*, a man of wit, etc. We cannot doubt that the younger son of the family is playing a role here: to call his heavy irony wit is a distortion. As for drinking, he practiced that, no doubt, under the influence of Alfred, a solitary drinker. But he was afraid of going too far, having

---

71. *Correspondance* 1:35, 30 November 1838. The incorrect grammar (the belief of . . . [*la croyance de*]), the abrupt changes (*belief of* is transformed without warning into *belief in*, etc.) are sufficient indication that he is upset.

inherited the Flaubert prudence—desperate, yes, but not reckless. As for skepticism, couldn't it be said, reading him, that he turns it into aristocratic nonchalance? A person drinks and then laughs at everything, like Mathurin. But in that very year, 1838—probably at the beginning of the summer—he had just finished *Mémoires d'un fou*, which was originally, as he writes in the preface, supposed "to be an intimate novel in which skepticism *would be pushed to the limits of despair.*" What has changed, he explains then, is not the theme, but the novel has become *Mémoires*, "the personal impression broke through the story." Skepticism is therefore not, for Gustave, the soft pillow of the honest man; it is the awful desolation born of his "belief in nothing." In other words, in order more effectively to mock Chevalier and his idiotic religiosity, Gustave changes the signs: could he, the lacerated child of the Hôtel-Dieu, convince Ernest if he countered the agreeable moments religion already provides for his friend by reciting his own tribulations, his horror of life, his painful and vain efforts *to believe?* At once he disguises himself as an eighteenth-century libertine. A man of wit and breeding, too shrewd to give in to religious obscurantism, he believes in nothing, but he does so joyfully; expecting neither punishment nor reward, he amuses himself with his own intelligence, enjoys the present without fear, and—the height of elegance—knows how to drink. Is this Gustave, this libertine lord? No, it is the character he has chosen to play in order to shame Ernest most effectively. We might say that his transported pen makes him into this character. Necessarily, so that Chevalier should be stung by his irony. And necessarily, therefore, Gustave must *believe* in that agnostic scoffer who vampirizes him. He does believe in him, but *only while he is mocking his friend;* in the next paragraph he is already someone else: "Poor Rousseau, who was so slandered, your heart was nobler than the hearts of others." This time we recognize the child cast down below the others "by his very superiority."

In a few years, the "man of wit" will become his *bête noire.* This character, assimilated by Gustave's provincialism to the Parisian who shines in the salons, annoyed him precisely by the narrowness of his views: he flies close to earth and amuses himself demolishing molehills, leaving creation as a whole untouched; Flaubert, the wholesaler of corrosion, can have only contempt for this retailer. Between the ages of sixteen and eighteen, however, he mentions him favorably and recognizes himself in him: "A joke is the most powerful, the most terrible thing, it is irresistible—there is no tribunal to call it to account in the name of either reason or feeling—a thing held in derision is a dead thing, a man who laughs is stronger than one who is afflicted. Voltaire was the king of his century because he knew how to laugh— that was his entire genius, it was everything."[72] The note following bears on the same subject, and in it we find that same gaiety Flaubert had previously flaunted, the better to humiliate Ernest: "Gaiety is the essence of wit—a witty man is a man of gaiety, an ironic, skeptical man who knows life, philosophy, and mathematics; reason means power, the fatality of ideas—the poet is flesh and tears. The facetious man is a fire that burns."[73] Shall we fall into the trap? Shall we think, as he wants us to, that the witty man is a man of gaiety? In this case we should not have read *Smarh*, in which he writes, speaking of his own time: "One laughed, but the laughter was anguished, men were weak and wicked, the world was mad." We should rather have noted the violence of certain phrases: "A thing held in derision is a dead thing," and "the facetious man is a fire that burns." They foreshadow the article on Rabelais (1839, Flaubert was seventeen):

> All at once a man arrived unexpectedly . . . who set himself to writing a book . . . full of mordant and cruel derision . . . Everything that had hitherto been respected over the centuries, philosophy, science, magic, fame, renown, power, ideas, beliefs, all that is knocked off its pedestal, humanity is stripped of its state robes . . . it trembles quite naked in the impure breath of the grotesque . . . it is ugly and repulsive, Panurge throws his jugs of wine at its head and begins to laugh . . . [A] real laugh, strong, brutal, the laughter that shatters and smashes, that laughter which, with Luther and '93, struck down the Middle Ages . . . Gargantua is terrible and monstrous in his gaiety.

And he concludes, apropos the nineteenth century: "Now a man named Rabelais comes along . . . If the poet could hide his tears and start laughing, I assure you that his book would be more terrible and more sublime than any before." Derision kills, facetiousness is a fire that burns, hilarity shatters and smashes. Fine; and now we understand this passage from a letter to Ernest, written in 1838: "I deeply value only two men, Rabelais and Byron, the only two who have written with the intention of hurting the human race and laughing in its face. What a tremendous position a man occupies who places himself in that relation to the world."[74] But precisely because of that—for the

72. *Souvenirs*, p. 172.
73. *Souvenirs*, pp. 72–73.
74. *Correspondance* 1:29, 13 September 1838.

very reasons he articulates—this painful, fierce, devastating laughter cannot, we are now certain, be the laughter of gaiety. Gustave the poet spills tears of rage; if he "hides his tears and starts laughing," do they stop burning inside him?

His project, however, is more evident to us: the raptures-stupors had, among other functions, that of nourishing his scornful indifference toward men; this purely internal attitude no longer suffices. The fact is that his classmates laugh at him while he is busy scorning them. He knows only too well that this ataraxia is imaginary; to tell the truth, his indifference must be externalized by a *counter-laugh* all the more gigantic as it must crush the endless jeering of the scholarly collective. The giant leans over the Myrmidons and bursts out laughing to see them killing each other. To give one's life, to take that of others, for illusions, lies, or idiotic passions, or goods which presuppose that we live in order to enjoy them—that is farcical. The human race is *comical,* and since "the thing held in derision is a dead thing," Gustave's cosmic laughter is, in his eyes, the accomplishment of a fantasied genocide. As he claims not to share any human ends, it is easy for him to base his hilarity on his "belief in nothing," on absolute nihilism. The difficulties are otherwise: they come from the grandiose and unrealizable conception his pride has whispered to him. The first is purely theological: it is difficult to see how a "brahmin lost in the idea" can concern himself with mocking men; in other words, how can the infinite *which is ignorant of them* know them well enough simultaneously to hold them in derision? Gustave is incapable of enlightening us; but we know that his ataraxia is feigned, that he is burning with rage and turns to the ecstasies to annihilate his classmates; if he has never really experienced indifference, his laughter will be merely another way of escaping the violence that strangles him by *externalizing* it in the form of defensive aggression. Something more serious is involved. I have demonstrated that the laugh is a collective and serial reaction, and that as a lesser lynching its aim was to denounce in a troublesome man the subman who takes himself seriously. Yet such is Gustave's pride that he, the one excluded, pretends to laugh *alone* and at the whole human race. This is what he calls, in another letter, "philosophizing and pantagruelizing." Let us note in passing these words in his Rabelais: "Gargantua is terrible and *monstrous* in his gaiety." Obviously, then, his laughter is a *retort*: this adolescent wants to laugh insofar as he is *alone,* nonintegrated, desperate; this monster pretends to laugh *insofar as he is a monster* of society who turns his anomalies into derision. Is this possible? I answer, no, *on principle:* he who is exiled by the ostracism of laughter hasn't the means to turn that derision against the community that exiles him. And, furthermore, the laughers play the parts *of men* by laughing at the submen who falsely claim to be part of the human race. One could laugh at this race only if one found oneself situated *above it:* man, that sub-giant, would be laughable for the Gargantuas and Pantagruels only if, unaware of his rank as sub-giant, he claimed to be a member of the race of giants. Moreover, the laughers would have to be plural and to be allied, all of them, to the community of giants.

Gustave cuts through these Gordian knots rather than untying them. Since his comrades' laughter cuts him off from human nature, he claims to have the choice: subman *or* superman. And his rage and pride lead him to opt for the unrecognized superman. He is a monster, fine: but a monster for the human race. Not for Gargantua, who is of his kind and who, attacked by men, "pisses on them so stingingly that he kills them all." His ecstasies have shown him that he is "as big as the world" and that he can mock the "narrow minds" who dare to laugh at him. Laughter becomes at all levels the superior race's lesser lynching of an inferior race that takes itself seriously. In these circumstances, it is men, small natures too weary to drink, to eat, to struggle, to jog along on the shell of the earth, who take themselves for giants, and it is giants—laughable themselves in relation to the negative infinite—who laugh at men. Gustave *elaborates the laughter:* we have described *primary* hilarity when—masochistic and sadistic—he wanted only to make men laugh at him. His fury led him to *secondary* hilarity: reversing the terms, he pretends to "pantagruelize," meaning, to direct his corrosive derision not only toward the failures of the human race but toward humanity itself insofar as it is merely a failure of being. No sooner has he ridiculed a young believer, a termite fatuous enough to believe that he possesses the infinite, than his laughter unmasks the incredible stupidity of the gluttons for work; such ants care for nothing but getting ahold of a first prize, when in other establishments in the same town, in other schools in other provinces, other insects are occupied with the same ambition, and when nature, boundless, indifferent to human ends, has produced them by chance in order to crush them without reason.

This first point, then, is quite clear: Gustave grants himself the right to laugh because he judges himself qualified to take the cosmic point of view toward our race. He has had predecessors: Voltaire before him laughed at man by looking at him through the eyes of Micromégas. And he will have successors: Queneau more skillfully describes our mores *from the outside* in *Saint-Glinglin,* and in this regard it can be said that science fiction is, among other things, a huge mockery mixed with the darkest anguish. Moreover, none of these authors, tempted by *secondary* hilarity, laughs *first:* they are won over, in the last instance, by the laughter they have provoked in their readers. Gustave's weakness at his point of departure is that he wants to laugh *alone* and at *everyone,* which is on principle an impossibility. Were he Gargantua leaning over the human vermin, he would not cheer up if he did not refer, at least in thought, to his pals, the Titans. Yet there is only one Titan, himself, and he is still only an imaginary one. Would his laughter not remain imaginary as well? If so, what has he gained by externalizing the internalized laughter of others?

Nothing, if he limits himself to laughing up his sleeve, alone—he would be playing a role without objective efficacy. But I have mentioned above a stroke of genius: he is going to *make laughter.* At himself. But even as he offers himself as a spectacle, he arranges things such that his classmates are obliged to laugh at themselves and at human nature when they believe they are amused at him. To laugh in the face of humanity makes no sense, or else it means laughing uncontrollably at humanity at the sight of one's own nakedness. No, Gustave has no wit; when he believes he is being ironic, he is mistaken; he is betrayed by a word, the woebegone little monster who suffers from taking everything seriously; the man of wit, he tells us, is *"facetious."* And this is just what the Flaubert younger son is going to be from now on. Jokes, cock-and-bull stories, puns, and nonsense. He is the life of the party, in brief, a jester, always laughing, always ready to make others roll with laughter, a clown: this is the role he plays at school and even in his family, to the point of sickening his parents and sometimes even his sister. But let us take care: his farces are venomous—each is a vignette suggesting that man is grotesque; the spectators, caught in the trap, must first laugh at Gustave, the subman, and then find that they are laughing at themselves. This is why he will demand his comrades' concurrence in creating, with them and against them, that combative character the *Garçon.*

Birth of the Garçon

The first time Flaubert refers to him in his correspondence is on 24 March 1837: "When I think of the proctor's mug, caught in the act . . . I cry out, I laugh, I drink, I chant, ha! ha! ha! ha! ha! and I let the Garçon's laughter ring out." Yet the letter immediately preceding this one is dated 24 August 1835; his silence of eighteen months remains unexplained, but whatever the reason for it—letters Chevalier lost or burned, etc.—it is clear that the character made his appearance during this period at a date we can determine very approximately by rereading the previous letters.

Until the summer holidays of 1834, these letters have the naïveté, the seriousness of childhood.[75] Gustave scarcely smiles and willingly moves from righteous indignation to commonplace and sometimes elegiac sententiousness.[76] From 29 August 1834 on, he gives evidence of the most vivid and brutal frenzies; if he didn't have "a queen of France at the end of his pen" (he is writing a novel about Isabeau de Bavière), a bullet would long since have delivered him from this farcical joke called life. The first totalization through laughter: life is a farce; there are only two ways out, suicide or literature. Yuk does not yet exist, but he is very close to being born and dethroning Satan. The change is emphasized with the letter from the following 28 September: until now, Gustave has used the proper phrases of a well-bred child. Yet here he raises his voice, the language becomes coarser: "derision" makes its entrance. The publisher—unless it was Ernest—has taken it upon himself to delete two passages (this is the first time but not the last); happily, what remains gives us the measure of what was removed: "Here's the start of school again *r'arriving* with its bloody affected air . . . Well, dogshit on it." From this point on, his writing will alternate between the clownish and the serious, and he will ever more frequently express the nastiness of resentment (we know what *that* means) by laughter: "You will be pleased to learn that our friend Delhomme has a black eye, his right one, but in a strange way, so wierd and brutal that the whole side of his face is swollen as a result . . . He was in the infirmary, they put ten leeches on the shiner. Ah, poor Livarot, a damned good joke! That'll give us something to laugh about for two or three days at least."[77] And it is striking that Gustave's reaction is so close to the one he will have nineteen months later upon learning, on 24 March 1837, that the proctor has been caught in a brothel. In '35: "You will be pleased to learn . . ." In '37: "I

75. Cf. 26 August 1834. To Ernest, *Correspondance* 1:13. Here Flaubert tells the story of a drowning and the comments it inspires.
76. An exception, however, is the letter of 31 March 1832: "One student at Père Langlois's nearly . . . fell into the privy . . . If he had not pulled himself out, he would have fallen into Père Langlois's excrement." Here we find once more the scatological vein of the "Explication de la fameuse constipation."
77. *Correspondance* 1:16–17, 2 July 1835.

have a pleasant bit of news to tell you . . ." In both cases the account of the event follows, laced with exclamation marks, with insults to the victim. Then comes the jubilation; in 1835: "a damned good joke!"; in 1837: "Now there's a good trick!" Each of the two paragraphs ends with a burst of laughter; in 1835, Gustave promises to "laugh about it for two or three days at least"; in 1837, the description is more epic: "I am rolling on the ground, tearing my hair out, it's so good," etc. But of course the news is much funnier: a broken jaw is an ordinary occurrence; a proctor caught at a brothel—that's a rare treat. The only notable difference between the two texts is that in the first one the Garçon is not named. From this we can conclude that he was not yet born in July 1835: since the two attitudes are basically identical, why wouldn't Flaubert have mentioned him? But by the same token we must recognize that everything is in place and everyone is waiting just for him: the *persona* is being gestated through whom cosmic laughter will have the means to become a singular universal. Other signs announce the appearance of the persona: it is at this period, indeed, that Gustave's tendency to clothe himself in pseudonyms so as to maintain his inner experience between the "I" and the "He" is manifest for the first time in his correspondence. In the same letter he writes: "I forgot to tell you a new bit of news, that my poetic incognito is 'Gustave Koclott.' I hope this will suffice to baffle the most cunning and vicious tongue in our good town of Rouen." And he signs: "Gustave Antuoskothi Koclott."

2 July: the schoolboys are about to leave on vacation; it seems unlikely that in the last days of the school year the students of the upper seventh term would have taken the time to forge a myth. We must suppose that the creation took place after the "October reunion." Not later, in any case, than the end of autumn 1835 or than the beginning of January 1836. Since the summer, Gustave had been in confinement: he was going on fourteen and knew that he had lost the game, but the flattering encouragement of Chéruel and Gourgaud gave him the inner strength to do an about-face; he remained surrounded, ill, but instead of charging at random, he deliberately marched forward and tried to give as good as he got. Between July and October, he discovered laughter as the disqualification of the finite by the infinite and of being by nothingness. No doubt the shock provoked by the return to school, "r'arriving with its bloody affected air," sufficed to induce the birth.

This does not of course mean that one day Gustave could have cried out, "Suddenly, there was the Garçon," as Cocteau would do—

"Suddenly, there was Eugène"—in *Le Potomak*. We know that there were "Garçonnades" in which this character did not figure at all. For example, that procession of skeletons for which Flaubert acted as master of ceremonies—the Garçon would have adored this mockery of life by death and death by life; there is no doubt that he would have taken part in the ceremony if not for one major obstacle: he had not yet been born. Gustave made a new beginning, he returned to school determined to assert himself by his "buffoonery"; certain of his classmates made themselves his accomplices, and their buffoonery remained impersonal until they claimed a *collective subject*, the symbol and unity of these desperate pranksters.

Here the question of paternity arises: who created the Garçon? Gustave? His gang? The two together? What share of the responsibility should be given to the group, what to the individual? The Goncourts' text is quite clear: they note on 10 April 1860: "Flaubert . . . spoke to us at length about a creation that deeply occupied his early youth. With several comrades and with one in particular, Le Poittevin, a school friend. . . , they had invented an imaginary character . . . They took turns putting themselves in his shoes, and their joking spirit into his voice." [78] Unfortunately, these few sentences are swarming with errors: Le Poittevin was not and never had been "Gustave's schoolmate." He left the *collège* in July, 1834, after his year of Rhetoric. Besides, in none of the letters we possess does he claim paternity or copaternity of the Garçon. The rare times that, to my knowledge, he speaks of him, he keeps his distance and seems to regard him as a creature belonging to Flaubert. If at times Alfred behaves in the style of this mythic hero, it is without ever referring to him. We have seen him imitate the cries of "the woman being pleasured." And when he laughs at Lengliné, his "strange" laugh, reflexive and secondary, which denounces the foolish cynicism of the young bourgeois's primary and spontaneous laughter, is not without analogy, at least in its meaning, to the laughter of the Garçon, but Alfred is far removed from the frantic violence and the gigantism that characterize the invented persona. He prefers aesthetic detachment, which he no doubt judges more "elegant," and a number of times comes close to faulting the "extravagances" of his comrade. [79] If he "shamelessly" questions passersby and acts out "the woman being pleasured," it is on his own account, for no other reason than his whim and circumstance: this in-

78. Edition de Monaco, 3:247.
79. As the dedications of *Agonies* and the *Mémoires* prove.

dividualist is not at all tempted to escape from himself, to leave his own skin and put himself into the skin of a collective, ritual being. We have seen that he is constitutionally allergic to ceremonies—except those that are celebrated in the family. Moreover, even when he unwinds, he remains cold and lucid: "We have committed, as is reasonable, not a little nonsense." And he adds that he has come home weary of others and of himself. If he was sometimes able, out of complacency, to adopt what the Goncourts call "a heavy, obstinate, enduring joke," I doubt that he ever took much interest in it or could be ranked among its "coauthors." The Thursday conversations, moreover, and Gustave explicitly says so, revolved around "elevated" subjects—"we flew so high"—and if the two friends ridiculed the whole of Creation they claimed, at least, to do it as "philosophers" and not as "buffoons."

Ernest himself "*did the Garçon*," we can be sure. He bowed at times to the tyranny of the Garçonic "freemasonry"—which allows Gustave to fault the serious young deputy magistrate of Calvi *in the name of his hero*. Ernest's contribution to *Art et Progrès* proves that the future card-carrying bourgeois began, like anyone else, by despising his class of origin; the national guardsman whose cowardice he ridicules in his story is none other than the bourgeoisie under Louis-Philippe, meaning, more or less directly—did he know it?—his father. We are aware, as well, that he carried a knife in his pocket "like Antony." Only the friends were neither in the same year nor in the same class at school. Ernest was beginning the tenth term when Gustave was starting the eighth. Certainly they saw each other often at school; the journal that was the fruit of their collaboration is proof of that. But for them to have collaborated in the collective creation as well, to have spontaneously invented and imposed their inventions on Gustave's comrades, would have required Ernest's being around them every day, which is hardly credible. Gustave himself, in his correspondence, mentions neither Chevalier nor Le Poittevin among the creators. In point of fact, he names only one of them, Pagnerre, in a line that implies that there were others, "one *of the* creators . . ." But the collaboration with Pagnerre seems somehow to exclude the possibility that Gustave's two childhood friends would have contributed much to the invention of the character: Pagnerre, in fact, never counted among Flaubert's "intimates"; he was a good pal, that's all. We must conclude that the Garçon, far from being a hothouse product cultivated in the intimacy of the Hôtel-Dieu by three inseparable friends, first saw the light of day outdoors, in the course of quarrels and practical jokes, and that he was created out in the open (at recess, in the refectories and dormitories) by those same boys who took him as a symbol of universal mockery: a group of "scamps" belonging to the upper half of the eighth-year class.

Gustave himself insists on the character's collective or, as the Goncourts say, *generic* character. He is called *the* Garçon in the same way Genet speaks of "*the* Thief." This effectively makes the character—though individuated by a personality, habits, a history—a "type" (this is the word the two brothers use), like *the* Misanthrope or *the* Miser. But the strongest proof of his *plural* origin is that—in contrast to the two Molière characters—he cannot be made the object of a concept[80] or even of a *notion.* Genet's Thief, a singular universal that is grasped only within a temporalization, pertains to notional knowledge; at least that knowledge can be made explicit by the fact that it is constituted as a transcendence of the concept of *theft.* This concept, preserved in the project which transcends it, illuminates *from within* the movement by which a thief, assuming responsibility for himself, becomes *the* thief. The Garçon, on the other hand, is not an object of *knowledge*—not at first, in any case. After the conversation of 10 April 1860, the Goncourts declare him "rather difficult to understand," and the context proves in fact that they did not understand him at all: they report precious bits of information in which they see no unity. Otherwise, would they be stupid enough to write that Monsieur Homais seems to them to be "the figure of the Garçon reduced for the needs of the novel"? The creators themselves—beginning with Gustave—appear unable to *explain* their creature. "To be situated at a certain point of view," writes Merleau-Ponty, "is necessarily not to see it oneself, not to possess it as a visual object except in a virtual signification."[81] And, at first, the Garçon is just that: a point of view on the world. Impossible to be there and to see it at the same time. Let us not conclude, however, that the character is simply a bunch of poorly strung together, heterogeneous clownings: those who act out the character undoubtedly *understand* him, for they *invent aptly;* if by chance their invention does not hold together, the group rejects it—whether by protest or by letting it slide quickly into oblivion. There is a Garçon's Word and Deed, that is, a collection of appropriate and acknowledged improvisations which tend to be preserved in the form of

---

80. Certainly the author of *l'Avare* [The Miser] goes beyond the concept, enriches it with his experience or inventions; but for him, for Plautus his model, and for the audience, *avarice* is the object of conceptual knowledge.
81. *Structure du comportement,* p. 234.

a liturgy. This obscurity of *meaning*—implicitly, but never explicitly, understood—in conjunction with the permanent control exercised by their public over the creators, is sufficient evidence that the character is a *collective property:* each one regards this obscurity from the outside to the extent that he knows how to slip inside as soon as he wants or feels inspired to do so. For lack of knowing *to what* they should relate the scene they are witnessing (as one does, for example, when one judges an actor by his role, that is, by the author's intentions, by previous interpretations of the same character, etc.), the schoolboys make themselves its critics insofar as they are themselves creators, that is, in terms of their own past discoveries, "virtual significations" which therefore served as guiding schemes to their imagination. Better, in virtue of these same schemes they collaborate in the present improvisation by regarding it from the Garçon's point of view: they support and exalt the improviser by their approbation, and they intuit his next inventions, which amounts to inventing them halfway. This explains why the archetype is never minted in multiple copies. Cocteau, the solitary designer, discovers Eugène, then *the* Eugènes. At the Rouen *collège,* there was only *one* Garçon, of whom a little community of initiates made themselves the guardians; all the members of the group in turn had the right to identify with him—no order in this, at least in theory, no privilege. Some, no doubt, less frenzied or more timid, more often remained spectators or played "supportive" characters; for the others, inspiration was the decisive factor. Someone fell into a trance, the group recognized him as being possessed, the provisional incarnation of the Archetype; they organized to feed him lines, he would outdo himself, go beyond the limits of his powers, finally collapse, and all fell back into the silence of seriality unless another instantly took his place. The reason for this is simple: the Garçon's point of view, considered in its most abstract nakedness, is laughter. Not the notion of laughter but laughter as *Weltanschauung.* And laughter is a collective behavior: it is therefore impossible to create the "Master of Laughter" without this individuated character being in each one successively the unification of a collectivity that laughs. The Garçon *makes* laughter, that is, he captures it in its dispersal and makes a *display* of it. We shall return to this.

   We shall never know the part each boy took in this collective creation. The very name "Garçon"—though I think it highly unlikely—could have been contributed by an unknown schoolmate of Flaubert's. Gustave certainly considered himself the producer, the ringmaster, and the principal inventor of this "enduring joke": with what occasionally annoying insistence he reminds his former schoolmates of their "common" work! The family is kept abreast of this: his sister Caroline considers the Garçon a common property of the group and at the same time Gustave's private property. Reporting an episode of the sort to gladden her brother's pride, she asks, him, "Have I sufficiently flattered the vanity of the Garçon?" as if this character were Gustave himself in the third person singular. The process of identification—which will later make Saint Polycarpe Flaubert's being-for-others—begins here quite early: Caroline, insidiously solicited, lends herself with good grace to her brother's demands and makes herself the mediator between the "I" and the "He," reflecting to the former the other-being he suggests to her. Gustave consequently considers himself the preserver and executor of the huge, hilarious Idol, as if the group of schoolboys, before dispersing, had given him their mandate. See how he uses it with Chevalier, whose spirit of seriousness begins to aggravate him. *First stage:* "Perhaps you will soon have enough [of Corsica, of your job], and will miss the valley of Cléry *where I made you roll with laughter?*" [82] Gustave poses as the man of "mad Rabelaisian gaiety"; he "pantagruelized," Ernest "rolled with laughter." This was not reciprocal, however—at least there is no mention of its being so: Ernest was not amusing, he didn't have to be; the crazy laughter was Gustave's ritual impact on his friend. *Second stage:* "So there you are, you've become a sober man . . . look at yourself in the mirror . . . and tell me if you haven't a great urge to laugh . . . Always preserve a philosophical irony *out of love for me,* don't take yourself seriously." [83] Gustave becomes insistent; he reveals himself: out of love for me. He is no longer minister of the cult, he has become the high priest of laughter. Alms are thus owed to him, at this time, "for the love of God."

Let us go further: if the deputy magistrate submits, he will laugh at himself *in* Gustave, as Christians love one another in God; the mirror—a favorite theme of the Flaubert younger son—reveals to each one his being-for-others, meaning, for this inhabited soul, his being-in-itself. Ernest will see himself in his mirror [*psyché*] as to himself his friend's gaze changed him;* the mirror is Gustave himself: a mocking reflection in a glass eye is all that will remain of a future prosecutor. *Third stage,* 13 July, 1847: "I would like . . . to fall into your office one

82. *Correspondance* 1:175, 13 May 1845. My italics.
83. *Correspondance* 1:182–83, 15 June 1845. My italics.
*Parody of a line from Mallarmé's "Le tombeau de Edgar Poe": "As to himself eternity's changed him."—Trans.

fine morning to break and destroy everything, belch behind the door, overturn the ink wells, shit in front of the bust of His Majesty, indeed, make an entrance worthy of the Garçon." This time the priest of laughter is really irritated: he doesn't even try to coax a smile from the pompous ass who was his friend; he threatens to appear in Corsica himself to lead Ernest back to health, that is, to self-contempt. Certainly he doesn't say that he is, or that he will be, the *Garçon in person:* he will *make an entrance worthy of him.* Nonetheless, his insolent assurance must derive from an old customary right that goes back to his school years: between the creators of the Archetype there is, he writes later with regard to Pagnerre, "a freemasonry that is not forgotten." Freemasonry: a half-secret society whose source is an archaic "terror fraternity," a group-in-fusion which was constituted around Gustave, then transformed against all dispersal (school vacations, etc.) into a sworn group. At least this is how Gustave understands it: in his eyes it is a commitment for life, and he is charged with making that commitment respected by all the confederates. Elected by the group, his position, he imagines, gives him a *real* hold on his former schoolmates: by transforming himself into the Garçon before the very eyes of any freemason who might be tempted by self-importance, Gustave has the *recognized* power to help him. Of course, no one takes him seriously anymore; those angry young bourgeois have no sooner left school than they are concerned only with becoming increasingly bourgeois. He suspects as much, but that hardly displeases him: the Garçon is only a role, let us not forget; if Gustave were going to shit in front of the bust of Louis-Philippe, he would risk legal proceedings against him, and Flaubert prudence forbids any criminal act. This means that the character must constantly threaten but never cross the boundaries of his unreality. And then, under cover of the reconstituted freemasonry, Gustave can fire off vitriolic remarks while claiming the complicity of the victim: he knows very well that for Ernest, becoming increasingly bourgeois is an inexorable process, and that the poor deputy magistrate long since quit the party of the laughers—who are powerless children—and placed himself on the side of the powerful—those who are mocked and don't care. But Flaubert enjoys using their past complicity, resorting to a myth that Chevalier cannot repudiate without denying the happiest hours of his adolescence. The evocation of the Garçon obliges the deputy magistrate, though deeply wounded, to keep up appearances, to respond with humor to what is presented to him as a manifestation of *their* humor. Black humor, forced laughter: this delights Gustave's sadism and reveals to us the negative aspect of the freemasonry, the meanness of the Garçon, to which we shall continually return.

Gustave is soon the only one who remembers the Garçon; no matter, he talks about him to anyone who cares to listen. From the time his niece Caroline is old enough to understand, he hastens to initiate her; the Goncourts, as we know, will not be spared. Nor will Maupassant. A letter to him, dated 15 August 1878, reveals to us that less than two years before Flaubert's death the process of assimilation was finally complete (*since when*—we shall never know): "Look here! my dear boy, chin up! What good does it do to wallow in your sadness? You must act the part of a strong man to yourself: that is the way to become one. A little more pride, damn it! The 'Garçon' was pluckier. What you're lacking are 'principles.'"[84] There can be no mistake: the Garçon replaces an "I" that Gustave does not want, or is not able, to say. The meaning is clear: "When I was your age, I was pluckier than you are." This is all the more manifest in that the "principles" he enumerates are his: the Artist must sacrifice everything for Art, life is only a means, one mustn't give a damn for anyone, especially oneself. Thus a veritable osmosis has been accomplished between the king of laughter and the "hermit of Croisset," the qualities of the one passing to the other, and vice versa. The hermit's voluntary sequestration is assimilated to the Garçon's disdainful mockery; inversely, under the influence of the latter the former loses part of his obscene violence and his meanness, or rather he gives it a positive, ethical interpretation: I had the urge to cry, like you, but I refused to give in to that weakness and was quick to ridicule the causes of my sufferings *and those sufferings themselves.* I killed myself with laughter in order to give birth to the Artist. It was hard: the strong man is *primarily a role*, I forced myself to play it. I *did the Garçon*—for *the man who laughs* is strong among the strong. And then, after a long ascesis, my *persona* became my truth. Does Gustave believe what he so proudly proclaims? Yes and no: anxious, grown old before his time, sapped by money worries, he knows he suffers from the insane nervousness of "a hysterical old woman" and cannot be unaware that he is playing at inner strength. But he knows too that the Garçon was a step along the path that led him to neurosis and, through it, to relative serenity. The collective aspect of the character remains, but at the price of several distortions and a certain simplification. Flaubert has entirely appropriated it for himself.

84. *Correspondance* 8:136.

From these brief investigations, one conclusion clearly emerges: Gustave always considered the Garçon his personal property; no doubt he recognized the contribution of Pagnerre and others, he takes the side of collective creation, but he remains convinced that the "scamps" would have *risked* nothing if he had not assembled them around him and directed them. They enriched the character by a few apt contributions, but Flaubert claims never to have lost control of the ceremonies and to have been the instigator of most of them. His comrades seem to have recognized his authority in the matter: aside from moments when the Garçon was incarnate in a boy who was suddenly seized with inspiration, Gustave remained its executor; besides, he thought about the character continually or, better, he continually practiced thinking *like a Garçon*. This constant preoccupation made him inclined to play the role more often than the others and to elaborate the inventions of his making. But above all he did not doubt for an instant that the Garçon was his idea; we shall show that he was right.

When little Flaubert reentered school in October 1835, firmly resolved to give as good as he got and to laugh at the laughers, his persecutors' hilarity remained serial, as it had been before the summer vacation. The ridiculous alone can provoke only scattered guffaws and spasms. Gustave was so conscious of it that he has described the "uproar" sparked by the arrival of Charles as the sudden flight of a flock of birds,[85] using an explosive-analytic metaphor to characterize the *atomization* beneath the false collective unity:

> At first there was a supreme uproar that released itself with a single bound, then subsided in distinct cascades, rolled like dropping sparks, calmed, yet bright, and despite the *pensums* . . . sometimes caught fire again suddenly along one bench . . . Like a flock of birds released in a drawing room, which at first make a great rustling, knock at the corners with the muffled sound of their wings, peck at the window panes, and are caught *one after the other.*[86]

The contagion remains mechanical; every individual has his own timing, his own higher or lower threshold for laughter which is determined both externally by the sudden, deafening outburst around him and internally by his immediate relation to Charles and his personal

85. In an unpublished passage from *Madame Bovary.* Cf. *Ebauches et fragments* (Leleu), p. 8.
86. *Ebauches et fragments,* p. 9. My italics.

118

motivations—the stage of common solitude has not been passed. With this atomizing descriptions of laughter *"in the state of nature,"* Gustave no doubt meant to avenge himself on his comrades who had mocked him *before* the invention of the Garçon: he presents this uproar to us, in short, as *nonsignifying*. As long as they remain separate, none of these conflicting spasms can comprehend the intention that produces them—in each boy there is a rejection of solidarity whose object is Charles, but, by his rejection, each one acting in solitude finds himself out of solidarity with the others and therefore never grasps himself in his collective dimension. I have said above, however, that he refers tacitly to an exquisite community which does not exist but which the laughers affirm and for which they feel nostalgia.

It is this *realized* community that Gustave is going to present to them as a spectacle. As we have seen, his immediate, naive sadness and bitter bewilderment have gradually given way to vehemence and fits of passion. He will exercise his "somber irony" on the "despotism of all." But in this serious, credulous, and contemplative child, laughter is not spontaneous. He was never more painfully serious than at eight years old, when he wanted to *make laughter*. If he wants to be a laugher now, he must steal the laughter of others. Or he must *imitate* it. Previously, if he allowed himself to be overtaken by contagious hilarity in study hall or in class, he did so as an individual, serialized by withdrawing his solidarity from a particular object. Now it is quite a different matter: for *everyone* to laugh at a single person is normal; it is impossible for a single person to laugh at everyone else. Yet this is what Gustave wants to do: to set himself against the little society of children and balance their collective laughter by the solitary force of *his* own, enclosed in his person, to release at the right moment a vast "flock of birds."

A final trump card: his physical power. He properly discovered it between the seventh and the eighth terms. From his thirteenth year this solid and muscular boy must have seemed a worthy adversary, even to the "big boys." He felt it, he felt the new respect his biceps commanded. This would have been the moment to settle a few debts with his fists. Such a thing didn't occur to him. If he happened to threaten an assistant master, it was all boasting and swagger. He would show his strength so as not to have to use it; it was a threat, nothing more: you will swallow my rude retorts without flinching; if anyone takes offense, I'll knock his block off. After each offensive remark he would burst into a gigantic laugh—he could do it—which would cover any protests. But from the earliest days, when he ap-

119

proached his comrades determined to pay them back, and dearly, for all their rotten tricks, conscious of the eyes turned toward him, he suddenly felt himself *in danger*. Not that he was afraid of being beaten: it seemed to him, in some obscure way, that he did not believe enough in his gigantism. Certainly he was the tallest in his class, perhaps in the school—only the cursed Bouilhet was the same size, but Gustave was still half an inch taller. The problem was otherwise: it was a question of the credibility of the signals his organs sent him.

Through the experience of its own structures, the body produces specious evidence; in particular the aptitude and limitations of our anatomy, internalized—and reexternalized by our actions—reveal to us our immediate hold on the world. Flaubert's gesticulations are *also* the unhampered development of his physical person; his long strides are prompted by his long legs. His condescending benevolence or his contempt for his interlocutors first presents itself as the internalization of a physical relation of nonreciprocity: he leans over the others, they shrink their necks into their shoulders in order to meet his gaze with an upturned face, defenseless. His dimensions determine his hodological space; from the proximity of a wall, of a sofa, distances are shortened; his muscles determine the coefficient of fragility in tools and even in men. If he enjoys obstructing a class, a study hall— later Mathilde's salon—with his presence, it is chiefly because he feels voluminous: his ringing voice, the sonorous symbol of his stature, crushes all other voices effortlessly. When his body goes to his head, he experiences the "intoxication" for which the Goncourts would reproach him.

Still, this powerful organism thwarts him more than it persuades him: superior height can prove anything you like—the timid would regard it as confirmation of their timidity, they would never dare to unfold themselves for fear of their strength; to draw from it the certainty of being superior to others, the wish to dominate must be already present. And we know very well that, by contrast, a body of reduced dimensions, far from preventing pride, the will to power, and aggression, often favors them, even as a mode of compensation. Here we must think of a dialectic of the experienced organism and its options. These preexist, since they are rooted in prehistory, but they remain abstract, implicit, until the organism, deciphered *as a function of those options*, discovers them for themselves by proposing itself as their concrete confirmation. Flaubert's body is hyperbolic only in the light of the project that leads him to choose hyperbole. Yet at the same time, his constitutional passivity contradicts the pithiatic evidence

120

offered by internalized anatomy: hypernervous, often prostrate, the young Hercules plunges willingly into a stupor and spends hours on end staring at nothing, without will or desire. His magnificent skeleton inclines him to exuberance, his musculature is the outline of an act, violence in repose; the flaccidity of his flesh is the suggestion of a swoon. That is the trap: *kinesthesia* persuades, *coenesthesia* denies. He is already very close to the group he wants to summon and still wonders if he dare *provoke;* he will soon depict this uncertainty in Garcia, poor devil, who dreams of scratching and biting and ends by falling into a faint. He understands this much, in any case: incapable of direct aggression, he will never make practical use of his strength; in other words, he is not even sure of his meanness. He immediately reacts with behavior of extreme urgency, in which he has indulged habitually since the Fall: powerless to *make laughter* at the expense of someone other than himself (to denigrate a comrade in the presence of others), he will play them the role of the Giant laughing at man. The Garçon has just been born; about him, indeed, all witnesses agree: the Goncourts compare him to Pantagruel and declare him endowed with "enormous bodily strength"; Caroline Franklin Groult calls him a "modern Gargantua of Homeric exploits." Gargantua, Pantagruel, these names strike us in passing: neglecting Rabelais's humanism, Gustave is pleased to believe that he "laughed in the face of humanity." This author, *in order to disparage men,* supposedly took it upon himself to place some giants in their midst.[87] The Garçon's primary feature, then, is a gigantism of contempt: Gustave unrealizes himself *in him.* So he falls into the hands of others: it is the others, down there, who will give him his truth, providing he can impose himself in their eyes as that Gargantua he claims to be and can only act out.

How can he, by himself, provoke that crazy laughter and put the laughers on his side? How can he mock things and people in their generality without attacking real individuals and targeting their particularity? Only one way: laugh at *everything*—and thus claim the collective laughter for himself; to laugh at everything, one must put oneself into *everyone.* But if Gustave wants to make this boundless hilarity his individual vengeance, it must, while preserving its power of multiplicity, emanate *unified* from his idiosyncrasy. Such is the source of gigantism: by playing the Giant, in whom Gustave incarnates

---

87. Gustave seems unaware of the popular literature which provided Rabelais with his details.

the laughter of everyone at everything, he transforms this laughter into that of the All laughing at everyone—in short, a cosmic uproar. We know this giant quite well, we have seen him leaning over the schoolboys of Rouen, contemplating their antlike bustle. He wasn't laughing then: he represented the painful contempt that a misunderstood boy, perched on a summit, felt for the "little society of men." Caryatid of a heaven blind and deaf to our prayers, this mediator's physical constitution was the symbol of Gustave's spiritual superiority, ravished as he was by an eagle and borne to the summit of Mount Atlas. We need only change the signs and we have the Garçon flinging his mechanical laughter in the face of humanity. But as soon as he is transformed into the Garçon we find him laughing at man and consequently at himself: we shall soon see how this comes about. But we cannot describe the Garçon and offer keys to understanding him without coming back to Gustave himself. This is not merely a trap the victim sets for his executioners; the actor lets himself be possessed by his role, the Garçon represents a more elevated stage of his unrealization and a new spiral of movement which personalizes it. In these crucial years (1835–38) Gustave was not content simply to act out a new character; he chose one that would take him to the very outer limits of his persona, the "He" that others had to reflect back to him as his most intimate being if he found the right gestures to convince them. We must understand that he had now determined his relations with others once and for all: he knew what he gave them and what he demanded of them. *Generosity* (secret dependence), *laughter* (or masochism turned into sadism): these two basic characteristics must claim our attention.

Generosity

Simply by giving his classmates the Garçon, Flaubert won the first place outside that he could not achieve in class. A poisoned gift—we shall return to this—but a gift all the same. With it he manages to reconstitute the feudal hierarchy in which he will be prince—*princeps* and not *primus inter pares;* the latter, as we know, can establish himself only by a lordly gift eliciting the homage of vassals. And what can we shamans give if not the invisible, or, as Eluard says, the other world inherent in this one? This gift is imaginary, and Gustave, illusory lord of illusions, does not escape the rule: he gives his persona to the youth of Rouen as the prince gave his to France. When, seemingly indifferent to their attention, he inaugurates his street hawker's mime-dramas in the presence of his astonished classmates, who are initially mistrustful, then seduced, his rapport with them *in reality* remains governed strictly by the principle of exteriority. He mimics strength, "the mysterious emblem of God," in vain; he will never be the gang leader or high priest of a secret society, using his biceps neither for nor against anyone. *In the imaginary,* on the other hand, this same principle, once *surpassed,* allows the establishment of bonds of interiority between the little boy, who offers—*at a distance*—the spectacle of the universe, and his classmates, whom this unbridgeable moment transforms into spectators even as it awakens their need to deny the passive role in which they are cast and to leap headlong into unreality so as to join the buffoon who is beckoning them. The public's invasion of his drama transforms Gustave, not into a real lord but rather—less honorable but more suitable—into the leader of a young theatrical troup. Nonetheless, he now has the right to *spend* himself, to turn himself at once into trainer, creator, director, to give real orders that are really heard in relation to imaginary actions. In short, he measures his generosity by the violence of his trances and the exhaustion that follows them. Thus, he gives and *feels himself* giving. Not out of love, or truly out of hate—although his embittered passion has by no means diminished—but in order to assert himself. Certainly he does not forget that he is leading his followers toward the abyss, that is, toward self-contempt. But now he is intoxicated with his lofty power: they walk, they walked, they ran, they recognize—at last!—his superiority: he is their example and model, they fight over who is to play *his* character, in other words, who is *to be Flaubert.*

And what does he give? His persona, born of his scandalous anomaly, begins with a transference of scandal: in order to conceal the young boy's humiliating inadequacies, his persona is dedicated to showing men the original and infinite scandal of creation. Why is there being rather than nothing? Why is this so-called being only a determination of the nothing? Why is there nothing rather than being? Why is the infinite only a pulverulence of solitudes? Why does the absolute-subject in each finite individual allow itself to be degraded, disqualified by the indeterminate infinite? Why is there suffering rather than a calm, silent nothingness? Why is each of our sufferings swallowed, digested, dissolved by universal nothingness? In short the cosmos, infinite or finite, illusory or real, created or uncreated, remains wholly in the state of scandal. Gustave's persona is generous insofar as it publicly denounces radical evil, not by reasoning and not by a Byronic torrent of blaspheming eloquence, but by embodying it for everyone; it is the singular display of a universal wound. This persona lives out the farcical drama, laughing: the explosive presence of the All in the part, symbolized by the presence of the giant in a manchild. This occurs whether the All tumultuously denounces the inadequacy of the part to the point of bursting it, or whether this infinitesimal particle, maddened by the visitation of the All, spills over into an absurd agitation, ridiculing simultaneously the acrimony that feeds on its *difference* and the folly of the infinite that produced it, giving birth to a mouse—that same infinity which stubbornly persists in spilling over through its unlimited expansion *and* residing in the particle.

In other words, Gustave's *persona* is the individualized possession of man by nature. Confronted by his comrades, Gustave pursues a familiar enterprise: in order to compensate for negative pride, he claims to break out of his limitations, calling the crowd to his aid in order to denounce the shabbiness of his all too human ambitions and to crush his pitiful self-esteem. He has successfully conducted this contestatory and unrealizing movement in the subjective setting: by means of ascesis, he was dying to his body. But if he wants to *represent* it so that others reflect it back to him, everything changes: in the setting of objectivity, only objective determinations and forces exist. If Gustave should *make visible* the religious infinite present in his finitude and breaking through it, negative as it may be, he must necessarily degrade it: it would have to be in some way determined, which is the death of any determination. This empty and sacred immensity will manifest itself as a *visible* essence in the form of unadorned nature, an aggregate of the physico-chemical forces explosively present in each of its parts. The Garçon is initially this: Gustave as prey to the cosmos. And we should certainly not apply the "paradox of the player" to this actor dominated by his persona. The Goncourts report that, according to Flaubert, "this strange creation . . . took veritable possession of them, drove them mad." Even if it "drove" Pagnerre and the other freemasons a little less mad than he says, it is certain that Gustave was possessed by it. He believes in this manufactured "He" in order *to give* it; he believes in it because he catches its reflection in everyone's eyes; he believes in it although the character is imaginary, or rather because it is: sustained by the laughter it creates, the persona casts a very real spell that keeps him prisoner in the realm of imagination. In brief, his immediate rapport with others is the *trance*, indissolubly acted and suffered, fictive and specious, a gift of himself, a generosity-spectacle. In their presence, immensity takes hold of him;

he cannot resist this spontaneous unrealization. Behold the Garçon, tormented by telluric and celestial forces; the first slip inside him and distend him, swelling his feelings and desires to gigantic proportions, and the second, lightning, thunder, hurricane, swoop down on him, as if he were a giant plum tree, and shake him without respite. He is a medium, a Pythia: unintelligibly, he prophesies the systematic destruction of the human race by Stepmother Nature, who has nonetheless produced it. This cursed Adam portrays the curse of Adam, which is expressed by roarings, kickings, an irrepressible but codified laughter that shatters the eardrums. Let us add that this gigantism is rigorously opposed to praxis; rather, it expresses unleashed passion: the Garçon *cannot act*. Violent but submissive, gestures and cries are born on the outside, whistlings of the wind, harsh bursts of deafening thunder enter him like a tempest in order to tear him away from himself; then they exist again, inhuman or rather dehumanizing howls, convulsions, sudden flailing of the arms. Or he issues a combination of neighing, last gasps, and crazy laughter: ecstasies and raptures, impossible to "*render*" as they are, find before a public an objective symbol in the pantomime of *abandon*, swooned consent to the invasion of the cosmic into the microcosm.

The Goncourts will later regard this abandon, so characteristic of Gustave's "style of life," of his passivity, as mere vulgarity. And certainly the naive acceptance of the natural in its most brutal form is contrary to the "distinction" of these titled bourgeois in their vain attempt to *contain* nature. Gustave "breaks wind" with enthusiasm, takes in "snoutfuls," "bellyfuls." Myopic, grumpy, and dry, the Goncourts confuse this actor feigning a noisy and forcible return to an encumbering materiality with a badly bred provincial who allows himself to be dominated in public by his natural needs. Nothing could be more false. In truth, Flaubert despises physical needs. But, as we shall see more clearly later on, naturalism and antiphysis coexist in this "Artist." And if the actor, as the Garçon, is consigned to capture Nature publicly, obviously "[his] desires are measureless."[88] But it is merely a question of materializing Great Desire, which is in essence unsatisfied, by lowering it to the level of organic need. Gustave will give it a natural image by assimilating it to the pantagruelesque, insatiable claims of a giant's organism; the Garçon—and Gustave himself when he plays *himself* in his correspondence—feels only "rages,"

88. To Louis Bouilhet, December 1853, between the 15th and the 27th. He is speaking about himself, of course.

125

"frenzies," "itchings." These appetites in their boundlessness burst the niggardly barriers in utilitarianism: one must eat to live, say the thrifty bourgeois; it could not be said of the Garçon that he lives to eat, but rather that the boundlessness of his "famines" make them almost totally gratuitous. And their violence destroys self-esteem, that is, the choice of particularity: they are pure desire for everything through the coveted object. Thus, whatever he does, whatever he says, they are "Avalanches of Azure," landslides, volcanic eruptions, and earthquakes which are echoed in the voice of his character. Shouting and gesticulating, congested, beside himself, Flaubert tries to convince his comrades—in order to convince himself through them—that an excess of power makes him feel he is at the outer limits of the human and already on the side of the superhuman. For this reason, Gustave's persona of the excessive, even when the Garçon is no more than a memory, will continue to vampirize him under other names. If we glance quickly beyond the *collège* to the years of his maturity, we will come to a better understanding of the creation of his adolescence and we will grasp its other meanings, which were implicit in 1835 but later largely explicit.

Gustave is forty years old; he knows the "literati," and, when for three months of the year he resides in Paris, he frequents the literary salons. The rest of the time, alone in Croisset, he stews in his vapid contingency: stupors, capricious laziness, "emptiness," boredom; he judges himself limited but without contours, hence without character. As soon as he has crossed the threshold of a Parisian salon, however, he is prey to a strange overexcitement; becomes irritable, congested; gesticulates wildly, bursts out laughing, or thunders. What possesses him? A dizziness: he rediscovers the egalitarianism of his school years, an archipelago of bourgeois solitudes, atoms *without real ties*. But he is now among the "elite," the "cream," "true gentlemen," "men of Art." There is nothing to be done, however; real relations are only of the practical kind, and these good people who spend their evenings at Saint-Gratien, at rue de Courcelles, do nothing. In this respect these artists' gatherings are the very image of bourgeois receptions. Everyone goes to experience his absolute separation in the guise of specific difference; everyone is an audience for everyone else; the unbridgeable distance that separates each molecule from all the others becomes the orchestra pit that separates the stage from the rest of the theater. The social actor circumvents the judgment of his public by signs, symbols; through mime and recitation he offers as a model the character he wants recognized. *Is he* this character? Certainly not. His reality is elsewhere, in his real activity. But he wants to seem like it, to realize, thanks to the audience, the impossible coincidence of his being with his persona. In this sense, the bourgeois is an imaginary being. Reciprocity exists, however—the reciprocity of these impersonations. Everyone permits himself to be easily convinced by others so that it will be easier to convince them—a tacit agreement. It often happens that someone convinces by seniority because he always puts on the same *show*. Edmond de Goncourt was "born" into the nobility, and the nobility *is* military. This diarist, without ever having commanded a regiment even in barracks, applied himself so early and with such perseverance to playing the military man in mufti that his peers, who certainly knew his style of life, ended by respecting in him the bearing of a retired officer.[89]

So everyone is willing to recognize the specific difference of everyone else provided they recognize his own—this is the rule of the game. But it would be bad form to claim more. A negative society; beneath its aspects of caste, it dissimulates a universality of refusal: everyone rests on his difference like a landowner on his property. Mutual recognition is in fact a negation: don't step on my flowerbeds, and I won't step on yours; let us affirm our mutual superiority over everyone else, but let us never establish a qualitative hierarchy between ourselves. By means of which, each one can choose his persona, manifest it continually, maintain it to the end; and all the others—one good turn deserves another—will take it for his *real being*. Save for venting their spleen in private journals or to their wives. A burdensome egalitarianism: this fundamental equality is elating to writers when they come upon its reflection *elsewhere*, in the eyes of a dazzled admirer: it becomes the common power to create, to illuminate France. But they are exasperated by it at Princess Mathilde's when they *realize* it as their social status, as the common limits their origin imposes on their ascent. Drawn to the rue de Courcelles or to Saint-Gratien by the vain hope of gaining access to the aristocracy, their illusion is dispelled when they are introduced, since they find they are among themselves, just as before. In their disappointment they blame everyone, even the Princess, everyone reproaching everyone else for giving

---

89. The Goncourots' nobility is itself questionable. In 1786 their great-grandfather, Antoine Huot, had acquired by way of trade a small house, "La Papoterie" ["The Chatterbox"], and the title connected with it, "Seigneur de Goncourt et de Noncourt." See André Billy, Preface to the *Journal*, Monaco edition.

127

a bourgeois tone to these gatherings by his presence, in effect condemning in the other his own vulgarity.[90] At Saint-Gratien, at the Magny dinners, superiorities become quite secondary: it is merely a matter of *primus inter pares*. On these evenings the Goncourts tearfully confide to their journal that they have surpassed everyone. But how could they believe such a thing? And then, their timorous vanity does not dare to pronounce the word "genius"—every day they bitterly reaffirm their *talent*. Well? Everyone has talent in this small elite, that is understood; their genius, however, goes *unacknowledged*.

When Gustave, after eight or nine months of separation, finds himself once more in his Parisian "circle," he suffocates. At a distance, he could imagine being integrated into this hierarchy of immortals—isn't Art an aristocracy? Close up, he suspects a mob-rule democracy based on the principle of exteriority. At the same time it seems to him that all eyes are on him: he has made Charbovary's entrance, surgical gazes scrutinize him, pierce him; they will judge him, discover his "anomaly," still worse, mock him; he is defenseless. Nothing could be truer: these gentlemen are not gentle with newcomers. Each time a rookie makes his appearance at Magny's—I am thinking of Taine, and especially of Renan—the Goncourts are infuriated and observe him cruelly, taking a definite satisfaction in pointing out his physical defects. After several months the system of mutual recognition goes into effect, the newcomer is adopted; they note what he says, what he does, nothing more, except for scratching him or tearing him apart when seized with a neurotic urge to do so.

Still, the newly admitted are Parisians—an infamous title in our times, a glorious one under Napoleon III; they meet continually until they no longer really see each other. Flaubert himself, that provincial hermit, would never be a "veteran," even when he became the elder statesman among Mathilde's guests; he reappeared every year burdened with nine months of solitude, forgotten, a bit suspect; he

90. The Goncourts set the tone: these bourgeois gentlemen were wild with joy when the Princess asked to make their acquaintance. They note: "Here we are with the best literary relations in the world . . . Only our talent . . . holds us back." But from the second dinner at rue de Courcelles, we see them disenchanted: "A princess like that would never do anything more extraordinary than have you to dinner . . . Even when they are whores they are well-bred. *You foolishly believe you're in a novel when it's really a salon.*" But their disappointment does not prevent them later from reproaching newcomers for degrading these get-togethers: "The Princess's salon," writes Edmond in 1873, "that salon of letters and art, that salon ringing with the fine speech of Sainte-Beuve, with the Rabelaisian eloquence of Gautier, the knifelike thrusts of Flaubert . . . that salon which . . . echoed with profound paradoxes, elevated ideas, ingenious *aperçus* . . . was extinguished like fireworks in the rain."

needed to reaccustom people to his voluminous presence. In short, each year when he made his entrance once again, he felt subjected to a qualifying examination; this scrutiny quickly stripped him of his subjective certainties: he would lose his head and react, as in school, with the feudal performance—that is, by pantagruelizing. From the first day he would indicate his princely generosity by encumbering the salons with his instantly summoned persona; he would give himself as a spectacle: in his feigned violence, his loud-mouthed turbulence, his willed vulgarities, he expects the involuntary excesses of his titanic temperament to be recognized. There he is, heading off into the imaginary; he does it for three months. Quite in vain: how could these petty natures recognize the giant's superiority in Gustave? A silent battle begins whose only echo is found in the Goncourts' *Journal*; Gustave senses a tacit but general rejection: without really being conscious of it, he is exasperated by this resistance. He overdoes it—less to convince than *to displease*.

On every occasion we see him boast of an insolent good health: if the Goncourts are irritated, it is because he secretly intends to irritate. One day he exclaims in front of them: "I'm amazing, it seems that I'm just inheriting the *vigors* of all my sick friends!" And the two old maids purse their lips: how tactless! They fall into the trap: does this mean they are unaware that the braggart is himself a sick person, a great neurotic? That this display of strength and health *in front of others* is dictated by the role he plays, and that he proclaims his *"vigors"* in order to reassure himself?[91] Gustave understands himself better and would one day write this admirable sentence to George Sand: "This winter I was vaguely quite ill." Could there be a better description of the *lived experience* of a neurotic? Which doesn't prevent him from posing everywhere as the Alcidamas of the marketplace.[92] It is amusing to imagine Jules's and Edmond's sulks when they received this invitation (to the reading of *Salammbô*): "First, I will begin to declaim at precisely four o'clock. So come around 3. Second, at 7 o'clock, an Oriental dinner. You will be served human flesh, bourgeois brains, and clitoris of tigress sauteed in rhinoceros butter. Third, after coffee, recommencement of the punic rant until the audience keels over." What could the unfortunate man have had in mind, addressing this

91. We have seen above that from the age of sixteen, in the *Mémoires*, Gustave dares to admit his insane nervousness only after proclaiming his "excellent health."

92. In the last years of his life, he was *at the same time* "a hysterical old woman"—a "She" that came to him like the meaning of lived experience from the declarations of his doctor—and Laporte's Giant, the facetious reincarnation of the Garçon.

note to those two sourpusses? Was he determined to shock them or simply ignorant of their characters? Both, I believe: he rathar enjoys shocking his lapdogs, but he hasn't any idea of the loathing he will inspire. We hasten to note that these good apostles, so distressed at not being able to attach their atoms to Flaubert's, worked relentlessly to demolish him—and that Gustave never wrote a malicious word against them. And of course I am not trying to defend the Goncourts. Yet curiosity is already a human relation, although a malicious one. For Edmond and Jules, Flaubert counted sufficiently for them to want to observe and understand him; in spite of their sourness and their jealousy—or perhaps because of them—they were able to grasp and specify certain significations of his behavior. For them, he is a man—a man you want to get rid of as quickly as possible by destroying him because he is irritating—but, in spite of everything, like them: they are closer to Flaubert than Flaubert is to them.[93] For him, of course, they are uniquely *actor-spectators*. If he never says anything bad about them, it is because he could not care less about *seeing* them; he wants to *be seen by them*. He scatters over the literary circles he frequents a kind of vague benevolence—which disappears when he is devoured by envy—because he does not want to tarnish in advance the mirrors bearing his reflection.

The truth is that his persona of the generous but intolerable fellow, the good-giant-who-cannot-take-a-step-without-innocently-crushing-people-underfoot, takes hold of him, imposes itself, *forces itself to be represented*, and he has neither the means nor the wish to escape: he is condemned to truculence the way the maniacal life-of-the-party is condemned to gaiety. "You will be served human flesh." It is a *joke* (in case you hadn't noticed), but good God, how heavy-handed! Doesn't he sense it? He does, but he must convince the *lapdogs* that his mad, sadistic imagination has a taste only for extreme inventions; he must reveal it to them hyperbolically in order to "flaunt" his fantasies of cannibalism; he has to worry them—the good giant *is an ogre*. As for the "punic rant," it took place, we can be sure, on the appointed day, at the appointed hour: a man in the grip of nature is beyond talking, the cosmos rants through his mouth. Gustave infinitely regrets deaf-

93. And then, although Edmond was profoundly exasperated by Gustave's success and lost no opportunity to knock his colleague's works, he considered him a peer, an artist, a worker in art. When it was a question of upholding the respect for beauty and even the sensibility that he believed characteristic of his generation as against the barbarity of the young, he always wrote: "We and Flaubert . . ." Gustave's solitude and pride were such that he would never write: "The Goncourts and I . . ."

ening his public by useless vocal outbursts, but how should he stop himself? The last words reveal his deliberate intention to impose his physical superiority on his friends: "until the audience keels over." Oh yes, he is terribly concerned, he knows the fragility of his peers, he knows they will be stunned, flattened by this interminable reading; he himself could carry on until morning, until the end of his book; after they have gone, crammed with food and words, he will remain alone, still fresh, undaunted. Tactless? If you like—but intentionally so. Gustave's persona is characterized by poisoned generosity, let us not forget: it was born like this around 1835; it was revived like this during his Parisian visits. Therefore, his gifts *must* be displeasing; the resistance of others exasperates him, but he sees nothing abnormal in it—since he *must* displease and demoralize! Look: first he *will give* them an excellent dinner, and then he will shout himself hoarse *to give* them the joys of incomparable art. Oh well, these people will leave discontented; what can be done about it? Men will always be crushed by the gifts of giants: they will be unable to avoid comparing themselves to the donors or feeling small.

On Sundays at the boulevard du Temple, the Garçon once again welcomes the guests. Once again it is a question of making himself "henormous" in order to incarnate the "Fecundity of the Earth," the *Alma Venus* who has produced beasts and men, as well as Stepmother Nature who destroys them: Eros and Thanatos. Gustave the possessed has only to open his mouth: instantly there is an incredible proliferation of discourse, maxims, paradoxes, dizzying *aperçus* tossed off in a ringing voice accompanied by pantomime; this time, what is being *represented* is gigantism of thought. At first the Goncourt brothers go along with it: "These Sundays spent at the boulevard du Temple, at Flaubert's, spare us the Sunday doldrums. There is talk that leaps from one peak to another, harks back to the origins of the world, examines religions, reviews ideas and men, runs from Oriental legends to Hugo's lyricism, from Buddha to Goethe." But later we find in the *Journal:* "They pretend to stir up paradoxes . . ." These two texts, one dazzled, the other disenchanted, sound the same note: nothing is discussed at Flaubert's, everyone goes over his routine in his head while waiting for the "previously billed" talker to finish his. You avail yourself of one idea or another as you would use a trampoline to jump and bounce higher and higher. You mimic sacred exultation, the superabundance of ideas. You pronounce obscenities for the sake of boasting: "Flaubert's Sundays might be called disquisitions on the art of lovemaking." No one is fooled, no one listens to anyone else; they pantagruelize among the vases and end tables: the spectators swoon, *they are all actors*. Even the Goncourts, at least in the first days; for we cannot doubt—given the fatuousness that shows through their enthusiasm—that they took part in the "talk that leaps from one peak to another." They report to us *not one word* on the content of the talk, as if the essential matter at the boulevard du Temple were never the act of thought but stories about it, as if, at the end of the performance, the actors forgot their text until the following Sunday, as if the "paradoxes" and maxims neither should nor could have been—the tacitly agreed rule of the game—anything but dreams of ideas, brilliant mirages without content.[94] In any case, this was the only time in the week when Gustave found himself once more producer, leader, improviser, and director, as in the days of the Garçon. Moreover, here is how the two brothers depict him when they have recovered from their first dazzlement:

> Full of paradoxes, his paradoxes, like his vanity, reek of the provinces. They are gross, heavy-handed, labored, forced, graceless. He has a foul cynicism. On love, which he often talks about, he has . . . theses that are merely posturing and repartee. The man has basically a great deal of the rhetorician and the sophist about him. He is at once gross and precious in his obscenity. . . ; on things that are quite simple he imposes the complicated and the recherché, the staging and ordering of a forceful man.

There is no doubt that they are describing the Garçon without knowing it, unable to understand that Gustave *wills himself* to be gross and paradoxical; it is part of his assumed character.

At Mathilde's, on the other hand, Gustave with all his efforts would never succeed in imposing himself as master of ceremonies. At Saint-Gratien there are other rules, a semblance of etiquette; and above all Her Highness, violent and capricious, who represents princely generosity and dispenses it as she pleases (small gifts, protection—it was she who mounted a play of the Goncourts' at the Comédie-Française—official honors, and even, for Sainte-Beuve, the Senate). The gifts of the Princess, trivial as they may be, are superior to the Gift mimed by Flaubert by virtue of their *real* substance. Nonetheless, the persona takes hold of him, he will play the role all alone, raising

94. As for the Magny dinners, on the other hand, the brothers tried conscientiously, but without much success, to note after the fact what was said. We shall soon see that Gustave himself knew quite well that no one *thought* at his "Sundays"—that a company got together at his instigation to *act out the drama of thought*.

his voice, drowning out the others. The *Journal* of 11 March 1869 contains the lapdogs' sour reproaches: "Truly, Sainte-Beuve was sorely missed at the Princess's salon. Ideas subside, voices grow louder, and Flaubert, who plays the fool, turns the place into a provincial salon. For every story you tell, you can be sure in advance that he will say, whether the story is finished or not: Oh, I know a better one, and for any person you mention: *I* know him better than you." The reason for their irritation is clear: at the home of the Princess, who receives, gives, distinguishes, there is no place for a giant; everyone is servile, Saint-Victor more so than the others, but certainly the Goncourts as much as Gustave himself, who was perhaps the most sincere because he loved Mathilde. As a result, Gargantua importunes and above all plays false: how can one be a real vassal and an imaginary lord at the same time? So the Goncourts denounce his insincerity: "At bottom, this frank and loyal nature . . . lacks those hooked atoms that lead an acquaintance to friendship." Moreover: "He lacks heart, at bottom . . . this boy so open in appearance, so exuberant on the surface." One step more and they charge him with hypocrisy: they remark that in the proclamation of his hatreds, as in his enthusiasms, there is always something that rings false. They describe Gustave at Saint-Gratien "with wild theories, bawlings about independence, a vulgar pose of anarchy with the excess of a famulus, a provincial courtier." How could it be otherwise? This unhappy Hercules at the feet of Queen Omphale must know just how far he can go. Herculean, so be it, but without breaking anything: he must stop his paradoxes the moment they might be taken for convictions; his discourse must denounce itself as *imaginary*, just like that of an actor who passionately recites some incendiary monologue but has declared the evening before to the press that he takes no responsibility for the opinions of his character. Thus Flaubert plays his role of "Excessive" nowhere as badly as he does at the home of the Princess, that obdurate Bonaparte who reserved the monopoly on excess for herself.

But those refined observers, those profound connoisseurs of the human heart, are mistaken when they criticize his "vulgar nature." For Gustave—lacerated, gloomy, devoured by envy, rancor, and indelible humiliations, stupefied in solitude, submissive and respectful in his public dealings, dreaming beneath his "bawlings about independence" of being only a happy vassal, haunted by the fear of being deficient, fascinated by failure, terrorized by his peers to the point of sequestering himself nine months out of twelve—is the very opposite of a vulgar nature. The two blockheads don't realize that his carnival antics exhaust him and are followed by prostration, that after the Sunday improvisations he throws himself onto a sofa and restores his strength with several hours' sleep, that even those long months of a slow, vegetative life are insufficient to compensate for the depredations wrought in his organism by his brief Parisian sojourns.

They can't say, however, that he didn't warn them: 6 May 1866, he confides to them: "There are two men in me. The one, you see, narrow-chested, with a sagging ass, the man made to sit hunched over a table; the other, a traveling salesman with the genuine gaiety of a traveling salesman on the road, and a taste for violent practices." A traveling salesman? Isn't this how Caroline Commanville defined the Garçon: "A sort of modern Gargantua of Homeric exploits in the skin of a traveling salesman"? Let us note the "you see" in the confidence of 1866; the meaning is transparent: the one whom you see, the one who really is narrow-chested, *as you can verify;* the other, by contrast, is never *seen*—except when he breaks loose. Of the two men, one is real and the other imaginary; the second from time to time vampirizes the first. From time to time: every time he enters into contact with his peers.

And why, it may be asked, does he burden himself with a painful and thankless task that only succeeds in alienating his audience? What need has he to go and play the vulgarian among those petty natures, the "artists"? Why does he choose to encumber, to pester, to call continual attention to himself, not by his ideas or his acts but by his gesticulations and bawlings? Interrupting his interlocutors or drowning them out, deafening them with his shouting, sickening them with his paradoxes, continually putting himself forward until they "keel over"—is this giving, giving of himself? Well, yes, for Gustave it is; for the simple reason that his generosity is *acted.*

Generous behavior originally defined the *social* relation of the superior to the inferior. It must be described as the superstructure of the feudal world if we want to understand its full development and its objective function, which is to *affirm* publicly, as the free product of spontaneity, the hierarchy instituted as the dominant relationship in terms of infrastructures and maintained at need by the forces of repression. Generosity, when praxis, is transcendent; if we examine it on the level of the feudal relationship, properly speaking, it merely inaugurates an exchange: I give land, you give me your life. But the moment of the first gift, though inseparable from the second to which it is intentionally tied, is isolated and presented for itself ceremonially when the recipient becomes *obliged* to the donor; in this sense, although the vassal who gives his life for his lord is always honored, there is no doubt that this second gift is held to be relative, induced, tied to a strict imperative that is nothing more than the internalization of the first.[95] Or, if you like, the generous Gift is the dominant, independent variable; homage is a dependent and dominated gift. The notion of generosity as a practical affirmation of independence was developed in the feudal period to the extent that nearly everywhere the nobility became indebted and paved the way for its own ruin by deliberately unproductive investments or spectacular destruction. We know by what concatenation of circumstances—unproductive expenditures are not the least—wealth was to become concentrated in the hands of princes. By the same means they were to become the chief repositories of generosity—although the entire aristocracy held this to be its fundamental virtue.

If we see it not as a certain mode of exchange—which objectively it is—but as a prince experienced it, as he believed he practiced it, generosity expresses in the first place, in the subject, the tacit commitment *never to be an object.* Nothing restrains him, nothing binds him. The gift raises him above necessity since he considers himself permanently capable of ridding himself of the necessary. But by the same postulation he is convinced that when he gives, he escapes all motivation. His gifts are *gracious,* that is, gratuitous; conditioned by charity, the prescriptions of a Church, the right of others, his act belongs to him no more than if it had been determined by mean calculations, fear, or interest. His sole motive must be freedom itself as it rids itself of all motives by an absolute divestiture which at the same time commits the beneficiary and enslaves him, precisely if we grant that this freedom is colored by love to the extent that the prince's relation to his subjects is conceived as a father's relation to his children in a patriarchal family. Yet this very love must be conceived as generosity: God freely loves His creature, He freely gives him life, He freely gives or refuses His grace. He knows that the love He bears His creature is not deserved: thus His infinite bounty is the supreme generosity, that is, creative freedom; to make the gift of an object that already exists, even

95. This imperative, insofar as it is *other* (any internal obligation manifests the presence of the Other in me) and *inert* (a "duty" is the inert extension of a maxim, one's entirely material refusal to *adapt oneself* to changing conditions: "I don't want to know it"), represents in the vassal *the land itself as fief,* the presence of the lord in the very possession of the property insofar as the property is *held* by him.

of one's own life, is but a pale reflection of the infinitely gratuitous act that gave this object being, or produced it, and that maintains life in order that it can fill the cosmos, constituted *ex nihilo*, with love.

That freedom is certainly not ours, it is the freedom of the Prince who affirms himself by his detachment from others. To constitute himself as *absolute-subject*, the lord must transform the recipient into an object: "You owe me gratitude, which means that you recognize my freedom; I was not obliged to be obliging, and as for you, my obliged servant, your conduct toward me will be henceforth governed by an inert imperative. I am, by my kindness, situated by a single stroke outside all norms since I have no obligation to do what I have done; but as for you, I become your norm, I maintain you by the Gift in the sphere of obligations and, at the same time, in that of the all too human passions which I oblige you to curb, of the interests you must combat in order to serve me. My generosity is the choice of angelism, the rejection of human nature, thus the manifestation in me of the supernatural." Of course I have described a *notion*, the *eidos* of the generous act as it was constituted historically under the Old Regime. Under these conditions, no one was generous, ever. Nonetheless, every *intention* of generosity, however imperfect and mixed it may have been, referred implicitly to the structures we have described: affirmation of the absolute-subject, gratuitous act, transformation of others into objects.

On condition, of course, that the gift is real. It is praxis alone that allows the basic intention to be realized, at least in part. Yet for Flaubert everything is reversed: surrounded by his peers, he unrealizes himself as lord by reflex; he will *represent* in his person, to this egalitarian horde, what he takes to be the deed of the prince, generous ardor. But if in fact he *displays* it, it becomes an object for the spectators who, far from feeling its constraining weight and from divining the transcendence of the absolute-subject through their new obligations, observe the *donation* at a distance as Gustave's objective determination. They are the true subjects, for Flaubert, dominated by the Other, can only recognize himself in his being-for-others; no doubt he expends his energy to fascinate them, but they remain free, it is their approbation that will give the consistency to his *persona*; by their reprobation, they will strip him even of his apparent dignity. In effect, the persona *imposes itself* on Gustave, and the audience is *free*, in the eyes of the actor who knocks himself out to please it, to accept or to reject that persona. Part of his distraction can be attributed to the fact that he must make himself into an object in the presence of these impenetrable and sovereign freedoms. Here is the Prince offering himself to the judgment of his subjects; and what kind of generosity exhibits itself? What is a generosity-object if not an affection, a pathos, the very contrary of that savage *practical* intention of raising oneself to an absolute-subject? Thus freedom, which wanted to be supranatural, loses itself in the process of externalization, becomes naturalized nature: it no longer seems beyond all motivation but a matter of disposition.

Submitting to his generosity—and his freedom, which is a contradiction *in adjecto*—Gustave was compelled to act out a character whose philosophical portrait would later be drawn by Guyau, who did not suspect that for half a century a novelist had exhausted himself trying to represent and impose this character: the man who is generous out of an excess of vital force. Guyau indeed sought to preserve generosity's character as gratuitous expenditure in the complete absence of egocentric motivation, even while *naturalizing* it. In certain beings, according to Guyau, the surplus of biological energy must expand itself gratuitously so as to reestablish the equilibrium of the organism; people of that kind will therefore give, for in them it is life that gives, that is given—part of its force is always available for ludic or princely activities. Gustave is compelled to adopt just such a role; his persona suffers continually from an *excess of life*, which it must expend or burst. His gigantism manifests itself not only by extension, by size, but intensively, by the overabundant resources of an athletic organism. He suffers from a hypertrophy of fuel, he *is* an overflowing surplus, and this incredible vitality ought—this is the meaning of the role—to be communicated to those around him, to penetrate them, to make them burn with a more ardent fire, to carry them away in a great whirlwind of exuberance and fecundity where they would all expend, in paradoxes, leaping from summit to summit, the unbearable plenitude with which Gustave had crammed them.

This is what he *once* succeeded in doing with his classmates: through their adherence to it, his persona became a collective creation without ceasing to be his. By taking turns acting out the Garçon, the young men did better than *believing* in the character; they internalized Flaubert's "He" as their most intimate fictive being; refracted through all these consciousnesses, existing for each of them as their alter ego, Gustave acquired the consistency of the innumerable in the third person singular. We shall have to return to this strange relationship, multiple and one. Let us merely note that it lasted for a limited time, and that he remembered it with profound nostalgia. He tries to revive this relationship with his colleagues—in vain. Perhaps on Sundays, at the

137

boulevard du Temple, he sometimes succeeds. But never for long; the spirit is broken, everyone is strictly concerned with playing himself. Everywhere else, he fails: these artists have no wish to enter the dance and to elect him master of ceremonies. They will never be anything but his audience, and the worst one possible. Observers more than spectators, they return him to his solitude of the actor reduced to silence.

Thus praxis is definitively turned into exis: from a distance, Gustave shows his peers his big breasts swollen with milk. Since no one would dream of drinking from them, all he does is *offer himself as a spectacle*. And as this gift cannot have any real impact on the life of his peers, he drives his performance to the utmost, as if his hyperbolism passing into the infinite managed to compensate for the inconsistency of the gesture, conferred upon it the reality of an act, and ended by carrying with it the adherence of the spectator: Gustave publicly dramatizes a human sacrifice. Since only the destruction of an organized group of interests, bodies in motion, and motivations by the irruption of the cosmos can provide a physical image of a freedom disqualifying all particular motives by an act of pure generosity, Gustave will publicly destroy himself as a particular determination by displaying himself to his peers as the martyr of the infinite. Gestures and cries are torn from him. Through his twitches and gasps the possessed will mime the deluge, he will show himself to be the grievous victim of a macrocosm where man has no place. The telluric powers crush his peers in his person. What the good giant wants is to make an intolerable gift: he will fatigue his listeners with his bounty, cram them until they keel over. The basic fact of the matter is this: if you play-act generosity, it must be excessive, otherwise the audience will not feel its weight; Gustave's presence must be an overpresence with which his peers *must be* oversaturated: when he drinks, when he eats, when he breathes, they must hear him drink, eat, breathe; to give, he must encumber. Therefore, dead tired, he will encumber.

Doesn't he know he is making himself intolerable? He *wants* to be. Out of sadism, out of masochism: his bellowings too contain an intention of failure, as Edmond's irritated entries in his Journal demonstrate—which also suggest the listener's reactions:[96] "Flaubert's mania to have always done and experienced things more enormous than others was the final buffoonery this evening. He battled violently and nearly wrangled with the sculptor Jacquemart to prove that he had had

96. *Journal*, 17 December, 1873.

more lice in Egypt than Jacquemart, that he was superior to him in vermin." And Edmond concludes: "Flaubert gives off such nervousness, such combative violence, that wherever he is, the company immediately becomes turbulent, everyone is overtaken by a certain aggressiveness. At the false exaggeration and boasting of his words, I saw bourgeois good sense grow angrier, angrier, angrier." The scene takes place at the home of the Princess: it is therefore in Edmond, Mathilde, and Popelin that "bourgeois good sense grows angrier." Isn't this just what Gustave wanted? And the cautious sparring with Jacquemart to determine which of them had more lice in Egypt, isn't this precisely in the style of the Garçon? The result: the audience's exasperation. But Goncourt does not say [97] that this exasperation is directed toward Gustave; he maintains rather that it primarily sets the spectators against each other. Indeed, the whole thing concludes with a thunderous bang: the Princess thunders at Popelin, her lover, and flings this last remark *at everyone:* "You are a bunch of rotten pigs." After all, Flaubert fulfills the vow of the second half of the third-year class at the *collège* of Rouen: *épater le bourgeois;*[98] by his exclamations and his paradoxes, he invokes the bourgeois that these highnesses and artists are hiding beneath their skin. They simply don't like to be shown their true origins: unmasked, provoked, they feel like biting— real potential lynchers. They are restrained by the twin facts that Gustave's "combative" transport is imaginary and that by the common agreement of good sense, the performance separates them, making each one the other's "bad smell." Can we believe that Gustave himself doesn't catch a whiff of it? Damn it, of course he does: his aggressiveness, as I have said, is not direct; part of it is turned against himself, and another part evaporates in the persona. But finally the drama of the gift *must* cause displeasure, in part because it isn't convincing, in part because it obscures: it is the gigantism of triviality. Since it is displeasing, it must displease Gustave: he plays his role with disgust. He wears himself out—from the time of *Novembre,* he tells us—being always the same man; read: the same character. In the eyes of others, in their expectation, we glimpse a "He" always equal to himself, dictating our future gestures. One expects Gustave, in irritation and hostility, to display an exuberance that will exhaust him in advance, paradoxes that he knows are already familiar and simply awaited as signals marking the end of his routine. Harassing, he harasses him-

97. It is implied.
98. We shall return to this.

self. It is a cycle: a few months before, Edmond, more discerning than usual, noted: "Is he absolutely lying when he is in such utter contradiction to his inner judgment?[99] No . . . First of all, give me a Norman and I'll show you a Garçon, a bit of a braggart. Besides, our Norman is quite ready by nature to quibble. Indeed, the poor boy's blood rises violently to his head when he speaks. This done, I believe that with one-third bragging, one-third quibbling, one-third congestion, my friend Flaubert almost succeeds in getting sincerely intoxicated with his recitation of paradoxes."[100] This is exactly what Gustave feels when he pushes hubris to the point of congestion: blood drumming in his temples, headaches, the risk of being struck down. In sum, all these great organic movements represent for him the analogue of a conviction; this is what *for him alone* gives a hysterical consistency to the persona. But at the time when he seems to consume his life for that prince he is not, and whom he cannot help playing until death— at the time, if you will, when his overly zealous body, through suffocation and spasms, through increasing congestion, offers him the imaginary equivalent of conviction—Flaubert is perfectly conscious of the general incredulity; he knows very well that Edmond, hostile and starchy, sees him merely as a prolix and red-faced man threatened by apoplexy. This contrast between external incredulity, which reduces his performance to nothingness without sparing the spectators the revelation of their bourgeois baseness, and the captious docility of his own body, which burns up his reserves to feed the persona, is a contrast that Gustave is seeking—at least in the salons of the Second Empire. The grating, maddening game of belief as a physiological fact and of skepticism as an external and social determination, knocking himself out at the task before the bored indifference of the egalitarian brotherhood—this is what repels and attracts him. And then, when he goes home or his guests leave, the evening itself is resumed as he made it and as others made it for him, with the veneer of objectivity they throw over it. Just when it becomes irretrievable, he rediscovers his bitterness and his boredom, his real fatigue, his apathy, his mists:

99. The reason for this contradiction, according to Goncourt: "He wants to conceal his fundamental lack of originality by inventing 'truculent paradoxes.' I am talking about a particular originality that is always the mark of the superior man." Meaning Edmond, the refined collector of Japanese curios. It will be recalled that at school, Gustave scorned his comrades for having *such common* minds. But *he* had the temerity to add, "such narrow minds." Goncourt's originality is his specific difference. Flaubert's genius is to be cosmic and common, both together, and to know it. The result will be *Madame Bovary*.
100. *Journal* (Monaco edition) 10:128–29, 3 May, 1873.

how could he recognize himself in that loud-mouthed, red-faced, obscene, drunken braggart? He cannot even conceive that he could have been its incarnation: it is an Other, another falsely proclaimed who appears only in the presence of Others, engendered by Flaubert's overstimulation and unmasked by their disbelief. It is *his being*, yes, because in solitude he finds nothing with which to counter it but stupor, atrophy, forms of absence, but it is his *imaginary* being: he must bow to the evidence or flee from it into sleep, which is a way of accepting it.

This drama, however, painful to him and irritating to onlookers, has another, more positive meaning in his eyes, which I mentioned a moment ago; still only implicit in the Garçon of the 1835 period, it was later made more explicit, so much so that it did not escape the Goncourts. Quite unjustly they reproached him for wanting "so modestly to rush into face-to-face competition with Hugo." Gustave always admired Hugo, although he was bothered early on by the exile's political ideas. And above all he had too much pride to want to compete with anyone—comparisons were all very well for the Goncourts. But the two old maids are onto him: to the extent that Gustave assimilates himself to his persona, his gigantism intoxicates him, the man is effaced before the superman; what he makes visible by the intensely felt determinations of his passivity is that one cannot receive the terrifying and grotesque visitations of the cosmos without being oneself a force of nature. "Petty natures" have only "petty needs." The Garçon, on the contrary, is *in thrall to himself;* his submission to nature, whose menacing presence he manifests through bawlings and gesticulations, can be experienced inwardly only in the form of an abandonment to *his* nature.[101] We rediscover the child who felt "as big as the world": indeed, the lordly gift he makes to his friends and acquaintances is infinite nature as the pitiless negation of the human order, meaning that the dark, "derisive" exuberance of a man *possessed* is the degraded, materialized image of the destructive and demoralizing genius he would like to possess. When he plays Pantagruel in the presence of the Goncourts, it is indeed *his genius* he wants to make them recognize in the hope that their conviction will convince him. And in a way he has the ability to present his princely superiority to them in the form of a simple specific difference. In the early days of

101. When Louise calls him her "force of nature," she knows what she is doing: he is exultant. And, as we know, he signs his letters to Laporte—who is as tall as he is, or nearly—"Your Giant," pleased to equivocate (giant in size, giant in spirit) what elsewhere Laporte is pleased to maintain.

their acquaintance, the two brothers met him halfway; it is difficult to read the portrait of Flaubert they sketched in *Charles Demailly* without smiling: " . . . a tall boy, ravaged but powerful, capable of anything, twenty-seven hours on horseback or seven months of forced labor in his room . . . a strong voice, loud and martial . . . a man in whom something had been killed in his youth, an illusion, a dream, I don't know . . . His cold-blooded scrutiny digs deep into man to the very bowels . . . the grip of a surgeon . . . the greatest propensity of his spirit is [however] to the purple, to the sun, to the gold. He is a poet before all else." "That's it!" cries Monsieur Dumesnil, ravished, "That's it, indeed!" Yes, *that's* it, indeed. But *that* represents neither what Flaubert was in reality, nor what he claimed to be, nor altogether what the Goncourts then believed he was. It was a loyal and gallant effort by the two brothers to reflect back to him his gigantism reduced to the dimensions of a simple specific difference; *that* is a miniature Gargantua, *primus inter pares*, like all other members of the elite. They would very quickly perceive that this "reduction" was impossible: a giant cannot be contained in a salon. They willingly admit that he prefers the ancients to the moderns, that he knew Sanskrit, that he detested the English: these tastes sufficed to particularize him. But if he turns himself into nature, pretends to play the *Alma Venus* or the raging sea, his place is "down there on the Island" with the Father and not in Paris. One cannot be Hugo, converse familiarly with God, and dine at Magny's. If Flaubert boasts, he is a third-rate actor, a bore; but if there is a chance that he might truly be a medium, then it's every man for himself; the egalitarian elite is dead, a prince and his subjects remain. Indeed, Gustave would wish for a *consensus* that would confirm him *in his own eyes* as the Prince of Letters. He would like the bubblings of his *blue blood*, the mark of his Flaubert birth, to be recognized in this *suffered* generosity. In a sense, what he mimes on Sundays at the boulevard du Temple is the mysterious fecundity that he denies and that resists him at Croisset—we shall speak of it again— namely, *inspiration*.

Let us return for a moment to the invitation he sends to the Goncourts. It seems to be merely a question of Gustave's physical superiority to his guests: Gustave will flatten the listeners because he can "tolerate twenty-seven hours on horseback." Hence the acknowledgment: this "strapping guy" has greater strength, Sainte-Beuve will have greater critical acumen, Edmond and Jules greater artistic sensibility, greater psychological penetration; everyone is superior to the others in his sphere, therefore they are equal. But it doesn't take long to read between the lines that Flaubert is in fact postulating his absolute superiority; he is going "to rant" his work, fine, and his colleagues will be unable to endure the reading until the end. But is it to be supposed that *just any novel* would be suited to such ranting? A naive idyll, a reverie, a study in manners would be poorly served by such an expenditure of energy: you don't rant *Daphnis and Chloe* or *Paul et Virginie*. The work, therefore, must *of itself demand* this deployment of force; in other words, it is the work that makes the listeners "keel over." A note of Gustave's on his return from Carthage manages to enlighten us: he invokes the telluric divinities; let the heat, the vivid colors of the desert, the winds, the fecundity of the cultivated earth penetrate and inspire him. To me, Cosmos, give me your power. *Salammbô* is the reexternalization of the chthonic energies Gustave internalized in Tunisia. It is the intolerable dazzle of this masterpiece that overwhelms the listeners. Only Flaubert can give a reading of it—Ulysses alone can draw his bow—because only he could write it. It is therefore quite true that the physical qualities of the author, hyperbolized, are only hypostases of his genius. And the Goncourt brothers are to some extent justified in withdrawing while he reads, refusing to listen, and quickly running to their Journal to tear apart the work he tried to impose on them. They felt that Flaubert desired greatness; to demolish him they will attempt to replace the *height* of ambition by the *grossness* of the result: he has conjured the *"vulgar* Orient," the Orient of shoddy merchandise, of the bazaar, and—the main thrust—of barbaric violence. What Edmond has not understood, however, when he charges Gustave with buffoonery is that the grotesque-verging-on-the-base is a procedure knowingly utilized to show indirectly the presence of the sublime and to force its acceptance. Under my shirt I've carried all the lice in Egypt—this *also* means: I am the hardiest of travelers who, in order to know the incomparable joys of art, came closest to the wretched life of the natives, and with that kind of courage I could appreciate Karnak and Luxor better than anyone. The traveling salesman infested with vermin is the reverse of an exquisite artist. Only that? No, he is also the artist ridiculed by the real. In this circular movement, no one—neither the resident joker nor the poet—has the last word. Let us not forget, in fact, that even as he had contempt for his classmates in the name of his poetic ecstasies, Gustave denounced along with them the vanity of art and the imposture of the artist, false creator who knows how to produce nothing but phantoms. What makes the Garçon difficult to pin down is the circular structure that is basic to his "nature" and makes him shift at every level from mocked to mocker and vice versa. By anticipating the future avatars of Flaubert's persona we have, I hope, further clarified the *character* of the years around 1835. He is a devil in a bottle, a ferocious Gargantua, mad with rage, squeezed into a flask of human skin, ridiculing the Liliputians who hold him captive; and he is at the same time a man, an immense traveling salesman who is intentionally vulgar because Nature in "her high and mighty majesty," when she makes herself visible in a man who coughs, spits, sneezes, belches, farts, shits, and copulates like all "higher" mammals, can be only the triumph of vulgarity. He is generous by disposition and spiteful as hell because the aforesaid Nature pursues our species, and because he represents Nature as mediator of the infinite. For this reason his gifts are comparable to those of Corneille, of whom Gustave said in the "Eloge" that he abased the human race with the immortal gifts he had bestowed upon it. And, principally, he is the sublime below, the ignoble, an indirect allusion to the sublime above, out of reach. When Gustave denounces the budding importance and spirit of seriousness that he attributes to the deputy magistrate of Calvi, it is in the name of Great Desire, of dissatisfaction, of the horror of being man, of an obscure "religious instinct." He doesn't breathe a word of this and instead has the Garçon, practical joker and carouser, go shit in front of the bust of His Majesty—the ignoble is the executor of the base works of the sublime. In order to enter further into this complex creation, however, we must leave the theme of generosity for a moment and follow that other Ariadne's thread, derision.

Laughter as the Fundamental Structure of the Garçon
(or the sadism of a masochist)

Let us return to the years around 1835. When Gustave approaches his comrades and feels incapable of confronting each of them directly, what does he do? He is quick to laugh publicly at himself so as to forestall and assume the hilarity he fears to provoke. However, this collective laughter cannot *really* be produced by one person alone, and little Flaubert cannot be mocking his *true self*: he unrealizes himself in a character that is merely his caricature; distorting his features, Gustave publicly makes himself the comic object he has a horror of being. When unforgotten rancors tear that arrogant cry, "*They*, laugh at *me!*" from the solitary sixteen-year-old, he has long since chosen to play himself in the comic mode, making visible to others a merciless burden of self. And because one can laugh only at a character who takes

144

himself seriously, Gustave plays the Garçon as the man for whom the serious exists only to be cut through *at once*, as if by a knife, by bursts of a Homeric laughter that is born *elsewhere*, above him, and is finally torn, voluminous, from his own mouth. Hence the curious quality of his creature: the man-who-laughs-at-himself is never on reflexive terrain; he is absorbed in doing what he is doing as gravely as can be, without ever challenging his objectives or the means he employs to attain them. And yet he *is* reflected, for he is indissolubly the subject of his affects and his acts, the object of a reflection that is simultaneously his and other and manifests itself in a permanent attempt to withdraw solidarity. As though Gustave wanted to recuperate his visibility.

On this level we can see that his laughter has a dual function: the hilarity he steals from his classmates is that of common sense mocking his anomaly; but he is going to dramatize for them this trick of derision through the aggrandizement of that mocked particularity, human nature in general and common laughter itself, in the name of a higher and larger derision—a little like Alfred laughing at Lengliné, who was laughing at Gustave. In other words, the laughter of the common man is disqualified by the Giant's laughter. But instead of directly mocking his comrades—"You are no better than I am, the same narrow viewpoint, the same physical, mental, moral weakness, the same vanity, the same comic claim to be the navel of the world"— he derides them indirectly by revealing in this own hyperbolized determinations the portion of darkness and nothingness that is in each of us. As if he were saying to them: As for *me*, I feel the infinite gaze that crushes me, and you, proud or ashamed of your miserable differences, you don't feel it. By the same token, he is the man who immoderately inflates himself: the Christian, that relative and finite being, despite his weakness becomes an absolute through the distinguishing love the absolute Being bears him; in the same way, the Flaubert son, a reverse Christian, becomes comic and contemptible through the sneers he wrests from the immensity. The Garçon is "henormous": the Infinite must look at him through a magnifying glass and show him to men as the terrifying enlargement of their wretchedness.

From this point of view we shall see a hyper-Gustave in the Garçon. Gustave doesn't like himself much, as we know; his novel enterprise won't be hampered by narcissism. To the contrary, he takes great pleasure exulting in the disgust he inspires, outdoing his own faults, his horror of life. Through the eyes of the invisible Giant, he will make himself into a formidable insect, like Kafka, so as to transform man in his own person into a louse. This malevolent hyperbole becomes a permanent characteristic of his personalization. He strains to imitate the stupors of senility or the seizures of an old epileptic; but these stupors are his, and he knows how to turn them, in the solitude of interiority, to quite another account; in the epilepsy of the "Journaliste de Nevers" he is really fascinated by his own nascent neurosis and wants to carry it to excess *in order to worry his father,* who finally prohibits these exhibitions—proving that they were conceived especially for the family and that Gustave yielded to them with the purpose both of challenging and reinforcing the overprotection to which he was subjected.[102] A quadragenarian, he tucks up his coat, plays dead, lets his jaw drop and dances the idiot's ballet for his peers—a highly studied and regulated performance from the time of his adolescence—which causes the Goncourts a strange, admiring discomfort. The Garçon is an idiot, that's obvious: Gustave tells the Goncourts that he had, "along with his friends, attributed a complete personality [to this character] . . . complicated with every kind of provincial stupidity." We can be sure that the Garçon had an "infinite depth" of stupidity, like Charles Bovary's cap. But doesn't Gustave suffer from being the family idiot, the simpleton whose naïvetés provoked his comrades' offensive epithets? Doesn't he boast of attracting idiots, children, and animals? At seven years old, silent in front of his alphabet, he felt "brushed by the wing of imbecility"; at twelve he was shaken by the same anxious shudder when, initiated into the exact disciplines, his head became foggy and he was persuaded that the center of logical connections in his cranial box was atrophied. In his writing[103] he never embodies himself in laughable heroes; in public the impulse is too much for him, he must turn on himself and in the presence of witnesses play out that crushing stupidity he is convinced of being afflicted with, and of which he is deeply ashamed.

Gustave goes still further by making the Garçon a robot. "He had the gestures of an automaton," he confides to the Goncourts. His laughter itself, "broken, strident," has something mechanical about it. For this reason too it "is not laughter at all": rather than a human

---

102. We shall come back to this in chapter 14.

103. Yet *once* his taste for the grotesque triumphs, in his last years. *Bouvard et Pécuchet* is the doubling of the terrible Idiot. The title of this work was supposed to be "The Two Cockroaches": the two cockroaches together, plus the world's immense derision ridiculing their efforts—the last avatar of the Garçon. But it is no accident that this book of vengeance was undertaken only at the end of his life.

reaction to an event, to a spectacle, it seems to be the product of a machine set in motion by a physical stimulus. And as we know, Flaubert was haunted by the scientistic idea: if man is a system in exteriority—moved by the exterior, exterior to himself—the best metaphor will be automatism. Almaroës—that is, the half of the cursed couple in which the author has embodied himself—is an electronic machine, as we have seen. Moreover, Gustave is delighted to discern in pure bourgeois stupidity the movements of an enormous machine. When he writes *Le Château des coeurs*, he imagines that "gnomes cannot live without the heart of man, for in order to feed on it they steal it by putting in its place some sort of mechanical movement of their invention which perfectly imitates the movements of nature." Unresisting, men "abandon themselves to the exigencies of matter." This is the general theme of the piece. These automatons, of course, are stupid: someone regulates them, someone winds them up; they mouth commonplaces, make appropriate gestures without ever diverging from the strictest conformity because—and this was obvious in Flaubert's time but not in ours—a machine, whatever the number and arrangement of its elements and of their combination, cannot be unpredictable. Extreme intelligence—the intelligence of Achille-Cléophas, of Achille, and of the *prix d'excellence* students—reduces men to the state of a mechanical system, and this too produces extreme stupidity: two ways of "abandoning oneself to the exigencies of materiality." By his automaton's gestures the Garçon will symbolize both, ridiculing simultaneously and paradoxically the obtuse and limited clumsiness of the family idiot and the electronic intelligence of big brother Achille. But if the Giant mocks the two postulations of man this way, what is the Garçon? An idiot or a prophet? To my mind, both—I will explain in a moment. For now we are and should remain at that stage of the operation where Gustave, *heautontimoroumenos*, offers his comrades the *display* of his hyperbolized defects.

See, for example, how he denigrates his pride. Caroline writes to him that she keenly feels his absence (11 November 1841). She adds: "I hope that I am sufficiently flattering the vanity of the Garçon, and that you will be pleased with me." This means that Gustave is profoundly vain, conceited even, but *in the Garçon*. Yet at the time he received this letter, Gustave, having tried to present pride as the basic motive of our actions, had long since come to recognize that this general law was applicable only to him: I am mad with pride, he noted a little earlier. Indeed, negative pride consumes him, it is his illness. But when in solitude he confides this admission to a notebook which should have no reader but himself, he is quite far from condemning himself: I shall undoubtedly be more virtuous than most people because I have more pride, he writes one day. Moreover, he sees in this sentiment the source of all his sufferings and—he implies—the source of his future greatness. But once he finds himself an audience, it is stronger than he is: laugh, then, clown! White turns to black, noble to ignoble; Gustave's pride—which he rightly, as we shall see, considers the best part of himself—is transposed in the Garçon into vanity. This is not without several noteworthy mutations: pride, arrogant demand, dissatisfaction with himself and the world, become repeated foolishness, smugness, the narcissistic love of finite being for its determination, sanctimonious satisfaction. As we shall see, this involves an exchange of positive for negative; Gustave, the dolorist, establishes his greatness (as if he were saying: stripped of everything, I haven't the means to be modest). The Garçon, a pleasure seeker, shows the baseness (negative quality) of his vanity when it is (*positive* aspect) fully satisfied, that is, all the time. The Garçon is certainly not difficult; almost anything flatters him; if flatterers are lacking, he flatters himself. Hence he is *comic*, for what is more laughable than this great booby, fatuously naive, who wags his head at calculated compliments and outdoes those that have been made to him? Yet Gustave is *also* vain. Like everyone, more than everyone—and he knows it. Vanity in him is a failing of pride: weary of asking for the moon, he lowers his pretensions a moment and ends by accepting merely its reflection in a pond. Gustave's wholly naive vanity is touching; one feels that he yearns to escape for a moment from his inner hell when in his letters he seizes on a banal compliment made by one of his correspondents, swells up immoderately, and cries out astonished: is it really true? Do you know that you are going to make me mad with pride? At Constantinople in December 1850, he receives a letter from his mother congratulating him on the tone and style of the letters he has sent her. This is somewhat solicited praise, for several weeks earlier he apologized for writing to her off the cuff. Besides, he hardly admired her tastes in literature, and Madame Flaubert had no pretensions in that area. Yet here is how he answers her:

> Do you know that you will end, dear old thing, by making me immoderately vain, I who witness the progressive decline of this quality which is generally not denied me? You pay me such compliments on my letters that I believe maternal love has utterly blinded you. For the lines I send you seem to me quite insipid, badly written, especially . . . Since I know it is not quality but

quantity that is important to you, I dispatch to you as many as I can.[104]

This passage speaks for itself and needs no comment; I would remark only that Flaubert was suffering the blow of a terrible literary disappointment, which in part spoiled his journey and began to set him at odds with Maxime; Du Camp and Bouilhet, after he had given them a reading of the first *Saint Antoine,* declared straight out that the work was good only to be shelved. Imagine his disarray, his anguish: how hard it must have been for him to take pleasure in the appreciative comments of a woman whose judgment he challenged on this subject concerning letters that are indeed lively and quite colorful but obviously written in haste, which constitutes their charm *for us* but sufficed, *for him,* according to his aesthetic conceptions, to deprive them of all literary value.

Yet he will pillory this touching, naive vanity by giving himself in the Garçon both the immensity of an unhappy, hence insatiable, pride and the pitiable pleasures of smug self-esteem. An undated remark—but one which seems likely to go back to his seventeenth year—shows us both his method and his lack of self-deception: "I am conceited, they say—and why, then, do I have such doubt about each of my actions?"[105] He himself knows very well that pride is infinite demand and is expressed most of the time by doubt—did I really have to do that to become equal to my ambitions? Since others, however, fooled by a surface self-assurance, reproach him with being conceited, it is conceit itself, carried to excess, that he will represent in his persona. As if he were saying to the others: you think I'm vain; that needn't be a problem—I will make my vanity Gargantuan, and the Garçon will make you roll with laughter at his pretensions. This phony imbecile, moreover, has always desired and dreaded the tranquillity he believes accompanies true imbecility. Thus the Garçon is the hyperbolization not only of what Gustave is for others but also of what he would like to be and fears to become. By acting out his character, fierce and always satisfied, he grants himself at moments a respite, an imaginary fulfillment, at the very time when his prickly conscience condemns its stupid materiality.

It is not just his pronounced taste for scatology that we rediscover, amplified, in his persona. The Garçon belches behind the door, shits

104. *Correspondance* 2:263–64, 4 December 1850.
105. *Souvenirs,* p. 59.

beneath the bust of His Majesty; as we shall see, Gustave keeps a "Hoax Hotel" to which his clients come to eat shit by the bucketful. This wildman, possessed by violence and gesticulation, can take pleasure only in the lowest and filthiest jokes. *Like Gustave himself.* How do we know? "He was," says Caroline Commanville, " . . . a traveling salesman." And Gustave, to the Goncourts: there are two men in me, a bookworm and "a traveling salesman, a veritable wanton of a traveling salesman on the road with a taste for violent practices." [106] Very well; yet whom does he despise most after grocers but traveling salesmen with their gross "jokes," their commonplaces, their low bourgeois vulgarity? Yet he wanted to present to this comrades not only the caricature of his persona but that of the caricaturist as well. The Gaudissart side of the Garçon is the author's self-criticism through his creature: I know that I am not amusing, that I am too excited and to no purpose, that I importune and encumber, that all my bawlings are not worth as much as a well-aimed witticism. Furthermore, wit is hardly to be met with in the provinces, Gustave is convinced of that: he detests his provincialism and presents it as fodder to his comrades, provincials that they are. He tells the Goncourts, who repeat it with their usual touch of malevolence: "It was a heavy-handed joke, stubborn, patient, uninterrupted, heroic, unending, like a small-town or German joke." The circle is complete, the myth itself is judged: not only is the Garçon a traveling salesman on a spree, but his inventors would be inconceivable in a capital city; to extend this "German joke" over several years required the dullness of time that falls over small towns, and the slowness as well: nothing happens, everything repeats itself, everyone knows everyone else. If we add to this a good pinch of bourgeois faults—the Garçon loves comfort, he seems miserly, he takes pleasure in dining on his own—it all seems quite clear: a bourgeois laughs at himself in a sufficiently bourgeois fashion to provoke the gross laughter of a bourgeois public.

Nothing is clear. Indeed, how can we allow that Gustave's comrades were fascinated by this character if he was nothing but the Flaubert younger son to the tenth power? How can we believe that each of them wanted to slip into his skin and *feel he was the Garçon* at least for a few minutes? The features we have reported cannot be considered universal: little actors are not all, nor do they judge themselves to be, idiots, mean, vain, vulgar; not all of them have that suspect taste for filth and baseness, nor is it even clear that the "bour-

106. *Journal*, 6 May 1866.

geois," a myth of the nineteenth century, might be the model for this portrait. A line of Gustave's implies that the *general* interest of the Garçon is situated elsewhere: the Garçon, he tells the Goncourts, "represented a spoof of materialism and Romanticism, the caricature of Holbach's philosophy." The text is clear, though the Goncourts did not understand a word of what they were reporting. Who had mocked the materialism of the philistines and of the future Monsieur Prudhomme better than the Romantics themselves? And to counter the Romantics the bourgeoisie, not daring in these prejudiced times to call Helvétius and Holbach to the rescue, employed Voltairean irony and, more discreetly, scientistic mechanism. These counterattacks secretly aimed to destroy the idealism of the young noblemen-poets, and hence the ideology of the priestly party, by using the materialism of the eighteenth century as a battering ram. Thus the spoof of materialism is Romanticism, and the spoof of Romanticism is scientistic materialism. So the Garçon is no bourgeois laughing at himself. Or, if he is, only on a certain level. To the contrary, he is inhabited by an endless round of laughter: in him Romanticism mocks materialism and vice versa. What is left, in this case? We shall see. Certainly, we are encountering once again the conflict of the two contemporary ideologies—bourgeois scientism, aristocratic religiosity— transformed into an endless circle of dispute. We know that this contradiction tore Gustave apart. There is no doubt that it tormented most of his classmates. Little Flaubert entrusted the Garçon with freeing him of it publicly by allowing the two theses to ridicule each other—that is what interested his spectators. The Goncourts in their shrewd Parisian stupidity did not grasp the depth of the "heavy-handed provincial joke," nor did they see laughter as an imaginary solution to the antinomy of the century. They could not complain, however, that Gustave had not tried to help them out of the difficulty. He cited them at least one example: the "consecrated caricature every time one passed a [sic] Rouen cathedral."

"Right away someone would say: 'This Gothic architecture is beautiful, it elevates the soul.' Whoever was doing the Garçon would immediately start acting up, laughing and gesticulating: 'Yes, it is beautiful . . . and so is Saint Bartholemew's Day! And the Edict of Nantes[107] and the massacres by Louis XIV's dragoons, they are beautiful too!'" What is being mocked here? Materialism or Romanticism? Materialism, think the Goncourts, who see in the Garçon a prefigura-

107. The revocation of the Edict, obviously.

tion of Monsieur Homais.[108] Are we dealing with a philanthropic and nationalistic Prudhomme who is being ridiculed for his desire to use a few massacres as an argument to condemn Holy Religion and the works of art it inspires? Are we really invited to laugh at his laughter? Perhaps, but let us take a closer look.

The companion's line is obviously conceived to provoke the Garçon's reply. But it is self-sufficient: as reported, it is of *itself* and without any commentary a grotesque commonplace which might figure in the *Dictionnaire des Idées reçues:* "Gothic: say that it elevates the soul." Now let us ask *who* says this, who is the Monsieur Loyal to this Auguste. A Romantic, without any doubt; or, better, a pious bourgeois woman who has been touched by Romanticism and is delighted to enjoy in church what we would today call the ecstasies of consummation. A fool, obviously, and one who takes himself for an aristocrat. Good, we know who she is: Gustave in person. Let us recall the symbol of the holy water reflecting the high Gothic vaults of the nave. In any event, we have seen that he often experiences religion as a call from above—the bells, the rise of the walls up to the ogive. A disappointing call, since God keeps quiet up there, but one that facilitates spiritual exercises, particularly "raptures." After all, don't we know from Gustave's own words that he would have liked to be a mystic, "to die a martyr"? In his notebook of *Souvenirs,* it is not the Gothic that disposes him to these elevating sensations, it is the "waves of incense," and he adds: "It is a beautiful thing, the altar covered with embalming flowers." But doesn't this line elicit the *same* reply from the Garçon: "Oh yes! It is a beautiful thing! And so is Saint Bartholemew's Day," etc., etc. Thus Gustave mocks himself publicly for sentiments that affect him in private. But here again he only attempts to construct his character by appropriating the collective laughter in order to direct it toward his immediate feelings: he was that timid adolescent who furtively entered churches in order to seek faith without finding it. What

---

108. This conjecture seems to me quite idiotic. In Homais, everything is clear, precise, intelligent, but petty. In this cunning pharmacist, Gustave wanted to show the *stupidity of intelligence.* And precisely for this reason he presents him as a sharp little arriviste, prudent and efficient, who knows how to guard against excess and doggedly pursue his enterprise. Where is Pantagruel? Where is the laughter of the Garçon? And, above all, where is the *denied despair* hidden beneath that laughter? The "falsehood of Romanticism"—where is that? Homais's stupidity is nothing but his satisfaction. All one can say is that Bournisien and Homais represent the reexternalized contradiction of the two ideologies. With this addition: they are both equally stupid. The Garçon is *among other things* Bournisien *and* Homais—two materialisms—but radicalized, hyperbolized to cosmic stature, which—quality depends on quantity—is enough to make them unrecognizable.

is more, at those moments, as we have remarked in a preceding chapter, he felt disarmed, terribly exposed, and laughable: if my comrades could see me, how they would laugh at me! In this hopeless quest, everything is given at once: the stupidity of Monsieur Loyal, who seeks an absent or nonexistent God, and the ferocious laughter of the Garçon—that is, of his comrades. The laughter, moreover, is only virtual, therefore unreal, for Gustave's *risibility* does not in fact provoke any laughter: visible, he is not *seen* except hypothetically and in the imaginary. Nonetheless, the two moments are given together as the reflected and the reflexive that is disengaged from it, the latter, Gustave's *real* look at himself, masquerading as the Other's imaginary look at him.

Moreover, why does the Garçon laugh at the "consecrated caricature"? As his behavior is described, his gestures and his laughter seem to *urge him on,* signs of considerable excitation, and he recalls another aspect of Christianity: religion produced builders of cathedrals but also Grand Inquisitors. Elevations of the soul have as their counterpart fanaticism and holy wars. On this point everyone might agree, even a priest, who would simply remark that the faults of men cannot be held against that great body, the Church. But the Garçon is not of this opinion: he puts autos-da-fé and masterpieces of religious art on the same plane. This is tenable provided they are seen as products of the same culture, in the same society, at the same moment of history. From this point of view his reply is rather weak: massacres by the Sun King's dragoons have nothing much to do with the Gothic. Never mind, let us take the statement as whole; it amounts to saying that faith alone can move mountains and could construct these vast edifices for the assembly of the people; but such faith can only be fanatical: those who built the temples of God and those who burned schismatics in His Name were motivated by the same kind of intolerance. "It's beautiful, Saint Bartholemew's Day!" Is Gustave mocking his interlocutor? Where does he find—as the Garçon—beauty in massacres? We must not attempt to answer this without reference to the position taken by the "performer of himself" who is hyperbolized in this character: Gustave always declared that religious convictions were not conceived without fanaticism. Is this a defect? Not at all: instinct—or thirst for the infinite, for the absolute—impels man to produce those pathetic fables called religions, which cannot satisfy him because finite being has need of the infinite, but his weakness is such that he cannot imagine infinity. In sum, whatever the myth, it will never be anything but a finite representation of the infinite; from

153

this point of view, fetishism is neither more nor less valuable than Christian monotheism. What saves these mythologies from ridicule is that believers, for want of anything better, are attached to them with all the violence of their insatiable thirst for the absolute. The content is not important but rather the mobilization of all our energies by faith. In this sense fanaticism and intolerance represent what is best in man. The martyr and the inquisitor are brothers; both destroy the human species in themselves and in the other so that the kingdom of God might come into being. Inquisitors would make excellent martyrs, and martyrs, when they survive, are the best inquisitors. They obey the original imperative of the religious instinct, which is entirely negative: even if God is not, shatter the finite determination in yourself and in your neighbor in order to prove, beneath His empty heaven, your need of Him. The fanaticism of man for man is good: sacrifice and hierarchy complete each other; the fanaticism of man for God is better: it realizes at the same time the hierarchy of the human race and, at least when taken to its extreme, its abolition.

We must look at this abolition through Gustave's eyes and remember that it was not at all displeasing to his misanthropy and that he frequently wished for it. As for massacres, we know that he dreamed of committing them. At this period his favorite heroes were Nero the pyromaniac, Tamberlaine, Genghis Khan; soon he would invoke Attila and beg him to destroy both Rouen and Paris. Resentment and humiliation, of course, are what enrage him to the point where he embraces the most exhaustive idea of genocide, the murder of the human race as a whole. But he must have thought about it continually, because his anger has never abated. He has even established, in imagination, a set of values whose explicitly admitted principle is Thanatos: there is nothing more sensuous than making love while the servants are busy killing and torturing; there is nothing more beautiful than "making art" on a hilltop while a Capital of Pain rears up and burns to ashes, lashed by a conflagration of one's own making.

At the time, he is not content with these mastubatory dreams: in the street, in public places, wherever he encounters crowds, he has murderous impulses: sometimes he wants to punch his neighbor to death; sometimes, overcome with fury, he feels the need to make heads roll. We should not, I know, be overly impressed by this: unable to open the way to revolt, his great passive rage unrealizes itself in the desire to kill. For it is simply those nearest at hand that he wants to kill, passersby whose faces he doesn't like, nothing serious. Nevertheless, shame, impotence, the horror of living sometimes lead those the press calls "fanatics" to commit the simplest surrealistic act, that is, to go into a populated street and fire into the crowd. Gustave will never reach the point of action: he is protected against these desperate gestures by his condition as bourgeois. But his constituted passivity would not alone prevent him from committing them: these little massacres, frequently followed by a suicide, cannot rightly have any author but a passive agent. In any case, he is delighted with the role of powerful homicide, of a man who "no longer knows himself"—he loves to frighten himself. Be that as it may, the homicidal impulse is one of his fantasies—it cannot last; I am going to do something desperate! How could he fail to project it onto his persona? The formidable size of the Giant kept prisoner in the Garçon is already a genocide. But the Garçon is mean as well. Mean as the devil. As Marguerite, as Garcia, Satan, Mazza, as the young author himself. The first time that Gustave speaks to us of this famous laughter, we have seen, is 24 March 1837; the proctor was caught in a brothel. What puts Gustave in such a joyous state and for a moment makes him the equal of his hyperbolic caricature is the poor man's crestfallen look, in other words, the expression of his suffering. This functionary immediately understands the consequences: he will be the shame of the *collège*, an object of scorn to his colleagues and of derision to the schoolboys, and furthermore he will lose his job. This is just what delights the Garçon: the degradation, the vilification of a man and his *nearly* physical liquidation: he will not be killed but he will disappear and vegetate elsewhere with his odious memories.

If he is mean, would the Garçon—or rather the giant incensed at being shut up in the skin of a man—be likely to have such repugnance for massacres? It is true that the beautiful beasts he would like to take as his model—Lacenaire is the most recent—kill, according to him, for the pleasure of killing. Misanthropy, sadism pushed to the point of cannibalism, these, he believes, are their motives—which he pretends to approve unconditionally. Oh yes, the Garçon would say excitedly, the blood of man is beautiful when other men make it flow: death is beautiful when it comes by the sword and sinks with the sword into the heart of the condemned; the suffering of so-called innocent victims (one is never innocent of being man) is beautiful when the tormentors—calmly committed and certain of their rights—inflict it on them. But to massacre in the name of God, is this amusing as well? In the Saint Bartholomew's Day massacre, for example, there is either colossal blindness or immense deceit: people cut each other's throats in the name of a deaf, dumb, hidden divinity, which in any case, whether it exists or not, has nothing in common with the vulgar idol fashioned by the Catholics, nor indeed with what the Protestants offer as an alternative. This is no longer pure sadism: an "ideal" intervenes, in the name of which "justice is seen to be done." Well, it just so happens that for the Garçon these farces are the best. First of all, nothing of what he loved about the Neroesque festivities is lost: is the river of blood running in the streets of Paris any less red? As for sadism, a good conscience, far from stifling it, exalts it: what a pleasure to disembowel a young girl for the love of the Good! Above all, religious wars are much more farcical! Nero doesn't lend himself to laughter—he kills for his own pleasure. But when on both sides there is pillage, torture, and killing in the name of the God of justice and love, the Garçon is transfixed. Man is revealed at last in the perfection of his nature: he is either a ridiculous executioner or a laughable victim. Epernon, who massacred for pleasure, is less "henormous" than Torquemada, that imbecile who burned his neighbors out of virtue, that hypocrite who got an erection making others suffer and didn't want to know it. The Garçon goes still further: if man's sole value lies in his religious instinct, and if this instinct finds its human fulfillment only in fanaticism which leads inevitably to genocide, this monster is so constructed that his love of Being pushes him directly toward Nothingness. At the theater I laugh when a husband, by the very precautions he takes to defend his wife's virtue, lands her in spite of himself, in spite of her, in his neighbor's bed; shouldn't I laugh all the more if I see an animal species, the better to affirm itself *in the absolute,* set in motion the surest means of its own liquidation? By falling into agreement with his interlocutor, the Garçon intends to reveal beneath their apparent contradiction the dialectical unity of sentimental mysticism and fanaticism. If he mocks him, however, if he demoralizes him, it is by smearing his interlocutor's tender, quietistic raptures with blood; whether he likes it or not, Monsieur Loyal is an accomplice to the savagery of the massacres that have made his ecstasies possible. Gustave is all the more convinced of this as his *own* ecstasies are not in the least innocent: as we have shown above, they are rancorous flights that flatten men to the ground and end by eliminating them. In this sense the bloody history of religious wars serves only to reveal the secret savagery of ecstasies—Gustave's and, according to him, those of all the great mystics. What pushes his hilarity to excess is that the perpetrators of these massacres who use the name of God are right: in piously exterminating itself, our species is only executing the sentence brought against it on high; for that Elegant

Principle of Indifference, the *absolute*, we *absolutely* do not exist. We shall notice the resemblance between the curse of Adam, intent *by nature* on annihilating himself along with the entire species, and the curse of Gustave dreaming of eliminating himself in order to execute the orders of the Father. Gustave's personalizing reaction suggests a new spiral: all the themes of his constitution are taken up again and turned back on themselves in a new order, which is that of *laughter*, a new reaction that attempts to go beyond them.

In March 1836 he writes *Un parfum à sentir*, which he will finish writing on the first of April, and in the "Two Words" that serve as a preface to this "philosophic tale" he takes care to define the mean laughter that has become his best defense: "that dark divinity . . . that laughs in its savagery as it looks at philosophy and the way men contort themselves with sophistries to deny its existence while it crushes them in its iron fist." This dark God is *Fatum*, as we know. It crushes men—so much the better; but its sadistic savagery is merry, for as it leads men to genocide, it is enchanted by their blindness. An all-powerful Creator who loves them, a world made for them, the bounty of human nature, and if that is not enough, Grace, a discreet assistant to Providence, which respects their free will—what won't they invent to hide from themselves the fact that they are killing one another, that they are put into the world to suffer, to disgrace themselves, and to die! This was long after the global creation of the Garçon had taken place in the courtyard of the *collège*—and we recognize his laughter in Anankê's throat. Does this mean that Gustave assimilated his earlier invention to this divinity? No, but in *Un parfum à sentir* he made a reflexive effort to gain a better understanding of his new character. Destiny necessarily makes men laughable on the three following conditions: that the laugher does not belong to the human race; that it is misanthropic (laughter expresses the racism of the supermen); that it contains a presentiment of the horrible end toward which individuals are headed. All three conditions are fulfilled by the divine pleasure of seeing each of us realize his fate by the same maneuvers we use in our attempt to escape it. Let us recall Marguerite's suicide: the crowd goes after her, she strikes her forehead: "'Death,' she says *laughing*." Laughter arises here out of a flash of intuition, unfortunately retrospective, about her past life: what laughable obstinacy to allow oneself to love when one has been created unlovable! Her efforts are comic as their only result is to make her hated even more. The Garçon's trumpet bursts forth, not without causing us some surprise, from Marguerite's poor withered throat; yet she must kill herself:

157

she will escape universal derision only by consciously and deliberately realizing the destiny reserved for her. Thus we have Gustave assuming the hilarity he believes he provokes and reexternalizing it through a broken laughter that publicly manifests his suicidal genocide.

The idea instantly comes to mind that the Garçon *is right to be stupid*. Or rather that his feigned stupidity is the only viable mode of comprehension when what is at issue is the relation of the totalization in progress to a moment of itself which tries to assert itself for its own sake. Let us say that this relation is like a double refusal to comprehend: the part, affirming its sufficiency, refuses to comprehend the whole that produces it and simultaneously denies it to the degree that it is wholly present in it and wholly outside it; the whole has no capacity to see the part, even if it constitutes a necessary moment of totalization. In this double lack of recognition, whose positive reverse side is affirmative power—the power of totalization or of infinite being; the power of the part, which, borrowed from the whole and deviated, tries to assert for its own sake its finite determination—the relations of cosmos and microcosm are resumed. We might say that cosmos and microcosm represent the grotesque reversal of pantheistic effusion (which the young Flaubert often tried), in which the part and the whole are exterior to one another only *in appearance;* ecstasy, destroying the determination of the finite mode, makes apparent the bond of *interiority* which binds it to the infinite substance; if this is reversed, their reciprocal exteriority is asserted for its own sake by the ridiculous and double negation of the relation of interiority. In relation to its part, the whole, which is pure adherence to itself, assumes the role of non-knowledge; in its relation to the whole, the part rests on false knowledge. It grasps that knowledge *through its determination* as an aggregate of particularities exterior to one another, endowed by themselves with affirmative power and gathering together in decomposable systems; this is nothing but knowledge in exteriority or knowledge of detail, also called *analytic reason.* Just how laughable this double ignorance is, from which there is no escape, pantheism denied, depends on whether it is envisaged on the level of the whole or on the level of detail. In the first case, in effect, blindness arises from plenitude: the whole, pure affirmation, hasn't a glance to spare for the particularizing negation. It envelops the intelligent world, penetrates it, and secretly resolves it in itself, just as the night of non-knowledge envelops and dissolves in nocturnal uniformity all the scattered and winking lights called knowledge, which analytic reason aspires in vain to organize into a system. As for the part, unaware that its provi-

FROM LEGEND TO ROLE

sional being is only a specification of the All and consequently rests on a bond of interiority with it, it affirms at once its internal cohesion, its perenniality, from the consciousness it has of this internal relation and sets about decomposing the cosmos around it into finite elements which it is theoretically incapable of recomposing. This would be a drama or, as we say of Hegelian thought, a pan-tragicism if the All had a meaning or if, presenting and destroying finite moments in a *directed* order, totalization were progressing toward an end—the absolute-subject, for example. But when he plays the Garçon, Gustave opts for absolute pessimism: the universe possesses at best the inert, immobile unity of Parmenidian substance, at worst the underlying unity of infinite material dispersion. It is nothingness; creation and destruction are only one and the same thing. In other words, man is grotesque, but also being itself may be absurd, namely, stripped of meaning. At this moment—we shall return to it later—Gustave hesitates between two conceptions: on the one hand, "there is a meaning" (as Alfred says), there is an order, but this order is not at all concerned with man and is established only by crushing the human race; the human race is only a means of means, never an end. On the other, there is neither meaning nor order (the influence of scientist mechanism), nothing but the sterile games of the being of nonbeing and the nonbeing of being. But Gustave cannot resist giving an obscure unity to these very concepts (at bottom, man remains an absolute end and the universe exists only to mystify him). In any event, Gustave holds laughter to be the fundamental relation of the infinite and the finite. But the infinite in its impersonality cannot mock the particulars without first embodying itself in an infinite-subject, its first hypostasis. Such as the function Gustave assigns in *Smarh* to Yuk, god of the Grotesque. This god makes a thousand pernicious jokes.

> And after that he laughed, with a laughter of the damned, but a long, Homeric, inextinguishable laughter, a laughter as indestructible as time, a laughter vast as the infinite, cruel as death, long as eternity, for it was eternity itself. And in that laughter, through a dark night on a boundless ocean stirred by an eternal tempest, there floated empires, peoples, worlds, souls and bodies, skeletons, and living corpses . . . It was all there, oscillating in the shifting and eternal wave of the infinite."

A little further on, this same Yuk, affirming his superiority over death itself, exclaims: "I am the true, I am the eternal, I am the clown, the grotesque, the ugly. . . ; I am what is, what was, what will be; I am all of eternity in myself alone." The laughter is cosmic, it is a frozen spasm, "shifting and eternal wave where everything oscillates." But it does not become actual until a consciousness perceives from above, *mechanically*, that the carnivorous flies savor the lips of a royal carcass quite as much as those of paupers, until a judgment—contemplative, we notice, and not at all creative [109]—is diverted to ascertain that finite modes, buttressed by their determination, are laughable because they take themselves seriously; in sum, until an immense but *himself determined* person takes inventory of the world and transforms the indifference of the negative infinite into cruelty. Let us note in passing that this first hypostasis is risible by its very nature: since determination itself is derisory, Yuk, who is the determined infinite—equivalent to the infinite mode in Spinoza—seems at once the subject of laughter and its first object. [110] The God of the Grotesque is himself grotesque. His fundamental project is at the same time his being. Let us say even his martyrdom. Soon we shall see more clearly that the condemnation to laughter has as a direct consequence the impossibility of taking experienced suffering seriously. Hence Yuk's "laughter of the *damned*."

Yuk is not the Garçon; he was born at least three years later. Let us say that he is the Garçon's theodicy. Gustave has had all the time in the world to reflect and to spin out pataphysics on the persona of his fourteenth year. The Garçon is in himself hyperbolic, and the god of the grotesque is the hyperbole of this hyperbole. But all the themes evoked in *Smarh* are already implicit in the "collective" creature invented by the schoolboys of Rouen, so much so that we might call the Garçon the hypostasis of Yuk: man and giant, captive giant in a man's skin, he is the real mediator between the infinite and our finitude. He is immensely stupid, like matter, which neither thinks nor is thinkable. At the age of sixteen, Gustave says in the *Mémoires:* "It would be wrong to see in this book anything but the amusements of a madman!" But several lines earlier he specifies what he meant by this word: "a madman, that is, the world, that great idiot turning for so many centuries in space without going anywhere, shouting and drooling and tearing itself apart." The figure who best represents cosmic

---

109. Yuk, delegated by the infinite to hold being in derision, is posterior to being and confined to posting affidavits of bankruptcy. This sufficiently demonstrates that he was engendered in the brain of a "man of resentment" who passively contemplates the world and rejoices when circumstances are organized such that, without his lifting a hand, its absurdity is revealed.

110. Let us take note that the god Yuk, unlike Satan, is cursed by *no one* since there is *no one* above him. In him, the curse is simply a sign of his determination.

reality is neither the astronomer, nor the geologist, nor the physicist, nor any of those good souls who believe they hear the harmony of the spheres: an idiot trembling and drooling is the microcosm the world has chosen to represent it. Initially the Garçon is this gigantic and sorrowful idiot in whom the cosmos has descended, whose jovial ferocity will always conceal his suffering and whose inflexible stupidity, always aware of itself, overrunning everything, beats vigilant reason to the ground. But at the same time he is stupid like a man; stingily, for a short term at a high interest—and because his human particularity is stupidity. He neither reasons nor judges; he lives the contradiction of these two stupidities, which means that he understands them from the inside, being at once infinite and finite, and his mode of comprehension *is nothing but laughter.* Later, Hugo would invent the character of Gwynplaine, the Man who Laughs, a hero highly serious by nature but whose lips have been slashed by kidnappers and who is thus condemned to express himself forever by a hilarity he hardly feels. Gustave, more cruelly, has carved laughter into the soul of the Garçon; for the Garçon, living and laughing are the same thing. When he is amused by his own cruel, filthy jokes, it is as a finite determination of matter; a man among men, he perpetrates his farces in order to become an object of scandal, in order to provoke the indignant reactions of common sense, of morality, of our arrogant and minuscule intelligence, in short to exasperate the vain and Lilliputian *nature* in each of us. The reaction of the onlookers is laughter—an immediate attempt to withdraw solidarity: this Garçon is a subman! But the very instant we reveal ourselves, our hilarity is suppressed by a thunderclap: the messenger of the cosmos is laughing at our idiotic conceit; *in him, matter-as-subject* denounces our fakery, *through him* the explosive contact of the All and the part is finally produced. Man is a subgiant who takes himself seriously. The Garçon belches and farts, his comrades are indignant, and while he laughs they discover the laughable absurdity of their indignation: *in the name of what* should I, a mere sack of stench, withdraw solidarity from this other sack of filth? He displays it and I hide it. So I am the comical one. In short, his obscene and scatalogical stupidity manifests itself only to reveal our stupid hypocrisy as a material determination that takes itself for a pure spirit and whose ends have meaning only if it takes its ephemeral, relative, and finite being for an absolute. Thus the onlooker who laughs at the Garçon suddenly find that he is laughing at himself. Or rather, as one does not laugh alone, the various onlookers are taken to laughing *together* at the one among them who is slow to express his

161

indignation or his lynching-laughter; the Garçon can retire—mission accomplished: by enacting his Passion, he has led man to laugh at man.

It really is a kind of Passion, for he is man and God, like Jesus, of whom he is the reverse image. Jesus came to earth to save us, the Garçon to damn us: one expiates our sins, the other has purposely taken human form so that our species might withdraw solidarity from itself. His marvelously lucid stupidity is merely a refusal to *play the game*. Exterminating angel, he indeed had to give himself a character in order to descend among us—just as Christ had to have a specific hair color, dark or fair, a flat or an aqualine nose. And the Garçon has chosen to borrow the features of the Flaubert younger son, which he has distended and inflated until his human envelope threatens to burst. But he has descended in this *individual* in order to withdraw solidarity from him publicly and to laugh at his sufferings. This is something we shall understand better by means of another example. This time the persona no longer bears the name of the Garçon, but its structure has not changed—it is Gustave in full Garçon regalia. In 1862, Flaubert recalls for the Goncourts the beginnings of his liaison with Louise: "He told us the story of his coupling with Colet, initiated in a drive home in a carriage, painting himself as playing the role of someone disgusted with life, the dark, handsome stranger, the suicidal romantic, which so amused and cheered him that he put his face out the window from time to time to laugh at his ease."[111] Poorly received, this confidence nonetheless hits its mark: it shocks the two bourgeois Parisians, who transcribe it that very evening without concealing their discomfort, a discomfort the two simpletons try to allay by insinuating that the narrative is faked, that Gustave invented his character after the fact: he "paints himself as playing . . ." The ambiguity of the verb "to paint" implies that the man of forty, out of an affectation of cynicism, wants to believe and have it believed that in his youth he was capable of playing a double game: that of dark Romanticism, à la Petrus Borel, which is in its way a destruction of the human, and that of the dark laughter, which denies man even the sad privilege of his suffering. For us, on the other hand, having all the texts in front of us, the initiated "coupling" bears an odd, singular resemblance to the "caricature" in front of the cathedral, except that Gustave in the carriage is at once Monsieur Loyal and the laughing giant.

One fact is rigorously established by the correspondence. Gustave

111. *Journal* (Monaco edition) 5:219, 6 December, 1862.

really has embodied himself in the "dark, handsome stranger," as we can see in *all* the letters he sends to Louise, from the first one, dated 4 August 1846, until his journey to the Orient.[112] That is not all: beginning on 6 August, he reminds her of remarks made *before* their first night of love: "I had warned you about it: my misery is contagious. I am contaminated! Woe to whoever touches me!"[113] He returns to this on 11 August: "You tell me that I did not show myself to be like this at first; on the contrary, search your memory. I began by showing my wounds; remember everything I said at our first dinner; you even cried out: So you make excuses for everything? Is there no more good or evil for you?"

Was Gustave playing a part? In any event, he was being played with and he knew it. The sculptor Pradier had long been saying to friends: Let him take a mistress, there's nothing like it for curing nervous afflictions. Alfred collected these remarks and passed them on to Flaubert, who, weary of his chastity, replied that he felt tempted in the flesh but that if he were to deviate in any particular from the way of life he had imposed on himself since the "attack" at Pont-l'Evêque, he would be lost. A year went by and the proposal was not renewed, but "Phidias" had not abandoned his project: his choice lighted upon Louise, a beautiful, experienced woman who would know how to handle a new recruit to love. It seems unlikely that the sculptor would not have informed her of the stratagem when he saw that she was interested in the young man.[114] She willingly undertook the affair— Gustave was handsome, after all. So there was a siege according to the rules, but the Lovelace was not the conventional sort: he was wearing skirts. Before succumbing, the young man suspected a conspiracy: there was a dinner at Pradier's and then another invitation he did not honor, afraid of an involvement and of finding himself stuck with an unwanted entanglement. Too late—he was caught. He paid a visit to Louise, who led things briskly along, for we now find them in a hotel room, with Louise in bed, "her hair spread out on [Gustave's] pillow, eyes turned up to heaven, pale, her hands clasped, babbling foolishness [to him]." An excellent and rare description of the feminine *post coitum* in the last years of Louis-Philippe. Eyes turned up to heaven? Foolish babbling? For God's sake, if there was a performance,

112. Upon his return, he draws closer to her and the tone changes—we shall see why in another chapter.

113. *Correspondance* 1:215.

114. Had he only declared, as it is reported, "This young man is in need of your literary advice," the Muse would have immediately understood; Gustave too, perhaps.

Flaubert was not the only actor. That he felt bitter and uneasy about it, that he judged himself ridiculous, we shall soon demonstrate by examining a famous passage from *Madame Bovary;* in any event, we understand his resistance. First of all, the victim of seduction is himself; Louise takes him, puts one over on him. In a sense, this is what he wants—his partner's activities provoke waves of desire in his constitutional passivity. But she awakens in him the old ambivalence of his feelings for his mother, the all too skillful wet nurse, all too stingy with her tenderness. To be sure, Louise shows him tenderness. Her role demands it, but Gustave is mistrustful. It was therefore in a carriage driving Louise home or taking them to the hotel that he initiated the coupling. The Muse was too expert to take the initiative openly: while he bragged, she led things briskly along but without showing her hand, and since he insisted on playing the boastful rake and the suicide, she opened her eyes wide, shocked, misty with desire, contradicted him to indicate her alarm, and repeated, proffering him her charming bosom: "What! Then there is no such thing as good or evil?"

At this moment Gustave is convinced that they are acting out a bad comedy under the impulse of "that gallant genital organ," and that the objective of this long boring scene is to lead them to the following scene, which must take place at the hotel and will inevitably be followed by Louise's monologue—foolish words, eyes turned up to heaven, idealism. It has to be this way: in 1846, when a woman of bourgeois society has just played the beast, she must then play the angel. How does he react? By playing the worst of devils. The more he feels she is winding her veils around him, the more he reacts by exhibiting the ashes of his deadened heart. At first out of prudence: if there is no more good or evil, if his "belief in nothing" is right, then love does not exist; coitus is the only *real* relation between a man and a woman; if she protests, he answers that, at least as far as he is concerned, broken as he is by great misfortunes, tender attachments are forbidden him. He invites the young woman to get away from him while there is still time; he does not hesitate to borrow a few tirades from *Hernani,* "I bring unhappiness to everyone around me," but by adapting them to current taste: "I am contaminated." In short, he takes all possible precautions to prevent Louise, after the coupling, from blackmailing him with sentiment. Everything has been set up so that he may say to her one day: "Poor child, you take your ass for your heart." But he adds to prudence—not *bourgeois* prudence but the neurotic fear of committing himself—a sadism of resentment: she is beginning to cling to him, this glutton, and he knows it all the better as he is beginning to cling to her. Whatever the eventual course of their long liaison, the first letters he wrote to her are clearly those of a dazzled lover. Behind the fakery, there is sincerity in them both. And it is precisely Louise's sincerity he wants to reach in order to make her pay for her excess of seductive cunning. He cannot resist the pleasure of shocking her and trying to hurt her: go away, you will suffer, I am the dark, handsome stranger, the widower, inconsolable; my heart is dead, you will love me, perhaps, but as for me, I no longer have the power to love you. I am an old man, everything is over for me, go away! go away, then! If the two Goncourts had had the least intelligence—the least sensibility—they would have understood that this entirely negative role is not the role of the seducer but, to the contrary, serves as an embittered defense for someone who feels himself seduced. On this still very superficial level of interpretation, it must also be noted that his vanity comes into play: Louise is older; a Parisian, she knows life better than he; above all, through her numerous liaisons she has acquired an experience of people that Gustave lacks. What is his immediate ploy? The same one he later uses at Mathilde's salon: "Life, oh I know it better than you!" Through suffering, of course. And this is how he raises himself to that cosmic totality, whose reverse he found in the ecstasies, in order to condemn the movements and aims of our species. The Muse's trifling, particular experience is swallowed up by this totalization of experience whose conclusion is at once disgust with life and that supreme act, suicide, to which he has not yet had recourse but might as well have done.

This said, to the extent that he truly loves Louise he must *also* let himself go and speak of himself sincerely. Or almost. Let us say that insofar as he is acting, it is himself he is acting. After all, in 1846 the adolescent who in October 1842, in *Novembre,* had written, "I was born with the desire to die," had not entirely disappeared. And wasn't he right to paint himself as a Romantic about suicide who recalled "having often scratched off the verdigris of old coins to poison himself, tried to swallow pins, approached the attic window to throw himself down to the street"? And who concludes: "Man loves death with a devouring love . . . He does nothing but dream about it as long as he lives." And much later, in the *Préface aux Dernières Chansons,* when he seeks to contrast his generation to the republican youth, he recalls with naive fatuity two of his former schoolmates who voluntarily embraced death. We read that these young heroes killed themselves out of "disgust with life," and these are the same words Gustave pronounced in the presence of the Goncourts; how could he, in Louise's presence, play "cynically," as a "caricature," that deep disgust, felt since childhood, which would never leave him? As for the "dark, handsome stranger," all right—the phrase is Romantic, it belongs to Nerval more than to Flaubert. But what does it mean for him? That there is darkness in the depths of his soul, simultaneously the "terrifying depths" he mentions in *Novembre* as well and the obscurity of an "unspeakable" secret. And hasn't he written to the Muse that after reading this work she must have guessed everything "unspeakable" that it contained? What is this secret, then? A sorrow, of course, one of those immense sorrows that bring you to the summit of Mount Atlas and shrink the universe. The droll aspect of all this is that he really put one over on the Goncourts: in *Charles Demailly*, their *roman à clef*, they say that he is "a man in whom something was killed in his youth, an illusion, a dream, I don't know what . . ." For the two brothers to decide to paint him in these flattering colors, he must have carefully hidden the Garçon from them early in their acquaintance and instead given them a discreet glimpse of the dark, romantic stranger he wanted to be. Was he fooling them, then? That is unlikely. We should not, however, take him to be entirely sincere: he carefully promoted his publicity, sketched with bold lines the character he wanted to be in the eyes of the Parisian men of letters; a *dramatic* character, beyond despair. For Flaubert to allow the comic side of resentment to be seen he needed to be secure in his position in Paris, in the Princess's salon, and among his peers. *Even then*, the despairing figure of *Novembre*, discreet and taciturn, sometimes reappears and with no intermediary replaces the traveling salesman. We read in *Novembre*, in 1842: "When the crowd was jostling him, a new hatred claimed his heart; he brought to it, to that crowd, the heart of a wild beast cornered in its den, the heart of a wolf." The Goncourts' *Journal*, 6 December 1862, twenty years later, on the day he told them about his coupling with Louise: "He protested to us that he feels no contact with the people he meets . . . that a redskin is a hundred times closer to him than all those people we see on the boulevard." [115] A redskin, naturally: in order to compensate for the blue blood he lacked, Gustave had long since boasted of his Indian blood; some of his maternal ancestors had lived in Canada—that was good enough for him. The two brothers rejoice: they will note the same evening that Flaubert is ignoble—we shall shortly see that this is what he wanted—and they are so enchanted by the idea that they stroll gaily down the boulevard in

115. *Journal* (Monaco edition) 5:219, 6 December, 1862.

the company of the last of the Mohicans, a noble barbarian whom the sight of the French crowds plunges into a sacred fury.

The noble and the ignoble: Gustave continually moves from one to the other; in him they are complementary and can even coexist. For Flaubert is *primarily* and fundamentally that wretched, gloomy boy, "born" without being "wellborn," who has internalized the family ambition and success as negative pride. In the carriage he tells Louise what he *was:* and of course one *is* nothing on this level; being is a signification one tries to objectify for the other and, through the other's gaze, for oneself by means of words and actions meant to fascinate. Be that as it may, this performance will be sincere if it strains to release and firmly fix the constantly fleeing meaning of lived experience. Flaubert talks a great deal during the ride: he wants to postpone the moment of dreaded coitus and, of course, to prepare for the "coupling" by "paying court" to Louise, as was the rule at the time; it is not a question of seducing her but of showing by calculated confidences that he has as much respect for a woman he is prepared to screw as for an "honest woman." But, more fundamentally, it is sexual desire that pushes him to this "seizure of speech"; communication by the Word symbolizes penetration; in Gustave the *organ* is his bronze voice, which he grasps like an erect phallus. Conversely, however, and despite what he says about it, he does not regard the coitus in preparation as merely the contact of two epidermises and the blind pleasure born of their friction; solitary as Gustave may be in this first moment of an already irreversible adventure, the meaning of the feared and desired penetration is communication. Chamfort's absurdity is to employ the word "contact," which applies to caresses—and not even to all—when the essential aspect of love is that a man *enters entirely* into a woman who receives him *entirely*, which supposes that in welcoming him she closes around him, contains him, and penetrates him in her turn with what Doña Prouhèze calls "the taste of me." Love is not mute, especially when it falls silent: through flesh, "taste," odors, elasticity, colors, and forms, through the texture of skin, the distribution of hair, the total but unspeakable meaning of one person is transmitted to the other. On both sides, meaning becomes a material and silent condensation of all language, of all sentences spoken and to be spoken, of all actions taken and to be taken. The two naked bodies at this moment are equivalent to an infinite discourse, which they promise, surpass, then render useless. Therefore, in this pre-coitus through the Word, Gustave must enter into Louise by means of a monologue as sincere as his organ and his organism

167

will soon be, today or tomorrow. He is seriously playing a part: in order to paint himself more effectively, he borrows the principle features he has marked out in the autobiographical works. *Agonies, Mémoires d'un fou, Novembre,* it's all there—one more reason for thinking he is a performer of himself, pushing sincerity as far as he can. Was he lying when he wrote his books? Was he mocking Alfred when he dedicated them to him? Was he mocking Maxime and, twenty years later, the Goncourts when he lent them the manuscript of *Novembre,* of which he was so proud? What then? Someone in the carriage is laughing. Who? And at whom? And what does this laughter represent? What is its purpose?

The answers to these questions are provided by another carriage, lurching with "blinds drawn" through the streets of Rouen, sheltering the first frolics of Emma and Léon. The young clerk is no Hernani; he is still timid, but his Parisian polish gives him a certain self-assurance. Emma is not cynical but she is certainly experienced. It is her provincial snobbery that has convinced her to take the last step: Léon, opening the carriage door for her, has assured her that "it was done in Paris." And this "irresistible argument convinced her." Be that as it may, she had written "an interminable letter" the evening before in which she had canceled the rendezvous: "Everything was over now, and for their own happiness they ought no longer to meet." Not knowing the clerk's address, she has decided to give the letter to him herself at the cathedral. She has come, has handed Léon the letter, then has withdrawn her hand as he was about to take it, and has knelt to pray in the chapel of the Virgin. All this clearly signifies that virtue is ready to succumb but not without some oratorical sparring: Léon must do his share by preaching to this convert. We know in advance what they will say to each other—Flaubert has reported to us their conversation of the evening before. Léon said that three years earlier Emma had been for him "an incomprehensible force that captivated my life." Delighted, she cried out: "How is it that no one . . . ever expressed such feelings to me before?" He answered her that "ideal natures were difficult to understand"; he was often in despair thinking of the happiness they might have had if chance had allowed them to be united by indissoluble bonds. She confessed that she too dreamed of their union, then suddenly: "I am too old . . ." He would love others. And Léon was indignant: "Not like you!" It's all there: Léon's love will remain unique because there can never be another Emma. Moreover, she is an angel, an ideal nature whose very purity is a mystery for poor human beings. To assure her of the purity of his intentions, the young clerk transforms his desire to make her an adulteress into an inconsolable regret at not having married her. Two kindred souls made to marry, frustrated by bad luck: in short, they are *already* married. It is difficult to see how their discourse could go much further; in the carriage they can only keep repeating it by lingering over considerations of detail, over arguments that they hadn't had time to develop the night before, while their hands squeeze each other, forgotten, clandestine, or a furtive and totally unforeseen kiss, cutting off their conversation for a moment, joins their astonished lips. This will last for as long as it has to, until the work of mating has been completed in each of them. But despite Léon's nascent boorishness and Emma's self-assurance in her certainty that she is in charge, they are at least credulous, if not sincere. They are both of them trying, by their poor words, by leaps of the soul that issue in commonplaces, by an effort of imagination that breaks itself against the wall of language, by an angelism that expresses their animality in spite of themselves, to surpass the materiality of carnal desire and the copulation they know to be inevitable; every phrase is a vain attempt to transcend the inspiration of the "gallant genital organ" and fly toward beauty, purity. Surpassing, transcendence, this is what they aspire to display once more by an eloquence whose source they know only too well. Emma, without illusion but fooled again by the eternal mirage, tries to "take her ass for her heart." This means that she wills herself a woman and free against the animal lust[116] she feels her body will impose on her, whether she aspires to ennoble that lust by presenting it as a generous and lordly gift of her person to her faithful Léon, or aims to distract his attention and succumb by a surprise turn that will put her at the mercy of her lover without any preparation on her part and will thus relieve her of all responsibility. In other words, what they both want to preserve in the *imago* that each makes for himself and his human dignity conceived as inner freedom, not as a system external to the self and moved by external compulsions. What facilitates their enterprise is that they are alone and already bound together by bonds of interiority. No one looking on, only four walls; neither of the two is an object for a third party or entirely an object for the other; they take this intersubjectivity of isolated souls for their absolute being; you desire me, therefore I am; I desire you, therefore you are; it is scarcely surprising that each one is convinced of his tran-

116. I am saying what Flaubert thinks and what he makes Emma think, not what I think.

scendence by the faith his partner shows in him. Madame Bovary is an angel in a very real sense.

What is Flaubert up to? He yields to his creatures: they have drawn the blinds so as not to be seen by anyone? That needn't be a problem, no one shall see them, not even the author. Indeed, he takes his distance; his gaze embraces all of Rouen, the port, the countryside, and along the road, along the highway, along a major thoroughfare in the vicinity he tracks the "lumbering machine" containing the two lovers; he will stick with it uninterrupted for six hours and will gradually trace its itinerary for us. This will do. Until this point the amorous activities of Léon and Emma have prompted only a smile; now they become obscene and grotesque. What trick has he played on them, the wretch? Well, he has taken a man and a woman hot with desire, wholly alive, convinced of giving themselves freely to one another, and he has metamorphosed this entwined couple into a mere carriage. The transition is worked by means of an adroitly chosen commonplace: "The lumbering machine set off on its way." This line—like "the church bells struck midnight"—is so familiar that one scarcely reads it, yet it presents an ambiguous meaning. In the following paragraph we might just as well find ourselves *inside* the cab, face to face with the lovers; but the subject of the statement supposes that we have remained outside, that we have seen the doors closed, the blinds drawn. Flaubert need only maintain the same subject in the lines that follow to work this imperceptible transubstantiation: "It set off downhill . . . crossed . . . stopped. The cab resumed its course . . . It went . . . it dashed forward with a bound," etc. Without going as far as anthropomorphism, the verbs discreetly indicate human actions (it dashed forward), or at the least those proper to draught animals (the cab trotted). This is done in such a way that finally the object becomes the subject of the story without losing its properties as object; and the former subjects themselves become pure objects since their actions are revealed to us as the actions of the object. Still, the author takes great care to exempt the living, breathing team—the coachman, "demoralized and nearly weeping from thirst, from fatigue and depression," and the two hacks "dripping with sweat." The lovers, their eloquence, their caresses, their coupling, have been changed into that enchanted object, a black box on four wheels, hermetically sealed, perfectly inert and at the same time possessed by what the coachman calls, uncomprehending, a "fury of locomotion." Indeed, this thing has a voice:

The [machine] stopped short before the statue of Pierre
Corneille.

"Go on," cried a voice from inside.

The cab went on again, and . . . entered the station at a gallop.

"No, straight on!" cried the same voice.

. . . It made its third stop in front of the Jardin des Plantes.

"Get on, will you?" cried the voice more furiously.

In the course of the afternoon, the coachman tries several times to
stop, "and at once exclamations of anger burst forth behind him."

A simple but effective procedure. The coachman is presented to us
as a man: he has the simple but urgent needs we've all felt, he would
like a rest, he is hungry, he would like a drink at the tavern; at the
same time we see him working at his job, accepting without protest a
trial that is hard to endure, because he must earn his living. A banal
and anonymous character, but one who offers us a reasonable and
sound image of our species: he is the one who, humbly but totally,
represents transcendence and surpassing. The box, by contrast, is a
robot: every time the carriage stops, a furious mechanical voice issues
from it, enjoining the coachman to resume his course. The repetition
of the effect, like a running joke, is deliberate and meant to convince
us. We know quite well, of course, what is going on inside the cab and
that these reiterated injunctions are not meaningless. Seen from the
outside, however, the "coupling" is nothing but the "fury of locomotion" which has taken hold of an inert object. We know the story:
Gustave likes to envisage life as a brief madness of the inorganic. He
was inspired by this fantasy to change two perspiring organisms,
whose sexuality is nothing but pure life, into a fragment of inanimate
matter whose inertia is suddenly possessed by the rage of motivity
without the means of spontaneous movement: hence the voice that
mechanically demands an impetus from the exterior, in exteriority;
hence the "demoralization" of the coachman, who becomes the slave
of his own material.

Gustave's purpose is clear: if he were to show the interior of the box
and two lovers making love, Emma and Léon would have retained
the same human face as the coachman. And if prudence alone had
prompted him to pass over in silence the frolics the reader so easily
imagines, he could have ended the chapter at the moment Léon makes
Emma enter the carriage. But in this case we would have remained in
a bond of interiority with the young clerk and his mistress, as close to
them as we were in the cathedral and as we are in the following chap-

ter. Gustave has described at length the meanderings of the carriage—*which imparts no new information,* and consequently answers to
none of the internal requirements of the narrative—in order to provide a view of the "coupling" as the grotesque and terrifying transport of a material object—he deliberately forces us to adopt an *exterior*
view of human relations. He breaks our ties with the couple and leads
us to withdraw our solidarity with their aims, to have only a glancing
acquaintance with them. And certainly their bad faith is striking;
in the scene in the cathedral, which is intentionally "caricatured,"
Flaubert wanted to "make fun of" the follies of love. But to make the
lovers ridiculous he had no need to perch on a roofbeam and contemplate them from above. And as for us, to appreciate the comic aspect
of the situation, we didn't have to climb up onto a giant's shoulders.
Léon's impatience is comic: after such a long wait, he is afraid to keep
still when Emma finally yields;[117] comic as well is the show of interest
la Bovary affects and the lorgnette she takes from her purse to look at
the funerary slabs. We laugh at them, at their maneuvers, and not at
the entire human race. And if we had followed them into the carriage,
we would have continued to enjoy their petty hypocrisies *from an even
closer vantage point.* This is not Gustave's purpose; their insincerity, of
course, has the effect of annihilating discourse, reducing it to a string
of sonorous inanities. But, despite everything, the bad faith reveals
their transcendence, their intentions, their aims to the same extent
that it derails the one and masks the others. And it is *human transcendence* that the author wants to beat to the ground, it is the human
project he wants to abolish, human aims he wants to reduce to an enchantment of inanimate bodies. For that he must distance himself, in-

117. Pléiade, *Oeuvres* (Pléiade Edition) 1:547. It will be noted that the author limits
himself to saying: "It seemed to him that his love . . . was going to evaporate." But the
metaphor supporting this statement is so crudely and deliberately phallic that no one
can mistake it. (His love "that for two hours now had become petrified in the church
like the stones . . . [it was his erection—he had been erect for two hours] . . . was
going to vanish like a vapor through that strange kind of truncated funnel, or oblong
cage, or open chimney that rises so grotesquely from the cathedral") The grotesque
funnel could stand without comment, I would say, if the adverb "grotesquely" were
not there—as so often in Flaubert—to introduce the idea that the scene is grotesque.
Grotesque, too, is the fear of losing an erection. The adverb designates a material object—the open chimney—which has merely a relationship of contiguity with the reported events; by its mere presence, however, and at the same time on the level of the
metaphor—by which it links itself to the "kind of truncated funnel"—it is as though
this adverb had no other function than to reveal the absurdities of the organ with
which the males of our species have been rigged out. Gustave has the same raging hatred for his penis—and consequently for those of others—that the female sexual apparatus inspires in so many women.

flate himself, elevate himself: seen from above, Léon and Emma are plunged into the anonymity of matter, their names are no longer even uttered, the carriage and its rolling motion represent copulation in general and the human race without intermediary contemplated *from a distance* by a being who can no longer comprehend its doings and thus takes his place outside humanity. Once dehumanized, the reader has no more than a "glancing acquaintance" with this couple—which has become *all couples:* he sums them up in this box, whose joltings typify the frenzied movements of the beast with two backs. As if we pretended to reduce all the orgies of the world to the movements of all mattresses simultaneously registered by an ultrasensitive seismograph, giving fornication the blind and stupid nonmeaning of a natural force.

In fact, Gustave goes further. A natural force is still too beautiful—coitus is neither a storm nor an earthquake nor a tidal wave. Flaubert enjoys presenting it as an implement gone mad. The carriage is a product of labor and the instrument of another kind of labor: men are *objectified* in it. Gustave will make love a counterfinality, not the absence of all aim but the destruction of a human aim by a diabolic and anonymous one, which is manifest only through its fierce determination to distort the implement incomprehensibly. The carriage is a means of transportation: people use it to get themselves from one well-defined place to another. Beginning with the moment when Léon, asked by the coachman, "Where to, sir?" answers, "Wherever you like," the instrumentality of the carriage, that is, its rational meaning, is abolished. The first changes of place, however, preserve a trace of rationality because the coachman, left to himself, takes certain habitual routes at random: perhaps the customers want to visit the town? Perhaps they have a train to catch? Or they wish to stroll under the trees in the Jardin des Plantes? He tries; he stops in front of the statue of Corneille, at the station, in front of the main gate of the Jardin. But at every attempt the box goes into a frenzy behind his back; so he gives up trying to understand, and the cab, abandoned to itself "wanders" without purpose or direction, at "random," up and down the same streets, leaving the town only to reenter it. This tool was made to take *the shortest way,* to conduct the customer *at the least expense* to the address indicated; here it is, going nowhere, or what amounts to the same thing; it wears itself out, it wears out its coachman and his horses, dragging them along anywhere at all, demanding to go from one point to the other by the longest route. Labor is nonetheless involved: the horses are drenched with sweat, the coachman is worn

173

out but knows he will be paid. Paid to sell out his profession systematically, to obey his carriage instead of commanding it, to do in all respects the contrary of what his professional conscience orders him to do: this particularly is what *demoralizes* him. To the point "that he ran up against things here and there, not caring if he did." This huge, vague nonsense, this long tribulation of a vehicle, this jolting trajectory, this revolt of a tool against its worker, this abolition of practical order for the sake of something nonsensical, a disordered aberration, this hearse "shut tighter than a tomb" lurching at the rumps of two exhausted hacks, all this has only one meaning: it is love grasped in its *practico-inert* materiality as an absurd revolt of inanimate matter against the imprint imposed on it by human work. And also as a counterwork, in the sense that a piece of woodwork "works."

Thus these two lovers, transformed into a crazy vehicle, are more naked than they would be in bed since they no longer have anything to protect them. Their coupling is public: they are carved tomb figures gone mad; their transports are reduced to the unique character of a single transport whose essence is to go from nowhere to nowhere; the energy they expend in the sexual act equals that furnished by two indifferent hacks to execute an idiotic labor. Like the coachman, disoriented, constantly passing the same places, the copulation they wanted to conceal is transformed into an obscene exhibition: "At the harbor, in the midst of the drays and casks, and in the streets, at the corners, the good bourgeois folk opened their eyes wide, awestruck at this sight, so extraordinary in the provinces . . . continually appearing . . . tossing about like a boat." Everything, then, is *seen:* the good bourgeois see the couple screwing, they see them in their most obscene denudedness; the whole town can watch them pass by. That solitude which was so dear to them has vanished; before, they were *almost subjects* for one another, their bond of interiority gave each of them *absolute being;* now, metamorphosed into this strange and sinister thing, a hearse, and "tossing about like a boat," they become a pure object. Not entirely an object of scandal—"it is done in Paris"—but not yet in the provinces; those good bourgeois see carnal love passing by in its hideous nakedness but do not recognize it. Yet Emma and Léon are the object of malice and laughter. And their adventure, which seems to them an entirely new beginning, with irreversible, unforeseeable consequence, is objectified by the wearying, obstinate reappearance of the rickety old carriage in the same places in the form of an absurd cycle of repetitions.

Everything has been said; Gustave can be happy, he has unrealized, dehumanized, two human beings. Why these two more than others? Rodolphe, after all, is a rather repugnant character, and when Emma gives herself to him she may be more innocent but she is not exempt from bad faith. Yet the coupling in the woods, far from being ridiculous, is consecrated by a kind of pantheistic effusion: "She gave herself up to him. The shades of night were falling; the horizontal sun . . . dazzled her eyes . . . luminous spots trembled . . . Silence was everywhere; something sweet seemed to come forth from the trees . . . Then from far away she heard . . . a vague prolonged cry, a lingering voice, and in silence she heard it mingling like music with the last pulsations of her throbbing nerves." [118]

Although Gustave has always betrayed a certain repugnance, almost fear, when speaking of "matings," it is quite clear that this one seems to him neither wretched nor ridiculous. This is first of all because coitus, here, is rid of all the idealistic mystifications that pave the way to it and justify it. Rodolphe is a professional seducer; he takes all responsibility upon himself, to the point of ignominiousness, thereby relieving Emma of it. She is conquered according to the rules of the art, and when she surrenders, the reader understands that she has been manipulated. So she screws innocently—that innocence which she is determined, futilely, to recapture in Léon's arms—*there are no words in her head*; but instead of the silly, vague sentimentality which if it were present would compel her to toss off "cant remarks" about purity, poetry, and the charms of nature, Nature is simply there, mute, enclosing and penetrating her. We might say that Rodolphe is the means chosen by the cosmos to enter this woman, just as the All manifests itself in the part at the risk of bursting it. The handsome gentleman's erect member, the blunted pleasure (this will be specified for us a little later) he procures for himself—these are inessential; this deceiver is the world's dupe, the instrument chosen by it, on the occasion of a very maculate conception, to take into this woman a consciousness of self. Observe as well how Emma, alone in her room that evening, recalls the first embrace: "At first she felt stunned; she saw the trees, the paths, the ditches, Rodolphe, and she felt again his encircling arms while the leaves rustled and the reeds whistled." She sees herself in the mirror and is astonished: "Never had her eyes been so large, so black, full of such depth." The highly adept use of narrated monologue and the abrupt introduction of the pluperfect have the carefully calculated effect of keeping us forever uncertain: does

118. *Madame Bovary* (Pléiade edition) 1:472.

she *really* have eyes that have been widened and deepened by this experience, or is she merely imagining it? It seems to me that inauthenticity begins for her with the return of language, that is, in the following paragraph: "She repeated to herself, 'I have a lover! a lover!'" While she remains at the level of wordless memories and unadorned perceptions, she preserves within herself something of that world which filled her and withdrew. What is certain is that, in her memory, Rodolphe's embrace is not separable from the forest that surrounds them ("she saw the trees, the paths, the ditches") or from the rustling of the leaves or the whistling of the reeds. The cosmos is there, all around her; yet this enormous presence does not crush the young woman because the author has taken the cosmic point of view *from close up:* the setting of the "coupling" refers to everything, but implicitly; the regard of the Infinite turns itself into "something sweet"; the connections between outside and inside are relations of interiority. She cannot see the "luminous spots" that tremble around her, but she is intimately bound to these glistenings, for "the horizontal sun . . . dazzled her eyes," and her face is itself a spot of light. The horizontal sun, the azure, the interstellar spaces, this earth that turns and is enveloped by the shades of night: the All is there but it is discreet, restrained, gently internalized in this enraptured woman and at the same time gathered around her, totalizing and totalized in this privileged moment when language is dead, when the infinite silence of being is everywhere, even inside her—delivered from the commonplaces that haunt her—when the mute consciousness of a dazzlement and the dazzling setting sun are one. On her back, her body plowed by a man's member, her eyes burned by the fire from a star, Emma is very close to realizing the vow of the last *Saint Antoine:* "to be matter." It is clear, in any case, that she does not experience orgasm; nor does Mazza when she gives herself to Ernest for the first time. But Mazza's initial frigidity left a disappointment for which nothing would compensate. Emma does not even perceive that she hasn't had pleasure—she has become the world.

The second adultery is another matter. Gustave does not like Léon, who is too much like Ernest Chevalier: like him, Léon was popular with grisettes, who "thought he had a *distinguished air,*" and in Paris he was "the most proper of students." Above all, Flaubert views life as a cycle of involuted repetitions: everything always begins over again but in increasingly degraded form. He would gladly have taken Marx's statement, made somewhat later, touching on the great circumstances of history, and applied it to the events of an individual life: events reproduce themselves, the first time as tragedy, the second as farce—no more agents, only actors in whom praxis is caricatured. Thus, by giving herself to the young clerk, Emma parodies herself: this mating is a caricature, a hysterical imitation of the single instant, lost forever, when a movement that made her leap beyond her finite determination reintegrated her into the infinite, while by a reverse movement the macrocosm penetrated her and was entirely concentrated there. This time, everything is played out in advance: in this new mating neither the mature woman nor the young clerk denies the condition of determination; rather, each of them, while buttressed by it, dreams only of exalting it; intolerable prattling is substituted for the eternal silence of infinite spaces. How can the author render the absurdity of this recurrence without showing his hand? How will he indicate that he is withdrawing solidarity from his characters without leaving the impersonal mode behind and without adding subjective commentaries to his narrative? He believes he has found the way: since laughter is the refusal to understand and to participate, he will render them *objectively laughable*.

These observations do not answer the chief question; they merely allow it to be formulated with greater precision. As I have said, Gustave narrated the scene in the cathedral *in the comic mode*. Did he *need* to trace the itinerary of the carriage and replace a *particularized* couple with a couple human solely in its generality? Or did some searing memory prompt him to introduce into his novel a cosmic episode that had no business there? These questions cannot be answered without first answering this other question: did he achieve his purpose? Did he succeed, invisibly, in making an anonymous, disembodied laughter run on from page to page, imposing itself on its readers, without abandoning his "impersonalism" or doing anything but offer them the itinerary of a certain carriage during the afternoon of a certain day in a certain year?

The answer is clear: rereading, we shall see that he failed. Certainly *Madame Bovary* is a cosmic novel—this will be demonstrated later, and, as we know, Baudelaire was not wrong about it—but the power and depth of this work come from the fact that the macrocosm nearly always appears on the horizon of microcosms that are grasped from closer by. *Nearly* always: except in a few cases, the most important of which is the long circuit of the carriage, in which the perspective is reversed. In the darkness of the cathedral we were so close to Emma that we saw her "take out her lorgnette" and heard, when she walked, "a rustle of silk on the flagstones." All of a sudden, the box—a change

177

of perspective, a downward view. At the end of the chapter, the lumbering machine that has swallowed two singular persons will give us back Emma generalized in this form: "a veiled woman . . . who walked with her veil lowered, and without turning her head"; Léon will not be given back to us at all. As we see, there has been a camera movement whose *gratuitousness* reminds us of the author's malicious intent. This is what happen when the writing of a movie director is aestheticizing. The protagonists are framed in close-up—the spectator is among them; and then, suddenly, the camera flies off, we are at the camera end of a long shot for no good reason, we are looking at them from above. Well, there is one reason—the image is good. But it is the death of illusion: there are no more characters, merely dummies manipulated by a cinematographer.

This is how it works in the carriage episode. Someone appears and takes up the narration from Flaubert while pantagruelizing. Let us note what is required of the new narrator: above all, he must have a field of vision broad enough to contain the town and its environs; a sufficiently precise memory, sufficiently critical, to allow him to evoke Parisian customs in all their stupidity, an imagination satirical enough to invent the consequences of their being transplanted to Rouen by a young moron and the snobbery of his provincial mistress:[119] a sufficiently thorough comprehension of Rouen customs to be able to locate specifically the perambulations of the funerary box not only in the space but also in the time of the town's daily life.[120] More than all other qualities, the one most striking in this jocular narrator is the formidable ubiquity of his gaze, which spots the cab wherever it is,

119. Let us imagine that the "coupling" had taken place in Paris; many things would have been changed. In the first place, "It was done"; so the coachman would have been in the know. Far from letting himself get "demoralized," he would have been overjoyed: a long ride, a good tip. Second, for the same reason the pedestrians would recognize what was going on—at most, they would cast a conspiratorial glance at the coachman. Third, the city is so big that the team would not have needed to drive through the same streets again—one source of ridicule would have been spared that derisory, funereal box. But the essential thing would not be touched: the carriage would remain an inert demand, an object-subject, carrying the man-object in its belly; its joltings would remain the projection in the practico-inert of the spasmodic movements of copulation.

120. It was a stroke of genius to make it go "behind the hospital gardens, where old people dressed in black were strolling in the sun along a terrace all green with ivy." The line of fire of a grotesque and finally desperate *furia* crosses the mortuary calm of old age, of hopeless repetition, of ancient and taciturn nature. Conversely, the poignant poetry of this terrace disqualifies the two lovers because, wholly occupied with mingling their perspiration, they *do not see it*. Blinds drawn—communication denied. This is the opposite of the "coupling" with Rodolphe.

comes down in a thunderclap, and, even while crushing it to earth among thousands of cabs and houses, falling from such a height, possesses the incredible acuity to render it in detail. For a look that will allow him to laugh at the two lovers, Gustave has chosen to take a cosmic point of view—or, if you like, the world has chosen an intermediary, a giant possessed by the negative infinite who wants to preserve only a "glancing acquaintance" with men. The disconcerted reader suddenly hears the laughter of a misanthropic and sadistic Titan mocking humanity: he is invited to share in this laughter: all he has to do is raise himself up and bother to take a turn playing the *Garçon*. But no sooner has he slipped under the character's skin than he finds himself mocking his own sexuality. Like the schoolboys of Rouen in 1836.

Later we shall see that Gustave, the author, often acts out by writing the role of an author in the process of writing. Over and over again in *Madame Bovary* it is the Garçon who takes up the pen, breaking the illusion, though never so overtly as in this episode. We must therefore ask ourselves why Flaubert, so concerned with *unity*, allowed himself this abrupt break, why he could not refrain from becoming once again the Giant leaning over the Myrmidons. And we have to conclude that he was compelled to do it, but not by art. He has hardly chosen the point of view of the negative infinite out of necessity— that is, to promote our further knowledge of the characters and to advance the action; rather, he lingers to describe the sinister perambulation of that obscene hearse because he needs to render the feeling he himself once experienced, at the time of the "carriage ride home" with Colet. The coupling with Emma reproduces the one with Louise. Art is the loser here, since the author prefers himself and reveals himself; the man gains, however, by finally assuaging his resentment. The "drive home" must have weighed heavily on his heart for him to have been so inexcusably boorish as to paint in the colors of a tart in heat, simply for the lapdogs' amusement, a woman he had loved and esteemed for more than eight years.[121] This elephant's grudge manages to convince us: it is Louise's carriage that has entered *Madame Bovary*.

It will be pointed out, however, that there is no small difference between the box in the novel, hermetically closed, sealed like a coffin,

121. It is appropriate to recall that the Muse frequented literary clubs and that the Goncourts sometimes met her in such places. So Gustave, usually benevolent out of prudence, knows very well what he is doing and counts on the fact that the two brothers, when they see her again, will have to restrain their raucous laughter.

seen from the outside, and the carriage of 1846 *in which* Gustave and Louise Colet found themselves enclosed. Precisely! That giant who pantagruelizes while Emma makes love is what Flaubert *would have liked to be* in order to escape a frightening intimacy. Lacking the power to identify completely with him, at least he attempts to play the role or, more accurately, he plays the man regarded by the giant who is at once outside and inside him, a prisoner of his human envelope. What is he afraid of, then? Of the inevitable coupling he desires, of the entanglement that will follow, which he is not yet certain he wants, of the woman, undoubtedly, but chiefly of himself. After all, he plays this role of the doomed in order to defend himself but also for the purposes of seduction—what is more fascinating for Eloa than Satan's incurable sadness? Besides, it is *his role;* in a sense he has lived through what he is talking about, he is living it still. If he takes what he is saying seriously, he is done for: he is hooked, he surrenders, the Muse will simply gobble him up. At once the giant is summoned: seducer or seduced, if the young man laughs at himself and at Louise, he will not be fooled. Can he laugh? No, but the Garçon will laugh for him. Gustave makes himself seen from the outside; his face, his body are charged with a fictive visibility which isn't at all what appears to Louise's eyes; it is an opposing visibility, or better, a countervisibility. In a sense he is calling to his aid a fictive reflection whose primary intention is to withdraw solidarity from the reflected. Gustave proceeds masked, and his look from above unmasks him. On the primary level of spontaneity, the dark, handsome stranger, actor of himself, invites the young woman to take part in the joint suicide of copulation. On the reflexive level, he is the giant holding his sides, enjoying himself immensely, highly amused. So what is he laughing at, *in the first place?* I would say that, *fundamentally,* it is the young man's dolorism. To the extent that Gustave is sincere, he is *already laughable:* he takes himself seriously, his fine despair seeks to give this molecule an importance which the mediator of the negative infinite strikes with buffoonish inanity. What, then? Should man be a disaster? And afterward? That is exactly what must provoke our laughter: the grand airs of this pretentious termite are part of the mystification. To suffer, if God exists, is to show his wounds to heaven and blaspheme. Blaspheme! says the giant, if only you knew how little God gives a damn! And if heaven is empty, to suffer is to play the lone wolf: "Suffer and die without speaking!" Stoicism, precisely—the giant cannot think of anything more amusing: these pygmies twisting and turning on a white hot grid claim that they deserve to say "I": "I

180

suffer, therefore I am!" "I die, therefore I am!" Derisory sophistries that Gustave denounced earlier in *Un parfum:* "They twisted and turned in their sophistries to deny the existence [of fatality], even as it crushed them in its hand." Therefore suffering is our lot. But whatever our attitude toward our suffering, it is necessarily *comic.* To shriek, to demand grace, to roll about on the ground groaning—all this is quite droll in the eyes of the personified infinite. That miserable mite makes the great mistake of believing he exists; besides, if he did not believe it, he would be no less laughable for his determination. But he provokes peals of laughter when he claims *to make good use* of his maladies or his mishaps. One must *undergo* unhappiness—the original comedy—but there is no *way of living it:* protest is as stupid as consent (protest against *whom,* in the name of *what? And what a farce to consent to something one cannot refuse!). There is something funnier still. During the winter of 1841, Gustave jots down in his notebooks: "I believe that humanity has only one purpose, to suffer." At this moment he is quite serious. But at others, when he becomes the Garçon, he finds this aphorism—which certainly meant something *to him* ("I do not wish to be consoled")—unbelievably clownish: then you mean it's not enough for people to be tortured from birth, *they must reconcile themselves to it,* strive against themselves? Such indeed is the meaning of the statements Gustave, the dark, handsome stranger, makes to Louise: I suffer, I have suffered and cause suffering, I am beyond suffering because I have drunk it to the dregs, I welcome it all, it is my lot, my purpose, and my supreme dignity; I love death, I hate life. And *at the same time* a reflexive laughter denounces these statements: there is a comfort in despair that leads to the narcissistic satisfaction of dissatisfaction.

But the comedy is at its height when surreptitiously, hypocritically, the *Desdichado* moves on to the systematic exploitation of his disaster. He begins by pitying himself and granting himself small pleasures: he deserves them since he is *so* unhappy; an then, imperceptibly, he comes to use his unhappiness to obtain terrestrial satisfactions. What could be more droll than Gustave making a show of his "devouring love of death" in the presence of those beautiful literary thighs which are a bit slow to open? The partner is comic if she accepts it all as gospel; more comic still if, having decided to give herself *in her own good time* after a carefully measured resistance, she forces herself, from nobility of soul, to believe the nonsense dished out to her. Isn't this suicidal disgust with life that he proclaims while his member becomes superbly erect exasperated by an "itch" that pushes him precisely to reproduce life? To the ears of the giant, the discourse pursued in the carriage reveals its perfect inanity: beneath this reciprocity of rhetoric he hears confused sounds, emitted by a "gallant genital organ," which have no answer but the muffled intestinal rumblings of an "indiscreet jewel." Certainly, Léon and Emma pursue a different discourse: they have chosen to cover their rutting with the cloak of an angelism that Louise was alone in donning in 1846, while her partner played the disillusioned, boastful rake; there is no doubt, however, that for Flaubert *the same* bad faith is at work in both cases.[122] Thus the two scenes perfectly correspond, and the second is inspired by the first.

We still need to know the identity of this fictive and noncomplicit reflection that Gustave calls to his aid. The answer is clear: originally it is the father's gaze, which never ceases to penetrate his illusions and his lies. In August 1846, however, the place is empty, the progenitor has just died. At once Gustave installs replacements on the ramparts: leaning over Louise, he hears the collective laughter of his comrades exactly as in the time of his adolescence when, impelled by the humble need for belief to cross the threshold of a church, he *would see himself seen* by them and through this imaginary vision discover his *risibility*. The reflection at that time was an effort to know himself as a function of their laughter and to disqualify his spontaneous enthusiasm. No doubt in this case he called them to his aid in order to forbid himself that faith he so desired but was terrified of. Similarly, the Garçon's laughter, which pursues him in the carriage, spoiling his pleasure in preening, his pleasure in astonishing the poetess with his terrible confidences, and—who knows?—his secret desire to love, is the laughter of his pals. We have already spoken of the sexual life of young bourgeois men around 1840: they carried on with gullible grisettes who bored them or else they screwed whores. The result: a sadistic contempt for woman, a need to humiliate girls whom poverty had made venal, a willingness to sacrifice the other sex to their masculine friendships, which were homosexual around the edges, like all displays of masculinity. Deflowered by one of his mother's chambermaids, Gustave had no relations with women other than prostitutes apart from the brief encounter in Marseille. We know from Alfred's letters that he entered into the game and, like all his comrades, re-

122. Emma—like Louise—is a thorough seductress; like Gustave, Léon is manipulated.

garded things sexual as eminently laughable: he would later tell Louise—pure bragging but nonetheless significant—that he went into a brothel Christmas night, a cigar in his mouth, chose the ugliest whore, and made love to her without putting down his cigar to signal to his partner the extent of his contempt. For him as for his friends, copulation was eminently *public.* Whores were collective property: the young men indulged in joint debaucheries, recounted their orgies to each other in the grossest terms, exchanged good addresses. When he meets Colet, there is no middle ground for him: either women are inaccessible (friends of his mother or sister) or they are "creatures"— the sordid truth of love. Yet Louise belongs to neither of these categories: she is easy—like Eulalie Foucault—and openly kept, but she *chooses* her lovers, and in particular she offers herself to Gustave because she likes him, without asking anything from him in return. And then her bad verse (which he does not think so bad) gives her a certain prestige; above all, she is on familiar footing with writers whom Gustave admires. He can neither completely respect her nor completely scorn her; in short, he does not know what to make of her or how to classify her. In a way she intimidates him; he is infuriated and afraid of failing her. Léon's anxiety in the cathedral translates a major concern of Gustave's. In fact, the coupling was only *initiated* in the carriage in August 1846, and we have proof that the first time he had to execute it he was impotent.[123] For Louise offered him another image of love, more insidious, and he was afraid of letting himself be tempted. "Where would I stop? If I were to take it seriously and really throw myself into physical pleasure, I'd be humiliated . . . A normal, regular, rich, hearty love affair would take me too much out of myself, disturb my peace. I would be reentering active life . . . in the ordinary

---

123. He wrote to Louise, 6 August 1846: "What a poor lover I make, don't I? Do you know that what happened to me with you never happened to me before? (I was so shattered for three days and was as taut as a cello string.) If I had been a man who held himself in great esteem, I would have been sorely vexed. I was for you. I feared suppositions on your part that would be odious for you; others, perhaps, would have believed that I had abused them. They would have judged me cold, disgusted, or worn out. I was grateful to you for [your] intelligence . . . As for me, I was astonished by what happened as by some unheard-of monstrosity. Therefore I must love you, and powerfully, since I felt the opposite of what I was from the start with all the others, no matter whom." *Correspondance* 1:217. He subsequently takes his revenge, as we know from a previously cited poem by his mistress. Even more revealing than the weakness itself—common enough—is the way he explains it: if he failed her, when he always gallantly "serviced" the others, it is certainly because she is *other,* because she belongs to a troubling category of women with whom he hasn't learned to deal.

sense . . . and that is what has been detrimental to me each time I've tried it."[124] So his urgently summoned comrades glide above the carriage, just as they previously appeared in the churches, and in the name of their "philosophical love of whores" roundly mock the couple's words and embraces. In the name of their whoremongers' freemasonry they declare that Gustave is a traitor to their cause, grotesque and distressing, like Monsieur Loyal when he waxes enthusiastic over the Gothic. This is just what he demands of them: far from setting the seriousness of his desire against their insulting laughter, he is delighted to participate in their hilarity, to take it on himself so as to lighten his burdened body, to disarm the all too indulgent exhibition of his despair, and above all so as no longer to be alone with Louise, the praying mantis who terrorized him, the more so because, as we know, he wanted less to make her submit than to swoon in her arms. And so the Garçon appears, the brothel-mates' collective, the Alumni Friendship Society of the *collège* of Rouen who have come to shoot their wad in the capital. How *reassuring* he is, this crazy imbecile, man and giant all in one, who swoons for a lady of quality and sneers at the same time: all asses are the same; why put on such airs when you can have a slut's for a hundred sous?

The Garçon was born of a doubling: sometimes there really are two actors—as in the "consecrated caricature"—but one of them acts out unreflecting spontaneity and the other the reflection on that spontaneity. At other times—as in the carriage of 1846—it is Gustave himself who acts out the two roles at the same time; he is both the finite and the infinite reflection that disqualifies it. Here the advantage is double. First, with his pantagruelesque laughter at himself, Gustave arms himself against the mirages of sex and the vertigo of despair; he no longer believes a single word he says—he is playing a good trick on a woman of letters. And if he believes it just a little, the joke is even better: acting out his spleen, his dissatisfaction, his nihilism, his experienced misfortunes in order to invite this woman to fornication, he has the grating pleasure of becoming completely ignoble, since he uses what he takes for the noblest part of his soul to procure for himself the most ordinary, the most basely material pleasure. In this, the misanthropy and misogyny of the *heautontimoroumenos* find their satisfaction. Second, and conversely, the giant's alibi allows our young man to put himself inside the role, to let himself go, to feel the charm

124. Letter to Alfred of "June-July 1845," *one year* before the meeting with Louise. These reflections are made apropos "Pradier's advice." *Correspondance* 1:185–86.

of beautiful, startled eyes: this naive spontaneity is the necessary nourishment of reflexive cynicism. Hence he can permit himself a certain sincerity as *raw material*; he fears nothing: if he should abandon himself excessively, the glacial laughter from above would bring him to his senses. Thanks to this doubling, Gustave does what he likes, feels whatever gives him pleasure—changing the emphasis is all it takes. We see why the Garçon makes his appearance as Gustave's Passion: he has created this figure for the sole purpose of permanently withdrawing solidarity from himself. Born of a vitriolic pride, his character will bear its mark forever; what could be more unbearable than laughing at his own unhappiness and making others laugh at it too? Let us carry the argument a step further. This laughter belongs to an immense imbecile, and the imbecile *is right*; humiliated, crucified, the man he laughs at is wrong to the core: he has the extreme absurdity to postulate by his every action a human order, when there is nothing but a diabolical order or a natural disorder. In 1862, when Flaubert recounted his "coupling" to the Goncourts, he displaced the ridicule: in his story, the laughing figure is not the giant, it is Gustave the traveling salesman, and the object of mockery is Louise, the eternal feminine with her abject credulity. In 1846, the Giant—unified laughter of the Rouen schoolboys and mediator of the infinite—was at the rendezvous, and he was laughing *first* at Flaubert; the enterprising lover felt transformed in the carriage beneath his gaze: in the lurching "vagabondage" of the cab he felt the expression of the pretentious non-sense hidden in its belly.

The carriage episode will allow us to determine more precisely the *internal* connection between Monsieur Loyal and the Giant. Let us not forget that the Garçon was in fact *improvised*: the "consecrated caricatures" were at first happy inventions, which the group subsequently preserved in the form of rituals. Under such conditions it is not surprising that this character, depending on the occasions and probably his interpreters as well (or Gustave's whim), could present himself in three different guises. Sometimes the doubling is rigorous: Monsieur Loyal and the Garçon are *distinct* individuals; in this case the Garçon is merely playing a role: he is identified with the Giant himself and becomes a monument of "derisive" and triumphant stupidity. In other cases the two roles interpenetrate in a sort of syncretism: the Giant's human envelope is itself gigantesque; or, if you like, Pantagruel has come down into the skin of a traveling salesman; this figure remains a man, but, though never attaining the dimensions of his occupant, he symbolizes those dimensions by physical qualities that raise

185

him above the ordinary. There is nothing romantic about him now: a joker and vulgarian, he manifests the omnipotence and ubiquitousness of matter by the baseness of his materialism and the violence of his "material" needs; laughing and laughable, this grotesque figure resembles the god Yuk himself. His clumsy jokes inevitably provoke laughter, but this ignoble laughter is summoned expressly to provoke another kind, of the second degree: the laughers surprise themselves by laughing and, shocked by their hilarity, withdraw their solidarity from it out of derision. But radical dichotomy and syncretism are merely extreme forms of improvisation. The fundamental structure of the character is a doubling that is *actualized* but remains *internal* and claims to take place in the mode of reflexive scissiparity. "There are two men in me," says Flaubert to the Goncourts; *two in one*—this much is clear. A bookworm, a traveling salesman. Let us say that the Garçon, originally, is the salesman deriding the worm; the latter represents reflected consciousness, the former embodies the reflection. In this case it is permissible to inquire into the synthetic connection between the two roles, since they are played *both at the same time,* which introduces a new problematic that I shall call the ego-ology of the Garçon. The persona being a subject, it must *at least* be furnished with an ego; being double, of course, it should perhaps have two of them. Yet if we establish that this quasi-object is unique, whom does it designate? In what circumstances does one say "I" and "Me"? In principle, as I have shown elsewhere, the ego appears to the reflexive consciousness as pole X of the reflected, or, if you will, as the transcendent unity of feelings, states, and acts. The "I" does not set itself against the ego; on the contrary, it is part of it and binds itself more particularly to the ipseity, properly speaking, than to the diverse areas of praxis. The "I" and the "Me" have the same content since the question is one of different designations of the same ego. In fact, we are *project*, that is, *the surpassing of what is suffered;* as a consequence, according to the circumstances and our particular intentions, it is permissible to consider ourselves *in our passivity* (and in this case, the project itself reveals *its passive mode:* it is flight conditioned by a certain given) or in our *activity* (in this case, even *passion* is the free negation of the given, surpassing toward . . . pro-ject).[125] In the first attitude the ego is revealed as

125. These remarks are somewhat sketchy, but I wanted to proceed quickly. Taking account of the fact that "I" and "Me" are determinations of the discourse and that, as such, they belong to a practico-inert whole, each part of which is conditioned by the evolution of the whole and, from this very fact, develops its counterfinalities in the very mouth of the speaker, a true ego-ology would have to demonstrate why "I" [*Je*]

"Me," in the second as "I." Who is saying "Me," who is saying "I," when the Garçon thinks and speaks? We are going to see that this question is not purely *formal* but allows us to enter more deeply into Gustave's persona and to state more precisely the meaning of his pessimism. One could, in effect—since it is the quasi-object of reflection and since the salesman is, in relation to the bibliomaniac, in a reflexive position—believe that the ego manifests itself in one or another of its forms only in the first of the "two men," as pole X of the *psyche* of the second. We shall see that this isn't so. Indeed, the Giant's ego cannot have the *psyche* of the bibliomaniac, that of pathetic, "narrow-chested" man, as its own. On the other hand, what is the bibliomaniac to do with a gigantic ego—how would he find in it the unity of his melancholies, of his pitiable passions? In other words, there is an incredible disproportion between the immense ego that should correspond to the appetites of a Pantagruel and the reflected consciousnesses through which it is passed. How can this disproportion be expressed?

Toward the middle of our century, a hundred years after the general dissemination of the Garçon, Jean Sarment saw fit to call one of his plays *I am Too Great for Myself*. Now *there's* an optimistic author! Certainly this statement has nothing jolly about it—the hero can only be a failure. But who would laugh at him? This is man, bowled over by the postulations that surpass him and finally cause his death; the important thing is that he can, if only by his vows, rise above himself. We have understood the disgraceful consolation being proposed to us here: *you are worth more than your life*, we are told. The "I," assimilated to an active principle, constitutes the essential of the person; his ascensional force is hampered by our earthly weight, which is here called the "Me," that's all. What counts, the author tells us, is the movement of trans-ascendance, the permanent openness to the Being

---

can be made passive *in words* ("I suffer," "I am lost") and "I / Me" [*Moi*] is related to the subject as agent ("Who did that?—*I* did") and can even be the subject of a transitive verb ("Me [*Moi*], betray you? He and I [*Lui et moi*] have decided . . ."), or of a participle ("With me [*moi*] gone, what will you do?"), or to an antecedent subject of the relative *who* and followed by the verb ("I [*Moi*], who loves you so!"), etc. It happens that "*I*" and "I/Me" in the same sentence *appear* to exercise the same signifying function ("As for me [*moi*], I [*je*], don't like that at all!" "*I* would have [*Moi, j'aurais*] preferred . . ."), etc. The study of all these *enriching* deviations of intention by the instrument—as it is handled by all others and as any modification, even local, of the conventional combination reverberates in itself—has no place in this book. I must limit myself to indicating here that it is indispensable to any *ego-ology* that claimed scientific rigor, at least as the starting point for philosophical research.

of the heights. Once again, secularized by Sarment, we encounter the holy Christian enterprise attempting to save the believer by his intentions: you would not seek me if you had not found me. In a way, the title of the play gives the "I" *reflexive* priority; the "Me" appears as the inert mass of the reflected, totalized by reflection. Obviously, this benevolent ruse has no bearing; between the "I" and the "Me," which, as I just said, are but two different designations of the same ego, there could be no such disproportion.

Gustave makes the same mistake, but in his pessimistic intention he reverses the terms: for trans-ascendence, which *honors*, he substitutes trans-descendence, which degrades. He might have written of the Garçon, if he had to define his essence: I am too small for *myself*. Indeed, *he did write it*.[126] The ego of the reflection appears as an *alter ego*: the use of the word "Me" to designate it does not claim to affect it with passivity but rather with *alterity:* in this line the "I" indeed indicates activity, properly speaking, but also ipseity, that is, lived experience as a perpetual *return-to-the-self* through time and space. Gustave indicates by the "I" that on this level he recognizes himself; in his eyes, the being that inhabits the reflection is objectified by its character as stranger, and the term "Me" does not designate inertia but the constituted character of the "I who is another," which is manifest at once by its impenetrability, its density, and its absence. Impalpable, out of reach, and yet indicated, like a weight, it is *a Flaubert who does not recognize himself,* or rather a pygmy who cannot recognize himself in the giant that he *is* and that at the same time inhabits him. This unhappy fellow can say of his occupant "That's me" to the extent that he grasps himself as the minuscule reflected image of this Titanic reflection. But it must be understood that this teratological intuition is purely imaginary: reflexive consciousness is not given, it is simply aimed at by a retaliatory intention, which constitutes it *as an image* by using Gustave's real reflection on himself as an analogue. Here he is, then, reflecting on lived experience by pretending that his reflection is intersected by a gaze of the second degree that is directed down onto his ego. We understand, then, that this ego appears to him as an "I": he grasps it in its practical aspect of projective transcendence so that his humble activities might be crushed, denied, made passive by a superior transcendence invoked expressly to make the "I" into a transcended transcendence. The giant's gaze is

126. This definition would fit the hero of *Novembre* and Madame Bovary, as we shall see. Of himself, didn't Flaubert say: "I am a great man *manqué*"?

a *Medusa's spell;* this absent force metamorphoses agent into patient, subject into object, as we have seen, disqualifying in advance their acts and their words, changing Emma-Léon into lurching pine wood. When he does the Garçon, Gustave takes the reflexive attitude and pretends that his own reflection is a conductive medium for the look of his pantagruelesque "Me." This means that he invents, on the reflexive level of the first degree, what his "Me" of the second degree is supposed to perceive from immediate and reflected consciousness. The game consists of taking his inventions for lightning flashes from above which pass through him and whose contents impose themselves on him as if they were intuitions of the alter ego regarding him from the heights, as if from the wrong end of a telescope. In short, he is affected by a pithiatic belief: he must feel seen, he must feel in himself the astringent power of "his" imaginary gaze. When he manages it, this fictive transcendence transforms the reflected ego in turn into an unreal object; in effect, the Giant is found to have a rapport only with Monsieur Loyal or the bookworm—and neither of these characters is *really* Gustave. They are caricatures of him, transformed in weight, selecting certain of his features and exaggerating them in order to provoke horror of the self. Thus, there is homogeneity between the "Me" of the heights and the "I," an earthworm, since both are imaginary. The whole recipe is made on the first degree level of reflection—the only one which is real *at the outset* but which Gustave does not hesitate to falsify in order to make it the analogue of the other. Here he is, then, reflecting on lived experience and pretending that his reflection is itself deciphered on a level of superior consciousness, even as he gives his reflected actions the surreptitious push that will make them the stupifying reactions of a belated Romantic or the pitiful reflexes of a petty nature aiming at greatness.

The sadistic and masochistic malice of "I am too small for myself" is striking: it means "Abandon all hope." Sarment leaves the question open: ascension is *possible in principle,* the proof being that I feel the need to attempt it; someone awaits me, perhaps, at the sublime summit and, seeing my efforts, will one day give me a hand. Gustave himself begins by making ascension *impossible*—because it *is already accomplished.* The alter ego has preemptorily installed itself at the sublime summit. As other. And this Giant, mediator of the negative infinite, teaches us that no one can join him there without being a giant himself. But what is to be found above if not the "vibrating disappearance" of the world swallowed up by nothingness? The positive infinite is on its way out. *Voler c'est survoler,* to steal away is to survey:

the gaze, turned downward, perceives only the pettiness of every-thing. In brief, man is closed, buckled up; the malevolent gaze of the superego, lowered onto him, affects him with double risibility—risible first through his great desire, his dissatisfaction, his religious "in-stinct," by everything that pushes him toward trans-ascendence since it is proven that to reach the peaks one must begin by having the di-mensions of a mountain. His sublime aspirations cause the Pantagruel coldly observing him to "roll with laughter"; why endlessly recom-mence his microscopic efforts since we will always fall back again and *he knows it?* Sarment saw our vain postulation as the sign of our great-ness. Flaubert, playing the Garçon, sees it as the mark of our stupidity. Besides, risibility comes to man from his fundamental intention: he tortures himself, bloodies himself, and kills himself trying to reach the sublime summit. And what does he hope to find there? Being. Well, supposing the impossible, were he to reach it he would merely dis-cover universal nonbeing and his own nothingness. Our Pantagruel knows it only too well; he has paid for the knowledge, and this is the underlying reason for his cosmic buffoonery: man is a crude mistake, and by seeking the good he heads straight for the worst. *By nature* he resembles those characters I described above, whom we see in slap-stick comedies, throwing themselves into the wolf's maw through the very precautions they take to avoid it. Gustave's sadism is given free rein; he has dishonored anguish: the greater it is, the more amusing it is—you could *die laughing*.

His masochism finds its satisfaction here as well: it is his own dolorism that he holds in fierce derision. When all is said and done, he acts both roles simultaneously primarily because—as we shall see more clearly when we read *Novembre*—his scholarly and, recently, lit-erary failures have convinced him that there is a disproportion be-tween his mad demands and his capabilities. "I am too small for myself," the Garçon's motto, is also Flaubert's motto from his fif-teenth year, when his imagination drained itself, until the attack at Pont-l'Evêque. At the source of the Garçon is an unhappy child who believes he is a failure and who is pushed by his own pride to dissoci-ate himself from his status of failure through laughter, thus making himself other than himself. Imaginary laughter, laughter "that is not laughter" but receives a certain consistency from the fact that the laugher is already *laughable* in his own eyes for having been *constituted such* by the terrible gaze of the chief surgeon, his original superego, and for having subsequently made himself the object of the collective laughter of his comrades (or for having believed he made himself its object). Reflection of the second degree does not exist, but he has no difficulty imagining it and making it the matrix of his mortifying inventions as it would be the laughter of the collective superego.[127] Nothing demonstrates more effectively that the Garçon, born of a vitriolic pride, is Flaubert's Passion: what is more unbearable than offering his own anguish *as an object of laughter?* Finally, in his view, fundamental laughter is the point of view of nothingness on being. In *Smarh,* laughter and radical evil are one and the same: thus, Yuk takes on scope; he swells himself up beyond all measure, he is stronger than Satan; Death is merely his wife. He does not say to their faces, "I am truth, I am eternal"; he takes it out especially on his old wife, shattering the illusions of that ravenous creature: "You believe you're sowing nothingness? As if after the corpse there were no putrescence?" Putrescence, scavenging flies—these are our guarantee that this doubtful metaphysic stems from a sincere inspiration. The flies fly out the windows of the amphitheater and buzz around the two children in the little garden. Old memories, still powerful, are at the source of these texts—the cadaver gives rise to laughter, death is not the end of our troubles, for something continues to exist, a caricature of life: the deceased is quite naked, more than naked; he is abandoned to gaping eyes, to flies, to worms, and his obscenity strikes a comic contrast to the seriousness of his face. This is basically what Yuk is: synthetic unity by means of the grotesque in death and life, each existing in the other as a caricatured presence and secondary reflection of a past or future state. We can now better understand the boy's horror of his future remains, for we know that, far from placing himself at the center of the world through an imperious cognito,[128] a mad, positive pride that allows all modesties, he receives his being only through the eyes of others: he condemns himself to exist insofar as he will be *seen.*[129] He will be carrion for the doctors, for his family,

127. *Les Funérailles du docteur Mathurin* suggests that collective laughter has not suppressed the laughter of the superego, for this admirable doctor is none other than Achille-Cléophas-doing-the-Garçon.

128. The cogito remains, of course, his immediate possibility. Besides, we have seen that the Garçon is at the level of *reflection.* But the deviation is made by the shift to the imaginary: through reflection, Gustave plays the role of the Other and, unrealizing himself, makes himself an observer through the Giant; thus his ego, in the unreal, appears to him as the object of the other.

129. And also as long as he exists in memories. Hence his romantic but sincere desire—at the time when he believed himself to be a "great man *manqué*"—to wipe out even his name; he hated the idea that years after his death people would discuss him, argue about his character, interpret his failure.

as present as he was when living. Indeed, he has made consciousness into a mystification and has put his being in *appearing*, in this case his post mortem appearance counts as much as his live *appearing*; the former is in effect the result, the resolution, perhaps the meaning, of the latter. What can be done about that? It is striking that Gustave, the unloved boy, thinking of his deathbed, never envisages the sorrow of his last companions but rather their laughter. "A stiff, that's a laugh!" Achille-Cléophas certainly did not give him the idea of attributing to cadavers a coefficient of risibility, although the philosophical practitioner's irony is at the source of Gustave's "pantagruelesque laughter." Doctor Flaubert was much too engrossed by his work to laugh at his raw material. But medical students, at least during their first dissections, frequently defend themselves against horror by laughter— which is in this case only a total but provisional denial of sympathy or solidarity: we shall never be this corpse we are gutting, doctors are not mortal. Gustave was acquainted with his father's students from an early age, and it is not impossible that he may have encountered this laughing cynicism in some of them; in any case, of course, he would have seen only the derision and not even understood the component of anguish it concealed. Whether he borrowed it from them or not, laughter will serve him as it has served them: as an exorcism. For him it is rather more complex, however, than for a medical student struggling not to faint. In order to defuse the future laughter of others at his future remains, Gustave steals it from them in order to laugh *in advance:* he will make himself into the Garçon, organizer of the funereal, grotesque parade; he will fascinate his comrades and force them to find amusement in his eventual purulence so as to lead them by the same stroke to laugh at their own. As if he were saying to future strangers who might be tempted to raise his shroud: "Don't bother deriding my corpse, *it's already been done.*" And as if he were gently warning his comrades: "Take your time, enjoy yourselves imagining how I'll look on my deathbed; you're having a good laugh at the way *you*'ll look."

It will no doubt be objected that *Yuk,* a late creation, is the one amused by our cadaverous survival. What is there to prove that the Garçon, around 1835, was similarly amused? I answer that the deriding of life by death and of death by life is part of Gustave's "program" from the outset. It began with that pre-Garçonic masquerade, the procession of skeletons with a dual objective: to mock the religious processions that exasperated the Voltairean bourgeoisie under the Restoration but were probably—and this is why he was set against them—not displeasing to Gustave in his early childhood; and to reveal to those dead on reprieve—his comrades and the passersby—their comic truth as walking skeletons. But what he confides to the Goncourts is especially convincing: the Garçon "pronounced . . . funeral orations on living persons." At the time he is referring to, the Garçon had become a collective imaginary figure: each of the students could act him out. There were competitions in eloquence—the Goncourts declare that these oratorical jousts took place at the Hôtel-Dieu, in the billiards room. This is hardly likely; what does seem evident, on the other hand, is that they required a large and relatively isolated locale; we may therefore suppose that the young men met together on holidays outside the *collège* in some hall lent to them by one of their fathers. The two brothers saw this as mere clowning; they lay special emphasis on the efforts of these adolescents to ridicule *discourse* by *discourses*. An acceptable interpretation: for many of them, and particularly for Gustave, *language was in question*. Can one speak, and about what? The answer given by this derisory eloquence is that speech is compromise; when one abandons silence, one is lost. But there is much more in these funeral orations:[130] to display the living person from the point of view of death, to report his acts, his feelings, his "good deeds," all his present activity, as orators will one day do standing before his tomb—showing that life is *already dead* when it expends itself, when, convinced of being eternal, it throws itself into enterprises which will have no end and proposes for itself ends it will not attain. Conversely, this perspective makes visible the grotesque impotence of the corpse: stupid speeches are inflicted upon it, it is bored to death by compliments that would have made it shout with rage *in its lifetime*, that *would make* it shout with rage if it heard them since it is still in working order, that is, in a state of life. But if death and life, those two faces of our condition, mutually ridicule each other, it is because both are avatars of being: to die is not to leave the world but to remain here in another form; being is everywhere—no one can escape it. As a result, nature is on trial *as being*: something different should have been created, or rather, as Satan suggests to God in *Rêve d'enfer, nothing at all*. Meaning, in this case, that Gustave should

---

130. If it were merely a question of disqualifying speech, it would suffice to "parody" real eulogies of real deceased persons. And that is what the Garçon does—according to the same testimony—when he parodies speeches or celebrated indictments.

not have seen the light of day. And when all these young "wags" get together, some competing with their impersonations, others "rolling with laughter," the sons of bourgeois Rouen cry out to their parents: we didn't ask to be born. I have dwelt at length on this funereal hilarity because it gives us the meaning of Yuk and his laughter: this god laughs at being because being is comic when glimpsed through the prism of Nothingness. We must understand here that Gustave wholeheartedly subscribed to these words of Satan's in *Ebauche d'un serpent:*

> Sun, sun! . . . dazzling defect
> You who mask death, Sun . . .
> You, boldest of my accomplices
> And of my snares the loftiest
> You keep hearts from knowing
> That the universe is only a blemish
> In the purity of Nonbeing . . .
> . . . As weary of its pure spectacle
> God himself has broken the obstacle
> Of his perfect eternity;
> He made himself into Him
> Who accordingly scatters
> His Principle in the stars,
> His Unity.
>
> Heavens, his mistake! Time, his ruin!
> And the animal abyss, gaping,
> What original fall
> Glitters in the place of Nothingness . . .[131]

But Yuk is not Satan: he hasn't the Serpent's hissing irony; he laughs openly at being—of which Valéry's serpent remains prisoner and accomplice even while despising it;[132] being, a monstrous incongruity, is the Garçon as such, blind substance laughing stupidly, wildly, at its finite determinations. Yuk, the hypostasis of nothingness, envelops with his infinity and penetrates on all sides that viscous *reality* which has committed the unpardonable fault of extricating itself with its own force from the infinite nonbeing and of gathering itself up into the absurd plenitude of a cosmos, *out of vanity*, so that "there might be something rather than nothing," and which is

131. Valéry (Pléiade edition) 1:138 ff.
132. The Satan in *Smarh* finds himself in the same boat.

roundly punished for it, that great whale, since it is merely an almost imperceptible blemish in the purity of nonbeing. As we shall see later, the artist for Flaubert is he who views being from the perspective of nothingness, life from the perspective of death. We see this conception—which is at the source of all his great novels—taking shape here through the *practical* investigation of his persona.

Still, there are two laughters. The first is the laughter of the giant, of the traveling salesman who represents the enormous fatuousness of being, what we might call *ontic ideology:* Long live strength, God's symbol! Nothing is beautiful that is not big, fat, and juicy! Long live matter, which is pure being! In the name of being I scorn, mock, and destroy all that is little—especially the human race. This involves a negation of the negative in the name of absolute positivity. From this point of view, what matters in the Garçon's hyperbolic exuberance is less the vain satisfaction of being gigantic than the intoxication of belittling, disparaging, destroying. But this cosmic laughter is shot through by a glacial, hypercosmic hilarity: the hilarity of nothingness mocking Being; that great lunker who laughs at beings doesn't realize that he is big only *by comparison,* and that, as a mere blemish in the purity of nonbeing, he is enveloped and paralyzed by negation. We must recognize that these two laughters are hardly compatible; certainly they both have bearing on the finite that believes itself infinite, on the determination that takes itself seriously; nonetheless, the colossus laughs in the name of being, and Yuk mocks the colossus in the name of nothingness. We could say that Yuk does not realize he is laughing *in the name of the colossus*—of which he is the hypostasis. Derision of the first degree, as of the second degree, aims at denouncing the nonbeing of being. But such an observation, satisfying as it may be in the abstract, does not help us understand how the three roles (Monsieur Loyal, Pantagruel, Yuk) can be acted out simultaneously by the same person. We shall press the problem further if we recall that Flaubert's generosity is poisoned and that the Garçon—that gift he makes to his schoolmates—is booby-trapped. It is time to examine this aspect of the character. Perhaps we shall perceive that he is actually quite different from what he seems.

The Trap

What is the relationship between laughter and truth? Does Gustave really believe that the grotesque is the truth of being, that laughter

195

reveals to us the mysteries of all reality? He posed this question for himself in *Smarh* and several pages later provided two contradictory answers.

The first is *yes*. In his dialogue with Death, Yuk declares: "I am the true, I am the eternal, I am the clown, the grotesque, the ugly." A scarcely tenable affirmation: even if the cosmos is a defect of nothingness, it is hard to laugh at it unless one incarnates nothingness itself. The character thus constructed will be nothing but a man-who-laughs, hence a role played by an actor *who pretends to laugh*. If we return to our point of departure, we shall recall that Gustave was (or believed himself to be) the object of the laughter of others; when he decides to steal their collective hilarity and turn it against them, he does so in anger and in order to defend himself. The pantagruelesque and doleful laughter he forces on them, with the intention of drawing them into a trap, can be nothing but an act of mimicry aimed at representing an emotion he does not feel. This formidable laugher had never laughed, and the objects of his laughter have never been laughable except in his imagination. Gustave is so conscious of this that he gives a second answer, a more developed one, and in order to underscore its importance he reserved a place of honor for it: it will be the conclusion of *Smarh*. In the summary he writes for Ernest, 18 March 1839, he recounts: "At the end [of the work] a woman comes on the scene. Smarh loves her. He has become beautiful again, but Satan has fallen in love with her too. Then they seduce her, each in turn. Who will be victorious? Satan, you think? No—Yuk, the grotesque. This woman is Truth; and it all ends with a monstrous coupling." These few lines seem at first to confirm that laughter itself is being, inasmuch as it is devoured by nonbeing. But on rereading, nothing seems quite satisfying. First of all, why does Truth come so late? For two hundred pages, Yuk and the Devil have been leading Smarh everywhere: he has been experiencing the human condition; in palaces, in humble cottages, he has—thanks to his two Virgils—probed the innermost depths of the damned; then, baptism by air and a visit to celestial realms, and again descent, landing, and a series of complementary experiences. What did they show him, then, if Truth was so conspicuously absent? Mirages? Should we believe that the two cronies who have plunged him into despair were really conjurers? In this case, pessimism and misanthropy would be merely *temptations*. They *tempt* Smarh, and Truth hides herself: why come forward when all has been consummated? And then, there is that suspect adjective *"monstrous."* No doubt Yuk is grotesque, while the woman he possesses is beautiful enough to provoke the love of a poet and of the Prince of Darkness. But what is this all about? Should Truth be beautiful? Then Yuk is not "the true." But we must not forget that this is an allegory,[133] the characters are symbols. In this case, there is a choice to be made: *Either* beauty is *authentic*, hence the coupling is not monstrous but is simply impossible on the level of ideas; the *eidos* of the beautiful and the ugly are antithetical; certainly they condition each other by their opposition, and one can imagine a Hegelian *Aufhebung* that will surpass them while preserving them, but this surpassing cannot be symbolized by copulation. *Or*, as with the amorous Devil, beauty is only an appearance masking some quite hideous demon, so that the union of ugliness and the grotesque, repulsive as it may seem to us, cannot be considered *monstrous:* it is not a matter of uniting, unmediated, two contradictory terms, but, quite the opposite, of yoking like terms together.

If we go back to the work itself as it was completed in April 1839, one month after the summary Gustave sent to Ernest, our suspicions will be confirmed. Truth is an angel, but not an innocent one: men "have chased her, driven her away"; she has wings that don't do her much good since her feet are bloody. We understand from this that she is not something men like to hear. Yet she comes to Smarh and calls him "my beloved" because she leads her lovers to despair, and because Smarh is *already* despairing; so once again he becomes not beautiful but a poet; as if poetry began beyond despair, he glimpses the mysteries of being: "Something resplendent and eternal!" Satan appears and interposes himself: "That woman is mine!" Will poetry be the measure of the world? Or will the principle of evil alone use Truth to devastate the hopeless souls of the damned? What is at stake seems important, as the earth, prey to the Accursed One, implores the young woman to give herself to the poet. Must this fable be seen as merely a tissue of nonsense and clichés, as Gustave himself, rereading his work a year later, will see it? I am rather inclined to find in it the awkward outline of a kind of Catharism: the earth remains

---

133. We know that it has affective roots: the monstrous coupling is that of Maurice Schlésinger and Elisa, which the young boy would picture to himself at night in Trouville, his bitter jealousy prompting him to take pleasure in placing the woman he loved in obscene and ridiculous postures. Maurice is a sorry jester, a practical joker. It is no surprise that he is promoted here to the dignity of the God of Jokes. He will be brought down to more accurate proportions in the first *Education*, where he is cast as a third-rate actor. But if this "monstrous" union informs us of Gustave's misogyny, its affective charge prevents it from appropriately symbolizing the dialectical investigations of man and truth.

Satan's, this is the *first truth,* which is surely cause for despair; but he who is convinced of it, if he succeeds in breaking the accursed circle of human passions, will perhaps reach resplendent eternity through poetic intuition. In any event, the Manichean and Romantic solution is abruptly set aside: the moment Smarh is about to become a poet, the dark, disconsolate stranger Yuk appears and wins all: "Yuk began to laugh, and jumped on her and clasped her in an embrace so strong, so terrible, that she suffocated in the arms of the eternal monster."

Gustave was right: the coupling was indeed quite monstrous, for the poor woman died of it. This new metaphor is obscure. We shall return to it. What should be noted here is that the world *has lost its truth.* Nothing is false, nothing is true: Smarh turns in the void, in his belief in nothing. The grotesque is not the true: he has the right to take Truth's virginity but cannot do it *without killing her.* Let us recall that Gustave, a year earlier, was declaring himself to be "antitruth." At the time, he was setting poetry against science, against prose, as the unreal against reality. *Smarh* shows some traces of an attempt to reconcile poetry and truth, poetry being born of the despair into which we are plunged by the discovery of truth. But finally Truth bothers him: *since it is science,* it is on the side of his father and his older brother. He is prepared, therefore, to suppress it; only it will no longer be with a beautiful lie, a line from Lamartine or Hugo: the criminal weapon is laughter.[134] The Garçon's laughter does not burst forth from an abrupt, spasmodic intuition of the truth: quite to the contrary, its function is to turn us away from it. A strange, unknowable cosmos—it has been stripped of the fundamental categories that permit knowledge. Let us be clear: he is not saying that the true hides itself but that laughter suffocates it. Two categories remain: the real and the unreal. The unreal is invented, deployed, its insubstantial splendor folded back on itself; the real is touched, seen; it weighs on us, obsesses, importunes. But it has no more truth than the other.

---

134. Curiously, Flaubert declared to the Goncourts that the Garçon, far from being an archetypal and immutable character, "had a history." From this we understand that he is a product of his own history: in effect, he begins by making poetry and ends as proprietor of the Hoax Hotel, where the Festival of Shit is celebrated every year. Doesn't this mean that he has moved from poetic antitruth to cynical and "pantragruelesque" antitruth? The first, or the *idealist,* negation of the true, engenders from disappointment a negation by comic ultramaterialism. If they hadn't been affected by the confidences of 1862, we would take these features of the Garçon for the temporal development of the contradiction that is embodied later in the brief moment of "coupling" in the carriage. In any event, Gustave intimates that the cynical buffoon is born of a murdered poet.

The source of this conception is Gustave's passive constitution, which deprives him of the power to deny and affirm, forbids him any certainty, and leaves him only belief: at the conclusion of *Smarh* he is merely speaking from experience. But there is more: this fable contains a practical intention. In the merciless struggle that Flaubert mounts against reality in the name of the unreal, reality must be stripped of its chief weapon; it must be conceded an obtuse, material presence, opacity, the frightening power to crush us, nothing more: without truth, the being of the real is merely an appearance of being, and its deceptive cohesion an infinite dispersion; the atoms themselves lose their indivisibility. This pulverization is somewhat reminiscent of the astonishing plays of being and nothingness in the eighth hypothesis of Parmenides: "If the One is not, what becomes of other things?" [135] and we shall have to return to this at length.

Nevertheless, well before he has stifled Truth, Yuk's intentions are highly explicit: "When he opened his mouth, there was a tangle of calumnies, lies, poetries, chimeras, parodies, and they always ended by entering someone's ear, planting themselves somewhere, building something, destroying something else, burying or exhuming . . . If he stretched out his foot, he would kick over a crown, a belief, an honest soul, a conviction."

"I am the True," he said to Death. Yet according to the long passage we have just cited and the conclusion of the work, he should have declared, on the contrary: "I am the False." Was he lying, then? That is not said, but where would the god of illusion and sleight-of-hand find the means to enunciate a truth? Is he perhaps deceiving himself? In any case, let us note Gustave's implicit admission: the world is not really grotesque; that is Yuk's finest and most complete calumny. The Garçon cannot be assimilated to the cosmos. What is he, then, but calumny itself, that tangle of "lies, poetries, chimeras, parodies," whose consistency derives precisely from the fact that whoever hears it is lost, incapable of leaving this labyrinth of sophistries and counter-truths? There is a complex and aberrant unity to the unreal; it is a complete world with its own paths, its swirling movements, its curving lines: only being is lacking. Or, rather, the unreal possesses a certain being, that of appearance as such, the being of nonbeing. Yuk the grotesque, the god of appearance, is also the god of those workers of the imaginary, artists. The Garçon derives from him: that great cosmic idiot is a caricature of creation. Indeed, what comes out of Yuk's

135. Plato (Pléiade edition) 2:252–54.

mouth is precisely the discourse of the Garçon. The Garçon "made poetries," the Goncourts report. His parodies we already know: false funeral orations, caricatures of speeches, of indictments, comic imitations of trials. As for his slanders, let us recall Gustave's jubilation at demoralizing Père Eudes's boarder with groundless accusations. If the Garçon is the slander of the world, if he gives Yuk's tangle of clownings the organic unity of his personal "history," we can conceive that the god of nonbeing and his hypostasis might be two simultaneous hilarities that would be contradictory if they existed *in reality*.

The lusty, idiotic laughter of the traveling salesman is the laughter of an imaginary cosmos that would push absurdity to the point of mocking in itself the grotesque determinations it produced in order to destroy them. The function of this character is fascination: "posted" in front of humankind, this deceiver clucks, drools, slaps his thighs, in order to hypnotize. If the operation should succeed, the cosmos would see in this mirage its own oneiric image; thrown into confusion, the universe would live in a nightmare.

Yuk, the Father, is not unaware that his Son is ridiculous: after all, he wished him so. However, he does not mock his son but rather reality, to the degree that he senses it will fall into the trap; hence it is understandable that the great, mad laughter of Matter is traversed by the silent, glacial, infinite laughter of nothingness: the matter, the laughter, the nothingness are not real. I demonstrated earlier that nonbeing is the mockery of being—that is surely the underlying meaning of this comedy. Provided we add that nothingness must be touched by a certain kind of being in order to take on the appearance of a laugher. The Garçon, king of appearances, is alone qualified to deride the nonbeing of being. Again we have just seen that this mockery has no reality: it will "take" only if *being* allows itself to be taken in and, by its *real* reactions, makes such mockery effective. When Gustave shocks Père Eudes's boarder, what matters to him is the action of the unreal on reality; the sycophant savors the poor pious boy's blushes, his beads of sweat, because they are the *true products* of notorious lies. And that is the most radical subversion: Being mystified by Nonbeing, what *is* affected by what is not. Yuk can rest content: he has "built" and "destroyed." Ideally, young Eliacin should lose his faith; then the grotesque and wicked god would have "stretched out his foot and [kicked over] a belief, an honest soul, a conviction." His basic purpose is "demoralization," but what matters to him even more than the ravaging of souls is the way he has done it. To destroy a conviction by valid arguments is to undeceive, perhaps, but surely not to demoralize. But if someone undermines beliefs by slander, by lines of reasoning he knows quite well to be false, if we lose our faith fraudulently and if, subsequently, without recovering it, we expose the sophisms and lies that have led us astray, then we can say that we have been demoralized.

In order to understand the meaning of this term, let us turn to the military, who have long been acquainted with it. Demoralization, in their eyes, is not immorality properly speaking but the loss of morale, the loss of the tension demanded by soldierly virtues and, if one is to believe the military, by ethical life in general. *Morale* would consist of a high degree of psychic integration, permanent mobilization of all our energies, confidence in oneself and in the cause to be defended based on a healthy Manichaeism and on the principle of authority. If morale is high, it is because the soldier is commanded well; if after certain reversals his morale is lowered, it is because civilians are attempting to demoralize the army. *By means of sophisms,* obviously. If the little hypocrite were losing his faith out of curiosity, unformulated lust, a strange overheating that certain images, *taken as such,* provoked in him, he would not even have recourse to agnosticism or atheism: demobilized by concupiscence and shame, this soul would remain certain that God exists but would no longer have the strength to believe in His existence.

To demoralize is therefore to ruin an existence by manipulating it through fantasms, to produce collapses, irrecoverable losses, shatterings, a deficit in reality through the representation of the unreal. But for the operation to be perfect, it is not enough to employ deceptions and fakeries: it is indispensable that the victim become conscious of their nonbeing—if not at the beginning of the process at least as quickly as possible—for it is at this moment of sudden consciousness that he will discover the being of nonbeing and the nonbeing of being, and that he will perceive in a stupor that all this was *nothing* and that this nothing has inexplicably corroded his life. It is at this moment that laughter will take hold of him, the laughter of an Other, a Laughter that is other, purely imaginary and yet fascinating. This determination of lived experience is familiar to us: it is that of the dupe—and who isn't one?—who cries out, too late, haunted by the huge, phantom laughter of his manipulators, "I've been fooled! How they must be laughing at me!" Indeed, they are slapping their thighs, saying to each other, not "he took himself seriously" (primary laughter), but "he took *us* seriously" (secondary laughter).

The process is perfectly described in an episode in *Smarh.* It is true that Satan, in this particular case, collaborates with Yuk, but this complicity has nothing to do with it.[136] The two cronies, dressed in work clothes, present themselves to a poor man. The poor man has nothing in his heart but envy and hatred of the rich.[137] He is not demoralized, however: his anger possesses an incomparable power of integration: "I have treasures of hatred for them . . . and when it gets cold, when I am hungry, I am unhappy and wretched, I take nourishment from that hatred and it does me good." To give proof of this strength of soul is to tempt the Devil. The demoralization, quickly undertaken, goes well. Satan sits in the beggar's ear and begins by exalting his hatred, then he points to Yuk and says: "Kill him. He is a hard-hearted rich man." At the same time, Yuk opens his cloak, revealing a purse studded with diamonds. The poor man hesitates a little: "Kill someone?" Satan gives him a final shove and the unhappy man, "*fascinated*," throws himself on the grotesque god with a dagger the Devil has slipped into his hand. Yuk falls, "covered with wounds." At the same moment, called by the Evil One, the police appear and lead the pauper away. To be sure, Yuk gets up unscathed, but, since there must be a victim, "the body of the workingman remained on the ground, covered with wounds." What workingman? The one whose role Yuk played and who was only a phantom. There he is, falsely dead, since he never lived, but with real blood streaming from false arteries. Mission accomplished; what interests Gustave is not so much Satan's *temptation* of the pauper as the sleight of hand that accompanies it. Which is it, a false workingman or a false rich man? It's difficult to say; if the workingman reveals himself as a rich man in disguise, the rich man is no less a mirage, for it is the workingman who remains on the pavement, a corpse revealing his true identity. Not true— Yuk has played all the roles. By the same token, the murderer, caught

136. One of the weaknesses of *Smarh* is that Flaubert has given Yuk omnipotence and Satan seems to be merely his pale double, finally having nothing more to do in this story. In the same way, in certain religions a dethroned God continues to exist, distant, impotent, as the sign of some very ancient evolution (or revolution or invasion), which is accompanied by a certain syncretistic tolerance: in 1839, the preeminence of Yuk marks the violence of the counteroffensive within Gustave. He has moved from tears (the world is Hell) to mad laughter, and of his former convictions he retains only one, which can make you laugh or cry: the worst is always certain.
137. In his notebook of *Souvenirs*, a comment of Flaubert's that seems nearly contemporaneous with *Smarh* would remind us, if we needed to be reminded, that he is far from disapproving of these sentiments: "I have no love for the proletariat, and I do not sympathize with its poverty, but I understand and enter into its hatred of the rich." Therefore, whatever is best in the worker causes Satan and Yuk to attack him.

red-handed, has killed no one: it has all been imaginary, even his willingness to kill, prompted and manipulated by Satan. In contrast, the consequences of the false crime are real. First of all, demoralization: the beggar, having staked his life on an illusion, will wonder even at the gallows by what aberration his hatred of the rich pushed him to murder a brother in wretchedness whom he *knew* worked with his hands. The hanging afterward is so perfectly ineluctable that Satan—who is bored—gives the pseudo-criminal the chance to escape. Having *done nothing*, in effect, he is not yet damned. But the (erroneous) conviction of having committed a first crime and the certainty of being tracked down by the police (who take him, *wrongly*, for a gallows bird) will soon transform him, through a chain of motivations which no longer have anything to do with phantasmagoria, into a real highwayman: assuming his imaginary crime, he decides to commit others—real ones—and to follow the road to Hell. We see the technique: take a powerful feeling in a strong soul and, by the fascination of a "fabulous opera," make it the irresistible moving force of behavior that radically contradicts it. I hate the rich, *therefore* I cut a poor man's throat. On the level of this *therefore*, mystification slips in: the man no longer recognizes himself in his acts, he is engulfed by a great demoralizing laughter (this behavior is itself provoked by something exterior: his practical objectification makes him withdraw solidarity from his inner certainty and *render himself laughable* in his own eyes).

The pleasure of the "eternal monster" is more immediate, more brutal, but, in the end, more cynically subtle than Satan's. Satan wants to damn God's creatures—he is not particular about the means. Yuk will never refuse to deliver his dupes to his crony, but for him damnation is merely a secondary objective. What matters is *the joke;* those he mystifies will be damned *for nothing;* wandering in a miraculous labyrinth they take for reality, they make oneiric decisions that have real consequences in the real world, which a curtain of images was masking from them. But the monster's victims are not sleepwalkers, nor are they dreamers; he wants them to have their eyes wide open and focused on the holes in the curtain. Unlike Queen Mab, whose nocturnal power may have inspired Gustave, Yuk reigns over a solar, diurnal world. He begins his work in broad daylight; he does not act directly on minds but rather falsifies the environment just enough so that appearance is momentarily substituted for reality. Hence, unrealized without their knowledge, men take themselves for

203

what they are not, act accordingly, and find that they have fallen into an all too real ditch, their backs broken, without understanding how they got there.

Such trickery has a name and is practiced on a small scale in families, in society; everyone laughs, and the victim, even if torn apart inside, must be the first to be cheerful: these are *practical jokes,* they are sold in specialty shops. The principle is simple: a small group, by choosing a victim to be fooled "for laughs," tries to exorcise the anguish of being-in-the-world. This anguish, a specific instance of a fundamental anguish which is simply our freedom itself, is born of an insoluble contradiction of our praxis. Indeed, no one is unaware that "appearances are deceptive" and that "clothes don't make the man," but whatever our vigilance, the necessities of action—scarcity of time, for example—force us to consider "appearances" as the manifestations of being. It is, in effect, convenient—and conforms to an original relation of concurrence with the world—to take that man going by in a brown cassock, bareheaded, tonsured, for a Franciscan or a barefoot Carmelite. Especially if I am absorbed in my enterprise and "have no time to lose." But this concurrence, always contestable and silently contested, is not lived without anguish save in each particular case, at any rate as the global feeling of our insertion in the world. It is not a matter of doubt—explicit and methodical doubt is reassuring, at least to a certain extent—but of a more or less actualized *"estrangement."* Most of the time we mask this anguish from ourselves by staying on the surface of the self and attaching ourselves to "securing" constants that are manifest in external sequences; the estrangement is concealed by custom or purely and simply *repressed.* I come to myself "from other horizons"; the world is what separates me from myself and announces me to myself, so that in every "mundane" appearance there is a disturbing menace and a still more suspect promise that is addressed to me in the depths of my existence.[138] Moreover, daily work, through its raw materials and its tools, reveals to us the "coefficient of adversity" in things. This is variable and defined by the means of production and consequently by society, whose type of integration is extrapolated and projected as an objective unification onto the aggregate of mundane facts ("nature" is defined in every era as materials and the limit of techniques in current use). Thus the environment

138. I am not speaking here of *common* dangers (the peril of death, the risk of accident, etc.) but of the menacing promise of discovering for myself at a distance *what I am* through a transformation of some object insofar as each of them puts in question the world as totality and consequently myself, as I come to myself from the horizons.

announces me as coming *also* to myself through others, that is, as alienation and destiny. In particular, connection-with-the-world is experienced from birth, beginning with our relation to our surroundings: the text of the world is the meaning of the family context, itself conditioned by institutions; we are *at ease* in the world only to the extent that we are *at ease* in our own family—and "ease," in truth, is only the least possible degree of being "ill at ease." For this reason, all being that reveals its appearance and all appearance that confesses its nonbeing risk exposing us as *pure appearance* or disclosing our "deepest being" as base or terrifying. Thus, when a mundane object seems dubious to us, it is the whole world, ourselves, and our relation to the world that become suspect: what went unsaid no longer goes without saying; compromised to the very mysteries of existence, we glimpse a monstrous *alterity of being* that is the truth of the cosmos and of our person.

Someone hands me a sugarbowl; *trustingly*, distractedly, I take a cube of sugar apparently the same as all the others; look how it weighs in my hand like a piece of marble or else, on the contrary, how it floats in my cup of coffee without sinking to the bottom. In either case I have done nothing but behave as millions of other people are behaving at the same moment: a habitual action, prescribed, guaranteed. The local revolt of matter merely has a better chance to take me unawares: everything becomes possible, this room is the site of the most radical unpredictability: *I don't believe my eyes*, I seem a stranger to myself, my habits are disqualified, my past abolished; I am naked in a new present that is lost in an unknown future. To tell the truth, I suspected it, I suspected it all my life: my connection to being, to *my* being, was only an appearance; the *true* relation reveals itself, and it is horrible, I come to myself, a terrifying monster, across a monstrous world. The jolly prankster who offered me some sugar is not unaware of my feelings: in order *to laugh at it*, he wanted to trigger that feeling of being ill at ease which, if prolonged, would soon drive me crazy; to laugh at it, to make others laugh at it—for the perfectly good reason that he has often felt it himself. What he doesn't know is that his underlying intention is to trigger the feeling in another so as to be able to dissociate himself from it through collective hilarity. In fact, while I marvel at the object in question, which suspends the legitimacy of matter, he *proves* to himself by laughing that everything is in order, that the cosmic constants have not changed; and—by extrapolation—that they will never change; that what to idiots—that is, to me, mystified as I am—looks like a sudden mutation has only the *ap-*

pearance of an exception: to the laughers, the joke is a demonstration by absurdity of the rationality of the world and the permanence of the laws of nature. That sugar *was not sugar* except to the ninny excluded by the laughter. It felt like marble? Nothing surprising about that, it *was* marble. It floated like celluloid? Of course, it *was* celluloid. The two materials behaved just as they always do. This instantaneous minishock seems therefore like a vaccine against the anguish of existing: actualized in the mystified victim, its only cause is clearly human stupidity. And, by the same token, the laughers—supermen of rationality—believe they are mocking the "ancestral terrors" of humanity in the name of reason. The vaccine always takes. Unfortunately, the effect does not last; it must be continually renewed: the practical joker is a man filled with anxiety.

He is malicious: he delights in infecting me with his anguish. He has accomplices: one offers me tea, the other distracts my attention when I help myself, etc.; everyone knows he *is playing a role* but me, yet I am the principal actor—since I make a spectacle of myself, and my surprise, though sincere, verges on unreality. In fact, they have obtained the complicity of my freedom: by freely accepting their offers, by freely sticking to my habitual conduct, I have fallen into their trap; my freedom, manipulated from a distance in its own name, has turned against me as a destiny. A new antinomy: my freedom is merely the means of my subjection; through it they have manipulated me by remote control; those nasty jokers affirm their own freedom by laughing at my enslaved will: freedom, anguish, illusions that are only too human. Man is their real target: I can recover the *reality* of the marble sugar only by exposing the essentially human as a mirage. Even my incredulity, provoked by nothing, was nothing. Or, rather, since they *made me play a role*, I must disown my immediate past and affirm with them that for *five imaginary minutes* I have lived under their control.[139]

One practical joke is not serious. Ten, twenty, a hundred jokes played by the same laughers on the same victim end by inducing an artificial psychosis and compelling the victim to live his adaptation—which is normal—to the real as a permanent disadaptation. Yuk, a

---

139. This is not true, of course: I have had a *true* reaction to a false object. But put yourself in my shoes! In fact, I was not doing what I thought I was doing, I was not what I thought I was: a mistaken perception, when it is not intentionally provoked, cannot derealize me in my own eyes. Here, by contrast, derealization affects me objectively because it comes to me *through others*, and if I want to join with the laughers I must internalize it.

practical joker by definition, doesn't stop playing jokes on his distraught scapegoat, the human race; nor does the Garçon, his hypostasis, stop mystifying the schoolboys at Rouen. The two of them can
make only one hyperbolic joke, which contains within it all others—
"a heavy-handed joke, patient, continuous," says Gustave to the
Goncourts, " . . . a small-town joke." I would call it the *practical joke
of the world*. To tell the truth, every practical joke is cosmic to the extent that the faked object seems to suspend natural laws: it is always a
miracle against nature. But the miracle takes place in the midst of the
world and engages it only to the extent that it produces and totalizes
the recalcitrant part; the person mystified cannot decide whether that
part escapes the All or reveals its deepest being. In this form, the trap
corresponds in Gustave to what I will call in a later chapter interior
totalization. But for one who believes he has an overview of being,
exterior totalization always seems possible as well: he believes he is
able to totalize the cosmos from the outside by synthetic intuition.
Such is Yuk, such is the Garçon: instead of compromising the world
with a false sugar cube, they go right to the crux of the matter and
mystify their victims by presenting them with a false world, which
the victims confuse with the true one. The fake object in this case is
the Garçon himself. Certainly he makes a hundred separate jokes and
caricatures, but these are in the name of universal principles and a
priori. Being is laughable by definition, creation is one of God's blem-
ishes; the worst is always certain; whatever you do, once you are em-
barked on this wretched life the result will be grotesque: Romanticism
is stupid, materialism is stupid, etc., etc. As soon as one of the schoolboys, fascinated by the gigantic idiot's convulsions or the traveling
salesman's cynicism, slips into the character's skin, he is cornered: he
adopts the vision of the world proposed to him on the sly, he barters
his moderate, eclectic convictions for an absolute pessimism that does
not spare even his own person. He is then condemned to express his
despair with a defiant "laugh of the damned" or, if he intends to express it directly, with sobs, to unleash the mad laughter of the audience. Cornered like a rat: if he plays the angel, the beast in him will
laugh at his beautiful soul and at the nastiness that hypocritically
produces his ecstasies. If he plays the beast, farting, pissing, shitting
everywhere, his baseness provokes the laughter of desolidarity, at
which he scoffs in turn by demanding from *what point of view* these
laughers can challenge him except that of nothingness? Hilarity in
this case expresses the radical condemnation of being and suggests a
destructiveness that should be followed by collective suicide.

207

But the Garçon is a mirage: Gustave would have everyone believe that in creating this character he tried to achieve the real through the imaginary, or, as is said of writers and artists today, that he lied in order to tell the truth. The hypocrite! He lied in order to lie, he cannot be unaware of this, and the world we see through his eyes *is false*. Flaubert's underlying intention is to poison his comrades by a cosmic lie that compels them to adopt it; and he gave the Goncourts information that permits us a better understanding of his enterprise: "The Garçon, he says, had a whole history to which everyone contributed something. He made poetry and ended by running a *Hoax Hotel* where there was a Festival of Shit at sewer-draining time, and where you heard the following orders echo through the corridors: 'Three buckets of shit for Room 14. Twelve dildos for Room 18!' This creation was reminiscent of de Sade . . . He asserts he had not read him at the time."

It will be noted that Gustave claims the invention of this festival, whatever may have been the importance of other, previous contributions. The Goncourts state it clearly, exclaiming, "It's from de Sade!" and are astonished by the marquis's influence on their colleague; they take it for granted, *according to his own story*, that he is the author of the final episode. And Gustave, instead of protesting that he hadn't much to do with it, that the credit should go especially to Pagnerre or to others, implicitly confirms their hypothesis by answering them very simply: "I had not yet read him." Moreover, the process of the creation is easily reconstructed, and we recognize in it the style of the young Flaubert. First of all, the scatology. This goes back to his childhood; we cannot forget that at nine years old he wrote "La belle explication de la constipation." And then, the punning—he was crazy about it all his life. The origin of this festival is *verbal:* voiding, vintage. At harvest time, when the new vintage is gathered, we celebrate the grape, product and material of labor; at sewer-draining time, why not celebrate shit, the product of man and the material of repugnant laborers? Beginning with this approximation, Gustave throws himself into hyperbole and pangagruelizes; the shit runs in torrents, it is ordered by the bucketful, they stuff themselves with it. After anthropophagy, coprophagy.

Indeed, from Gustave's point of view it is the same thing. To eat man in order to shit him out, or ceremoniously to eat the shit of others, is making excrement the reality of the human race. Gustave's taste for scatological humor manifests his horror of the natural functions. From the moment animals and plants are transformed in us and by us into that putrid matter, we are shitpots; it hardly matters what we do with our excrement subsequently. The most honest thing would be to eat it again; then man would become what he is: a fecal cycle. The first alimentary bolus is ingested, digested; its unassimilable elements are excreted, and these, carefully assembled, constitute the second bolus. Surely some nutritive substances remain that a second digestion will be able to integrate. A third, perhaps . . . ? This is never said; the main thing is to let nothing be lost. The maxim certainly implies that we are shit-eaters *in a figurative sense* when in our avarice and egotism we insist on recuperating and recycling all the waste products of our activity. Thus coprophagy is *also* bourgeois utilitarianism: practical man returns unceasingly to himself in excremental form. Gustave's derision has an even deeper thrust: at the Hoax Hotel, Shit Day is celebrated as a holiday;[140] by this ceremony, Gustave wants to show the absurd stupidity of the great feast days. The organizer of this solemn festival is the same fellow who as a child wrote to Ernest: "You were right to say that New Year's day is stupid."

Before examining the contents of this caricature, let us acknowledge that it does not seem to have been *acted*. In any case, it is not said, and the way the Goncourts report to us the "history" of the Garçon indicates that his Deed consisted of recounted episodes. We know, moreover, that there must have been a Garçon "drama," and it can rightly be supposed that it was a written piece. The being of the Garçon, always unreal, could manifest itself in different ways: improvisation, liturgy, written literature, and oral literature. The episode of the Hoax Hotel alludes, in my opinion, to an oral tradition. It hardly matters. They told each other the Garçon's adventures, taking turns playing the role; they invented a happening, a detail; the creation passed from the dramatic to the novelistic mode; they spoke of the Garçon in the third person, but this did not change anything because, being originally a persona, the character remained even for his interpreters a "He" who said "I" through their mouths. The purpose remained the same: they had to invent the epic of the ignoble. Whether expressed as an imaginary stage setting around the little actors—let us recall Ubu and his companions: they too ate shit, not at a festival but

---

140. This does not mean, from his point of view, that shit is tasted only once a year. The vintage harvest festival [Vendanges] is an annual affair, but we drink wine every way.

at a private dinner—or whether described in the course of a collective fabulation, the Hoax Hotel remains the unreal container of the entire company: that is, it compromises them.

Let us promptly note the first trap. Gustave knows very well, and pretends to be unaware, that the essential object of a peasant and pagan festival celebrating human labor is to ensure the renewal of the exhausted earth and the return of the seasons *by expense.* Wine from the vats of former years is drunk, which means that this year's labor is consecrated by squandering a little from that of previous years. Sacrifice and gift, a provisional reversal of the norms, the Festival, whatever else it is, is inappropriate as an image of the avarice that economizes and recuperates. Undoubtedly the Garçon, master of ceremonies, was amused to create this contradiction: an expense that preserves.

Another trap: what are the dildos doing here? The Garçon is willingly scatological but, curiously, hardly tempted by pornography—at least according to the information we have on him. Let us admit, however, that the Festival of Shit is accompanied—like the Roman *lupercalia*—by an outburst of sexuality. These adolescents are not tormented—except for Alfred—by the fear of impotence. Whether the gallant company gave themselves over to pederastic frolics or dredged up a few prostitutes, such substitute tools would be useless to him. They might conceivably have been of use to some "accursed women," but Gustave was never interested in Sapphic love; besides, those who frequent the Hoax Hotel are not lesbians but Flaubert's teachers and classmates.[141] So there is only one explanation: these instruments can be of use only to the whores taken by the schoolboys from the sidewalks of Rouen and to a few instructors, perhaps, in the event that the fellows might like to be sodomized by their women. At its source, as we see, there is the fantasy—very widespread but particularly pronounced in Gustave—of maternal virility. The matrix of these joyous inventions is fetishism, which expresses his desire to have himself, feminine man, taken by a virile woman, a mother-goddess, who would subject him to the rigidity of her imaginary phallus. Twelve dildos: twelve men penetrated one by one by the same matron or by twelve different ones. Nothing demonstrates better

---

141. Perhaps a first sketch of this Hotel should be seen in the letter to Ernest of 13 September, 1839: "The Garçon, that beautiful creation so curious to observe from the perspective of the philosophy of history, has undergone a fine addition, the Garçon's house where Horbach, Podesta, Fournier, etc., and other brutes are reunited; you shall see the rest." (*Correspondance* 1:56. Horbach was a professor at the *collège* at Rouen.

Flaubert's fetishism; nothing expresses more clearly the dreams of his passivity and the fact that his homosexuality is indirect and secondary. But since the Garçon is involved, that is not what is at issue here: having noted the matrix of his phantasmagorias, we must see them *in themselves*, as we are given them, within the Garçonic Legend. In this light, the dildos, abruptly and, in a sense, gratuitously evoked, have something suspect about them. Gustave, at the time, knows quite well that Madame Flaubert's phallus is imaginary—"I know very well, but all the same . . ." And if he orders it here by the dozen, it is certainly not *despite* its unreality but *because of it*. A magnificent hoax! These fakes have only the appearance of the masculine member: they represent man's domination by woman, the fetishization of the penis, and at the same time its mystifying metamorphosis into an inanimate object. In short, traps: if some unsuspecting companion happened to touch one under a dress, he would be disturbed, like the man with the floating sugar cube, like Père Eudes's boarder. And everyone would roar with laughter: "It's wooden! It's wooden!" But the laughers are themselves victims: they are made fools of, they are castrated, the dildo is a caricature of life, sexual impulses, erection. Gustave effects here the reification of man that he will later accomplish in the carriage scene. The virility we're so proud of, what is it but the power to hang a wooden twig between our legs that won't even bloom? And if that's all it is, why shouldn't a woman have the right to do the same? The result: Gustave and his comrades are the object of a mystification that takes place at the moment of penetration, but Flaubert is perfectly conscious of the unreality into which he leads his classmates. Everything is false in these orgies: possessed by women by means of false masculine members, the companions are perhaps pleasured, but they are mistaken: it isn't the Mother-goddess that penetrates them but a piece of wood. As for the prostitutes who skewer them, they may be unrealized as man-tamers but have no sexual pleasure. What remains is a hoax subverting Gustave's oneiric sexuality, a fraudulent and mystifying figuration of coupling: the producer persuades the men of his troop that the male dream is to have oneself ridden by the female, and that this reversal of customary roles takes place at least once a year in the private rooms of the Hoax Hotel.[142]

But if the dildos, like the marble sugar cubes, are traps, if they are

142. The relation between anal coitus and coprophagy is clear: it refers to certain of Gustave's infantile fixations. It must be added that one finds a distant echo of it in Huysmanns's *Against the Grain*. Everything here is "against the grain": the woman takes the man, the anus becomes an entrance, excrement becomes food.

evoked here as disturbing signs of a generalized erosion of being by unreality, isn't the entire Festival perhaps simply a hoax? We can hardly doubt it when we remember that it takes place at the *Hoax Hotel,* and that the Garçon, as innkeeper, is master of ceremonies. So the great and sacred coprophagy takes place only in the deliberately provoked, directed oneirism of certain schoolboys. Besides, where is the proprietor? How is it that he never shows himself and that we do not know if he participates in the festivities? Maybe he has shut himself up in his office to eat a good steak accompanied by a good bordeaux, laughing in his drunkenness at the joke he is playing on his clients. They too remain invisible: not a soul stirring, corridors with voices thundering out indecent orders; as for the staff, no sign of them at all: there is not a single bellboy hurrying through the corridors, carrying buckets full of the precious food. Empty corridors, mechanical voices: this evocation is meant to be grotesque; there is something sinister about it—the flight of those long, deserted galleries is troubling. It would be wrong to point out that this presentation concerns only the Goncourts, that Gustave might have described a scene of coprophagy that was later omitted by the two brothers out of forgetfulness or an abridgment of the account. This is *possible,* of course, but highly improbable: if Flaubert had given such an account, they would have hastened to transcribe it for the pleasure of exclaiming; for the same reason, when they have almost forgotten the events of their day, the confidences of their "friend" are the last to be effaced, for these bear witness—irrefutably in their eyes—to the vulgarity of his "gross nature" and his provincialism. Besides, they wrote it up the same evening, when their memory was fresh; a *double* memory: they could compare their recollections. But above all, as little as we know of Gustave, we recognize his style. Let us recall the carriage and the robotlike voice of the invisible Léon: a box speaking. On the other hand, Gustave knows how to show the anguishing absence of men in the buildings they have constructed to live in, and this absence becomes the very meaning of the edifice. Among a hundred examples, let me recall only Baptisto at the beginning of *Bibliomanie:* "How proud and powerful he was when he gazed down into the vast galleries where his eyes were lost in books! If he raised his head? Books! If he lowered it? Books! To the right, to the left, still more!" Galleries, books: nothing but human products. Man is there, however, he *is* this desert, the inert product of his own products. The Hoax Hotel resembles this library: it represents the collectivization of a single thought that preserves the austerity and the spareness of autism. Gustave might well say, I *am* the Hoax Hotel—or, rather, the Hoax Hotel and the Garçon are one and the same. Which explains the absence of the proprietor: he cannot be summed up in any particular room because he is identified with the building that contains them all. The young man transforms himself into wells of shit before the eyes of his classmates who lean over the rim, fascinated, fall into the hole, and drown in the filth.

There is a catch: an ostensible human sacrifice followed by a secret genocide. If we want to grasp the mechanics of it, let us reread the text one more time: "The Garçon had a whole history to which everyone contributed something. He made poetry and ended by keeping a Hoax Hotel," etc. To his two colleagues Flaubert insists on two particular points: the Garçon is a *character,* he has a *history;* in other words, whatever he represents, he is a concrete and singular being. History is temporalization: we know that for Gustave it is involuted; evoking the life of his character, he does not hesitate to show it as a process of degradation. Despite the ambiguity of the construction, the use of the verb *to end* is not a mistake: the Garçon *began* with poems and *ended* with the Festival of Shit.

Gustave at this time is in the midst of a long and violent crisis that will lead him from pre-neurosis to the attack at Pont-l'Evêque and to neurosis properly speaking: the poet is effaced to the advantage of the artist in the course of a painful mutation whose steps we shall retrace in a subsequent chapter. For the moment, he at once doubts himself ("Fire is burning my soul but my head is made of ice; formerly, I had thoughts, now not one . . . And yet all has not been said. Nothing to say, to stand there mute in the presence of this idiot world looking at us . . ."), doubts language, which he judges incapable of rendering his ecstasies ("The more I think, the less I speak"), doubts poetry itself ("What to say? Is that the limit of art? And is poetry another world *every bit as false as the other?"*). The three citations between parentheses are taken from *Smarh:* that unhappy hermit would like to be a poet but discovers that he is too small for himself; at the same time he wonders if poetry is not a practical joke, and the conclusion of the work seems to be an affirmative answer. Thenceforth it also issues from Yuk; the Muse who whispers to Musset, "Poet, take up your lute," is Yuk disguised as a naked woman. Let us recall that this god no sooner opens his mouth than he lets lose "a tangle of calumnies, lies, chimeras, *and poetries."* Gustave considers himself—as he often repeats in his *Souvenirs*—a "great man manqué"; for him, the practical joke is double: poetry is only appearance; it has offered itself to him and suddenly evaporated, he has mistaken his pride for genius

213

("Pride—Pride! Blood of the poet!"). This is the moment he begins to fear *ending* as a notary in Brittany or a deputy prosecutor in Yvetot.

One fine day, dreaming of the adventure of living, one Sunday, no doubt, or during vacation, in the solitude of his room at the Hôtel-Dieu, he discovers the last avatar of the Garçon; he will be an inn-keeper, like Gustave the notary, in order to put an end to things. Inventing the Hoax Hotel was all it needed for the morose and anx-ious adolescent to direct the collective laughter of his comrades at his melancholy. His own end appears to him, transposed from tragic to comic, as he will soon retell it with great ferocity while attributing it to his characters. Yuk inspired the Garçon's poems. What poems? Dirty rhymes or elegies? We don't know, but it's all the same. In the first case, poetry is ridiculed on the spot as Lamartinian verse is subjected to scatological ends;[143] in the second, it can create an illusion for a time, but its comic quality resembles the business of the Gothic ec-stasies: a deluded turd mistakes its stink for perfume. Nothing is lost in waiting, and its essence will be unveiled at the Hoax Hotel by the annual festival which sums up an experience and a whole life: the truth of poetry is coprophagy. Gustave's ambivalence is revealed, however, in the fact that the passage from poetry to business is pre-sented as a failure. When the Garçon becomes an innkeeper, he *is finished*. Such is the first moment of the operation he attempts at the beginning of term to work on his comrades; it is the Passion of Gustave the failure, the human sacrifice for which they are greedy and which he never tires of representing to them. But genocide is not far off: "It's from de Sade!" exclaim the bewildered Goncourts. And it is true that his masochism becomes the means of his sadism: the schoolboys laugh, some play the Garçon, others provide the repartee, they are all demoralized.

Astonishing. A piece of slander, a lie, can harm on the condition that the interlocutor takes it, if only for a moment, for truth or at least remains uncertain and cannot decide what is false and what is true. But the Garçon? All the members of the troop know that he is a fiction and that they are its authors; nothing he says is believed or believable, it is a game, the Festival of Shit is a *Commedia dell'Arte* scenario. How could they suffer from this "perpetual joke"? Well, precisely: they suffer from it because it is only a joke and because it is perpetual,

---

143. Or pornographic: Alfred sometimes distracted himself from his boredom by versifying his sexual exploits or Gustave's. His obvious purpose was to humiliate Ro-mantic—and classical—poetry by using the high style for treating low subjects (or those held to be such).

214

meaning that it possesses them and compels them to perpetuate it. Demoralization, the unique function and sole passion of the "eternal monster," reaches perfection when a fable known as such and, better still, invented in common, has the effect of tormenting its authors and degrading them in their own eyes. This can happen only in certain groups in which the collective makes itself the guardian of a particular fiction and forces each individual member to perpetuate it through the perpetual unrealization of his person. This is the case with the Garçon, a kind of totem, unique symbol of the integration of the "jokers" with what Gustave calls their "freemasonry." In fact, this semisecret little society has no purpose other than the Garçonic ceremonies; the scamps, who are all "Garçon"[144]—as the members of the same clan are all Lizard or all Tortoise—cannot stop actualizing this character and his universe through daily inventions, even though they are afraid of what they invent. Their membership in a small, sworn group (the vow is implicit) means that each of them is unrealized by all the others and unrealizes them by unrealizing himself. As a result, the imaginary creation of the group acquires a social consistency and is, *for this particular society,* the collective dimension of each of them; unreal as object, the imaginary is real as a bond, whereby it governs and vampirizes the individuals who perpetuate its being. Somehow it is always *elsewhere,* and, as a result, each one can be integrated into the community only by internalizing the general fiction, by making himself its coauthor. Hence, the gestures and repartee he invents are adapted to the situation of the group—which is at once fictive and constraining—and are determined as a function of previous inventions. Without ceasing to be pure appearance, these previous inventions acquire, because of their irreversibility, that particular being which belongs to past events and might be defined as the impossibility of not having been; these jests took place, no part of them can be altered, and their *ne variatur* becomes their exigency: it is up to everyone today to change himself in order to remain faithful to them. And, of course, those who watch the spectacle *from the outside* without participating in it will say more correctly: you cannot change anything *in what Pagnerre* brought to the Garçon the other day. But *on the inside* there is no more Pagnerre, there is only the Garçon and his ministers; the actor today must refer to the Garçon's former words and gestures. His anxiety grows: will he ever escape from this matrix of unreality? Will he ever find the real again? Will he come to believe

---

144. Even those who never acted out the character.

in this "tangle of chimeras" and seriously take himself for the character he is playing? Moreover, he plays his role with a strange, fascinated certainty: how can he do otherwise when he senses that he is believed? Each one, indeed, to unrealize himself better, believes as an unreal being in the reality of the others' unreality. At this point Yuk has won: the imaginary, socialized, becomes a prison and a gentle anguish. Even if it is produced *for laughs*, the laughter itself is unrealized and imposes itself on the laughers as the single admissible reaction in circumstances which have been defined in common. Gustave, the consummate ringleader, need only propose the most unpleasant themes with a straight face: a discomfort settles in and perpetuates itself, unacknowledged.

This is what he's done, the traitor, with his Hoax Hotel. The Festival of Shit is in itself a trap: he would have us believe that through this foul ceremony, man reaches the deepest level of human nature and, reentering himself in the form of excrement, *consecrates* his ignominiousness. Certainly his comrades are not unaware that this is merely an image, a symbol—none of them will really taste the sacred food; coprophagy, they know too, has its ardent defenders, but these are too few in number for it to be seen as a general practice of humanity. Gustave, however, uses his art to persuade them that by participating fictively in this fiction of ceremony, they will give an epic but basically correct representation of the human condition. It is as though he were telling them: "If men are not as we depict them, it is out of inadequacy of being and bloodlessness: if they dared to follow their inclinations to the end, they would eat their shit with jubilation. The Garçon, man and giant in one, is *man as he should be*. By hyperbolizing his stupidity—which is none other than his materiality—we are raising him to his *eidos* without ever leaving the realm of the imaginary, for the Idea, virtual and nonrealized truth, can be actualized only if it is acted out." To depict man "as he should be" was the aim two centuries earlier of an illustrious fellow-citizen; he can therefore be taken as a model. In order "to disparage the human race," however, he made use of the sublime above, whereas his great grandnephews more willingly use the sublime below. Don Quixote, adds Gustave's embodiment of Yuk, is undeniably Man; yet there were far fewer knights errant in the seventeenth century than coprophagics in the nineteenth century. So, to our task! Work, make the effort, and be assured that the Garçon will be for our time what the noble *hidalgo* was for the time of Cervantes.

He has tricked them, he's got them: he has launched them, they walk, they run; whether acting or story telling, the unfortunate boys are in the midst of a nightmare; they throw themselves voraciously onto platters of excrement, shamming coprophagy with hearty truculence, or else they take a close look at the stuff, pick at it, act the gourmet: in Bordeaux, *it* is much better than in Rouen. Each of them, gripped by a dark collective enthusiasm, is perfectly conscious of fabricating a directed nightmare, but despite the horror they feel, the unity of the group is so strong that they plunge into the toilets, madly determined to go the whole hog; they vie to be most ignoble in order to expose what they believe to be the Idea of man. Thinking that what they are doing is truer than the true, they reinvent a human race—*their* race—which repels them, and these children of man are constrained to laugh at it as soon as possible in order to withdraw solidarity from the man they have forged, all of them excited, laughing in horror, all shouting, running around from one "caricature" to another, to avoid recognizing themselves in the monster they enact in vain. This is the moment of demoralization: alone, each of them would resurface, would find himself again, *real*, in the light of reality; together, they are at once overexcited and crushed by the terrible consistency of filth—which is nothing but the vow each of them made to be the *filthiest* of the group. An infernal contest is instituted, a black reflection of scholarly competition; they will not get out of it—the unreal sticks to their skins.

Gustave does not interfere: everything will happen of its own accord. It is enough if he intervenes from time to time to compel the "caricature" or, when resolution is foundering, to set it back on the right track. What vengeance! We recall with what a bitter mixture of envy and obscure respect he had verified the *reality* of his schoolmates; those future physicians, lawyers, engineers showed themselves to be quick, positive, efficient; they had eyes only for being and truth; those pint-sized Achilles scorned the Flauberts' younger son, mocked his ecstasies and his great staring eyes, saw him merely as a future tamer of shadows, a maker of books. In sum, what they condemned unconditionally in the family idiot was imagination, an "exultation of the brain akin to madness." That needn't be a problem: he has decided to take them all and damn them *through imagination;* in their limited minds, which are so practical and reasonable, that faculty, though crude and rudimentary, is not entirely atrophied. That is all he asks: he sets to work right away, patiently awakens their imagination, develops it, exalts it, then exasperates it by the laughter he has stolen from them; as soon as they want to take part in the spectacle, they become images in their turn. Do you sense, Alfred would say, the beauty of this trap: Doctor Achille Flaubert, *caught by imagination?* Achille: no, alas! He escapes. But his future emulators have fallen into the snare: fascinated by the gigantic laughter of the Garçon, each of them wanted to embody the character in order to laugh at him all alone, like a crowd. And no sooner had one of them entered into the monster's skin than he discovered—too late—that his laughter "was not laughter" but an imaginary hilarity. As for the object of this forced derision, he thought he perceived that this was man, and that consequently he was laughing at himself. So be it; he has put his rage into it; guided by a bad angel, he has invented a grotesque monster, he has laughed the way a mangy dog scratches—until he bleeds. Gustave has condemned them to their laughter. And the funniest thing, the little avenger thinks, is that they are laughing at a creature that does not exist. The Garçon is not man, not even the idea of man. He is a three-stage construction comprising a false man mocked by a fictive giant who represents being and is mocked in turn by Yuk, the image of nothingness. Flaubert knows this but does not say so. Hence the Garçon, played by Pagnerre, has nothing in common with the Garçon played by Gustave. When Gustave takes the role, it is a perfect totalization: three laughters in one; or, if you like, the laughter is mocking itself, knows itself to be an imposture, and is delighted to be one yet does not rehabilitate the fake of the first stage, who is stupid enough to take himself for a man. When one of the schoolboys ventures to pantagruelize, the two first stages evaporate; what remains is an idiotic monster who makes himself hoarse with feigned hilarity, convinced that the human race, in his person as in anyone's, is basically this possessed character struggling and shouting to escape the horror of an imaginary character he believes himself to be and whom, in fact, he is limited to inventing. The monster thinks, I have driven these realists crazy, and he is thoroughly cheered.

What shall we conclude from this first sorting? If Gustave mystifies his comrades, if radical evil is only a fiction, what does he hold to be the truth of man and of the universe? Does he believe that we live in the best of all possible worlds? Or, in any event, that there might be worse ones? Shall we allow that this purveyor of bad jokes is an optimist? We wouldn't know him very well in that case. Under the circumstances, however, we must pose the question of his relations with truth.

The answer is simple, and we have already given it in other chapters apropos of other problems: Flaubert's constituted passivity forbids him any practical relation to truth; to be frank, he cannot even conceive of what a true idea might be. When the word *truth* appears in his discourse, it refers either to the judgments of others—principally to those of scientists and practitioners which he knows are founded on methodical inquiries—or else to a certain subjective state, that is, to a vivid and transitory belief. In the first case, scientific truths are imposed on him by virtue of the principle of authority without ever convincing him completely; in the second, just when his subjective adherence represents the idea to him as true, it denounces itself as a simple belief without revealing to him what certainty might be: "There is no such thing as a true idea or a false idea. At first you eagerly adopt things, then you reflect, then doubt, and there you remain."[145] What is left? Nothing. By raping Truth, Yuk has broken her neck. The real is not *true*, the unreal is not *false*. Then, it will be asked, isn't the Garçon a *false* image of man? Doesn't he mean to deceive his comrades? Let us say that *for Gustave* this character is neither true nor false: he is unreal, that is all. The trap comes into play when his comrades, believing in Truth and Error, take their creation for a myth—a hyperbolic or epic metaphor—that restores man *in his truth*. They are the ones who trap themselves because *in their system of thought* the imaginary is at the service of praxis and, consequently, of truth. When in sound mind, they resort to images only in order to determine, in the course of a mental experiment, the consequences of a possible action. The imaginary child, who takes the image for an end in itself, whatever its relation to the real, is delighted by the vicious circle he has imposed on his comrades by forcing them to interpret through their realistic categories (truth, utility, etc.) their total and veritably mad unrealization. These unfortunates, subjected to a monstrous idol, are sufficiently insane to believe that the "tangle of calumnies" that demoralizes them can *be of use*, that laughter is a means of knowledge, and that the ignoble the best approach to man. To man *as he should be*, in any case. Gustave enjoys himself immensely: speaking their language, he has put this madness into their heads; the *should-being* of man, what does this mean if God does not exist? If the cosmos is nothing but a great heap of matter, adrift and uncreated? These overexcited schoolboys ought rather to speak of the should-being of God. In the mechanistic universe, fact is king; an absolute nominal-

145. *Souvenirs*, p. 96.

ism: no *eidos;* man is what he is, nothing more, nothing less, since no one in Heaven demands that he come close to an essence that doesn't even exist.

Such is what I shall call one *attitude* of Gustave's toward his own creature. But there are others that he adopts by turns, according to his whim and the circumstances. For, as we know, he is a materialist out of spite, and two ideologies never cease contesting each other within him. After all, he too has reproached, still reproaches, God for His absence; he too, in his bitter agnosticism, condemns the human race—quite unjustly—because it is without God. He too, in his solitary exultations, has in utter seriousness played the mediator between the infinite negative and our Lilliput. The difference between these ascensions—which originate in rage and shame—and the Garçon, a three-stage strategy, can be summed up in a single word: laughter. While he clowns in public, mocking even his own dolorism, he weeps in secret and draws some consolation from the stories he tells himself: he will be greater thàn all of them, like the Garçon; he will make heads roll, he will be cruel, merciless, like Yuk; he will demoralize the human race, like the Garçonic trinity. Sobs, forced cries of triumph, hate-filled broodings, dreams of vengeance: this is what we find in the dark and sinister tales he shows to no one but two childhood friends. This is the same adolescent who writes, at several months' interval, the two "formulas," as he calls them: "I believe that humanity has only one purpose, to suffer," and: "I love to see humanity debased, this spectacle gives me pleasure when I am weary."[146] Comparing these two maxims, we find the explanation of the Garçonic joke: since that wretched strumpet loves to suffer, since—like me—she draws her dignity from suffering, let's debase her by infecting her with a colossal laughter that will ridicule her pain, let us make the unhappiest and the proudest man unable to look at himself in a mirror without seeing an obscene, grotesque monkey he will be forced to laugh at. Through phantasms, let us compel the entire race to be penetrated by an unreal but tenacious baseness, and let us through various stratagems induce the race to become really ignoble in order to conform to its image. In those moments, as we can see, Gustave does not aim so much to *expose* our baseness to us as to *affect* us with an *artificial* baseness that will end by becoming habitual. Men are not commonly attracted to their excrement; yet rather ordinary illusions will persuade them to regard themselves as turds. In this second attitude, Gustave

146. *Souvenirs,* pp. 90 and 109.

does not scorn his peers out of hand; he even recognizes that dolorism—of which he is proud—is a practice common to everyone; he simply hates them and attempts to change them into swine precisely because he does not succeed in finding them sufficiently repugnant.

He often takes part in the game himself. Then he goes mad like his comrades; fascinated by his invented character, he bustles around, gesticulates, becomes intoxicated by his own paradoxes, takes pleasure in his gigantic strength as much as in his vileness. If the other actors respond to his attempt, if the spectators laugh, he feels that he is asserting himself and is enclosing, like a gigantic folktale figure, all his comrades in his loins. In those moments, author, actor, and director, he rejoices: he returns to his old passion, the theater; he plays the Garçon as he played Pourceaugnac: the malicious intention becomes secondary; the essential thing is to have genius. Conscious of his generosity, he makes a gift of his person, unrealizing himself in order to give his comrades the unity of a group-in-fusion. The intention to do harm is nearly forgotten: he is leading the realists to the superior spheres of unreality, and he feels real sympathy for the scamps he has overwhelmed and who, in return, agree to play the supporting roles so that he can play the main character. In sum, he keeps play-acting, now diabolical and now possessed, now mystifier and now simple actor, now sadist, now *heautontimoroumenos;* and what matters to him is that his comrades, as satellites, revolve and play-act with him.

At least, this is how Gustave presents the thing. He does not entirely convince us. What we are missing is the *others' point of view.* How did the Garçon come to hold such fascination for Pagnerre and his pals for so long? Did they let themselves fall into the trap in complete ignorance, like birds in a snare? Were they so heedless? I can hardly believe that: since they pursued this heavy-handed joke, which must have horrified them, for *at least* five years, they must have found something in it. In this case, perhaps the anomaly on which Gustave prided himself, and of which he deeply regretted being the sole victim, is, contrary to what he thought, really the most widespread thing in the world. If that should be true, if Gustave's classmates resemble him, then he has partially misunderstood them and has not *situated* himself in relation to them. And this necessarily means that he has escaped himself. We shall completely understand the Garçon as a collective enterprise and the personalizing movement of its principal creator at this stage only if we attempt to reconstruct the totalizing temporalization that led all these adolescents toward the 1848 revolu-

tion and the coup d'état of 2 December, in short, toward the destiny
that awaited them. What was a Rouen schoolboy like between 1830
and 1840? There is no need to depict Flaubert's classmates one by one,
but we shall give them, through a narrative based on the school ar-
chives, a dimension that their comrade couldn't see, or didn't want to
see: historicity.

When Gustave entered the *collège*, something had just occurred: in
the spring of 1831, the students staged an act of rebellion, and this in
turn threw them into a lengthy undertaking, which was sealed by
eventual failure. They had discovered their own *Fatum*, their being-in-
danger-in-history; they would continue to give themselves over to
rearguard actions against the administration, which represented the
"forces of order," and against an invisible enemy—we shall mention
it soon again—that sought to atomize them. March 1831: expulsion of
the student Clouet; December 1839: expulsion of the student Flaubert;
between these two events, eight years of struggle, a pitiless involution of the group, internalizing and singularizing the history of
French society.[147] If this was the case, Gustave did not see that he was
entering a community instituted by hatred, by the determination to
resist the vanquishing enemy to the last man. Having eyes only for
cyclical returns, he did not notice the adventure which, cutting across
the circles of repetition, was twisting and transforming them into *a
single spiral*, symbol of historical temporalization. For this reason he
did not do justice to his comrades, who were inventing and suffering
their history; what he describes as natural qualities in individuals are
the moments of a collective withdrawal. The Garçon must therefore
be *made temporal* insofar as he is a collective creation. Who is to say
that he did not appear at the very moment when the Rouen schoolboys needed him? Perhaps these young men, conditioned by the
whole of their history, embodied themselves, toward the end, in an
imaginary character in order to effect through the mediation of the
unreal an impossible and necessary insight. Let us look at the facts.

B. HISTORY AS PSYCHODRAMA

Until 1830, the *collège* had no internal history. Altered by every change
of regime but always *from outside*, it remained purely an object of
national history, an inert container, a poor conductor, incapable of

147. Lacking connections with the real forces of the country, these children who believed for a moment that they were subjects of history were never more than its objects.

transmitting to the students the great movements agitating French society. Not that nothing gets through: what does get through is distorted; the children periodically, inexplicably, receive powerful and violent shock waves. They learn about history in the making from their families or, perhaps, in the street. The school establishment, moreover, knows no historical time, and the students live there in wholesome, cyclical monotony, receiving an education defined in the Royal Almanac thus: "The rule, the manner, and the objects of instruction received by the students are the same in all secondary schools. Students shall be taught religion, ancient and modern languages, belles-lettres, philosophy, mathematics, physics, chemistry, natural history, geography, etc." Religion comes first—the Catholic religion, of course. It is *taught:* isn't it the religion of the vast majority of the French? And how can it be taught without compelling the student to practice it? No one will understand the divine gift Christ made us without receiving his body and his blood; since communion is included in the tutorial system, the boys are sent every week to confession. Therefore, the church reigns supreme at the *collège,* it imposes its dogmas and its rites on the sons of liberals, it tries to discipline their hearts; and the heads of the families, former Jacobins, are not embarrassed to accuse the church in private of "kidnapping." The sons fulfill their religious duties, but many, closing their minds to the insidious discourse of clerics, are conscious of remaining faithful to their bourgeois origins.

The July Revolution at first seemed to them a dazzling confirmation of their views: with liberalism in power, it was the end of state religion; the citizen-king, consecrated by La Fayette, given a plebiscite by the crowd, could not be the elder son of the Church. This meant that the arrogant swagger of parish priests and bigots, idol carriers, would no longer be seen in the streets and, concomitantly, that religious practices at the *collège,* though not forbidden, would become optional. The first part of the program was realized without difficulty: the regime cleaned the streets and street corners; the Congrégation, flabbergasted, retreated underground. But at the start of the school year in October 1830, the schoolboys were taken down a peg: it was still a theocracy at school, as before, and the chaplain maintained his power over souls. The boys did not understand at all: the party of the liberals had taken power, their fathers had triumphed; why leave their sons to rot in darkness? Was it negligence? Treason? These children lived uneasily through the first trimester; they interrogated their families, who were evasive, who counseled patience; they were two steps away from suspecting their parents, which would have broken their hearts. Happily, after a sullen trimester, in December the sword falls, La Fayette is dismissed. On the last day of the year, a child who has not yet left his family home writes to a comrade eighteen months his senior, who is already a *collégien:* "My friend, they have just sent packing the bravest of the brave, white-haired La Fayette, the freedom of two worlds; friend, I will send you my political disquisitions of a constitutional liberal." If the event is this troubling to little Gustave, ordinarily moved chiefly by his personal problems, what must its effect have been on the schoolboys? For most of these already politicized adolescents, La Fayette, the "kingmaker," appears to be the champion of liberalism and the qualified representative of their fathers. Everything is clarified—or so they believe: their fathers have not betrayed them, the sole traitor is the citizen-king. By dismissing his benefactor, this monarch is attacking their families; he pretended to adopt liberal doctrine, but now that he is on the throne he is going to suppress, one by one, each of the liberties won by the people. It is now up to the sons to descend into the arena and fly to the aid of the Revolution.

On this erroneous assumption, the student Clouet, a little political genius, forms a plan of action. Since the liberals are sleeping, they must be shocked awake. Freedoms are indivisible: you cannot stifle one without strangling the others. To highlight the danger threatening the press and political rights, it will be enough to expose the fraudulent operation that in certain sectors has deprived future citizens of their freedom of thought; the Church no longer controls the streets, but its grip on public instruction has not been loosened. The schoolboys are going to take the initiative by setting themselves against it, as they are the first to suffer. Clouet secretly conspires with four or five comrades: they will publicly refuse to make confession. What can a chaplain do when several boys say no to him? Have them dismissed from school? So much the better: he will fall into the trap the confederates have laid for him. To obtain the expulsion of four children who refuse the rites of Catholicism is to proclaim that religious freedom does not exist in the institutions of the State. A provocation, in short. And the most vicious one: the chaplain and the headmaster, if the boys persist, *must* expel them or lose face. Clouet and his friends count on this blunder and the disturbance that will follow to awaken the dozing liberals in the two Chambers, even in the innermost circle of the government: summonses, a press campaign, the fall of the ministry . . . At this point the children will withdraw, saying to their fathers: "Your turn to play! Take the power from our feeble hands."

The first part of the program is executed without difficulty. At the beginning of March, the conspirators refuse confession. The chaplain informs the headmaster, who meets with the rebels: they persist in their refusal. The headmaster is at a loss. He resigns himself to expelling the guilty, but clear evidence that Clouet's calculation was not so stupid is the reason the headmaster invokes in his report to the rector to justify his decision: they have been guilty, he writes, of an "act of insubordination," of a "plot intended to compromise order." The *religious* aspect of their crime, hastily mentioned, figures not at all among the official considerations. Well, all right! the poor man seems to say, these sorry individuals have flouted the chaplain and challenged his sacred authority. But the sacred is none of *my* business, I know nothing about it, I don't take sides, I am merely stating that the *lay* order has been disturbed to the extent that this priest is part of the staff and, as such, possesses powers that must be respected: I am not the one who has packed this institution with priests, but since they are here, I must make sure that they remain here unless the government retires them and gives me orders to prevent their return. So soon after the three glorious days of July, it would have been foolhardy to express oneself otherwise; for some months the government seemed bent on a prudent conservatism, but the liberals remained in power.

The same phase of the operation surpasses their wildest hopes: the school revolts out of solidarity with Clouet. Reprisals: the rhetoric students spurn the chaplain, the eighth-year class verbally abuses the English teacher; the teacher of philosophy, Abbé Denize, is sorely abused several days in a row because he is a churchman and an accomplice of the priestly party. A short while later, the boarding students of the eighth year are at it again, bombarding the proctor with eggs; in his distress he forgets himself sufficiently to strike two of the students. The tumult redoubles; the two victims publicly accuse their adversary: blows and injuries! It is hastily established that they are the guilty ones—they threw the eggs with their own hands. Immediate expulsion. The tension grows. On the morning of 6 March, the day students of the eighth unite and declare solidarity with the boarding students: they vow on their honor to get their two comrades readmitted or themselves expelled along with them. On the 7th, in the early hours, they go into action with a determination that takes the administrators unawares; a sit-down strike, occupation of various sites; they rejoin the boarding students in the dormitory, refuse to go to class, and barricade themselves. The proctor tries to parry as quickly as possible: he "rushes around among the upperclassmen," according to his own account, negotiates with them for three hours, obtains their neutrality by the narrowest margin. During this time, the strikers coolly give themselves over to the most criminal depredations: they tear up the flagstones: through the shattered windows they bombard the building in which the august Academic Council—including the "notables" of Rouen, in particular Doctor Flaubert—is deliberating, having been convened in an emergency session. Supported by this constituted body, the administration calls the forces of order to its aid. Not the police: the cops must not enter the school, nor must they strike the offspring of the rising class. The administration calls the firemen and the national guard. The national guardsmen are the fathers and older brothers of the mutineers. So we have the fathers against the sons—and highly discomfited: if they were to storm the barricades, they would be put in the position of slaughtering their own children, which would have been thought barbarous at the time. But what can be done without bludgeoning? The place is surrounded, the troops are massed in the corridors, blocking the entrances—and then an attempt is made to negotiate. In vain. The insurgents go only as far as to make their conditions known: the two boys expelled will be readmitted, no sanction will be taken against those who supported them. The administration having declared it will not give in to blackmail, the occupation continues.

What a celebration! From the fourth year to the last, there is not a single student who is not waiting, holding his breath: they dared! They are standing up against the grown-ups and commanding a certain respect, unmasking the weakness of authority. On this day there is a firm belief, at the *collège*, in the reversibility of merits: the strikers are in the process of changing life: if they win, all students will be subjects, the administrators and teachers will become their approved objects. Power to the children!

They are not going to win: in this third moment of the enterprise, the difficulties begin. One wonders if the older students, who this very morning admired the younger ones without following them, feel some remorse. Can those students from rhetoric and philosophy imagine what would have happened if the school had been occupied by all the boys together? If they can, it is not without discomfort: it would have taken nothing for them to join the rebels that morning when the headmaster had them in a stalling action; they now know that his purpose was not so much to convince them as to give the national guard time to take up its positions.

Night falls. The strikers appraise the situation and ascertain that they are isolated: enclosed in the ghetto they themselves have chosen, they can expect nothing from the outside. Give themselves up? Never! Therefore, negotiations: they demand the readmission of the two boarding students, and for themselves immunity. Of their two demands, the authorities accept only the second: no sanction will be taken against the strikers. They had better be content with this lame compromise. In a way, they have failed; their comrades remain in exile, the entire eighth year class has not been reunited with them. But, taking things *politically*, their action, without aiming to, has attained much more important objectives: they have shown their comrades that a general insurrection is possible at the *collège*. The eighth-year class has ridiculed its tyrants: so as not to give in to this handful of adolescents, the administration had to resort to calling the national guard into a temple of culture; the headmaster—who was in constant communication with the rectorate—wound up, despite a massive support of shopkeepers in uniform, by concluding a wretched truce, as though he were crying out to everyone: "I am only a paper tiger." When the administration expelled Clouet for "having been the brains behind a kind of plot to compromise seriously the prevailing order" and the two boarders of the eighth-year class for having thrown a couple of eggs at the Proctor's topcoat, it marked the boundaries of what was tolerable and what was not. The strikers, in consequence of their vow, deliberately transgressed those boundaries and came down immediately on the side of the intolerable, in a plot not to "compromise seriously" the established order but radically to destroy it to the advantage of a spectacular disorder, prelude to an unknown and terrible order. This was a premeditated mutiny, an astounding refusal of obedience; it was depredations, vandalism, and bombardment, not just of the proctor but of the whole Academic Council, something that would justify the expulsion of the least guilty. And the strikers retire with the honors of war, unpunished, unvanquished. Therefore the administration is at fault: "Either it was wrong to punish our comrades, or it was wrong not to punish us." An exemplary revolt: it showed that power is weak when it is unjust. This is not true, of course, and power, whatever it is, is unjust to the same degree that it defines its own justice; but it makes an impression on these young bourgeois, who are badly in need of idealism: the cause of the schoolboys is just; let them unite, they will triumph. Not one of the strikers wants to stop just as things are going so well: it's only a beginning, let's keep up the fight. And why, indeed, shouldn't they keep it up? The next day, when they return to school, their comrades, charged up, arrange a triumphal celebration for them. The agitation continues and spreads. The moderates are won over; the upperclassmen want to take things in hand and reestablish their authority by their feats of daring. Just let the headmaster take it into his head to cajole them again! They would let him have it this time, he would know he was in real trouble.

He already knew it; it was evident from the first: his magnanimity, far from appeasing the rebels, encouraged them; he ran through the classrooms, saw sparkling eyes everywhere, came back to his office to write up his report to the rector with great urgency: without quick and decisive action, everything was going to blow up, it was a matter of hours. It did not take the Academic Council long to understand either. They informed the parents, who were enraged to discover that their offspring were putting them in danger. Measures and overtures, confidential messages, clandestine meetings: now it was the adults conspiring against the children. The schoolboys would learn the result of these counterrevolutionary plots early in the morning of 10 March, from the notices posted on the closed doors of the *collège:* this institution is "temporarily dismissed."

They should have thought about that! To expel everyone "temporarily" is to expel no one; the promise has been kept. At the same time, by means of a sudden decompression they are atomized, and every little atom is sent home to his family and submitted to brainwashing. The reopening of school is scheduled, but they are not notified: Easter is approaching, the vacation tends to demobilize their zeal, classes can resume at the beginning of April without danger. And if, after consultation of dossiers, secret meetings, the discreet intervention of notables with regard to their fathers, certain students are not at the reunion, no one will be able to blame the administration.

After Easter the schoolboys return, dumbfounded. They have lost none of their anger, but confused by these entanglements they no longer even know where the enemy is. They will fight without understanding, without even discovering whom they are fighting against; for the group they have constituted for a while, it is the end of the Apocalypse and the beginning of the reflux. They will pass through various *defensive* phases that I shall attempt to describe, and then after 1835, when they have understood and it is too late, they will burst out laughing; and the Garçon, evoked by a despair new to history, will come to fulfill their last vows.

The Counterrevolution. What stupified the mutineers of March was the welcome they received from their families: they had believed they were fighting for them; they now learned they had betrayed them. The indignant fathers boast of being the source of the general dismissal; sermons, rage, mothers' tears, sanctions, nothing is spared the children during this gloomy vacation. They have tried to explain their problem: can a state religion be tolerated at the *collège?* And the progenitors have turned a deaf ear: discipline first, no freedom without a rigorous and voluntary order. Yet these were the same men who, two years earlier, were reading Voltaire to their sons and whispering to them, smiling: crush the villains! The same men who professed that the chief virtue of the liberal must be religious tolerance. The boys cannot believe their ears: have their fathers changed? Or did the sons misunderstand their teachings? In any case they quickly learn that their parents, in this affair, are their real enemies. For four years the parents express their rage: they want a strong man at the *collège* to keep their offspring in line. And as this cannot be done without first liquidating the current administration, they give the headmaster and the proctor a difficult time of it. For four years, complaints and petitions flood the rectorate, the ministry: no one tires of signaling that the administration has lost the confidence of the good bourgeois of Rouen; they bring an inspector all the way from Paris expressly to conduct an inquiry with the parents of students. He reports that they blame the headmaster, "a good man but weak," for having "ruined discipline, having let the studies weaken . . . and having done nothing to prevent the corruption of morals." They come on strong, these sycophants. So their progeny have a poor attitude? They don't hesitate to accuse them of poor morals. Are they all thieves? Homosexuals? Not much is known; the fact is that these adolescents are corrupt. It is true that they raise Cain at school; but we shall see that this is a matter of desperate, rearguard battles. The aggressor is the father, without question. At the Academic Council, Achille-Cléophas takes personal charge of having the proctor transferred: he asks the rector for the proctor's head, judging him responsible—these are his own words—"for the decay of the *collège.*" He too, as we see, cannot control his words; discipline ruined, morals corrupted, the decay of a temple of culture—bourgeois humanism is in danger. Poor Clouet: he wanted a scandal and got one. But this was not what he had in mind: the newspapers clam up, the Assemblies are silent, and if the liberals

229

of Rouen press the government, it is to obtain administrative sanctions. Paris is scarcely disturbed, it seems, by these provincial disorders; it will wait four years before intervening.

What are we to make of these ogres of Rouen, eager to consume their own progeny? Yet they really do detest the Church and really are liberals. The explanation lies in a number of dates. Eighteen thirty: the revolution is a victory of the people that the bourgeoisie managed to snatch away from them; the bourgeois are not unaware that agitation continues in the streets: the Orleanist solution seems quite fragile to them; they are afraid. They couldn't care less about La Fayette. He was useful in July—now let him get out; Louis-Philippe is the man for them. Eighteen thirty-one: revolt of the Canuts; they are practically the masters of Lyon for forty-eight hours. Emile de Girardin is amazed to discover the "new barbarians" and candidly translates the panic of the rich in the *Journal des Débats* of 8 December, 1831:

> The sedition at Lyon has revealed a grave secret, the civil struggle that takes place in society between the class that has and the class that has not . . . No factory without workers, and with an ever-growing and always needy population of workers, no rest for society. Take away commerce, society languishes, stops moving, and dies . . . Multiply commerce and you will at the same time multiply a proletarian population that lives from day to day, and which the least incident can deprive of its means of subsistence . . .
> Every factory owner lives in his factory like the colonial plantation owners in the midst of their slaves, one against a hundred, and the sedition at Lyon is a kind of Santo Domingo insurrection . . . the middle class should know its position: it has below it a population of proletarians who agitate and simmer without knowing what they want, without knowing where they will go. What does it matter to them? They suffer. They want to change. It is from these ranks that we shall see issue forth the Barbarians who will destroy it [the middle class].

The article ends with a call to holy union: monarchists, republican, all friends! Forget your political differences: class against class!

This text, naive and cynical, represents the equivalent of a genuine insight. Saint-Marc Girardin willingly admits that "commerce" (in other words, profit) demands the multiplication of the proletariat and that *in itself* it engenders the workers' wretchedness. He also recognizes that the workers are the secret of the bourgeois class and is not afraid to call the class struggle by its name. Further, the comparison of manual workers to barbarians is significant: the barbarians owed their triumph to the decadence of the Roman empire; however tragic the death throes of the ancient world, the barbarians are the source of modern nations. Girardin knows very well that the word "barbarian" simultaneously suggests the decomposition, the chaos of a society and the painful gestation of a new society. Eighteen years later, in almost the same terms, Tocqueville will calmly predict the end of bourgeois domination. And this is certainly what is suggested in 1831, in the article in the *Journal des Débats*. Girardin's conclusion is clear: since the bourgeoisie must one day be overthrown, let's pull together, let's join forces with all the rich, *let us maintain ourselves by force* as long as possible, and after us—the deluge. His readers agree; they agree with Metternich, too, who writes on the same date: "In Germany we still have a strong attack by the middle class against the throne and the upper classes; in France, where these last two elements have nearly disappeared, the population is now in revolt against the middle class. This is only logical."[1] The "middle class" has understood: it risks losing its "security blanket," as Marx says; it pulls it close and hides beneath it. Let us restore the upper classes!

Eighteen thirty-two: more social troubles, the funeral of General Lamarque, the "affair" of the Saint-Merri monastery. Eighteen thirty-three: a tailors' strike. Eighteen thirty-four: recrudescence of the social and political agitation in Paris and Lyon. Meanwhile, the king gets rid of his liberal ministers: the government is looking for the first opportunity to take a tough stance. At Lyon, the repression is severe; in Paris, the capital, there is nothing less than a massacre: it takes place in rue Transnonain. Eighteen thirty-five: the forces of order have won the day; pursuing its advantage, the executive throws the republicans into disarray by the trials of April '35 and votes in villainous laws reestablishing censorship. This same year, as we shall see, the Rouen heads of families will have the hides of the headmaster and the proctor.

These proper folk are not so much afraid of socialism as of the Republic. In 1830, the great majority of the French had not taken part in the first Revolution; those under thirty were born under the Consulat or the Empire; those in their forties were scarcely five years old during the Terror. Yet their memories are overloaded with recollections, true or false. And witnesses are still numerous: a sixty-year-old in 1830 had already reached his majority in 1789. The adults were quite aware of the errors of their fathers inasmuch as the fathers, if they survived,

1. Letter of 10 December 1831.

did not have to be begged to tell their stories. The bourgeoisie despised 1793, in other words, the whole Revolution. Napoleon they adored; he had only one fault: he was too expensive. They draw the lessons of paternal experience and put them to use to prevent the same thing happening all over again. They hold power, true, but they will not be so stupid as to share it with the disadvantaged classes; the best way to avoid this is to hide what power they have. What good is it to drive out the aristocracy if it is replaced by an ostensible plutocracy which sooner or later will lead, through disturbances, to the aberration of democracy? The electorally qualified members of the bourgeoisie know that unless extreme caution is exercised, they are in danger of giving birth to the Republic. They know it because it has already happened. Better to associate the nobility with the exercise of power. After July 1830, the necessity of a compromise stares them in the face. Thus, even before giving themselves a constitution, the victorious bourgeoisie will hide behind the vanquished nobility: "Nothing has changed," they say. "The principle of monarchy is preserved; the aristocrats will have one Chamber for themselves alone—with the exception of a handful of commoners who do honor to France and who will be chosen by the king." These bankers, these industrialists who pull the strings of the royal puppet, the son of a regicide committed to Equality, would have it believed that the two sources of sovereignty reside in him, harmoniously married because he is the *heir*, sworn to rule by blood, by the will of God, and is also the *elect*, the sovereign whom the nation has freely given itself. This king defends the bourgeoisie against itself or, if you like, defends the liberal against the republican temptation. His monarchy is also the gold powder the bank and industry throw into the eyes of passive citizens, preserving some kind of colorful sacred pomp.

The nobility and the rich have one privilege in common: they alone can vote, hence their complicity. But their solidarity is inadequate. If the bourgeoisie wants to win over the nobility, it must take care to do nothing alarming, nor to attack its respectable beliefs, its faith; moreover, since the bourgeoisie pretends to recognize the primacy of the aristocracy, it is fitting that the aristocracy should be recognized as well in its ideology, which means, *in the first instance,* in education. The victors of July judge it politic not to touch the curriculum. The teachers will teach, as before, the acquired truths, and the chaplains the revealed ones; the children will go to confession and will take communion as before. Secondary studies will continue to be called the "humanities" and will be limited to bringing some small improvements to their object, Man. These slight precautions, which were beginning to be taken around 1825, when the two dominant classes seemed in equilibrium, will enter into history under the well-chosen name of eclecticism. In the curious pot-pourri that is the ideology of Louis-Philippe at the outset, the old monarchist thought and liberalism loosely overlap without achieving any synthesis: there is movement without transition from charismatic power to popular sovereignty, from feudal generosity to utilitarianism, from quantity to quality, from inherited rights to the rights of the citizen. The philanthropists of this compromise effortlessly reconcile two kinds of optimism: the supernatural naturalism of the aristocracy, a particularism of blood, and the bourgeois universalism of the previous century. In any case, man is good: by nature or by divine right, it's all the same because nature is only another name for the creation.

The bourgeoisie accepts this double-duty humanism all the more willingly as it has lost a considerable illusion in the course of its journey: in 1789 it considered itself the universal class, now it begins to understand that it is a particular class with its own special interests. It sorely needs a covering to hide its nakedness, gratefully takes what the Orleanists hand it, and wraps itself up. Just imagine the amazement and indignation of families when they perceive that this ruse has convinced no one. Neither the legitimist aristocracy, nor the republicans, nor the people, *nor even their own children.* When the sons declare, in March 1831, "We are not going along with the farce," the fathers understand that these scamps see the emperor quite naked,[2] and their heads swim at the idea that the hideous Republic can become, from one day to the next, the highest priority to the flesh of their flesh.

2. As we have seen, Gustave retains a dazzling memory of his encounter with the duchesse de Berry, and at the age of eleven he quite effectively translates the general contempt of the younger generation for their sovereign: "Louis-Philippe is now with his family in the city that saw the birth of Corneille. How stupid men are, how limited the people are . . . ! To run after a king, to vote 30 million francs for holidays . . . to put yourself out, for whom? For a king! . . . Oh!!! how stupid everyone is. As for me, I've seen nothing, viewed nothing, neither the king's arrival, nor the princes, nor the princesses. I went out yesterday evening only to see the fireworks, again because they pestered me." From this period on, little Flaubert detaches himself from politics: he laughs at kings, but he laughs at the republic too because the people are stupid enough, servile enough, to stand in line for their masters to pass by. Be that as it may, it is *at the collège* that he learned to scorn the monarch. His anger and the last words, "again because they pestered me," indicate that a more conciliatory Achille-Cléophas urged him to mingle with the curious and, as usual, mocked his son's grand airs. We can see in this incident a very attenuated image—neither the father nor the son were really interested in politics—of the embryonic conflict that divided these two generations.

Are the bourgeois of Rouen right to be afraid? Yes and no. Flaubert intimates—but without otherwise stating it precisely—that there were some republicans among his schoolmates. But the heroes of March '31 only thought of flying to the aid of their fathers by crushing the eclectic compromise, which they could not suspect was the work of the bourgeoisie itself. Moreover, they placed themselves under the banner of the universal and good Man of the *philosophes*—just as their parents, when they were in the opposition, had had the imprudence to evoke in the family circle the old egalitarian myth of '89 against the arrogance of the nobility. The weakness of liberalism is its instability: if left to itself, it will go on to demand universal suffrage. Therefore, in fighting for the advent of (bourgeois) Man, the children will sooner or later be led to claim equal rights for all citizens. They hardly know this; their parents know it, however, and recognize their sons with abhorrence as the forerunners of a new Terror. During the violent days of March, the adolescents had experienced direct democracy; in the course of the disturbances that followed the expulsion of Clouet, something was born that began to emerge into full daylight at the time of the vow of 6 March: an insurrectional practice aimed at replacing the hierarchical authority with the sovereignty of the sworn group over each of its members. These young bourgeois were, of course, inspired by the bourgeois vow of the Jeu de Paume. But by the sudden explosion of that terror-fraternity which is the dictatorship of freedom they had simply demonstrated that a revolutionary order is possible and legitimate, whatever the social unity envisaged, so long as it remains the living and intimate product of the group; in other words, as long as it is nothing but the totalization of human relations produced in this community and experienced—all for one, one for all—*internally*. The schoolboys did not know how to decipher their experience: they did not know that for thirty-six hours—from the vow until the truce—they had exercised and maintained against all an inalienable power that was abolished only with their dispersal. Even more than the abolition of the electoral tax, their fathers dreaded popular power; when they saw it revived within the four walls of a dormitory, they resolved to crush it. This is one of the most amusing aspects of the misunderstanding: the parents reproached their children for constituting themselves without a mandate; the children, amazed, responded that they had been mandated by their parents. Dialogues between the deaf, which ended with a double accusation: the fathers accused their sons of betraying their families and their class; the sons reproached their fathers for disowning themselves and, as a direct consequence, betraying their children. The sons were right: they had betrayed no one, and their parents in the course of a few months had demoralized them forever.

It is time to abandon these treacherous Moseses of the bourgeoisie in order to return to their little victims: these boys thought they were going crazy between '31 and '35, and they thought so for two reasons, each of which necessitates the other.

1. *The reflux.* During the last school trimester, they put their heads together. These proud combatants try to preserve—out of voluntarism, loyalty?—the conviction that they are the elect of history, that they serve the most righteous of causes. They have merely lost a battle, not the war; they are young, the future is theirs, this is only a beginning. They may be making plans for the opening of the new school year in October. When the summer holidays come, they are dispersed; once they are alone, doubt penetrates them, or rather they internalize in the form of doubt the triumphant certainties announced by a hostile environment: and what if we had lost the war? Still, nothing is lost; they will continue to fight. What is happening inside them is deeper, more obscure, unsayable. I cannot evoke their defeat without thinking of the original drama as Mallarmé retraces it: "He throws the dice, the bet is made . . . He who created finds himself again to be matter, blocks, dice."[3] Between July and October the schoolboys have lived, each on his own account, the Mallarméan moment, pebble of eternity, *paradox;* these children believed they were historical agents, they threw the dice, made their bet, and—he who created finds himself matter once again—these subjects have once again, through the necessary failure of their enterprise, become the objects of history, inert barrels buffeted by its waves. They believed that just causes always prevail (you cannot be a revolutionary without optimism: the advent of Man is near, this will be the end of history, virtue, happiness; it will be done by their hands). However, they discover their defeat: history continues *without them*, what they took as the end of history was only their own end; as historical subjects, they have fallen into a pit, whether because their mistakes ruined their enterprise or because the targeted object was beyond reach. In this last case, Man, the supreme purpose of men, chose these scamps in order to manifest in principle his impossibility: he appeared at the *collège* only to collapse beneath the blows of an all-powerful enemy. A cruel

3. *Igitur* (Pléiade edition), scholium IV, p. 451.

235

alternative: either Man will be made later, elsewhere, *without them*, or he is a mirage and his reign will not take place. In any event, he is bleeding, he is dying on the paving stones of the courtyards, real and unreal, a twilight bogeyman, dead and alive; dismayed, the children glimpse beyond the crushing of their insurrection the triumph of an inhumane order. The worst thing is that they can no longer fully recognize themselves. To recall what they were in March, they would have to have a clear understanding of what they did. But the inertia of the vanquished reduced to impotence progressively blurs their capacity for practical thought. They must internalize the passivity imposed on them. Within their families, no one shrinks from describing the sovereign act that was their pride as if it were the unreasonable product of their passions: youth is impatient, it does not know how to wait, they were the victims of their turbulence and their heedlessness, etc., etc. This pernicious talk always ends with a promise: you will engage in politics *when you are grown up*. But from the beginning of the reprimand to the end, they have taken care to speak of *acting* in terms of *suffering;* hence the children have lost the means even to conceive a future praxis. The future and the past escape them together; the parents have deliberately unleashed in them what psychiatrists sometimes call an identity crisis. When they find each other again, at the reopening of school in October, it is pandemonium between four walls. The violence has grown, but it has lost its meaning.

At this very time—or perhaps three months later, not more—Gustave enters school. What does he see there? Desperate mutineers? Not at all; we find nowhere—neither in his work nor in his correspondence—the least allusion to the events of March. Yet it is *perfectly impossible* that he should be unaware of them: his father took part in the counterrevolution; Ernest, an eyewitness, certainly spoke to him about it; finally, the glorious eighth year class had become the ninth, the *collège* was filled with veterans, telling of their exploits. Be that as it may, Gustave denies these beaten-down children a history, *their* history. He says that he found in the *collège* "a model of the world, its vices in miniature, its seeds of ridicule, its petty passions, its little coteries, its petty cruelty . . . faults that would later become vices, vices that would be crimes, and children who would be men." He presents his schoolmates' reactions as the eternal traits of human nature, still barely developed, which an inevitable maturation will push to their full potential: a little fish will become a big one, that's all. The schoolboys' agitation, far from having its source in their common adventure, is explained by the universal and immutable characteristics of the species, merely an outline in miniature of the absurd cataclysms that destroy cities and overturn thrones. These children of men are potential men, unhappy, stupid, and vicious. Gustave adopts the adults' view of his comrades: "Later . . . when you are grown up . . . when you are done with doing . . ." Just one difference: for eclectic humanism, the adult—if he is a property owner—realizes in himself the harmonious equilibrium of the passions and reason; for the Flaubert younger son, he is a completed monster. Moreover, his permanent predisposition prevents him from comprehending that he has just left the cruel and sweet time of repetition to enter into the adventure of others; he finds himself in a madhouse—his schoolmates are animals sick with history, bewildered, depersonalized, unhinged. They know neither what they want nor what they are; they no longer recognize their comrades. Those who are on their side they see coming at them as their indecipherable reflections; with the others, the law-abiding ones, it's a scuffle: they reproach the fighters for making them lose a trimester, to which the heroes of March reply that they would have won if not for the treason of the Marais who did not follow them. Among the rebels, several extremists flee in defiance, in anguish, beforehand and swear to "get their own back" when they have the chance. A permanent conflict sets them against a majority already discouraged, still proud of its role, that refuses to forswear the revolution but who would not begin it again at any price, *at least in this form:* reflux, times of discord, coteries. The strong torment the weak, and the big boys torment the little ones? That goes without saying; when a terror-fraternity is broken, certain of its fragments are transformed into tyrants who institute a reign of terror without fraternity. By crushing their neighbor, by reducing him to slavery, they revive for a moment the lost joy, give themselves the illusion of acting, of exercising once again the sovereignty they yearn to recapture; they choke with rage, they will burst if they don't find a scapegoat. It is not surprising if these children, victims of adults, make other children pay; this is not a matter of human nature but a moment of the revolt: when the oppressor is, or appears to be, invincible, the oppressed go at each other.

Yet Gustave had to *live* this interminable collective defeat; like the others, he had to pass through the same phases of the same process of degradation, and he had to submit to the same pressures exercised on each of its members by the revolutionary community which, all hope lost, was determined not to die; he had to participate in the aberrant and courageous resistance of this lost generation against a victorious enemy. But although he gives an exact account of the moments of the conflict, he describes them without placing them in the movement as a whole and without even attempting to connect them to each other, in short, as a succession of *tableaux vivants*. His already inveterate misanthropy makes him see, instead of the historic hatred the schoolboys felt for a still ungraspable adversary, a nontemporal, universal animosity of all against all, which he is convinced is at the root of human relations.

The chief reason for this misconstrual, however, is that he enters school as an aristocrat in order to take his rightful place there. The son of one of the powerful of this world, he sees equality, like Auguste Comte, as merely an "ignoble lie," hence his indifference to the unhappy enterprise of 31 March. What does he have in common with the little Brutuses of liberalism, and wouldn't he hate it if all men were equal, he who bears in his heart the frustrated but avid desire for a feudal society, his father its king? He still prefers to suffer hell *unjustly* rather than rid himself of his evil, rather than confess that he has lived in error and that there is neither first nor last among men. How could he not be on his guard with these school troublemakers, champions of an abstract universalism, who would strip him, if they won, of his noble misfortunes, the irrefutable signs of his quality? The trouble is, the Flaubert younger son does not cut such a fine figure in class; these sons of the bourgeoisie treat him like one of them, like a son of the bourgeoisie. If he lets himself be ranked according to their rules, he is lost: Achille-Cléophas was right to chase him out of paradise. Thus, paradoxically, what prevents him from understanding their true problem is that it is also his own, but experienced differently; for him as for them, the basic issue is the *relation to the father*. But the Flaubert younger son's misfortune is to take himself for a son of the nobility; that of the former insurgents is to have discovered that they are the sons of the bourgeoisie.

2. *The impossible insight.* Listening to the small-minded sermons lavished on them the previous summer by their families, the schoolboys were seized by a terrible suspicion: what if the bourgeoisie *were not* that universal class it prided itself on being? What if it were a particular caste, ambitious, niggardly, and vicious? What should they do in this case, those who were born into it, to sever their ties to it? In the light of their defeat, they glimpsed the possibility that the enemy of Man, that enemy they swore to hate, might very well be their own fathers. As a result, the hatred skids and slides; during the reign of

Louis-Philippe, how could the *juniors* of the ruling class condemn the *seniors* without at the same time passing judgment on themselves? They *think* the bourgeoisie is hateful, and they *say* so, but being incapable of seeing it, they do not *feel* it. One cannot be a challenger or even an observer without *situating* oneself in relation to the object under consideration. And this is precisely what is forbidden to these adolescents produced and reproduced unceasingly by an infinite milieu of non-knowledge and non-challenge which is the very object of their futile search: the bourgeoisie has fed them at their mothers' breasts, kneaded them, penetrated them with their first actions, their first steps, their first words. The things that stand before us, gigantic, visible, offered, are also behind us and in us, maneuvering and conditioning us down to the very judgments we make on the illuminated face they turn toward us. Such are bourgeois institutions for the Rouen schoolboys. At first they seem to be objective determinations of the external world; the children can look at them, they are shown their workings, but when they try to *evaluate* them by placing them in their social context, their eyes cloud over; these institutions suddenly seem so natural, so self-evident, so familiar, so strange in spite of not being foreign to them that they no longer know what to say about them. By the time the children think to question them with regard to external realities, these institutions have long since been ingested and digested in a more assimilable form; the internalization of the external, when it takes place in early childhood, transforms the external, manifesting itself in its objective exteriority, into a quasi-object. Why should they be astonished by real property, these young legatees who have been told by their fathers from the time they could first understand: you are my heir, I have given you life so that you might take up the patrimony and pass it on to your children? We have already noted, with regard to Gustave, that these heirs have internalized property as their fundamental bond to their creator; from on high down, it is the patronizing *gift*, generosity, love; from below up, it is love, recognition. Before possessing anything, even before being born, a Rouen schoolboy is a constituted property owner; his being and his duty-being are defined by *having*; he lives to inherit, from submission, from gratitude as much as from interest: it is the amorous expectation of destiny that his progenitor has prepared him for. How could he stand up against the system and judge it, he who is the system *in person*, the system-subject?

As for utilitarianism, we might say that they have the clearest view of it: they *discern* their fathers' avarice. The work of the "disadvantaged" classes and their families' economies have modified the environment. The chief task will long remain one of accumulation, but unproductive services increase in number. The parents do not even perceive the slight change that affects their budgetary options; the sons glimpse new possibilities: they will administer the patrimony more rationally, by modern methods, and unproductive expenditure will thereby increase: they will live better. This veiled annunciation is made to them by things themselves, whose inert prophecy they have internalized: the idea of comfort, specifically bourgeois but still unknown to the bourgeoisie, could be seen on the horizon. The juniors contest paternal avarice—failing to see that it is not a character trait but a product of the times—and the utilitarian ethic that justifies it.[4] Yet their indignation will never go very far. First of all, far from questioning the objective to which the seniors subscribe, namely profit, they cannot even imagine that production could have any other purpose. Their disagreement is therefore limited since it bears on the means, not on the end. Above all, this contradiction sets the son against himself even more than it sets him against his father, because he was made a utilitarian from his cradle. For a child, nowhere is the utilitarian "art of living" better manifest than in domestic economics, that is, through the maternal praxis; loving restrictions, austerity, deprivations, keeping accounts, perpetual concern with preserving

---

4. There is more: their age constitutes them provisionally as the family's incidental expenses—later they will make money. In the meantime, they are costly; these bourgeois apprentices will not reach their majority without their fragility being protected by heavy investments, provisionally unproductive, which—in the case of nothing more than a bad turn, a bad case of the flu, a piece of bad luck—may remain so permanently; a mediocre investment, then, and hardly secure. Never mind if the sacrifices seem necessary to the one who makes them; this is not the case. Strictly speaking, one can calculate in the abstract precisely what it will cost for the enterprise to become profitable and for the child to be amortized; but the name of existence not being necessity but the necessity of contingency, all disbursements are contingent, even when inevitable. From the moment smallpox becomes evident, it becomes necessary to cure the little patient, but whatever the parents' hopes for their child, the expense remains tainted with inutility because it was not useful or, indeed, inevitable that the child should catch this contagious disease (his roommate wasn't sick). As an individual of a certain class, the son can become the object of a rational and calculated estimate. As a singularity (insanity, ailments, difficulties in physical and mental development, etc.) defined by a certain anchorage, he is constituted by his father as a permanent occasion for superfluous expenses. This is never said, it is felt, and so the mother does not hesitate to "make comments" whose meaning is only too clear: "You're costing us a fortune, you're bleeding us dry." Through the progenitor's constant efforts to balance the family budget and reduce the costs of his progeny, the future heir is led to internalize his objective condition in guilt: he is, by definition—and even if he feels loved—the superfluous man.

and restoring the least expense—this is what loving one's mother means; loving one's father is to consider the principle of utility an absolute norm. All this is not said or thought but registered nonetheless, it is the matrix that produces feelings and ideas. When the adolescent, a little later, reads the text of the world in his own way, under the influence of extravagant impulses tied to the youthful virulence of unfulfilled sexuality, he still does not cease to "think useful," for this is how he is made. The future and the past conspire to make a fool of this angry young man: he would like to condemn his family's vaunted avarice, but how could he become conscious of the infection that has tainted his blood, that disposition to curb costs and thus preserve competitive prices, and how could he free himself of it? This is merely a family recipe, merely a normative vision of the world and society: *"Take life seriously,"* depressing advice which, while sometimes appearing to lose its normative aspect, passes for a summation of universal experience, the very taste of lived experience—"life is not a novel." But this, indeed, is the maxim of bourgeois alienation, and it means: act always in such a way that you sacrifice the man in yourself to the property owner, that is, to the thing possessed. Infected as they are, these adolescents are not even inclined to introduce expense and gratuity into a world they have not for a moment ceased to take seriously: generosity is futile, sheer folly, because natural laws are ironclad. So all is shrouded in an ambiguous fog; they would like to denounce the calculating, avaricious puritanism of their parents in the name of prodigal impulses, yet here they are, passing judgment on their irresponsible and frenetic dreams of prodigality in the name of that puritanism with which they too are possessed. The fathers' parsimony is effaced, it is merely an adult response to the seriousness of life; the sons stick by it to the extent that they stick by themselves, though later they condemn themselves for it in a flash of fury when they demand pocket money and see their demand denied: they will not resolve the dilemma before adjusting their extravagant tastes to their economic status, which they will do only much later, under the Second Empire. It is very clear: even though they would like to do so, they will never hate their fathers enough; this is not to say that a few of them might not despise the pair of individuals who bore them: this aversion, when it exists, has roots going farther and deeper than the March rebellion; they must be sought in childhood, at the source of the idiosyncratic adventure. But as for swearing to the heads of their families a *common* and *socialized* repugnance addressing itself to their class-being, they are incapable of such a thing. Yet the concept of

241

"bourgeoisie" has existed for quite some time; under the Restoration it took on a pejorative sense, they know, but for them it remains emptied of all content. In order to fill it, they would have had to be of another class, or to see their parents through the eyes of *others*— the nobility or the disinherited. And far from being able to borrow such an outside perspective, they have no contact with the other classes: school and family are two connected, self-enclosed vessels from which there is no exit.[5]

We would be wrong to believe, however, that nothing had happened from March to October, and that nothing would happen in the following years: the rupture between the two generations took place, sometimes in disguised form, always masked, irreparable. The fathers aggravated it—they unleashed the repression; the shabby inquisition and the systematic frustration of the schoolboys up to the catastrophe of 1835 serve only to exasperate them. Embittered affection is part of it; they reproach the grown-ups, whom they have so much loved, for having tried to break them. They have the almost unbearable feeling that the family circle regards them as black sheep: not so long ago those very parents who now treat them with such mistrust, and at times with annoyed contempt, were recognized as having total authority, the absolute right to decide what is good or bad for the entire family group. Such old habits are not so easily broken, and, recognized or challenged, the paternal power remains unshaken. At the same time, the son cannot help internalizing the blame and becoming suspect in his own eyes; what if he were merely the errant son of a good family? This permanent interrogation does not make his self-appointed task any easier: how should an accused man judge his judge, sitting at the bench in all his majesty? The adolescent is haunted

5. The spectacle of poverty does not seem to trouble them: the rich and the poor have always been around, always will be. It is not society but stepmother Nature who is responsible for the inequality among men. A beggar is an exquisite piece of luck, the opportunity for a rich man to be good, hence an object of generosity. These children are exalted by giving alms; they have charity in their blood. Little Gustave left us valuable comments on this subject: "I remember that, while still a small child, I loved to empty my pockets into a poor man's. What smiles greeted me as I passed, and what pleasure, too, I had in doing good" (*Mémoires d'un fou*). The order of motifs is noteworthy: he gives alms in order to be greeted as a benefactor and, "too" (this word is revealing), for the pleasure of doing good. When he writes these lines, he has already confided to Ernest that the most powerful motive of charity is nothing but pride. An angry admission, a taste for self-destruction: he goes after his former joys and destroys them. But *in the past*, when he evokes his early childhood, they preserve a purity for which he feels nostalgia. Is it not the best of worlds, in which the laws of nature give rise to philanthropists who temper the severity of those laws?

by the fear of sacrilege. But this very fear makes him irritated with those who provoke it. Above all it throws him into a confusion which the progenitors have not foreseen: when the adolescent in his uncertainty asks if he has betrayed, he cannot avoid asking himself at the same time the crucial question: *to whom, to what* am I a traitor? The adults have a ready answer: you have betrayed your own class, felon! you have preferred Man, a deadly abstraction, to the parents who have sacrificed themselves in order to make you into a perfect bourgeois; shame on you! In fact, the prodigal son is dying of shame; but in thinking over the paternal anathema, he succeeds in reversing the terms: he blushes not at being disloyal to his class but at being its issue and still a part of it. Beneath the reproaches heaped upon him, which touch him in spite of himself, this humanist withdraws into himself: if I am affected by their accusations, if I secretly grant that they are right, it is because I am grist for their mill, a bourgeois enemy of Man just like them. Here he has arrived on the verge of an insight: What is a bourgeois? Or, rather, as a bourgeois, what am I? Unfortunately he will go no further, for the same reason that prevents him from perceiving the "class-bound individual" in his father. In order to *see himself* bourgeois, as well as to unmask the bourgeois hiding under the skin of the grown-ups, he would have to borrow other eyes, for the parents have structured even his reflexive vision; what reflection wants to grasp in that which is reflected is already in reflection, deciding what it *can* see and *how* it sees.[6] An obscure but constant adherence to the self prevents him from discovering his own anchorage. In the absence of a foreign mediation, his class-being will remain something "unrealizable" for him.[7]

Here he is put in question. Is he a traitor to his class or enemy of Man? He must choose. No! Why should he not be both? Maybe his treason was short-circuited because he did not want it *enough*? How can he answer without *encountering* himself and *recognizing* himself? How can he encounter himself without getting outside himself? He will remain in this state of hesitant disquiet; the shame will not go away: this revolutionary feeling is at the source of what is often

6. Because reflexive consciousness is not an *other* consciousness, and is born of a scissiparity of the immediate (or unreflected) consciousness.

7. It goes without saying that the possibility exists for him, at least in principle, to form some idea of his objective reality; but it is an idea cut short since it focuses its objectivity strictly *within the class* for other individuals who are equally a part of it, or for organizations, socioprofessional groups, constituted bodies, etc., which the class as such has produced.

243

called the "second *mal du siècle*." The first—we shall return to this—begins with a flood of tears: young, subsidized monarchists weep over the trials of the Bourbons. The second will be completed in an anxious burst of laughter: the bourgeoisie discovering itself through the eyes of its youngest children like a shameful and inaccessible disease. An unreasonable shame, the abstract conviction that they cannot condemn the enemy without crushing themselves, and that his guilt—like their own—though obvious, remains undemonstrable, a merciless hatred but one without a definite object, the permanent desire to tear oneself away from oneself, to escape into noise and uproar—it would be enough to madden the hardest of hearts. At the beginning of every new school year, for four years, the *collège* is filled with wild boys who are no longer privy to the secret of their folly and will not stop until they have destroyed everything. Gustave's schoolmates are really convulsives; this is the state in which he found them.

His testimony will be valuable to us—in particular certain personal recollections in the *Sketches and Framents* from *Madame Bovary*[8]—provided it is given a historic dimension.[9] In the first chapter Flaubert made a curious, quickly abandoned attempt to sketch what must be called a "negative portrait" of Charles Bovary. He tries to portray him during his school years in terms not of what he is or what he does but rather of what he is not and does not do. The author, still speaking in the first person plural, wants to show the isolation of this country boy in the midst of the city boys who, though they don't exclude him entirely, don't try to integrate him either. This leads Gustave to elaborate for us in detail the mores of the schoolboys in order to show to what extent they remained foreign to Charles. Which gives us a remarkable picture of the life of boarding students in Rouen after 1830. "How

8. Collected by Mademoiselle Leleu (Conard edition).

9. He wanted to believe that the unbridled, manic violence of these lost children had nothing abnormal about it and might be found in all French schools. I grant he may be right on one point: you could probably count on the fingers of one hand the scholarly establishments where the news of La Fayette's dismissal met with an indifferent reception; numerous, on the other hand, were those where it provoked serious disturbances. In some, the students *perhaps* pushed their indignation to the point of mutiny: after all, they had to wait more than a century for Monsieur Labracherie to reestablish the events of March 1831 as they really happened. Still, it served merely to clarify a rather obscure period in Flaubert's adolescence. Not all the *collèges* were lucky enough to shelter an illustrious childhood, and nothing prevents us, if we are so inclined, from supposing that a certain number of them might have had their moment of glory, now forever lost. There is no doubt, in any case, that the second *mal du siècle* was pervasive. But for this very reason it must be seen as a product of history and not as a fact of nature. Other than in periods of counterrevolution—in 1970, for example—where could we find fathers pursuing their sons with such animosity?

little he resembled us *in everything*.[10] He did not want the school to burn down . . . He never dreamed of Paris, he did not see . . . as we did, as if at the end of a funereal avenue each class one of its cypresses, some great sun of freedom shining with love, resplendent with inexplicable beauties." This much is clear: for these boys "whose minds were compromised by their provincial milieu," the only hope—Rouen having no university—was to complete their studies in the capital. Then they would be full-fledged. Still, the two texts are disturbing: fire, death, death by fire. The second, which is metaphorical, is illuminated by the first, which reveals to us that the children are united by dump. In order to express the feelings of these pyromaniacs, Flaubert uses the imperfect indicative [*ne souhaitait pas*, "did not want"; *ne rêvait point*, "never dreamed"; *ne voyait (pas)*, "did not see"], which in his hand takes on the value of a frequentative. This is his "favorite" tense, one that best renders the cyclical duration of repetition. Still, he usually takes care to specify by an adverb (often, sometimes) the frequency of the returns. Here, nothing of the kind—which is equivalent to writing "we wanted it *all the time*." Flaubert understood that the schoolboys—he is one of them—vow the *collège* a suicidal hatred that never falters in its vigilance: let it burn, even if they must burn with it. We rediscover their desire, masked but recognizable, in the metaphor that follows a little further on, the dark, explosive dream of the boarding student sleepwalking along that funereal avenue and gazing at the ascent of a sun on the horizon—it is a dream of hatred. The star is Paris, all right; but it is also *empyrosis*, the tongue of fire licking at the cypresses and the tombs before devouring the whole world. These incendiary reveries conceal beneath their rather modest ambitions—burning *one* school, so what?—an arrogant nihilism that demands the abolition of being in a universal conflagration. When we examine the image closely, it seems to be overdetermined or, if you like, *saturated* with significations. That Gustave implicitly compares his school years to a way of the cross, its stations marked by cypresses, is not surprising; the sentence is obviously governed from afar by a ready-made expression, "It was a Calvary!"—an old metaphor, worn out with overuse, which is here paraphrased in the hope of being rejuvenated. We shall see that Gustave is a veritable fountain of youth for old proverbs and dead images: he loves to take them for the subjects of vast, colorful compositions. At first glance, then, there is nothing "felt" in the "thing" he

10. My italics.

has just painted, which remains as abstract as the proverbial locution it merely makes explicit. But when we look closely at this elaborated picture, several words strike us that cannot be explained by rhetoric and have surely forced themselves upon the author. Why is this way of the cross bordered by cypress trees and, as the adjective "funereal" suggests, tombs? The "great sun of freedom" shines from a distance, for him alone, and does not illuminate: it is the "city of light" that plunders the provinces and leaves them stagnating in shadow. The *collège* is a provincial cemetery at nightfall; bewildered children waste their best years there in twilight. The image ends by imposing itself in its mysterious absurdity: who are those deceased? Do all schoolboys everywhere regard their school years as a sepulchral stroll along tomb-lined lanes? Surely not; some of the boarders cannot bear the confinement, others do not adapt to it easily, but monastic life is not without its charm, at least for certain children who adapt themselves to it from the start; the majority move fairly quickly from resignation to habituation. With the metaphor of the cemetery, Gustave has offered a faithful interpretation of his schoolmates in spite of himself: they are the living dead, torn between rancor, disgust with life, raging confusion, and ennui, wandering interminably in the gloom toward the only two options left to them: Paris, flaming with love and freedom,[11] or suicide. The sworn group of 1831, crushed by an iron fist,

---

11. By the time he wrote *Madame Bovary*, Gustave had long since been disabused of this notion. Paris is only a myth of provincial and bourgeois stupidity: unless he has an income of a hundred thousand francs, like the young gentlemen who dine at Tortoni's, the student in Paris will find only ugliness and discomfort, those inseparable elements, tedious work, conventional knowledge through courses recited *ex cathedra* that he must learn by heart, the foolishness of grisettes and the syphilis of whores. Between 1842 and 1844 Gustave spent two "deadly" years in the capital, and these years catapulted him into neurosis. But he does not condemn the savage dreams of the children sequestered in the school; it is the people of Rouen he mocks, young or old, who "have lived it up" in the Latin Quarter and persist, out of vanity, despite a negative experience in encouraging the schoolboys' hopes that one day they *will find themselves* in a café on a boulevard in the "modern Babylon."

In the autumn of 1842 he had written from Paris, he was settled, to his friend Alfred: "If Lengliné or Baudry knew how I felt, what an idea they would have of me." Alfred answers, 15 November: "You have truly intuited it: you have excited Lengliné's pity . . . My mother had spoken again at dinner of your sadness. Lengliné was present. He laughed with pity, but a benevolent pity, like a father laughing at his child's small sorrows. He predicted that Paris would quickly console you; that was during dinner; and afterward he whispered to me in confidence that the *little girls* would cure you. He was laughing a good deal and made fun of you, but I laughed louder, apparently with a strange laugh, for . . . he quickly squelched his." In *Alfred Le Poittevin*, by René Descharmes, p. 169. Flaubert was not the man to forget insults. He remembers them in *Madame Bovary*, when he paints Léon's foolish dreams and his departure for Paris. He entrusts Homais with the role of *Lengliné:* " 'That poor boy,' repeated the health officer,

has entered its painful death throes, complete with misfired and convulsive delirium. What has died for them is the Revolution, hope, optimism: they see in the instituted repression the concerted murder of their youth. Unable to condemn the culprits, their fathers, they have transferred their hatred to two objects: the school and the province.

The first, with its authoritarian institutions, its moral order, its admitted knowledge, its hypocritical humanism, its competitive structures, the fate it assigns to the future bourgeois elite—what is it but the reification of their parents transformed into an inert prison? They will be able to despise them all the better in this petrified form inasmuch as they *understand* but *do not know* the intention that presides over the transference; it is not surprising that their first defense is to consign to death *as if they were things* (fire, depredations, damages of all kinds) those cruel progenitors whom they were not capable of hating as men, and even less as bourgeois. The second object, the province, defines them on a level of objectivity that is accessible to them: there are the mediating factors of centralization and the proximity of the capital. The third mediators are the Parisian cousins—who *see* them during vacations, when the bourgeois of Rouen embark in their carriages to pay a visit to the Parisian branch of the family—and the administrators, who constitute them as second-class Frenchmen, the best men and the best products being drained away from Normandy. Thus, while the central organs of the "tentacled city" despoil them and dull them, in short, *provincialize* them, the Parisian beneficiaries of the process verify the result by scoffing at their Norman cousins. The schoolboys of Rouen seize the opportunity; a new displacement of hatred: instead of the decidedly inaccessible bourgeoisie, what they

---

looking sad. 'Don't go pitying him,' said the pharmacist . . .' He will amuse himself there . . . He will gradually do as the others. You don't know how those pranksters carry on in their Latin quarter! Sometimes they even go too far. Besides, students in Paris are held in high esteem because they are so much fun. Provided they belong to a good family . . . one asks nothing better than to admit them into the best society.'" *Ebauches et fragments,* p. 481. What follows are the familiar allusions to flattering liaisons formed there, and to "chances to make very advantageous marriages." Homais adds, moreover, that "one is surrounded there by all sorts of traps: that is the other side of the coin."

Of course, the pranks and indecencies to which Homais reduces the joyous Parisian student life have no more in common with the hope of the schoolboys, who want only to live—to know freedom and love in their highest forms—than Lengliné's little girls have in common with the sun revolving in the sky at the end of the lane of cypresses. But what is striking—and we shall return to this—is that Gustave's burning desire to tear himself away from the provinces is replaced, the moment it is realized, by the anguish of leaving his family. We are soon going to find this ambivalence again.

247

will hate in their fathers and in themselves is their provincialism, *too obvious a defect*[12] (the love they bring to the capital, on the other hand, will never be free of bitterness: they know that it despoils them and cynically mocks them).[13] The transposition of class-being to provincial-being is a stroke of genius that gives them back hope: as bourgeois, they are damned, one never leaves one's class; as provincials, they have a chance to leave the provinces. Thus they can smugly hate the vulgarity of their fathers without entirely condemning it in themselves: in the adult it has become ingrained; in the child it is a simple disposition, which he has the means to efface. It may be suggested that these young provincials are wrong, under such conditions, to hate the *collège*, since it seems to be their only access to the capital. In fact, they are quite prepared for such an objection. This filthy dump is itself a second-rate establishment: the teaching is mediocre; no sooner has a young teacher given proof of talent than Paris calls him; he is found at Versailles, like Gourgaud, at the Sorbonne, like Chéruel. Those who remain are old pedants and idiots. Their prison offers the schoolboys the image of all they detest in the provinces: suspicion,

---

12. Gustave is perfectly conscious of his provincialism. When he leaves for Paris, he is sure that he is carrying with him his baggage of indestructible Norman vulgarity, and this feeling is in part the source of the truculent and dominating character he plays in the Parisian salons. Had he known that his "lapdogs," his good friends the Goncourts, described him in their Journal as "a great man of the provinces," he might have been wounded, I imagine, but he would have subscribed to their judgment. Early on, indeed, Achille-Cléophas, hurling recriminations at Dupuytren, had convinced him that the province meant exile. Here he is, then, doubly and unjustly frustrated: born in exile, he too the victim of his father's executioner, Gustave reckoned he was not rich enough to settle in the capital and live comfortably. After 4 September 1870, his animosity toward Paris would narrow to hatred: he would go so far as to wish that a conflagration might destroy the city. Fire again! Perhaps the same fire, the sun of love, that he saw revolving thirty-five years earlier above the City. Of course, he despises the people of Rouen: they remind him of his own image and, as Genet says, his "bad smell." But Rouen, the place of his exile, is also his refuge—hence the ambivalence of his feelings toward his home town.

13. We see the metamorphosis and the degradation to which Clouet's purpose has been subjected. For him as well, man was defined by freedom and love. But he was *to be made*, or at least to be conquered, by slaves mystified by their tyrants. His optimism was based on a bourgeois myth that was just beginning its brilliant career, the idea of Progress. But if Man seemed to him the necessary end of historical temporalization, the young leader was not unaware that Man's advent would not take place without persistent battles. During the reflux, the schoolboys' thought becomes confused: the Ideal is no longer in the future; space has replaced time; love and freedom are 110 kilometers from Rouen. Certainly they are separated from it by a certain duration, but they will pass the next few years passively or—as we shall see—in a useless revolt. After five years, four years, three years of waiting, they will be *Man* in their turn—which means students, Parisians, adults. And certainly there is nothing base in their conception of freedom except that, for them, it is *given*.

spying, scandals, repressive violence, foolish knowledge with no connection to their real aspirations. So the *collège*, an exasperated province, leads the students toward Parisian life even as it contrives to make them forever unfit for such a life by provincializing them. They are in danger there; the school is doubly their enemy: it embodies their parents as bourgeois and as provincials. It is the school they will set about attacking first. They are prepared to make a perpetual uproar that is bound to reach their parents' ears; unable to liquidate the royal establishment by a fire they dare not set, they try to ruin it by discrediting the teachers and the administration. Flaubert bears witness to this as well: "He would say 'Sir' when speaking to the study master and did not continually complain about the food . . . If he did not participate in our daily pranks and even refused to help us in great undertakings that required a certain audacity, he certainly never denounced anyone, even lending his homework when necessary, and did not abuse his power to tyrannize over the smaller children."[14] The intentionally destructive character of these "pranks" need not be demonstrated; they challenged everything by violence: the established order, power, and knowledge. A merciless struggle ensued between the fighters and the administration: the former were content with depredations, symbolic minidestructions; the latter packed their gangs with informers—Gustave acknowledges this, taking the trouble to congratulate Charles for not "giving anyone away." From time to time the agitation tends to become insurrectionary: it demands "a certain audacity"—a real surprise attack. We shall see that Flaubert junior will get himself expelled in 1839 for participating in a collective act of this kind. This unrestrained and uninterrupted turbulence will not be futile, for in 1835 the schoolboys will succeed in having the hides of the headmaster and the proctor. A Pyrrhic victory, followed by a counterrevolution that institutes a bloodless Terror. But although they have sworn to follow their action to its conclusion, although they have assumed the risk of being expelled, as in the heroic old days, these children no longer know what they are doing. For lack of a purpose like Clouet's, or specific claims, they exhaust themselves perpetuating disorder, and the meaning of their enterprise escapes them. They are no longer capable of conducting a collective and concerted action. When one outbreak is over, another begins elsewhere, but there is no plan connecting them; two motives persist: blind fury and emulation. In the dining hall, Flaubert tells us, the thrice-weekly sight

14. *Ebauches et fragments*, p. 24.

of "a piece of cod swimming in a yellowish sauce" unleashes an uproar. But do they really want their usual fare improved? Not at all: they would lose a chance to fume. The result is that their rows lose all interest for them. *Before*, they expected the infinite—suicide, homicide, conflagration of the universe; they would be Samsons, they would pull down the columns of the temple onto their own heads in order to crush the Philistines; *afterward*, they perceive, disenchanted, that nothing has happened except the repetition of a common little wrongdoing—a wall is spotted with ink, a chair overturned, a windowpane broken; they are showered with exercises, and afterward? There is nothing to do but begin again. In any case, their action no longer has any *political* meaning: the failure of 1831 has soured them on politics. It's a jungle. This pessimism will stay with them, and the news coming from Paris gives them no comfort. These forced laborers have two objectives: to maintain by means of a perpetual guerrilla war the unity of the historic group against the forces that attempt to atomize it, and to perpetrate symbolically the murder of the father by dismantling the *collège*. Unfortunately, this itself is merely symbolic: every day they must repeat, through surprise attacks, the *deed* of radical destruction.

They have chosen as scapegoat, we are told, the natural history teacher: the row is directed, in principle, against the system through the person of one of its representatives. Is this a good choice? Are there not more formidable suppressors, well known to the inspectors, respected by the families? There are, but these petty tyrants are intimidating, the mutineers admire them, secretly approve of their severity. And then, in spite of everything, competition is a factor: it is rare that the classes of the most important teachers are disturbed. It is obvious, therefore, that they have decided not to torment a qualified spokesman for the regime but that their victim is merely one man, scorned by his colleagues and by the administration, an outcast like them, dregs, a man they accuse of lacking authority. Why take the trouble to break him? Because it is easy. The ailment of these stricken children, placed in the lazaretto by their own parents, finds an outlet in the torments they inflict on discredited teachers or on the needy study masters who oversee them for starvation wages. So their agitation becomes suspect even in their own eyes. *Who* are they? For *whom* do they have contempt, and why? Should we see them as the castaways of liberalism, carrying on a permanent carnival to display their profound disdain for Voltaire's old-fashioned humanism thrown into an eclectic pot? Or are they rich kids, heirs, proud offspring of the dominant class, demonstrating not against bourgeois knowledge but against the insufficiently qualified wretches who are paid to dispense that knowledge to them? To tell the truth—we shall see more of this—they are both, and, to their misfortune, *they suspect it.*

Moreover, if it is difficult to consider these poor devils the representatives of the teaching staff or the administration, it is still harder to see the administration, after 1831, as having the parents' mandate. The parents continually rage against the administration, denounce it to the rector, vilify it in front of their children, and criticize it for its weakness; as a result, the "scamps" regard the headmaster and the proctor as enemies at school but feel obliged to defend them from attack within the family. I offer a curious anecdote as evidence, in which Gustave and Achille-Cléophas are the protagonists.[15] We have seen that Doctor Flaubert had joined the often slanderous campaign waged so high-handedly by the parents against the administrators. He imprudently believed a rumor from an unknown source: the proctor was remiss in his duties, failing to inspect the students' written work and to monitor their acquisition of knowledge with daily quizzes. The philosophical practitioner did not hesitate to report this to the rector. The proctor was at great risk—the complaint had all the more weight as it was made against him by one of the outstanding citizens of Rouen. He was saved by Gustave, who protested to the paterfamilias that everything was just fine, and that the proctor was determined to fulfill all his obligations. Convinced, the medical director wrote a letter of repentance to the rector which smacks of embarrassment: his good faith had been found to be in error: on being questioned, his son had proved to him that his accusations were groundless. Did he question Gustave, as he claims? I do not believe he did. If he had been likely to request the testimony of this witness, wouldn't such an emotional but honest man have done so *before* communicating to the authorities a slander based on hearsay? He wrote in blind anger and without consulting anyone; his son intervened on his own authority and spoke so clearly that he persuaded him. Why? From the goodness of his heart? He is not good. From a love of truth? He despises it. From sympathy with the proctor? He hasn't the least bit—this is the period when he is editing, with Ernest, a "literary journal" in which he heaps abuse on certain teachers and their families. We have even speculated that after the paper was seized, he avoided dismissal by the skin of his teeth. Passive and bitter, he generally avoids meddling in other people's business and is not worried

15. Reported by Monsieur Labracherie.

when innocents are punished. The only conceivable reason for his intervention is that the proctor, persecuted by Achille-Cléophas, no longer seems like the authorized representative of the paterfamilias's power and has descended to the rank of his victims—the most illustrious and pitiable being Gustave himself. Whether they were unable to cope, or whether they wanted to be humane, the headmaster and the proctor failed to repress the student disturbances with the ferocity the families demanded of them; and the anecdote I just reported shows that in 1835, when everyone sensed that the drama was approaching its turning point, the schoolboys had come—yet without ceasing their uproars—to defend *their* headmaster and *their* proctor against the enemies of Man. Proof that they no longer knew what they were doing.

These children were waging a battle on shaky ground. Indeed, they were no longer battling, they were struggling, and their disordered spasms legitimized the repression. Eighteen thirty-five: everywhere in France the forces of order went onto the attack; the government, in process of liquidating the republicans, finally gave in to the entreaties of the Rouen families: the headmaster and the proctor were transferred; their replacements were strong men who imposed an iron discipline, crushing the rebels by surprise. Several weeks later, a general inspector hid in a dormitory to witness the rising of the boarders; in his report he declared that he was dazzled by "this metamorphosis of the school in less than a month." He saw them jump out of bed, wash up, dress, get in line; it was marvelous: "I can only compare the dignity and precision of the movement to the maneuver of an armed regiment." This is what they wanted for their children, the good bourgeois of Rouen—barracks. They rejoiced. According to the same inspector, the schoolboys were no longer discontent: "The morale of this youth is good, they ask only to be governed well." The revolts became less frequent—their hearts were no longer in it. Vanquished but unbroken, burning with rage and hatred, "this youth" would take the battle to another ground: its morale was good but it read bad books.

Passage to the imaginary. In the *Préface aux Dernières Chansons,* Gustave goes so far as to acknowledge that his schoolmates were continually under extreme pressure. He does not limit himself, as he usually does, to confirming that fact; he tries to offer an explanation. "The last flowerings of Romanticism reached even us . . . [and], compressed by the provincial setting, provoked strange agitations in our brains." This implies that Romanticism, elaborated in the capital, was experienced nowhere with such violence as in the provinces.[16] Certain words, however, make us suspicious: first of all, in Paris the movement is in its death throes when it reaches Rouen; this time-lag necessarily implies an alteration of its "message": affected by its "*last flowerings*," the Rouen schoolboys are beginning at the end; they are reacting, first of all, to Late Romanticism. And the "strangeness" of their reactions comes from the fact that these are not the pure effects of new conceptions on unprejudiced minds: the agitations are strange *in relation to Romanticism itself*; penetrating into a highly structured setting, it is immediately thrown off course, refracted, polarized. The "flowerings" close up, become condensed as soon as they enter these narrow minds that are squeezed, crushed, afflicted by a permanent contraction, by a tetanus triggered by provincial venom. The schoolboys, says Flaubert, absorbed a concentration of Romanticism that turned them completely crazy. Okay. Except that he once more denies the historical interpretation. Put another way, history exists, at least as an irreversible succession, but it is made *elsewhere*, in Paris. In Paris the movement was born, evolved, aged, and will die. In Rouen it makes an impression on inert matrices, passive subproducts of the social environment who will deform it according to their *received* constitutions. We cannot accept this purely structural conception of the phenomenon: certainly the schoolboys are very far from being subjects of history, and we have seen that they struggle in vain not to become its objects; be that as it may, they make what they suffer to the extent that they suffer what they make. They have constructed and affirmed their provincialism, as we have seen, as a substitute for their inaccessible class-being to the same degree that third-party mediators—agents and witnesses—have affected them with it. Besides, even granting Flaubert's interpretation, we would be justified in asking him why the chief event that overwhelms the schoolboys should be Late Romanticism rather than the July Revolution. We know that Gustave is silent concerning the mutiny of 1831. But that mutiny is indispensable to our understanding of the events that followed it. Would the works of a particular literary school be greeted with such emotion if they were not understood on the basis of prior circumstances? It is the veterans of March who adopt the language of

16. Obviously, we are not speaking here of Romanticism as such: this immense upheaval cannot be described in a few pages. We are examining only the way it might have been received in the provinces by the first "post-Romantic" generation.

Romanticism and believe they have found in it a solution to their problems.

"Never in the yellow glimmer of the smoking lamp did [Charles] spend the night hours of winter immobile, devouring some thick novel from a lending library that ravaged our hearts. Melancholy of my school dormitories, he did not know you."[17] These unpublished lines confirm the famous passage from the *Préface aux Dernières Chansons:* "The exercises finished, literature began, and in the dormitories one ruined one's eyes reading novels." This "one" no longer designates all the schoolboys, but, as Flaubert specifies at the beginning of the next paragraph, "a small group of the exalted." The "we" of the negative portrait of Charles seems larger: the circle of reading enthusiasts seems to have narrowed, in Gustave's memory, with the years; unless his subject—the apology for Bouilhet—led him to present as the "unpunished vice" of an elite what was in fact a much more widespread practice. However understood, the text clearly indicates that the new defensive did not have the breadth of the preceding counterattacks. The use of force in 1835 had broken their courage: many submitted; we shall no longer have occasion to speak of them. Others, more hardened or more deeply affected, continued the school history: to read forbidden and controversial authors secretly, at night, was to perpetuate proscribed violations, to pursue their war when the victors thought they had deprived them of the means to do so. "The exercises finished, literature began." The exercises were *everything:* day, the sun, waking, the natural needs that were never fully satisfied: they were classical teaching, Livy, Ovid, La Fontaine, Fénelon, Bossuet, Massillon: they were competition, dismal bourgeois boredom. Literature was night, it was solitude and hypnosis, it was the imaginary. The students tell each other they are going to construct a formidable strategy that will force their enemies to retreat. But to penetrate their intentions more effectively, it is fitting to pose a preliminary question: what are you reading? To tell the truth, they don't answer. But, once again, Gustave will answer for them—we shall take an inventory of his library with him. We shall be forced to acknowledge that Romanticism did not make a splash at the *collège* when it was already in its death throes in Paris but, quite the contrary, that it insinuated itself little by little, beginning in 1832, and probably even earlier.

17. *Ebauches et fragments,* p. 24.

The text of the *Préface* contains a single name: Hugo. The correspondence confirms that he was the first "Romantic" Gustave and Ernest had discovered. And Flaubert, a man of the theater, knew Hugo first from his plays. During the summer vacation of 1833, he writes to his friend: "At Nangis we saw the old castle . . . It is the castle that belonged to the marquis of Nangis who is mentioned in *Marion Delorme*."[18] He is not even twelve years old, and he is already speaking of Hugo like a fan. He is not the only one either: Ernest is in on it, that is clear; he will be suitably delighted to learn that Gustave saw a castle that the magnificent bard deigned to mention. Others, we can be sure, many others, shared their admiration. Certainly Ernest and Gustave showed that they were the most precocious, but Romanticism was at the same time taking root among the "big boys." *Marion Delorme* offered them a select assortment of Hugo characters: the courtesan with the heart of gold, the charming and wise fool, the gloomy, bored king, and "the man in red passing by"—Richelieu, the future Torquemada. What struck them first was his protagonists' greatness of soul—including the villains—and the force of their passions. The boys observed, astonished, the marriage of genres, the comic coupled before their very eyes with the dramatic, and the grotesque with the sublime—they couldn't get over it. Nor could they forget having seen onstage the Cardinal's litter borne by twenty-four guards on foot, surrounded by "twenty other guards with halbards and torches," "scarlet" and "gigantic." Above all, for the first time these children felt that someone was speaking to them: discarding unworthy parents, an older brother came onto the stage and leaned toward his younger brothers, addressing them directly: "This was the hour," says the preface to *Marion Delorme*, "for him whom God may have endowed with genius to create a new theater, a theater vast and simple, one and various, national in its history, popular in its truth, human, natural, universal in its passion. Dramatic poets, to work!" The adolescents learned that the play, written in June 1829, had been proscribed by censorship on the personal intervention of Charles X. The author spoke frankly of his liberalism, and he added: "Censorship was an integral part of the Restoration. One could not disappear without the other. Therefore, the social revolution had to be completed for the revolution of art to be achieved. Some day, July 1830 will be no less a literary date than a political one." It was the perfect language for

18. *Correspondance* 1:9.

those angry adolescents on their way to being depoliticized: for the Three Glorious Days of July to have the sparkle restored to their memory, they had to be saved by their consequences, and the political revolution had to be made a means to the literary revolution. That isn't exactly what Hugo says, and we can also understand that the political and social upheaval of 1830 was, according to him, an immense event that is going to transform simultaneously all sectors of national activity. But we know how the children of Rouen received that ambiguous sentence: "The social revolution *had* to be completed *for* the revolution of art to be achieved," and what they took from it. "One was above all an artist; the exercises finished, literature began." Now we more clearly understand these "exercises": they were *active life*, which begins with daylight and ends with daylight. What the "exalted" few have Hugo say is that action is intolerable unless one feels that it is in the service of the dream. The soldiers of March '31 recovered a certain pride; their enterprise, so generally disgraced that they had preferred to forget it, was resurfacing, dazzling in the sunlight, *legitimized by Art*.

We shall find it difficult to regard Hugo's *Marion Delorme*, written shortly before and performed shortly after *Hernani*, as one of the "last flowerings" of Romanticism. Moreover, Rouen was not so provincial that a child of eleven could not speak familiarly—as of an old acquaintance—of a drama of the new school less than two years after it was presented for the first time to the Parisian public. Curiously, we have to wait until 1845 for Gustave to mention *Hernani* in his correspondence. But on 2 April of that year, he reminds Alfred that he was reading "*Hernani* or *Renée*" to the Collier sisters—encouraging the young English girls to share his earliest enthusiasms. Be that as it may, Hernani—grandee of Spain and an honorable outlaw, a conspirator who always misses his shot and owes his life to his most obliging enemies, a passive and passionate hero, extracting from his failures an inexhaustible, sublime, and ineffective eloquence, a banished man, a wanderer (the mountains of Aragon, Galicia, Estramadura, ah!), bearing misfortune to all those around him—was without doubt a prestigious model for the inert Flaubert and for the hobbled youth around him, as these words in the second letter to Louise testify: "I have the plague! Misfortune to him who touches me!" Moreover, Gustave has known the term "Romanticism" since 1833 and uses it when he writes to Ernest, certain of being understood by his reader. In the course of a journey the horses run away, the Flauberts' carriage is borne off; happily, the coachman recovers the reins . . . "this was the finish to our grotesque and romantic adventure." A little while later, he cites a play by Delamier entitled *Romanticism Thwarts All,* which shows that he was well acquainted with the disputes raised by the Creed. Two years later, in July 1835, he writes to Chevalier: "My poetic and productive incognito is . . . Gustave Antuoskothi [*sic*] Koclott . . . There's a bit of cute romanticism." Certainly a kind of awkwardness comes through the assurance, and the word is never taken entirely seriously. But the irony, always superficial, is nothing more than a gesture of modesty; Flaubert distances himself, even from Ernest; he does not want to offer himself unreservedly. And even the awkwardness does not prevent him from *getting it right.* A purist might find fault, for example, with the pairing of "grotesque and romantic," since Romanticism contains precisely both the grotesque and the dramatic. But it is a true and profound intuition that shows Gustave the comic side of the adventure (crazed beasts, the creaking of the practico-inert as it is shaken about, everything he will later describe in the Rouen carriage scene) and its properly Romantic aspect (dumb animals becoming *Fatum* for human beings and leading them, *passive,* toward their death, which is glimpsed for a moment through his fear and his impotence in spite of his pride's denial.

In short, there was no *invasion* but an *infiltration,* and this began in 1830. What happened in 1835, after the militarization of the *collège* and because of it, is that the language of Romanticism—with which the old establishment was already impregnated—was definitively chosen by the schoolboys as *their* language. It ceases to be a discreet commentary on their struggle against the bourgeoisie and becomes the *struggle itself,* the counterattack launched by the vanquished *as such,* who believe they can find in it the means to conceive of their defeat; it is ink that dries black. In Paris, the language is black and white and has never ceased to be so; in Rouen it is exclusively *nocturnal,* the consequence of a deliberate choice. The children, victims of a show of force which they will never accept, choose their readings as a function of their anger and their bitterness; they demand to be shown the inhumane world that crushes them, and demand that it be denounced to the vault of the heavens. In fact, beginning from that fatal year, Gustave's readings increase and darken: he buys *Antony* on 2 July, *Catherine Howard* on the 23d; 14 August he announces to Ernest that he has just read *La Tour de Nesles,* a dark melodrama in which everyone is wicked. In the same letter he indicates that he is "completely absorbed in old Shakespeare," and that he has begun to read *Othello.* But along with the dramatic works, historical studies now make their appearance. He takes Walter Scott's three volumes of the *History of Scotland* as reading matter for his travels. It is not until 24 March 1837 that he mentions Byron, of whom he will say in September of the same year: "I truly admire only two men in the world, Byron and Rabelais." But it is clear that this poet has long been familiar to him: "I hardly know any kid who would have a Byron. It is true that I might take Alfred's . . ." It is quite likely that Flaubert may have come to *Childe Harold* under Le Poittevin's influence, in 1835 at the latest: infatuated with Byron, whom Gustave calls in 1835–36 "the son of the century,"[19] Alfred had just written *Satan*, which shows obvious Byronic influence and appeared in the *Revue de Rouen et de Normandie* during the first semester of 1836. With Byron, Gustave discovers another aspect of Romanticism, perhaps the most important for him and his comrades: the theme of arrogant refusal and revolt against Creation, defiance of God. We shall grasp more clearly the reversal of motifs and signs if we go back to *Mémoires d'un fou*, which he wrote at sixteen. In it, the boy offers us a sample of his readings. This selection is of the greatest interest, for he drew it up himself and kept only works that nourished his "bitter passions": three men, five works. Byron, Goethe, Shakespeare; *Childe Harold* and *The Infidel*, *Werther*, *Hamlet* and *Romeo and Juliet*. Why this choice? Because, he says, "a quality of such burning passion joined with such profound irony must act strongly upon an ardent and virgin nature . . . This great poetry . . . makes your head spin and makes you fall into the bottomless gulf of the infinite." No doubt. And we shall return to this. But note that Victor Hugo, his first love, is not even mentioned. It is because the majestic infinite of the poet is not an empty gulf[20]—you must see God himself in it, in his *presence*. And after 1835, Flaubert demands that Romanticism sumptuously consecrate his defeat by satisfying his rancor. *Childe Harolde*: the revolt against being.

19. In his "Portrait of Lord Byron" written that year. Monsieur Bruneau says, somewhat lightly in my opinion, that Flaubert could have penned it without having read a line of Byron. I agree with him that nothing in the text in itself indicates that this younger son of a proper bourgeois family was familiar at the time with the work of the man he depicted. But when Bruneau adds that Gustave has not given the title of a single work, I cannot help answering: and what if he had cited them all, what would that prove? It is suggested that he might have copied a biographical notice: taking things in the abstract, why not? But in this case, in order to perfect his work he could also have copied a bibliography. And how could this adolescent who considers himself a poet, whose only joy is in reading, and who is fascinated by Byron, resist the pleasure of reading this author when Alfred possesses a collection of his poems and has just written *Satan*?

20. Even though the words "gulf" and "abyss" are found constantly in his writing.

Werther: suicide out of boredom with living. *Hamlet:* a good young man, driven mad by sordid family affairs, ungifted for action, incapable of revolt, takes revenge through monologue, ruminates indefinitely over the impossible and necessary murder of a usurper who has stolen the love of his sluttish mother, and finally kills him by accident. *Romeo and Juliet:* yet another family history; this time there are two protagonists who dream only of killing each other, and the two fathers' stupid hatred for each other will merely result in the deaths of the loveliest of their children. Deadly and sublime impotence of beauty, love, noble desires: the sons are lost angels because they live in the world of their parents.

Theater and poetry are Gustave's path, but there are other ways to reach the new Art. And in particular there is prose. When Flaubert speaks in the name of the "exalted," he says: "*We* read novels." Nothing more, either in the *Mémoires* or in the *Préface.* But it is not impossible to cite several names. These works are in general quite gloomy; sometimes utterly dark. Moreover, in the unpublished fragment of *Madame Bovary,* Gustave states clearly that they "ravaged our hearts." We shall see below the precise meaning of this phrase; it is clear, in any case, that young readers sought such ravages. Much later, Flaubert, irritated with Hennique, who claimed to "satirize Romanticism," take up the defense of the men of 1830. "Note that I am speaking to you of things I know personally." The word "personally" can have only one meaning here: I am speaking to you of my youth, of works I discovered then, which allowed me to discover myself when they still preserved their virulent novelty. And he adds: "You should read Petrus Borel, the early plays of Alexandre Dumas and Anicet Bourgeois, the novels of Lassailly and Eugène Sue, *Trialph* and *La Salamandre.* As a parody of this genre, see *Les Jeune-France* by Théo, a novel by Charles de Bernard, *Gerfaut,* and some of the *Mémoires du Diable* by Soulié, the artist."[21] Petrus Borel, Charles Lassailly: black Romanticism, skulls "still yellow with a kind of human rust."[22] Soulié: cynical Romanticism, a devil who reveals to a damned soul all the vileness of contemporary society. Hell and damnation, laughter of the damned, flood of tears, solitude, steely contempt. His resentment is satisfied by these readings: they denude the rich and powerful, pull the covers off the bourgeoisie: the fathers will go naked before the amused eyes of the sons. The sons will nonetheless remain their vic-

21. *Correspondance* 8:369–70.
22. *Trialph,* p. 57.

tims: there are the wicked and the damned; Gustave is delighted to rediscover, clearly formulated at last, his own pessimism, skepticism, and misanthropy. Monsieur Bruneau cleverly established that in July 1835 he must have been under the influence of a very recent reading of *Notre-Dame de Paris*, and I cannot imagine that this bookworm hadn't known Hugo's previous novels, *Han d'Islande* and *Bug-Jargal:* in these sinister and baroque worlds, it isn't good to be alive. No more than in the world of Balzac, of whom Flaubert will later remark that "his perverse heroes [Rastignac and Rubempré] have turned many peoples' heads." Eugène Sue, in *Les Mystères de Paris*, taking up the myth of the Great City outlined by Restif de La Bretonne, confirms his readers in their admiration for the capital and, at the same time, in their raging disgust for the provinces. Even Musset and Vigny are adapted to the current taste. Flaubert liked Musset's *La Confession d'un enfant du siècle*, as we can see from his autobiographical works, particularly *Mémoires d'un fou;* he saw in it especially the distress of man without God and the lengthy complaints addressed by his young elder to the Jacobin bourgeoisie that had dechristianized him. It might be called the antidote to Byron. But, in fact, the agnostic's despair is the necessary complement to the angels' revolt, as we already know. As for Vigny, Flaubert kept *Chatterton:* the total shipwreck of this poet murdered by bourgeois society could only flatter his sadistic masochism.

I know an objection will be raised: what gives you the right to cite Gustave's readings as *representative*? You are taking an inventory of *his* library: his schoolmates had neither the desire nor the capacity to digest such a quantity of works, and works of such diversity. Besides, the choices of the Flaubert younger son are dictated by a personalizing movement that assumes and surpasses a constitution whose origins are anterior—and by far—to the insurrection of March 1831, in which he certainly took no part since he entered the *collège* only in October. If, as you claim, his comrades' options were conditioned by their defeat, how could they coincide with his and, above all, issue from the same intentions? In 1835, Gustave identifies so little with the vanquished group that he doesn't breathe a word, *anywhere*, of the repression exercised by the new headmaster.

I admit it. I do not claim that the list of works he "devoured" represents anything but the *maximum of possible readings* for a Rouen schoolboy in 1835. Be that as it may, the *average "exalted"* schoolboy read all the crucial works. The books circulate, the boys lend them to each other; Gustave knows no one who owns a Byron, but Ernest finds it quite natural that his friend should borrow books of this author's poetry and pass them on to him. And isn't it likely that boarders at the same dormitory would pass around the "thick novels" from the reading rooms? On his own, or thanks to Le Poittevin, Gustave discovered certain novelists and poets, but others were surely made known to him by comrades burning with the same Romantic fever.

Gustave's individual adventure and the history of the school community are, admittedly, profoundly dissimilar. But while he is blind to his historicity, the younger Flaubert son is nonetheless caught up in the general reflux. Others, who due to their young age could not participate in the mutiny, are nonetheless literally maddened by the hypertension suffered by their seniors and become convulsives in their turn, without knowing why. And, above all, although Gustave and the veterans of March have followed different paths, their options at the time are identical.

The young Flaubert's passivity, constituted from early childhood, structures his vision of the world and his consciousness of himself, forbids him from affirming, from denying, more generally from acting and from understanding the action of others. None of his comrades, perhaps, senses this sudden paralysis in his muscles that comes over Gustave whenever the question of taking practical action arises (although the *collège* probably contained clearly defined proportions of active and passive boys). But as members of a sworn group that will crumble into particles at the end of its degradation, they are fettered, reduced to impotence. Just as in a group in fusion each serialized individual is seen to come to it as social activity—to the extent that every member comes to every other member as the same and not as another—and tears himself away from the *pervasive* seriality, so, in the dismantled group falling back into a state of seriality, each one again becomes progressively *the other*—for the moment, *oneself as other*; the individual senses in his neighbor their common impotence to struggle against serialization and the loss of their sovereignty. After the counterrevolution of 1835, the schoolboys felt like the *patients of history*. They wanted to deny the group's dying by organizing disturbances, but that denial, far from appearing a limited and practical challenge of factual state that *might be changed*, seemed to them transformed, despite their efforts, into a denial of reality. Their violent acts now served the single purpose of delaying the moment of abdication: they were not yet dreams, but neither were they any longer acts. There they were, stripped of their transcendence. Not that it was reached in principle; their common aims were simply con-

261

jured away and the field of their collective possibilities razed. Passive, they no longer recognize their former objectives, but they preserve what Monsieur Delay calls an autistic memory of them, by which we understand that these memories, unrecognized, unrecognizable, haunt them as what has not been and never will be attained, determining in them a permanent consciousness of their impotence and a permanent denial of the aims proposed to them. Is this really a denial? Rather, would such aims not seem strange to them? To learn Greek and Latin, get married, take after their fathers—these are possibilities, no doubt, but certainly not *their* possibilities. How could they pro-ject themselves toward what does not in the least concern them? These are external *events* that will happen to them, perhaps, like an illness, or an accident, or death, but which they will do nothing to hasten. Therefore, no projects, no surpassing except in the realm of the immediate; their revolt stays inside them, a suffocating, incomprehensible fury that keeps turning and cannot even be named since it is not externalized as an act.

Rational thought is forged in action: or, rather, it is action itself producing its own illumination. Therefore, if a thought of inaction, of impotence, exists, it can be only a dream. In autism, an extreme form of passivity, desire is unable to go beyond itself toward the real and so turns back on itself as its own image, as imaginary satisfaction or, if you will, as transcendence bent back in immanence, the way parallel lines in a curved space bend toward each other and meet. As we have seen, Gustave has long since become an imaginary child; in him the dream is the empty and gaping site of impossible praxis. For this pithiatic soul, we understand, reading is a veritable magic spell: he allows himself to be possessed by another's dream in which he is featured in the name and traits of a sinister, princely hero who will avenge his humiliations by debasing the human race. But Gustave's comrades, although their passivity is provisional and circumstantial, are no less potential dreamers. Their bitterness, their resentment, their "ideal" can find neither issue from the self nor even expression, endlessly circling each other and consequently resulting in confused images to which the dreamers have no key; they know neither what they are dreaming about nor what to dream. Swept by oneiric gusts that vanish in an instant and seem to have the purpose of mitigating the absence of practical mediation by presenting desire through its imaginary satisfaction, these children are struck by the apparent incoherence and poverty of their fantasms, which, once dissipated, leave them in the grip of a stange unease. They will be prey to the first *other dream* of directed oneirism that shows them their underlying demands precisely by gratifying them. Since the Fall, Gustave has had all the time in the world to ruminate on his shame, he is to some extent acquainted with his needs, he knows in general what he wants from literature. The others, taken by surprise, have no opinions: how should they know that they are awaiting a dream in which they might recognize that part of themselves which their ponderings have rendered unrecognizable and which was once their pride? For a better understanding of the meaning of their "reading," we shall here attempt to describe the oneiric postulation they carry within them, which, in order to crystallize into a dream, is only waiting to make contact with external crystals.

As was said at the time, their "ideal"—though still shadowy—was Man. Clouet and his friends wanted to hasten his advent by a political action that would compel the adults to keep the promises of the July Revolution. They did not consider themselves finished examples of humanity—since the City of ends was not yet built—but rather builders; if the dignity of man should one day be conferred upon them, it would not come to reward their merits, but they would receive it, like everyone else, as members entirely outside the society they had helped to construct. Nothing could be more realistic, as we see: these young politicos wanted to *realize* the ideal of the French Revolution. We know the result of their attempt: Man having appeared at the doors of the *collège* only to collapse, revealing his impossibility, the schoolboys, deprived of Clouet and the most conscientious of their leaders, were convinced that Man neither was nor could be fashioned. In short, they gave up trying to *realize* him. He remained in them, however, this unrealizable ideal, like a permanent demand, a sense of remorse, a bitter regret. What could they do but unrealize themselves in him? Impotence leads to autism, one of whose basic characteristics is that autistic thought, having lost practical categories, confuses the end with the means, the agent with the end or with the instruments that allow its attainment. A mental patient who *dreams* of escaping has no means to put a rational plan into operation. Is the aim to open the door and flee into the country? Very good: the means and the end adhere, form a sticky and formless mass. A proverbial saying facilitates this interpenetration: he "will take the key to the fields." Lacking a structure through praxis, the key and the fields vaguely constitute the same, single objective: the key gives the fields, it *is* the fields: it is enough to hold the key in one's hand to possess the entire countryside enclosed in a single fist. The countryside, which *is* freedom. In other words, the operation is simplified: the key is no longer a means, it is the absolute end. All the patient has to do is steal the key from the psychiatric hospital, but even if he succeeded, why would he use it? Let him hide it under his mattress and resume his dream. Yet it must be stolen; this means reorganizing the practical field, calculating the opportunities and the risks; the dreamer, however, is quite incapable not only of succeeding in these undertakings but even of conceiving them. The desire is there, nonetheless, and it has not in the least diminished. Happily, to the same extent that autistic thought prevents its *real* gratification, it procures him a symbolic satisfaction: by replacing "doing" and "having" with the inert category of "being," so well adapted to his impotence, it allows him to become unreally the key itself through a gelatinous fusion of ends and means: "I *am* the key," says the patient. He *is* the key, that *is* the open door, that *is* the countryside, that *is* freedom.

The schoolboys are less affected; they work—more or less—and busy themselves, absorbed by a thousand daily affairs. Their autism is *social*; born of an identity crisis, their relation to Man in the depths of their being has continually been modified, a relation which was originally a practical and communal demand: they had to *make* it. The unity of the group being broken, the categories of collective praxis are dissolved; they can no longer even conceive the meaning of the inert postulation that remains inside them; the meaning of their autistic dream, vague and incomprehensible, forever shattered, an illusion that never "takes"—it is upset by practical tasks—is that they *are* unreally Man, whom they cannot *realize* in objectivity. It is not a matter of building a humane society together but, quite the contrary, of every man for himself, building at night, while asleep, the most inhumane of societies, magically identifying with the great solitary, hollow image they preserve inside them. These children are all disposed to transfer their resistance *to the terrain of the imaginary*. But since they haven't the good fortune to be mad, they will not effect the mutation of categories *alone*: no sooner would they attempt it than they would fall back into the insipid inconsistency of their subjective selves. They must have the mediation of a third party, which provokes an artificial autism by hypnosis; in other words, the autistic mode must be presented to them simultaneously as the subjective movement of their imagination and as a temporal determination of objectivity—which is possible only if *someone other* sets to dreaming of Man inside them and for them. Therefore it is *fiction*—novelistic, dramatic, or poetic—that they unwittingly await. It comes, gets passed around the *collège* as contraband. They pick up that material object, a book, open it, and discover on the materiality of the white page very real, impenetrable striations. Convinced that the work is a reality, since it gives itself through the opacity of things, they *read:* reviving a defunct intention, rewriting, reassembling, animating this heap of inertias, giving a future to this presence by projecting themselves forward to the end of the book, the end of the chapter, the last moments of the sick man, the last day of the man condemned to death; lending their own future to the fictive adventure in order to illuminate the present by future lights, awaiting. A double-faced expectation: the future and the expectation of the reader, captured by words, are also the fatality that furiously pursues the characters in their anguish or their impatience, the unexpected event that disappoints their expectation and ours. In short, the Romantic reader is temporalized by lending his temporality to the protagonists; these, conversely, impose singular but inflexible rules on his oneirism: the rhythm of duration, its orientation, the speed of the narrative, the slower passages, the shifts of speed—he submits to them to the very extent that it is he who has awakened them in an inanimate object, and so he is trapped. Is ip the dream of another that he is compelled to internalize and that is substituted for his subjectivity? Or isn't it perhaps his own dream externalizing itself and generating its own strict laws in order to impose them on the world? This time, the illusion prevails; the schoolboy is vampirized by this monster, an image that is reality.

This is the moment of *incarnation.* Some works of fiction do not require it: they cast a spell but only *allow seeing;* the reader, prisoner of a fictive world, remains purely a witness to what happens there. The Romantics lay claim to the reader's complicity: he is compromised; jolted by the imaginary events his reading constitutes, is taken by surprise, overwhelmed, crushed; it is he who rescues a fair lady in a stagecoach, he who suffers, gets himself killed, or kills. The Rouen schoolboys, enraptured and amazed, have not even finished arranging the scenery—a Spanish road at nightfall—when along comes a character they have never seen or heard of, yet they immediately know his name, his age, where he comes from, where he is going, what conjunction of circumstances led him to this place. At first sight he scarcely bears any resemblance to them: he lives in the sixteenth century, he is a hard-eyed Castilian who is searching for another Castilian in order to plunge his sword into the fellow's chest to avenge his dishonored sister. Moreover, he is referred to in the third person, as if to make it clearer to them that he is a stranger who leads his life as he

265

intends, a consistent and opaque being, absorbed in his own thoughts, who has not even perceived their presence and has no need of them. Be that as it may, this individual ends by imposing himself; they get into his head, discover his feelings, his thoughts; they are forced to see what he sees and the way he sees it, to know only what he knows of the world, to share his cares, his desires; all at once they are dazzled by the perception that this stranger is one other than themselves, and that he is also Man in his plenitude, and that the sole means of *being* fully a man is by projecting their ego into him. Now when they read "he" or "him," these words take on a new and complex meaning: without losing their power of distancing, they appear as the "I" or the "Me" that dares not speak its name; for these readers, the Castilian avenger is at once the object of an imaginary perception and the ego, a quasi-object of reflection. In other words, reading seems to be an imaginary reflection, of which the reflected-on is the Castilian's *lived experience*, and in which, pushing the reflexive dichotomy to the extreme, the imaginary reflection makes the ego *its object* without thereby depriving the reflected consciousness of its transparency. For the schoolboy who ruins his eyes reading, the Castilian is that reader appearing to himself at last as the object he is in the world, and at the same time he is the reader's own subjectivity as it would appear *in itself* to an impartial and omniscient observer. What we have, in short, is the in-itself-for-itself finally realized.[23]

Incarnated! They feel deliciously free because they are the ones who recompose this imaginary world by joining letters and words together, by awakening meanings, by losing themselves so that this material should make sense. But this complete freedom has the effect of constituting a rigorous destiny for them: they will follow in the Castilian's footsteps; they will go where he goes, never elsewhere; they will suffer his sufferings, bleed from his wounds, submit to the consequences of his acts, and will be inflexibly led through a hundred episodes toward 16 June 1567, the day of his death and of their sad awakening. The full employment of the imagination absorbs all power to imagine: real life is viscous but slack; we can pull ourselves away from it, the time of an image; no one can escape the fiction of novels except by throwing away the book and finding once again the reality that lies in wait. The reader is no longer available to form even a single image for himself: he is mobilized to produce those images proposed to him, and those alone; in short, the *written* imaginary, torrid, piti-

23. This, as the reader will have understood, is the illusion proper to incarnations.

less, is a total image, and utterly virulent. It excludes all freedom to conceive something other than it, even while claiming a plenary freedom that grasps the real and maintains it outside of nonbeing by a continuous creation. It is as if the dream had abolished the revery, as we see in nocturnal dreams, where all deliberation on possibilities is forbidden since possibility does not exist in dreams—which means that all conjecture is immediately transformed into belief. In this sense, oneirism might be defined as the triumph of imaginary engagement over the free play of imagination. Such is reading as well, and this is what abuses our schoolboys: struck by the abyss that separates the poverty, the evanescence of mental images from the organization, the richness, the unpredictability, the indestructibility of the written imaginary (the duel on page 112 is a *fact* since it can be found again, precisely the same, each time the book is reopened at that page), they are convinced that they have lost their imagination and that reading is eminently perception. Do they imagine that they are actually perceiving the duelists? It is not so simple; but the death of one of them, unexpected, inevitable, *leaps from the page* like an event in the real world: if they don't actually claim to have seen this death, at least they would swear they have witnessed it and even intuited it. Hence the certainty—inarticulable because language, too, is totally mobilized—that if the mental image is unreal, the novelistic image is *on the side* of reality. This error is inevitable: he who does not commit it cannot give himself to his reading. However, it is a confusion of the real with the necessary. And the bond of necessity unites abstract propositions; the more one approaches the concrete, the more this connection tends to disappear: on the level of lived experience—which is also that of Romantic fiction—it is dissolved. In fact, the question is not so much *what* constitute the real events of our lives as *how* they offer themselves and *how* we receive them. And they seem to appear in the immediacy as gratuitous consequences—obviously, since the contingency of the visible refers us to our contingency as seers. Moreover, observant thought is practical, it is born of action and is made explicit when action is already there, carrying it along and erecting it as its self-regulation. This thought participates, therefore, in the wager of praxis, which, surpassing every situation toward *possible* transformations, holds that every situation is surpassable on principle. The wager is often lost, but it must not be considered an error, a "transcendental illusion"; it is, in fact, the very structure of the existential project. Thus, facticity and transcendence—which are, moreover, dialectically connected—have the effect of revealing the event that pounces on us as something that might have been produced differently or not at all, and above all as something we might have been able to avoid had we been more vigilant or more clever. In short, it is the contingency of fact that is the best indication of its reality.[24]

Autistic thought, on the other hand, is inflexible because the dreamer is affected by impotence: no possibles, as I have said, no freedom, neither means nor end, the crushing of the dreamer by the dream; images come to the dreamer and are affirmed through him. He is the one who creates them, certainly, but he cannot distinguish what is from what can be; he suffers them in the manner in which they burst forth, mingled with a desire, an anguish, coiled back on themselves. Similarly, when autism is provoked by reading, what undeniably marks the unreality of the fictional object is the iron necessity that is imposed on our freedom and compels it to produce the dream of another in a preestablished order in which the smallest detail cannot be changed. And that necessity, precisely, appeared to the adolescents of 1835 as a criterion of truth. The error was inevitable, above all because they needed to make it.

Here they are, then, rigorously conditioned by the words they awaken. Even as they submit to such domination, they are conscious—as I mentioned earlier—that their freedom is on loan. Yet instead of being an enslaved will, conscious of its servitude and terrorized by it, as in the case of pathological autism, this freedom does not lose the feeling that it can revoke its commitments: it is always possible, at least in principle, to throw the book aside, to wake up— even if the adventure is deeply engaging. The Romantic reader's dual relation to the novel—submission, surmounting—makes him all the more captive: it reassures him and elates him; above all, he has the inimitable joy of being at once the cruel demiurge and the creature whose destiny he organizes, who will live out that destiny until he dies of it. Through this demiurgic inflexibility he escapes his true progenitor, the contingency that comes to him from the fact that his being has been given him without his opinion asked; he makes himself the basis of his own existence and of his being-in-the-world. Moreover, the fictional narrative does not suppress all possibles: the hero often wonders if he will take this or that step, which one will best serve his designs. Thus—save in certain fantastic tales where everything is possible, which disqualifies and suppresses all possibil-

24. When someone reports an incident he claims to have witnessed, don't we say, "That is too well constructed, it is contrived, I do not believe it"?

ity—the fictional world is less frightening than the dream world: the reader knows that he will not be invaded by horrible phantasms that come from his own dark side.[25] When the schoolboys read, spellbound, they escape from grown-ups, from parents, from the slack and inexorable universe in which they are enclosed: they recreate themselves *in objectivity*, begetting themselves as Manfred or Rolla. Do they think they really are? Yes: in those black and blasphemous masses which they celebrate against everyone and everything, they are convinced, evening after evening, that something has finally happened to them.

We must therefore distinguish three dialectically related levels of consciousness in Romantic reading, which are conditioned by the form and content of the grapheme. On the surface, the reader assumes a quasi-reflexive consciousness of an imaginary ego, which, in the form of an alter ego, is presented as its *Fatum* and its necessity. Just beneath the surface he is conscious of intentionally abandoning himself to passivity in order to produce the dream of others as *his* dream, in other words, of maintaining himself continuously in a certain pithiatic state that is the necessary condition of all directed oneirism. On this level, however, what is intuited is not so much the consent to powerlessness as powerlessness itself, recognized by the schoolboy as *his* powerlessness (which always silently affects him). At the deepest level (the level of non-thetic consciousness), he grasps himself as a freedom that *lends itself* and makes itself demiurgic in the process of exercising the demiurgic prerogative. This triplicity has important consequences: through it, in effect, Man—resuscitated for the first time after the collapse of 1831—is constituted as *Romantic* and becomes the imaginary being of the little readers of Rouen. Indeed, we would have trouble recognizing in Hernani, Didier, Antony, Manfred, and other avengers the free citizen that Clouet wanted to release from his chrysalis. Yet it is Man they incarnate to the extent that the

25. The result, however, is the same: in pathological oneirism or in the nocturnal dream, the possible is purely and simply suppressed. In reading, possibles exist, they are numerous, but they impose themselves neither more nor less than recounted events. These are the possibles that the author has given his character in the *other-dream* with which he has infected his readers; they are fixed in advance; it is them or nothing. The constraint on this point is as clear as it is in autism, it is simply taken to the second degree: we are accorded these possibles, but we are captured by them and in them. The reader is forbidden to create possibilities from others that would be *his own*, forbidden to dream of what the Castilian knight *might* have become if the author had not decreed his death. Closing the book, we will do as we like, but while we are reading we divest ourselves of all our possibilities in order to slip naked into the skin of the character, who will impose his immutable possibilities on us.

hobbled children, depoliticized, reduced to autism, claim the valorization of both their fundamental freedom and the impotence to which their fathers' counterattack has reduced them. In other words, the Romantic hero is Man, in whom the reader, projecting himself, rediscovers his facticity in the form of necessity, and his being in the form of duty-being. This "man" is neither a future being who represents the end of a concerted enterprise, nor a simple *specimen* of the human race, but simply an existing being whose spontaneous actions are in themselves norms, produce values—a being in whom *lived experience* is immediately ethical.

Can powerlessness, the permanent state of the vanquished schoolboys, be valorized? Yes, it can. First of all, on the very level of writing: the inspired poet is overcome by inertia in order to produce the poem that will make these children weep. Does he not weep himself? His creative delirium—the waxlike flexibility of the writer—and the nocturnal displays to which it gives rise at the *collège*—the waxlike flexibility of the reader—proceed from the same core of passivity, all the enchantments and all the "possessions" of which are merely particular determinations. Writer and reader meet on the level of the character whom they raise up by their joint efforts: for each of them, the dream that inhabits them—the *same* dream—is the dream of another. The writer—is he sincere?—in any case continues to pretend that it is: "There, inside his burning head, something like a volcano took shape and grew. The fire smolders silently and slowly in the crater and lets its harmonious lava escape, spewing it out of itself into the divine form of verse. But does he know the day of eruption? One would think it's as a stranger that he witnesses what is happening inside him, so unforeseen and celestial it is! . . . He listens to the harmonies slowly forming in his soul."[26] At the moment of creation, "I" is another. The reader is cordially invited to rediscover the profound otherness of his being so that the "harmonious lava" should seem to burst from it. Reading is a "listening"; he who abandons himself to it will have the sudden revelation of his savage being: if he can *be dreamed* it is because, more profoundly, he *is thought* and, at the basic level, *existed:* his desires and his dreams are posed for themselves only on the surface, yet they retain the mark of the subterranean nets where being and meaning come to him. Here we have the first glorification of passivity: it is the basis of all oneirism and, in consequence, of all poetry. But this is still merely a formal aspect of the Roman-

26. Vigny, Preface to *Chatterton* (Pléiade edition) 1:817.

tic oeuvre: it will be *pathetic* or it will not exist, for the imaginary is *suffered*. The contents of the poem or the novel redouble the reader's passivization: the adolescent embodies himself in dark figures that capture his *consentual* inertia and return it to him as if it were the law of their being—as if the possession of the child by the dream of others corresponded to the possession of the hero by his *other-being*. The hero suffers his life just as his creator claims to suffer his creation; his rule is *pathos* in the Hegelian sense of the term, that is, a right lived as a passion. He lacks the means either to affirm his ethical exigency or to compel others to satisfy it: he *suffers* it, he *endures* it, he is martyred by it.

By definition, therefore, he is an *outlaw*. Better, he is the son of an exile, exiled himself, *born in exile*, whose rages or melancholy his father's goods or—who knows?—his crown; dragging his incurable ennui on foreign soil, he bears the permanent consequences of a match he lost without playing, even before being born. Everything he sees, everything he feels, everything he does is framed by the world of exile and is produced necessarily against that original right—which is merely one with himself and yet is other than he (his title of duke, for example, is *inherited*)—so lived experience can only be an *endurance* for him. A stranger, he witnesses the flow of his life, just as the poet-prophet, his creator, witnesses the slow formation of the volcano from which the "harmonious lava" flows. Indeed, action demands adherence to oneself—for this reason it can be called Manichaean. But the dark hero rejects action a priori, or, if he attempts a show of force, he bungles it. He will therefore legitimize his demands at once by the violence of his passion and by the deep certainty that he must die of it. It is this futile death, the inevitable end of the passional journey, the meaning of the entire process, that haunts love, ambition, hatred like a prophecy, revealing their true nature: being-to-die. On this point we have Flaubert's testimony. In the second *Education*[27] he writes: "In these last days [Frédéric] had written nothing, his literary opinions had changed: above all, he esteemed passion; Werther, René, Frank, Lara, Lelia, and others more mediocre roused his enthusiasm almost equally."[28] There is some malice in presenting Romanticism as a fad, the object of a passing infatuation. But the two verbs, as always carefully chosen, do justice to what was pathos for the

27. According to the context, this change would have occurred between thirty-six and thirty-seven. According to the correspondence and the youthful works, it must be situated a little earlier.
28. *Oeuvres* (Pléiade edition), 2:46–47.

schoolboys of Rouen. How can one *esteem* passion if it is not an ethical commitment? How can one's *enthusiasm be roused* for Werther if this character, by an exemplary suicide, does not offer himself as a model of morality? From the point of view of common sense and of utilitarianism, nothing is more absurd than this death if it is not the fact that all these angry young men agree to a process which they make fixed and fatal by their refusal to do anything to stop it.

Indeed, one is sometimes tempted to believe that these characters have *chosen failure* even more than passivity. Look at Hernani: what a bungler! It is impossible to be so stupid: he must do it on purpose. When, from defeat to defeat, he ends by falling into the hands of the enemy, he will surpass himself. He has a mandate: vengeance,

> . . . who keeps watch
> With him always walks and speaks in his ear.

As he is arrested incognito, he still has a chance to get out of this scrape and one day become the avenger he has sworn to be. What does he do? He steps forward and enumerates his titles and qualities:

> I am Jean of Aragon, king, executioners and
> valets.
> And if your gallows are small, change them.

Perfect: by indicating a disdainful solidarity with the conspirators, he has made his execution inevitable. Thus he renders himself incapable of accomplishing his mission; he has betrayed honor for vainglory—can one imagine behavior more typically doomed to failure? But Hugo goes further; this fine declaration is ineffective for when Jean of Aragon offers him his head, Don Carlos has decided to be merciful to the conspirators. Poor Hernani: dead, he could have carried his hatred to the tomb unassuaged; living, his rival disarms him by giving him back his titles and Doña Sol besides—blowing on his hatred and extinguishing it. "Oh!" says the unhappy man, "my hatred has vanished!" He throws down his knife and betrays his father for the second time.

At least that is what the bourgeois Voltaireans of 1830 would say. Their sons see things quite differently: Hernani has not fashioned his destiny; an *other will* has prescribed it for him—his dead father's. By demanding to be executed, he *assumes it:* through lofty words and sentiments he dissolves the other-being of Fatum and transforms it into free choice; by revealing his name and rank he validates his blood right for the first and last time, claiming the right *to die as a Spanish grandee.* Hernani, the object of history, becomes a *sublime-object* by giving a *verbal* body to his dream of being its subject. He wants his horrible death to be a stunning demonstration that he indeed merits the status he claims but at the same time to make it impossible for him to enjoy his newly recovered dignity. And this is precisely what fires Frédéric, Gustave, and their comrades with "enthusiasm." No more double-entry bookkeeping, *debits* and *credits;* the impassioned man has nothing, owes nothing: he is a torch, a public solitude, consuming himself in front of everyone until he dies. In this sense, passion is opposed to bourgeois virtue as *expense* is to *savings:* what the *desdichados* claim is the right to be pure consumers in a society that is built on the production of goods and the accumulation of capital. And what have these outlaws got to consume but their own lives, all that remains to them? They are *giving* it: to everyone, to the world, to heaven, to anyone; they give it *gratuitously* and in order to affirm the perfect gratuitousness of their sacrifice: "conspicuous consumption" must take place before the crowd; but let no one try to derive any benefit from it—other than the advice to go off and be burned at the stake in their turn—otherwise, this spectacular self-destruction just might be useful to someone or something, and utilitarianism just might recuperate it. A useless, ineffective process of annihilation, a burning stake, kindling heaven and with its light, crackling and grandiose sentence escaping from it like stars, addressed to no one except perhaps to a deaf God; Romantic passion is *generosity itself.* Extravagant and baroque, hyperbolic, it continually extrapolates, becomes intoxicated with sorrows, which it *acts* in order to feel them in the extreme; it lives beyond its means; perpetual tension of lived experience, maniacal insistence on not departing from the prescribed route, it is life squandered in the name of death, it is love devouring existence for nonbeing, it is the realization of nothingness posing as the supreme purpose of being. This is why Lara, Rolla, a hundred other "more mediocre" protagonists fire their young readers with such enthusiasm. In the impassioned Romantic figure, generosity appears nowhere as praxis, that is, as a sovereign act placing the agent beyond nature; it is nature still, and nature saturated, for authentic Man is fated to be generous. But this very nature is supernatural as well, for contrary to all the affirmative essences that are manifest through the tendency of being to persevere in its being, Romantic generosity demonstrates a negative rapport to the future, as a tendency of being to invest its plenitude in the abolition of its being. In short, rather than a having-to-be, it is a having-not-to-be, a kind of intelligible choice that escapes as such and is nonetheless reflected in the empirical character of the generous person, through the directed rigor of the passional connection, as the mark and seal of freedom. In other words, the egocentric determinism of submen alienated from their being, that is, from the preservation, for and against all, of their particularity, is contrasted in Man with Passion, or the *conatus* toward death, which defines him as the effort of an obscure freedom set on denying any singular determination. Man poses his being in order to destroy it and is affirmed in his plenitude only at the very moment of its abolition; he lives the sovereign decision of his free will hidden like an irresistible impulse that hurls him toward death; his "being-to-die" is natural in that it can be grasped, within the involutive process or from the outside, as a simple observed fact and appears as a reality in the midst of the world, but it remains inexplicable without recourse to the supernatural because it is opposed in its very essence to natural law. With this inevitable consequence: that the "passional" is the deepest reality of man, while reason is merely a surface phenomenon, a methodical exploitation of human forces, the mobilization and canalization of our affects for the capture of nature. For Frédéric and for the Rouen schoolboys, reason and passion were no longer opposites, as they were in the classical centuries when one represented pure thought, the part of our soul that is not dependent on the body, and the other represented imagination, the place where the body and the soul unite. Quite to the contrary: reason, unmasked by this conversion to passivity, loses its rights; far from having the governing of souls conceded to it, it is revealed as purely utilitarian: it is a tool. This very thing degrades it: the Romantics of 1830 boast the same contempt for utilitarian undertakings that medieval barons had for work: he who wants to earn his living will lose it.

To assume "endurance" without holding back, to abandon oneself to it, to exalt it, to exaggerate it, can only mean to build an ontology and an ethic on passivity. The Romantic hero regards his life as a renewed Passion of Christ. He is Jesus returned to earth, condemned by the will of the Other (an Other who is himself and his father at the same time) to expiate a sin he has not committed. He knows it, he knows in advance the stations of his cross, the detail of his sufferings. Born in exile, a mocked God, he *endures his provisional humanity* and lets himself be beaten and murdered by the very souls he has come to save. The Passion, the proclaimed meaning of every Romantic life, is the consent to failure; it is sacred passivity. Truthfully, subversion somewhat corrodes the myth: among the Christs of the time we find numerous perverts and several Anti-Christs; Melmoth is one of the former. Be that as it may, all are both damned and redeemers; un-less—which amounts to the same thing—they damn themselves in order to drag the human race down with them in their fall and doom it more surely to Hell.

Such is the message the schoolboys receive when they are on the verge of despair. The failure of revolt, the triumph of order, their im-potence—they discover to their amazement that these are the signs of their election. Angels murmur to them that they are heading in the right direction: let yourselves sink straight to the bottom, the great-ness of the human race begins with defeat, and the saintly life is simply an endless shipwreck. Man will never happen: his very perfec-tion prevents him from existing; but he allows us to sense his pres-ence in the final challenge of a man condemned to death(in the invincible, futile pride of the vanquished, in the gasping victim's scorn for his executioners. They fall the more easily into the trap as they are readers and as they are conscious of awakening the hidden meaning beneath the inertia of signs: demiurges, their freedom lends itself so that Lara might exist and embody them; the presence of the human, which they divine between the lines of the recomposed dis-course, is their own; together, they are the fascinated, despairing incarnation and the benevolent creator who keeps him from anni-hilating himself and smiles on him with love. When the hero believes he is lost, they know he is saved: let him die, they tell themselves, we will receive his final message in order to make it the golden rule of our lives. He is Man, he is unaware of it, but we who incarnate ourselves in him have no doubt about it: through consensual failure, divine pas-sivity, the desperate love of death by which we are affected *in him and by him,* freely, we are reunited with our pathos as vanquished. Oh yes, it is true, we are born in exile, and our failure, lived in convulsive violence, is the Failure; the new headmaster is merely an agent of des-tiny; in crushing us with his iron fist, he has revealed to us our being-to-die.

The bad angels listen, satisfied, to the soliloquies of these ensnared rascals: "You," they whisper to them, "who could not *see* your par-ents in their terrible objectivity and who dared not judge them for fear of condemning yourselves along with them, fear no more! Slip into Chatterton, look at them with his eyes, resuscitate his impotence and his despair, lend him your scalding but aimless hatred, he will concentrate it on the single hateful being, your father, the bourgeois. Being incarnate in this murdered poet, you will discover that monster in all his baseness and will judge him without the least worry: for although you are the issue of his flesh, you are not of his species. The image of Christ, an innocent and sumptuous victim whose freely consented failure was, as God, to be born of a human womb, you have endured from birth that basic defeat which is at the source of your Passion. Men, you have been born of bourgeois wombs."

What a marvelous celebration they propose to these schoolboys! It is all there: the children are infected by their enthusiasm, leap, and fly up into the air, rolling in a field of stars. It seems to them that the incarnation has put an end to the identity crisis that was overwhelming them. Romantic reading is therapy: it puts them in possession of an ego and of that cardinal virtue, generosity. A transsubstantiation is effected that reveals the norm beneath the fact and, beyond the pleasure principle and the principle of interest, initiates the reader into the majestic mysteries of the death wish. Reading, at this time and for these young men, is meant to celebrate a rite of passage (from child to adult, from bourgeois to Man, from the every day to the sublime, from being to having-to-be, from inertia as the internalization of an induced impotence to passion as the sovereign choice of pathos, from real object to imaginary subject, etc.), to rejuvenate the Christian myth of the Incarnation; they celebrate in solitude a sacred festival, a black mass, shivering with cold and enthusiasm, tense and somnolent, extralucid and overtaken by marginal hallucinations. Black, yes, because the cross, that pair of sacred planks raised behind the altar, worshiped as a symbol of power and life, is in reality the emblem of punishment, of physical suffering, of spilled blood, of human wickedness and of the abandonment of the martyrs, of death, finally, the meaning and supreme aim of life. Indeed, a whole life, the brief and magnificent life of Chatterton, of Werther, is lent to the adolescent each night and makes itself lived from beginning to end, death being present from birth, a mournful and magnificent consecration of every moment, and birth present in death as well, if not as the path to eternal life at least as the entrance to the imaginary. Reading is murder of the father; at the same time it is a *"rehearsal."* They have given their life to nourish fictional worlds; it will be given back to them a hundredfold, reworked, molded, compressed, rid of its dross, pure as only an imaginary can be and beautiful enough to break their hearts. It is Adventure, wholly predictable even in its unpredictability, which is deciphered beginning with the end and whose least event, strictly the product of future and past, is at once premonition and prophecy, like the notes of a melody. Ultimately, reading is the magnified internalization of childish gratuitousness; it puts an end to their unease by teaching them that one must be superfluous, and that this is their finest claim to glory. Let them make their fathers fork it over from the cradle, let them get all the dough they can, and let them squander it wherever and however they may for the pleasure of being the angels of the bourgeoisie, in themselves and by themselves. "I will destroy everything," thinks the nocturnal reader, exultant at rediscovering his old dreams of pyromania: "That great flame in the distance is that *myself*? I, the Great Expense, the cursed part, I, the last sun launched by the pyrotechnicians, spinning before bursting, I, who neither am nor want to be anything but the destruction of my body, of my soul, and of the goods of this world by frenetic and fatal abuse of pleasures."

Revenge of the aristocrats. They race to their doom: the machine is not running smoothly, it is going to break, the damage will be considerable; how can they not perceive it? It is not for lack of alarm bells. First of all, are they really *theirs*, the partis pris imposed on them, the arrogant denial of the discursive, of logical connections, the absolute condemnation of that utilitarian thought, reason, the contempt for the concept that arrests the movement of the soul, the systematic quietism that claims to free the thinking substance from the structures imposed on it by praxis? Aren't the Rouen schoolboys surprised when they are incarnated in Lara, Didier, Hernani, never to have *ideas*, in the proper sense of the term, but only feelings that claim to think, or thoughts that suffer? The Romantic *idea* is an ecstasy or an anguish, but it is never a determination of discourse: it must be surrounded by a multiplicity of images, none of which is entirely fitting; you do not deign to reason and, to tell the truth, you are incapable of it. Oneiric thought is *occupied, manipulated* in shadow; it goes from intuition to intuition by gliding or drifting, which happens to it under an *impulse that is other.* Thought is often, here, merely the dream chosen as the lived ideology of nonpower and of disconnaction; the book dreams in its readers, produces *images of unthinkable ideas.* And when the image takes itself for a thought, all thoughts take themselves for images, and the ones that have a valid content manifest themselves—in the author as in the reader—only by symbols borrowed from the external world, which necessarily distort them. The Romantic "text" is merely an immense metaphor: what is expressed in it is a thought that dreams itself, or a dream that believes it is thought.

This does not mean that such oneirism is not clearly structured; Romantic reading can assert itself with imperious plainness, *provided* one has adopted its system of references, which is merely the diurnal system in reverse. The Romantic mirror offers these adolescents a world similar to our own, except that No is pervasively substituted for Yes, and Yes for No. Oneiric thought is nocturnal: in these dark, hypnotic novels, our young owls find a little of everything, even sunny landscapes, but nothing may be seen, neither the sun nor the dazzling beauty of women, except through the smoked glass of night. It is the world upside down: you take on the eyes of death to look at life, those of madness to observe reason, nonknowledge envelops and penetrates knowledge, action is merely a glitter on the surface of universal passion, perhaps merely a passion that is unaware of itself, just as knowledge is merely ignorance that does not know itself. You lose before playing the game, and you can do nothing but trail your grievances from cypress to cypress the length of the funereal grove, searching desperately for thistles and thorns on which to tear yourself and bleed, ah! to bleed even more, for victory is trivial and belongs only to the Other; it offers itself to Man only to be rejected and to make him know the bitter splendor of failure. There is nothing to do but destroy, and destroy yourself, to dream of a conflagration that would reduce us all to ashes; such is generosity, the supreme value of the nocturnal world in which man, king of creation, appears on the last page only to be abolished along with the dream that engendered him. Why do the schoolboys fail to perceive that this ethic offers the most obvious example of perversion? That it would make no sense if a solar world did not exist *first*, in which life appeared as the supreme good, and death as the absolute evil? I answer that they do perceive it. If not all of the time, at least quite often, but that *precisely* in those moments they renew their vow of allegiance to Romanticism out of a willingness to be perverse. They know that the bourgeoisie reigns and that they are vanquished: *therefore*, its ideas are true, its values are just, its acts efficacious; the bourgeoisie is the subject of history, it is *reality*. What is there to do but submit or *unrealize oneself*? They will unrealize themselves; after a false submission, when their fathers, reassured, triumphant, go to sleep thinking that "this youth asks only to be well governed"; they will go strolling in another world, a deception, a fixed mirage inscribed in books, whose underlying and blasphemous meaning is to deny the real in full knowledge and to give nothingness ontological priority over being. In reading, they affirm their freedom to say no *in the imaginary*; they opt for the false, the illusory, the insubstantial, and win insofar as the real can do nothing against unreality. Assuming their failure—which is a nonbeing—they become incarnate in the phantoms that vampirize them, jubilant to *be* in Lara, in Childe Harold, that nonbeing of being to which they have been reduced. "Determined not to open their fists," like Mallarmé's Old Man, they dig themselves in, proud to be error, sin, death, and to condemn the entire world. Lara, Frank, are merely tools: the chief incarnation, the only one worthy of them, is Satan. Never has he been so fashionable, this Prince of Darkness, who will never cease to fall or to despair or to be infinitely wrong—having in vain attempted to carry wrong to infinity—or proudly to proclaim his crime and his revolt, or to mock the creation by deceiving men with phantasms that borrow their consistency from the being they deny. They will become incubi, these lost schoolboys; they delight in feeling that reading is scandalous for the simple reason that it sometimes scandalizes the bourgeois inside them; to read is to commit every evening the inexpiable sin of despair, to give one's soul to the Devil and to condemn the divine work by deliberately preferring the uncreated, night, the impossible—in a word, the imaginary.

Is Man the Devil, then? someone will ask. Wasn't he Jesus a moment ago? I agree that he is now one, now the other, and sometimes the two simultaneously. It depends on the depth of the pithiatic slumber: if the young reader is at this point so fascinated that he almost forgets what he is doing, the written dream closes around him; he remains conscious of being incarnate in a persecuted hero but regards this incarnation as the supreme sign of his generosity; a demiurge made man, he lives the Passion of Jesus. Let interest give way, let him be disconcerted or shocked by a paradox that requires his immediate attention, and he is engaged in the passive act of losing himself and of damning himself so that Rolla, reanimated, should curse the bourgeoisie in his name. At this moment, reading and at the same time reflecting on his reading—which is, as we have seen, a quasi-reflection—the Man-Christ suddenly reveals himself for what he is: a dirty trick played by the Demon. Will he wake up completely? No; on the contrary, he rejoices in doing ill and in being pledged to the Devil in order to learn from him those sleights of hand that challenge the real in its totality. One can conceive an infinite number of stages between total sleep and lucidity, and Romantic reading is the continual movement from one stage to the next. Thus, the Man-Christ is never entirely Catholic nor the Man-Satan entirely unworthy. This nightmare Jesus is poisonous around the edges; and what grandeur in the Accursed One! Be that as it may, the sleepers would quickly awaken if

279

their most extravagant dreams were not guaranteed by beings of flesh and blood, by their older brothers, proud and generous lions who write as they live, no holds barred, and who do them the honor of addressing them. Man exists, that is certain: what other name should be given the poet who went off to die at Missolonghi out of generosity? And to countless others who, at the height of riches or in the pomp of power, did not cease to dream? Yes, Byron is worthy of Lara, Chateaubriand of René—the adventurers of Greece and the Americas have no cause to envy their heroes. Man, that impossible creature, is at hand, he awaits his provincial younger brothers, next year or in five years, a few miles from Rouen, in the capital. Through the pen of *his* writers he is giving them a sign; a novel is a message that concerns them alone: you are chosen, you will enter this career when your elders are no longer there, you will live as they live, you will know luxury and money the better to measure their vanity, you will have power and glory to suffer solitude the more mercilessly, you will feel the painful ecstasies of love, you will travel, you will be given the moon, first of all because you deserve it and then to develop in you that properly human quality, infinite desire, which is not satiated by the possession of all.

The children were exquisitely impatient: through this incarnation they gave themselves the pleasure of joining their favorite authors in the imaginary. Indeed, those authors too were only recently incarnated in the sorrowful and noble creature they had produced with their sorrows, their passions, their superb nostalgia. And the children could not reanimate that creature without lending him in turn their own sorrows and passions, without nourishing him with their temporality; nor could they understand him without projecting into him their own nostalgia. Dreaming the *other dream* that imposed itself on Vigny, the young reader, without ceasing to be Chatterton, rediscovered in himself the author's creative generosity, felt that he was a natured Vigny being modeled by a naturing Vigny: he became the author's imaginary creature *against the author*—for as Chatterton he closed in on himself with the hostility of the creature *set* against his creator—and at the same time identified with the poet by allowing himself to be *occupied* by the imagery that had only recently invaded him. Being a passive activity, Romantic reading becomes, as passivity, a provoked and voluntary unrealization; as activity it turns the reader into a hypostasis of the author.

Still, for the operation to succeed, the reader must truly like what he knows of the writer, what he senses of the man through his work.

If the little Rollas of Rouen should one day perceive that Musset has deliberately deceived them, that their big brothers, "sweet as bad angels," were leading them by the hand toward a hidden precipice, the illusion would be broken, a swarm of vampires would fly out, startled, the sons of the bourgeoisie would find themselves bourgeois once more and would exchange an exquisite desperation, full of promises and healthy tears, for a a dry despair, closer to laughter than to tears. This is what will happen between 1835 and 1840. But we shall understand better the scope of their misunderstanding if we compare what the adolescents hoped to gain from Romanticism with what Gustave asked of it and with the objectives the authors actually set themselves.

What Flaubert asks of his readings corresponds quite precisely to what he seeks in his spiritual exercises: that they should rescue him from the egalitarian world of quantity where every unit is worth as much as every other, that they should restore to him, in the imaginary, his *qualitative* supremacy. Life would not be livable if Gustave could not, for lack of other claims, consider himself Injustice's chosen. The *only* chosen, the only one to whom God denies himself, the only one to know the weight of Adam's curse, the only one banished, a gentleman of science in exile among the peasants—in a word, the only victim of an ordered society, of a monarchy where the father reigns, a prince who is kind to everyone and the pitiless persecutor of his only younger son. As we see, Gustave adopts all the Romantic themes. At the outset, there is the theme of failure, an obscure pre-natal sentence he is compelled to realize in all its iniquity, day after day, by *suffering* his life and groaning with Byron: "I was born a child of wrath," and also, "I am my own hell." Impotent, abandoned, condemned to perpetual dissatisfaction, this arrogant, dark nostalgia gives proof of the *quality* that others are vainly bent on denying him. He is the first in a secret hierarchy, and, assuming his condition of humiliated schoolboy, applying himself to live it as a Passion, he is very close to Christ, that other consenting victim of another Father's will. He suffers for everyone—in vain, as all is vanity, superbly, as he redeems everything through sublime transports—and makes a gift of himself, denouncing the scandal of the creation out of pure generosity. Therefore, he is also Satan; he will make men jump into the frying pan of style, and in the pure gratuitousness of art he will be the Great Demoralizer. This is the image of himself he wants to glimpse as he leans over the Romantic mirror. It is familiar—the portrait of Gustave as a young aristocrat. He will learn nothing from the "thick novels" he devours, his character is already completely formed; but while he reads, his imaginary face benefits from the objective rigor that gives the protagonists an appearance of reality. Unlike his classmates, he asks the other to dream his own dream so that *his* dreams, returning as *others* to inhabit him, compel him to observe himself, to await himself, to understand himself in joyous amazement, as though he were a stranger. He existed concretely for himself only to the extent that he was an object for others. Through the rare happiness of reading, Gustave becomes an object for himself, yet without ceasing to be at one with himself; he observes himself but knows himself, he awaits himself but foresees himself; everything he does, feels, and declares in the novel he reads is always what he wanted to say, do, and feel. He recognizes his birth and his blood, his race: for him, reading is a certificate of nobility, and at the same time it allows him to affirm his implacable contempt for the bourgeoisie. Not that he wants to dissociate himself from his class or that he intends to condemn Achille-Cléophas for his bourgeois habits—father and son are both lords. No; when the adolescent proclaims his disgust for the calculating, utilitarian, greedy, and stupidly sententious bourgeois, he is taking revenge on his classmates and their fathers by stigmatizing their plebeian condition from the height of his noble generosity: he denounces the plebeian Louis Bouilhet by dying of misery every evening while the commoner, a sly careerist, accumulates his laurel wreaths.

So when a child convinced of being *"wellborn"* asks the Romantics to confirm him in his belief, they hurry to satisfy him. On the magic mirror they hold up to him, a majestic face appears, his own, that of a superman who surveys the world and has merely a glancing acquaintance with our species. How can such a character inspire the same enthusiasm in Flaubert, bent upon incarnation as an aristocratic hero who will reflect his blue blood, and in his classmates who only recently claimed, along with Clouet, the advent of universal man? How can the same fiction at once exalt his classmates' humanism and Gustave's misanthropy? We shall not understand this without investigating the Romantics themselves. Indeed, they present their creatures in a highly ambiguous manner, something they would not choose to do, it seems, had they not planned to create and maintain the misunderstanding we mentioned. They like to speak of Man, the fallen god who remembers Heaven, and their protagonists appear to be at once the qualified representatives of the species and the empirical manifestation of Man-as-he-ought-to-be. Hence there is something of Corneille's influence in their works—with one reservation, as we shall see, which is paramount. But what is striking in their works, as in the old trage-dian's, is that "Man-as-he-ought-to-be" turns out to be the aristocrat. Let us say that Corneille and the Romantics depict the nobility and its aspirations at two moments of its involution.

In order to fight the ascension of *his* class, the mercantile bour-geoisie, which the monarchy associated early on with the government of public property, Corneille depicts for us, as in a dream, the mar-velous equilibrium that would be produced by the union of the throne and the aristocracy. The wisdom of the sovereign would temper the chivalric impetuosity of his great vassals, and their fierce demands— "respect our rights"—would act as a brake, when necessary, to the ambitions of the king. His hero, as we know, is characterized by gen-erosity, the institutional virtue of the nobility. The nobleman, in effect, gives his life to defend the honor of his House, his lord, his king, and his God. He is a military man whose function is to kill, to be killed when necessary, and who defines himself as the supreme spendthrift by his permanent project of going beyond his practical field toward violent death—given or received. The contempt in which this career soldier holds workingmen derives from a prejudice: they knock themselves out to reproduce life for themselves and for others, their labor is in essence a refusal to die; since they define themselves by it, they can have no more value than the property, so vile and com-mon, that they have chosen as an absolute end. By contrast, he who gives his life without expecting anything in return, he whose very birth is a right and an obligation—since he is born-to-die—must as Spendthrift be the Great Consumer. In the light of his future death, he regards consumption, providing it is gratuitous, as a sacred cere-mony: the systematic destruction of goods symbolizes the killing of man in the things he possesses or produces. Whether you burn an enemy town or gorge on food or squander an inheritance, the prin-ciple is the same: you render the goods of this world to their primitive materiality by effacing the traces of human labor. All worldly riches— whether given or taken—eminently belong to the generous man, that exterminating angel who explodes while blowing up the earth, since he uses them not to reproduce his life but to reproduce his death and the death of the enemy by means of a symbolic destruction. He takes food only to preserve the strength that will allow him to make war and get killed. And of course he also fights to preserve or increase his patrimony, but he derives that patrimony from the dead and sets it apart for his eldest son, dead on reprieve. The circle is closed: death governs all human relations through the dominant class; the funerary sacralization in feudal regimes corresponds to the reification that characterizes human relations in bourgeois societies. Through etiquette and ritual, through the very gestures and style of life of the aristocracy, death *emerges* as the meaning and purpose of all praxis, the hierarchical connection of the superior and the inferior, the foundation of all powers, and the majesty of all attitudes: all ceremony is funerary.[29]

In the feudal period and in the tragedies of Corneille, the great vassals, bound to the monarch by sworn faith, are *actively* generous: they consider themselves agents of history, and they are not altogether wrong; it must be recognized, too, that they give their lives *in effect*, that in any case they risk their lives in the course of concerted undertakings. Moreover, in order to reconstitute an ideology that is disappearing, Corneille aims at the *practical* sublime: it is acts that are admirable, and resolutions are exalted only if they are related to acts. In 1830, on the other hand, the sublime is verbal. It reaches its climax when the situation makes all praxis impossible or, what amounts to the same thing, useless. Nonetheless, after the fall of Charles X, Man-as-he-ought-to-be is contrasted to the triumphant bourgeoisie just as Corneille's hero was contrasted to the rising bourgeoisie; condemned by failure to passivity, generosity, as we have seen, remains his essence: he gives nothing, to anyone, he can be merely a useless passion and he knows it. Be that as it may, his fundamental quality remains the gratuitous surpassing of life toward death, although it is severed from everything that gave it its efficacy. Born to die, these outcasts look at life from the point of view of death; the passion that destroys them without profit is pure consumption. They consider themselves Great Spendthrifts banished by a parsimonious society. They have replaced death on the field of honor with suicide, but sui-

29. After that the nobility could be avaricious, calculating, hungry for honors or gain, indulgent, lewd, and salacious; I am describing their ideology or, rather, what is sometimes called their false class consciousness. They thought and lived in the name of death, and their most egotistical appetites could appear to them only in the guise of generosity. It is impossible to understand the Crusades without grasping the Crusaders' conquering ambition, which was thought of as the noble desire to give one's life to deliver the Holy Sepulchre. As for deciding in each case to what extent this religious devotion is pure appearance and to what extent it contains some *reality*, this can be done only by an examination of actions. It is certain, however, that generosity as an interpretation—more or less false, more or less true—of impulses is bound to have a real effect on those impulses and, consequently, to modify them.

cide is their honor; every moment of their life is worth something only through their future death, through the death that at the same moment totalizes them. For them, sworn faith is a vow to die for nothing. It has lost its institutional meaning: Hernani does not die *for the king;* he poisons himself in order to keep the promise that a jealous and cruel old man has extorted from him. In other words, he tears himself from life stupidly, just as he was touching happiness, to prove that he is by nature (read: by his royal blood, by his prenatal choice) superior to all gratification, to all happiness. The Romantic hero is a lost soldier who wants to make his life into an epic of solitude as a reminder of the victories his ancestors really accomplished on the field of battle; he is a nobleman in exile in a society of bourgeois who have killed his king. Nothing surprising here: the *Desdichado,* that collective character adored by the schoolboys of Rouen, was especially conceived by monarchist authors for a monarchist public, preferably a titled one. The masters were called Chateaubriand and Lamartine. The younger ones had begun their careers in the twenties, determined to tie their fortunes to the regime.

Everything tempted them to do it, and primarily birth. Most of them belonged to the nobility: from infancy they had seen the throne overturned, power usurped by a "Corsican with slicked-down hair," religion flouted, their caste dispersed. They were, they thought during their adolescence, the losers of a game others had played; doomed to prenatal failure from the day Louis XVI's head rolled, exiled not in some Koblenz but in their own country amidst regicides; as sons of an irreparable disaster, they had grown in hatred of the bourgeoisie, who had robbed them of their future, and in loyalty to the dead king. For them, the Restoration was a divine surprise: the monarchy returned when they no longer believed in it; they found a mandate again, a mission, a future—they would serve it.

Those of their confederates and friends who are not titled think they should be and, like Hugo, add the particle to their names. Monarchists, they are also imperialists;[30] Napoleon fed them on glory. For them, there was no prenatal failure: the disaster came later, on a day the eagle soared to the heavens and a gust of wind broke its wings. They too regard greatness as military: death, victory, the sun on the bone-littered field: "Death itself was so beautiful, then, so grand, so

---

30. We also find this double allegiance in certain young noblemen; in Musset, for example, who, more sensitive to military successes than to usurpation, wrote: "Never were there suns so pure as those that dried all this blood. It is as if God made them for this man."

magnificent in its smoking shroud . . . There were no more . . . old men, there were only corpses and demigods."[31] At the time, it was enough to be French, the son of a dead man or a *moriturus,* in order to be noble: "all children were drops of burning blood that had flooded the earth." As the son of a general of the Empire, the comte de Siguenza, and of a woman from the Vendée, Hugo loves two nobilities at once, both won on the field of battle, and judges himself, through his father, to be the equal of the sons and grandsons of the exiled aristocracy. Be that as it may, the Emperor is dead, long live the King: these young bourgeois will put their zeal into loving the gouty old man who reigns by divine right. Victor de Hugo will make himself the bard of the nobility. His bourgeois friends and confederates hasten to believe in revealed religion: protected by the monarch and the Church, they seek and are accorded the divine right to be geniuses. These elect no longer have anything in common with the ordinary people who gave birth to them: God whispers in their ears. They aspire only to hobnob with those other elect, the aristocrats, in the salons of high society. Who else, they think, could understand them? To whom else could they speak of death and generosity?

For readers, and no doubt for themselves, these lofty considerations mask the most realistic ambitions. The eighteenth century was pure gold: enlightened despots, princes of the blood, dukes appreciated literature and made writers their companions. Crowned with honors, exquisite attentions, sumptuous gifts, intoxicated by the company of the great, these writers had in return only one obligation, an agreeable one: to sing the praises of their benefactors. Revolutionary barbarism put an end to that, but since the legitimate monarchy has been restored, couldn't one hope that the fabulous age of Maecenas might be revived? If, in return, one had to supply a little propaganda, where would be the harm? After all, Voltaire was not unaware that Frederick II and Catherine of Russia used him for public relations purposes, which may have prevented him from writing everything he thought but certainly not from thinking everything he wrote.

Immediately after the duc de Berry's assassination, the marquis de Fontanes, the marquis d'Herbouville, and Chateaubriand, feeling the need to intensify monarchist propaganda and win the intellectuals to the cause, establish the Royal Society of Letters, whose name is its program. Victor and Abel Hugo are delighted to recite their poems there; an eager public calls them "children of the royalist muses."

31. Alfred de Musset, *La Confession d'un enfant du siècle.*

And when Hugo, Vigny, and others found *The French Muse*, Henri de Latouche refuses to "join a phalanx of ultras." The *Odes* are saturated with Christian spirit, marrying the poetic sentiment to the religious one; the preface recalls "the cross raised by Chateaubriand on all the works of human intelligence." Lamartine judges it opportune "to enshrine himself in the established order"; in return, the king reads the *Méditations* and congratulates him. Encouraged, the poet connects himself with *Conservateur*, a review that gathers together the heads of the royalist party; he agrees to replace the final lines of "Bonaparte" in the *Nouvelles Méditations*, anodine as they are, with a conclusion that is duller and harder on the emperor. The young poetry aims to go back to the "national sources of French inspiration"; this is a rather crude maneuver intended to fight the universalism of the bourgeois eighteenth century and identify the personality of France with the Restoration monarchy. In a more picturesque and more publicized form, a "return to the Middle Ages" is initiated, officially patronized by the duchesse de Berry, who in fact makes it the theme of her costume balls. The operation is accomplished *at the expense of the bourgeoisie;* weary and vanquished, turned in on itself, the bourgeoisie contents itself with a precarious agreement with the aristocrats: if the regime is viable, it will be accepted. For the young *arrivistes* of the Restoration, this criminal rabble would not be worthy of constituting a public if they did not judge themselves bound to confirm its feeling of guilt, to point out its uncurable baseness, and to uphold its respect for its king and its fear of God. These authors write with pleasure only for the aristocracy.

The annoying thing is that the aristocracy does not read. Or scarcely. They have considered intellectuals suspect since 1789.[32] After all, they are the ones who carefully prepared and fomented the revolutionary troubles: "Voltaire is to blame, Rousseau is to blame." The disappointments begin: after several small favors, the collaborators of *La Muse française* understand that they will not be the beneficiaries of the regime. Of course, in 1825 Charles X inducts Lamartine and Hugo, who is twenty-three years old, into the Legion of Honor. But Chateaubriand, the idol, is in a rage: after his resounding fall, he quits the political scene and shuts himself up in a scornful silence; he is reduced to the solitude of René the *Desdichado*, while affecting to remain faithful, as sublime vassal, to the kings who abandoned him. Vigny, who long thought he could reconcile literature and a military career,

---

32. The duc de Richelieu put the "young nobility" on guard: "Distrust intelligence."

resigns in 1827, disheartened by the ingratitude of the sovereign and the political blunders of the government. *Marion Delorme* is censored; Hugo seeks an audience with the king, who graciously consents, asks to read the piece, upholds the censorship, and commits the unpardonable error of making known what he thinks of writers in general and of Hugo in particular: he grants Hugo a pension of two thousand livres. Hugo never refuses a pension when he can persuade himself that it is in reward for his merit; indeed, he is already pensioned. But this one is an attempt to buy him off—he does not accept it. These insults endured by the children of the royalist muses put them in mind of their prenatal failure; they believed, in the light of their first successes, that the return of the Bourbons had effaced it; but the old men who govern have nothing but their name in common with the proud monarchs of former centuries. The noble writers, however, will remain loyal to them since sworn faith is part of the fundamental project which is at the source of their aristocratic *quality;* but they begin to understand that their loyalty—as in the time of their adolescence—is addressed to *nothing,* or perhaps to the old men, now dead, whom they never knew and who disappeared without leaving any heirs or any heritage. Death paralyzes them: they will be faithful until death to those voluntary-dead. Hugo, however, returns to Napoleon, another deceased: henceforth he will no longer hide his admiration for him.

In the meantime, the July days sweeping away the Bourbons give power to the bourgeois rabble they have so scorned and who haven't forgotten it. They discover that their adolescence was prophetic: their destiny was indeed exile. They will live and die as they were born, in the midst of this sacrilegious third estate which has twice renounced its legitimate sovereigns, killing one, banishing the other, and which, overthrowing the natural hierarchy to its advantage, has despoiled the "young nobility" of its heritage. These gentle lords have lost all hope of leaving penury behind: Vigny, a resigned officer, will have to be content with a meager income from his properties; Musset, his brilliant junior, only recently enrolled in the phalanx of his elders, is enraged at the age of twenty to be merely an employee.[33] But this is not the worst of it. They suffer above all from a loss of substance, the withering of the "older branch" forbids them to give themselves to the usurper—no double allegiance—but their loyalty to an old mon-

---

33. And even through this profession he is linked to the arms business. Messieurs Féburel et Cie, his employers, dealt in heating for the military.

arch in flight is merely an absurd, ineffectual sulk. In the new society, their values no longer have currency, they are congealed; stripped of meaning, they sink to the level of futile postulations, and yet the young writers cannot change them because they express their being-in-class. This is how Vigny, while no longer practicing the military profession, remains nonetheless the military man he was by birth, but he will henceforth be merely an abstraction of a soldier: his funereal majesty stinks of death. A gratuitous death, for his sovereign has, alas, no more need of his services; a death he hopes will haunt the witnesses to his life all the more as he imagines neither giving it nor receiving it; a death that was a concrete project until 1827, and even until 1830 (while a Bourbon reigned, the poet could, in case of national danger, don his uniform once more), and which was subsequently changed, without his having anything to do with it, into a dark comedy compelling him, a wounded wolf, to suffer-and-die-in-public-without-a-word. Does he not feel that his generosity has moved into the realm of the imaginary and is in no way different from that of an actor playing the role of a prince? And yet it is undeniable that he was born to die, and that he is playing what he is—he is unreal only because the new society, in rearranging its structures and institutions, has unrealized him. He has seen his praxis changed into *legend* and dies from not dying. In compensation, he considers himself the permanent representative of the "sacrificed" nobility. To be convinced of this, simply reread *Stello:* "Nobility . . . betrayed, undermined by its greatest kings, who emerged from its midst . . . hounded, exiled, more than decimated and always devoted, sometimes to the prince who is ruining it . . . sometimes to the people who misunderstand it . . . always bleeding and smiling, like the martyrs, a race today crossed off the books, looked at askance, like the Jews."[34] This time, we've got it: the *Desdichado* incarnates the entire nobility, and his singular failure resumes in itself the drama of a moribund class, or rather—as he says, as Boulainvilliers has said, as Gobineau will say—of a *race*. Reduced to impotence, loyal to its vows, this race lavishly spends its blood with a mad generosity which will simply have the effect of eliminating it from history.

Madly generous, perhaps. But not to the point of forgiving the bourgeoisie. These military men preserve a fierce hatred for the enemy class that has changed them into literary men. Nonetheless, literature will make itself militant; since the sword stays in the scab-

34. Vigny, *Oeuvres* (Pléiade edition) 2:797–98.

bard, the pen becomes a sword; words will tear apart; the haughty academic spirituality of the royal muse will be replaced—gall, bile, horror, my God—by the vociferations of fury and despair. The misfortunes of the Romantics are profitable for Romanticism: toward 1830, it turns black. Visible or invisible, the Third Estate is present in their work. And it is ugly. The portrait of the bourgeois that will be imposed on the nineteenth century will issue later from the pens of Henri Monnier and Emile Augier; it was the vanquished aristocratic and legitimist writers, however, who first drew its outlines, and those who subsequently took it up could add nothing to it. *Chatterton*, in particular, describes for us the customs and character of a certain John Bell, the ancestor of Messieurs Poirier and Perrichon as well as of Isidore Lechat. In order to establish the magnitude of the misunderstanding that separates the black Romantics from their Rouen readers, we should return for a moment to that somber drama published in February 1835.

Flaubert seems to have read it only in 1836, at the earliest, and no doubt in 1837. The fact is seventeen or eighteen years later he still preserves a glowing recollection of it: "I am grateful [to Vigny] for the enthusiasm I previously felt in reading *Chatterton* (the subject accounted for much of it)." [35] The subject is the assassination of a poet by the bourgeoisie. At this period Gustave considers himself a poet rather than an artist. And Vigny's preface, which he must have devoured, characterizes the man of action, the great writer, and the poet: in the last, the adolescent believed he had discovered his own portrait; unqualified for anything but divine work, he is born to be a burden to others, and imagination entirely devours him. This possessed being observes as a stranger the movements of his own soul; his human relationships deteriorate and are finally severed; it is essential "that he do nothing useful or ordinary," that he be spared the "rude din of positive and regular work." Flaubert heartily applauded this question: "Is the only science of the mind the science of numbers?" Isn't he, precisely, "a spiritualist stifled by a materialist society in which the avaricious calculator pitilessly exploits intelligence and labor"? He is grateful to the poet for having sacrificed the particle in his name signifying nobility and for allowing himself to be represented by a sublime young plebeian: in the family of Achille-Cléophas, there is blue blood but no title; what is inherited is genius. In short, he is filled with enthusiasm, and his naive exultation carries him a hun-

---

35. To Louise Colet, 7 April, 1854, *Correspondance* 4:53.

dred miles away from the author's real intentions. This is understand-able, of course. He was fifteen or sixteen years old, Chatterton was eighteen, both were born with the desire to die; the elder gives him-self up to death at the end of the last act; the younger will save it for tomorrow, at the latest for next week; both, while they are alive, are terrified of dying without being completed. With what bitter joy the little schoolboy, recognizing his own fatalities in the destiny of his En-glish confederate, dies with him, uncompleted victim of his fatal gifts, of an impossible love, of the wickedness of the bourgeoisie. Following what we said above, we understand that nocturnal reading is the deep place that unites Gustave with his classmates: he ponders an in-dividual failure that has made him what he is, they live in fever and bitterness a collective failure that has smashed their group to pieces. Avid to compensate for their misfortune, the "individual" veteran and the fragmented team, reading the same novels, find a common denominator in the historical failure of the former ruling class; in other words, they all live that failure, *as if it were their own.* Or, if you will, they aspire to grasp their defect *through that failure* as a Passion, as their destiny, the unique source of their greatness. They are not unaware, of course, that Vigny embodied himself in Chatterton. But they never think of asking the primary question: Why does this gentle-man of thirty-eight, at the height of his glory yet embittered, interest himself in the fate of an ill-born child who kills himself without having done his work? Why did this future academician,[36] this *chevalier* of the Legion of Honor,[37] choose to incarnate himself in a luckless child whom adults treat as good for nothing and society refuses to recog-nize? Must we believe that he was thinking of "his wandering and military life," of the young poet in uniform that he was in the 1820s? Or, as he has the cheek to claim, that he, a writer who had "arrived," wanted to take advantage of his credit to "address to all of France an appeal in favor of the unhappy young men [whom he] was pained to be unable to help himself and [whom he] saw ready to succumb"? If

36. He made his first academic "visits" in 1841. Are we to believe that six years ear-lier he was hostile to becoming "immortal"? At eighteen months—Gustave is the one to say it—everything is already played out: a person has *already* opted for honors and shame or for dishonor and glory. Vigny is a cop. Hugo, Guillemin has shown, was tempted to become one around 1845. His formidable "constitution" and the 2 De-cember coup reminded him of his foolish pride.
37. In 1833, Vigny did not spit on the cross timidly offered by the Usurper. He was decorated by the Minister of Commerce and Public Works, which would have greatly astonished Chatterton, allergic to "all positive and regular work," an enemy of com-merce and profit.

they reflected on it, the poor boys, they would understand that Monsieur de Vigny, a legitimist, is slyly rallying to the younger branch, and that in order to mask the operation by a literary smoke screen, he wants to cry out "to all of France" his disgust for the pitiless peasants who wrested power from the nobility and are trying to accomplish its demise. His "appeal for the young men who succumb" is, in truth, an indictment against the Orléanist shipwreckers who killed the chivalric virtues and the generosity of the French gentry. This aristocrat takes up the defense of the wretched. Chatterton is as much the people as a prince. He is surely not the younger Flaubert son, that young bourgeois who lives in comfort and who is serving at school an apprenticeship in the virtues of his class. Count Alfred de Vigny, *desdichado* number 1, harbors no sympathy for the heirs of commoners. Just as he sells himself for a fistful of honors to their qualified representative, so he incarnates himself spectacularly in Thomas Chatterton—not in his singularity, but insofar as he judges he has received (no one has given it to him) the formidable privilege of personifying the entire legitimist nobility gathered into a single martyr, a single "innocent victim" of bourgeois society, a murdered poet. I have shown elsewhere that saints are made from would-be heroes. That is also true of those occasionally repugnant saints, always suspect, that we see swarming in literature after the July Revolution. In Vigny, in any case, from 1818 on, the poet is engendered by the mishaps of the military man; literary ambitions succeed disappointed class ambitions, and aristocratic pride is unrealized the moment the aristocracy loses its privileges. For Vigny, for the young Musset, an aristocrat conscious of his shipwreck can only be a poet, a poet can be born only of a shipwrecked aristocrat. Indeed, the aristocrat knows that his generosity gave him the *quality* to "read in the stars the way shown us by the finger of the Lord"; immolated in advance, living in the company of death, his abnegation raises him above all particular interests, all egotisms. In the name of a voluntary death, he aspires to exercise the noble function of "pilot," he has tried his hand at it, he has named the stars and the route, but no one lent an ear. And his sacrifice draws a new qualification from his gratuitous anguish: useless, unmotivated, untiringly pursued beneath a Heaven "deaf, dumb, and blind to the cries of creatures," this nobleman as pure witness transforms his lost efficacy into beauty. This explains the aristocratic origins of a literary doctrine born around 1830, which would survive the nineteenth century: art has no other end than itself because from the early period of French

Romanticism its only mission was to render futile the sacrifice of Man—that is, of military man. The genius of the poet and the blood of the nobleman are the same thing: their predestination. Dedicated, both of them, to despair, to death, they are equally banished by a vicious bourgeoisie. Chatterton is the Great Spendthrift: he consumes his life because one must die in order to speak properly of death, the vocation of the soldier; this explains his contempt for "useful work." For him, as for the barons of the thirteenth century, labor is aimed merely at reproducing life, the useful is based merely on egotism and on the craven fear of want. The young poet cannot even understand what is at issue here: dead on reprieve, everything is uselss to him, the useless is his vocation, he can create nothing without harming himself, without reviving his funereal phantoms and hastening the hour of his demise.

A legitimist swan song, an exaltation of the loyalty that conceals a sulky attempt to rally the forces, *Chatterton* is not written solely to pay the author's dues in the eyes of the partisans of the older branch: the bard's heart is foul with rancor, he wants to drag the bourgeoisie into the dirt; and on this point he is sincere. Or nearly. His play is a war machine. Analytic reason and its product, mechanism, were dangerous weapons in the hands of the *philosophes* and the encyclopedists; determinism, social and psychological atomism, the pleasure principle, and utilitarianism helped them deny freedom, generosity, and heroism, and at the same time it helped them deny the gentry their "quality," that certain something that justifies privilege. Vigny rebuts the argument: there are *men of quality,* such as Chatterton; therefore the bourgeoisie takes the baseness that belongs to its own class for a universal trait of nature. If the analytic method and the "materialist calculation" have succeeded so well, it is because the bourgeois have used them first of all to know themselves. The object and the method are one.

Vigny goes farther; with the clairvoyance of hatred, he shows John Bell, a rich manufacturer, as a merciless exploiter, just as the Southerners at the time of the Civil War would denounce the exploitation of man by man in the factories of the North. Whatever the viciousness of a landowner, he is well placed to perceive the "reification" of human relations in bourgeois society; the relationship between the squire and his peasants remains direct as long as mechanical inertia and atomization have not come to alter it. In act 1, scene 2, Vigny the property owner accuses the *real* proprietor of sacrificing his workers and

293

devoting himself exclusively to the god of profit—in other words, to the human Thing.[38] Are we to believe that he truly understood the way in which production, institutional structures, and praxis were connected to the interests, analytic thought, exis, and ethic of the bourgeois class? Certainly not. John Bell is not, in Vigny's eyes, a pure product of social contradictions; the proprietor is wicked, of course, because he is a manufacturer, but if he is this manufacturer, the absolute master of his enterprise, hard and egotistical, just according to the law instituted by his peers in order to protect their interests, it is because he is wicked *by nature* or, if you will, by his membership in the third estate. For egotism, the appetite for gain, a hard heart, economy pushed to the point of avarice, and the instinct for domination are in the nature of the commoner when he is not constrained by the authority of a monarch, by the generosity of the aristocracy, by the commandments of religion. The bourgeoisie has not *become* wicked, it has always been that way: all evil has come from allowing it to take power. In short, Vigny regards the bourgeoisie as a race. The result—disastrous for our schoolboys—is that his books, intentionally or not, are booby traps: if genius is a form of generosity, and if the nobility alone is generous, they are going to suffer great pain, these sons of the bourgeoisie who shed sweet tears, murmuring: "And I too am a poet!" The bourgeois race produces merchants, bankers, manufacturers, doctors, mathematicians, and—why not?—prose writers.[39] It is forbidden to produce poets because it is defined by its appetite for living and its will to power, and because its baseness makes it perfectly incapable of understanding the gift of self, being-to-die, and consensual failure. The schoolboys absorb this racism like a fatal

38. See especially Vigny, *Oeuvres* (Pléiade edition) 1:832: 832; John Bell claims: "The land is mine because I bought it; the houses because I built them; the inhabitants because I lodge them; and their work because I pay them. I am just according to the law." His interlocuter remarks with irony: "You are the absolute baron of your feudal factory." Meaning: Was it worth substituting you for the aristocrats when you are harder than the most ruthless barons of the feudal centuries?

39. In the first pages of *Souvenirs*, etc.—at the latest in 1839—Flaubert contrasted the poet to the artist. This passage is directly inspired by the preface to *Chatterton:* the artist corresponds trait for trait to the prose writer whom Vigny names the great writer. "The judgment [of the great writer] is healthy, exempt from troubles other than those he seeks . . . He is studious and calm. His genius is attention carried to the highest level, it is good sense in its most magnificent expression . . . He has above all a need for order and clarity." Vigny, *Oeuvres* (Pléiade edition) 2:815–16). "Between the artist and the poet there is a vast difference; one feels, the other speaks, one is the heart, the other the head." Flaubert, *Souvenirs*, p. 52.

poison, and curiously it awakens in them the Jansenism of their ancestors: all bourgeois are damned *by nature* and *their own fault*—because they are only free to choose Evil. If, every hundred years or so, one of them escapes from this rigidly enslaved will, his dismayed mother, cursing, shakes her fists at God, crying: Oh that I had spawned a nest of vipers rather than nurturing this mockery, this stunted monster! In other words, only the Almighty in His incomprehensible and infinite Goodness can choose to grant a plebeian child a perfectly undeserved salvation. "It *can only be a miracle;* the annunciation made to some Bastard-Mary, wife of a grocer": "You will give birth to *a nobleman*" seems to her some kind of curse. As for the chosen monster, his miseries will surpass the most sadistic imagination until the bourgeoisie, sickened at having given birth to a class enemy, puts an end to his brief existence.

Now begins the famous mystification that is called the second *mal du siècle*. A prestigious author presents to these schoolboys, battered by the animosity of their fathers, an untitled but sublime beggar and invites them to become incarnate in him: he is just a poor child like you! But no sooner have they entered the role than their ecstasy is troubled by an inexplicable uneasiness: something tells them that they "are not the character," that he is a foil, and that the character of John Bell would fit them like a glove. This has worked before—look at Hernani, that bold highwayman, a son of the people. They recognized themselves in him trustingly, flattered all the same at finding such a sense of honor, such magnanimous ideas, in this peasant whom they took for their spokesman and at being familiar, in his person, with kings and emperors. Unfortunately for them, there was that theatrical twist in the fourth act; the brigand throws off his mask—he is Jean of Aragon! Everything is explained; it is no longer astonishing that he knows how to answer the great in their own language, for it is his as well. The voice of blood. He is of their race, the traitor, he belongs to the military caste. By birthright. Suddenly, the little reader who is not *wellborn* lets go and tumbles back into his plebeian condition: he is not the one who has uttered these sublime words, and no one has spoken them *in his name.* He has understood the warning: if he likes, he may witness from the audience the sacred drama that sets a Spanish grandee against the heir to the throne, but he may not take it into his head to mix in. Noble sentiments are not his affair (what does he know of honor? and how could he practice clemency?); it is good enough if he manages an approximate comprehension of such sentiments; he surely cannot share them. Where was he misled, the poor boy? Lara and Manfred are sons of lords; Rolla, Chatterton, sons of counts; a viscount fathered Abencérage, the last of his line. A little bourgeois boy is not allowed to play with the lord of the manor's children. Jean of Aragon, if he should recognize him, would have nothing to say to him and doubtless, brooding on his vengeance and his love, would not even notice him. Others, more cruel, would spit in his face. For the simple reason—he is not unaware of it—that their fathers scorn and despise his own. For Messieurs de Vigny and de Chateaubriand, the young boy has inherited the guilt of the revolutionaries; regicide, an inexpiable crime, will stain the criminal class until the last generation. What a terrible misfortune, to love René so much and to be loved so little in return.[40]

The Rouen schoolboys believed themselves to be victims of a generational conflict: the fathers had taken the right road but had stopped en route; the sons had tried to continue the march, to push liberalism to the end; they blamed their parents in the name of Man as he should be and as they wanted to make him. And here a specious discourse induced them to change their struggle into a class conflict and to unrealize themselves as aristocrats in order to look down on the bourgeoisie with the scornful gaze of the upper caste, the caste which their grandfathers had fought, which their vanquished fathers despised in silence, which the Glorious Revolution had overturned, which Clouet and his friends wanted to finish, which the insurgents of March reproached their parents for sparing.

The most serious thing is that they are complicit in the dirty trick being played on them. In 1830 the attitude of the bourgeoisie toward the nobility is highly ambiguous. The bourgeoisie needs the nobility, as we have seen. But this is not all: the bourgeoisie "manufactures" an inferiority complex. Industrialization has scarcely begun—there is no need to look for new markets in underdeveloped countries; nationalism is yet to be born: the loyal subjects of the citizen-king are resolutely pacifist; war, they think, must give way to external trade. Yet they openly admire the military virtues of "their" aristocracy. The army is their luxury, their ideal, their generosity, their prestige: they support it with their last pennies. It represents, so to speak, the "ac-

40. There is of course Ruy Blas. This character seems to have been conceived to show that valor does not depend on birth. Unfortunately, what emerges from the play is that a lackey *can have the heart of a nobleman*. Again, a disguise.

cursed part" of their gains. Besides, many of them would like to have a title: in the past, every time a commoner could betray his class, he did it, and it could be said—an incomplete explanation but not a false one—that the notables of the Third Estate stood against the nobility in 1789 because it refused to integrate them. The result: in the second half of the eighteenth century, the Third Estate, being oppressed, *rightly* considered itself the truth of the nobility. As the victors in the first half of the nineteenth century, they thought *wrongly* that the roles were reversed: the defeated class posed as the truth of the triumphant class, and the bourgeoisie, while challenging the judgments made against it by its former masters, recognized their unique right to judge. They could not have been more deceived: the truth of the bourgeoisie, as other eyes were discovering, in Lyon, in Rouen, in Paris, would burst forth in June 1848—it was the proletariat itself. But the rich cannot even imagine that the "new barbarians," who can neither read nor write and who sell themselves each morning like merchandise, might raise their heads and stare them down.

The sons have internalized their fathers' attitude; but their ambivalence is more marked. To borrow Freudian terminology, we could say that for them there is a real nobility, bigoted and limited, whom they despise, and a symbolic nobility whom they admire, and they are unable to separate the two or decide whether they want to abolish all privilege or are sorry they were not born into it. And here they are offered a chance of being incarnated for the space of a dream in true aristocrats worthy of the name. Of course, it's a trap; but who can say that they are not in some obscure way conscious of it and that they have not seen in their readings, without admitting it to themselves, the chance for a temporary and secret ennoblement? At any event, victims or accomplices or—most likely—both, the little Judases will be terribly punished.

As we have seen, for a while—one year, two years perhaps—they could deceive themselves without much difficulty: the discovery of reading-hypnosis was too unexpected not to overwhelm them. But the frustration, when they felt it, took hold in them as a permanent exis; yet they pursued their sessions of directed oneirism despite the disappointment they now knew awaited them, not only upon waking but in the very heart of their dream, like shipwrecked mariners overcome by thirst who cannot prevent themselves from drinking sea water, knowing all along that it will burn their throats. In a previously cited fragment from *Madame Bovary*, Flaubert bears witness to this

compulsion when he shows them "sitting on their beds, heads lowered, backs hunched, spending the winter nights devouring, immobi-
lized, some thick novel that ravaged their hearts." It is impossible to
be mistaken, for we know the care Gustave takes in choosing his
words: the ravages caused irreparable damage. In the *Préface aux
Dernières Chansons,* he spoke of the great conflagrations ignited by Romanticism in these doubly compromised minds: we know now that
the shattering shock waves produced disasters, splitting the hard material in which they spawned; seismic tremors, cave-ins. After the Romantic Attilas have swept through the good town of Rouen, nothing
will remain as before; devastated hearts will never grow green again.
This can have only one meaning: a splendid and disappointing illusion left them disgusted with themselves but unable to give up their
need for it. The children of the night will undergo, at their own expense, the experience of what Flaubert calls, at around the same period, "demoralization."

Let us take a schoolmate of Flaubert's, one of the boys who are
going to create with him the freemasonry of the Garçon—Pagnerre,
for example, whom we encounter again in 1863 as "a shareholder of
the new society who owns popular theaters." Let us suppose he is
reading *Chatterton* and attempt to describe the effects of this reading
on his daily life. In other words, how will he behave *during his waking hours after* a night of imaginary orgies, *before* the next nocturnal
orgy? What has become, for him and in him, of the poet who embodied him yesterday, who will embody him this evening? The answer is
simple: while reading, while reviving the signs, Pagnerre *was inside*
Chatterton to the same degree that he signified him and his English
environment. Now it is Chatterton who resides in Pagnerre, inaccessible transcendence at the heart of immanence, unassimilable kernel
of exteriority, remnants of a discourse no longer going on. *To be inside*
Pagnerre cannot mean to be incarnate in him; quite to the contrary, it is
to make oneself, inside him, the inaccessible Other *who signifies him* as
a wordly being, as an organism, as suspect. In short, as someone who
is not Chatterton, someone Chatterton cannot be and is constrained to
designate doubly, as the imperative showing him the path to follow
and as the supreme magistrate judging him on what he does.

The reader has no sooner come out of the Romantic hypnosis than
the *Desdichado* takes on a different ontological status: without becoming *real* he nonetheless loses the dimension of the imaginary. Of
course, Chatterton continues to suffer in the imaginary: the book is

there, the drama slumbers inside it, and anyone can waken it. But for Pagnerre, who now willy-nilly *realizes himself*, this imaginary is no longer imagined except *elsewhere:* elsewhere, in other dormitories, perhaps, other exultant schoolboys sacrifice themselves to institute the character. This surely has the effect of substituting for the lost imaginary state a collective dimension that seems to Pagnerre to be Chatterton's *objective being:* he who can appear everywhere *except here*, in this mind that remembers but temporarily cannot imagine. In short, for the fallen child, Chatterton's being is his virtual ubiquity, he is inside Pagnerre as an innumerable absence. The character becomes for his former reader what I have called a *collective*, a social object that draws its being from nonbeing, from the distance, from the noncommunication of the social agents who refer themselves to it. It appears to them in its inflexible inertia as the *index of separation* that characterizes the serial whole of which they are part—or, if you will, as the reason for the serialization. Hence it is of little consequence whether Chatterton is real or imaginary; his being comes to him from the fact that he infinitely overflows all consciousness, though he can only exist through it.

In truth, this relation to other readers—past, present, and future— was already present in veiled form during the hypnosis. But the implicit consciousness that for other readers other "readings" were possible, basically identical but differentiated by details, could only increase the sensuousness of reading by consolidating the imaginary and lending it unexplored depths, ineffable richness, "truth," an agreement demanded a priori from all sensible minds on the basis and with the firm intention of denouncing all readers who would not rally to this commonly held opinion as "enemies of Truth," old-fashioned and philistine. Upon waking, however, the serial relation can only increase the schoolboy's anguish by convincing him of his loss. As he was reading, *the others* were those who, *like him*, were unrealizing themselves in Chatterton; now the others are those who, by a consensual sacrifice, perpetuate the radiant incarnation and lend the Disinherited One a hundred thousand bodies. Through those absent others, Chatterton is *instituted in Pagnerre* as otherness, he is raised in his abstraction to the rank of alter ego—of superego, indeed—pitiless and sacred. This collective structure is tied in the Protagonist to his character as temporalized apparition: he presents himself to the former reader as a being in this sense, so that the being of the existing person is the past surpassed. The incarnation *has taken place*, it is, it will always be—at least as having been—an indestructible event. Thus the *pathos* of Romanticism has been *lived* in imagination, and the *norms* of Romanticism have been applied in the imaginary;[41] both attain the dignity of archetypes, of a primary and sacred experience that can be reproduced but in no way altered, and still less surpassed.

The memory, it should be added, being penetrated with nonbeing and finding itself therefore in a homogeneous relation to the imagination, does not on its own—that is, without a complex system of mediations—possess the means to distinguish between the past that was really lived and that which, at the same period, was simply imagined. Each of us can verify this by our own experience. Who among us has not hesitated before a fragmentary memory, undated, unclassifiable, and, unable to integrate it into past experience, has let it escape without deciding whether it was the resurrection of a dream or of a real event? How many people, betrayed in a dream by someone close to them, an intimate and perfectly loyal friend, can prevent themselves next morning on waking, and often all day, from feeling a bitter mistrust of "the traitor" that even they are surprised at? In this case, in spite of honest efforts, the reasoned conviction that this is just an oneiric phantasm remains superficial and cannot reach the deepest level where beliefs are forged.[42] To this triple root of his ontological status—collective being, past being, remembered being—the disincarnate incarnation adds the ek-static and future structure of awaited being. What is poor Pagnerre doing, in fact, during the "pensums" of the day but *hoping* for the night? Night and the lion's skin he slips on. So Chatterton is there in his pure abstraction, wordless, imageless, like a tension of the soul, a singular imperative: revive me in reality as I am in the eternity of a work, *realize* the man that I am, die endlessly and pass judgment in my name against the bourgeois assassins, beginning with your father. Let it no longer be the dream that tears you from your class but the inflexible and real verdict you render against it.

41. Pagnerre, the imaginary hero, conformed his behavior to the set of values to which Vigny implicitly refers; an imaginary magistrate, he is in agreement with the Quaker in condemning John Bell.

42. It would do little good to object that the contents of this dream bear witness to a secret hostility toward the friend whom the dreamer forces to betray—this is obvious. And it is true, too, that the following morning this hostility, revealed to itself in a dream, uses the dream as a pretext for persisting during the waking hours while dissimulating its true nature. What is striking is that the hostility should be able to fool itself and continue to take a phantasm *exposed as such* for a reality.

The child feels he has a mandate, but people have hestiated to tell him that the verdict, while theoretically possible, cannot in fact be given unless it be in the imaginary and through the mediation of reading. The trap closes on him: the imperative mission to condemn all hominids in the name of imaginary men is but a pretence; Pagnerre takes for a real command what is only a perpetual incitement to *read*, as if a voice were whispering to some bourgeois of flesh and blood: "Pick up your book, go back to sleep, become Chatterton again in your dream so as to condemn the imaginary John Bell." Unfortunately, the ontological dignity of the former incarnation and its serial universality as *collective* gives professed values an abstract and deceptive consistency. The *being-elsewhere*, the universal absence of the *Desdichado*, manifests itself to Pagnerre as the having-to-be of Romantic norms. Being-elsewhere, having-to-be: two unrealizable guises demanding realization. As the common character of the imaginary ethic and the real ethic is their being-beyond-being, the first can easily pose as the second. The error is inevitable and necessarily results in the "You must, therefore you cannot!" that we have already encountered, which characterizes the historical situation of a bourgeois son between 1830 and 1840. Even if Pagnerre wanted to betray his family and view them as the military views civilians, how could he, since he was not put into the world and raised to be a soldier? A bourgeois son, the bourgeoisie is his anchorage, the setting of his life; his tacit complicity with the people of his class is a custom that has become natural, his most intimate and hidden reality is the color blindness that makes him blind to the bourgeois in others, a collection of principles that pose as facts. The praxis of grown-ups has shaped him; he has made himself their accomplice in reshaping himself; he has internalized suffered modifications through a proprioceptive transformation which changes them into *habitus*, into exis: he is the return of the seasons, of vacations, of holidays, of family ceremonies; the return of the school year in October, of supervised studies, competitions, and exercises; and, through repetitive time, the irresistible spurts toward the death of the father and the inheritance. From Monday to Saturday, every night, a novel takes possession of him and compels him to challenge the bourgeoisie, but Sunday evening, after twenty-four hours spent "at home," it is a dutiful son who reenters the dormitory, his head full of bourgeois memories. Gustave describes it effectively in the same fragment from *Madame Bovary:* "When we had returned, we talked of what we had heard in our families, of the news of the town, the performance we had been to, the singer we had seen, and especially the little dance that left us with our hair still curled the next day.[43]

Bourgeois sweetness, little bourgeois pleasures, the bourgeois poetry of family dancing parties, self-indulgent comfort, security—this is what the dreaming bourgeoisie misses on coming back to school, what Gustave will miss so bitterly as he leaves Rouen for Paris. Up close it is not so easy to hate a father, especially if he smiles at you; the charms of the sedentary life are a permanent temptation for these cloistered adolescents because they become confused with the charms of freedom and amorous intrigues. Why travel? Why not remain all their lives in their native town, in the house where their father's grandfather had already lived? Later on they would take up business, marry the cousin who danced with them the evening before, they would have children . . . Such are the domestic dreams the little gentlemen bring back to the dormitory. Dreams? Not at all: *it is their lot*, and they know it; they tease their destiny and quite complacently *make themselves* bourgeois. Where have they gone, the Laras, the Fra Diavolos, the Hernanis? Have no fear: they will return in force the following day. But are they sound asleep on Sunday, when the young gentlemen testify to such domestic inclinations? No, they are in retreat, in shadow, but they are awake, intent upon reminding the children of the fierce nomads they were two nights ago so as more surely to spoil their pleasure. The children born at the turn of the century were "drops of burning blood that watered the earth"; "raised in the schools to the rolling of drums," they "flexed their puny muscles," "looking at each other darkly." For their fathers were living and returned from time to time "to raise them to their chests bedecked with gold"; Ceasar reigned, destiny of all the fathers and all the sons. When the sons, "ardent, pale, nervous," dreamed "of the snows of Moscow or the sun of the Pyramids," they were only prophesying their destiny: like their bloody progenitors, "they knew they were destined for the hecatombs," they wanted it. Death was in them, they called it the "sun of Austerlitz." But the children of these children were definitely *made to live*; with the exception of Gustave and a few other originals, they throw themselves with all their young strength into the conquest of happiness. Their defeat in '31, the rearguard actions, the bloodless Terror that followed led them to dream of murder and, often, of suicide; they are haunted by the idea of death, easy

43. *Ebauches et fragments*, p. 25.

prey to the demons of the new art. But in most of them the being-to-die, so loudly proclaimed, is only a borrowed being, an occasional and peripheral response to the difficulties of adolescence, to the events of the little history of school, while their being-to-live is a much deeper postulation that can be taken as their practical truth. Reading their thick novels, they have no trouble unrealizing themselves as a dead soldier by taking as an analogue their superficial death wish and looking at the contemptible little world of life through eyes that are already corrupted. But nothing works any more when, yielding to treacherous entreaties, they try to *realize* during their waking hours, at school, in the family, the funereal character who vampirizes them. They tried it a hundred times, we can be sure of that. The sun shines, Pagnerre sets aside the story: no more pirates, no more Indians or "Lords of Latency"; in the school courtyards there is only the legitimate and entirely plebeian son of Monsieur and Madame Pagnerre, who, as such, is seeking to practice the virtues of a Spanish grandee, an honorable outlaw, an exile. In this fish pond of solitude, can he give proof of an admirable and terrible generosity on the occasion of minute, daily events? To renounce life, happiness, for the honor of his name, in order to keep his word, for nothing? Oh no! He cannot do it: these children have every reason to *dream* they are prodigal sons, they have no reason to remain so; spendthrifts, if you like—as each of them is the object of expenses, of long-term investments—but on condition that prodigality itself is an intensification of life and not an offering to death. They give, but they contain their gift within "reasonable" limits: this means that they consent to depriving themselves, not to losing themselves.

At sixteen, Gustave shares with Ernest his painful discovery: egotism and vanity are the source of the finest actions; certain of being understood he does not hesitate a moment to choose alms as an example. And he mentions alms again in *Mémoires d'un fou*, when he laments his lost goodness. Alms, a wise bourgeois folly: I owe nothing to the poor, but I have the graciousness to provide them with necessities by granting them a calculated part of my superfluous earnings. These measured gifts, whose purpose is to preserve the domination of the bourgeois class, cannot in any case be claimed as generosity: the disinterestedness of the bourgeois is basically interested; he wants to save his life, whereas the sullen and vanquished aristocrat wants to lose his. Thus, every time Pagnerre or Flaubert, having vainly sought occasion for a bursting prodigality, resolve in desperation to give alms, it is inevitable that they should discover egotistical motives for

303

this measured expense. And this does not mean that all generosity is interested but simply that death is not their destination, and that radical expense of self does not constitute their fundamental project and their permanent possibility. If it were the case, indeed, far from being explained by motives, whatever they might be, the generous act would refer directly to the original structure, being-to-die, as the matrix of all prodigality, and motives, in contrast, would appear as the concrete historical singularizations of the surpassing of the self toward death.

Flaubert's disappointment—we shall soon return to his personal evolution—could be found in all these chimerical schoolboys in one form or another, but more or less as follows: to give, to give myself, I need reasons, therefore I will never know the gratuitousness of the military act; I will never leave the world of utilitarianism. Intoxicated with their splendid nocturnal incarnations, they want to affirm themselves against the familial utilitarianism by a purely unproductive expense; but generosity, when it has no other motive than the hatred of "greedy calculation," finds itself based on egocentric aims; the dice roll, the act is accomplished and, just because it was conceived from the original utilitarianism and as its negation, *is found to be utilitarian*. They will not escape—it is their lot; generosity is not a virtue, it is an institution, an *instituted* relation, in certain regimes, between giver and receiver. And then, go try to practice it at school: in a competitve setting you do not give gifts, you must win to survive—the weak are eaten, as Gustave effectively observed. Besides, the scholarly apparatus isolates and serializes, it breaks the properly human relationship: the practico-inert, here, denies the gift of self. Man was defined for them by this imperative: "Don't build your life, burn it." [44] These future builders—sworn to building well before their birth—understand with discomfort that having-to-be, which for them is *imaginary*, makes Man their most intimate impossibility, one that illuminates them privately and constitutes them, in relation to the titled military, *relative beings*, larvae created to resemble humankind but deprived of ontological dignity, whose only purpose is to clothe and feed the superior caste. From this point of view, even their mad desire to demonstrate their generosity cannot be admired: the valet envies his master. Just as Pagnerre is about to joyously condemn his father for the crime of subhumanity, he is abruptly challenged: he was wrongly taken for

44. This formula of Camus's effectively defines the Romantic and aristocratic imperative.

a judge; let him go and join the mass of the accused. A strange verdict is rendered, doubt is not permitted: this floating, evanescent sentence haunts him and chills him; inapplicable to the details of his subjective life, it nonetheless poses as the truth of his being.

Where does this inert, unverifiable verdict come from? What is the source, for example, of the fixed reproach, "You think basely," which his real thoughts, even anxiously scrutinized, can neither confirm nor deny? It must be that *an other,* transcendent in the heart of immanence, has the inconceivable power to judge him. And who is this pitiless observer of his life but Chatterton, the irreducible poet on whom he had thought to model himself and who remains inside him, an inert, enclosed figure, the painful and cruel memory of a dream. In fact, Chatterton says nothing, does nothing: he remains invisibly at his observation post; it is Pagnerre, now unable either to become incarnate in the poet or to communicate with him, who tries to see himself as the character sees him, to know himself and appraise himself as the Other knows and judges him. In the presence of his alter ego, Pagnerre cannot feel anything, conceive of anything, imagine anything without forming innumerable conjectures about the *other object* he is, at this very moment, for the Other, without reviving the contempt his incarnation evidenced for John Bell, and without striving in vain to be overcome by it.

In vain: the uselessness of these efforts throws him into confusion. The contempt is there, he is sure of it; he can *think* it—he still recalls the disgust the London manufacturer aroused in him—but he cannot *experience* it: surely contemptible, he can neither feel contempt for himself (that is, internalize actively the other's contempt and assume it) nor feel himself held in contempt (internalize it passively through shame). He must acknowledge the facts: Chatterton is his worst enemy; but unfortunately this deceased poet, who considers him with the fixed eyes of death, is deceased Man, descended in Pagnerre, who declares him, in turn, guilty of treason against society. So everything reverses itself again: the schoolboy is angry at being damned from birth—is it just to bear the crushing weight of original sin without having done anything? God has sent a Redeemer to the children of Adam. So who played this bitter joke on the children of the Third Estate, presenting them with a savior whose wild generosity would redeem them, inviting them to become incarnate in him, to live his Passion, and then establishing it in them, as a divine flame, guide and director of conscience, only to reveal to them subsequently, when the time for self-defense has passed, that they have opened their door to the exterminating angel? Should the torments he inflicts on them be taken for gracious gifts? Before the coming of the revered Lord who inhabits them, the schoolboys, disabused by their failures, held the conviction that Man was impossible. Why undeceive them only to reveal, when they have reached the height of exultation, that it is impossible *for them*? Are we speaking of ordeals to be surmounted? No, for they are presented as intrinsically insurmountable. So this Christ who inhabits them scarcely seems Catholic: is he perhaps the Antichrist? If they wondered *who* sent him, they might easily trace him back to the new authors. Monsieur de Vigny, writing his play in a flood of tears, declared, in short, that he was the man with divine right and that Pagnerre was not and never would be. Why not? When these children ask themselves this question, they are not far from discovering the truth. "How is he different from us?" wonders Pagnerre. "What gives him the right to set himself up as judge? Why is he *my* judge when I am forbidden, a priori and whatever he might do, from becoming his? Because he is a poet? But who has decided that I will never be one? If it is God who inspires him, why doesn't He inspire me? If the author declares that he owes this divine grace to his eminent merit and, singularly, to that generosity he possesses from birth and I am denied, it must be that Man, that so-called universal, is merely a collection of privileges, which by definition can only belong to some if they are denied to all others."

In this case, we must return to our point of departure: if the human condition is inaccessible to the greater part of the human race, Man is in essence unrealizable; he is the impossible dream of the whole species or the title that a few of the privileged wrongly give themselves. Have these poor children understood that the vatic poet of Romanticism aspired to express the grievances of a racist and suicidal nobility? They have glimpsed it several times, perhaps, but they cannot admit that Monsieur de Vigny has taken the trouble to write, in a flood of tears, works they still admire with the avowed intention of demoralizing the children of his vanquishers. It seems to them, rather, that this retired officer and most of his contemporaries have tried to create a knighthood of the heart from which the sons of the bourgeoisie are inexplicably excluded. I have said that the schoolboys of Rouen are victims and accomplices; this is why they do not follow their insight to its conclusion: their aristocratic postulation disposes them to find it natural that Man should be by definition an aristocrat. They are quite illogically indignant that the greater part of the human race—and most particularly the future citizens of Rouen—should be excluded from this new knighthood. If the Romantics had no intention of constructing war machines against Pagnerre and his schoolmates, they must have wanted to conceal the hideousness of the century by enveloping themselves in the magnificent shroud of illusion. These adolescents escape the horror of feeling hated by their favorite poets only by insisting on the purely oneiric character of the Romantic cosmos. Be that as it may, they certainly sense that these poets, by their standing invitation to the dream, are leading them, intentionally or not, toward perversion.

The parents are there to finish the work: they will kill the fatted calf, provided the prodigal son is willing to recognize his error in seeking virtue at the far corners of the earth when his humble duty awaited him at home, under the paternal roof. Since one must live and reproduce life, the progenitors are right to accumulate wealth. To cut costs in order to increase profits—that is true altruism, true devotion to the family. What is the answer? If Man is a pernicious dream and generosity a phantasm of pride, an imbecilic revolt against the natural laws of economy, then the only practicable ethic, the only sensible one, is utilitarian puritanism. The adolescents remain nonplussed. Will they settle down? Will they bury their anger and their noble despair—which has not helped them? Will they say, "My father was right"? Suddenly their writers seem to be in league with their families; Vigny and Monsieur Pagnerre are both saying to Pagnerre junior: "You will never be a superman or even fully a man; you will not make history and you will not restore the splendors of the Old Regime; you are the worthy son of your father and have no other task in this life than to resign yourself humbly to being a mere bourgeois, like him." Will they accept this monstrous alliance? No: the parents would put an account book in their heads and the poets would fill them with dreadful regrets. Since everyone is in league to destroy them, they will do battle on two fronts at once.

The Angry Young Men. Their tactic consists of making unrealization, which was merely a moment of reading, their absolute end. As we have seen, this moment tended to be posed for itself; however, the reader surpassed it since autistic *being-man* was his aim. He sought incarnation *in spite* of its unreality; he will henceforth seek it *because* of it. Turning the Romantics' own weapons against them, he devalorizes being in favor of nothingness. The Parisian poets believe in the reality of aristocratic norms, in the good, the beautiful, the true: they limit themselves to declaring that the bourgeoisie understands nothing of this. Rejecting at once the familial utilitarianism to which everyone

307

wants to condemn them and the ethic of the privileged caste, the schoolboys are about to decide that the good and the beautiful are merely mirages; they find universality in the negative by decreeing that, since generosity and passion are not of this world, such values are as inaccessible to the retired officer who writes verses as they are to the son of a clothmaker. This new option exhibits all the characteristics of a *conversion*, except that most converts claim to move from lesser being to being, while the schoolboys deserting the real—the being they can perceive, experience, know, and modify practically— demand that the practiced dream give them access to nonbeing, because nothing is beautiful, nothing is good except what does not exist. This is ontological proof in reverse. They will pursue their nocturnal readings, but instead of asking of the readings a prefiguration of what they will one day be, they demand the imaginary intuition of an ethical-aesthetic world to which no *real* man can have access. Chatterton is a mirage, all right, but not only for them: for Count Alfred de Vigny—who is a nasty piece of work like themselves—and even for the poor child from London who took himself for Chatterton and has died as a result.

The meaning of this operation is complex. First of all, it must be viewed as defiance: unable to offer themselves the luxury of a gratuitous act that is real, they will opt—over against the bourgeois who never do anything for nothing, and over against the Romantics who are victims of their own maneuver and believe themselves truly sublime—for *absolute gratuitousness*. They will deliberately *waste* their time imagining the impossible and being devoured by the dream, not despite its perfect inanity but in order to incite the world and their own person to destroy themselves together. Since generosity is a military and destructive gift, their attitude is at once a reaffirmation of it and its caricature. Taking the real as analogue of an infinite, dark image, they offer up being in its totality to *nothing*, or, if you like, they sacrifice the world so that nothingness should become nothing. Can a more regal gift be conceived of? Note that the ethic of Romanticism is preserved—they still love it, these poor little cuckolds—but it becomes the object of an ironic and desperate radicalization: "Lose yourself under an empty heaven to bear witness to the impossible." All imaging consciousness detaches itself from the real because it aims at absences. Defiance situates itself on the level of detachment. Moreover, it is also an escape. The scamps are wounded; they suffer from knowing that they are bourgeois and will remain bourgeois until death in their thoughts, their affections, and their real conduct: they might as well flee into nothingness since they horrify themselves. They cease to see, to see *themselves,* and put all the faculties of their soul at the service of an absenteeism the more easily maintained as the "sickening returns" to reality frighten them.

But there is another aspect of the imaging act: one dissociates oneself *in order to form an image.* On this level, conversion is felt by the converts themselves as an intentional *perversion:* it preserves within it the demoralization that gave rise to it. As long as he could believe that history testified to the existence of Man somewhere on this earth, in Paris, in Missolonghi, the little reader maintained a *white* relationship with the authors consisting of amorous abandon and awestruck confidence: the Book was the Bible, evangelical in the proper sense of the term since it announced the good news. But now he knows that "nothing" is announced to him; reading is drugging oneself. His rapport with the author turns *black:* he borrows the Romantic writer's satanic powers against his victorious parents; he makes a pact with the Devil. But at the same time he sets out to fool the Evil One: "This time, the deceiver will not deceive me, I know very well that the coins in the purse he is handing me are only appearances of coins and that they will change into dead leaves. But if I take them, it is precisely because I like false appearances, booby traps, illusions, and because I like them for the nothingness they contain." In the sulphurous and grinding pleasure he takes in his reading, there is a good dose of resentment: it is not pure nothingness that pleases him, it is nonbeing insofar as it vampirizes being, insofar as appearance makes itself both the being of nonbeing (being borrowed from being) and the nonbeing of being (negation of the dead leaf which is effaced by the false shine of false gold). It seems to him that he is playing a good joke on the real by submitting it to unreality. Sainte-Beuve, who during the 1820s was fascinated with Chateaubriand, later wrote, not without rancor, that "René," the artist's portrait of himself, was "a kind of incubus with a fatal embrace." This is just what the schoolboys demand: an incubus, a drop of sperm shed by a sleeper; an evil nonbeing seizes it, feeds on its being, and, diverting it from its natural ends, uses it to fertilize, a thousand miles away, an innocent sleeping female. Chateaubriand, Vigny, are the sleepers, their heroes the incubi that will possess the young sleeping males and impregnate them with a dream. The boys allow it: they love the clownish embrace because it is against nature. This is how they join in the satanism of their favorite authors: to dream *in order to dream,* to give themselves in onanistic solitude a satisfaction they are denied—they are convinced that this is *doing wrong;*

309

the strict ethic of this conversion is, finally, merely a system of *anti-values*. It is clear that these children give themselves over each evening to the most radical genocide: in the name of impossible Man, they exterminate the subhuman race that populates the planet.

The modification of the reader is the initial moment of the conversion, but not the most important: the conversion, in fact, runs beyond the night and extends itself into the diurnal world. The scamps listen to the teacher, sneering and distracted, learn their lessons as well as they can, do what they must so as not to be expelled, no more, and take refuge in absence when they can. Gustave is not alone, whatever he thinks, in "drowning himself" in the infinite; in these moments, they are no longer anyone but quite simply an abstract, shriveled negation, a suicidal detachment without its counterpart, incarnation. But when the bell or the drum recalls them to life, they hasten to revive in daylight the vampires that engender their nocturnal oneirism. Without a written text, without words, they incarnate themselves publicly. Pagnerre knows now that he will never be Jean of Aragon, a Spanish grandee. Nor Man. Too bad: better to *play* Hernani than to *be* Pagnerre, son of Pagnerre. They strike poses; each of them asks his body to reanimate his nocturnal convictions through borrowed postures, asks his comrades to consolidate this phantom of belief through their assent. It is a new incarnation, less convincing than reading—for it is not accompanied by hypnosis—but more radical: it seeks out the individual fully awake and derealizes him in the heart of reality by forbidding him to give responses adapted to the demands of the external world. Lacking the power to annihilate themselves, these tragic actors replace acts with gestures, thus condemning themselves to permanent distraction, to never experiencing real feelings again, to no longer being anything but a *"chargé de rôle,"* like a *chargé d'affaires.* But they care nothing for this: haunted by the fear of actualizing by their actions and affections the bourgeois they potentially are, they have chosen never to do or feel anything for real. Internalizing the No they encounter on all sides, they appropriate it and take the implicit nihilism of the Romantics to its extreme in order to make it their permanent exis: they will be the negation of everything; indeed, they have entered post-Romanticism, and their old hatreds, increased tenfold but diverted, are in the process of making them utterly enraged.

To *whom* are you referring? someone will ask. To *all* the schoolboys? No. The time has come to be more precise: there is the mass of well-behaved children who do not read at all and hardly ever torment themselves; and then there are the honor students, the good boys proud of their scholarly success: "The strong regarded [Charles] as beneath them, and he was too good a boy to mix with the scamps." The strong: those who stole from Gustave the honors that rightfully should have come to him. Sure of themselves, scornful, they form a caste; they are the elect and do not deign to mix with the mediocre. Bouilhet was one of them: he had not yet lost his faith and didn't care about being bourgeois provided he lived on intimate terms with the nobility: he liked the calm and pious aristocrats who tempted the Muse better than the fanatics whose nihilism he found less shocking than their triviality. The scamps, by contrast, mediocre or passable students, sublime dreamers, were wild and crazy. These boys do not lower themselves to breaking windows, to making a ruckus, except out of solidarity; they nonetheless enjoy a solemn prestige among their comrades: these are the "young madcaps" whose "superb extravagances" Flaubert will vaunt. Who are they? Avengers. For the first time, in this slow evolution, they bear witness to that misanthropy which is one of the chief characteristics of the bourgeois nineteenth century. With them, Man will submit to a new avatar: realizable, with Clouet, then impossible, then aristocratic, and finally imaginary, he becomes profoundly hateful: it is on him that the angry young men ultimately want to take revenge. Let us reread the *Préface aux Dernières Chansons*, which traces the figures of a chimerical ballet whose sole meaning is a homicidal and suicidal hatred:

> Enthusiastic hearts would have wished for dramatic love affairs with gondolas, black masks, and great ladies languishing in post chaises in the middle of Calabria . . . Some darker characters . . . aspired to the uproar of the press or of the tribunal, the glory of conspirators. A rhetorician composed an *Apologie de Robespierre,* which circulated outside the school and scandalized one gentleman, resulting in an exchange of letters and an invitation to a duel in which the gentleman behaved badly. One good boy [was] always gotten up in a red cap; another promised himself to live later as a Mohican; one of my close friends wanted to become a renegade in the service of Abd el-Kader . . . ; you carried a knife in your pocket, like Antony. Out of disgust with existence, Bar—— blew his brains out . . . And—— hanged himself.

The gradation is obvious: Gustave begins with the "enthusiasts": this is Léon, the notary's clerk, this is Ernest Chevalier. When he tells us the dreams of his childhood friend, Flaubert has long considered him a certified bourgeois. Still, he makes him figure among the prize-winners; absenteeism is never contemptible: absent from himself,

Ernest was worth more, whatever the silliness of his dreams, than Chevalier, the prosecutor, who was all there. Very well(someone will say, but why speak of extravagance? At fifteen years old, with the blood coursing through their veins, dreaming of women is normal. Of women, yes. Of rich women, strictly speaking, especially if the dreamer is poor. Of great ladies, no. These amorous dreams are dated: around the same period, Julien, the poor peasant boy of Verrières, having seduced a titled, respectable mother, married the daughter of a duke. So in the good old times of colonialism, the colonized sometimes dreamed of avenging themselves on the colonists by taking their women; these ponderings of hate-filled eroticism are one step along the road that leads to armed organization. In 1835, *after* the bourgeois victory, these fantasies exult "enthusiastic hearts" because the privileged have kept "most of their privileges, and their vanquished arrogance exasperates their vanquishers. Our flouted schoolboys burn to avenge the Romantic outrage by cuckolding the gentry.

Since they are forbidden to be Jean of Aragon, they will prove they are worthy of him by using main force to rescue a noblewoman from the brigands; this is stealing from the military their congenital virtues—generosity, martial prowess, virility. Fooled by this behavior, the princesses open themselves up; the young bourgeois penetrates them. Not having issued from the member of a princely family, he will enter such a family through his own member—intercourse will replace birth. A stupid kind of oneirism, someone will say. No, they are killing two birds with one stone: disowning the bourgeoisie and ridiculing the nobility. Gustave probably had little appreciation for such trifles. If he cites them, however, it is because he finds some charm in their perversity; they seem comic to him and disturbing, these candid bourgeois, torn from their class out of folly, pursuing an interminable schizophrenic rumination in which the nobility of the sword is conferred upon them by the opportune use of a weapon, meaning their phallus, and by the licentiousness of a felonous princess. These innocents justify his misanthropy and are themselves misanthropes: dreaming their impossible heroism (are they going to drag the princesses to Calabria?) and, conscious of its impossibility, they give evidence in their persons that Man is merely a swaggering woodlouse.

Next come the ambitious; Gustave considers them coolly: they want to be politicians or journalists, two professions he will despise all his life. They are worth more, however, than the rescuers of duchesses: their comrade concedes that they have a "more serious" character, and this means that they are inflamed by passion, that their insatiable pride will never be content, that they will not deign to attain power and glory except through the dangerous ways of contestation. Above all, they despise men and want to "debase" them, like Corneille, or dominate them, like Nero or Tamberlaine, *out of pure misanthropy,* according to Flaubert. They are, Gustave insists, under the influence of Armand Carrel, and their dearest desire is to stigmatize the regime, to expose abuses and crimes everywhere, finally to reach renown and fortune by making themselves the titled censors of French society. It will take nothing less to cure the Romantic malady: humiliated by the aristocrats, shameful of being ill-born, they mean before all else to criticize bourgeois power, in other words, the power of papa. But the nobility must not expect them to be their patsies: defying their parents and the privileged caste, they will go, if necessary, so far as to call themselves revolutionaries, to praise the Republic. Are they Clouet's disciples, the continuers of his work?[45] Not at all; Clouet was no pessimist; he believed in the possibility of Man and sought to compel his fellow citizens to realize that possibility. The bitterness of Flaubert's classmates can be explained, on the contrary, by their skepticism: Man is an imposter. Clouet thought he was committing a political *act;* if he failed, it was not his fault; his successors have scandalous political *opinions* and have adopted them in order to *scandalize:* convinced of their impotence, they are horrified by action. Shall we say, at least, that they act *in their dreams?* Not even there: their pessimism deters them from playing reformers. They see themselves rather in the guise of a Savonarola, discovering the wounds, the abscesses, the gangrene, but curing nothing. They will plunge their contemporaries into shame, they will make them disgusted with themselves. Politics—never: they are demoralizers. From the time they come of age, they will conspire like the *Carbonari,* or like those mysterious characters feared by the bourgeoisie—is it certain they exist?—and who, it is claimed, are the organizers of secret societies that want to overturn the monarchy with the support of the workers. But the schoolboys of Rouen have neither the means nor the desire to organize themselves: they *are organized* from the beginning of their dream. The Republic, for them, is insurrection: they give the signal,

45. However, there is nothing to prevent us from believing that many among them—in particular, Robespierre's apologist—took part in the days of March 1831. They were optimists then. But we have shown the succession of defeats which led them to misanthropy.

313

the people rise up, the king flees, our young revolutionaries come out of the shadows, heroic and victorious, in order to hit out wildly at the institutions of July. These institutions are broken, and so the boys twist between their iron hands the ideologies of both the bourgeoisie and the Old Regime and reestablish universal suffrage. Will the world be better for it? They sincerely doubt it, as our species is not perfectable. Besides, the new order is not their business. These men of disorder are not concerned with building; they dream of demolition, of perpetual violence: for them, the Revolution is 1793. It is no accident that these sons of Girondins have chosen to glorify Robespierre among all the Montagnards. Dead, he has preserved the great honor of being the Number One enemy for the entire bourgeoisie—beginning with Michelet—and simultaneously for the aristocracy; in short, he realizes the holy union of the enemies of Man against him. Man being in their eyes merely a chimera, his little worshipers are incapable of appreciating Robespierre's revolutionary politics. What do they admire, then? The Terror. Unaware of the complex dialectic that led to it and the central role played by the masses, they attribute all its merit to the Incorruptible. What blood! It flows from all veins, red and blue, the heads of the bourgeoisie roll in the dust along with the heads of the *aristos*. At Robespierre's command, the bourgeoisie undertakes to exterminate itself, the Jacobins kill each other off. Why did they stop when they were doing so well? Long live the Terror, and let it come again as quickly as possible: with a little luck, the sons will see the venerable heads of their fathers pop like corks, and like the pirate's fiancée they will say: Hop la! Yet see how they are, these little republicans; if someone were inclined to protest, if a "gentleman" were to criticize their idol, they would aristocratically draw their swords and call him out. In their hearts, then, they remain faithful to the great military dreams of their Romantic period. In their new fables they kill and are killed, they recount their deaths a hundred times, always noble. It's the same when they play a role: haughty duellists, they do not hesitate a moment to risk their lives to kill the gentlemen who have looked at them askance and who will, of course, show their bourgeois baseness by refusing to fight. Robespierre's apologist has dealt a double blow: writing, he performed the movements of writing and played the part of passionate hagiographer (perhaps also of the hero he claimed to resurrect); this comedy has required, however, that he trace words on his piece of paper, and those words were fortunate enough to shock an adult: no sooner has the adult made a grimace of protest than he finds himself brutally requested to give proof that he prefers honor to life and that he is one of those-who-are-born-to-die; by his evasion, he makes himself ridiculous, demonstrates his plebeian nature, and at once throws into relief the *quality* of his adversary. The young duellist, on the other hand, has shown that the mystery of his birth is far from clear: is he really son of the bourgeois who claims to be his father? Might he not rather be an aristocrat who has become republican out of generosity? All that has happened is an uproar at the *collège;* yet the little actor has found the means to get up on the stage and take a stand against both the class that denies him and the class that produces him.

There is really no need for him to make so much of it, to invent a new installment daily in which he is the hero, or, being unreal, to walk through the secular world, encumbering it with his chronicle of exploits. For these adolescents, the thing to do will be to invest in the unreal, if possible permanently, with the being that comes to them *de jure* and is denied them *de facto.* They had believed, until now, in making themselves incarnate in a character *read about* or *acted* whose exploits might reveal their *nature;* they were wasting their time. What good are these details, appeals, complex intrigues, what good is the *dramatic* or the *fictional,* if they are merely to make themselves into the calm and fixed image of an unbridled violence? A wise economy allows certain individuals to unrealize themselves at less expense. Since they want only to *be the Terror,* an unvarying *habitus,* an inert mortage on their future, a threatening claim on the future of the world, since they intend that this ontological structure be given unreally to their inner meaning as a sort of "fixed explosion," as *their very being,* signifying itself to them as nontemporal and instantaneous presence, it will be easy for them to simplify the rites of incarnation and designate themselves by the inertia of an unvarying accessory, the way kings are designated in their power by the crown and the scepter. Suppressing the character as intermediary, they become manifest to themselves by the simple mediation of an inanimate thing: "You carried a dagger in your pocket, like Antony." The willed anonymity of the "you" implies that this was a very widespread habit.[46] Still it contained—ultimate residue of Romantic reading—a reference to a particular Character. But look at that "good boy" down there, he is

---

46. The letter of 15 December 1850 informs us that Ernest "carried a dagger." But these two observations"—*He too* wanted to be an artist," and "he followed . . . the normal path" (by moving from Romantic exultation to the "comic seriousness" of the bourgeois)—are sufficient evidence that he was following fashion by walking about with his knife in his pocket.

modestly content with a red cap: calm, candid with his teachers, he is undoubtedly one of those average students of whom the assistant headmaster says that they "could do better," which in his case is undoubtedly true as he literally does nothing but wear a cap, think that he is wearing it, and, when he removes it, think that he will wear it again as soon as possible. There is nothing extravagant in decking oneself melancholicly in a Phrygian cap to signify that one is faithful to certain political principles which the head covering openly symbolizes; there is a great deal of extravagance, however, in putting the Terror on his head as the sign and symbol of himself. At other times he must have dreamed of beautiful massacres, even of a genocide that he had organized, of a flood of tears and blood; in short, he told himself stories with words, with images. He is no longer dreaming: what good would it do since the red is there, once and for all, on top of his head. Another schizo, someone will say, and I admit that autistic thought offers few more successful performances. What economy of means, what elegance: rather than *make* the Terror *reign* each night, the little fellow has preferred to *be* it; he sums *himself* up in this cap to the same degree that the cap sums up the Terror, condenses it in a unique quality, *spilled blood*. The blood that he spilled? Yes. And he will make it flow tomorrow and is spreading it this very moment and in all eternity. Through the fetishized cap, that blood, which is drunk by the earth, and dry, an inert coat of arms, designates him to himself, *in his being*, as *Human Thing;* through the light pressure of the headgear on his temples, gentle as a loving caress, he comes to himself from the outside, empty and sacred; he internalizes his fundamental project that preserves, in the heart of immanence, the unvarying consistency, opacity, impenetrability of the *in-itself*, he is his own fetish. A tempest provisionally withheld, always about to unleash its thunderbolts, a terrible calm at the center of a cyclone, this symbol tears him loose from the human race: the deluge has happened, will happen, never stops happening; he has seen, he sees, he will see the scarlet blades at the storming of Mount Ararat; he surveys a massacre that is simultaneously the object of a memory, of a perception, and of an oracle because the good fellow has given himself the *time of the thing*, and at once the ek-stases of human temporality are crushed in the homogeneity and continuity of physical duration. Through this memorable extermination of which he is overjoyed to become the author and to have been the author, and which is his nontemporal vocation, he gives himself, in a carefully maintained vagueness, the dumb present tense of the atom and the eternity of the angel. For all that, the best son in the world.

This said, let us not be in a hurry to take him for a fool. Perhaps he is one—what do we know about him? But his attitude, far from contrasting with the social behavior of the period as the singular contrasts with the universal and the extraordinary with the particular, merely recovers the meaning of the most common rite of appropriation. To base *being* on *having:* isn't this the same as to cede the proprietor to his property and, hence, man to the thing? The bourgeois, we know, advertises himself by what he possesses; and his "interest" is himself in danger in the external world: thus, when the cunning scamp asks *his* cap to reveal *his* essence to him in terms of exteriority, he does credit to the wrought matter he has acquired, for it can be only him, being his, and therefore could not deceive him. So his faith in the practico-inert oracle is sustained by the confidence that his class accords to the human thing, confidence of which it represents merely a particular moment. How uncertain of themselves these young people are! Victims of an evil genius, they are their own traps, and everything in them is a mirage: they have all decided to kill their fathers and the lords of the region, indiscriminately, but we have seen one of them make himself incorruptible in order to guillotine the nobility and then, drawing his sword at the first opportunity, to find himself standing against the bourgeoisie in the skin of a nobleman. Now it is the other way around: in order to massacre the criminal class that gave him life, an agent of justice finds nothing better than to become bourgeois in the extreme by ceding himself to his hat. For this reason, our angry young men, like their enemies the Romantics although for opposite reasons, do nothing but die and ponder their deaths. To die: to mineralize their lives, to take negation to the point of radical self-destruction. The two scamps who come next on the list, unable to remove themselves from the family influence, will at least immolate themselves before our very eyes so that it may be understood that they "no longer have a human face."

The first prefers the society of savages to that of the wealthy[47] he meets in his parents' living room: he arrests his life with a vow; he will pass his baccalaureat and perhaps take a law degree, then he will be-

47. This schoolboy is perhaps Gustave in person, proud of his Indian blood, who will tell the Goncourts much later that he feels closer to the savages than to the Parisian crowds. Let us note, however, that the attitude must have been widespread: the name "Mohican" clearly marks the influence of James Fenimore Cooper.

317

come a Mohican. There is nothing positive in this solemn commitment: that Mohican doesn't want the company of men, even if they
were Mohicans by birth; he dreamed about Rousseau but doesn't believe in the noble savage—his heart is no longer in it. He will go
searching in Connecticut, not for the human race in its original purity, but for the desert and inhumanity. He hates the bourgeois, the
Europeans, the civilized: since by burning schools, libraries, and mu-
seums he cannot eradicate the hideous culture they secrete, he will
carefully destroy its traces in his thought as well as in his heart. How
he envies those Indians who can neither read nor write nor count;
once in contact with them, he will forget everything; with a little luck,
he may even unlearn how to speak: then he will find the nature that
was hidden from him. Not the nature of man, which is itself a product
of culture, an artifice, but that of the wild beast, the illiterate solitude
of Djalioh's paternal ancestors. Yet Gustave endowed his apeman
with a rare sensibility. There is nothing similar in this dry, angry
dream; everything is negative: I swear that when the day comes, I
will turn on myself, I will mutilate myself, I will tear out my eyes, I will
spill molten lead on my wounds simply because man is hateful, because I hate him and want to abolish him in my person; I swear that
when the operation is over, nothing will remain of the "me" you gave
me, which sickens me because it is too much like yours; I swear I will
do everything to make myself into a helpless idiot.

The vow most striking to me, however, is the other, the one an
"intimate" friend of Flaubert's made to himself. But which friend?
Frenzy is not usual with Alfred, who has in any case left school; it is
still less usual with Ernest. Perhaps Gustave is telling us "the story
of one of his own follies." Well, no matter—they lent each other their
dreams. This second option does not initially seem very different
from the first: the same future proscribed by sworn faith. The same
voluntary exile, the same abandonment of old Europe: in another desert, other Mohicans await the traveler. But what matters is that the
hatred is exacerbated: the emigrant, not content to deny his fatherland, now goes out into the wilderness looking for a chance to betray
it. A gratuitous and perfect betrayal which has no end but itself. Certainly the victories of Abd el-Kader compelled the admiration of the
French, but what sparks the enthusiasm of the young traitor is not the
Algerians' tenacious resistance to colonization: he is not going to go
to Maghreb to support a just cause—for the misanthropes of the
collège, just causes do not exist. What fascinates him is the imagined
opportunity to slaughter his compatriots. And why slaughter them?

Because it is evil. Who knows how this young renegade will end up? As a notary, perhaps, or a textile manufacturer. Nonetheless, in the years around 1835 he sat in the tribunal of the imaginary damned and showed himself to be the most radical of them all: he counted not only on destroying French lives by firing on the soldiers of Bugeaud but on destroying his own purity as well. Man arouses such horror in him that he would not even deign to kill him if he could not do it *traitorously;* he damns him in his own person by an inexpiable act; after which, this unreconciled Melmoth will burn in Hell, his head high, without a complaint, drunk with pride. This bourgeois has become a *military* traitor; to accomplish his wickedness, he must give his life—*for nothing.* When dreaming of his countrymen—and for the sole pleasure of affirming his freedom-for-Evil he lay in ambush with a good chance of losing his skin—what did he do but show his total generosity and at the same time *ennoble himself* beneath the benevolent eye of the *noble emir* Abd el-Kader? This is the final word: his traitorous dream is to change class. Let us not believe, however, that he is denying only his parents: in the French army, most of the officers are titled; he will know the supreme pleasure of creating a black knighthood, of which he will be the only member, by making the aristocrats his target.

Death is the key. For everyone. The *Préface aux Dernières Chansons* tells how you go from the dream to art and to suicide: "You were above all an artist; exercises finished, literature began; and you ruined your eyes reading novels in the dormitory; you carried a knife in your pocket, like Antony; *you did more:* out of disgust with existence, *Bar——* blew his brains out . . . *And——* hanged himself." I have italicized this strange connection; it is significant. Reading, as we know, is dying a little; playing a character is dying a great deal; you can *do more* and hang yourself to finish the job. What is astonishing here is that Flaubert presents as a *gradation* what is in fact a qualitative leap, a break in continuity. For these young men, reading is certainly an invitation to expire: those who are still reading and go to sleep toward midnight, ravaged—dying of sorrow—awaken dead; they see day from the point of view of night; others no longer read: the knife that lies heavy in their pocket is well worth twenty novels. Their noble death, however, remains imaginary. Why does Gustave present real and deliberate self-destruction as the highest degree of unrealization? If carrying a dagger is sufficient to plunge one into a savage nothingness that has the good fortune to be self-conscious as well, why draw the dagger from one's pocket and turn it against oneself?

I would answer, first of all, that neither Bar—— nor And—— made known their real reasons; perhaps they did not know themselves. In any case, these reasons have not been preserved, and Gustave sovereignly decides, more than thirty years later, that they killed themselves "out of disgust with existence." Besides, even if this were true, there is no proof that they went, as he claims, from imaginary death to suicide; suicide is obviously a rejection of reality, but it is nonetheless a response to real stimuli, which assumes generally that the desperate person, by virtue of his constituted characters or the situation, has regarded himself as forbidden to resort to the techniques of derealization. It may even be thought that evasion-in-a-role[48] and voluntary death are two possible reactions to despair which are in fact opposed, and therefore incompatible. In contrast, *Gustave's* interpretation of the facts will be particularly interesting; no doubt it reflects the opinion current at the time among the scamps. In their comrades' suicide they admired the radicalization of their own choice of sleep standing up and, finally, its *truth*.

Absenteeism, think the adolescents, is one step along the royal road that leads to voluntary death. The Mohicans, the Incorruptibles, the Avengers, the Agents of Justice, and the two comrades whom they are ready to canonize have, in any case, something in common: refusal to live. All put their greatness in their disgust with existence, that is, with themselves first.

For they are disgusted with *themselves*. Once they saw in derealization an ultimate but effective resistance: pursued, they would leap into nonbeing, leaving their hides to the forces of order. Now, they have understood that directed oneirism, far from being a real negation, presupposes a consent to defeat. As we know, the human object when reduced to impotence, reified, can only dream; conversely, however, he will dream only if he submits to his condition as human thing. A *real* refusal is surely not sufficient to remove him; he is forbidden, in any case, an escape outside humanity and is constrained to seek tirelessly for a *practical* outlet to a *definite*, even desperate, situation, at the risk of sinking at last into convulsions with no other purpose than to delay as long as possible the moment when the victim accepts his fate. Between 1831 and 1835, the absurd convulsive violence of the schoolboys bore witness, at least, to their persistence in saying no. No to impotence, no to their class-being, no to their prefabricated destiny, no to authority. Reading itself was the continua-

48. This means, strictly speaking, mental illness.

tion of their revolt as long as they could believe that it taught them the truth of the human condition. But now, having understood the perfect unreality of their incarnations, they know they are seeking the imaginary for itself; rejected by history, these agents have changed themselves into actors: it is the end of their resistance. Certainly they still manage some fine passions, rages—but everything is acted. They proclaim the same determination to challenge, but on the deepest level they are resigned: have they not chosen to disqualify *all* reality by an imaginary leap into nothingness? To reject everything, to accept everything—it's the same thing. In both cases one renounces praxis, which recognizes certain givens and assumes them in order to modify others. The boys identify with the *Desdichado* without believing in him and proclaim that he is Man *personified* but unrealizable, and that his reign will never come. It is a tacit confession that mechanistic determinism, social atomism, and the molecular theory of society are right, that egotism is the basic motivation of all behavior and, hence, of their own actions—including their derealizing maneuvers. This is rallying to the paternal ideology. They gain by it, for they are paying Vigny back in kind: noblemen and bourgeois vanish together, all that remains are solitary particles; but this is exactly what liberal thought affirms, and the equality of these interchangeable molecules resides in their incurable mediocrity. If the human condition cannot be ameliorated, if, as Flaubert will say later, no one can do anything for anyone, and if humanity, which is uniformly vile, is not worth the trouble anyway, such futile disturbances—so-called praxis in all its forms—must be roundly condemned. These adolescents are tacitly committed to disavow the future Clouets, and if they took part in the rebellion of March '31, they are disavowing themselves: demobilized by oneirism, they renounce the idea of "changing life" forever. Apolitical, they will *decline to intervene:* they will leave the management of public affairs to their parents; taking refuge in the all too easy alibi of the dream, they loudly declare that they are not interested in the secular. So they will leave everything as it is: the idiotic rules of the *collège,* the abusive power of the Church, the monarchy, the electoral tax—they will not touch it; their acted absence allows them to ignore what goes on around them and to wash their hands of it. They cannot ignore the fact that this is the alibi of a cad. They are absorbed in playing at being what they know they are not, in order to avoid seeing what they truly are. Yet they still have memories of things they do not recognize and are anguished that they no longer understand their past: how could these quietists of the imginary see things with the eyes of the little fighters they once were? Terrified, they sometimes wonder if their sumptuous oneirism is not quite simply the surest way to become the bourgeois they are. At school, at home, they are being prepared to manage the patrimony; reading and drama would serve as compensation for their austere studies, and these safety valves would be tolerated by the grown-ups themselves if they knew about them. Since these children find themselves constrained by circumstances to serve in shame their apprenticeship to their class-being, they are allowed at certain times to be Manfred, Faust, that is, a great crippled lord, incestuous and magnificent, or the Olympian prime minister of a German principality. While they absent themselves, the process of bourgeoisification is pursued in their deserted souls without encountering the least resistance; when they come back to themselves, they will find they are a bit more bourgeois than before. Is this not the beginning of the return to order? Are they not in the process of becoming adults unworthy of the adolescents they are? Gustave shares this anxiety—at least as it concerns others; as we have seen, he prophesied quite early, peevish and scared, the bourgeoisification of Alfred. There is but one remedy for this slow and sure metamorphosis: eliminate both the bourgeois dreamer and his corrupting dream. They had chosen to move into the imaginary, a year or two earlier, because it gave them the means to unrealize themselves as grown-ups stirred by grand passions and lofty sentiments; now, disappointed, they see the imaginary as nothing but negative interest: imagination is absence from the world, derealization. Unfortunately, experience teaches them that one absents oneself in fits and starts, continually falling back into the filth of the real. Escape is nothing inasmuch as it is provisional; worse, it is a form of complicity; and as death alone is likely to fix it for eternity, suicide clearly seems to them the underlying meaning of unrealization, its requirement and its justification. To dream is *to be committed to die:* therefore they dream that they are so committed; like Saint And—— and Saint Bar—— they have death in their souls; the only difference is that they keep it there, waiting for an opportunity to make it move into their bodies. They know now that they must choose between abject resignation and suicide, and that if one does not kill oneself one is not fit to live. But, after all, they *have killed themselves:* "it's as if it were done." They followed Camus's advice a century before it was given: "There is only one really serious problem. To judge whether life is or is not worth the trouble of living is to answer the fundamental question of philosophy. Everything else . . . comes later. These are games; first of all, one must answer." They have answered. Or rather, they are grateful to the two Saints for having answered in their stead—one with his pistol, the other with his suspenders. These two decided that *for this generation of bourgeois children*, born around 1820, life was not livable. And I admit they were right. By killing themselves, they structured for everyone the "fatal years" at the *collège*. We shall see in the third part of this work that the answer will remain valid when the children have become men. There is, however, a way of escaping the dilemma, whether to resign oneself or to relinquish life; Gustave sensed it at sixteen. When as an adult he would write a preface for the work of a poet who died *naturally*, he had long known it: it is literature. Not the literature one reads but the literature one makes. The artist perpetuates derealization; by initiating a cycle of eternal images, he *institutes* and *sanctifies* the imaginary; for this reason, he has the right to survive. We shall also see that art, according to Flaubert, requires its ministers to suffer the experience of death—he will undergo it himself in January '44—so that they might look at the world with the bewildered eyes of those who have come back from the beyond. In 1837 this was not so clear: all artists? Why? and how to become one? This has been *his* business for a long time and for personal reasons; it is difficult to admit that art, a substitute for suicide, should be his schoolmates' business as well. And—— and Bar—— confront most of them with death as their fundamental possibility, without mediation.

Such is the penultimate avatar of the school community. The time of humanism is past, as is that of Romanticism; the time of sanctity is beginning. Until then, death was only the most sumptuous of their chimeras; that is over: you no longer die protesting on the gallows, slain by society; you must really kill oneself, all alone, in a closed room, with a bullet or a rope. Poor boys! It is true, they did not ask to be born, and it is atrocious for a child of man to be *born bourgeois*. But since they are made to live, since their young appetites compel them to reproduce their lives, they cheat themselves once more and refuse to decide whether to regard And—— and Bar—— as examples to *imitate* or as redeemers who have offered themselves in martyrdom in order to redeem their schoolmates. In this second hypothesis, the dead have killed themselves *instead* of their comrades and for them; the Communion of Saints allows all the merits acquired by their fatal gesture to be showered upon the others' heads; for these kids, who are all honorary dead men, suicide suddenly becomes optional. Preserving these two interpretations inside them, syncretic and undifferentiated, they can accord themselves the mournful importance of the

323

young elect, inhabited by their death insofar as another has already realized it and condemned them to survive to bear witness. They have contrived it such that they should be able to integrate voluntary death with their dream and surpass it by acting out this new character, the *suicide*, permanently designated by a loaded pistol stuck in his pocket.

Unfortunately, and for the first time, their insincerity does not pay off. The beginning is good, but no sooner have they gotten underway than the illusion crumbles and they are faced with undertaking an act. Simply because *the pistol is real*. Until then, their oneirism was protected by the decision to dream only the impossible: impossible for Pagnerre, for Baudry, to be Jean of Aragon or Ruy Blas, to become a Mohican, to join Abd el-Kader so as to betray the duke of Aumale and one's fatherland—impossible, quite simply, to become a cavalry officer. But suicide, on the contrary, is possible: a weapon in their pocket, they can kill themselves at any time. No one is committed to the impossible: we can't blame them for rejecting resignation, for maintaining their eminent rights, for persisting in playing at the character they will never be. But they would be ridiculous *playing at* suicides since they always have the possibility of "calling it quits with the point of a knife." If they proclaim their disgust with life, the possible becomes the basis of a strict imperative: you can, therefore you must, change your imaginary demise into a real and irreversible death. The unhappy boys discover their imposture not in the abstract and reflexively—which would be less painful—but while absorbed in acting their new character: a concrete perception smashes the whole drama to pieces. No one, in effect, is suicidal unless he has often caught himself pondering the way he will choose to end his days. The candidates are therefore prepared to catch themselves leaning over a razor and meditating; the most conscientious push the muzzle of a gun deep into their throats and leave it there a few moments: if they change their minds and pull it out again, it is understood that their resolution remains unshaken but that they have not entirely decided on the moment of its execution. Unfortunately for them, in the game of voluntary death the accessories are not semblances but real and threatening instruments. How could someone who handles a loaded pistol to give himself a momentary illusion that he will use it prevent the unquestionable reality of the tool from transforming his feeble attempts, in spite of himself, into the demands of the practico-inert? How could he prevent the weapon from designating him, from *aiming* at him, in every sense of the word? How could he prevent acts that are real, but remain *to be done*, from announcing themselves through his gestures, and himself from being the signified of that signifier? He is up against the wall; under his index finger, teasing it, the trigger conducts its own interrogation: has he finally decided? He need only increase the pressure of his finger. Nothing, literally, now separates the actor from the "fatal moment," everything invites him to take the leap; it is unbearable: maddened, he opens his hand and drops the pistol. The child was afraid of himself; or, rather, the Sancho Panza who inhabits him, his real ego, suddenly feared that his alter ego, the famous actor from La Mancha, might end by catching himself at his own game, or, still worse, that his Character might become his truth. He leans on the table, perspires, shivers; his teeth are chattering: a blunder would have been enough—this time I really thought I was going to do it. What terrorizes him still is the lingering sensation of dizziness: the weapon at his feet, he need merely stoop down . . . At this moment the Character dies, the scamps all have the same reaction: discovering their real persons, they burst out laughing. Sancho, sinister but liberated, cheers up at the disappearance of the old vagabond who terrorized him; the squire, weeping with laughter, savors with sharp sensuality the feeling of baseness and rejoices to have found a viable solution to the puzzle that has obsessed him for five years.

The seriousness of the comic. In these turbulent years, protest by laughter makes its appearance and coexists for a moment with protest by dream, of which it is the result and which it ends by replacing. Toward 1837 we note the existence at the *collège* of a group of adolescents—nonchalant, cynical, disillusioned by everything, before they've even been there—who are sickened by the Creation but have taken the tack of laughing at it rather than crying over it; they have dubbed themselves the *Blasés*. We know almost nothing about them except that they are united by rather loose ties—affinities, similarities—and not by that terror-fraternity which is forged in battle (what battle would they lead? No human aim is worth the trouble) or by the common vow that establishes secret societies. A lucidity that claims to be implacable, a nihilistic quietism, such is their exis—which is usually expressed by black humor accompanied by forced laughter. This laughter, which manifests itself as an all-encompassing view of the world, is in fact the particular relationship of the young bourgeois generation with itself. It is the first moment of an insight that is diverted, duped, that will lead these restive adolescents to accept themselves fully as bourgeois, and later as heads of families. This last

325

phase of involution, begun in March '31 and ending in 1840, is defined quite well by Flaubert in his letter of 15 March 1850. Coolly summing up the life of poor Ernest, former freemason of the Garçonic order, of whose marriage Madame Flaubert has just informed him, Gustave writes that he "followed the usual route" and progressed "from the seriousness of the comic to the comedy of the serious." We shall try to join them in their "normal course"; in the course of this new episode, the so-called Angry Young Men, having become Blasés, are going to encounter Gustave, and from this encounter the Garçon will be born.

What makes these adolescents laugh? The world, or their failed suicide? Both. Their failure has unmasked their imposture; their being-in-the-world-to-die was a comedy: they are in it *to live*. This disgrace renders them *comic* in their own eyes. Not risible: risibility, as we have seen, is an immediate characteristic that can be attached to any individual by a defensive and spontaneous reaction of his circle of friends. The comic, by contrast, is mediated, elaborated. It is encountered, like the tragic, its opposite, in the form of a finished product. Both appear as relational systems so carefully arranged that they seem to intellectual intuition like the truth of human life finally unencumbered by that jungle of appearances, facticity, and considered on the level at which premises engender their consequences according to imperative norms. To better exclude from these "models" everything that might smack of contingency, both comic and tragic writers must forbid themselves any recourse to the categories of the possible and the real; the only ones they make use of are those of the impossible and the necessary, like geometers. For comic and tragic writers alike, the individual, being always unnecessary, is revealed as an impossibility, or, if you will, his death is a necessity. Each of their works is a system in which human life appears only to be suppressed, every intrigue is an example of the inflexible contradiction that sets the macrocosm against the microcosm and microcosms against each other. The difference that separates the two genres is that in the one—save for the intervention of a mediator, a *deus ex machina* monarch, placed above humankind—the impossibility of being leads ineluctably to the abolition of the hero, the qualified representative of Man, whereas in the other this same impossibility produces quite as inflexibly the reverse consequence: impossibility maintains the life of the comic character, who is, moreover, the typical representative of our species. The tragic hero surmounts the contradiction by dying—even if his death is inflicted on him by another, he is responsible. The comic character is enclosed in an insurmountable contradiction, which manifests itself as a vicious circle, as every term produces its opposite. In *Modern Times*, Charlie Chaplin, atop a scaffolding, spies a packing case resting on the platform of an *invisible* lift; bending his knees, sticking out his buttocks, he is about to sit down when the lift starts to move: packing case and platform disappear; in their place, a black hole. Death *becomes visible*, ineluctable. But someone hails him, he stands up, saved by luck. After a brief conversation, however, there he is, at it again. This time, nothing can save him: death is *necessary*, we *see* him already losing his balance and falling twenty stories. But just as he is about to tumble into the void, the packing case reappears, rising to meet him, and is found under his bottom just in time for him to sit down without becoming conscious of the mortal peril that has threatened him. The gag begins again several times; the same device that *should doom him* is found, for reasons perfectly alien to the character, to save him: there is a fortuitous synchronism between the rhythm of the lift (it comes and goes according to the necessities of the work) and Charlie Chaplin's maneuverings (he sits down, gets up, sits down again for reasons that are always obvious). But this synchronism *announces death* in its very perfection: if the packing case were to rise a fraction of a second later, the unfortunate man, at the price of a rather rude shock, would perceive the danger. By keeping him in ignorance, the malicious precision of the mechanism preserves to the end his status as a man condemned to death: he has escaped unharmed *this time*; *nothing* guarantees that he will escape the same way next time. Conversely, we have to admit that the ignorance that *should doom him* actually protects him, under the circumstances: if he had taken a look behind him with his knees already bent, there is no doubt that the shock would have made him fall into the hole.[49]

But where, it will be asked, is the rigor here? It is only a game of chance. Agreed. But chance, excluded from tragedy, appears in comic constructions as the negative principle par excellence: it passes judgment and decrees that man is impossible. It is not by chance that everything happens by chance. The human person at first affirms himself as sovereign, convinced he is acting on the world and controlling his life. Chance comes afterward, exposing this illusion: the world is allergic to man, the *comic* makes us witnesses to a process of rejec-

49. This is a theme often found in Chaplin's films. In *The Circus*, for example, he is an improvised tightrope-walker, dancing marvelously on the rope while thinking he is attached to the roof by a line (which has, in fact, broken a moment ago), and just misses killing himself when he perceives that nothing is supporting him.

tion. The physical liquidation of the character is necessary, and he is spared only by the substitution of his moral liquidation; if chance reigns, man is lost in advance unless he is saved by chance. In the lift from *Modern Times*, these two opposite characters manifest their underlying unity: whether the macrocosm seized as pure *exteriority* crushes the microcosm, or a fortuitous convergence of external circumstances intervenes in time to save him without his being aware of it, man is *killed*; he leaves the adventure dehumanized because his ends have been stolen from him and restored at the last moment by things. He can survive for some time as an object of the world, but any ideas of praxis and interiority are shown to be the dream of a dream, and the *human object*, an accidental assemblage preserved by accident and which another accident will disassemble, is shown to be external to itself. It has been cleverly arranged to let us see the inflexible connections that are the *truth* of what he takes for his free decisions. Chaplin's lift must persuade us by laughter that we cannot even sit down without unbelievable luck. The possible and the real being excluded, chance here represents necessity; the comic appears, therefore, as the side taken to make analytic reason triumph over the syncretic idealism of the aristocracy by reducing the interior to the exterior, the subjective to the objective, the *doxa* to science, historical temporalization to physical temporality. This reduction is not disintegration: the illusion remains; we are left endlessly disqualifying it.

I have taken the most abstract, the simplest example, one in which death is directly *visible*.[50] Obviously, in most cases the impossibility of living is veiled. Be that as it may, the comedy of situation or the comedy of character both refer to the basic contradiction, or the ontological comedy; author, actors, spectators explicitly refer to it. An enterprise, an amour, bound to fail by their accidental nature, are triumphant by accident (the lovers are lucky enough to marry, the dupe is lucky enough to find his money) but are by the same stroke devalorized. The impossibility of acting or loving (of committing one's life with a vow) manifests the impossibility of being man.[51] We see the path followed from *risibility*: spontaneous laughter denounces *this* in-

50. I have simplified it myself. The comedy of Charlie Chaplin is never purely comic: there is a "humanism" in his films that shows us the vagabond struggling humbly against chance in order to affirm, in spite of everything, the possibility of being man. But we need not examine here the complex forms of the comic.

51. It is understood that the comic is a bias. Its share of truth is immediately apparent, and its partial character can be surpassed only on the level of dialectical reason.

dividual—who takes himself seriously—as a mere subman. Laughter provoked (by the comic) aims to reveal to us that *every man* is a subman who takes himself seriously.

From this point of view, the schoolboys of Rouen are spoiled: they are directly connected to the comedy of being, as if an invisible director had manipulated them. And—— and Bar—— have concluded that "life is impossible, therefore I die," and Man has affirmed himself in the memory of the survivors as the permanent meaning of their suicides; he has emerged at the "fatal moment" when, assuming their own impossibility, they have rejoined his impossible-being. But these false saints, far from bestowing their merits on those who have not killed themselves, denounce them; their schoolmates are living because Man, for them, is an impossibility—because they are too cowardly to kill themselves. We see the circle being drawn: there is no Man but tragic man, ineffectual beyond the deliberate abolition of submen conscious of their subhumanity. The schoolmates of And—— and of Bar—— are thorough submen, and it is their criminal appetite for living that defines them as such. This is comic because it is equally impossible for them to continue their dog's existence and to deprive themselves of life, and also because their very subhumanity seems to them the sign of their status as men, affecting in the unreal the lofty sentiments they haven't the means to experience in actuality, an imaginary being-to-die that obscures their consent to the inhuman world of analytic reason. Incapable of choosing nothingness, they have chosen the nonreal, its symbol, and *play* military men in order to forget that they are bourgeois. Can military men be men? No, the comic is universal; those bullies are *playacting* as well; they are cowards, unless their feigned courage is merely ignorance of danger—as though we should call it heroic when Charlie Chaplin, sitting down in the void, risks death unawares. It *must* be this way. Aristocratic syncretism is a dismal illusion maintained by bad faith and continually breached by analytic reason; nobles are bourgeois without knowing it. Atomism, determinism, mechanism—these are the truth. But what about And—— and Bar——? What are they? Does the exception prove the rule? The tightening circle leaves no hope; in the first place, their deaths have pointed to the only possible choice: to kill oneself or to laugh at everything, and first at oneself. But the bitter discovery they have provoked turns against them: their gesture could not be the realization of their being-to-die because that being is only a dream; it must therefore be explained by some *bourgeois* disappointment. Unless, while playing the role of suicides, death came to them inadvertently: that would be a good joke, and one could laugh at the suicide himself. The wheel turns again. The adolescents laugh more than ever, but at their own baseness—aren't they like dogs laughing at dead lions? Doesn't the idea that everything is vile, even their martyrs, give them a kind of abject gratification? And—— and Bar—— are reestablished in their earlier dignity, but the circular movement still does not stop; in a moment, the Blasés will once again find themselves laughing at those two imbeciles who, somehow or other, killed themselves *by mistake*, etc.

They have returned to the illusion of their grandfathers, who took the bourgeoisie for the universal class; they go even further, for they confuse it with the human race; the only difference—which is big enough—is that the bourgeois of 1789 made this mistake the basis of an optimistic humanism, while their grandsons, reversing the signs, make it the basis of their misanthropy and of a universal pessimism. Their laughter avenges them, first of all, on those imposters the *Romantics:* it is Werther, not Goethe, who blew his brains out; it is Chatterton, not Vigny, who poisoned himself. The Gentlemen of Paris would have it believed that one dies of love or of spleen; that is false: they *live* by those lofty sentiments, or rather they live by writing about them, for such fatal passions do not exist. Flaubert retrieves the laughter of the Blasés when he writes of *Graziella:* "There should have been a way of making a good book from this story by showing us what undoubtedly happened: a young man in Naples, in the midst of other distractions, happens to sleep with the daughter of a fisherman and then sends her away; she does not die but consoles herself, which is more common and more galling."[52] It is also the Blasé who, in the same letter, tries to demystify romantic love. "And first of all, speaking frankly, does he screw her or not? They are not human beings but mannequins. How charming they are, those love stories where the chief thing is so shrouded in mystery that one doesn't know what to think; sexual union was relegated systematically to the shadows, like drinking, eating, pissing, etc."[53] The Romantics, like women, are wrong "to take their ass for their heart"; those "hypocrites" experience all human needs, for they are organisms pushed by an underlying *conatus* to produce, to reproduce life, not death; like everyone else, then, they are interested, greedy, egotistical, calculating. They put on a good face, saying that they have fallen from the

52. *Correspondance*, p. 193, 24 April 1852.
53. *Correspondance*, p. 193, 24 April 1852.

heavens and still remember it: their nature is limited, certainly, but in direct consequence their vows are no less so. They pretend to aspire to the infinite, inconceivable as it is, in order to mask their true desires, which are mediocre, trifling, relatively easy to satisfy: give them money, applause, a pretty whore, good health, they will ask for nothing more. It is their profession, of course, to act insatiable, but that is why they are comic. They have made their living from Man, the transcendental illusion of men: as cynics they would be merely odious; as victims of their own lie, they are objects of laughter. In this they are the accredited representatives of the human race, which is entirely laughable since it can neither free itself from this constitutional illusion nor conform to this supposed model.

But bourgeois man remains the principal target. The schoolboys have not forgotten the persecutions of the earlier years, and their savage rancor has increased, for they are afraid of resembling their fathers. As long as they could believe that their generosity, their being-to-die, tore them away from their family, their class, they reproached their parents for misunderstanding their greatness and persecuting them; now they rebuke them for having put them into the world. Those monsters did not understand at the time, or did not want to understand, that they were making the children *in their image;* monsters, they engendered monsters who did not ask to be born and for whom they ordained a monstrous destiny. Laughter avenges them: the bourgeois is comic because he has his own way of taking himself seriously; utilitarian puritanism hides John Bell's base appetites and rapacity; a fetishist, he rejects Christianity and replaces it with the religion of property. They will laugh at this solemn pedant, at this philistine and his humanist pretensions.

These children have double reason to laugh at themselves. They have been fooled by the Romantics; they believed they were the sons of Man and were merely false aristocrats—with the sole excuse that there are no true ones. As sons of the bourgeoisie, they will inherit their fathers' seriousness, that pedantry which Flaubert will call "the comedy of the serious." Those provincial bourgeois were victims of the Parisian bourgeois: laughing at their own silliness, they perceive that they are laughing at it in bourgeois fashion, in the name of paternal baseness, and there they are, laughing at Joseph Prudhomme's pompous absurdities, which they too harbor just beneath the skin. Laughter of the damned, Gustave would say. And indeed it is the result of despair. But it must be recalled that it is also an intentional behavior, by which the laugher breaks solidarity with the object of

331

his laughter. They ask of this hilarity—which they exercise against the self—that it be *cathartic*, that it free them from themselves. It is ersatz suicide in the sense that the adolescents refuse to be serious about their own seriousness and even about the despair from which it issued and from which any hope might be reborn. So we see them withdrawing from themselves and pretending once more to escape their class-being, this time by denying themselves, by mocking their ignominiousness, their dreams, and their anguish which hasn't even the power to make them die. They will be suicides and "judge-penitents,"[54] for they are seeking to rid themselves if not of life at least of *being*, and are at the same time attempting to punish themselves for having passed judgment on others. Derision, as we have seen, is a minor lynching. Each of them is trying to lynch himself so that he can lynch the others.

But here a legitimate question arises: *who* is laughing? In other words, can the mocker and the mocked be the same person? I would answer no, unless he has forcibly internalized a collective derision of which he is now the object—which is not the case here, as each of them is laughing at the others while laughing at himself. Certainly, since every *other* is targeted, and since everyone is himself and other at the same time, we have the makings of a seriality. But the series does not succeed in constituting itself because it is not primarily a matter of internalizing one's other-being (as the chief examiner in his mortarboard does, compelled by his fall and the great roar of laughter from the crowd to see himself as others see him) but rather of instituting laughter as the connection of self to self. And derision being a serial connection with the Other, they can laugh alone neither at themselves nor at each other. They can mock their parents in theory, but since they have removed their aristocrats' glasses, they see them no better than before, for the bourgeois experienced in intersubjectivity is merely the color blindness that prevents them from perceiving the bourgeois in others. Details, yes, anecdotes: you can offer a father's avarice as fodder to the collectivity. But you can't see the bourgeois as a type without falling back into the slogans of Romanticism—John Bell, Prudhomme—or the trite sayings of abstract misanthropy. In consequence, no one really laughs among the Blasés. These poor children have even more trouble: they *playact laughter* and fail to perceive that they have once more crossed over the line that separates the real from the imaginary. Here they are again, unrealiz-

54. The word is Camus's. Cf. *La Chute*.

ing themselves; dry and dour despite their great bursts of false laughter, they have chosen to be *nothing but the fetishized impossibility of living,* and they mock in themselves and in everyone else humanity's will-to-live *from the point of view of death.* We have come back to the beginning. They turn endlessly from the nihilism of the Angry Young Man to the nihilism of the Blasé, and vice versa, now choking with rage, now dying of laughter, without ever bringing about the catharsis they so badly need.

Psychodrama. The Garçon is born of a memorable misapprehension, prefiguring the one that will lead to the success of *Madame Bovary.* We have retraced the involution of the schoolboys since its inception, so it is now possible to find the reasons for this quid pro quo and its meaning.

Gustave is not unaware that he is of bourgeois origins, and we shall see in the next chapter that his class-being will soon horrify him. In the 1830s, however, it is the least of his concerns. Son of a prince of science, he enters school proud of his birth: when his schoolmates dream, they think of themselves as gentlemen-bourgeois; Gustave is convinced of being a bourgeois gentleman. After the Fall, and especially after his scholarly disappointments, he replaced the aristocracy of men of science—the only *real* aristocracy in his eyes—by that of poets, which is based on failure. In any event, it is a matter of proving to himself that he is of a different species from the bourgeois sons who surround him. Pondering his problems—which are exclusively of the familial kind—puts him in a state of permanent distraction and prevents him from understanding the school history we have just recounted. At the time of the nocturnal readings, he unrealizes himself furiously, like the others, more than the others, but for opposite reasons: in Chatterton, his incarnation, Pagnerre seeks to escape his class of origin; Flaubert, certain of being "wellborn," seeks to recover his. Chatterton is Flaubert: a murdered poet, he dies, the victim of bourgeois competition, every time the teacher evaluates the trimester's compositions in front of the John Bells of the class. Like his comrades, he is his father's victim, but according to him these bourgeois sons are themselves bourgeois, and their family conflicts are mere gossip, while Achille-Cléophas, the *noble* progenitor, has exiled him, the cursed but always noble son, among the wild beasts of the common folk. He can in good faith identify with Stello's tirade on the nobility, "cheated, exiled . . . still devoted to the prince who is ruining it"; he knows the rage and anguish of awakenings after reading or revery, but not the nausea of disillusionment, for he finds himself

333

once again martyred. If Gustave had won first place in all his subjects, the Garçon would never have seen the light of day. He was born when Gustave, offering himself up to the derision of his ferocious classmates, played Chatterton's trick on them. Vigny has arranged things such that, believing themselves to be poets, they find themselves in the skin of John Bell seen through the scornful eyes of the nobility; little Flaubert arranges things such that, laughing *with good reason* at a child dying of shame, they suddenly perceive that their good sense, their realism, their pretensions, their importance are chilled by the glacial wind of universal laughter. What the doomed soldier succeeded in doing unknowingly, perhaps, Gustave wants to do deliberately, and to his own advantage: he will demoralize his comrades.

The annoying thing is that they are *already* demoralized. At first they believed that the bourgeoisie had received a historical mandate to create Man, then that the bourgeoisie was the mortal enemy but that its sons, rising up against it, could contribute to the advent of the human reign; rebuffed, they embodied Man in the dream, then, conscious of their imposture, they convinced themselves that the bourgeois is constitutionally ignoble. Now, unable to see their class through the eyes of the "new barbarians" who are privy to its secret, they have come to consider the bourgeoisie as a natural species; in other words, there is no escape; willy-nilly, through their thoughts and actions, they will perpetuate the specific ignominy of the species. Gustave does not understand that they need laughter as a final escape, but that they will not succeed *alone* in laughing at themselves: thinking to kill them, he fulfills them.

They will mock themselves only if they see themselves as objects, as others for others. Now, the trap Gustave offers implies that he proposes the Garçon as his own caricature. Have they recognized the model? This hardly matters; they have recognized their own contradictions externalized. The Same comes toward them, laughable, beneath the mask of the Other. So much the better if it differs from Pagnerre or Baudry in the details of its character: the act of breaking solidarity will be facilitated. And representing an *individual*, the character will not manifest itself as a *type*—unlike Joseph Prudhomme, for example—as the easily dissolved unity of general faults and vices, but rather as a mythic singularity, scarcely decipherable and all the more fascinating. It seems to them that when they act it out, they will not know the constraint of precise and abstract rules (those that impose themselves on the author, or on the actor when they want "to type" a miser), but will be engaged in the free play of imagination. In the story of the Garçon's life (he begins as a poet and ends as an inn-keeper), they recover their school history: they too began with the dream and ended, or will end, like their fathers, in trade or manufac-turing. All the phases of their pitiful revolt are given in the unity of an imaginary temporalization. In the Garçon, Gustave shows himself as a failed poet who takes revenge by becoming the cynical organizer of shit festivals. That's us, say his victims, "rolling with laughter," that's really us; and, according to their mood, they will eat this eminently bourgeois food or make their parents eat it. There, I've caught them, thinks Gustave: what a coup! Not at all. Cosmic laughter, far from chilling their senses, fires their enthusiasm and reassures them: they believed that baseness belonged to the *bourgeois* race; so, even if blasé, they were anything but certain that lofty sentiments existed nowhere else, in no other men of any other species. Now, in his peevishness, Flaubert has gone too far: so that their loathing should be complete, he wanted to stigmatize the *human* race in the person of the Garçon. What a relief! The ignoble is everywhere, baseness is the most com-mon thing in the world; to laugh at oneself is to laugh at men, at creation, at God, if He exists, at matter itself, to denounce the per-petuation of life with the declared impossibility of living.

Gustave rejoiced at making these *realists* fall into the trap of the imaginary. But what does it matter to them? What counts for them is that their laughter is at last *real*. He didn't see, or didn't want to see, the role of the dream in those poor heads. Antony is a role. And Robespierre. And the Terror in a red cap. They are offered another role. They are not mistaken about it: it involves playing the micro-cosm as prey to the laughing macrocosm. It will be pantagruelesque. Perfect! Of course, it is not entirely *like that* in reality. But the Garçon attracts them; not *in spite* of his unreality but because of it.

These judge-penitents need to be incarnate in him by turns, so that each of them, through a new, black Passion, might make himself laughed at as other and might thus acquire the right to withdraw soli-darity from the human race when, a moment later, another is inclined to play the character. For this very reason, the Garçon *must* be a fic-tion. For the actor, it is a matter of exaggerating baseness and stu-pidity, of *inventing the ignoble* in oneself, of forcing hyperbole to the point of the "sublime below." He will act well only if he fulfills him-self through filth, for the new ceremony contains *simultaneously* a symbolic murder of the Father, the chastizing of the Romantics—by capital punishment—and the public confession of a hideous heir. The

difficulty for the actor is that he invents himself such as he is: the ignoble is in him (as it is in us all, only he has the intention of privileg-
ing it); it is proper, then, to reassure him. Which the heavy idol, the
fierce, gigantic traveling salesman, succeeds marvelously in doing.
He hypnotizes them, this colossus, by his sovereign frivolity: say anything that comes to mind, do anything, *it's for laughs;* your inventions
don't commit you; if it amuses you to choose coprophagy, I'm the
one, the Garçon, who will eat shit. The young actor knows, moreover,
that the character is not *his* creature: it is collective property, and
nothing will remain of what each of them brings to it without unani-
mous consent. By incarnating the Garçon, the actor for the day, or for
the hour, makes a vow to defile himself to excess so that his sacrifice
might allow his comrades to save themselves with crazy laughter; he
is acting *under control,* and the sacred character of the representation
frees him and justifies him. Thus the unreality of the Garçon and
his collective character breaks censures and inhibitions—not all, of
course—and lances internal tumors; unknown desires are revealed
and fictively satisfied; impulses born in the "hideous depths" dare to
affirm themselves in broad daylight (the actor declines all responsibility); the inarticulable is articulated; the actor frees his impulses in anonymity, adding his personal touch to the *common* ego of the persona.

If these performances had a real audience separated from the actors
by footlights, if the actors were unremittingly devoted to self-criticism
and parricide, and if their audience watched and judged without
taking part in the action, there would be serious trouble. In the best
case, the illusion would not "take"; in the worst, it would be heart-
rending—both for the spectators excluded from the ceremony by the
adamantine hardness of the imaginary, and, even more so, for those
of the actors devoted to representing indefinitely the ignominiousness of the human race to others without the release of laughter themselves. For this reason—and for many others that need not be dealt
with here—therapeutic psychodramas take place without an audience: all those present are possible actors. And this is precisely the
case with our primitive psychodrama: the spectators are Garçons in
progress; the character is *performed* by a single person and invented by
everyone, as those who permanently control it are waiting their turn
to perform. In this sworn group the Other does not exist, since each
one is *the same* in relation to each other one; or, rather, the Other *for
everyone is none other* than the character, the geometric site of all al-
terities. Their laughter remains serial, it is true, but beyond the laughter is their "freemasonry," which is experienced by all of them as a

bond of interiority, as the human relation that is indispensable to them if they want to manage the common enterprise of representing for themselves their being-in-exteriority—in order to recognize and deny it. We have remarked in an earlier chapter that laughter, even while serializing the laughers, reflected an integrated society that did not in fact exist. It was a question of the fortuitously risible. Here, the common production of the comic *realizes* the integration of the actor-spectators. The cathartic invention therefore has the double virtue of being genocidal and integrating, for on the basis of this sworn community each one produces his specific being (or what he takes as such) in order to deliver others from it, *on condition that this action is reciprocal,* in a movement of improvization that seems to emanate from their collective spontaneity: at times the group's movement, like a tidal wave, sweeps Pagnerre away; at other times it is Pagnerre who rises to the crest of the wave and appropriates the organization of the performance. This does not happen without teeth-clenching, since these grisly workers mix the shit by hand, but they are doing this to get rid of it. And the joy they believed was dead after March '31 is reborn: *to make themselves* the Garçon, to give him his cue or control his intentions, is to surpass their boasted misanthropy by instituting true human relations without knowing it. In these inspired moments, it is no longer from the point of view of nothingness that they mock the creation: they are deriding liberalism, humanism, mechanism, and Romanticism from the point of view of a real, integrated and *free* society that exists *in fact* and through them.

Has catharsis, then, put an end to their demoralization? Not at the deepest level. Escape through comedy could not sustain them in their real class destiny. An armchair awaits Baudry at the Institute; a deputy prosecutor's mandate is reserved for Ernest; Pagnerre, when public companies are created, is singled out to receive a portfolio filled with judiciously selected shares. For the moment, they amuse themselves by rejecting their class-being because they are not yet resigned to accepting it. But this imaginary and, despite appearances, idealistic rejection is exclusively motivated by the very ideology of the bourgeois class. Moreover, the "rising class" is in the full swing of mutation. Flaubert's classmates, like the sons of Noah, incited by Romanticism to discover their father's nakedness, are shocked by its vulgarity. When they laugh at his belly and his lower parts, this vengeful hilarity seems to suppress their intestines, their urogenital organs. In fact, they are simply disposed to hide them by that puritanical hypocrisy, *distinction,* a bourgeois virtue if there ever was one. The Garçon is vul-

337

garity itself; he belches, farts, shits under the bust of Louis-Philippe: his interpreters are pleased to reinvent this scatalogical triviality both because it is *their* birthright and in order to withdraw solidarity from it. In vain; these new gentlemen want to give their class a polish that corresponds to its recent power, but they discover themselves in the very same way that they denounce the faults of that class: vulgarity and distinction, as I have shown elsewhere, are two aspects of an identical reality.[55] The nineteenth-century bourgeois does not think to distinguish himself *by his nature* from the workers he exploits (unlike the nobility, who have the assurance of being "wellborn"); he must therefore distinguish himself by concealing his body, erasing his needs, denying nature in his own person. In short, the class of exploiters refuses to share the materiality of the exploited: distinction creates vulgarity—just as the law, according to Saint Paul, created sin—but since needs can be condemned, covered up, but not got rid of, vulgarity,

---

55. Gustave is the first to pick up these bad habits. The use he makes of the word "vulgar" would itself deserve an entire study: "[Emile]," he said of his comrade Hamard, "is vulgarity itself." And this estimate cannot surprise us: for the aristocrat Flaubert, a bourgeois *must* be vulgar. But in fitting retribution—he is indignant about it, however—*La Gironde*, 1871–72, treats him as a banal bourgeois, and Barbey d'Aurevilly says of *L'Education sentimentale*, "The central character of this novel is above all vulgarity." The man himself irritated the Goncourts by "his traveling salesman side," his taste for "slovenliness, for his unbuttoned style of dress and thought." "Gross, decidedly, a very gross nature." "Flaubert's alacrity," Jean-Pierre Richard quite aptly notes in *Littérature et Sensation*, "preserves something gross and even fundamentally vulgar." In the same tone he relishes the meals he is going to have (with Chevalier), "We'll eat to our heart's content," and the journey he dreams of, "I promise myself a binge with Greece and Sicily." He "crams himself full" of the Latin poets. He will "give himself a bellyful" of colors, etc. Yet it is a willed grossness, an unhappy quest for truculence. But even as he condemns Hamard so severely, isn't he bringing round the whole "grocery" to the *distinguished* conception he erects for himself of the "Artist's" life? "What a fine thing it would be, a little brotherhood of good fellows, all art people, living together and meeting two or three times a week for a good bite to eat, moistened by a good wine, while savoring some succulent poet" (letter to Louis de Cormenin, 7 June 1844). There is something fecal in this alimentary use of poetry: the dream will be realized in those famous Magny dinners where Taine vomited in his beard and George Sand on the feet of her chair.
Conversely, he despises bodily needs and is determined to deny them, going many days without eating, dreaming of castrating himself. His disgust with the body—with his own body—is, whatever the idiosyncratic motivations, a way of *making himself bourgeois* by a puritanical denial of his own nature. We see the circle: distinguished as he is, he discovers and condemns the vulgarity of others, but this refers him to his own, which horrifies him. He is skewered on his distinction and thus *made bourgeois*. So when he believes he is leaning over his own class from on high, his contempt, which is burgeois, anchors him firmly to his seat as galley slave. From here he leaps into the imaginary; the Garçon appears, the triumph of need over distinction: Gustave plays Gargantuas and mimes cosmic violence in order to ennoble his natural functions and at the same time to make them derisive.

turning back on distinction, compels the bourgeois to seek endless compromises with his body; what then appears is the vulgarity of distinction. At the time we are speaking of, the vicious circle has just been installed; it is the result of the slight cultural gap that separates the two generations: the parents are "nature"; the children, discovering the paternal vulgarity, invent the Garçon in order to wallow in their own vulgarity and at the same time withdraw solidarity from it.

The fact remains that, while they are acting, the unity of the group, *on the level of lived experience*, is established against class and is *really* felt. The value of the Garçon is that he allows these young men to love each other. The consequence is obvious: Gustave's relations to the Blasés are overturned. More precisely, there are no more blasés, just a delirious troupe of actor-spectators that cannot be created *without integrating him*. The solitary child, the one excluded, the murdered poet becomes the Grand Sorcerer of a sworn group. By appropriating his creation, of course, the little society has stripped him of his rights as author; in exchange, he has received merely the right to incarnate the Garçon, *like the others*—when it is his turn or by priority in moments of inspiration. The young freemasons have quickly forgotten that he made them a gift of the character. What they *acknowledge* is that he is its permanent guarantee. First of all, he has the right physique. A few of the actors must have been discouraged in advance: they were too small, their voice was too weak, so they resigned themselves to playing secondary roles; others, better endowed, would risk taking the lead role but had to inflate their voices, puff out their chests to *symbolize* the gigantism they could not *show*; they *carried on* but quickly got out of breath, and even in their best performances they could not stand comparison with Gustave. And besides, there's no doubt he plays the role best: he has the calling (the "billiard room" at the Hôtel-Dieu gave him practice) as well as the flair. And how could anyone challenge his imagination when it is himself he invents? No one would dare to meddle with incarnating the collective persona if Gustave were not there to guide the improviser, to enrich the "caricature," to correct when necessary, and as a last resort to take the role from the failing hands and boost it into the sublime by hyperbolic radicalization. Hence, though the troupe recognizes no particular right to the collective property, he always remains—no matter who the *actual* interpreter may be—the virtual representative of the Garçon. We might call him its guardian; he serves as everyone's model and guarantee. To the extent that the "heavy-handed, heroic joke" contains something sacred, he fulfills the function of priest or Grand Sorcerer; it is agreed that he should exercise scarcely visible but dictatorial control over the convulsive inventors in the name of his strange but acknowledged acquaintance with nonbeing. He is respected now, *he is loved*—in the Garçon, of course, as Christians love each other in God. But he feels that this affection they bear him is particular, that the group loves each other in him, conscious that it would desist if Gustave were to disappear. In this sense, the young man *has made a gift of his person* to his grateful comrades. Isn't this what he wanted? Hasn't he, the generous lord, reestablished the just hierarchy? Does he not now occupy his rightful place, which his teachers persist in denying him? The unexpected friendship of his subjects ought to be a balm to the wounds of the unloved boy. Is he at least content?

Less discontent, perhaps, and he may experience occasional bursts of pride. Content, no. Things are less simple than they seem at first glance. To begin with, he is neither king nor lord except in the imaginary. By denying him first place, the masters did him a *real* wrong; they rendered him *really* inferior to Bouilhet. To compensate for this inferiority, he would have to exercise a real and secular power over his classmates in the courtyard and the dining hall, like any other gang leader who organizes disturbances, launches his men in an attack on the kitchens, or orders them to kidnap a study master. And they listen religiously to Gustave, imitate him, follow him on condition that he does not try to give them orders: let him inspire, let him animate, okay; but let him never demand. Moreover, his authority, to the extent that it is tacitly recognized, has bearing only on gestures. On acts, never. He is the grand master of the imaginary provided he is imaginary himself: to impose, to orient, to control he must first of all unrealize himself or, at the very least, be considered a permanently virtual image. As an image, he commands only images. Not Pagnerre, the son of Pagnerre, but the Garçon, Monsieur Loyal, insofar as these images vampirize Pagnerre, who is in any case an ordinary analogue and always replaceable. Gustave's authority is always limited by the free inspiration of his partners as much as by the *habitus* of the Garçon, by inventions past and surpassed, sanctioned and retained by the whole group (even if these inventions come from him). Indeed, he again finds himself as he was in the "billiard room," the director of a little troupe composed of Caroline and Ernest, the slave of a written role, whoever the author (it might be himself), and sometimes outflanked by the initiatives of his sister or his friend. The difference is primarily quantitative: in the era of the Garçon, there are more actors. Hence, there are several qualitative modifications: specifically, they are not bound to Gustave by blood or childhood friendship; some of them are known to him only to the extent that, coming from the outside, they have applied for and obtained integration into the group; in this sense, the young man's authority is *extended*. On the other hand, all the interpreters being theoretically interchangeable, Flaubert participates in this interchangeability: his power of control is superior to that of any other actor-spectator, yet he does not escape the collective surveillance. He must continually prove that he is worthy of the privileges tacitly accorded him; for him, as for the others, the possibility of "being a flop" accompanies every improvization. In short, the imaginary child remains imaginary in his new function: he is king on the boards, and his crown is made of paper. We must go further: this new office increases his unreality. From the time he entered school he has unrealized himself only in solitude. As curator of the Garçon, his unreality takes on a new dimension: it is public, instituted; his profound and intimate relation to nonbeing, recognized by his peers, makes him an *objective* determination of the collective imagination, something approaching—all things considered—the great popular myths of Don Quixote or Don Juan. To be more precise, the group integrates him only in the name of the permanent possibility of his transformation into myth. And as he exists in his own eyes only as the other whom others see, it is as if his instituted-being (or, if you like, his absolute being) came to him "from afar" as imaginary being. The re-internalization of this external being represents a new spiral in the movement of personalization, for it tends to make everyday reality (schoolwork, family relations) a materiality without being, an inconsistent object of the *doxa* and very close to the Platonic *hyle*, and to place his true being in the brilliant, rigorous game of appearances bound by rules produced and preserved by a community.

As we have noted in passing, the ludic activity of the little actors has an underlying purpose, catharsis, which represents the "seriousness of the comic." It has also created real fraternal bonds among them. Even if Gustave is integrated as a technician of the imaginary, should he not be overjoyed at the reality of his integration into the group? Here we return to the basic question: did he love his comrades? Did the members of his troupe seem to him "narrow-minded" bourgeois or superbly extravagant young madcaps? But this time we have all the elements of the answer, which need merely be articulated.

The situation is reversed to his advantage—it is so obvious, he cannot fail to notice it. But this change disconcerts him insofar as it reveals to him the misapprehension at its source and his own contradiction. In

341

fact, he had two opposite objectives at the outset: with deepest humility he sought integration; pushed by pride and resentment, he sought to outdo his exile. Was he not still excluded yesterday, when those idiots were laughing at him? He has come toward them in order to return their laughter and deliver them up that monster, the Garçon. This presupposes that he should strut *in front of* these goslings and fascinate them until he affects them with an unreal taint, his own anomaly hyperbolized. When the Baudrys, the Pagnerres, those solid bourgeois, future masters of the earth possessed by his dreams, become the hallucinated characters of a play he has authored, he will laugh in their faces, as Byron and Rabelais laughed in the face of humanity. He does them injury, so he can be neither among them nor with them; the exile avenges himself without leaving the place of his exile. But his deepest desire, corrupted by rancor, is to become their black lord by making them the gift of his person and his misfortune. And they are delighted, they rejoice, they adopt Gustave and institute him as Grand Sorcerer. They have no sooner integrated him than he perceives in a daze that his two postulations are in conflict: the bad boy is *outside*, the lord is *inside*, at the top of the hierarchy but *within it*. Does he entirely understand the misapprehension? No; he remains convinced, at least for a time, that he is injuring his comrades, that they so gaily agree to being coprophagists out of pure stupidity, that their laughter is superficial and conceals their real horror at the image enveloping them, a devouring tunic of Nessus. Since they love their tormentor, since they have introduced him into their assemblies, and since Gustave utilizes the love they bear him to damn them, the bad boy regards himself, not without pleasure, as the *traitor*. To betray implicates exteriority at the heart of interiority, using powers that are instituted and effective only inside the group—in short, its very freedom—to make it fall into an external trap of which the traitor *has knowledge*. He is therefore at once an accomplice to the exterior (knowledge of that kind is connivance) and a retainer of free power which the group produces in immanence: leading the group to its doom, he becomes its freedom-to-be-alienated. That he might assume it, however, the traitor's contradiction never loses its virulence, nor is it surpassed even by the felony that delivers his community to the enemy; in fact, he is ordinarily an early expression of the disintegration of the collective and lives this nascent conflict in love (unity maintained) and hatred (discord, fissure that appears only in the synthetic foundation of interiority). He hates what he loves to the extent that he loves what he hates. Which means—at least in principle—that he is born into the community—or has entered it with the intention of perpetuating it, and that love (terror-fraternity or sworn group) has preceded hatred. But in Gustave's case it is the reverse: hatred—if the word is not too strong—has preceded love; from the outside he has conditioned the transformation of the Blasés into a troupe of actor-spectators and consequently finds himself integrated into this little society. But from that time forth he has lost all acquaintance with exteriority: he cannot be bound to the enemies of the group since, in this case, the enemy transcendence was merely himself. Having entered into immanence, this transcendence can be maintained only with difficulty because it has no further relation to the outside. No doubt Gustave brings with him Vigny's scornful gaze. But as we have seen, it is an imaginary and abstract point of view. Moreover, if the little band expresses the underlying and impassable contradiction of the younger generation of bourgeois with previous generations—which is experienced by each of them as his personal contradiction—no *real* conflict divides it from the interior, which would allow Gustave to play them against each other. Perhaps a certain tension exists between those who are the acknowledged interpreters of the Garçon and the weaker sorts who are relegated to secondary roles. But the contempt of the former for the latter is tempered by the necessity to make provisions for the "supporting" cast; and the jealousy of the weaker ones is tempered by the fact that their right to play the central role is recognized in principle, and only physical or mental disadvantages prevent them from doing so. Between 1835 and 1839, the persona, far from becoming fixed, a mere collection of stereotypical ceremonies reflecting the internal dissensions and growing disaffection of certain members of the group, is continually enriched and radicalized, which presupposes perfect accord among the actors: Gustave has no choice but to participate fully since he must do so to pursue the enterprise. This presupposes that the Great Producer and his troupe understand each other at a word and even without speech: when the game begins, all are united by a prospective comprehension of the intentions of whoever does the Garçon. This divining expectation of the "magic word" that will suddenly give meaning to the improvised scene is one of the highest forms of *empathy* that unites each one to the others, and particularly Gustave to his actors: he needs it when he acts; he feels it when he is not acting, or when he takes a secondary role. In short, not every would-be traitor becomes one. He is loved, he must love; he cannot take for himself the aspirations, the anticipations of the group and fulfill them without being in full personal accord with his com-

343

rades. Gustave the traitor, sustained by everyone's friendship, makes the passage to the imaginary a gracious gift of friendship. He must realize this: he has not betrayed; their gaiety demonstrates that he gave them what they desired. If this misanthrope ever felt a deep, warm feeling for a community of equals, it was certainly not at the Magny dinners, nor at Mathilde's, nor the boulevard du Temple, but during those four years, in the moments of glory and love when he was inventing himself, ignoble and sublime, in order to answer the diffuse demands of his peers. He will never forget it: something took place, an order was instituted, a black knighthood was born that he will vainly attempt to revive in the Parisian salons.

Is his hatred therefore disarmed? Does love efface the unloved boy's resentment? Certainly not. For he persists in detesting the *collège*, arranges at the beginning of the school year in 1838 to return as a day student, and succeeds in getting himself expelled at the beginning of the school year of 1839–40.[56] By 1841, the Garçon is no more than a memory. The Grand Sorcerer has unhesitatingly taken the group he used to animate and has sacrificed it to his taste for domestic sequestration. Another indication: when he writes *Mémoires d'un fou*, the masquerade of the Garçon is in full swing; the Flaubert younger son therefore fully enjoyed the friendship of his accomplices; yet it was in this work that he denounced *without exception* his comrades' imbecility. But in 1838, as I believe I have established, no one has mocked him for a long time. The young author is evoking distant but still keen, memories. He has forgotten nothing, forgiven nothing; the extravagant madcaps and the "narrow minds" *are the same boys:* from one moment to the other the lense changes, at the whim of circumstance and his mood.

First of all, he *suffers* the friendship he bears them; I have shown that he is the victim of a sleight of hand: caught in his own trap, he creates the group, integrates himself in it, and feels frustrated in his anger; he will take up its thread when he can, when daily tasks disperse the little community. In short, a hundred times a day, during studies, compositions, etc., his friends again become his rivals, solidarity gives way to competition. Not that the "extravagants" are

56. It is perhaps at this time, if the Goncourts are not mistaken, that his partners come to the Hôtel-Dieu during the vacation and attempt, in the resurrected "billiard room," to prolong the agony of the character. The next chapter will demonstrate why chance factors (bad health, unforeseen scandal) cannot be used to explain his becoming a day student, and then his expulsion, and why we are in fact dealing with a veritable *strategy.*

particularly threatening competitors: we have seen that they were recruited from among the "scamps," more rarely from among the "strong." Be that as it may, while their grades may be inferior to his in general, there is no guarantee that they will not get the better of him *this time*. I have described above that circular antagonism created by the competitive system: every man for himself. And even if he is certain to prevail, they will nonetheless be witnesses to his defeat; they will see Icarus, who flew so high toward the sun, do a sudden nosedive and tumble down into the bourgeois mire: first, Louis Bouilhet.

There is worse to come. The Garçon, as I have said, is for each of the actors that "He" whom everyone disowns and whom, by a veritable human sacrifice, they incarnate by turns so that the entire group can withdraw solidarity from him. This collective character may be called cathartic in that he represents the group's being-in-exteriority: the one who interprets him accepts provisional and fictive exclusion from the community. Even as he is esteemed, as his performance is perhaps admired, he creates a minor scandal and becomes the object of a symbolic lynching. For those who have never suffered exile, this is not serious: they lend themselves to this imaginary ostracism to gain the right to pass judgment him their turn on the next incarnation; while they are acting, moreover, the Garçon exists in the third person for them too: they animate him with their passions, they lend him their secret inclinations, but as *an Other*. Alterity everywhere: this "He" has no subjective density. Except for Gustave. First, when he interprets the Garçon, it is his former exile he is representing; second, he is the only one to know he is exhibiting *his own anomaly*, hyperbolized, of course, and grotesque, but *his*; finally, as we have seen, it is futile for him to insist on the collective character of the Garçon— when he is caught off guard, he admits that he has always considered the monster his work and his property. Thus the Garçon, for him, is not so much an other whom he must animate as an alter ego for whom he feels solidarity. The reason he remains continually watchful, always ready to correct, to set to rights, to guide, is that even as a spectator he is perpetually conscious of being the martyr from whom the crowd is withdrawing solidarity. Pagnerre is unaware that he is playing Gustave, that he is delivering Gustave to the laughers; Gustave himself knows it and suffers from it; he recognizes his solitude, his inexpiable singularity, his impotent ferocity, his resentful malice. It often seems to him that, like Cocteau's photographer—"since these mysteries are beyond us, let us pretend to be their organizer"—he has done nothing but pretend to organize the division of spoils and his own death scene. The Garçon—his creation—does *not laugh:* his laugh—mechanical and gutteral—"is not a laugh," it is a hyperbolic and cold representation of collective hilarity. And his interpreter of the moment is the only one not to laugh. The only one *along with Gustave,* even when he is not playing, or when he is playing one of the "supporting" roles. The Flaubert younger son is unceasingly absorbed in representing or controlling those who represent the group's *being in exteriority;* he identifies with this objective; being repulsed by laughter, he judges himself responsible for it; he is unconditionally exterior, he assumes his role as the comic object, the instigator of the hilarity, and so he is permanently compelled to dwell in the *seriousness of the comic.* As far as he is concerned, he is the secret fissure of immanence: in the heart of the community he pretends to laugh, he makes laughter, his comrades are grateful to him for the provoked laughter, he feels it, at moments he is exalted by it. His solitude comes to him because he never laughs; when someone else plays the Garçon, Gustave watches him anxiously, and in the community of laughers he *feigns* hilarity merely to seem *one of them.* But his endeavored mimicry—he makes more noise than all the others put together—distances him from his peers: at once *superior*—since he raises or rules the laughter—and phony—since he pretends to feel what they are feeling—he is *with them* when they invent the character together and separate from them when they unanimously reap the rewards of their inventions. Hence his instability: there is nothing to prevent him, at the least provocations, from cutting himself off entirely from the group and regarding the laughers as both dupes and apes mimicking a man. The Garçon is the comic reverse of his sorrowful ecstasies, of his gigantesque contempt for these Liliputians; thus, even when he plays him, he can rage against his audience: *they,* the idiots, laugh at *me!* The next moment, of course, he is overwhelmed by the jubilation of the actor-spectators, moved by their congratulations; his superiority is acknowledged, he is at the top of the hierarchy, *inside,* loved, loving—as a lord can love his vassals—forgetting, in his success, the misapprehension that separates him from them, ready to give them credit for their superb extravagance but still bitter that their fealty is only in the imaginary. When he emerges, stunned, from the "heavy-handed, heroic joke," he understands at once that the farce of the Garçon has made amends for nothing: Achille remains unequaled, unequalable. Gustave is a dreamer who rules over woolgatherers. But tomorrow, very soon, he will once again don the harness of the imaginary: it is stronger than he is, stronger than they are; the Garçon has

FROM LEGEND TO ROLE

taken possession of the entire troupe and its animator; he possesses them and condemns them to reproduce him endlessly. These prisoners of the ignoble are like raving maniacs: they are bound forever to their nightmarish gaiety.

Consent, or the comedy of seriousness. Neither Gustave nor his classmates are conscious that their laughter, the final avatar of the schoolboys' involution, a desperate denial of the bourgeois condition, is at the same time the ultimate step in the inflexible process that is leading them to *consent*. Already, as we have seen, when they were fleeing from their class into the dream, their absenteeism implied a veiled abdication: leaping into the field of stars, they abandoned the real to their parents. The move from Romanticism to cynical hilarity changes nothing of that: they have reversed the signs but have not left the imaginary. While they are laughing at the Garçon, at an *invented* humanity, the conservative bourgeoisie has consolidated its power, repression has been established, the republican party, dismantled, becomes clandestine; the workers, uncertain, bludgeoned, seem stymied. Universal laughter, prompted by a gigantesque shadow, is like signing a blank check. But, even more serious, it cannot be denied that the misanthropy which is at the source of this laughter marks the beginning of complicity with the established order. Since lofty sentiments are simply impostures that conceal sordid interests, since all men, rich or poor, are wild beasts, since, as a direct consequence, no regime is good, and since the plebeians, if by some impossibility they were to seize power, would only oppress their former oppressors while their leaders tore each other apart—who needs to change the world? The bourgeois order is as good as any other, the essential thing being surely that an iron law, imposed from without, should intimidate the savage appetites of the populace. For these adolescents reduced to cynicism, there is no just cause; they will not have the naïveté to defend the widow and the orphan: the widow is abusive, the orphan, far from being innocent, whatever his age, has "the defects that will become vices," for he is "a child who will become a man." Who are these laughers, anyway, but future men? And from what are they withdrawing solidarity but *themselves*? What are they mocking but their own vain efforts to escape the bourgeois they are themselves beneath their skin? Certainly the bourgeois too, above all, perhaps, are laughable. But what does that mean? If they laugh at a fictive and hyperbolic character who is charged with representing the typical bourgeois, isn't this proof that they could not hold him in derision *in his reality* because he is none other than *themselves*? To laugh at a phantom is to defer the inevitable and foreseen acceptance of their class-being. The freemasonry of the Garçon, their last refuge, certainly reproduces in its interiority the sworn group of the rebels of March 1831; it differs from it in that its revolt is imaginary and it has neither enemies nor a real base—hence its fragility. It protects them but does not change them; when it is abolished, what do they find? The charms of a bourgeois Sunday, of the dance at which they courted their cousin, the poetry of family comfort, all the temptations of the bourgeoisie. Laughter becomes an alibi: they will abandon themselves to their class-being complacently, sure of purifying themselves the day after tomorrow by *doing the Garçon*. Not to take themselves seriously; to banter; to practice mental restriction; to disqualify in advance all their compromises with a wink to themselves, to the freemasonry of yesterday, to that of the day after tomorrow, and, protected by this imaginary connivance ("If they were there, they would have had a good laugh!"), to compromise themselves utterly; to wallow in the family mire; to consent to the comedy of seriousness by mentally referring to the seriousness of the comic; to do with nonchalance, with ease, everything their fathers do on the pretext that they have seen everything and finally come around, and being home after this long journey they want to begin cultivating their garden so as not to be fooled: this, for these post-romantics, is their way of endorsing their class-being, for which they compensate by moderate absenteeism. A provisional solution; it will take no more than three years for them to embrace it completely. Paris will complete the metamorphosis: there they will be wanton students, and they will return as dutiful sons.

This pitiful history, begun in 1831 with Clouet's dismissal, ends in 1839 with Gustave's. What a difference between the two revolts! We know about the first, and here is the second. When the Flaubert younger son enters the philosophy class, the chief teacher, Monsieur Mallet, a respected master, recognizes his merit. Unfortunately, this excellent pedagogue is in delicate health: he has to take a leave of absence from the first trimester. His substitute, Bezout, has neither his titles nor his culture. The students are indignant: their parents pay dearly enough that their children might not be dispensed cut-rate teaching. They will show this Bezout the contempt in which they hold him:

> The students entered very noisily, talking at the tops of their voices, and it was only after I succeeded, with difficulty, in obtaining silence that I could begin the lesson, which was interrupted three

times by the students Flaubert, Scentrenie, and Poittevin,[57] whom I was forced to punish separately. the disorder continuing throughout, the students fidgeting with their feet and murmuring, and my being obliged to follow a rather difficult explication, it was impossible for me to distinguish the guilty parties. I found myself compelled, regretfully, to inflict a general punishment . . . I hesitated a long time and it was only at the third warning that I gave a thousand lines to the whole class . . . The disorder having continued, I had to stand by the punishment.[58]

The little gentlemen are not going to let themselves be punished by a common assistant master unjustifiably raised to the rank of teacher. They send a letter to the administration protesting against Bezout: "The students whose names follow refuse to do the exercise . . ."[59] The proctor chooses three "insubordinates"—Flaubert, Piédelièvre, and Dumont—and threatens them with expulsion. A new letter— thirteen signatures, including Bouilhet's—was sent to the headmaster. Here are some extracts:

You have been told that we were children, that we were acting like children; we are going to try by our moderation and our loyalty to convince you otherwise. We sent the Proctor a letter from all the students who refused to do the exercise. Without regard for this list, the Proctor [has chosen] three students whom he threatens with nothing less than total exclusion from the collège, which means destroying their future and prohibiting them from ever pursuing the career they might have embraced . . . We herewith sign our names again, and state, Headmaster, that first of all we are prepared to give you the reasons for our actions today and then, if notwithstanding these reasons you continue to decimate the class, that we claim for all of us, the undersigned, the exercise if there is an exercise, exclusion if there is exclusion . . . If the whole class can be given a thousand lines, the whole philosophy class can also be dismissed . . . We leave it . . . to your justice and your impartiality, which, we know, likes to be exercised on behalf of students who deserve it, students of philosophy who are not acting impulsively like seventh-year children but who have reflected, meditated deeply before taking a measure that seems to them just and which they have resolved to pursue to the end.

57. This student has nothing to do with Alfred, of course.
58. Report to the proctor: 11 December 1839. *Bulletin des amis de Flaubert*, 10.
59. Thirty-one signatories, including Bouilhet.

349

Nothing is done about it: Flaubert, Piédelièvre, and Dumont are expelled. But this is not—at least for the moment—what interests us. Examination of the collective protest is more significant; it allows us to measure the distance covered in eight years. In 1831, Clouet was fighting the Church; in December 1839, the philosophy students were after the skin of a poor devil who hadn't enough diplomas to merit their respect and seemed to them unworthy of teaching the sons of the Rouen bourgeoisie. They are bent not so much on annoying him as on giving him insolent indication that he hasn't the right to speak. They drown out his voice as soon as they enter the classroom, conversing among themselves as if he did not exist. Calm is no sooner established, no sooner does he open his mouth, than Flaubert and several others interrupt him, no doubt mocking his diction or the nonsense he is uttering. The poor man is his own undoing, as he candidly acknowledges, and is lost in a "rather difficult explication." This time the students scrape their shoes on the floor. Warnings. Then Monsieur Bezout loses his head and punishes the whole class; seized with fear, he begs them: stay quiet and I will lift the punishment. In vain: the young gentlemen, divining his weakness and his disarray, pursue their advantage ad nauseum. Saved by the bell. These are the games of the rich: the prey is a poor man they want to assault. The rebels of March, betrayed by their parents, fought them courageously. The insubordinates of December are proud of being respectable sons. Rich kids, they want their money's worth; it is in the name of the rising bourgeoisie that they demand, when they no longer believe in man, to do their "humanities." These desperate children, who earlier believed they were suicidal, now have a "future"—their letter proves it—a *fine* future which they accuse the proctor of destroying. Competition, selection—these are things they accept, even demand: why study if not to *have a career* and to give oneself the polish befitting their rank? Utilitarianism and a taste for prestige were the motives for their insubordination. Besides, they are hardly taking a chance: the whole class signed the first petition; but the proctor holds firm and they are deflated; only nine students declare their solidarity with the three who are threatened with expulsion: the follies of the 1831 "lawbreakers" are long gone. On the contrary, how full of their dignity they are in these words, not previously cited: "It would perhaps have been well, before taking a measure so grave, so decisive, to weigh impartially the equity or the injustice of an exercise that is so imperiously required of us today." This is the stiff, formal style of Royer-Collard. At heart, they want it known that they are grown-ups, they who used to detest adults: "[We are not acting] impulsively like seventh-year children but [have] reflected, meditated deeply before taking a measure that seems [to us] just." Where has their Romantic passion gone? Where are those mad extravagances? This time, it is their fathers they are imitating. Monsieur Flaubert purchasing a piece of land, Monsieur Le Poittevin making an investment or deciding to buy an English machine, certainly speak this language: a decision meditated, matured, weighed pro and con, an unshakable resolution—the language of Reason. The crazy adolescents have become rationalists; those bewildered victims of paternal injustice are now judicious, prudent; they publicly claim the family virtues for themselves and present their disorders as the beginning of a return to order. The long involution comes to an end: post-Romanticism begins, these children accept the bourgeois adventure; Melmoth reconciled approaches Joseph Prudhomme, he will live like everyone else, continuing to feel that he is worth more than his life, saving himself from abjection by constant, imponderable irony, by a preserved horror of the self. Poor children, who could reproach them for this implacable defeat? I have mentioned the reason they began as losers, cut off as they were from the working class— which was barely aware of itself. Their wretched destiny—whether they abdicate everything or persist in wishing themselves republicans—will be to stifle the popular revolt of 1848. Some of them will be among those national guardsmen who will descend on Paris, in June, to "put one over on" a few workers; others will take advantage of universal suffrage to send reactionary deputies to the capital as Napoleon III's quartermasters. Dedicated to crime, ineluctably, they will yet be guilty with no attenuating circumstances. We shall find them again later, gloomy and futile, under the Empire. Meanwhile, let us not waste our time pitying them; they have done what they could, it's true, but we can do nothing for them: history condemns them in advance. And the Garçon? He would have a good laugh, I think, seeing these freemasons of laughter taking themselves so very seriously. But, in fact, what becomes of him? And how is it possible that his qualified representative, the high priest of his cult, is one of the signatories, perhaps the instigator, of the bourgeois homily addressed by the "philosophers" to the headmaster? Well, as I have said, the Garçon is dying, his hour is past, the comedy of seriousness has taken hold everywhere. As for the younger son of Achille-Cléophas, the crisis has already begun that will make him the neurotic of 1844, the hermit of Croisset, and, eventually, Gustave Flaubert, the scandalous author of *Madame Bovary*. It begins badly: for various reasons and under the influence of various circumstances, this prince of the blood, this "aristocrat of the Good Lord," who will never accept his class-being and really did once take himself for Chatterton, comes to discover the bourgeois he is under his skin and the bourgeois destiny his father is reserving for him. What a shock! The poet will die of it. Now we must retrace the long march that will lead the survivor, a man without qualities, to the condition of artist.

PART TWO
_____

Personalization (continued)

BOOK THREE
Preneurosis

From Poet to Artist

(continued)

Between 1838 and the attack at Pont-l'Evêque, Flaubert is shaken and finally defeated by a crisis that I shall call—with no greater precision for the time being—psychosomatic. Many authors admit that Gustave was subject to ill-defined troubles during this period, which worried his family, but see these merely as discontinuous manifestations, separated from each other by "normal" years. I shall try to establish that a single and inflexible process is continually organizing itself, enriching and deepening, until the explosion of January 1844 becomes inevitable. I shall even claim that this crisis—which leaves him no respite—is a temporal organism, a directed movement that continually stirs up, sets and resets in perspective, Gustave's contradictions until, falling at his brother's feet, he reveals to us and to himself the underlying intentionality of his neurosis. I also propose to demonstrate that this illness, far from being simply suffered, is the object of a passive choice, and that Flaubert shapes himself in the same measure that he is shaped by the situation and events.

In this organizational unity, whose end is gradually confirmed as the establishment of what Flaubert will later call "a valid system for one man," we shall nonetheless distinguish, for the sake of clarity, two periods: the first goes from the last months of 1837 to 1840, the second from 1840 to January 1844. Of course this division is abstract, since all themes are present from the outset. On the other hand, in the first period the theme of "choice of a profession" and the theme of "literary disappointment" are not equally developed; after the winter of 1842 the first will become fully developed within the framework of the second. Therefore, even while drawing attention to the indissoluble, vectorial unity of the process, we can consider that the division—made for the requirements of a comprehensible exposition—is still not entirely arbitrary if viewed in relation to the object described.

A. LITERARY DISAPPOINTMENT (1838–1840)

If we look at the years 1838–1840 in the light of Flaubert's own testimony, and also in the light of the number and nature of the works he produced during this period and the events defining them, we are struck by the agreement between exterior and interior, that is, by evident "correspondences" and reciprocal symbolizations, as if an identical reality were being constituted and simultaneously expressed in various languages. I shall try to reconstitute these "utterances" before seeking their implicit and underlying meaning.

1. Flaubert's Testimony

There are retrospective accounts; others are contemporaneous with the crisis. They agree.

On 17 September 1846, Flaubert writes to Louise (in a letter already cited): "At fifteen I certainly had more imagination than I have now. As I advance I lose in verve, in originality, what I gain perhaps in critical acumen and in taste. I shall end, I'm afraid, by no longer daring to write a line. The passion for perfection makes you detest even what approaches it."

At the age of seventeen, on 24 February 1839, he declares to Chevalier that he will probably stop writing and will certainly not get himself published. And in the same letter we read: "I feel in a confused way, though, something stirring inside me; I am now in a period of transition and I am curious to see what will result, how I will come out of it." The *Souvenirs*, recently published, rarely carry precise dates. We know, however, that they were begun in 1838. And in the first pages we find these words: "It is not enough to have taste, one must have a palate. Boileau . . . had taste. Racine had a palate." Those immediately following are dated. "28 February 1840: I just reread this notebook and I pitied myself." This rereading allows us to suppose that Flaubert had abandoned his notebook some time before; hence that first reference to artistic "taste" must be situated between the end of 1838 and the end of 1839. From that time on, he never stopped tormenting himself, and we read on 8 February 1841—he is nineteen years old: "What I'm lacking above all is taste, I mean all."

The dates nearly agree. In 1846, Flaubert is speaking from memory, which generally tends to simplify. In 1839, he is speaking in the present; but he alludes to a maturational change that is obviously an ongoing process and of which he must have become conscious *before*

356

mentioning it to his friend. In general, then, we can situate the conscious concern with "taste" as a new and basic requirement between his sixteenth and seventeenth year. Is there a contradiction between his complaints of 1841 and his declarations of 1846? On the contrary, I contend that the latter confirm the former. In fact, both *tell* us that Gustave's creative spontaneity has been constrained, upon leaving adolescence, by a new conception of literature.[1] Between 1838 and 1841, Flaubert is distressed to be writing *less;* this is also what he asserts in 1846—in a rigorously objective tone. But although he then presents his relation to the work of art in a rather positive manner, the negative force of taste, its power to inhibit, is manifest: the young author notes, impassively, that he has lost his verve, his originality, his imagination. As he did beginning in 1838, he evokes the possibility of never writing again. And if we want to know what anguish and bitterness are hidden beneath this superficial impassivity, we need only refer to a subsequent letter. On 4 September 1850, Flaubert writes to Louis Bouilhet: "There is one thing that damns us, you see, one stupid thing that shackles us, and that is 'taste,' good taste. We have too much of it, I mean, we worry about it more than we should. The terror of bad taste invades us like a fog . . . So we dare not advance, but just stand still. Have you noticed how we are turning into critics? What we are lacking in is audacity . . . Let's not worry so much about the end product."

This passage must be read on many levels. Flaubert is writing from Damas, full of discouragement. Torn by the failure of the first *Saint Antoine*, he turns against taste, for it was in the name of taste that Maxime and Louis condemned that work. He profits from his friend's momentary depression to criticize the critical attitude: "If you had less taste and more audacity, you would be less unhappy." But he cannot prevent himself, at the same time, from questioning his own attitude: was it not in the name of "taste" that he submitted to the judgment of his two friends? And in these few lines, which seem— when compared to the letter of 1846—like a reversal of perspective, we read what have often been Flaubert's feelings in his periods of discouragement. "Taste" appears here as a sterilizing dictate: it prevents progress; set against it is an audacious spontaneity—which is the stuff of genius, perhaps, and which Louis, Maxime, and Gustave are dangerously close to having lost. Is this not the same contradiction

---

1. We have seen the role that his friendship for Alfred played in this crisis. We are examining here the objective reasons for it.

between spontaneity and reflection that we first discover in 1838 in the young author of *Souvenirs*? And in these same *Souvenirs*, do we not find, at some months distance, the assertion that taste in the literary object is *all*, as well as lively attacks against literary criticism, "an extremely stupid thing . . . whether good or bad"?[2]

In sum, all these texts confirm each other: until the end of 1837—influenced by the Romantics and because of his own inclinations—Flaubert conceives of literature as a product of inspiration. He writes to Ernest toward this period: "Oh, how much I prefer pure poetry, the cries of the soul, the sudden soarings and the deep sighs, the voices of the soul, the thoughts of the heart." He asserts this again in the very first page of the *Souvenirs:* "I like improvisation better than reflection, feeling better than reason." But almost immediately this tendency is challenged in him by a new conception of Art, which manifests itself as a kind of terrorism: as an adolescent he was a lyric writer; between sixteen and seventeen, he suddenly develops a reflective and critical idea of literature. And the appearance of this idea is less an enrichment than a catastrophe: between inspired eloquence and the rigors of censorship, a twenty-year war begins, characterized during its first period by the rout of inspiration.

A fundamental question must, therefore, be posed on this ground. Flaubert, so unfit to *see himself* or to examine the products of his impassioned rhetoric, is abruptly struck down, in the midst of his Romantic period, by a new malady: the conception of Beauty as the product of *reflected* Art. To tell the truth, he hesitates a little at the outset, and taste, like genius, seems merely a gift—"Racine had the palate for it." But what gradually comes to the fore is reflexive control, which means that the writer's reflection on the work is not distinguishable from his reflection on himself. Indeed, it is a historical and social fact of the nineteenth century that the powerlessness of the creator manifestly accompanied the advent of a "critical poetry." After Victor Hugo, the unquenchable, came Baudelaire and Mallarmé. We shall seek later the general reasons for these phenomena. But it must be noted for the moment that the metamorphosis of literature was effected *first* in the young Flaubert at a time when he had neither the instruments of thought that would later allow him to understand it completely, nor the required aesthetic means. The question, then, is this: for what *particular* reasons does the most unreflective of men cross over, around the age of sixteen, to the reflexive attitude? And

2. *Souvenirs*, p. 97.

358

what will be the consequences of taking up this position for him and for his work?

2. Objective Transformation of Writings between 1837 and 1843

Flaubert's writings of the period manifest this internal upheaval both in their objective contents and in their number.

First of all, quality. By this I am in no way referring to *value;* rather, I mean that he abandons—or almost abandons—certain genres and practices others. "At fifteen, I certainly had more imagination . . ." In fact, he had neither more nor less than at thirty. After all, we know the sources of the first works: from 1835 to 1838, Flaubert imitates as much as he invents; more precisely, his originality resides in his way of treating a borrowed content; conversely, the best passages of *Smarh* deserve attention, as those of the first *Saint Antoine* will do later, because of their abundance of "images."

Imagination is no longer a faculty of the mind but a finite source: this is a complex attitude toward the real—which will not change in Flaubert for the rest of his life, in the sense that the imaginary child of 1835–37 passes whole into the imaginary man who forges himself after 1844. What is evident, by contrast, is that the works of pure fiction (narrative, tales, etc.) tend to disappear. *Passion et Vertu* was completed on 10 December 1837.

From then until 1842 we find only two "stories": *Ivre et Mort* in June 1838, and in August 1839 *Les Funérailles du docteur Mathurin.* Again, in the second narrative the plot is entirely subservient to the general project, which is very consciously philosophical. Two in five years. In the same period, by contrast, Flaubert produced one drama and historical essays (*Loys XI,* March 1838; *Rome et les Cesars,* August 1839), brief critical pieces (*Rabelais; Mademoiselle Rachel*), "skeptical meditations" (*Agonies,* April 1838), allegories (*La Danse des morts,* May 1838), and autobiographical writings (*Mémoires d'un fou,* undoubtedly finished before the autumn of 1838; *Souvenirs,* intimate notes and meditations from 1838 to 1841, whose existence proves Gustave's anxiety when confronted with himself and his deliberate intention to know himself, or at least to situate himself). This enumeration shows clearly that the literary object has become *other* in his eyes.

Number. We are quickly convinced that this transformation is both the cause and the effect of a profound crisis when we consider Gustave's production in terms of *quantity. Before* the end of 1837, it is impressive; despite his schoolwork, hardly a month goes by that

359

Gustave does not give us some narrative. His works are short, true, but generally complete.[3] Beginning in April 1838 (*Smarh* is finished) and until September 1842, that is, in four and a half years, Gustave produces nothing, aside from *Les Funérailles*, two brief essays, the narrative *Voyage en Corse*, and some "reflective" notes hastily jotted down in the notebook of *Souvenirs*. He is certainly not lacking in the *desire* to write. In 1837, in *Agonies*, he writes: "Will I be condemned all my life to be like a mute who wants to speak and foams at the mouth with rage?" And on 21 May 1841 he curiously replays the same formula: ". . . it is a need to write, to pour out my heart, and I know neither what to write nor what to think. Yet this is how it always is, with confused instincts; I am a mute who wants to speak." But sometimes—as in *Agonies*—he thinks he has a great deal to say and insists on the difficulties of expression. Sometimes—as in this passage from *Souvenirs*—he is speaking of a naked need to pour out his heart. What is missing, then, is the Idea. We shall have to take account of these variations. We shall see they are merely complementary aspects of that "terror" he will later reveal to Bouilhet, which fills him with "fog" at the very moment when the reflexive attitude should cast some clarity into his "confused instincts."

3. Lived Experience.

Deep within him, Gustave experiences this overturning of his literary conceptions, and the quasi-powerlessness resulting from it, as a personal catastrophe. From 1837, as we have seen, he abhors his work and abandons barely outlined narratives. The same year, in *Agonies*, he confides to us that he is writing in "disgust," and several pages later he gives up. Little by little this "disgust" grows more marked. We shall come back to the "afterword" he adds to *Smarh* in 1840, after rereading it: here he quite frankly advises himself never to write again. From now on, silence and discouragement: this is what he calls his laziness and, in 1841, an "intermittent moral sickness." Several lines from *Souvenirs*, written at the beginning of the same year, seem to prove that the word "sickness" had not been chosen at random: "What a long time since this was written, my God! It was a Sunday afternoon, a time of boredom and anger; as harassed by remedies as by sickness, I put down my pen and went out." The turn of phrase

---

3. With the exceptions of *La Derniere Heure*, *La Main de fer*, and *Agonies*, for reasons that we shall see further on.

proves that this is not a matter of an accidental indisposition. No doubt the text is somewhat elliptical, as happens when one is speaking to oneself, but this is precisely what demonstrates that Gustave is evoking his "sickness" as a familiar acquaintance, a personal attachment, or an inner ailment, that asserts itself with such indiscretion and then at such length that it harasses him. No doubt he yields to it somewhat, settles into it perhaps, but from time to time he rebels, he walks out. His condition does not prevent him from hurling himself out of his bedroom and striding the streets of the town. In other words, Gustave is on the way to voluntary sequestration, but he does not keep to his bed. The mention of "remedies," however, confirms in our minds the existence of physical troubles. What sort? We shall attempt certain hypotheses a little further on. What is important is the double face of the "sickness" that must be attended by the body and that at the same time passes for a "moral sickness." Isn't this just what we call "psychosomatic"? This conjecture would seem hasty if it were not the only one capable of explaining several facts often mentioned but usually regarded as unimportant.

When Gustave enters his last year at the *collège*, Ernest and Alfred are long since in Paris; he counts on joining them there the following year, after taking his baccalaureat. Yet although he receives his diploma in August 1840, he doesn't leave for Paris until June 1842, that is, two years later than he had expected. It is inadequate to say that he doesn't write during these two years: he does nothing, or almost nothing, and we know from the correspondence that he doesn't open his law books before March 1842. Are we to believe that Doctor Flaubert would have put up with his son, in good health, dragging out two years in Rouen in complete idleness? Achille-Cléophas's anxiety, mentioned by certain biographers, becomes apparent several times. Why does he terminate his son's boarding at school in 1838? Is there a connection between this decision (signaled by a letter to Ernest on 11 October 1838) and the malaise Gustave speaks of on 28 October of the same year: "Here I am again, finally, back on my feet and at the [writing] table, the table I had been forced to leave for some time . . . You know that I lost nothing—but time . . . I swear to you that I will take vengeance on the mockery of heaven that has made me such an asshole."[4] Why did Doctor Flaubert unblinkingly accept the fact that his son—after his rather contrived dismissal from the *collège* in De-

4. "Mockery": Flaubert fell ill (or his illness was aggravated) at the moment Ernest had chosen to pay him a visit in Rouen before returning to Paris.

cember 1839—should continue preparing for his examination alone and in the bosom of his family? Is it true, as Bruneau would have it, that the trip to Corsica was simply a reward for Gustave's successful baccalaureat? Or should it be seen, as Dumesnil thinks and as I am inclined to believe, as a medical attempt to prevent or cure an illness unknown to us? Gustave returns from Corsica—where he was well entertained—gloomier and still more irritable: is this why Achille-Cléophas delays sending him to Paris to do his legal studies? And what is the meaning of the anecdote later reported by Flaubert: some time in 1841–42 he was imitating an epileptic beggar; his father, nervous and angry, ordered him to stop at once; why? I shall soon try to answer these questions. For the moment we shall be content merely to ask them; we had to prove that Gustave's sickness did not escape his father. This means that his drama, while manifesting itself at first by a crisis of creative inspiration, goes far beyond that: the young author is no longer entirely in control; he surprises those around him by the violence of his "nervous troubles." It must therefore be understood that he lives his malaise on all levels at once. It is in this framework that we shall resume our inquiry, try to retrace the evolution of this psychosomatic process, and offer an interpretation.

Death of the Poet

As was shown in the first part of this work, and emphasized in the preceding chapter, Gustave cannot grasp in himself the *class individual:* he is unaware of the reality of the bourgeoisie, its function in the society of 1830, and cannot discover in himself the bourgeois *habitus.* Unlike his comrades, who have a rudimentary class consciousness and turn themselves into aristocrats only through nocturnal escapes, certain of recovering their condition on waking, Gustave long preserves—let us say until 1837—the stubborn illusion of being "well-born." And at the moment he discovers his class, he "loses" his imagination. Is this conjunction a matter of chance? We shall not settle this question without establishing *how* he was able to discover his bourgeois-being and—as he is incapable of grasping it in its objective reality and in its internalization as exis—in what form this being manifested itself to him.

We recall that his relations with Alfred are deepened and intensified at this same period: he comes near to being rewarded for his efforts to build a lived friendship that will allow him to *communicate* with the man he places above everyone. Unfortunately, he feels perpetually hampered in this attempt at *participation:* by his familial seriousness, by the utilitarianism that he has internalized despite himself, in sum by the Flaubert spirit, Alfred's attitude remains inimitable; it delineates for Gustave the unbridgeable threshold separating the "professionals" (the upper level of the middle classes) from the capitalist bourgeoisie. Gustave, like an imp in a bottle, floats to the surface of his class and dives down again into the depths of the petite bourgeoisie; his movement, indefinitely repeated, allows him to discover outside and inside himself what we have called the man of the mean, or the average man. But one suspects that this perception would remain hazy if other factors did not clarify it: his hopes and his disillusionments have a character too personal (disappointed love is the dominant element) for him to glean from them a precise view of the social body that envelops him, conditions him, and denies him.

Let us say that he is alarmed at the apparent gratuitousness of the behavior his friend proposes to him and as a result, perhaps, resents these feelings of alarm. He understands, though very grudgingly, that there is within him a propensity to serve, to bind himself to a cause, an enterprise—that he will never be his own but always the means of an alien end; it is futile for him to rage at it, it is stronger than he is: he must have been injected with this poison at birth. He wouldn't go any further were he not convinced, around this time, that his subjective seriousness corresponded quite precisely to his objective destination: he wants to be a means because he was made the means of a singular enterprise. He becomes consciously aware of having been expected, created, raised in order to accomplish a mission that awaits him in the depths of the future, and that awaited him even before his parents had conceived him. They made him, in sum, so that he should *make himself* bourgeois by *choosing a profession.* Read: by choosing a career among those reserved for the sons of the bourgeoisie. Or rather—it's all the same to him, but a certain precision is fitting—among those reserved for the children of the middle classes.

What suddenly convinced him? Well, first of all, it was his age. His father must for some time have pondered his children's future aloud and in Gustave's presence; the boy scarcely paid attention—he had plenty of time to think about it. And then, suddenly, time is running out; 1837–38: he is in the tenth year; in two years he will have to chose an occupation. He doesn't much enjoy his schoolwork; yet it is bearable as long as it seems disinterested; after he has taken his baccalaureat, the work will become utilitarian. The cyclical duration becomes vectoral, it will be structured by irreversibility and imminence. But there is something else: in October 1838, his two best friends leave him to study law in Paris. He hopes to join them, but at the same time he cannot prevent himself from seeing their present activities as prefiguring those that await him. In his letter of 24 February 1839, he speaks *for the first time*—and in anguish—of his future;[5] he will not choose a profession, he says. But these alarming denials poorly conceal his anxiety: how can he resist the paternal will? Is he not defeated in advance?

What is a profession? I would call it a double-edged reality. Government, administration, or private industry create or suppress employment as a function of social needs (interpreted, of course, according to a certain optic). The determination of the number of jobs is, of course, a *practical* decision. But—as long as social stability is not challenged by demographic growth or some entirely different historical fact—the decisive moment is reduced to its simplest expression: numbers speak, their demands are transcribed, most often routinely. It is difficult to distinguish here between the fact and the law, for one can say either that twelve candidates *must* receive their degrees this year or that there *will be* twelve degrees received.[6] Even when it is a question of widespread need—which itself arises from an evolution leading to a certain conjunction—it is interpreted, quantified, defined on the basis of definite presuppositions by more or less constituted groups. In the nineteenth century a certain number of factors—in particular the possibility for the governing classes to reinvest a lesser proportion of surplus value in business—facilitated the appearance of a need which had until then been masked: the demand for doctors would be considerably greater. But it was a policy (of the medical Order, of administrators—municipalities, general councils, members of parliament, etc.) that would determine the possibility of opening an office in this or that location.

For the adolescent choosing a career, on the other hand, the factual decisions—which certain agencies make outside him—appear to determine the field of his possibilities (expanding, shrinking, qualitative transformations, etc.). Because he is bourgeois, his bourgeois-being is defined by the totality of careers that represent at once his opportunities and his duty to make himself the bourgeois that he is. This body of factors is complex: there are equivalences and hierarchies. It varies

5. The idea comes to him from considerations of Ernest's future.
6. In every human activity, act and right are inseparably mixed. The basic structure remains the hypothetical imperative, but it is more or less experienced as more or less reduced to a simple logical determination.

as a function of the place such a family occupies in the bourgeois class: certain professions are accessible, others proscribed (a "low-income" household, even if middle-class, cannot envisage having a physician son). The prejudices of the milieu have the effect of limiting possibilities even as the tenacious will to *rise* enlarges them. For all these reasons—and many others too that do not interest us here—a child, well before birth, is designated by a certain field of possibilities, fairly restricted and quite clearly organized, which reflect back to him the social needs defined by his class through the options of decision-making groups and ultimately through the will of his father. The father, one might say, is determined as accidental individual by the body of careers he judges accessible to his son. But the son himself, put into the world at a certain moment in social evolution, grasps that structured body through his father's choices as *his future reality*. And this reality presents itself at the same time as the limit of his horizon and as expectation, as an inert demand that calls him from the depths of the future, as a categorical imperative, indeed. So here he is, provided with a *being* that presents itself as both factual reality and as value. He is bourgeois because he was put into the world in order to make himself bourgeois by acquiring the necessary knowledge to exercise this or that occupation. Everything happens for him as though an end, working from the depths of future years, had created him in the belly of a woman expressly so that he might fulfill that end. Here the term of departure and the term of arrival are confused. And nowhere is this more visible than in the Flaubert family: a position as chief surgeon at the hospital of Rouen—which existed from Achille-Cléophas's childhood—has actually bred a certain Achille in order to be occupied by him in the 1850s (a move precipitated by the father's premature death). This position, the body of inert obligations as long as they are not fulfilled, is anterior to Achille and will survive him; in other words, in relation to this mortal the position is a determination of eternity. And Achille's bourgeois-being is internalized in him as his having-to-be-a-physician. In the case of the Flaubert's eldest son, this prenatal identification of his being and his destiny, of his actual existence and his value remain hidden to him: the reason for this blindness comes from his identification with the father. It is not that he is unaware of his destiny, but he grasps it differently, in pride, as his opportunity and his desert, as living testimony to the love of an adored father; it is, in his eyes, the *Mana* of the Flaubert blood. He believes he is shaping the future when he is merely maintaining the present to the extent that the future shapes him. Such are the polytechnic students in these celebrated families who condescend to produce only polytechnic students.

But what about the younger brother? Frustrated, he has quickly perceived the inert objective that awaits him on his way. He will have to *take up a profession*. Doctor, barrister, solicitor, magistrate, notary, subprefect, judge:[7] this is *his* field of possibilities but it is also the complex end that defines his having-to-be and his destiny, that is, his being. Of course, there is a play of differentiated options, and certain passages in *Souvenirs* seem to indicate that Gustave discerns some sort of hierarchy among them. Medicine and the law occupy the highest rank. The profession of notary seems to be the lowest. As for a judgeship, that is grotesque: "I will be . . . *a judge*, just that." In spite of this perspective—which is fuzzy and variable at best—these professions are interchangeable. First of all, "you will certainly have to be one of those, and there is no middle course."[8] In any event, they represent the same having-to-be, the same destiny. But he is struck above all by their equivalence: whether he should choose one or the other, he will in any case be made bourgeois. And a second-class bourgeois: the first being that of the rich and powerful (Achille will be one of them; usurping his father's legitimate glory, he will reign over Rouen). In short, at the age when Gustave discovers the bourgeoisie through the eyes of Vigny and passes judgment on them, the obligation to choose an occupation, that is, the structured body of objects that impose themselves with its choice, reveal to him better than any other experience the fatality of his *bourgeois-being*. The accidental individual is in him merely the means to realize the class individual. This "difference," which constitutes his unhappiness, his shame, sometimes his pride, but which he takes for his inner reality, is merely a superficial truth that will dissolve when he becomes what he must be, what he *is* deep down. He knows that he is going to be transformed into a woodlouse or a spider, and that everything making up his life today will be stifled, crushed by the inert function that lies in wait for him and whose agent he will become. About *the* bourgeois, we know, Gustave has little to say. And for good reason. Of *the* notary, on the other hand, he has a less schematic vision, for the simple reason that it represents an *other* determination of the same class-being; another function, another *habitus*, another milieu; the young man "sees" the profession of notary with the eyes of a doctor's son. He has a scien-

7. These are the professions he enumerates in the letter to Ernest of 23 July 1839, *Correspondance* 1:54.
8. Ibid.

tist's and clinician's contempt for those who exercise a *nonscientific* occupation— drawing up contracts, judging one's neighbor. Can he distinguish the class individual in them? Obviously not. But he believes he grasps it in their professional deformations: in other words, he thinks he is capable of writing a physiology of the notary, the magistrate, or the solicitor on the model of the *Physiology of the Traveling Salesman* he has recently completed. The bourgeoisie is a species; the traveling salesman, the judge, the magistrate represent families. And on this young man—who feels himself infinitely lacking in being, yet utterly defined—they want to impose a determination that will enclose him in a fixed matrix; you might as well say that he knows himself as *finished-in-the-future.* And it is not only this fall into finitude that horrifies him; he cannot bear the idea that the function and *habitus* that result from finitude are his future truth and consequently his present *vocation:* this is a new form of the paternal curse. Gustave will become *the* notary: he will do so because he *already is,* by virtue of a predestination that is none other than Achille-Cléophas's will. From this point of view, his personal impressions, his fits of despair, even his denials are disqualified *in the present* by the ineluctability of the process that compels him *to become what he is,* as if the chief surgeon had said to his wife one night: "Come here so that I can make a notary for you." The ragings of his distressed soul are, at best, inconsequential snivelings; at worst, dissimulations that conceal from him a shameful consent, or the means chosen by the end to realize itself more surely as such. In the bright light of his future, he is anguished to discover in himself that web of close complicities which he exhausts himself vainly denying, and which fashion him so that he will later coincide quite neatly with the imposed function. Is it really a question of *class* connivance? Yes and no. Objectively, it was impossible for a young bourgeois in the 1830s to *move outside his class*—neither above it, as we know, nor below. The solution taken up today by the sons of good families—to abandon their studies and "do factory work"—was practically inconceivable. When Gustave dreams of fleeing his bourgeois destiny, he does not even imagine becoming part of the working class: he will be a beggar or a camel driver in a hot country. This is taking a vow of poverty, nothing more: as a leper in Naples he will remain alone in the midst of the crowd, like a hermit; he will never find solidarity with other men from other backgrounds, with other interests than those of his class of origin. Instead, he will himself slip outside humanity to the level of the subhuman or the saint. The inconsistency of these daydreams indicates clearly that they represent the internalization of a factual situation. But another adolescent would live it otherwise: Gustave unrealizes himself as a beggar because his constitutional passivity forbids him to revolt, which does not mean that he is consenting. In short, he is not quite able to disentangle in himself the part played by historical necessity, the part played by complicit resignation, and the part played by his singular constitution. This is the era of suspicion: he waits and watches for Chevalier's, and even Alfred's, progressive transformation into a bourgeois. If he avoids speaking of his own, it is because he is too frightened of it. Must he become a "married man, orderly, moral"? Thus the "thoughts of a poor child of sixteen" are merely epiphenomena. But what can be done to escape his destiny if even the actions that deny it contain in them the class-being they attempt to surpass? If his average-man seriousness compels him to become the means of a class he denies?

We can now understand why the muddled discovery of his class-being is accompanied in him by the death of the poet. He used to take himself for Chatterton, who, born of a bourgeois belly, was raised by his genius above all classes; it seemed to him then that the bourgeoisie was merely a birthplace. After all, Jesus, who spoke for all mankind, was born of a Jewish woman; Flaubert's anti-Semitism lent all its weight to this odd argument. Yet the emulators of the young Englishman would have had to possess, as he did, an utterly pure heart, and a providential grace would have been needed to allow them to escape the specific characteristics of the species as well as the depredations of education. For Gustave, then, it was obvious: the thoughts that were instantly formed in his virgin soul reflected only the majesty of the infinite. In short, before 1838 he could not have been further from those who, today, consider poetry a verbal activity based on an original connection with language: for him it was a mental attitude close to a heightened mystical state. These "states of the soul" had a specific and irreducible quality; certainly he knew he was incapable of expressing them in words, but he hardly cared: "I knew what it was to be a poet. I had it inside me, at least in my soul, as all great hearts do . . . All my work was in me, and I never wrote one line of the lovely poem that delighted me."[9] What does it matter that poetry never surpasses the stage of subjective determination if that determination is the *essential* thing, if in the plenitude of the immediate it manifests itself as the fundamental relationship of an aristocratic nature with the infinite.

9. *Souvenirs*, pp. 56–57.

Nothing could be better. But he suddenly has the misfortune to discover that bourgeois sons participate in the bourgeois condition, that their spontaneous reactions are conditioned first of all by the class from which they come. What becomes of poetry if it is no longer the purity of the immediate? Nothing but a process of unrealization that nearly always manifests itself as a defensive tactic against becoming bourgeois. Gustave soon catches on: certainly he remains proud of those "states of the soul" that raise him above the vulgar; be that as it may, they are flights into the imaginary, the "lovely poem" is not the quintessence of his *reality;* rather than proceeding from it, it is dreamed against it as its systematic negation. Better: who knows if the escape does not conceal an acquiescence? As we have seen, Flaubert is far from reproaching imagination for its unreality; but on this occasion the issue is a different one: he would like his fabulous operas, fictive as they are and despite their insubstantiality, to express the *reality* of the one who has produced them; he would be only too happy to recount himself: to forge beautiful myths, one must be born. But he has just discovered the opposite. Only one of two possibilities can be true: if the poet is a bourgeois who dreams, poetry does not save him, and to find himself at the age of thirty in the skin of a verse-scribbling notary may even be the surest way to perdition; if in order to be Chatterton one must be an aristocrat, then poetry is denied to bourgeois souls. This is the choice: poetic ecstasy is a decoy, or else the ecstasies of the younger Flaubert son are not poetic. Experienced for themselves, they represent the exquisite death of the bourgeois; but this is a farce: the bourgeois is made to live and to reproduce life; he *playacts* being-to-die, that unique basis—supposing that it is really experienced—of Romantic poetry, and through this drama he ends by instituting himself as bourgeois. What can then be done to escape the destiny of "woodlouse" that awaits him? Nothing, surely, except to change his being.

The terrible crisis that shakes Flaubert between 1837 and 1844 has its sole source in the stupefying, rigorous, and finally abortive endeavor to change his being. This entails changing his end. Since the imposed end, the *other* end, structures him in his class-being, and since "moving out of one's class" upward—that is, acceding to the aristocracy—is impossible, the problem formulates itself thus: how to change one's end without once again substituting the caprices of the accidental individual for the rigorous objectives of the class individual (or of class in the individual)? In other words, for Flaubert the question is not deliberately to propose for himself another aim but to discover in the future the *true* inert demand that has conjured him. The ideology of the bourgeoisie in this first half of the nineteenth century included—though Flaubert *never* mentions it—individualism (as the theoretical and ethical consequence of economic liberalism; and at the same period a certain number of young bourgeois found recourse from class objectives in class-being itself. They will become notaries, fine, but in their inner life the most incomparable of beings. For Gustave this antidote is a failure: I have stated above why the structure of his family and his earliest relations with his mother permanently proscribed the egotism of a Stendhal, the narcissism of an Amiel; he scarcely likes himself, and his passivity forbids him to valorize the movements of his life, to conceal from himself his *other end* by discovering *his* own objectives, by giving an absolute value to his impulses just because they are his—spontaneous, exempt, at least in the beginning, from all alienation. Quite the opposite, the sole fact that a desire is his own reveals its insubstantiality; *recognized* spontaneity devalorizes him; his gigantism, from this point of view, is a way of combating the insignificance that he is only too inclined to find everywhere when his "personal" life is at issue. This permanent devalorization in him of the *self* by the *other* allows him to avoid the idealist traps of the inner life: even Great Desire, as we have seen, does not pull him out of his condition as average man; he knows that he is *playacting* fundamental dissatisfaction—and in vain. Even the simple inner denial of his bourgeois-being could not save him: deny it as he will, he is conscious at the same time that irresistible forces, with the complicity of his passive activity, are leading him to realize this bourgeois-being. But, by the same token, lucidity alienates him even more: he can replace the half-alien end that conditions him in his being only by discovering *another inert expectation* that designates him as its means. An inessential cog in the social machine, an inferior man, sacrificed as man to the effective working of the whole, he will pull himself out of his status if he binds himself and sacrifices to another end of the same nature—half-alien and presenting itself as something exterior to internalize—that has raised him in the very belly of his mother as the *essential means* of its realization. In other words, the child will escape—he thinks—from his class (namely from his creation by the retroactive action of a future end) if he discovers himself to be the sole means chosen by an end that escapes all class conditioning and even, as we shall see, transcends the species as a whole. If it can be proved that this end exists and is personally addressed to him, reclaiming his sufferings, his zeal in practice, and his sacrifice, he will escape from bourgeois alienation by living in painful happiness another alienation, more fundamental, that valorizes him by destroying him.

Until the age of sixteen Gustave likes nothing better than "improvization."[10] And then suddenly he hesitates: what is it, after all, that *inspires* his writings? If it is God whispering in his ear, well and good, but Gustave cannot bring himself to believe in God; if inspiration comes from a passionate impulse, it is worth no more than the subjective agitation that produced it: presto, it is disqualified, it was less the demand of an ever future end than an instantaneous and hence worthless exuberance. Transubstantiation will be accomplished by a retroactive election; it will be announced by a categorical imperative. Vocation is no longer based on the accidental riches of a contingent nature but, quite the contrary—like sainthood—on inner poverty. Lord, how could I, weak and ignorant as I am, with the little that I have at my disposal, satisfy Your demands? The poet is dead, long live the artist.

Birth of the Artist

At first Gustave limits himself to contrasting this newcomer with his old friend the poet: "Between artist and poet there is a vast difference: one feels, the other speaks, one is the heart, the other the head."[11] This maxim, inspired by Vigny, clearly indicates that his preferences still lean toward the poet. But with increasing frequency in the correspondence, the word Art tends to replace poetry: "Art is more useful than industry." In 1837 he is "antiprose, antireason, antitruth" and would gladly exchange "the senseless erudition of hair splitters, speculators, philosophers, novelists, etc.," for two lines of Lamartine. But from the end of 1838, art becomes his unique concern. "Art, Art, bitter disappointment, nameless phantom that glitters and sends you to perdition," and, on 15 April 1839, "Let us make sadness in Art, since we are more sensitive to that side of things . . . etc." The idea is certainly in the air. Gustave was not yet born when Victor Cousin, the Muse's future supporter, wrote: "We must have religion for religion's sake, morality for morality's sake, art for art's sake."[12] The "Philosophe" was merely trying to designate the autonomy of the three

10. Ibid., p. 54.
11. Ibid., p. 52.
12. Sometime in 1818.

sectors: "The Good and the Holy cannot be the path . . . of Beauty." But this formula, although anterior to the great works of French Romanticism, foreshadows post-Romanticism; strictly speaking, it denounces the Lamartinian confusion of religion and poetry. Poetry, losing its "ecstatic" character, is now ranked among works of art and is answerable only to the category of Beauty: it will henceforth be appreciated as a function of aesthetic norms and not for its potential for generating mystical effusions. We know what conclusion Theophile Gautier drew: "There is no real beauty except that which serves no purpose."[13] But the real reasons for this new terminology are fully illuminated only when it is taken up again by Flaubert's generation: one must escape bourgeois-being; "inspired" poetry is merely an admission of failure; the artist alone *institutes*.

Gustave is the first, perhaps, to grasp the ontological implications of the doctrine: "to make Art" is to *be* an artist. And what is an artist? He is first of all the poet denied, disowned. At least to the extent that the poet affirms the primacy of the subjective, Gustave refuses to judge himself according to his states of mind; these are in any case suspect because of their very spontaneity. Besides, the subject is both judge and contestant: as a bourgeois, how would he discern what is bourgeois in his personal experience? By a Copernican reversal, he poses the primacy of the objective over all subjectivity. For him as poet, the written poem, a vague reflection of his exultations, had only secondary importance, it was a "repercussion." As artist, the work alone counts: "worker of art"—as he will later be pleased to call himself—he becomes a worker whose efforts are geared to transforming a certain raw material, language, to produce an object. Shall we say that he *objectifies himself* in it? Yes and no. No, if, like the lyric poet, he claims to externalize his interiority, to express what he feels, what he is *for himself*. Yes, if it is understood that he objectifies himself in his product *as artist*—in other words, as technician of the Word, putting his sensibility and, in a general way, the whole of his experience in the service of the word *to be made*. Subjectivity is taken into consideration only to the extent that it is entirely mobilized as a *pure means of work*; it is found again in the finished product, but this product does not *translate* subjectivity: it exploits it, masters it, and in a sense denies it, since it refuses it all possibility of existing for itself. This is the first step toward what Flaubert will later call his "impersonalism." We shall examine this theory, and we shall have to ask ourselves if it

13. Preface to *Mademoiselle de Maupin*.

really accounts for his deep intentions and if he has really observed the rules he establishes. What we need to note here is that he crosses over from the immediate to the mediated, from the unreflected to reflection, from spontaneity to the critical attitude. Recognizing somehow that it is impossible for him to distinguish the accidental individual from the class individual, he uses the immediate givens of his consciousness as *raw material;* he is no longer one with those givens; observes them from above and sees what use he can make of them. His passions are no longer *his:* in this sense, if he discovers that they are bourgeois, he need no longer feel ashamed of them; he will turn them into objects of study and, if it seems worthwhile, into analogues through which he will imaginatively create a portrait of an immortal bourgeois. Imagination, here, no longer has anything in common with the poet's escape into the imaginary; it is a precise technique that finds its justification in the work. The artist escapes the bourgeois he is beneath his skin to the degree that, perched above himself, he is no longer anything but a *practical reflection,* solely concerned with achieving a certain end.

What end? This is the basic question. On this point, Gustave hesitates for some time: is the object of art more useful than the rest of our handiwork, or does it totally escape the category of utility? We find he harbors both ideas. In 1838, he writes, some days apart: "I prefer the beautiful to the useful,"[14] and "Art is more useful than industry, the beautiful is more useful than the good."[15] But in the strange example that follows the second affirmation, we read that "the first governments . . . are artists, poets, they build *useless* things like pyramids, cathedrals." And at other times he makes comparisons between the work of art and tools, which would imply that they belong to the same category: "If there is something superior to all else, it is Art. A book of poetry is worth more than a railroad." But gradually his thought consolidates itself. In January 1839, he writes *Les Arts et le Commerce,* and we understand the meaning of his vacillations: "Does the soul, too, not have its needs and its appetites . . . Do you not feel in yourself that instinct which demands . . . to satisfy that soul which has an immense thirst for the infinite and requires reveries, verses, melodies, ecstasies . . . ?" etc. The work of art fulfills a need of the soul; it can equally be said to be useful to the famished soul or useless for the satisfaction of material needs. Unfortunately, at this period

14. *Souvenirs,* p. 46.
15. Ibid., pp. 48–49.

Flaubert is working on *Smarh*, of which the least we can say is that this bitter, grinding, nihilistic work in no way resembles the "reveries, verses, melodies, ecstasies" that ought to satisfy our hunger for the infinite. No doubt the infinite is presented to us there, but it is indistinguishable from nothingness, from the void in which Smarh ends up, spinning eternally. No doubt Smarh produced poetry; but we have seen how much sense it made. These remarks allow us to understand that Flaubert is not entirely sincere when he claims that the purpose of a work of art is to satisfy the needs of the soul, or rather that he is not entirely detached from his "antiprose" passion. Indeed, when he claims to put the poet in the service of humanity, he forgets that he admired—four months earlier—"only two men, Rabelais and Byron; they alone wrote in a spirit of malice toward the human race." Yet he has not changed his mind in the meantime, for on 24 February 1839, he considers "taking an active part in the world . . . as demoralizer." Indeed, even as art becomes more profound, it loses in his eyes all utility, even spiritual utility; though superior to all means, a work of art is still a means, and man its end. What Gustave now asserts—in the course of the year 1839—is that the product of the artist is not the means to any end. This is simply the logical consequence of his misanthropy and the deliverance of beauty from its humanist bonds. For him, henceforth, art has no end but itself, and it is up to men to serve it. The finished product forces itself onto them, it is a source of indefinite obligations. In the presence of a work, aesthetic admiration is *required*. And it is in this sense that the artist institutes: a masterpiece "opens a cycle to the future";[16] the writer is a legislator, since his writing, if beautiful, appears to us as a complex of singular laws that assert themselves "with the authority of the instituted." The interest of this new conception will already have been understood: Gustave has long since refused to share human ends—which he confuses, most of the time, with those of the bourgeoisie. But if he wants to tear himself out of his milieu, a refusal is not enough; he must discover that his own end is inhuman: he is needed in order to attach men to creations that surpass them and are occasionally liable to harm them; this requirement consequently removes him from the middle classes. He remains the average man, but he escapes the infernal round of means-ends and ends-means: an absolute and chooses him as its unique and essential means; beauty, the binding of men to an inhuman end, is first of all the binding of the artist to his art. Gustave

16. Merleau-Ponty, *Signes*.

thinks that this rigid bond is his liberation from class-being. Not that it clears the way for an anarchic surpassing of his condition. But rather because it substitutes a radical and absolute bond for the relative attachment of the bourgeois to the bourgeoisie.

So he must know what is required of him: What must he institute, and how? At this period, Flaubert no longer hesitates: the *poetic* attitude was merely the flight from the real into the imaginary; *artistic* activity consists of devalorizing the real by realizing the imaginary. In state-of-the-soul poetry, the flight left reality intact: you escaped into the nonreal; the negation concerned Gustave's being-in-the-world and not the world itself. Now the movement inverts itself: Flaubert reconsiders the world in order to annihilate it, which can be done only by totalizing it.

At the age of fifteen he rereads his earliest works, written blindly, and discovers their meaning: they invariably tell the story of a failure, of the triumph of the crowd over a singularity. In sum, they reflect more or less clearly his own anomaly, not as a positive value but as a curse. But when Gustave sees this persistent and veiled subject with new eyes, he is horrified: here he discovers his "difference"—which he has tried so assiduously to hide—he designates himself from the outset as victim, which is repulsive to his pride. The prescribed transformation is a generalization of the Flaubert "case" by making it the truth of our species. What was the issue in these brief stories? A victim was dying, challenging his executioners with a futile denial. And whatever its futility, the denial was the mark of some kind of superiority: it was Marguerite's ineffable "sentient fragrance." By universalizing, Flaubert makes the *futile denial* the clarification of the world and the human condition. He will institute it by words, and even while preserving its powerlessness he will inscribe it in materiality as an irreducible imperative: crushed by the world, man invests his dignity in denying the fate the universe imposes on him. Literature is made so that this human protest should eternally survive the individual wreckage.

But how can wreckage and denial be used as principles of totalization? How can the fact that "the world is Hell" be made *aesthetically* visible? From 1838 to 1842, Flaubert gradually develops three operations, which he uses in turn. First, the totalizing of the universe as interiority: what is shown is the wreckage and death of a universal subject who summarizes human experiences in himself and dies from the totalization without ceasing to say *no*. But the universal subject, raised above the world and above his empirical ego, can witness in his impassivity—which is a stoical denial—the annihilation of this universe and his own person: totalizing in exteriority by an explicit overview. Finally, the author can effect a slow process of corrosion within a concrete singularity, revealing the vanity of our illusions, the explosive contradictions of being, and, through a systematic demoralization, pose the belief in nothingness as an aesthetic imperative—that is, make explicit in his readers the *futile denial* which, by and large, they live only implicitly. These three operations correspond to three *mental attitudes* with which we are already acquainted: passive activity, pride, and resentment. We shall study them in connection with these attitudes, which we shall see evolving from an original syncretism and then affirming themselves against each other; we shall then attempt to discover in each one the fundamental reasons for its failure, and we shall be able to determine the essential questions that the "art of writing" poses for the young Flaubert. In any event, art, at least for Gustave, has only one *subject,* which is total: totalizing the creation in order to show its futility, its nothingness. We shall see in this chapter and in the third part of this work that he has remained faithful to this purpose, and that his novels, from *Smarh* to *Bouvard et Pécuchet*, have no other meaning.

The Original Syncretism

When Gustave wrote *Agonies, Pensées sceptiques,* he was already conscious of his literary purpose and even claimed in a brief introduction to have begun one year earlier "this work . . so often thrown down, so often taken up again." In paragraph I, however, which immediately follows, he says: "So I take up this work, begun two years earlier." Is there some contradiction here? Not necessarily; the introduction may have been written a year *after* certain passages, a year *before* others. Paragraph XXV proves *in any case* that this interrupted work contains reworked pages which in their first version date back to 1835—it is really another rehashing of *Voyage d'enfer*. Certainly when he wrote this primary text at the age of thirteen for the school paper, the young writer did not intend to gather his "skeptical thoughts" into a book: he presented *Le Voyage* then as a self-contained whole. We should not believe, however, that he was trying to deceive us: at fifteen, rereading *Le Voyage*, he understood its movement and meaning; from the age of fourteen he wanted to effect a totalization, to show evil and unhappiness everywhere in order to conclude at the end of this exhaustive enumeration that human life is precisely equal to damnation.

He remains faithful to his initial project since he includes *Le Voyage* in *Agonies*. But he seems to think this allegorical totalization is inherently unconvincing by itself, for he adds a series of "thoughts," one of which is—or nearly is—itself an *exhaustive totalization*. The dedication ("You have seen them come to fruition, my dear Alfred") proves that they were born successively—in an order that we cannot reconstitute—as a young boy's desperate reactions to the distinguished pessimism of his elder. In this sense, there is no real progression from one thought to the other: everything is said, for example, in paragraph IV, which tells us that "the life of man is a curse . . ." Paragraphs XIV ("Oh yes, misery and unhappiness rule over man . . .") and XIX ("What is unhappiness? Life") add nothing. Yet the author preserves the progressive aspect of the idea; by setting these maxims, allegories, and confidences end to end, he pursues a precise objective which he defines twice in his introduction. He intends to entrust to us "a whole, immense summation of a quite hideous and black moral life" or—as he declares a little further on—"to unite in a few pages a whole immense abyss of skepticism and despair." Are the two formulas equivalent? To settle this question we must come back to paragraph XXV and compare it to *Le Voyage*: the corrections supplied by the author in the first text may allow us to grasp his reflection on the work and to retrieve the embryonic intuition from which the entire direction of the work issues.

Le Voyage is told in the first person. Someone says "I." Who? In truth, this Memnon is merely an abstract subject. From the outset, the author places him above the human race. What does he do? Nothing. He meditates. Inconclusively. Satan appears and carries him off: Memnon sees the false virtues of man, his vices, his misfortunes. He infers the conclusion that Satan himself does not refrain from drawing. Does he suffer? We don't know. Nor are we told if he is convinced. Why is he necessary then, this Kantian, inhuman subject without conviction or vice? Why write, "(In Europe), he showed *me* scholars . . . these were the maddest of all," rather than, "scholars are the maddest of all"? The reason is clear: purely objective totalization would be a nontemporal act that would make its author simply the synthesizing power to tie and bind. Even a pure, cold statement at the end of an inventory would be a determination of time: an inventory is made gradually. Satan, alone and speaking only to him, *knows* since the fall that the earth is his realm. This certitude can and must be expressed by a minimum of words: it summarizes an inventory *already made*. The expression of acquired truth can of course admit a connection with the subject: "The world is *my* property." But the subject here is allegorical—it is the Devil. Thus the most correct expression will be rigorously impersonal: it will be stated that the natural and social universe is corroded by radical evil.

The young Gustave introduces the first person singular because he wants to temporalize this immediate certitude, to transform it into *experience*. The knowledge Satan can evoke instantaneously must be made accessible, by Gustave, to someone who is ignorant of it, so that he can acquire it gradually. Taken as a nontemporal insight, the connection between the universe and evil resembles a maxim or "theory"—a synthesis of concepts. But Gustave is distrustful of concepts: in a synthetic judgment, this "passive nature" reveals a kind of activism, which it denies with all its passivity. He grasps experience as a *suffered progression* and thinks that the power of a conclusion comes from the fact that it forms itself in the subject without him and against him; it derives its obviousness only from the impossibility of its being avoided. In a word, "skeptical thought" is an acquired truth, the real and concrete result of which is temporal development. He will say later:[17] "My life is a thought." He does not see things so clearly in 1835, but he already senses that the totalizing conclusion—if we want to avoid making a theory of it—must be the progressively unveiled meaning of lived experience. But because this unveiling is never, in his eyes, the object of a *practical* attempt, because the heuristic quest is as remote as possible from his possibilities and concerns, he shows us the work of totalization effected in the setting of subjectivity by the strong hand *of an Other*. Satan is precisely *this absolute Other* (the Father, Alfred, and, as we shall see, Gustave himself at another level of existence) who realizes by violence the synthetic unity of subjective experiences until the transcendent meaning of lived experience ("The world is Hell") reveals and asserts itself. The difference between this methodical despair and Descartes's methodical doubt is that the latter is an enterprise of the subject against the "Evil Genius," whereas the former is an enterprise of the Evil Genius in the subject himself. Satan "shows," he *makes visible*, he is at once the *other unity* of the successive movements of subjectivity, the *other-orientation* of lived experience, and the imposed content of experiences. We find here, therefore, the strange coupling of an exterior totalization—simple objective knowledge concerning the world—and the slow realization of that same

17. *Mémoires d'un fou.*

synthesis through the "lived experience" of an appropriately guided subject. A nontemporal truth can impose its acquisition only by temporalizing itself in a manipulated soul.

In 1835, however, the child is writing blindly. The subjective movement of directed experience is still merely an insubstantial appearance that barely conceals a vast objective enumeration of our faults. From this moment, the exterior-interior totalization, still secret, contains the principles of radical divorce of the interior from the exterior. The abstract "I" is not Gustave's ego, insofar as it remains without qualities; but as universal subject it designates the young author as well as anyone else: he need merely give it a subjective content for it to embody and relate to Flaubert's own experience. But in this case, the subjective life risks closing in on itself, dissolving the activity of the Other in its own inner depths; if taken to an extreme, it would no longer be philosophy but autobiography. Conversely, insofar as it is Other, Satanic activity tends to be self-affirming, to become a theoretical knowledge manifested through a set of judgments. In *Le Voyage*, Flaubert tries to reveal by means of an allegory what might be called a *singular universal*. The task is difficult: by universalizing, totalization can fall into abstract generalities; by singularizing, lived experience can lose its universality.

Agonies marks at once the reflective deepening of original intuition and the vacillations that are its results. When Gustave rereads *Le Voyage* in 1837 or 1838, the meaning of his enterprise becomes clearer to him: it is still a matter of revealing the radical evil at the end of an exterior-interior totalization. But he sees the defects of his first draft and is no longer satisfied with this pseudo-temporalization of the nontemporal. Indeed, he will integrate it into *Agonies* only with extensive modification. And the essential change concerns the ego of the narrator:[18]

> And at the time when I was young and pure, when I believed in God, in love, in happiness, in the future, in the fatherland; at the time when my heart leaped at the word "liberty!"—then—oh, may God be cursed by his creatures!—then Satan appeared to me and said: Come, come to me; you have ambition in your heart and poetry in your soul, come, I will show you my world, *my* realm.

18. There is another change: the text is no longer written in verse form. This means that Flaubert is distancing himself from poetry.

The colossus has come down from Mount Atlas, he has lost his arrogance, which raised him above our species: now he is a manchild, a child full of illusions. Since he is part of the human race, he cannot remain indifferent to the surprises Satan has in store for him. It is his own damnation he must learn from the Devil: "The world is Hell." Now this means: you are a subject of my realm and I will make you suffer like all your kind. Two words indicate that this disappointed child is related to Gustave himself: like him, he is a poet and ambitious.[19] There is no doubt that Flaubert has decided to damn him *through his virtues*—he would have suffered in his sullied purity, in his disappointed ambition. In short, what was sketched out at the beginning of verse XXII was the cruel movement or disillusionment. The subject passes from faith to despair—isn't this what happened to Djalioh, to Mazza? Isn't the revelation of evil as omnipresent in the world at the same time the unveiling of his own subjective nature? If virtue is merely appearance, it is not only about others that he was mistaken but about himself as well: his purity was merely an appearance that concealed a hellish pride. The stage is set this time so that Satan's last words "assemble a whole abyss of skepticism and despair."

Yet these last words will not be written. Flaubert recopies twenty or so lines and then leaves it all unfinished. He measures the abyss that separates this ego, enriched as it may be, from his own person.

In fact, in the previous paragraphs he developed his thought alternately in one of the two opposite directions that his original intuition sketched out.

We encounter exterior and abstract totalizations like this:

"What? You don't believe in anything?"
"No."
"Not in fame?"
"What about envy."
"Not in generosity?"
"What about greed."
"Not in liberty?"
"Don't you see the despotism that bows the necks of the people?"
"Not in love?"
"And prostitution?"
"Not in immortality?"

19. Cf. *Souvenirs*, p. 66: "Oh, my God . . . why did You cause me to be born with such ambition?"

"In less than a year the worms tear a corpse to pieces, and then
it is dust, then nothingness; after nothingness . . . nothingness,
and that is all that remains."

Here dialogue still exists, but it is reduced to its simplest expression. One can just discern in the succession of lines an embryonic
temporality and recognize the first voice, if you like, as that of the believer and the second voice as that of the "spirit that always denies."
But the dialogue is really enumerating the goods of this world and
showing the secret corrosive acid in each of them. Still more "exterior" are the considerations of misery and unhappiness or the allegory of the lost traveler whom "the tigers tear apart"; the young
writer places himself outside the world and from this position shows
us its wounds. The reckoning takes shape before our very eyes with
no one doing the reckoning, and the total is always negative.

In other paragraphs, however, the totalization is developed in interiority, in the lived time of a subject, and affirms itself as the adventure of a singular person led inexorably to despair by the unfolding of
his life. Gustave hesitates: shall he write in the third person, as in the
introduction, or in the first person, as in the paragraphs that follow?
He is certain of only one thing: first or third, this person will be him.
And in spite of the nontemporal aggressiveness of the maxims he in-
serts into the warp of his work, the introduction reveals to us in precise terms his preference for subjective syntheses: "It will soon be a
year since the author [of this work] wrote the first page, and since
then this troublesome work has been flung down many times, taken
up again many times . . . Every time a death was effected in his
soul . . . every time . . . something painful and troubled happened in
his outwardly calm and peaceful life, then, I say, he cried out a few
times and spilled some tears . . ." So his task is to show the impersonal truth through the unhappy adventures of one person, through
the way in which a soul is destroyed by gradually internalizing that
truth. In short, one can talk about the world only by talking about
oneself, and, conversely, one can talk about oneself only by talking
about the world. For between the world and the ego there is a reciprocity of perspective. The ego finds its fate in the world, the world
finds its temporalizing unity of totalization in the becoming of the
ego. What Flaubert at this period calls his "belief in nothing"—which
means that he *does not believe* in anything and simultaneously that he
believes in nothingness as universal truth—on the pain of illusion or

folly—must be based on the objective reality of nothingness; but, on the other hand, nothingness as the basis of reality will grasp itself only through the torments of a subject that it totalizes through disillusionment. Flaubert, in the introduction to *Agonies,* puts the accent on inner impulse, on cries, tears. But although the subject speaks to us of his experience, of that death which gradually engulfs his entire soul, the writing must be like a double register, every sentence has a double meaning and a double import since it refers simultaneously to lived experience and to that which lives on. The subject then becomes, in the fullest meaning of the term, a martyr. If the author is skillful at inviting us to generalize, his torments bear witness: every admission of the subject has a double aim; an amorous complaint must be received by the reader as an individual confidence, but it must almost immediately be transformed into an objective denunciation of the deficiencies of love. It would be ideal if radical subjectivity induced us to grasp the evil suffered by a single man as a universal wound, that is, to pass spontaneously into the domain of absolute objectivity.

On this level, it is fitting that the literary confidence be *constructed,* that the writer imagine singular incidents with potential universality, and that his narrative, while remaining subjective, should contain paths that lead us inexorably to objectivity. Gustave discovers this construction through the reflection that it is his task. Indeed, we shall see that this is merely one of three dimensions. What could be more intoxicating? To take his own lived experience and to rebuild it through the art of writing so that it is transformed in the reader into a generality without losing its sharp singular taste—isn't this the best an artist can propose for himself?

But, as we already know, the singular universal can corrode its singularity, fall into pure universality, become a maxim, an axiom, or a simple rhetorical flourish. Conceptualization is done at the expense of becoming and temporalization: the young author throws himself into a declamation on wretchedness. Conversely, the confidence can remain subjective: it depicts the individual who is speaking, and not the world. When Gustave claims "to assemble a whole abyss of skepticism and despair," he gives the formula for the singular universal: despair and skepticism are subjective attitudes, but when he defines them as *abyss,* he is hoping to make the reader suffer from vertigo and fall into the abyss himself. By contrast, when in the same introduction the author proposes to himself to make us read "an immense summation of a quite hideous and black moral life," the very words he employs make us feel that there is a risk that this life will remain *his* and we shall learn nothing about our own:

Paragraph I

I therefore take up this work begun two years ago, a work that is sad and tedious, a symbol of life: sadness and tedium.

Why have I interrupted it so long? Why do I feel such disgust at doing it? What do I know of it?

Paragraph II

Then why does everything on this earth weary me? etc.

Paragraph IX

I am weary. I wish I were dead, or drunk, or God so that I could play tricks . . .

And shit!

These three paragraphs—there are many others—count among the most interesting. Indeed, the subject who is speaking is Gustave himself; he confides to us his particularity and gives us no way out. In paragraph I he makes an effort to generalize, but he does so by *comparing* his work as a writer to life. A comparison is not a reason. And when he asks himself, "Why do I feel such disgust [at working]," he offers us a singular determination of his "lived experience" that cannot possibly mirror our own since we write without disgust, perhaps, or we do not write at all. Paragraph IX seems to translate on immediate impression, a moment thrown down on paper, in short, the singularity of a mood in its least transmittable form. In a word, from the age of sixteen Flaubert conceived the *critical* idea of constructing a singular universal—entire pages of *Agonies* demonstrate this. But the content tends to detach itself in many other pages from the form and to present itself, through an objective totalization, as universal pessimism; by the same token, lived experience in its idiosyncrasy slips into the "I" of the narrator, and this new content transforms a universalizable testimony into a "cry," a "tear" that testifies to nothing. Gustave never stops oscillating between two exterior totalizations— one purely objective, which effected itself automatically, the other maintaining within itself the formal and rudimentary "I" of the totalizer—and two concrete singularities—one constructed with a view to communication, the other perfectly real, spontaneous, but designating only the concrete subject. He oscillates to the point of losing himself and giving up. It is natural that he should be shocked, rereading it, by the diversity of levels on which he places himself, by the heterogeneity of the "ego" that speaks to us. For example, when he interrupts paragraph XXV, isn't it because he has discovered that the concrete "I" who was saying, "I am weary, I wish I were dead . . . And shit!" is not reducible to the abstract subject that the ramshackle devil leads through Europe? He is not the same man who inclines the reader to conclude and who delivers ready-made conclusions; he is not the same man who *knows* the world or who suffers the course of things. This disparate aspect alarms him. In the introduction describing his work, he grudgingly tells us the reasons that will lead him to give up: "It is less than poetry, it is prose; less than prose, cries; but it has false cries, shrill, piercing, muffled cries, always true, rarely happy ones. It is a bizarre and indefinable work, like those grotesque, frightening masks." He reproaches himself, in sum, for having missed his mark: the work does not belong to any genre, it lacks unity, it is merely cries, tears, sometimes "false" but "always true." [20] The "I" that expresses itself here is sometimes abstract to the point of vanishing into the universal, and sometimes so concrete that it escapes all generality. At times the movement of temporalization is real, at others it is simply a matter of rhetoric or eloquence, and at still others it effaces itself altogether for the sake of the nontemporal maxim. These breaks and shifts of speed give the work the character of a "grotesque mask." This "is frightening," but above all Gustave is shocked by the disunity. He is so conscious of his oscillations between exterior and interior that he abruptly makes up his mind to drop this irregular work for the sake of an *exterior totalization*. In fact, on 18 May 1838, less than a month after dedicating *Agonies* to Alfred, he finishes an allegory he calls *La Danse des morts*, from which he tries to expunge any personal confidence, any allusion to the author. The characters are abstract and symbolic: there is the "Poor Man," the "Damned," "the Souls who go up to Heaven," "History," the soul that—for a moment—realizes in itself the movement of disillusion and despair, namely Christ. Totalization is effected by Satan and by death. Or, rather, there are two totalizations, which contradict each other since death claims to survive Satan ("When this world no longer exists, you will be able to rest, like it, and sleep in the void; and I, who have lived so much . . . I must endure"), and Satan claims to survive death ("You will die because the world must end; all except me"). In any

20. The contradiction is merely apparent. Flaubert relates "false" to the *contents;* by "true" he means "sincere." We shall soon see him ask himself if he does not exaggerate his unhappiness.

case, the point of view of exteriority is explicitly assimilated to that of the *other*. Theory and practice are one and the same: we are certainly not told that everything—man or empire—ends by collapsing into nothingness, but death speaks and tells us that it kills. Radical evil is not presented to us as a determination of being; we are shown Satan "giving vent to . . . a laugh of pride and joy, . . . swooping down to the earth, extending his two bat wings over it and enfolding it like a black shroud." Flaubert is partial to these symbolic figures not only because their dialogues, their confrontation, and their acts preserve for exterior totalization a semblance of temporal progression; it is also because radical evil does not appear to him in the simple guise of the objective absurdity of our condition: he sees it as the effect of a malign and inflexible will, which imposes destinies in order to realize in time the original curse.

Is he satisfied? No. Certainly he has made a homogeneous work that says more eloquently what *Agonies* was saying, only that and nothing more. But despite the presence of a pitiless Christ, the martyr fails. Allegories can struggle, vociferate all they want; they can be shown to us, absorbed in their gigantic work of demolition: they will never replace the ground on which progressive disappointment realizes evil as acquired reality. Thus—after completing *Ivre et Mort*, his last fiction [21] (which also attempts a totalization through the exterior)—he openly returns to interior totalization with *Mémoires d'un fou*: this time he has understood and tries to preserve subjective unity by describing the progress of despair in a concrete subject. In short, beginning in 1838, the two types of synthesis isolate themselves, and Flaubert oscillates between them, no longer in the same work—though we find subjective lyricism in *Smarh* and maxims in the *Mémoires*—but from one work to the other. After *La Danse*, the *Mémoires*; after the *Mémoires*, *Smarh*, where once again we encounter all the symbolic characters of *La Danse*; after *Smarh*, *Novembre* and the first *Education*; after these "autobiographical" works, the first *Temptation*, which totalizes the world in exteriority. We shall attempt to show directly that these oscillations in Flaubert not only translate the hesitations of the *artist* but correspond to two fundamental options *of the man*. For the moment, let us follow the "subjectivist" line, and let us see what happens to it in *Mémoires d'un fou*, Gustave's first rigorous attempt to totalize through the interior.

21. Because *Les Funérailles du docteur Mathurin* is hardly fiction.

Interior Totalization

He took this work to its logical conclusion, someone will say, so he couldn't have taken a dislike to it. I'm not so sure about that. To tell the truth, it seems neither finished nor interrupted. Chapters 22 and 23 do represent a conclusion. But the preceding chapters—oratorical flourishes and maxims—seem interpolated.

Gustave might have added ten more or cut them out altogether, they are scarcely relevant to the story of his amours: the evident despair is not the consequence of Maria's disappearance; the reflections on art, on the infinite, on freedom have no connection, when all is said and done, with the rest of the *Mémoires*. Flaubert seems to have unburdened himself of these reflections in order to complete, in spite of everything, a work he was prevented from continuing by internal difficulties. Besides, we find that he almost stopped along the way. He notes at the end of chapter 10:

> *After three weeks' interruption.*
> I am so weary that it is deeply distasteful to me to continue, having reread the preceding . . .

But he does add, taking up his pen once again: "Here the *Mémoires* truly begin."

So he resumed work on his manuscript again and—since he gave it to Alfred in January 1839—*decided* he had finished it. By examining the correspondence and the dedication, let us try to establish the attitude he adopts toward this work.

In June 1837, he writes to Ernest that he refuses "to analyze the human heart only to find it filled with egotism and to understand the world only to see its unhappiness." He adds: "Oh, how much I prefer pure poetry, the cries of the soul, sudden transports and then deep sights . . ." He would then give all of science "for two lines from Lamartine or Victor Hugo." Except for the short missive of 22 September 1837, there is nothing more in the *Correspondence* until 13 September 1838. This silence of fourteen months is in part comprehensible: the two friends saw each other nearly every day; vacations separated them, and they resumed their correspondence. During these fourteen months, however, Flaubert wrote *Agonies* and the *Mémoires*—which bear little resemblance to the *Méditations poétiques*. On 13 September, *Agonies* had long since been abandoned. But he had only recently finished the *Mémoires d'un fou*, was in early summer no doubt, for on 11 October he wrote to Ernest: "I have loafed rather enough this vacation."[22] And the note of 13 September shows us a Gustave bristling, gritting his teeth beneath an affected stoicism and launching into grandiloquence. He responds agressively to Chevalier, who has dared to offer his opinion of Hugo: "Your reflections on V. Hugo are as true as they are unoriginal," and he finishes with an arrogant flourish: "What is the world to me? I shall ask little of it, I shall let myself go the way of the heart and the imagination, and if people shout too loudly, I may turn back, like Phocion, and say: What is all this cackling about?" Reading between the lines, we can recover the flight of pride that lands him on the summits after each vexation. But the new preferences he affects are what best display his bitterness and his "meanness": "Really, I deeply admire only two men, Rabelais and Byron, the only two who wrote with the intention of harming the human race." He does not yet propose to adopt "their tremendous position *in relation to*[23] the world," for, as we have just seen, he prefers to turn his back on it. Yet he dreams of it—as we shall soon see. What interests us here is that he is uncomfortable with himself, irritated to the point of exasperation. This malaise comes strictly from discontent with himself, which means that Gustave is discontented with the *Mémoires*. He is disappointed with himself, once the work is finished; after rereading it, he puts it aside, "loafs," and writes not a line more. Toward mid-October, Ernest, who is leaving for Paris, pays a visit to the Flauberts and finds Gustave in bed. Gustave says nothing about this illness or his malaise except: "I swear to you that I shall avenge myself for the mockery of heaven that had made me such an ass." On his feet again, he still doesn't write. On 20 November we read: "As for writing, I don't write, or write almost nothing, I content myself with making plans, creating scenes, dreaming up situations, incoherent, imaginary, and immersing myself in them. Funny world, my head." In this same letter he declares: "I am still the same, more clownish than jolly, more inflated than great." We shall see further on the precise meaning of this bitter remark; I note it for the moment because it is an obvious indication that his exasperation of September, while turned against himself, has not diminished. It will last until mid-December when he abruptly changes his mood and feels "in the best state in the world"; he has finally made connections between the reveries and ruminations of October and November: he has con-

22. Thursday, 11 October 1838: Ernest and Gustave have not yet seen each other again.
23. My italics.

ceived *Smarh*. In short, laziness, moroseness, discouragement followed the *Mémoires*, that outline of interior totalization, and did not leave Gustave until the day when he frankly turned toward a new attempt at exterior totalization.

Yet he does not entirely deny his work of 1838, for on 4 January 1839 he dedicates it to Le Poittevin. This dedication should be examined. In the first lines Flaubert writes: "To you, my dear Alfred, these pages are dedicated and *given*." [24] Gustave does not stop at inscribing a name at the beginning of his work: he gives his friend—an act that is unique in his life—the only manuscript he possesses, which, as Louis Le Poittevin testifies, never gets back into his hands. He might have claimed it after Alfred's death, if only to make another copy; he didn't think of it. No gift more complete: the work will have only one reader, its owner, and may disappear with him. Already in *Agonies* we find a foreshadowing of this mad generosity: "Never did [the author] do this with the intention of publishing it later; he has put too much truth and too much good faith into his belief in nothing to tell it to men. He made it to show to one man, two at the most." [25] This text is clear evidence of Gustave's ambivalence over the question of publication: on the one hand, there is fame to be had, which presupposes a great number of readers; on the other there is that originality of the misfit which has made him suffer so, and which he lives sometimes in shame and sometimes in pride. The quest for fame must be hidden at any price; domestic seclusion is accompanied by literary seclusion. If, therefore, in 1839 he *gives* the *Mémoires* to "one man alone," it is because he has unburdened himself in this work more than in *Agonies*. Yet he has not written *for* Alfred: from the first lines, an aggressive plural "You" [*Vous*]—which continually recurs in the pages immediately following, then becomes less frequent without ever disappearing altogether—informs us that the book was conceived to address a *public*. This is what stands out, for example, in the last sentence of chapter 1: "And you readers, perhaps you have just gotten married or paid your debts?" This sentence—like so many others—cannot be addressed to Alfred. The only explanation for this double, contradictory conduct (he writes for everyone, he *gives* his writing to one man alone) is that the work gradually became transformed and is not what Gustave first planned. Discontent, he gets rid of it, and his magnificent gesture resembles, from a certain perspective, the abandonment

24. My italics.
25. Alfred first, Ernest to a lesser degree.

of a child. To give it forever to his best friend is better than tearing it up: by a feudal gesture, Flabuert offers himself to the man he still loves more than anyone else;[26] but the offering is also an annihilation: take my progeny and do what you like with it, I can neither suppress it nor keep it.

The dedication tells us what has happened: Flaubert confesses in it that he has not accomplished what he set out to do; the work transformed itself under his pen; it engaged him and revealed him to the point that he determined to confide it, like a secret, to his only friend: "I had at first wanted to create a *roman intime* in which skepticism would be pushed to the final limits of despair; but little by little in the process of writing, the personal impression pierced through the story."

Of course, we already know what he wants: from his point of view, the only thing that prevents him from being strictly adequate to his destiny is his "anomaly"; this will allow him, by a vigorous denial, to constitute himself as *artist* in the imaginary. But at the same time he is ashamed of it: it is a taint, a simple fissure in his bourgeois-being. Comparing it to the ontological density of the extraordinary Flaubert family, he sees the anomaly as a lesser-being. He wants neither to deny it, since it must serve as the basis of the totalizing unveiling of the "macrocosm," nor to assume it, since it has been a source of reproach and he would then have to accept the paternal curse with all its consequences. With the appearance of reflection, writing-as-gratification loses its oneiric character and becomes writing-as-plea: interior totalization absorbs his singularity, which is universalized by becoming the adequate perception of reality. In the name of this perception, he condemns his class without appeal: everyone is conscious of the impossibility of being man; he will call bourgeois those who systematically avoid thinking about it. All the difficulties of "autobiographical" works issue from this initial position, which claims to give universal man as his generic imperative the narrow "vision of the world" of the incomparable monster that Gustave believes, wants, and does not want himself to be. We shall see how the aesthetic transposition of the anomaly simultaneously demands and denies the development of self-knowledge in Gustave.

His purpose is to set up his "belief in nothing" as a categorical im-

---

26. However, the dedication already creaks—as we have seen above. Alfred is in Paris; Gustave cannot bear the thought that Alfred and Ernest see each other without him: this is a breaking-up gift.

perative. He must therefore show how the consumption of a soul starts from faith and arrives, with the blow of successive disappointments, at absolute skepticism. His hero must launch himself naively into life, and each of his transports must be repaid with a rebuff. The experience must be cumulative: every day he thinks he has touched bottom, and every other day he suffers a little more, death creeps further into his soul, devastating it bit by bit. In brief, he must replace repetitions—which are the negation of history—with a directed process; he must forge a historical subjectivity which must be all together particularized by details and reveal itself as *this* universal: the history of all subjectivity.

Therefore, he *will construct:* he must individuate by details on pain of finding himself in full totalization from the outside; but he must choose these details and work them in such a way that they become the vehicles of universality. This means that Gustave must invent *a* life—a subjective temporalization of disillusionment—that shall be *all lives.* He would have to be able to say of his *roman intime* what he will say later of *Madame Bovary:* "Everything invented is true, you can be sure. Poetry is as precise a thing as geometry. Induction is as valuable as deduction, and then, having reached a certain point, one is no longer mistaken about all that constitutes the soul. No doubt my poor *Bovary* is suffering and weeping in twenty French villages at once at this very hour."

According to Gustave, then, fiction has a precision that makes it prophetic. Does this involve creating a "type"? Certainly not; after all, Madame Bovary remains to the end an incomparable individual. But his work aims at creating nothing less than a singular universal. The singularity begins by reassuring the reader, and then fascinates him, and finally he perceives, too late, that it contains the universal and that the destiny recounted to him, despite innumerable and irreducible differences, was merely his own. In order to obtain this result, the strict dosage of the particularity of imagined detail must be determined and made at once resistant and soluble. Flaubert has understood this from 1838 on: if he must speak of himself and reveal the early history that produced his despair as a subjective certainty, he consequently undermines its generality. What would he prove? Only that at least *one* unhappy life exists and that others are *possible;* but not what he wants to demonstrate: "that the worst is always certain." He has learned from the mistakes in *Agonies.* In that work we saw the author himself, tormented by doubt and by the desire to believe, finally seek out a priest, whose ugliness and gluttony drove him away.

Flaubert concluded: "Tell me now, who was at fault? I went to find clarity in the midst of my doubts; well, the man who should have instructed me I thought ridiculous. Is it my fault, mine . . .? No, surely not, for I had entered his place with pious feelings. Yet it is no more that poor man's fault if his nose is misshapen and he loves potatoes; not at all, the fault is his who made hooked noses and potatoes." These few lines testify to the author's hesitation in the face of the anecdote he reports. It is not my fault, he says. Nor that of the priest. Fine: we must stop drawing conclusions. It is a matter of chance: other chance occurrences might have been possible, that's all. Unless we calmly decide that all priests are hooked-nosed gluttons. But all at once the author, refusing to admit defeat, starts generalizing: it is God's fault (or Satan's). He does not convince us and hardly convinces himself: for He (God, the Devil, or Nature, the young man is undecided) who makes hooked noses and gluttons also makes straight noses and ascetics. Gustave *has* met this priest: we admit it, and, since he sticks to his belief, we can say that this unhappy meeting was his personal misfortune. It is impossible to conclude, as he does a little further on: "You will wait for someone to help you. But no one will come . . . Oh, no! And the tigers . . . will tear you apart." The lesson he draws from this failure? Only the detailed invention and inflexible organization of a fictive life will permit the transmission of a priori truths in the guise of false contingency.

The *roman intime* is the form he chooses. He could not have found a better one. In 1838 it was usually presented as a literary fashion. It was really a genre. On 16 July 1837, *Le Colibri* publishes an unsigned article that states:

> According to certain practitioners, the *roman intime* is a conscientious, meticulous, microscopically detailed analysis of all the impulses of the heart, a physiology of thought; but they do not limit themselves to the discovery of feeling, they push their exploration to the point of establishing a physiology of its trappings. Hence . . . abundant tears spilled over bread and jam, adultery caused by an overcooked leg of lamb, separation caused by a botched mayonnaise . . .[27]

Despite the irony of the pamphleteer, the genre is perfectly defined, and we understand at once what convinces Gustave to adopt it. After *La Danse des morts*, he threw himself back on interior total-

27. Cited by Jean Bruneau, op. cit.

ization; but now he grasps its meaning better: if despair must be a concrete reality, one must show its progression through familiar encounters and familiar incidents. In this sense even *La Dernière Heure* announced itself as a *roman intime,* but the hero was led to suicide by an extraordinary event: the premature death of his sister. Still too much pomp and too much external tragedy; after all, the sister might not have died, and her decrease depends uniquely on the caprice of the author. What Flaubert really wants is "to spill tears over bread and jam and to make adultery the result of an overcooked leg of lamb." In other words, if nothingness is the truth of all, it should not reveal itself through copious catastrophes—which might equally have failed to happen—but should be grasped in the stuff of the most insignificant, therefore the most universal, things; it is very simply the taste of lived experience as such. When shaving, Flaubert cannot look at himself in the mirror without laughing: that is what he must show, since all men shave every day. We shall be convinced only if the author shows us our damnation through the intimate quality of our sensations, the absurdity of our most elementary behavior, the grotesque stupidity of things spoken, whatever they may be, that is, of language.

To invent an ordered succession of familiar scenes in which readers can recognize themselves and which dissolve in their minds, leaving a taste of nothingness—that is the aim. It goes without saying that Gustave is not yet capable of achieving it: he still lacks the tool. Is this why we find him again, after September 1838 when the work is behind him, so prickly, so bitter, so lost? Where does his bewilderment come from, the sharp sense of having met with failure? Is it that he hasn't found the appropriate form for interior totalization? I don't believe that in the least: the exigency of an apprentice writer hardly goes beyond what can be done by the instruments he has forged. We must seek elsewhere the underlying cause of this first crisis. He shows us the way himself in the preface written after the event: "the personal impression pierces through the story." In other words, the *roman intime,* constructed to draw Gustave out of his anomaly, plunges him back into it and becomes autobiography.

An adolescent, to escape his particularity, makes himself a universal subject. He decides to write in the first person, precisely because (as we glimpse in the introduction to *Agonies,* and find fully unveiled in the final pages of *Novembre*) the "He" singularizes: the third person is the object of inquiry, it is seen, examined, it is the Other for an Other who by his gaze reduces it to the idiosyncrasy of exteriority. Little Flaubert is above all a "He" for himself because others installed themselves in him from the start, and because their language inside him designates him. His anomaly comes to him through others: *he* is the family idiot; an integral skepticism reduces the transports of his subjectivity, everything, even his thought, to the rank of epiphenomena, the mere consequences of objective conditioning. Curiously, the "I" liberates him: as *subject* he can think the universal and grasp himself as the original source of his feelings and principles. Flaubert's "I" is a victory to the degree that he affirms himself as the locus of experience. It is a refusal to learn oneself through the mediation of others and the basic intention of preserving only a single link with the exterior: the synthetic link of the microcosm to the macrocosm. Thus, the "I" of *Agonies*, of *Novembre*, and of the *Mémoires* is the moment of repossessing the self. There was the monster; he expanded as generalized subjectivity. Yet the limits of this transformation must be marked: unlike the Kantian "I think," the subject here does not discover itself as the unifying principle of experience; Gustave changes nothing of his underlying structures; at this level he remains what he has always been: a passive activity. The monster was the object of the family; the pseudo-subject becomes the object of the cosmos: he—this is the hypothesis of the Evil Genius—chooses to produce himself in his totality as determinations linked to that subjectivity.

Experience itself is unified and totalized in the intimacy of a soul, and the subject witnesses the flow of passive syntheses in himself—produced by an *other-activity*. At least this activity is never mediated: the world *is made to suffer* in this subjectivity grasped as universal setting until the final conflagration, in which microcosm and macrocosm destroy each other.

Be that as it may, recourse to the "I" appears at the outset as an attempt at nonpersonalization of the subject. The subject is qualified only by the content that is unified through him, that is, by the suffered cosmos. Certainly this totality must be given a *false particularity*: it can indeed be temporalized only as *a* particular story. Faked anecdotes will be used to this end. But to the very degree that these must be invented, the subject particularizes himself only by unrealizing himself. It is not a question, nor can it be a question, of the author's ego: Gustave is not liberated from himself. On the other hand, he is perfectly conscious of drawing the reader into a trap: in order to accomplish the simplest operations of reading, the reader is constrained to identify with this "I," subject of all dimensions, and to become the ulcerated soul whom life consumes and who crumbles into ashes at the end of the totalization. Flaubert avenges himself: others have designated him a monster by that "He" which cannot be absorbed; through the reflexive "I" he compels them to designate themselves and discover their destiny among the damned. In constructing his novel, Gustave palms off his "anomaly" on us, making it our burden to transform it into that universal, the "human condition." At least this is what he wants. To his misfortune, things are such that he will fall head first into the trap he proffers to his public.

First of all, if he wants to fascinate his readers with this depersonalized ego, prudence demands that he never address himself to them. But spontaneity is not so easy to give up. Since he first began to write, the boy has been indulging in rages, in fits of indignation that *really* express him; against his malaise, against the class-being that defines him in spite of himself, he often defends himself with oratorical flourishes. He points to us with a false aggression: "You who are reading this book . . . ," and most of the time it is to insult us or to heap scorn on us. The *Mémoires* are no exception to the rule: from the beginning, he taunts us: "What are you, you reader? How do you rank yourself—among the idiots or the fools?" As a result, there we are, cast outside, the illusion is broken: there are *we* and there is *he*. Not only for the public: Gustave shifts, perhaps unintentionally, from the formal "I" to an already personalized "Me"; when he blames us, he is *self* for himself. Not yet the ego of the depths but no longer completely the universal subject; his rages define him by opposition: he is an angry young bourgeois. Angry at the other bourgeois. This anger is real, it is singular; he does not invent it, he lives it, and at that moment he turns himself, in defiance of everyone, into Gustave Flaubert; solitude lies in wait for him, the "monster" is not far off. I shall say the same about the "cries of the soul," the interjections, the vehement interrogations: all these movements of the pen lead the impersonal subject to his authorial singularity. Thus the "I" of the writer and the "I" of the character become separate; the writer reveals himself as the real ego of the fictive hero.

That's just a start. But he fulfills his resolution only by turning his back on the truth of his experience and his life. What he actually finds in himself is not a slow progression of unhappiness, an accumulation of disgusts, but, to the contrary, an affective a priori that accompanies all his perceptions and systematically alters their meaning. No sooner does he feel the dawn of a pleasure or enthusiasm than he predicts he will be disappointed, creating the disappointment on the strength of his expectation. In this sense, the movement of lived experience is effected against the grain of what he wants to describe. For a long time now, the *Vanitas vanitatum* has been the prefabricated grid that allows him to decipher the world. And it is precisely the highly precocious appearance of this grid that constitutes the anomaly to be dissolved: the child has "come back without ever having been away"; in other words, the disillusionment precedes the illusion and prevents it from being produced, yet never ceases to pass itself off as disillusionment. When he says to Louise that he had very early a complete premonition of life, he means a sudden, blinding insight; despair came in one fell swoop. His first stories confirm it: Djalioh goes directly from happiness to the pangs of jealousy; for Mazza, it is Ernest's departure that suddenly destroys her hopes and her life; better, Garcia has always been unhappy and mean, Marguerite always damned by her ugliness. We know Flaubert's motives for projecting himself into the other as *disillusioned in advance:* everything is played out for him at eight years old; despair is already there, with its double face, the one turned the outside, the *belief in nothing,* and the other taking charge and internalizing the paternal curse, *self-disgust.* School life reinforced these predispositions, it did not create them. Gustave's pessimism is really not the product of his history but of his *protohistory:* toward his eighth year, he appears as a totalization not of the cosmos but of his family life and of the consequences of that life for his character. For example, maternal handling constituted him from the first year as passive activity, which first contained in an implicit state a lack of appetite that would soon be explained as disgust with living,[28] boredom, "belief in nothing."[29] Thus Gustave is *formed,* but not by a conscious experience: by a set of processes that precede experience and condition it.

Certainly, even a priori, the affirmation of nothingness must be temporalized. In *Agonies* he is taken to pondering dreams of glory and quickly rebukes himself: "It's a lie. Ours is a foolish breed." The denial precedes the desire, but the desire is necessary for the denial to manifest itself as an inhibition. Every new experience admits in itself a minimum of faith and hope, which the negative principle comes to destroy in embryo. Flaubert, apropos of "ideas," has given a good description of his behavior: "At first you adopt things very enthusiastically, then you reflect, then you doubt and there you remain."[30] It goes without saying that these reactions are particular to him: others

28. "I was born with the desire to die."
29. The taste for life is based on a protohistorical development of *activity* (or of aggression).
30. *Souvenirs,* p. 96.

adopt ideas and stick to them; for others, doubt precedes and under-
lies conviction; yet others are constitutionally agnostic and adhere
only with difficulty to their opinions without ever having them challenged. For Flaubert, obviously, doubt preexists, unformulated but
conscious; it is *against doubt* that he throws himself into belief, in the
hope that the passionate *gesture* of faith will be capable of disarming
that doubt. But this transport leads to nothing, the adolescent knows
he is defeated in advance, as witnessed by that very maxim which
foresees the progress of his thought. In other words, faith for Flaubert
affects vivacity in order to mask its real nature: it is really a behavior of
failure and knows itself for such. This foreseen temporalization, destiny gathered into a moment, characterizes all the impulses of his
soul—for example, his rare moments of happiness. There are certain
people made in such a way that they take fright when they begin to
feel happy: "It is proof," they say, "that the worst is about to happen
to me." Thus they prove themselves right: joy is transformed into anguish. Flaubert is one of these people: he cannot prevent himself, at
fifteen, from having joyous awakenings; but since the worst is always
certain, the pleasure is merely a bad joke on the part of the Evil Genius. Scarcely felt, there it is, ruined. At least it must first be felt. In
other words, although the general movement of his life in these years
is repetition pure and simple (which is a kind of permanence), every
singular face of lived experience is *temporalized:* empirical novelty—a
posteriori—provokes in each case negation a priori, which is given
before experience but becomes concrete only during experience. In a
sense, Gustave is not wrong: the taste of nothingness is given to him
from the beginning of the process as the final meaning of temporalization. On the other hand, this apparent reversal of terms (the appearance of the a posteriori preceding the concretization of the a priori) is
at the source of his conception of the *roman intime:* in his view, experience is given *first;* friendship, love, glory manifest themselves as fascinating realities. And it is these resplendant gems that transform
themselves into dead leaves and produce, from disappointment to
disappointment, universal doubt as the totalization of experience in
generalized subjectivity.

Gustave therefore finds himself at a crossroads when he begins the
Mémoires: either he will seriously sit down to write the *roman intime* he
is considering and will show the inflexible growth of despair in a soul
who becomes conscious of the human condition, or he will describe
as a permanent foregone conclusion what the *roman intime* claims to
offer as the ultimate result of a life. In the first case, the truth will con-

tinually disturb him: it structures the imaginary, which aims at surpassing it; he will be discomfitted to find himself again in the child full of illusions (he totalizes *all* possible illusions since at the moment of death he must totalize *all* disillusions), whom he must, by virtue of the major theme of his book, establish from the first pages. In other words, the imaginary is no longer a mythic transposition, it becomes a systematic lie. And the subject is no longer an alter ego of the author, it is frankly his negation. But if he chooses to tell what is—even in the movement of an aesthetic totalization—he will merely be revealing to everyone that anomaly he wants to hide. Having written, "I was born with the desire to die," it is not the human condition he is illuminating but his particular conditioning. For he knows quite well, damn it, that the desire to die is ordinarily countered by the violent drives that impel us to live. By the same token, he allows us a glimpse of the *monster* and loses all possibility of generalizing. He does the opposite of what he wants: attempting to tear himself away from his facticity and catch us in the trap, he falls once more into his chains and frees us by revealing himself.

Gustave does not choose between these two possibilities. The question was whether to put the despair at the end (*roman intime*) or at the beginning (investigation of the self). But in the *Mémoires* he grows confused and puts it at both ends: it is an a priori and it is a conclusion. As early as chapter 2 he writes: "My life is not made up of deeds; my life is a thought . . . Oh, what a long thought it was! Like a hydra, it will devour me with all its mouths. A thought of grief and bitterness, a thought of the weeping buffoon, a thought of the meditating philosopher." Let us read carefully: it is not experience that produces the thought, it is the prefabricated thought that devours life. A thought: disenchantment, the complete premonition of existence, the intuitive grasp of our damnation, the contradiction, in a word, of bourgeois-being and of the bourgeois denial of the bourgeoisie. It is the "madman" speaking, now cursing the philistines, his readers, now offering himself as their laughing-stock through masochism, and now trying to move them to compassion. And as he is neither able nor willing to seek the underlying reasons for his hypochondria, he compels us to judge it congenital. What reason would we have for identifying ourselves with this kid, demoralized from birth? The chips are down in advance, "thought" corrodes life from the outset. So Flaubert's historicity is negated, and the novel collapses.

But in the same chapter, immediately after the paragraph we have just cited, the author takes up the *historical* narration: "Oh, how my childhood was filled with dreams . . . I was cheerful, full of laughter, loving life and my mother. Poor mother!" Here the fiction mingles with memory: Flaubert pretends that his mother is dead. No doubt this is reminiscent of *La Dernièe Heure*, in which the hero has just lost an adored sister and reviews his entire life in the black light of this grief. But it is significant that this theme had not been developed in the *Mémoires*—save in the narrative of a nightmare in which the author sees his mother drown before his eyes. This aborted motif reveals to us a striking contradiction in Gustave: he still intends to invent, but at the same time he is loath to construct. The death of the mother—conceived within the framework of the *roman intime* as a banal and tragic event that could give the hero a first intuition of death—is set aside just *because it is an event,* and because Gustave's first relations with death are quite anterior and of an entirely different sort. Yet the negative progression is sketched out for the first time: "As a child, I loved what is visible; as an adolescent, what is felt; as a man, I no longer love anything." But just when we believe he is going to give the underlying reasons for this involution, Flaubert stops short, and despair reappears as his personal lot: "Why such bitterness so young? What do I know? It was perhaps in my destiny to live thus, weary before having borne the burden, out of breath before having run."

This line bears witness to a rare lucidity: no better way to say that Flaubert's pessimism is an a priori. This time it is Gustave who is speaking—and speaking *about himself:* he tell us lyrically of his stupor when faced with himself, his "estrangement." No more novel: the monster, exhausted, confesses his sins. But this is merely so he can immediately disappear and make way for a first totalization: he wrote but *discovered* that words betrayed him; contemplated, but *recognized* the vanity of knowledge. He thus came to doubt God, hesitated before "embracing that faith in nothingness," then threw himself into the abyss to spin "in an immeasurable void." And, as if one did not imply the other in advance, from doubting God he comes to "doubt virtue." This brief enumeration, moreover, merely *looks* like an interior totalization: in reality we review from *the outside* (as Doctor Mathurin will soon do) the great values to which man, "poor spindly-legged insect, wants to cling": art, science, religion, virtue. Flaubert is aware of it, for he writes: "I will later recount to you all the phases of this dismal contemplative life . . . you will know the adventures of this placid life, so banal, so filled with feelings, so empty of deeds. And you will tell me, then, if everything is not derision and mockery." *Later:* so he knows he is not *recounting* but summarizing; and he returns to the idea of working out an interior totalization in detail for us, of recounting the *history* of a life. The chapter stops here: the author has not stopped vacillating between the idea that despair is his singularity and the idea that his experience has a universal value, between the denial of history in the name of his own permanence and historicity—as edifying construction. Curiously, his antihistoricism reveals the author to himself; he unrealizes himself and conceals his singularity from himself through narrative and temporalization.

Nonetheless, certain very powerful motives somehow incline him to *recount himself.* No doubt he was tempted, in the *Mémoires,* to totalize his own memory and recompose his past life. This desire was with him for a long time: in the *Souvenirs,* for 21 May 1841, he writes: "[The *collège* period] was a time of inconceivable boredom, and a dull sadness mingled with bouts of clownishness; I shall write that story some day, for I am eager to tell myself to myself; everything I do is to give myself pleasure." He will try again in *Novembre,* but with no more success, for he declares more than once to Louise Colet that he would like to write about his life from the age of seven to twenty-five. Thus the use of the "I" in the midst of subjective impersonality implies a permanent temptation to personalize the narrative. But why? Out of a taste for truth? And is there such pleasure in retracing "the boredom, the dull sadness and bouts of clownishness"? His real motive is rancor. Garcia, Marguerite, Djalioh, Mazza are what others have made them: they were not destined in themselves for unhappiness and meanness; the original curse, contempt, sarcasm, and injustice have transformed them. For Gustave, to recount himself is to enumerate his sufferings and blame them on his executioners.

There are two strategies for dissolving the *anomaly:* one, as we have seen, is to present it in the imaginary as the human condition and to generalize it by infecting the reader. The other is to make it simply the product of the cruelty of others, in brief, to place responsibility for it on certain specific persons. The autobiography that tempts the young Gustave is an exposé of bitterness. And from chapter 3 a new narrative gets started. The author is ten years old; he enters the *collège,* his first disappointment: "I was cast down to the lowest rung by my very superiority." But take care: Flaubert is afraid, he knows he is exposed. We should not expect him to take the risk of describing the real anomaly that defines him from his earliest years, nor to name those actually responsible, his parents. There is no longer any question of Garcia the envious, Mazza the criminal, or the hideous Marguerite.

Since he says "I," the author stays on the surface of himself: we shall certainly not see that malevolent martyr, the family idiot, but a "superior" being, a desperate adolescent. Dryness, boredom, desolation: these negative qualities serve to *suggest* monstrosity the way a discreet tailor to mature gentlemen suggests fashion without yielding to it. "I was good then . . . now I have a desiccated heart, my tears have dried. But may misfortune befall the men who made me corrupt and mean, good and pure as I was." The men "I" speaks of are his fellow students and his teachers: "I was at the *collège* from the age of ten, and there, quite early, I contracted a profound aversion to men." He repeats in chapter 5: "The *collège* was antipathetic to me. It would make a curious study, that profound disgust felt by noble and elevated souls as a result of contact and vexation with men."

As we see, we have a *story*, a temporalizing event, the encounter, heavy with consequences, between the hero and society. This time there is no place for astonishment at the way "thought" corrodes the life of the narrator; we know how it has happened to him: through commerce with men beginning at the age of ten. This explanation proves equal to Gustave's design: it is totalizing since the entire human race is implicated in this troublesome affair. At the same time it reduces the original anomaly to a simple matter of superiority: the child was simply better and more sensitive; he has fallen from the heights, that's all, and something in him was broken. Can he be lying? Certainly not; first of all, it is only too true that Gustave suffered at the *collège*. And then, *does he know* that his misfortunes go even further back? That this claimed "superiority" was merely a shriveled defense against a deep feeling of inferiority? It is certain, in any case, that he is restrained by fear: during this entire period the reminiscences of the *collège* function as a screen memories and allow a transfer of responsibilities.

This narrative, however, is in formal contradiction to the *roman intime*. The purpose of the latter is to incarnate the human condition in a subject, whereas this narrative aims to place the narrator above his kind. Hence the two types of narration collide. In the first, insincere but nonfictional, Gustave in anger and shame attributes his misfortunes to the meanness of others. In the second, which is invented, he explains his despair in terms of human weakness: "I have read, I have worked with ardor and enthusiasm, I have written . . . There again, disappointment . . . Weary of poetry, I launched myself into the field of contemplation . . . And weariness overtook me, I came to doubt everything . . ." etc. As we see it, is the human character that is at

400

issue. Inside and out. Curiously, he prefaces this narrative—which is supposed to show the successive stations of his Calvary—by a general maxim that summarizes them *in the nontemporal:* "Man, poor spindly-legged insect, who tries to cling to the edge of the abyss, to every branch, who grabs onto virtue, love, ambition, who clings desperately to God, and who always lets go and falls." It will suffice to compare these lines to those in the next paragraph—" . . . I came to doubt everything . . . life, love, glory, God . . . yet I had a natural horror of embracing that faith in nothingness; at the edge of the abyss, I closed my eyes; I fell"—to perceive that the "I" is introduced merely to give the universal the appearance of temporality.

Be that as it may, the timid impulse to recount himself, by working against the fictive succession whose purpose is to temporalize the nontemporal prompts two contradictory egos to appear in the same chapter, one of which owes its misfortunes to the baseness of others and the other to human nature in general. And the former is deeply conditioned by the concrete actions of particular individuals, while the latter is merely the medium of subjectivity and is determined only by the immediate relations of the microcosm to the cosmos.

The reason we are slow to notice the contrast between these two *selves* is that the real story, taking fright, conceals itself beneath the veil of generalizations as soon as it appears. The misfortunes of the student Flaubert suddenly lose their hard reality: "It would make a curious study, the disgust felt by noble and elevated souls . . ." etc. What we have here is an *example;* the concept is in the background. The *practical* meanness of singular persons is effaced: what remains is a contact provoking a universal reaction in "noble souls" who represent the ideal subjectivity. This passage to *eidos* misleads us and makes us believe that the two subjects are simply one. We are confusing the flight from temporalized idiosyncrasy toward the idea with the fictive historicization of an atemporal concept.

And Gustave? There is no question that he suffers—in bad faith— the same confusion. This adolescent regards himself as both historical and eternal because he is at the age when one has no history. True, he is launched by his birth into a singular adventure that must end with death, an adventure whose style and form were fashioned by his earliest years. But if he stays on the surface, he must recognize *that nothing happens to him,* that is life—at the *collège* and at the Hôtel-Dieu—is a "calm and peaceful existence." He adds: "I am young, I have a face without wrinkles and a heart without passion . . . I have scarcely lived . . . I have not known the world at all . . . I have not entered, as they say, society . . . my life is not deeds . . . my life is a thought." This means that he can easily confuse the wholly super- ficial indeterminacy of an existence without history with the deter- mination of universality. If he looks around him, inside him, what does he find? The eternal return of works and days. But his works are nothing but commerce with ideas, the internalization of an abstract and quintessential form of the culture. He has no need to reproduce his life—others take charge of it for him. He has no knowledge of the passions within him precisely because he is nothing but a terrible hid- den passion. In brief, he is a *young bourgeois:* his social reality (without needs, supported by his father) and his deepest inner reality (struc- tured by the particular and general structures of his family) are *latent.* On the surface, by contrast, he is everything and nothing, he regards himself as mind and plays, yawning, with the theories of others, which he takes for the movements of his own thought. In 1842, in *Novembre,* he will write this sentence, a summation of what he consid- ers the truth of his being for at least five years: "I was therefore what you all are, a certain man who lives, sleeps, eats, drinks, cries, laughs, very much enclosed in himself and finding in himself the same ruined hopes wherever he goes . . . the same paths recrossed a thousand times, the same unexplored depths, dreadful and disturbing." In these few lines we find his entire program; above all, to generalize: "I was what you all are." But in this definition of a *"certain* man" just like everyone else, we see what is missing: need[31] and work as much as dark ambition. He describes a son of good family while believing he speaks of man in general: the mistake is to take as universal what is simply abstract because it has not yet been explicitly determined. As a result, he lends to all members of the human race his own despair, which he does not hesitate to define as a repeition rather than an ad- vance: the same paths recrossed a thousand times symbolize the mo- notony of his ruminations. We shall note the adroitness of the last words of the enumeration: the monster is there, squatting in the "dreadful" depths of his soul. But although he honestly recognizes that he does not want to explore them, he arranges for us to agree that we are all monsters at bottom. Abysses are common to us all, and so is rejection of self-analysis. The idiosyncrasy itself he palms off on the species and generalizes, without probing deeper. Nothing of what he says is false; rather, everything is said. Except that he does not see

31. "Sleep . . . eat . . . drink . . ." But these activities mask hunger, thirst, fatigue by preventing them.

402

that his real indeterminacy—including its infrastructures—is a particularizing determination. Thus, his day-to-day reality, passively suffered and intentionally lived, represents the permanent setting in which the singularity of the historical ego and the universality of the "I" of subjectivity are continually substituted and mistaken for each other. So that Flaubert can say in the same paragraph: here is what they made me, and here is how a noble soul lives the human condition.

These perpetual substitutions are, however, both effect and cause of a malaise that becomes more evident from page to page. For the narration (inauthentic but in some sense truthful) stops abruptly. Chapters 6 and 7 are exterior totalizations or, more simply, tirades with no connection to the story we were being told: "And when will this degenerate society, filled with every kind of debauchery, end?" There is nothing authentic in these lines: as for debauchery, the young Gustave professes elsewhere that he hasn't the least aversion to it; he knows quite well, in any case, that if bourgeois society repels him, it is for its puritanical utilitarianism rather than its orgies. But then in chapter 8, without transition, Gustave himself is revealed to us: "And there are days when I feel an immense weariness, and a gloomy boredom envelops me like a shroud wherever I go." The *Correspondance* and the *Souvenirs* confirm it for us: this observation is *true*, and Gustave has willed it so, to the point of renouncing his usual hyperbole: this melancholy, he specifies, is not constant; it overwhelms him on certain days; on others, he is in a less gloomy mood and perhaps even cheerful, who knows? Aside from sweeping oratorical flourishes, this chapter contains valuable notations on the adolescent's feelings. Where does this come from? It seems that here, for the first time, "the soul guides the pen." What he offers us is neither an evolution nor the eternity of a concept but simply the present. It seems that the author can no longer resist the lyric desire to *lament*. In any event, these lines escape him because he feels a sudden desire to tear himself out of his overly subjective "estrangement," his silent rumination, and to "lay himself out on paper" and see himself face to face. Not that he seeks to understand his pain by studying its causes. He simply wants to give it the objectivity of the written word. But as a result, the monster reappears: "No sooner have I seen life than there is an immense disgust in my soul . . . Yes, I am dying, for is it living to see one's past as water flowing into the sea, the present as a cage, the future as a shroud?" Flaubert shoves himself into a corner: he must give up writing or explain this immense *premature* disgust that his "calm and peaceful" existence is incapable of justifying. In short, this lyric lament, this "moment of truth," drives the author to reject the ego of the fiction and that of insincerity and to throw himself into the perilous enterprise of *knowing himself*, of exploring his "dreadful depths."

Such an exploration is what he does *not* want, at any price. Here he is in chapter 9, setting out again to evoke memories: "There are trivial things that struck me deeply." He describes a "kind of château" and the old woman who lived there, ending with these words: "How long ago that was! The mistress is dead, the château is being used as a factory."

He is turning around in a circle: the château, the dead old woman, are merely illustrations of "the flowing of the past" which he laments on the preceding page. He feels he is marking time, yawning, growing bored with writing and consequently with living. He no longer comprehends his enterprise: this *roman intime* reveals too much and not enough of him; the subject "I" is sometimes himself and sometimes another. He senses that he must choose: either escape the anomaly by giving himself an unreal ego, or try to dissolve it through what must be called self-analysis. But he cannot decide, nor does he want to; he is now bored with inventing himself and terrfied of going deeply into himself. He abandons his manuscript and then, after three weeks, rereads it with disgust. Is he going to tear it up? No. He finds a way out, decides to relate a real episode from his life, his love for Elisa Schlésinger, whose acquaintance he made during the summer of 1836 or, more probably, 1837. Everything is changed, as we can see: it is no longer a matter of totalizing an existence through memory but of evoking a set of precise and dated memories. And the young author no longer seeks this set of memories in his early childhood but in his more recent past: he is writing at the age of sixteen, and his first encounter with Madame Schlésinger had taken place when he was fourteen or fifteen.[32]

Are we to say that the *Mémoires*, from their conception, were bound to include the Trouville episode? Everything suggests the opposite. First of all, it runs contrary to the principal design: since one must doubt everything, love, like virtue, must be mere nothingness. Yet the young author does not speak of his attachment without a certain satisfaction; quite to the contrary, he emphasizes its strength, its purity. He can love, then? Where is the desiccated heart in all this? Where is

32. Gérard-Gailly thinks that the meeting occurred in 1836. Sergio Cigoda places it in 1837. For my part, I would be inclined to accept the latter solution. The "I came back there two years later" is not at all conclusive—since in any event it contradicts the "I was then fifteen years old." If he saw her in 1836, Flaubert was only fourteen.

the skepticism and ennui? No doubt his love is unrequited. But does he really lament this fact? In any case, this charming and melancholy adventure in no way justifies absolute pessimism. He is so sure of it that he concludes the story with these words: "Adieu! and yet, when I saw you, if I had been four or five years older, bolder . . . perhaps . . . Oh no, I blushed each time you looked at me. Adieu!" In other words, if his loves have not been happy, it was because he was too young and too timid. These are merely accidental reasons: in effect, only the difference in age counts. A few years more and he would have been bolder; he even seems to believe, interpreting some attitude of Marie's, that if he had only dared, she would not have been cruel to him. Can this bit of bad luck serve as the basis for an affirmation that mutual love is impossible? When Flaubert articulates this maxim later on, he will support it more solidly and will endeavor to show that no two lovers ever love each other with the same love at the same time. There is nothing of this sort in the *Mémoires*. Certainly there is the fall: Gustave, once back in Rouen, loses his virginity with a chambermaid. He accuses himself harshly and goes so far as to reproach himself for having systematically seduced this willing young woman. "Nearly everyone [any other man] has followed the instinct of nature like a dog; but there was much more degradation in calculating it, becoming aroused at corruption, throwing oneself into the arms of a woman . . . only to rise and show one's impurities." But he admits, in equally pompous but clear terms, that he was relieved of his virginity out of pride in imitating his older or more knowledgeable comrades: "I had been chasing vice as though it were a duty, and then I bragged about it. I was fifteen years old, I spoke about women and mistresses." To sleep with a servant or a prostitute in order to enter the circle of the "initiated" was nothing very splendid for a bourgeois young man, but neither was it so reprehensible. How remorseful is he? Hardly at all, for a year later, coming back to Trouville when Maria is no longer there, he evokes her memory and determines "really to love her." If he had felt so guilty toward her, he would have lost her or at least would not have "found her again" with this tranquil spontaneity. He condemns himself so vividly merely to reintroduce the theme of human weakness and the vanity of all things. But the conclusion tallies poorly with the premises, and Flaubert is well aware of it, since he writes: "Dear angel of my youth, you whom I saw in the freshness of my feelings, you whom I loved with a love so gentle, so fragrant, so full of tender reveries . . ." All in all, this is giving the adventure a very optimistic ending: it all happened in the young man's mind; but this is just what delights him: "Ah, my soul melts in delight at all the follies my love invents." Is this Hell, then, this world where one can at least love? No, if we believe chapter 22, from which these citations are taken; yes, if we put our trust in the twenty-third and last chapter, in which the author, forgetting Maria, recovers the tone of his first pages.

Furthermore, if Gustave had expressly decided from the time of its *conception* to put the narrative of his first love at the center of his *Mémoires*, he would have placed the previously written fragment, which tells of the "tender feeling mixed with foolishness" that he felt at around the age of fourteen for a young Englishwoman, *before* the Maria episode. Both because the events reported preceded the meeting at Trouville and because this unimportant little crush did not survive that meeting. The reason he awkwardly interrupts the thread of his narrative at this point and introduces these few pages is that he threw himself into writing the "real" *Mémoires* without any plan, spontaneously, gathering the unsorted contents of his heart just as they came. When he suddenly makes up his mind to it, he begins with the first summer on the beach; along the way, he finds that he had other "heart throbs," judges it necessary to inform his readers of these (if only to emphasize by comparison the importance of his new attachment), recalls that he has previously sketched out the story of one of these crushes, connects this sketch as well as he can to chapter 14, and returns to Maria with these words: "[Her] gaze made the memory of that pale child vanish." This disorder is the most effective indication of his train of thought.

What is the significance of this abrupt change? To find the answer, we have merely to examine the words he uses to announce it: "Can the works of a world-weary man amuse the public? I shall, however, force myself to divert both of them. Here the *Mémoires* really begin." We shall note that it is the author himself who speaks. And his speech is *dated:* he has taken up the pen on a certain day in the summer of 1838, "after three weeks' pause." Here the absolute present irrupts in these *Mémoires,* which until now he was writing in the past tense, and we have the convergence of the narrator and his character.

What is he telling us? That he dislikes the first nine chapters of the *Mémoires:* they are the work of a world-weary man. This way, he dismisses on equal terms his effort to make explicit the a priori he calls "his thought" and his attempt to temporalize his pessimism in the imaginary by presenting it as the interior totalization of human experience. He no longer attempts to render cosmic nothingness and no longer attempts to understand himself. In brief, he abandons simultaneously the two divergent projects that maintained the tension of the first pages. The reason given: that he is merely depicting the universal void, or the void of his heart; he will bore, he will be bored. He will therefore leave these monotonous ruminations and tell us of a "real event." Does he perceive that he has brutally transformed his project? Perhaps. Let us say that he knows it but does not want to acknowledge it. Indeed, if he were acknowledging it, he would immediately abandon the first nine chapters and begin a new work, whose first chapter could be number 10 of the *Mémoires*. He does nothing of the kind. Not only that, but in the last pages he will again take up vast external-internal totalizations irrelevant to his little romantic novel. Thus the first chapters, however disavowed by those that follow, serve as their introduction. One word allows us to understand that the author is not unconscious of what he is doing: the word is "divert," which must be taken with its Pascalian overtone. Let us recall the adjectives in *Novembre*, "dreadful, boring": for Gustave, the dreadful is lived *in boredom*. He will "divert" himself from it—that is, he will deliberately escape it—by choosing, against the eternal return of doubt, to relate the truth of appearance, that which is *seen, heard, felt*. In brief, by recounting himself, Gustave has chosen to deny himself. But can we say that the man who feels his life "corroded" by a thought is definitely the same man who experiences his first love at Trouville? In truth, we cannot; for us to have *understood* that he is the same man, the feeling would have had to be replaced in its context, in Gustave's family situation; we would have had to make allowance for affective mediations that, coming from "dreadful depths," produced him and maintained his existence. The author does not conceal the fact that Elisa Schlésinger is a young mother, older than he, and that he surprises her in the act of nursing; we could recover the truth of his predilection for her if Gustave had been able to elucidate—and had actually done so—his relations with his own mother. Since he does not show the genesis of his love, it remains floating in air, neither true nor false, neither *his* nor other. Similarly, he reports to us frankly, and rather crudely, the effects of his jealously: "[she] aroused obscene and grotesque thoughts in me: so I defiled them both, I heaped the bitterest ridicule on them, and I forced myself to laugh pityingly at those images that had made me weep with envy." But he does not seek the reasons for this attitude: it belongs to him. We find it again, transposed, in all areas, and the *Souvenirs* inform us that during this period he was dwelling on the petty baseness of great men out of spite at being unable to equal them. And we already know that Djalioh's jealousy represents both that which Elisa aroused and his old rancor against the usurping brother. He does not compare his efforts to defile the couple with his penchant for the ignoble and the obscene that has its source in his abhorrence of the flesh. He speaks of this abhorrence in the *Mémoires* themselves, but it is the horror of a noble soul for the baser instincts. No link is established between these declarations against physical love and the allusion to obscene images that torment him—no doubt to the point of masturbation—and fill him with simultaneously sadistic and masochistic confusion. Yet, of that at least, of his "meanness," of "that feeling which impels man to become impassioned by what is hideous and bitterly grotesque," he is fully conscious. Why doesn't he breathe a word about it?

In reality, denying the dilemma that imposes itself on him, he rescues himself from distress by playing on words. His decision is simple: he was writing a hybrid work—semifiction, semiconfession—under the name of *Mémoires*; he has us believe he is conceding to the taste for truth, renouncing fiction and choosing autobiography. "Here the *Memoires really* begin." This means: My mistake was not to be completely truthful; I should have spoken only of myself." And of course it is by accusing himself of insincerity that he is most profoundly insincere: for it is not a question of deciding merely that you will tell the truth, but of what level you assume in order to tell it. His initial intention was "to push skepticism to the final limits of despair"; these words themselves indicate a will to hyperbole. Be that as it may, he wanted to achieve through fiction what I have called the superreality of the world, meaning its infernal character. He must abandon this superreality (the world, product of the Evil Genius, making itself live through human subjectivity to the point of absolute despair); if the facts he wants to report are true—and they are—they will not be *soluble,* they will not have been constructed so that their apparent particularity might vanish by revealing their universality. In sum, he pretends to forget his original project. But it is not to the advantage of *his* truth: nor does he want to remember the intermittent apparitions of the "incomparable monster" he tried allusively to indicate to us. His *roman intime* aimed to produce a singular universal; his anomalous truth announced itself as a singularity that is not universalizable (at least not immediately), but of a "dreadful depth." By refusing either to forge the one or to discover the other. Gustave chose, in the name of truth, his level of truth: that of the anecdote; he propels himself with great effort back to his own surface. The events he is going to recount cannot claim universality since they are singularized by irreducible chance happenings; but neither can they attach themselves *to the monster:* they are *related* rather than *analyzed.* A first love, told as it was lived, remains an intermediary between the generalizable and the idiosyncratic. For this narrative provokes certain *resonances* in readers: they find themselves in it without finding themselves. They cannot prune the details, since detail is essential in autobiography. On the other hand, through incidents that differ in all respects from their own memories, readers vaguely relive another, entirely dissimilar love that had other beginnings, other twists and turns, another ending, happier or more logical, that was addressed perhaps to a little girl or an adolescent girl of their own age but shares with the feeling recounted the fact that it was also their first. The *resonance* again prevents *acknowledgment* and *knowledge:* the reader will know neither the author nor himself because the author has chosen to recount himself *so as not to know himself* and to stick to descriptions of superficial psychology which never deliver anything but "consequences without premises," facts without interpretation, acts that are *significant and deprived of meaning.* The cosmos, universal subjectivity and anomaly, in short, phantasms and personal reality vanish together; what remains is one inadequately particularized adolescent.

He hesitates, not over the subject who experiences this love, but over the "I" who recounts it. And undoubtedly the narrator and the hero are one. But should this unity be reinforced or broken by introducing into it a temporal "distancing"? In short, will the author who says, "I was fifteen years old," be sixteen or sixty? In chapter 2 he wrote, "I am young," and although he spoke of his life as if it would soon be over, he converged with himself. But when the "real" *Mémoires* begin, in chapter 10, he says: "To tell you the precise year [of my meeting with Maria] would be impossible for me, but I was very young then; I was, I believe, fifteen years old." Fifteen years old: that was last year. But he pretends to be so old that he is not even sure of his age at the time. And several pages later: "I pause here, for the scoffing of the old man must not tarnish the virginity of the young man's feelings; I would be as indignant as you, reader, if I were pursued by such cruel language." As we know, Gustave considered himself an old man from the age of fourteen. But the words he uses to speak to his *young* readers prove that he does not consider old age, here, a quality of the soul but a time of life. Yet in chapter 22 we again find the identification of the two "I's": it is Flaubert himself who laments: "I shall always think of you, I shall be thrown into the vortex of the world . . . Where am I

409

going? I wish I were old, and had white hair." What is there to conclude but that Gustave's *intention* has been to make himself the Other
of his own life by recounting it with the disabused irony of a man of
experience *already disillusioned* with everything, but that when he must
conclude, he finds himself to be the young man he was at the beginning. Except that he no longer meditates on a life nearly over, but
suddenly, almost in spite of himself, one of the real reasons for his
torments is offered us: the anxiety he feels when he thinks about the
future. He had no future at all in the first chapters, for his "thought"
had corroded his young life; he *no longer has a future* when, as a hoary-
headed old man, he recounts his love for Maria. And this is how that
denied future reveals itself at the very end of his work: it is the number of years that separate him from that old age he claims to have attained, which appears here as the blessed age when passions are
spent. Toward the same period, the letters to Ernest and the *Souvenirs*
show that his future destiny is the object of his chief concern: will he
be a genius (therefore beyond class categories) or will he take up a
profession? We shall return at leisure to this anguish. It is enough to
indicate here that the *Mémoires* make mention of it *in passing*, almost
negligently, and that this allusion suffices to destroy his double intention, which is, on the one hand, to show his life from the point of
view of an imminent death—in those first pages doubt has consumed
everything; all attempts, all temptations have been reviewed, all illusions have vanished, so there is nothing more to do and nothing more
to hope for—and, on the other, to recount an episode from his youth
as it might appear to a cynical old man. In any event, the young man
is not comfortable in his role of narrator: his will to suppress the future dovetails with his enterprise of distancing, which compels him to
establish himself in real old age in order to recount an episode that
has only just happened. In short, even when he recounts himself,
Gustave remains insincere: he suppresses one of the temporal dimensions and claims to have only a *past* when the future is his real torment. This results in the strange business of reconstituting his real life
from the point of view of a fictive other (the old man he is not), and
consequently gives his memories—even precise ones—the character
of fiction. It is as if the young novelist could present reality only by
unrealizing himself in order to render it at least *formally imaginary*.

We know the negative motivation of this attitude: he wants to flee
from himself and hide; the present monster and the future bourgeois
are equally horrifying to him. But upon closer inspection we shall
find positive reasons as well. We have seen that Flaubert abandons

the *Mémoires* at the end of forty or so pages,[33] and that he rereads it
with distaste three weeks later. He sets to work again, however. In
the course of his rereading he must have discovered precise reasons
for overcoming his "lassitude" and for continuing to write by transforming his initial project. Is it an accident that chapter 9—which from
the point of view of the whole is merely a repetition—is found to be
the first that includes *concrete* memories? In it, Gustave describes the
"château" in the most precise way; he amuses himself showing the
furnishings "of embroidered silk," the park where "a goat grazes,"
the play of light and shadows ("On fine days, rays of sunlight passed
through the branches and gilded the moss here and there"). The "old
mistress" is given to us wholly through the objects she uses: "I can
still see her gold snuffbox full of the best Spanish tobacco, her pug
with the long white fur, and her adorable little foot encased in a
pretty, high-heeled shoe adorned with a black rose." It is striking to
see the first appearance of the theme of footwear, so important in
Gustave's life and work.[34] Thus, it would hardly be a mistake to consider chapter 9 as the hinge that joins Flaubert's first enterprise ("a
roman intime in which skepticism would be pushed to the final limits
of despair") to his second ("Here the *Mémoires* really begin"). In writing it, he found reasons for leaving the work unfinished: he merely
repeats himself, he does not advance; but in rereading the work he
found reasons for taking it up again: to restore things past is what is
"diverting." As he glanced through it, he was struck by a new tone,
by the still awkward will to find words to render things that have disappeared. We have already seen that he is fascinated by the objects of
his perception, that he "enters into them" or they "enter into him."
But until this point these fascinations have scarcely influenced his literary exercises. In chapter 9 of the *Mémoires* they finally appear in the
course of the narrative. Not the fascinations, moreover, but the memories they left him with: "There are insignificant things that struck me
powerfully and that I shall always keep, like the imprint of a branding
iron, be they banal and foolish." With these words, which begin the
chapter, Gustave gives his concrete and material reminiscences—the
singular quality of a noise, a color, a form—access to the literary work.
In this sense, despite the artificial conclusion ("the mistresss is dead,"
etc.) that is supposed to connect this description to the whole, the de-

33. Twenty printed pages in the Charpentier edition.
34. He adds: "How long ago that was! The mistress is dead . . . and the poor shoe
has been thrown into the river."

scription becomes isolated in a kind of gratuitousness. And when he finds it again after his initial recriminations, he takes sufficient pleasure in it to change his project: the irreducible flavor of the past is what he must render palpable. His first goal is not to recount *himself* but to find the words that will restore the immediate.

But let us pause a moment to consider this new direction. Does Gustave want to revive the past by reason of its *reality* or because it has *ceased to be real*? In fact, a memory is ambiguous: one remembers what *has been* and what *no longer is*. In this sense, any evocation of things past is at the intersection of the real and the imaginary. And it suffices to read the *Mémoires* attentively to understand what attracts Gustave. In chapter 15 he writes: "Of all the dreams of the past, memories of former times, and reminiscences of my youth, I have preserved a very small number, with which I amuse myself in hours of boredom. At the evocation of a name all the characters return, with their costumes and their language, to play their role as they played it in my life, and I see them act before me *like a God who amuses himself observing his created worlds.*" [35] The accent is put, as we see, on the creation (or re-creation) that characterizes in part each of our acts of memory. Flaubert avoids manipulating his images too overtly ("they play their role as they played it"), but he is conscious of their fundamental nothingness: not only does the memory exist in the latent state merely in his unique, particular memory, but the evocation takes its being merely from the will of the Demiurge. To remember the past, for Gustave, is to unrealize it. That this unrealizing intention is at the origin of his new project is clearly demonstrated by a curious passage in the *Mémoires*. Gustave has spoken to us at length of his love for Maria, the pangs of jealousy, their separation. He has written, in the same chapter: "If I told you that I have loved other women, I would be lying like a traitor." Yet, after two years, here he is again at Trouville; Maria has not come back to him, he is strolling along the beach alone. It is then that he cries out:

> How could she have seen that I loved her [two years earlier], for I did not love her then, and whatever I told you was a lie; it was now that I loved her, that I desired her; that, alone on the shore, in the woods or the fields, I would create her there, walking beside me, speaking to me, looking at me. When I lay down on the grass . . . I thought of her, and I reconstructed in my heart all the

35. My italics.

412

scenes in which she had acted, spoken. These memories were a passion.

Rarely has a visionary described more profoundly the process of unrealization. Presence irritates those who have chosen the imaginary: the richness of reality overwhelms them, they lose their footing, feel themselves constrained by the power of things and their inflexible course; overtaken by a swarm of details, they withdraw and grow bored. Besides, in Gustave's case, the presence of an undesirable—the husband—awakens the old jealousy, which torments him, reviving the primal scene, and transforms him into Djalioh.[36] But when the present has slipped away, what joy! One is pleased with its poverty and its tractability: *"I would create her,"* says Flaubert. In other words, the past will take its being only from me—since it is a nonbeing evoked—and as this past is myself, I will derive myself only from myself. Through this unrealization, Gustave realizes in the imaginary that uprooting of his class-being, which he seeks to effect through art: he becomes his own creator. With what skill does he manipulate himself and move imperceptibly from the "reconstruction of scenes in which [Maria] has acted, spoken . . ." to hallucinatory invention. Indeed, he continues:

> One day . . . I was walking quickly, I could hear only the sound of my step crushing the grass, I kept my head down and was looking at the ground. This regular movement lulled me almost to sleep, I thought I heard Maria walking near me; she held out her arm to me . . . it was she who was walking in the grass. *I knew very well that it was a hallucination I was animating myself, but I could not prevent myself from smiling and I felt happy.*[37]

In fact, he feels happy not *in spite* of the translucidity of the image—which offers itself as a fiction—but *because* of it. He smiles because he feels he is "animating" the phantasmagoria. Everything is a balance of nerves: he is at once tense and unconstrained. But it is the tension that dominates: the rustling of the grass will serve as an analogue; through this continuous noise another person or, more simply, feet treading the meadow will be evoked. But above all Gustave unrealizes

36. Flaubert, as we have seen, meets Madame Schlésinger during the summer of 1836 or 1837. *Quidquid volueris* is written in October 1837. It is likely that this description of the pangs of jealousy was done *in the heat of it*, that is, at the return to school just after the separation. Which tends to confirm that the meeting took place in 1837.

37. My italics.

himself in Maria: the movement of his legs becomes the movement of the young girl's legs: he does *not see* her since he keeps his head down; he plays her by a kind of doubling and becomes an imaginary woman (here again we find his desire to be female flesh) without ceasing to be himself. Better, she turns her head to see him. The young man uses his passivity—his being-there, if you like—on a whole side of himself as the analogue of a *being-observed* (and this reminds us of that need to be seen which we have previously described). Thus she is outside him—for this *felt* gaze holds him at a distance—and inside him—since she is his walk, the sound of his footsteps. The unreal consistency of the young woman—for whom he does not evoke any physical trait in this instance—issues precisely from that contradiction whose being he endeavors to sustain. At the same time, he affects *somnolence:* he denies any perceptive activity; all the signals his body sends him he elaborates into an image; the sounds of his walking reach him like the false sounds of another's walking. A bitter pleasure: he abandons himself to the void for the joy of maintaining at his side and even in his own flesh an impalpable, invisible presence. But this is just what he wants: not the *persona* that is the irreducible Other, but the *imago* that is other and his own, himself as other and the other in him. And it is at this instant, when he becomes the imaginary creator of the imaginary Maria, that he claims to love her. The deep meaning of this love, its power, its limits, we need not specify here. But it should be noted that it is not platonic love: Gustave *desired* Madame Schlésinger and does not hide it from himself. It would be more fitting to call it a mastubatory scheme. In this case, as we know, the image is the diaphanous meditation between the masturbator and the masturbated. What is certain is that he speaks of love only at the moment when memory is transformed into imagination: at this moment, as I have shown elsewhere, feelings themselves are unrealized. In other words, for Gustave true love can be only an imaginary feeling.[38]

When he decides to recount the Trouville episode, he is still not departing from fiction since he undertakes—against the future, which makes him anxious—to *imagine his past.* Thus, when "the personal impression pierces through the story," it is not so much—as he implies—that his present passions incline him to show his wounds, but

---

38. It is the same, for him, with desire: he will prefer to masturbate with Louise's slippers while evoking the Muse's beautiful body than really to sleep with her. And it is for this same reason *as well* that we must explain the perpetual breaking off of their meetings.

rather that his life already lived fascinates him by its absence. This nonbeing calls first for a reconstruction by mental exercises, then by words. He has lived this life like that of another: by reconstituting it half-true, half-forged, he appropriates it for himself. For him, to recount himself in this first moment is not to know himself but to produce himself and fix himself, an eternal lacuna, in written words. Hence we can conclude that the author of the *Mémoires*, even when telling the truth, hardly ever departs from fabulation. We are now in a better position to note the hybrid character of this work. Flaubert both wants and does not want to talk about himself in it. Originally conceived as an *Erziehungsroman*, these false confessions were to pull him out of his "anomaly" by presenting it as the ultimate result of interior totalization. On this level, the reflexive "I" is already *other* since it appears at the horizon of a fictive experience and represents the unity of generalized subjectivity; yet from another point of view it is the "I" of the author since it accompanies the particular enterprise of showing that his personal unhappiness is shared by everyone and thus of *legitimizing* his anomaly by presenting it as a more lucid consciousness of universal evil. But the result of this generalization seems to him disappointing to the extent that it has led merely to oratorical repetitions which reproduce the same inventory on every page, sometimes in the same terms. And he often falls back into the temptation of presenting his anomaly as the point of departure rather than a point of arrival. But even on this level he remains insincere: first of all, he stays on the surface and conceals his "dreadful depths," his protohistory; then he describes his "thought" as an acid that corrodes the present moment when, as we know, the object of his greatest anxiety is the future. The "I" who speaks is faked, mutilated: although it is that of the author, it remains *other*. In the face of these difficulties, Flaubert feels the need to go deeper, but once again avoids doing so by throwing himself into an autobiographical narrative that contradicts his first project. Scarcely engaged on this terrain, he again feels the need to cross over into the imaginary: the facts are true, but the "I" of the narrator is no longer his; he plays an old man and consequently lies while telling the truth. As we have seen, his truth is a mental exercise aimed at unrealizing the contents of his memory. The "I" of the narrator is unrealized in its turn to the extent that he becomes the imaginary creator of his life. This is a rather particular attempt. Proust, for example, who recounts "a symbolic story of his life" (as Painter says), modified all its details. So the story, being entirely imaginary, defines the narrator himself as a fictional character;

there is thus homogeneity between the invented "I" who recounts himself and the fictional events he reports. As a result, the real ego of the author disengages itself and defines itself on the horizon of a creative reflection on a totally unreal object in which the fiction closes around the character that presents it to the reader as his truth.[39] In Flaubert, on the other hand, the invention concerns the identity of the narrator, and the events, though unrealized, conform to the truth, such that the story refuses to absorb the teller, who remains floating in a kind of limbo, neither outside nor inside. However, by flashes a real "I" appears, that of the present, who confesses, for example, that he is scared of the future—or who insults and "demoralizes" us. But these moments of truth clash with the rest of the narrative precisely because they reveal a fretful and troubled present in the midst of a discourse which by various means tends to pose as a reconstruction of a past. Thus Gustave is sometimes the *madman* (the monster who counterattacks by saying: the world is mad and my anomaly is merely my lucidity), sometimes *Man*, sometimes the *Old Man*, and sometimes the *Adolescent*, but, save in rare moments and inadvertently, never *himself*. The result is the total failure of his enterprise; certainly not in our eyes, in his; he has not done what he wanted, he does not know what he did.

We have shown that Gustave experienced this sense of failure by an examination of his letters from the autumn of 1838: boredom, moroseness, discouragement. But the feeling appears already in the last chapters of the *Mémoires*, as Flaubert returns abruptly to pessimistic generalizations that are not justified by the anecdote just told. He forces the tone in order to show the vanity of the sexual act, of art, of human life. As a result, the "I" gives way to a rhetorical, familiar "you": "Open your eyes, man who is weak and full of pride . . . [And] first of all, why were you born? Is it you who wished it . . ." etc., etc. Who is this man so vividly interpolated? Anyone, Flaubert as well as another, with the slight difference that Flaubert claims to keep his eyes open. But this is sufficient for him to keep his distance from his interlocutor and to fall back, finally, into exterior totalization: again, Satan-Flaubert describes the human condition to a reader who is innocent or insincere.

This passage to panoramic objectivity presupposes that Gustave "places himself in relation to the world" with the intention of "laugh-

---

39. Naturally, the problem is more complex: Proust does not lie in order to conceal himself but in order to speak the truth *more truly*.

ing in the face of the human race." Doesn't this constitute the recognition that he has miscarried in his enterprise? Yet these long tirades do not satisfy him either: first he must conclude and take leave of Maria. We come back to her in chapters 21 and 22. But the change in tone is obvious—so much so that the apostrophe to "man" was probably written beforehand and inserted between two moments of the narrative. Finally, to close the circle, Gustave takes up the interior synthesis: the bells ring, "[his] soul takes flight toward eternity and the infinite and glides in the ocean of doubt at the sound of this voice heralding death." It was on death that he had to end: the totalization of subjective experience reveals the nothingness of the world and the necessity to die. However, he does not yet dare to *give himself death* as he will do in *Novembre:* he evokes it as his destiny, nothing more. After the panoramic "you," the "I" of doubt reappears, whose life is destroyed by a "long thought." These wide and sudden oscillations are evidence of the author's disarray: he has gotten lost along the way.

The dedication to Alfred, written a little later, is even more revealing. Gustave wrote the *Mémoires* so as not to examine himself; he examines himself now because he no longer recognizes his original intentions in his work: "[These pages] enclose an entire soul. Is it mine? Is it that of another?" He hereby signals his deep anxiety. While rereading himself, he falls back into that very *estrangement* he was trying to escape through generalization: did *I* really produce *that* in the heart of "my calm and peaceful" existence? Consequently, new questions pose themselves: do I *believe* in it? And *who am I* to believe in it? The work causes the defeat and itself becomes the problem.

This could, of course, be considered merely a rhetorical interrogation. And the line "I prefer to leave this in the mystery of conjecture; for you, you will not do it" could be seen as providing the answer straight out: others are always unaware, but you, Alfred, you *know* that *I* am speaking about *me.* But this interpretation does not satisfy me. On a certain level of signification it is valid: these ambiguous words politely remind Alfred that Gustave has no secrets from him. But when he writes the dedication, Flaubert has resolved to have only *one* reader, Alfred, to whom "these pages . . . are given." What good is it to speak of "mysterious conjectures" if he immediately adds that the only reader of the manuscript will not make any? Isn't it really the author himself who, looking at his work from the outside, can interpret it only conjecturally and, not daring to decide between hypotheses, leaves his best friend the responsibility of concluding? Let us go further: "you will not make any" is pure courtesy, for in the following line we read: "Only you will believe, perhaps rightly, that the expression is forced and the scene darkened at whim." In other words, the author fears precisely that his only reader might not recognize him in his work. And he is compelled to add: "*remember* that it is a madman who wrote these pages." In short: is it not *you*, Alfred, who will take me *for another* by forgetting that I am mad? But what does "madman" mean here? And isn't madness an escape hatch? Upon reflection on this obscure text it appears that Gustave is certain neither of Alfred nor of himself. He foresees that his friend's indolent skepticism will be astonished by this virulence: "You exaggerate." He is irritated by it all the more as he himself is not sure that he hasn't exaggerated his pessimism.

In fact, as early as the autumn of 1838—just after finishing the *Mémoires*—he writes to Ernest: "I am still the same, more inflated than great, more clownish than jolly." In short, he accuses himself of insincerity. In his eyes, clownishness characterizes his everyday behavior. But the inflation? Flaubert cannot conceive—at this period or at anytime in his life—of any greatness but that of writers. The inflation comes from his forcing and "contradicting the truth."[40]

We shall understand his feeling better if we go back to an undated jotting in a notebook written between late 1838 and late 1839: "I have already written a great deal, and perhaps I would have written well if instead of elevating my sentiments to carry them to the ideal and putting my thoughts on stage I had let them run free in the fields just as they are, fresh, rosy."[41] The two adjectives at the end of the sentence will surely surprise: does Flaubert mean that if he let himself go, he would find some sort of optimism that was his truth? Yes and no. I think he contrasts the *health* of feelings and real thoughts with the contorted meagerness of overextended ideas that are trying too hard to prove something, whatever their contents. The idea of familiarity,

40. These three words are taken from a page of the *Souvenirs* written two and a half years later, which quite certainly allude to his attempts at totalization—in the *Mémoires* and in *Smarh:* "If you begin your book by saying to yourself: it must prove this or that, whether religious, impious, or erotic, you will write a bad book because in composing it you have contradicted the truth, falsified the facts. Ideas flow of themselves by a natural and fatal bent. If with some purpose or other you want to make them take a turn that is not their own, it will all founder. You must let the characters take shape by their consequences, the facts be engendered by themselves." He cites examples: "*Les Martyrs, Gil Blas,* Béranger." But he is really the one who wants to take skepticism to the point of despair. He is the one—as we shall see—who dreams, in *Smarh,* of writing one burning page in order to push human animals into universal rutting, he again who wants to engender in his reader if not impiety at least the belief in nothingness.

41. *Souvenirs*, p. 66.

of the unadorned everyday, could already be found in his project of writing a *roman intime:* "intimism" requires the whisper rather than the shout. And the contradiction results when he assigns excessive goals to this modest genre. Be that as it may, the question of his sincerity is posed. He even comes to wonder if pessimism really expresses his truth; indeed, one year later he writes: "There is a bit of affectation . . . in my doings; I am always playing tragedy or comedy." A sentence that finds an echo as late as *Novembre:* "He was a man who was invested in the inaccurate, the unintelligible, and greatly abused epithets."

Tragedy, comedy: it is not just his works that are at issue; Gustave has long known that he is an actor down to his least gestures and especially when he has an audience. But it is his works—primarily the *Mémoires*—that lead him to wonder if he has not flung himself into a frantic amplification of his feelings. And the question has urgency for him only to the extent that it concerns art, that is, literature: it is of little importance that he clowns in society, but if absolute pessimism is no longer his message, then he has nothing to say. We note that he examines himself in the midst of a depression, and that the fear of exaggerating, by leading him to doubt himself, merely pushes him further into despair. He has so long been accustomed to seeing himself through the eyes of others, grasping himself as other *first*, that he comes to wonder if he is not in despair as other, if the despair of another has not slipped into his soul to haunt him. Indeed, his "thought" is there, irreducible, inexplicable: it inhabits him and devours him, but in order to prove equal to it he must heighten his feelings. Or, if you like, he can feel his thought only by playing it, either through tragic pessimism with its bits of eloquence or through the cynical buffoonery of the Garçon. He is condemned to play the unhappy man and, when the actor in him takes a breath, to return to a mere familial existence, tedious and quiet. On 8 February 1841 he writes in his notebook of *Souvenirs:* "I would have to attach myself more deeply than I do to everything around me, to the family, to the study of the world, *everything from which I turn aside and, I don't know why, that I would like to force myself not to love* [the world is superfluous in this sentence]." [42] The "world" being suppressed, what remains is study *in the family setting;* and it is precisely this setting he feels he needs, and from which an unknown motive turns him aside: he can feel his aversion for the family only by playacting it, by *forcing himself to produce it.*

42. Ibid., p. 100. My italics.

419

Yet the ambivalence is there, clearly observed—denial and need—with the two impulses, the one, very real, toward seclusion in the paternal house, and the other, unreal and yet invincible, toward flight and the malevolent negation of all kith and kin. The adolescent feels this already in 1838. He wonders, fascinated, why he can live with his most intimate tendencies only by means of insincerity and bad acting.

Two letters to Ernest (29 February and 15 April 1839), along with a note from almost the same period, are sufficient indications of his malaise. In the first letter he complains. Ernest falls into the trap and responds by commiserating. Gustave has a surge of pride: make Ernest, his inferior, pity him? Never. And he answers with these curious lines in which he tries to reestablish the truth in its ambiguity:

> You commiserate with me, dear Ernest, and yet should I complain, have I any reason to curse God? On the contrary, when I look around me, in the past, in the present, in my family, my friends, my affections, with few exceptions I should bless him. My circumstances are favorable rather than harmful. And for all that, I am not content; we make endless jeremiads, we create imaginary evils (alas, those are the worst); . . . we ourselves plant the obstacles along our way, and then the days pass, real evils occur, and then we die without having had a single ray of pure sunlight in our soul, a single calm day, a cloudless sky. No. I am happy. And why not? Who is tormenting me? The future may be black. Let us drink before the storm; so what if the tempest breaks us, the sea is calm now.

"Objective happiness" is rarely so powerfully contrasted to the misfortunes that come from our natural disposition. Gustave tries to specify—insincerely, since he must keep Ernest at a respectful distance, but with a positive impulse to be truthful—the inner reality of his torments. Even better, he puts that reality in question and would like to settle the matter without falling into either tragedy or buffoonery: honestly. *I have no reason*, he says, to be so unhappy. And it is true, on the level on which he situates himself. But if this is so, why doesn't he try to act on it and put his phantasms to flight? Ah well, this is what he does. The only affectation is a philosophy of the moment, which doesn't work smoothly. With Ernest, he limits himself to that. But in the notebook he keeps for himself, he notes with profundity that the *Carpe diem* is impossible. "The secret of being happy is to know how to take pleasure at the dining table, in bed, standing up, sitting down, to take pleasure in the nearest ray of sunlight, in the most insignificant landscape, that is, to love everything. In other words, to be happy, you must already be happy."[43]

In other words, to combat imaginary evils, you would have to take pleasure in the moment; and how could this be done since these very evils prevent us from doing it? It is a vicious circle: to denounce the subjective character of our troubles is to devalorize them, not to cure us of them. We are playacting them? So what? What does it matter if we are constrained to act them! Gide said something like: "Actor, so be it, but it is myself I am playing." Thus subjective evils are real because they are imaginary.

From an imaginary adolescent we cannot expect more. But Gustave is not so easily satisfied: the failure of the *Mémoires* filled him with the rage to know himself; a literary rage, but real nonetheless. To know *what he is,* for him, is to discover what he has *to express.* If there is nothing, he will be nothing: a "mute who tries to talk" and can only say words, a "great man manqué." The inquiry he undertakes seems to him of prime importance: in it he seeks his salvation.

That he was aware of it from the outset is not to be doubted. Beginning in the autumn of 1838—a month or two after "completing" the *Mémoires*—he begins to reflect on himself and carefully transcribes his observations in the personal notebook that Madame Franklin Groult will later entitle: *Souvenirs, notes et pensées.* On 26 December 1838 he writes these words to Ernest, which can only relate to his new enterprise: "For as you and Alfred are no longer with me, I analyze myself more, myself and others. I dissect unceasingly; this amuses me, and when at last I have discovered the rottenness in something that was believed to be pure and the gangrene in beautiful things, I throw back my head and laugh." This passage demands a close interpretation because it represents, to him alone, a whole nest of vipers, and we shall return to it. But we should note, to begin with, that it allows us to date Gustave's first attempts at analysis: it was in October 1838 that Ernest left for Paris; Alfred joined him there before 19 November. It may be that their departure prompted Flaubert to practice dissection more than before. But the principal motive is something different: he already knew that he would go no further in totalizing interiorization without first advancing in self-knowledge. But that will not happen without anguish, because he writes in order to escape

43. Ibid., p. 59.

421

from himself or to unrealize himself. Let us ask, therefore, whether he can really know himself and whether he wants to.

The only tool at his disposal is reflexive analysis. The object must be reduced to its elements. But with psychic facts, this reduction is a mental exercise. What he calls dissection is necessarily reduced to passive observation and—when the return of certain sequences seems to justify it—induction. You don't get far with this method. Again, Flaubert pauses along the way: what he discovers in himself he immediately seeks to generalize. For the terror of his "difference" torments him, and no sooner does he discover a particularity than he immediately makes it a trait of human nature. Thus, seeking Gustave, this Oedipus is prepared to encounter in himself no one but man. Nothing could be more telling in this respect than his reflexive relation to what he sometimes calls his vanity and sometimes his pride.

He has long known that he is proud. Garcia is tormented by pride, Mazza takes pride in her sufferings. But at this period it is difficult to establish what he invests of himself quite consciously in his characters and what passes from him to the other without his knowledge. The first mention he knowingly makes of his self-esteem occurs in paragraph 6 of *Agonies,* written between March and April 1838, perhaps even a little earlier. He is sixteen years old, perhaps fifteen:[44]

> Vanity, in my opinion, is the basis of all the actions of men. When I had spoken, acted, done anything in my life, and I analyzed my words or my actions, I always found that old madness lodged in my heart or mind. Many men are like me, few are equally frank. This last reflection may be true, vanity made me write it, the vanity not to seem vain might make me delete it.

It will be noticed that he begins with the universal: he is not afraid to put vanity at the basis of *all* actions. And when he introduces proof, he speaks only of his personal experience. This maxim is based on introspection. We shall see it at work toward the end of the paragraph: "Many men . . . few . . . This last reflection may be true, vanity made me write it." The ink is not dry when he rediscovers, either in the sentence itself or in the movement of his subjectivity, the self-esteem that he denounces. Is this, as he claims, *analysis*? Yes and no: it is true that he takes a reflexive attitude in order to consider either lived experience or the intentional meaning of his own products; it is

44. He writes in the introduction: "It will soon be a year since the author has written its first page." And following: "This work begun two years ago." Is paragraph 6 to be included in the "first page"?

true, as well, that this attitude is immediately and doubly inductive: all my acts . . . all men. There is an a priori intention to consider his singularity merely an example of the concept. But it is enough that he holds to it: the real motives of his action separate themselves out from those he has offered for himself in bad faith. "This reflection may be true." This means: even though it should be true, "vanity made me write it"; by tracing the words, he learns the real meaning of his act. In other words, for this *anticipated* subject, the selection was immediate. There is no methodical effort in it but, rather, a passive proposition issuing from a conditioned reflection that does not seek but knows what it must find. In the example cited, it is obvious to us, as it is to him, that the sentence in question expresses, among other things, his vanity since it aims to classify him from the outset as part of an elite. But what escapes him and seems clear to us is that he tries to accept his "difference" and to disarm it by placing it on the level of reflection. The reflected is the same in everyone; in me, he thinks, it is the reflexive look that is different, more lucid, more frank; in short, he cannot discover pride in himself without adding that it is characteristic of our species.

Similarly, in *Mémoires d'un fou*, when he asks himself—vaguely and inconclusively—"Is it out of vanity again? Ah, is love merely pride too?" it is not *his* penchant for Maria that he claims to "analyze" but Love, that Platonic entity. The premature shift to the universal prevents all conscious examination. On the chapter on pride, he will make little further progress. In his letter of 26 December 1838, in which he claims "to have arrived at the conviction that vanity is the basis of everything," following the "dissections" performed after the departure of Alfred and Ernest, he is merely repeating the core of the reflections from *Agonies*. This time, it is true, he first implicates himself: "It is friendship that deceives you and makes you see a superior greatness in my actions when there is only invincible pride." But the generalization is immediate: "For, since you are no longer with me . . . I analyze myself more, *myself and others* . . . Well, I have therefore come to hold the firm conviction that vanity is at the basis of everything." And immediately he uses a vengeful "you," which in part is generalizing but allows him also to designate Ernest: "Yes, when you give alms . . ." and to deny his own difference more concretely since he shares it, among others, with Chevalier. We must still try to understand why he presents as a completely new discovery a "thought" that has tormented him for at least a year, a thought he already expressed in 1837 in all its clarity. Had Ernest not read

423

Agonies? Perhaps not.⁴⁵ But this is not the question. Several lines at the end of the letter show that what is involved for Gustave himself is a persistently vivid anxiety: "This theory seems cruel to you, and it even disturbs me. First it seems false, but with closer attention, I sense that it is true." So he is still questioning himself on the validity of his analyses. Each time, his conclusions disturb him; each time, he goes beyond, defeats any resistance, and concludes again that pride is fundamental. What he offers here as a new theory is merely a new and entirely provisional decision to support and resume interest in a theory that has been abandoned, or is on the point of being abandoned. And his motive each time is the reappearance of *his* vanity as the original experience beneath the passive gaze of complicit reflection. On the spot, he wants to tear himself away from idiosyncrasy, from the concrete forms of lived experience, and to raise himself to the level of abstractions, to the human race. Occasionally, of course, he begins with the species. In a passage from the *Souvenirs* that is contemporaneous with the letter to Ernest—or that could have been written a few weeks before, in the autumn of 1838—he begins by distinguishing between two kinds of vanity: "public vanity and private vanity, which is called good conscience, human respect, self-esteem, such, it is true, that in every man there are two men, one who acts and one who criticizes. Inner life is the perpetual cajoling of the one who criticizes by the one who acts," etc. But these reflections, after lengthy developments, conclud with their author's abrupt return to the self: "I can speak of pride as a past master." In other words, it is *his* reflexive life that he has just described as the "inner life" of the whole species. The generalizing movement is *defensive*.

We shall gain a clearer perception of this by rereading the letter to Ernest. Unlike La Rochefoucauld, Gustave certainly does not try to reduce the apparent variety of our motivations to a single basic impulse manifesting itself beneath various disguises. Quite to the contrary, he recognizes the existence of feelings not reducible to vanity—adding simply that vanity plays a dominant part in the motives of our actions: "Yes, when you give alms, there is perhaps an impulse of sympathy, the sensation of pity, an abhorrence of ugliness and suffering, even egotism; but, more than all that, you do it so as to be able . . . to regard yourself as more tenderhearted, to have a sense of

---

45. Flaubert thought to show Ernest this writing *in the case of absolute necessity.* "He wrote it," he says, "to show to one man, two at the most." Perhaps he later renounced this intention.

self-esteem, which you prefer to all other kinds of esteem." This dosage of motivations transforms the analyst into a chef giving us a recipe. Curiously, we shall find the recipe again, unchanged, introduced by the same example, in the *Souvenirs*, dated 28 February 1840: "I say that when you have given a penny to a poor man and you then say you are happy, you are an imposter, you are fooling yourself. There is more than three-fourths pride in every good action, one-fourth remaining for interest, for inevitable animal impulse, for the need to fulfill, for real appetite." Comparison of these texts calls for two remarks. First, they both seem to present Flaubert's thesis with the maximum of concessions. The former might be written: "You will tell me, dear Ernest, that there are many other motivations, impulses of sympathy, etc., in us. I agree with you. But of all motives, pride is the strongest." And it can be argued that he presents his idea in this absurd form in order to convince, without alarming him, someone he already regards as a young "bourgeois." Virtue exists, agreed, and other sentiments; but their part in daily options is reduced. Yet does he really concede to Chevalier a point that must ultimately lead to the destruction of the doctrine?[46] We have only to read the note from *Souvenirs*—written, he specifies, for him alone, since it reproduces the recipe (almost like making a pound cake: one-fourth butter, three-fourths pride)—to know that the defensive and concessive attitude comes to him spontaneously. In short, he is afraid of his own theory. Is it so terrible? No; in principle the adolescent's pessimism finds expression in it. On condition that it is extended to the entire species. But analytic regression, if he really practiced it, would risk leading him too far: to affirm and to generalize his pride at one stroke is not something to worry about; man is a botched job, that's all; but if you try to reduce this or that impulse and rediscover pride at the bottom of it, who knows where the regression will stop? Who knows whether

46. It is theoretically possible to reduce by analysis (psychological atomism) all composite states to their elements (desire, pleasure), so why not pride? One might also show, by a dialectic and genetic progression, pride as infrastructure producing the claimed irreducible elements as its emanations (or, conversely, one could strip it of its masks by a regressive "analysis"). But if these methods are logically possible, they exclude Flaubert's dosages a priori. If I have not effected progressive genesis, regressive reduction or atomistic analysis, can I be permitted to affirm that the impulse of sympathy (which figures among the possible motives) is *always* inferior to pride? How can these independent forces be measured? And what is induction based on? If Gustave, moreover, admits qualitative irreducibility, he destroys both atomism and empiricism in the name of an idealist eclecticism which by definition admits *all* dosages, that is, conceives of psychic wholes in which the basic impulse might be provided by any of the components.

that discovered vanity will not reveal itself as a singular product of a particular situation?

This first observation implies a second, which is that our analyst is treading water. The first of the texts cited is from March, the second from December 1838, the third from February 1840. In short, more than two years have elapsed during this period. Yet, with very few exceptions, the second reproduces the first. The same "penny to the poor man," the same electicism of dosage. It will be noted that this abstractly outlined dosage does not even reproduce Gustave's experience. This is allusively revealed to us in the *Souvenirs* (late 1838 or early 1839); he describes reflexivity under the name of "critical" man and shows the reflected tampering with reflection in order to make it complicit. Why stop when he is doing so well? Because there is the risk that "inner life," if he describes it as solitude, may lead him to his own abandonment, to his particularity. In fact, when he writes in the same note, "How many poets . . . alone, hold their heads high, find they have genius in their eyes, on their forehead; how many people . . . smile to see themselves smile—talk while admiring themselves in a mirror . . . Haven't you ever been child enough to seek poses that suit you, enough in love with yourself to kiss your hand . . . ?" nothing but the will to generalize can guarantee him that this experience is not simply that of his singularity: indeed, by definition, everything that is produced here—as the permanent relation between the reflected and the reflexive—can take place only in the absence of any witness. And this description goes further than the author's doctrine: pride becomes a general enterprise, a defensive strategy to replace the esteem of others—which has failed—with the subject's own esteem, which he pretends to hold in the highest regard. The slope is a dangerous one: if he slips down it, he will end by discovering that pride is the solitary reaction of the "Family Idiot," that it is acted more than felt (he talks while admiring himself in the mirror), and that it is on a par with the imposed choice of preferring *oneself* (he kisses his own hand) precisely because he is the "unloved" child. The child who looks at himself in the mirror, who scrutinizes his eyes, his forehead, looking for a sign of genius, who caresses himself and kisses himself onanistically to compensate for feeling forlorn—we already know that this is Gustave and he alone. In other words: generalizations are possible, but if they take place they will be effectuated *by others* (this will later be psychoanalytic experience), who will compare this "inner life" *to others* from the outside; and the essential thing will no longer be pride but the internalization of protohistory. In this case it would be possible to refer to pessimism but at another level and for entirely other reasons. For him alone, and even if what we today call self-analysis were possible for him, Gustave descending into himself would only enclose himself in the singularity he wants to escape. For this reason he repeats himself: this theoretician of pride, who claims to speak "as a past master," barely advances. He admits, in spite of his personal experience and in the abstract, that other impulses are irreducible *in order to maintain* the irreducibility of pride, that generic given, against all temptation to go deeper. He has frozen his knowledge out of the desire to present every introspective discovery as a two-pronged thought leading on the one hand to the particular and on the other to the universal. He barely consents to note his individual difference, saying either that he is prouder than others or that he is more conscious of his pride—which amounts to the same thing, depending on whether we understand this to mean: if my reflexive consciousness of this motive is more developed, it is because this affect is in me more accentuated; or we construe it to mean: by my very lucidity I become The Proud Man, he who discovers that he is obsessed with Pride and connects everything to this irreducible impulse.

He really feels he is breaking loose: his theory always "embarrasses" him. On 21 May 1841 he writes in his notebook: "Ah! my pride, my pride, no one knows you, neither my family nor my friends nor myself. After all, I refer everything back to it and perhaps I am mistaken." He is no longer even certain that this pride, rooted in darkness, is his basic motivation. And isn't self-knowledge by definition a fraud?

> When I began this, I wanted to make it a faithful record of what I thought, felt, and it has not happened once, to such a degree does man lie to himself; you look at yourself in the mirror but your face is reversed; in short, it is impossible to tell the truth when you write. You make contact, you laugh at yourself, you simper, sometimes it happens that contrary thoughts come to you while you are writing the same sentence. You hurry, you cut things off; you hold yourself back, you overrefine and slacken.

In the vision of oneself there is already a play of reflections; and to know oneself is to *play oneself:* introspection should put an end to the drama but actually develops it, and reflexive sincerity is not possible. Doesn't this throw into question the value of all self-knowledge? What the adolescent tells us is that reflection challenges itself, that the

427

experimenter, with his habits, his desires, and his prejudices, becomes part of the reflexive experiment and must a priori falsify it. In fact, the known is an *object:* how, therefore, could one know *oneself* except as the object that one is for others? But the purpose of Flaubert's *Gnôthi seauton* is precisely to tear the self away from others, to deny the objectivity with which they prematurely affected him, and to play the part of knowing and known *subject*—which is, strictly speaking, impossible. The remarks we have just cited aim at demonstrating once again the impossibility of all reflexive knowledge. Flaubert's disgust is so great at this period that he incidentally comes to challenge the analytic method: "The sciences proceed by analysis—they believe that this constitutes their glory when it is their shame. Nature is a synthesis, and in order to study it you cut, you separate, you dissect, and when you want to make a whole of all these parts, the whole is artificial, you make the synthesis after having deflowered it, the links no longer exist: yours are imaginary and I daresay hypothetical." Such passages, it must be said, are rare in Flaubert's work. In this one, which deliberately attacks the paterfamilias and contains *Bouvard et Pécuchet* in embryo, there is undoubtedly an implicit opposition between science and Art, which alone can directly render the living synthesis, the connection between the microcosm and the macrocosm. More striking still is the secret disavowal of the psychology of analysis. An *Erlebnis* is a whole that is not reduced to the sum of its elements. Therefore the work that Gustave claims to do is merely a delusion. His reflection allows him to catch a glimpse of slippery syntheses that escape him when he tries to grasp them, that present themselves and disintegrate when he looks at them, but that seem to him the truth of lived experience. His critique of analysis ends with an incomplete sentence: "The science of the connections between things, the science of the passage from cause to effect, the science of impulse, of embryology, of articulation . . ." The meaning is clear: this discipline is yet to be created; it alone, however, would deserve the name of science, for it would allow us to understand the birth and development of its object. Applied to self-knowledge, this requirement becomes specific: we need a genetic psychology that retraces the dialectical progression of a psychic whole and describes its articulations for us.

He understands so well at this period that knowledge requires an object to know and that the systematic reduction of a whole to its unvarying elements falsifies concrete reality—in short, he is so conscious of the defects of his method and of his position—that he tries twice over to know himself *as other.* He will be other in relation to himself to the extent that time will make his thought of the day before yesterday the object of today's thought. In January 1841, on the advice of Doctor Cloquet, he tries "to put in writing and in the form of aphorisms all my ideas." The aim is to "seal up the paper and open it in fifteen years." What tempts him is the doctor's remark, "You will find another man." The slippage, the changes occurring in that gap of years, will allow him, after he has passed the age of thirty, to conjure up the young man he once was. He will see him as a strange reality, which will reveal itself to him in all its complexity. In this form, however, the attempt is desperate: he himself, today, at nineteen years old, is the one he wants to know; must he wait fifteen years to resolve what he is? He puts himself to the task with some haste, and then we see his zeal abate, and in the end the notebooks of the *Pensées intimes* are abandoned. What will remain of this attempt is a certain concern with observing himself from the outside, looking at himself in the third person as the object of an inquiry, traces of which we will find in *Novembre* with the doubling "I"/"He." But he realizes immediately that he is falsifying all the facts and that the "He" is not really an object (although he had forged a fictive witness—who is still himself). And from the first *Education sentimentale,* he will seek refuge in fictional invention. Jules, once again, *is Gustave to the extent that he is not Gustave.*

In short, Gustave is driven to know himself, but the analytic method deserts him in his enterprise, and the premature passage to the universal is a veritable swindle. As counterpart to an impossible *self-knowledge,* he possesses an exceptional *understanding* of his inner impulses. We need hardly emphasize the abyss that separates the two. Understanding is a silent adjunct to lived experience, a familiarity of the subjective enterprise with itself, a way of putting components and moments in perspective but without explanation; it is an obscure grasp of the meaning of a process beyond its significations. In other words, it is itself lived experience, and I shall call it *prereflexive* (and not unreflected) because it appears as an undistanced redoubling of internalization. Intermediary between nonthetic consciousness and reflexive thematization, it is the dawning of a reflection, but when it surges up with its verbal tools it frequently falsifies what is "understood": other forces come into play (in Flaubert, for example, the denial of the singular), which will divert it or compel it to replace meaning with a network of significations, depths glimpsed through verbal and superficial generalities.

Flaubert at sixteen is perfectly conscious of this difference. In chapter 13 of the *Mémoires* he writes: "How to render in words those things for which there is no language, those impressions of the heart, those mysteries of the soul unknown to the soul itself?"[47] But he does much more than mention it in passing. Between two eloquent flourishes or two fake analyses, strange reflections surge up in his works, which proceed from *understanding* but which, even in full daylight, remain obscure—suggestive allusions to an elusive meaning. I offer as examples only the two dreams he reports in chapter 4 of the *Mémoires*. If the narrative of the two dreams were replaced by "I had terrifying nightmares," the end of chapter 3 would be perfectly joined to chapter 5: "At night, I listened for a long time to the wind blowing heavily . . . I would fall asleep . . . half in dreams, half in tears, and I had terrifying nightmares. This is how I was," etc. At that period the dream as such had no right of entry into literature unless it furthered the complications of plot and integrated itself in the form, for example, of premonitory visions.[48] What, then, compelled Gustave to jot down two obviously selected nightmares without the least concern for breaking the thread of the narrative? No doubt they are related in their somber mood to the sadness of life at the *collège*, to the general pessimism of the *Mémoires*. But this should not have been sufficient because—according to the literary a prioris of the period—they do nothing to advance the story. There is no doubt that the young author must have sensed their secret importance. The one concerns his relations with his mother, the other his relations with his father: this last is incontestably—the comment has often been made—the first

47. We should note that Flaubert's thought, as often happens to him at this time, immediately goes astray. Indeed, he adds: "How could I tell you everything I've felt, everything I've thought, all the things I enjoyed that evening? . . . Could I ever tell you all the melodies of its voice," etc. There are two themes here: the first is the "mysteries of the soul unknown to itself," the second, quite different, is the inadequacy of words when it is matter of rendering sensation or feeling, even when they are the object of a clear reflexive consciousness.

48. Or unless it is offered, as in the German Romantics and in *Louis Lambert*, as a sign of our double nature. Indeed, Balzac writes: "How is it that men have reflected so little until now on the accidents of sleep which charge man with a double life . . . Shouldn't there be a double science in this phenomenon? . . . It indicates at least the frequent disharmony between our two natures." But we must not look for some presentiment of the Freudian *Interpretation of Dreams* in this text, since Balzac adds: "I have thus found at last a testimony to the superiority that distinguishes our latent senses from our apparent senses." The dream, for Louis Lambert, is really a means of access to the supernatural. To the contrary, the nightmares described by Flaubert are bitterly realistic and explicitly given as the effects of his nervous troubles and his anguish.

dream of castration[49] intentionally told in French literature. It is as if Gustave, neither able nor willing to speak about his family—he does not say a word about them when he tells of his Trouville loves, although all the Flauberts were present—had charged two dreams with expressing his relations with the couple who had engendered him in a form at once unknowable and understandable.

Let us be clear: first of all, the unknowable becomes the object of knowledge when one is in possession of a method of interpretation; *for us* twentieth-century readers, Flaubert's dreams are decipherable. But he leaves no doubt that the unknowable—always provisional—seemed to him definitive. On the other hand, we must not imagine Flaubert choosing with lucid determination to offer us information without the code that would permit us to decode it. He does not know this code himself. The oneiric intention is extended in the author by a vague feeling of the autobiographical *importance* of the two nightmares. We do not know what struck him: perhaps the dreams recurred frequently and he was moved by their repetition. Perhaps one occasion sufficed to give him a glimpse of the "abysses." What matters is the appropriateness of a spontaneous but unintellectual appreciation; the evaluation is not transparent to itself and undoubtedly presents itself as a literary choice or, more probably, as a suffered necessity—he *must* write *this*. Later, when Gustave continually repeats to us that one does not write what one wants, he is alluding to the category of options that are lived as compulsions for not having been recognized as choices. A half-century before the *Interpretation of Dreams*, when psychologists still saw dream life as simply a revival of the impressions of one's waking hours distorted by the organic life of the sleeper, Flaubert demonstrates that he somehow grasped the function of dream life as the route of access to himself by coupling two dreams (the father, the mother) together. Immediately, however, the diver makes a violent effort to rise to the surface again: *Novembre* and the correspondence inform us that his nights, following his years as a boarder and until the "attack," remain highly disturbed, but while the young man signals his nocturnal difficulties, he no longer describes them to us; the oyster has closed up.

The letters and the *Souvenirs*, however, are full of brief indications that Gustave lived his "estrangement" from himself as an under-

---

49. I add that the word "castration" is for me merely the expression of facts *in a certain discourse*.

standing that could not and would not be transformed into intellection. If these dreams astound him, it is because he sees them as the echo of *waking* inclinations and thoughts that are equally indecipherable. We know that he will write to Louise that his heart is exhausted by the "visitation of unhealthy things," and that he will voluntarily compare himself to a muddy pond that must not be disturbed for fear that stinking slime will rise to the surface. He therefore has a perception of the psychology of the depths. But well before, in 1841, he writes in the *Souvenirs:*

> If I have delicious desires for love, I have ardent ones, bloody ones, horrible ones. The most virtuous man has in his heart the glimmers of dreadful things. There are thoughts or actions that one admits to no one, not even to one's partner, not even to one's friend, that one does not say aloud to oneself. Have you sometimes blushed at secret, base impulses that rose in you and then abated, leaving you utterly astonished, utterly surprised to have had them?[50]

These secret impulses are his sadism and his masochism; they are his jealous rages, his black relations with the family. We are in the realm of understanding: he *lives* his anomaly, it astonishes him but he adheres to it; yet the moment he is about to open himself and see in depth the father's curse, he snaps shut. He escapes from understanding, as from knowledge, through generalization: *"The most virtuous man* . . . one admits to no one . . . Have *you* sometimes . . . ?"* Be that as it may, these thoughts are "glimmers": in other words, they are not only lived for themselves, they vaguely enlighten the person with regard to himself.

Let us summarize. Gustave has lived uncomfortably with his idiosyncrasy; for a long time an intimate participation with himself has allowed him to understand himself, to adhere to the impulses of his life and even, to a certain degree, to direct them. The shift to reflection, facilitated by Alfred's influence, leads him to schematize and to generalize certain determinations of lived experience: he will escape the bourgeois curse if his somber moods present themselves to him as the correct and unsophisticated evaluation of the human condition. The young author's primary intention, when he writes *Mémoires d'un fou,* is not to advance in self-knowledge but to realize the death of the soul in general by an interior totalization. The difficulties of the work and finally its total failure make it necessary for him to use re-

50. *Souvenirs,* p. 108.

flection in order to know himself. But the nature of his project—to escape the *self* as anomaly—his will to generalize, and the inadequacy of his tools lead him to challenge any possibility of introspactive knowledge. Therefore he will be ignorant of himself. But at the same time, his deepening understanding infuses him with the feeling that in spite of everything there is *someone* in him who must be known. He glimpses this *someone* in flashes but takes fright in the face of what he divines; the flashes of understanding cannot—in the absence of a method or a witness—be converted to intellection. Gustave can *experience himself* but not construct a *model of lived experience*. Moreover, he is fascinated by the "himself" that haunts him, but he dreads it and refuses to *admit himself to himself*. He will therefore live in increased discomfort: never is he more present to his subjective life than at the moment when self-knowledge seems impossible to him. The "glimmers" disturb him, reveal everything to him, and at the same time dazzle him: he sees himself unceasingly and sees nothing at all. The discomfort arises here from the fact that understanding permamently devalorizes knowledge, even while demanding it in a way. From the moment he ceases to think of it, the monster he does not want to be invades him, and when he finally dares to look at it, the filthy beast has disappeared. We might say that the censoring apparatus, on its usual level, functions poorly, and that repression is accomplished even on the level of reflection. He will explain himself on the matter sometime later in a letter to his sister that seems to be a conclusion to this long adventure. It is 1845; Caroline has married Hamard. They return from their honeymoon and remain in Paris "to find lodgings and furnishings." Flaubert is surprised that he isn't sad and recognizes that he does not know how to anticipate himself. In order not to be jealous, he says hypocritically, "I must love this good Emile." Nothing could be more false and he knows it: he detests and mistrusts his brother-in-law, of whom he wrote in 1840: "He is abysmally stupid." [51]

He gives us the truth unwittingly and in spite of himself—as he often does—with a simple turn of phrase: "If you love me it is only right, for I have loved you." In other words, he perceives or thinks he perceives that he no longer loves Caroline—rancor has stifled or masked love—and he is dumbfounded by it. He concludes:

> I am a strange character, as Chéruel used to say; I thought to know myself for a time, but by dint of analyzing myself, I no longer know

51. Ibid., p. 63.

at all what I am; also I have lost the silly pretense of wanting to grope about in that obscure chamber of the heart that is lit from time to time by a brief flash that reveals everything, it is true, but in return blinds you for a long time. You tell yourself: I have seen this or that, oh yes, I shall certainly find my way, and you set off and run up against all the corners, you lacerate yourself on all the angles. If I know where this analogy came from, I'll be damned. It has been a very long time since I have written anything, and from time to time I need to exercise a little style.[52]

This text is of capital importance—first of all because it retraces the moments of this evolution. Gustave has analyzed himself *too much*; he has lost the silly pretense of constructing self-knowledge on the silent flashes of understanding. Now he no longer knows himself, does not know what he is, and his reactions always surprise him. The moment he "believed he knew himself" corresponds to the first periods of re-flection. At that time—1837–38—he amassed several "introspective" discoveries; he caught himself in the act, his hand in the pot, in his reactions of exasperated pride. He then considers applying the ana-lytic method: it is a failure. Indeed, his purpose is tarnished with mor-alistic thinking, trying to separate the wheat from the chaff. In this sense, analysis is the movement of disillusionment: I believed I was good (when I was a child), I am not; which can also be expressed—in the light of his resentment—in these terms: I *was* good, they made me mean. But analysis leads him astray to the extent that it must by defi-nition reduce a particular whole to its universal elements. The pre-suppositions of the method serve his major aim only too well, which is to universalize himself through reflexive knowledge. Thus what he describes is his anxious quest in the years 1838–42. What he means here by the *abuse* of analysis is really the wrong use made of it. And reading between the lines we discover that he means its *use pure and simple:* psychological atomism falsifies the understanding of self by the universalizing will to reduce irreducibility to invariable elements whose combination alone varies. This analysis fascinates him (it is the father's gaze), horrifies him (dissection), serves him only too well (justification), and finally produces no result. Must it therefore be re-nounced? The word "too" shows here all the ambiguity of Flaubert's thought. In truth, he cannot condemn analysis entirely since he sees in it the scientific method. Yet the analytic knowledge he claims to possess hides his real *existence* from him; he is aware of it: those ab-

52. *Correspondance,* Supplement, 1:49.

stractions remaining in the bottom of the test tube have nothing in common with the syncretism of lived experience. Is he going to condemn analysis? No. At the last moment he recoils and prefers to condemn the abuse of it. This is slipping from one idea to another and essentially condemning—as does conventional wisdom—the use of reflection: I have too much observed myself living; I should have lived spontaneously. But he knows that this spontaneous life, unreflected or prereflected, which envelops his own understanding, does not by itself offer the tools that would permit knowledge of it. Therefore, rather than refute analysis as a psychological method, he prefers to declare that self-knowledge is *impossible* because understanding is not reducible to knowledge. But obviously this irreducibility makes the analytic method (in the eighteenth-century sense of the term) perfectly inapplicable.

What is striking in this letter, despite the emphasis—quite commendable—on style, is Flaubert's extraordinary consciousness of self-understanding. Of course, it is primarily intuition as opposed to the discursive, the sudden horrified pleasure in oneself as opposed to methodical research. Where does this perception of the whole person come from? No one can tell us. I suppose that it appears in certain states of *estrangement* in which Flaubert is surprised by his behavior: he tears himself open from top to bottom and sees himself. In general, we lack the facts to support this conjecture: Gustave gives us his experiences allusively; he speaks of thoughts that he is ashamed of, that he would not confide even to Alfred, "not even to yourself." But he hides their contents from us. Two passages of the *Souvenirs*, however, give us a hint as to what might occasion these revelatory flashes.

Here is the first. Flaubert is eighteen years old. Hamard, whose brother is dying, comes "to announce this dying to him": "He squeezed my hand affectionately, and as for me, I let him squeeze it; I left him laughing idiotically, the way I would have smiled in a salon. I didn't like it at all; that man humiliated me. It was because he was full of a feeling and I was empty of it—I saw him again yesterday—yet he is abysmally stupid, but I remember how much I loathed myself and thought myself detestable at that moment." And here is the other: "I am jealous of the life of great artists; the joy of money, the joy of art, the joy of opulence, are theirs . . . ," which is completed by this remark: "[If I wrote] a book, it would be on the turpitude of great men— I am glad that great men should have had any."

In both cases, Flaubert astonishes himself. His jealousy of great men makes him ashamed: he catches himself maliciously seeking out

435

their pettiness because he has convinced himself that he is a "great man manqué." But what particularly astounds him is that he should go so far as to envy the great sadness of an imbecile. Obviously he does not reproach himself for not suffering as much as his friend, under the circumstances; no, but he compares this overwhelming unhappiness to his own "emptiness," he senses his coldness and that in a similar case that he would be incapable of a sadness as dense, as profound. He loathes himself: he goes well beyond this particular behavior and takes it for the expression of his inner reality, of his concrete relations with the various members of his family. Undoubtedly it is so: the fact that he takes the trouble to note this particular and *dated* reaction, something so rare for him, is enough to show the importance he attaches to it. I would even say that this reaction is the only one—among many others, perhaps more important but, as he will say later, playing on the word, *unsayable*—that he had dared to put down in writing, and that it stands, in his mind, for all those he had to keep silent about, for fear of being read.

But did the sudden anguish that no doubt followed teach him something? No. And it is here that Gustave—in the letter to Caroline—shows his penetration: this brief flash "reveals everything, it is true, but in return blinds you for a long time." First of all, it will be noted that this inner truth *invades* Gustave. Intuition is never expected and cannot be reproduced; again we encounter the young man's underlying passivity—these are visitations. He thus underlines the syncretic indivisibility of this totalizing view. But there is more: it is dazzling. Meaning that this view *blinds* understanding. It is not simply irreducible; understanding and knowledge are not only incommensurate in principle, but the *dazzlement* demonstrates that understanding is the *denial of self-knowledge*. Restraints and inhibitions are immediately set in motion—they may even be said to be part of it—which makes understanding indecipherable: everything reveals and conceals itself at the same time. The passive activity of the young man limits itself to denying what is given to him. All the same, when the light is extinguished, it seems to Flaubert that he can profit from the experience. The work he undertakes, against himself, in anguish and in disgust, with the insincere but profound intention of knowing *what he is all about*, curiously resembles self-analysis (in the sense in which present-day analysts use the term). It is not a matter of dissection, this time, but of progressive reconstruction: an attempt to put the disappeared whole into perspective, a desire to discover its articulations and fix them through discourse. In this dark night, you think you are going forward, you try to remember a road that has never existed and that would have to be invented. You try to guide yourself, as by the stars, by visual impressions that the lightning flash has left in the memory, but which vanish when you use them as landmarks. You knock yourself out, batter yourself: you find within you resistances and indefinable sorrows, *unnamable* asperities, shames whose object cannot be identified. This remarkable text seems to confirm in advance the Freudian cautions against self-analysis. It rejects at once psychological atomism with its dissections and the possibility of retrieving the articulations of that subjective totality which occasionally offers itself, suddenly, in fear and trembling. It is all the more striking that Flaubert, in tracing these lines—as in the most revelatory passages in his correspondence—has only a very confused consciousness of their importance. He is astonished after the fact at having written them, and all at once, by a half-intentional error, explains them by his desire "to exercise a little style." Thus everything is obscured, including the impression of being obscure to himself. Only the conclusion is not obscure: *one must give up the idea of knowing oneself.*

Yet we should not take literally the historical sketch that Gustave has penned for Caroline, which begins with the abuse of analysis only to end in resignation. In general, the direction is correct: around the age of sixteen he tries to know himself; at twenty-four he knows that he will never know himself. But in fact it is all there at the same time, in every moment of the process: knowledge and its negation, analysis and understanding: only the *emphasis* varies. He both wants and does not want to reveal himself to himself. Rather, he is led to want it on the basis of an immutable denial. The acknowledged insincerity of the *Mémoires* prompts him to open a new notebook and to attempt to write down his introspective observations. But he has no sooner turned the first page than he seems to give up. Indeed, after a vengeful tirade against men ("I expect nothing good on [their] part"), he writes: "I have within me all contradictions, all absurdities, all stupidities." He adds, revealing his fears and proving that he does not yet consider himself finished, hence determined: "I do not even rely on myself, I may become a vile creature, mean and cowardly, how do I know?" Only to take himself in hand again immediately with the reassurance, "I believe, however, that I would be more virtuous than others because I have more pride." [53] And this bent toward agnosticism

53. *Souvenirs*, p. 46.

will express itself eight years later *in the same terms* when he tells the Muse: "I am a poor man, very simple and very easy and *very human,* 'all meandering and various,' made of bits and pieces, *full of contradictions and absurdities.* If you understand nothing about me, I do not understand much more myself."[54]

Meanwhile, how does he live this perpetual seesaw from 1838 to 1842? In discomfort. He passively *suffers* his pessimism and at the same time continually finds himself acting it out—which will later lead him to this confession: "My basic nature, whatever anyone says, is that of a mountebank." This perpetual exaggeration disconcerts and irritates him: hence the "deplorable mania for analysis," that morose tendency constantly to spy on himself in order to determine the respective shares of rigamarole and sincerity. But what *does he know* about himself? Nothing, except that he is dangerous and in danger. In vain does he want to flee from himself and look down at himself from above: he is at once the pond's calm surface and its muddy bottom; the least wrinkle on this smooth water has its source in the unseen movements of the slime and conversely perpetuates those deep disturbances. His understanding of himself constantly whispers to him that he is heading toward a great unhappiness, that he is running toward it and in some way seeking it out. What can he do? Turn the headlights on this destination that terrifies him? He would find no one there any more. Forget that "horrible worker"? But this is letting him take over: God knows what suicide he is preparing. Gustave has the uncomfortable feeling that he has fallen prey to someone unknown who is leading him to his doom. Someone unknown who is both closer and more distant than a twin brother, who wants the worst, who has already killed his soul by projecting an absurd "thought" into it, a pessimistic truth that devours him and exhausts him in order to justify itself. Gustave, prey to himself, is all the more desperate as he *does not like himself.* The *Souvenirs* are full of bitterness and grinding complaints against himself: "[Despite] an immense pride, I am increasingly in doubt. If you knew what anguish it is! If you knew my vanity. What a savage vulture, eating out my heart—how lonely I am, isolated, mistrustful, base, jealous, egotistical, fierce." We must take

---

54. *Correspondance* 1:405, 23 Novembre 1846. We note the flagrant contrast of this passage with others of the same period; with this one, for example (9 August 1846, *Correspondance* 1:231): "I had seen things and myself too clearly . . . I had understood everything in me, separated it, classified it [before seeing you—therefore before August 1846]." Flaubert never entirely makes up his mind either to know himself or not to know himself.

his pessimism literally: miserable and mean, he is ashamed of his misery and repelled by his meanness; cynicism, which he deplores and of which he does not want to know the causes, has taken hold in him, and he falls into a stupor when he glimpses the origin of that abstract, desperate repetition, not the objective situation or everyday experience but the secret intention of an invisible enemy who is none other than himself. On the surface, he is disgusted with himself; deep down, he dreads himself.

But let us remind ourselves that the terror of this haunted boy, the incessant battle in him between the determinations of his ipseity—class-being, the ego of basic intention, the alter ego that others denounce, the quasi-object of introspection, and the reflexive subject of knowledge—is not separable in 1838 from his literary failure. At the beginning of that autumn, he abandons—provisionally—interior totalization through the work of art and at the same time tries (in boredom and veiled refusal, in short in bad faith) to jot down in a notebook, without preparation, without style, therefore—he believes—without dramatization, the results of his introspective analysis. In literary terms, the result is that the "Artist" loses confidence in himself: to write, he must be sincere; to dissipate the spontaneous insincerity of the mountebank, he must know himself; yet self-knowledge is revealed to him as an impossibility in theory because he does not want it in reality. So he floats, cut off from his roots. But at the same time he gets ready to "bounce back." His reveries, the plans he outlines, the scenes he imagines, all lead him to *Smarh:* in other words, he returns, more decisively than ever, to exterior totalization.

Return to the Infinite

After the failure of the *Mémoires.* Gustave spends a long time dreaming. As usual, he blindly inverts particular scenes, becomes fixed on certain images, which he subsequently varies at whim; and all at once these disconnected efforts lead him to discover the whole. Boredom then gives way to sudden enthusiasm. He writes to Ernest, 26 December 1938: "Fifteen days ago I was in the best state in the world." [55] Fifteen days ago—at the moment of *conception:* at the beginning of the month there was this brief lightning flash; he was in doubt, and then, all at once, the "Mystery" organized itself. Never has he had such am-

---

55. *Correspondance* 1:37. The context indicates—we shall return to it—that he has since fallen back into stagnation because of the difficulties of *execution.*

bition: he wants to write "something extraordinary, gigantic, absurd, unintelligible to me and to others"; this will be a "mad work" in which "[his] mind [will be] extended to its full range" and which will be accomplished "in the highest regions of heaven." The afterword, which he adds in 1840, informs us that he "took himself for a little Goethe." In short, there is every indication that he wants to attempt a great coup. Let us not treat these aspirations lightly. Since the young man became conscious of the "thought" that devours him, since he took as his goal the communication of this thought through his writings, he has gone from failure to failure. He doubts his genius: nothing will free him from his disgust but a startling act of retaliation that will allow him to consider his previous works as *studies*—unsatisfying but *preliminary* efforts for a work that has finally "come together." During the autumn of 1838 he was vexed, embittered; his "immense pride" suffered. But this same pride, conscious of itself, is now going to save him. To understand this reversal, we must illuminate the cause by its effect: we shall anticipate and follow the developments of this mental exercise in the following years—we shall see him become more conscious, systematic. We shall then be entitled to come back to the Mystery of 1839 and to shed light on its author's design, to clarify the connection between pride and exterior totalization.

On 23 May 1852 he writes to the Muse: "One saves oneself from everything with pride. One must learn a lesson from every misfortune and *bounce back after falls*." He has indeed just applied the technique of bouncing back. On 20–21 March 1852 having confided the manuscript of *La Bretagne* Flaubert asks her to give it to Theophile Gautier to read: "As for *La Bretagne*, I would not be miffed if Gautier read it now. But if you are entirely involved in your comedy, stay with it, it is more important . . . In any case, just send *La Bretagne* to Gautier when you have read it, and let me know. I shall send you a little note to enclose in the package." He has been back in Paris for several days, and this is his first mention of Gautier, so we are not certain that Louise did not *first* suggest to him that she should play the role of intermediary. What is certain, in any case, is that he has taken the offer seriously: he admires Gautier and is burning to submit his work to him. The desire is only normal in a young man who has not published anything. But Louise, who in the meantime has become acquainted with the manuscript, flatly refuses to send it to "Theo." On 3 April Flaubert *thanks* her for it; that day, however, he naively acknowledges that he is "in a prodigiously bad humor . . . enraged, without knowing at what." Of course, Louise's judgment, which is that "jokes and vulgarities abound" in *La Bretagne*, has nothing to do with it. He is pleased to tell her, on the contrary: "What you have noticed in *La Bretagne* is also what I like best." And suddenly:

> May I hug you and kiss you on both cheeks and on your breast for something that escaped you and has deeply flattered me. You do not think *La Bretagne* exceptional enough to be shown to Gautier, and you would like his first impression of me to be a violent one. It is better to abstain. You recall me to my pride. Thank you. I have certainly played hard to get, with old Gautier. Here he has been asking me for a long time to show him something, and I keep promising. It is astonishing how modest I am in that respect . . . To wish to please is to stoop. From the moment one publishes, one descends from one's work. The thought of remaining all my life totally unknown does not sadden me in the least . . . It is a shame that I should require an extra large tomb: I would have [my manuscripts] buried with me, like a savage with his horse.

What a marvelous reversal! It is Gautier who begs and Flaubert who refuses, playing hard to get. And there he goes, meditating on his perhaps overly reserved nature: "It is astonishing how modest I am in that respect." The first impulse was an act of naive faith in his work; he wanted to show it to Gautier so as to impress him. Louise's criticism and her refusal are the fall. The bounce back immediately follows: Gustave internalizes the refusal and presents it as his own decision. Denying his legitimate desire to be read, he takes it for an absurd failing. And since, until now, he has shown his writings only to his close friends, he links this past conduct to Louise's present attitude; it is *his* haughty reserve that is expressed by the Muse's pen: "You recall me to my pride!" That is, to his profound truth. He has taken off now, he glides above Gautier, "old" Gautier, reproaching himself for being barely civil to him. Above Louise, too, to whom he explains the motives of the implacable No she has given *on his command* to Theo's beseechings: "To want to please is to stoop." But this is not yet sufficient. With renewed effort, Gustave gains height; his negation is universalized; now it is from the human race that he will hide his writings: "From the moment one publishes, one descends from one's work." This passage to the absolute permits him to judge *La Bretagne* harshly and to condemn the miserable failing of his constituted self. Seen from above, Flaubert's empirical ego and those of Louise and Gautier become confused with one another and disappear into space. The real subject is above them, has escaped from them, and has only a negative connection with the human race. All that re-

441

mains is to give a subjective value to the work whose objective value has just been challenged. Gustave takes this up in the next paragraph: "These poor pages have indeed helped me to cross the long plain . . . With them I have passed through storms, crying alone into the wind and walking dry-footed through swamps in which ordinary travelers remain mired to their chins." The trick is played: moral greatness is substituted for literary talent: for better or worse, *La Bretagne* is a talisman that allowed Gustave to avoid ambushes and to continue on his way, without stooping, as a solitary pilgrim.[56] Let us note that "these poor pages" were written between September and December 1847. First a misunderstanding with Louise and then the trip to the Orient prevented Gustave from showing them to the Muse. Three months, four at most: and should we not say that this slight work carried him across plains and tides as a steed would have done? There too, Flaubert amplifies and recapitulates: he moves from *La Bretagne* to his entire oeuvre thanks to the simple metaphor of the savage who has himself buried with his horse. The horse is the totality of his manuscripts. Does Gustave perceive that by this comparison he is making art a means of getting through life? Certainly, but this means becomes sacred to the extent that it has protected Flaubert from errors and vices; and above all the young author confers an *ethical* value on his works to the same extent that others argue their aesthetic value: poor pages, so be it; but I owe them my aristocratic dignity.

How, after this example, shall we define the technique of bouncing back? Let us note, first of all, that it is employed after "falls." But the "falls" are wounds of pride—and we can be sure that Flaubert roared with rage when he received Louise's letter. In short, one cures the wounds of passive pride by overdoing active pride. In the first moment, the bouncing back appears to be an intentional shift from the unreflected to the reflexive life: humiliated; Gustave withdraws to a high place and becomes purely a witness to his humiliation. He will use reflexive scissiparity to double himself: abandoning his self-object, as passive victim, to the hands of his tormentors, he makes himself the contemplative subject and watches with indifference as

56. The "bouncing back" will calm his rage but not his fits of rancor. In the same letter and in the one following, Louise will pay: she had sent him a comedy, which he tears to pieces. As for Gautier, he loses nothing by waiting. On 24 April of the same year, Flaubert writes to Louise: "Good old Gautier, he was yet a man born and made to be an exquisite artist. But journalism, the common course, poverty (no, let us not curse the milk of the strong), the prostitution of mind rather, for it is that, have often lowered him to the level of his contemporaries."

the inner object sinks down at his feet. Of course he is deceiving himself; the subject of reflection participates, from the time of its appearance, in the intentions of the reflected from which it is born; the moment we wish to see suffering and shame in ourselves, they are *already* in the reflexive consciousness, which grasps them simultaneously as a quasi-object, a provisional unity of lived experience. Be that as it may, the shift to reflection is usually motivated by the intention to break with the self, to keep one's distance from affects or inclinations that one denies. Gustave, who aims to break solidarity with the self by perching, a steely witness, above his life, has the same goal as those who, for example, believe in escaping guilt by acknowledging that they are guilty.

But the operation can only succeed for a moment if Gustave doubles it by another operation, which allows him to diminish the executioners while diminishing the victim; this earlier procedure is already familiar to us: as a very young boy on the benches of the *collège*, Gustave would lose himself in the infinite in order to escape the derision of his teachers and classmates. After 1836, he understood that recourse to the negative infinite is a tactic. By taking a superior point of view on the species of which he is part, he tears from the empirical Self—the unity of lived experience—the superhuman subject it is reputed to contain; it is with this subject that the young man then identifies. In other words, he assimilates simple *reflection* and vertical *ascension*, conferring on the latter a semblance of reality by what I shahl call the practices of *de-situating*. Without denying his roots or his facticity, he tries to challenge their importance and escape all conditioning by seizing on reflexive consciousness as the analogue of an imaginary "panoramic consciousness."

To de-situate himself, he must break the chains of space and time. First of all, place: he will minimize *being-there* until he makes it a point of negligible insertion, the child's finger to which is attached the long string that holds the red balloon. A captive balloon but one that glides, buffeted in every direction by the winds of heaven. To obtain this relative deconditioning, Flaubert makes use of two complementary procedures, which we have studied above: the drama of Great Desire, and the substitution of the imaginary for the real. Wherever he may be, he pretends to be *elsewhere*, and finally he is. His dreams of travel, so often declared, are only half-sincere: their aim is to show him that his facticity in no way expresses his truth, that his presence in Rouen is merely a pitiable contingency, and that it must somehow be lived *as an absence*; indeed, if the imaginary is a surreality, it is in

Asia, in Egypt that he really is when he describes what he wants to find there. To convince himself, he has constructed a curious theory: in our period of critical and conscious art, the well-directed imagination becomes visionary, it reveals the true structures of things never before seen; later on, perception merely registers recognition. In the letters from the Orient, he will claim to have *rediscovered* the monuments and landscapes as he had *invented* them in his room at the Hôtel-Dieu.

Conversely, however, this theory helps him to discredit the travels while he is making them: they are essentially *verifications*, they teach nothing to one who dreamed them in advance; for the rest, they must be seen merely as muddled experiences. A letter from Athens, which he writes to his mother in January 1851, tells us what he feels:

> You travel in vain, see landscapes and fragments of columns, there is no diversion. You live in a perfumed torpor, in a kind of somnolent state in which the backdrop changes before your eyes . . . But you are not happy; you day-dream too much for that. Nothing is more conducive to silence and laziness. Maxime and I sometimes spend whole days without feeling the need to open our mouths . . . Your mind . . . goes galloping through memories . . . stamping through dead leaves . . . [57]

A vague backdrop moves past, surrounds his somnolence; and since he *is* in the Orient, he escapes it by indifference. Another recourse against his presence in these highly desired places is the remembrance of things past. He abandons himself to nostalgia for his childhood, and, at a farm in the Bosphorus, evokes "the winter days when I would go with my father to patients' homes in the country." Wherever he is, the main thing is not to be there.

When he is certain of returning to Rouen, he is repossessed by his desire for "elsewheres" and feels exasperated. From Rome, where he is bored, he writes to Bouilhet: "I am going mad with unbridled desires, a book I read in Naples on the Sahara made me want to go to the Sudan with the Touaregs, who always have their faces veiled like women, to see the negro and elephant hunts." [58] And he confirms in a letter to Ernest: "Ah well, yes, I have seen the Orient and I am no further along, for I want to return to it." [59] Yet he had just refused Du Camp's offer to continue the trip (by way of Persia). Was it money, as

57. *Correspondance* 2:285.
58. Ibid., p. 304.
59. Ibid., p. 309.

444

he says to Bouilhet, or the fear of dismaying his mother, as he tells her? Or the revolt in Bagdad—the explanation given to Ernest? Or the "clap," caught in Egypt? The multiplicity of motives, and the fact that he offers only one to each correspondent, makes them all suspect. And what does he miss? The Orient and Persia (Ernest) or the Sahara and the Sudan (Bouilhet)? In reality, he is prepared to return to France and take up his dream behind the walls of Croisset, always de-situated, knowing full well, now, that all "elsewheres" resemble each other for the tourist who surveys monuments and landscapes without ever entering into the real life of the country. Flaubert's travels to the Orient demonstrate that his desire to be elsewhere is the radical con-testing of any displacement and can be accompanied only by the strictest immobility: this totalization is the permanent and revolving negation of an unvarying residence in which one hardly moves so as not to feel the bonds that hold you to it. Flaubert does not want Croisset to be a particular perspective; he rejects the material and hu-man expanse of works and days, and his "point of view of the abso-lute" becomes the affirmation of his presence *by right* in all the infinite and abstract space of equivalence.

The technique of de-situating appears still more clearly in his medi-tations on time. We know that he has some very specific reasons for turning toward the past. The future horrifies him (we shall come back to this), and he sees in it both the wretched realization of his destiny and the victory of a Voltairean and scientistic bourgeoisie over a social order that he could have "venerated," over beliefs that might have consoled him. But panoramic pride will generalize this relation to the past, making it the systematic negation of ties that unite him to his contemporaries. He writes, for example, to Louise Colet: "I have no more pity for the fate of the working classes of today than for the an-cient slaves who turned the grindstone; no more, just as much." The last words are put in to avoid the Muse reproaching him for his insen-sitivity. Flaubert customarily erases nothing: he corrects by careless addition. Be that as it may, the real thought is manifest; it is the nega-tion that counts: *no more,* and the positive turn is merely the negative in disguise. For we have no ties to the ancient slave. It is not even a question of remembering his sufferings; they must be reinvented. Consequently, pity and indignation become, in their turn, imaginary sentiments. By assimilating the Rouen proletariat—those living be-ings one exploits *during one's lifetime*—to defunct slaves, Gustave sys-tematically contaminates the living by the dead and with a single stroke lands all of humanity in the tomb. But his principal aim is not

445

to mask exploitation from himself, or to ease his discomfort—which in any event he does not feel; it is chiefly a matter of denying a solidarity that would situate him in history. So he concludes the paragraph we have just cited by declaring: "I am no more modern than ancient." In order to shore up these preconceptions, he often has recourse to metempsychosis: "I am sometimes subject to historic revelations such that certain things appear clearly to me—metempsychosis may be true—I sometimes believe that I have lived at different periods; indeed, I have memories of them."[60] In order to de-situate himself in space, he had invented the prophetic imagination that bridged dispances and revealed the essential structures of things before his experience of them. The same operation in time yields the visionary memory, which opens onto a lived past before birth and releases concrete memories of Rome or Carthage. Both kinds of memory are really *images* born of a culture (knowledge, graphic or plastic representations), but he has decided, by means of a subterranean intuition, that he *suffers* them instead of producing them. His passivity serves him in this particular case: other than self, he grasps them as *other-memories*, as *pre-perceptions* of the other manifesting themselves in him as the expression of an alien spontaneity. By the simple effect of this double negation, which renders all his real life inessential, Flaubert feels eternal, omnipresent; he can view the world from the "point of view of the absolute."

The basic aim of this technique of de-situating is to tear oneself as pure subject away from the species, even while leaving it one's human hide. The denial of any spatial-temporal location finds its unity in the total denial of man:

> I am no more modern than I am ancient, no more French than Chinese, and the idea of fatherland, the obligation to live in a corner of the earth marked in red or blue on the map and to detest the other corners . . . has always seemed to me narrow, limited, horribly stupid. I am the brother in God of all that lives, of the giraffe and the crocodile as much as of man, and I am the fellow citizen of all the inhabitants of the great boardinghouse of the Universe.[61]

He need only glide a little more, deny anthropomorphism, recall that the Creation is not made for man—a *scientific* idea, precisely, and bourgeois because it is not accompanied by a social consciousness—

60. *Souvenirs*, p. 51.
61. *Correspondance* 1:279.

and there he is, ready to identify with the hurricane, with the cyclone. The point of view of the absolute becomes that of the radical negation of the human:

> We makes ourselves the center of nature, the aim of creation and its supreme justification . . . There again, our pride! . . . In [the earthquake in Lisbon] there is a hidden meaning that we do not understand and no doubt a superior utility . . . Who knows if the wind that batters a roof does not swell an entire forest?[62]

Starting from this position, Flaubert's pride can satisfy itself in two ways: either by swallowing up all of reality in absolute negation, or by constituting itself as a totality transcending all barriers in the face of this parenthetical reality. But the two attitudes are very close. The second masks its radical negativity by words: it is true that Flaubert likes to speak of "identifying oneself with nature or with history";[63] it is also true that he quite often declares himself to be a "pantheist." There he is, then, the totality of the world, the totality of the human adventure, the totality of matter. But he has not for all that ceased to fidget over his formal and absolute negation, since history, for him, is the impossible resurrection of the past that challenges the reality of the present,[64] and since nature (we shall come back to this) is the systematic negation of anthropomorphism and of the preeminence of the human. He writes quite proudly one day ("bouncing back after a fall"): "The only way to live in peace is to place oneself with a single bound above humanity and to have nothing in common with it, merely a glancing acquaintance."[65] So that finally the negation takes on its full meaning: it is active negation, negation of the man in him, negation of man in the world through contempt and death. Two passages from his correspondences are striking, especially if we compare them. In the first, he limits himself to showing that love of humanity was substituted for the love of the fatherland and will disappear like it; then will come a Platonic civilization in which Justice will be loved for the sake of Justice, Beauty for the sake of Beauty, etc., in other words, Ideas as transcendent archetypes and not as bonds between men.

---

62. Ibid.
63. Ibid. 1:166 (1845).
64. The text cited shows quite clearly what the young Flaubert means by these great ecstasies. He has just seen again the arena at Nîmes: "I climbed up to the last tiers thinking of all those who bellowed and applauded there, and then it was time to leave it all. When one begins to identify with nature or with history, one is suddenly torn away from it" (*Correspondance* 1:166).
65. Ibid. 3:178.

And he takes up this same text a year later but in order to give it a completely different conclusion:

> One must be soul as much as possible, and it is through this detachment that the vast sympathy for things and beings will come most abundantly to us. France was constituted the day the provinces died, and humanitarian sentiment begins to be born on the ruins of the fatherland. There will come a time when something wider and loftier will replace it, and *man will then love nothingness itself* as he will feel a participant in it.

Meaning: the progressive universalization that permits man (according to Gustave) to escape his sexual condition,[66] his social condition, and even his human condition is ultimately the universality of nothingness.

Is de-situating merely a verbal procedure? Must vertical ascension be reduced to an oratorical flight? Sometimes. But when circumstances are appropriate, we discover behind the words that the "glancing acquaintance" is based on an *attitude*, and that although it is then expressed through speech, it can be lived silently and in a kind of joy, as if for Flaubert it realized a fundamental desire. A curious passage from the *Notes de voyage* provides testimony. We are in the desert:

> A caravan crosses our path; the men wrapped in kafiahs, the women heavily veiled leaning on the necks of dromedaries: they pass quite close to us, no one says anything; it is like a phantom in the clouds. I sense something like a wild feeling of terror and admiration running up my vertebrae; I giggle nervously, I must have been very pale, and I felt joy.[67]

Why should this apathetic fellow, who has seen all of Egypt without feeling moved, experience such joy at the passage of a caravan? Because it *presents* him with reality exactly as he wished it and the true connection to being that he dreams of. This encounter takes place in the form of simple coexistence. No contact is either indicated or possible with these men, who share none of Flaubert's concerns and who do not speak his language. In this caravan, humanity presents itself to him as a species whose *ends* he does not share, whose real aims remain alien to him. At the same time, the silence, the alienness of the group and its progressive disappearance provide him with an image

---

66. In this letter, as in fifty others, he entreats Louise Colet *to escape from her condition as woman*. To deny in her the "feminine element" because she "is on the male side!"
67. *Notes* (Edition du Centenaire) 1:242.

of a "phantom in the clouds"; this human society in motion offers itself, with the aid of background, as an *unreal reality,* man *out of reach,* sliding and disappearing into nothingness, being as apparition, apparition reduced to appearance, the essence of communication revealing itself as absolute noncommunication, the imaginary and the real confounded—this is what suddenly makes Flaubert tremble with terror and joy. We will have already understood that this joy is the joy of the *aesthete:* it is given to him when conditions converge so that the event *realizes the derealization of the real* and shows him the human race as a product of his imagination.

Thus Flaubert's fatal pride compels him to consider the life of others and his own from the point of view of death. Flaubert is well aware that this position is an ethical imperative which can be addressed only to the imagination. He writes to Louise: "*Poetry implies duties. It obliges us to regard ourselves as always on a throne and never to think that we are part of the crowd.*" De-situating, by Gustave's own admission, is the same thing, in the end, as unrealization. To take "the point of view of the absolute" is *to choose being imaginary.*

Now we can return to *Smarh.* For the impulse that prompts Gustave to conceive it is precisely the impulse to bounce back. To the extent that *Mémoires d'un fou* is a *roman intime* that veers toward autobiography, Gustave displays himself in it as martyr: he has his vulture— that Thought which devours him—and then the world crushes him, he takes its weight; in short, he is a passive victim, a being *from below* doomed to progressive destruction by the forces of Evil. The failure— in his eyes alone—of the *Mémoires* disconcerts him and at the same time humiliates him: it is not only his work that disgusts him, it is his passivity, his dependence, and his inferiority. He is ashamed to complain, both *in the book and in reality.* This is the moment of the fall: lacking as it is, the book reveals to him his masochism, which horrifies him, and all is lost. No, the Garçon saves him. This character has existed for several years, born of a recovery of pride. By the same token, Gustave understands the meaning of the role: since the world is Hell, and one suffers infinite torments in it, why not identify with the tormentor rather than with his foolish victim? Merely give the pen to the giant who is mocking the human creature. Until then, the Pantagruelesque and clownish traveling salesman appeared when Gustave had anything to do with others; the writings of his solitude, on the other hand, sinister and desperate, were merely the sorrowful cries of a martyr. Even when he attempted an exterior totalization of the world, the young author remained deplorably sad. The generative

449

ideas of *Smarh* is to write in one work the martyr and the buffoon, to make the first the victim of the second and above all, without negating his bonds to the first, to make himself the buffoon's accomplice through laughter. The first personal works (*La Dernière Heure*, the *Mémoires*) did not involve a distance from the self; the first totalizations from the outside do not enclose interior totalization within them: the subject of the *Voyage*, that Memnon leaning over men, is *already* a supernatural being; in *La Danse*, subjectivity distributes itself between the choir and the dead drawn from their tombs and Christ, a sad and passive thinker. Gustave imagines that *Smarh* will be the cosmic synthesis of the two totalizations. The subject is announced at the beginning of the work in four lines. Satan says to God: "I know a Holy Man who lives like a relic; you shall see how I plunge that man into evil in no time, and then you will tell me whether virtue is still on the earth, and if my hell has not long since melted that old icicle that was chilling him?" This wager is inspired by Faust's, but the stake is not the same: in this case Smarh must be made to commit the sin of despair, the only sin that is inexplicable and leads straight to Hell. And there is no doubt that Smarh represents Gustave—meaning Marguerite, Garcia, Djalioh, Mazza, and the young hero of the *Mémoires*. But the author has taken care to withdraw support from his incarnation: he considers him coldly, without the slightest pity; the more eloquent laments of the Holy Man (now mystic, now poet) are "distanced": Flaubert pronounces them, he wishes that the beauty of these tirades would compel admiration, but in contrast to his strategy in the tales, he never seeks to enlist our pity. Smarh really is an *object*: even when he laments, he is manipulated, guided by Yuk and Satan. And certainly the storyteller impassively claims to relate objective facts; but as he is the one who invents them, we feel in every line that this malicious creator is the hermit's real tempter, that he *is amusing himself* by making Smarh submit to the progressive experience of nothingness through interposed characters: if he incarnates himself, it is in Yuk, the Garçon hyperbolized. Yet everything is transposed, generalized. Smarh's sweetness, his original goodness ("Thank you, my God, for having made me a soul like yours and capable of loving"), are expressly mentioned in order to recall the state of innocence Flaubert claims to have known in his first years. But they indicate also that the temporal scheme of *Voyage en enfer* is deliberately repeated:[68]

68. In *La Danse des morts*, Gustave had abandoned it: the result was a certain confusion that he wants to avoid here.

Smarh is man grasped at the outset in the moment of illusion and slowly led to absolute skepticism less by the "natural" unfolding of life than by a malign will which mystifies him. The totalization that happens for the Holy Man is interior; but this internalization, seen from above, passes itself off as an element of cosmic exteriority. Yuk-Gustave and Gustave-Satan, the only active characters, parade brilliantly before Smarh. He, pure passivity—as the first *Saint Antoine* will be—can merely record what happens. This constantly manipulated object is presented to us as human subjectivity considered as a determination—among an infinity of others—of cosmic objectivity. Flaubert preserves the impulse of the soul that he has previously presented as his own, but at the same time he tears himself away from it by a reflexive bouncing back in order to regard it "from his throne" with an indifferent serenity. Or, better still, to mock it. This is at once the stoic attitude and—to the extent that Smarh represents *every* man—a form of sadistic behavior. For the very type of Flaubertian sadism is exterior totalization when it transforms a subject into an object. In this sense, *Smarh*, lacking in 1839, will find its issue in the famous carriage scene, when the Garçon transforms a couple in their carnal intimacy into inanimate matter.

It is not this formal scheme, however, that "dazzles" Gustave when he conceives his "Mystery." The reason for his terror and jubilation must be seen, rather, in the discovery that is at the source of his new enterprise: at the moment of bouncing back, he realizes that pride is an *ethico-aesthetic method:* a work of art cannot be achieved without its creator's practicing a strict morality with regard to himself, and, reciprocally, this morality is justified by the work it makes possible. The impulse of pride tears the individual away from his being and by the same token gives him artistic vision (exterior totalization). In tearing himself away from his masochistic and bourgeois subjectivity in which he thought he would be swallowed up, Gustave believes that he has *made himself other:* he has escaped his *finite* alienation by giving himself up to infinity. We have seen it before: this is the meaning of his ecstasies, and it is also the very structure of the Garçon. What he believes he understands in December 1838 is that his proud ascesis, provided it can be constantly repeated, defines the Artist. Such a person "extends his mind to its full range" in order to make himself at once a grain of sand among grains of sand and the qualified representative of the infinite; he makes himself inhabited by absolute reality and grasps himself, pure subject, as a finite incarnation of infinite thought. The irruption of this thought in his limited intelligence makes everything

451

burst: there is no common measure between his feeble intellectual resources, his linkages of ideas, his minuscule *man's* knowledge and
this unlimited explosion of being; thus, far from the vertical ascent
raising him to a degree of superior intellection, it tears him away from
all forms of human intellection: something is developed in him "that
thinks, other than this very intelligence, something that is convinced,
other than our reason,"[69] and that thinks Knowledge and Reason *as
other*. Reason, said Hegel, is not a bone. But that is just what it must
be for the artist, who sees it *from the outside* and integrates it in objective totalization: losing its translucence, its principles, and its certainties, it becomes a mechanism in the eyes of the nocturnal subject who
shares no human ends. For this reason, translating into words what
the nature of the human race is in the eyes of the absolute, he will
write "extraordinary, gigantic, absurd, unintelligible things for him
and for others." He is inhabited, like a Sibyl; the man who holds the
pen does not understand what the infinite dictates to him.

A difficult task. No God helps him; he must raise himself *all alone*
above himself, maintain contact with our species by means of the facticity that has plunged him into it—in short, understand it from the
inside—and at the same time reveal it as an alien species, despise it in
himself and outside himself, despise himself in it. He will not stop
living, that is, suffering. Standing above lived experience by means of
a lofty renunciation, he will refuse either to acknowledge himself or
to see in the jolts of his tortured vanity anything other than the
pitiful, ordinary old sorrows that are the common lot; in short, he refuses to validate his subjectivity except as the source of *general* information. As the reflexive subject issuing from pride, the artist must
in any event comport himself as if he had produced himself as ego
constituted in the flow of lived experience in order to give a content to
his art.

Gustave has not forgotten that his ascesis is unrealizing. It is *in the
imaginary* that he makes himself lieutenant of the infinite. The absolute itself is aspired to (ineffectually) by a trans-ascendent intention,
never attained. In this sense, he can say that the artist *is a role*. But
what does that matter if the proud *époché* allows him to escape his
bourgeois-being, and especially if it finds its confirmation and achievement in the work of art? And that, precisely, is the dazzling discovery
of December 1838: the ethical work he does on himself leads him necessarily to the *Weltanschauung* of the artist, that is, to consider reality

69. *Souvenirs*, p. 62.

from the point of view of the unreal, to see the world as the worst of all possible worlds, thus to grasp it in its finitude, imagination being by definition the infinite (the place of unrealized possibles); consequently, he is ready to produce what he takes for the essential objective of all literature: a "discourse on the world." But when he sets to work, *Smarh* does not appear to him to be merely a transcription of an already acquired intuitive contents. To the contrary, what exalts him is the idea of accomplishing simultaneously the work and the ascesis, the one by means of the other; the plan of *Smarh* is a plan for life, and vice versa. To raise himself to the "point of view of the absolute," he will help himself with words: he will say more than he thinks, more than he feels, so that these utterances might carry him beyond himself and serve him as a springboard. Conversely, at every stage of the climb, the infinite will send him "unintelligible" messages whose meanings he will divine well before deciphering the words that express them. In the end, the letters of credit on the absolute and the obscure messages caught by his pen will find, he thinks, their harmonious equilibrium in the unity of a work of art. *Smarh* will be the product and the expression of a metamorphosis: by changing his relationship with himself (with the constituted ego) and with all finite beings, the young man will integrate himself to the infinite and will transform his immediate intuition of the universe. Proof of his existential metamorphosis must be furnished by modification of the material contents of intuition, and this modification will manifest to itself only by being expressed through a new discourse. When Gustave glimpses his future work, he is exalted and stupefied by its amplitude. It will be The Book, for he will say everything in it; and if he can really say everything, he will prove that he is capable of placing himself above everything and keeping himself there in pride. The subtitle "Mystery" indicates the underlying meaning with which Gustave seeks to endow his attempt: to see the finite from the point of view of the infinite, and to render his vision in words—that is a *sacred* enterprise.

Art and the Sacred in *Smarh*

We are "anchored"—Gustave is deeply aware of it—and, to the extent that being-in-the-world is totalization, this silent, implicit totalization is in fact a putting in perspective, and the cosmos is merely a horizon; thus the totalizer is himself totalized, which is Leibnitz's message in his *Monadology*. The world is in front of us but also behind us; and, as Merleau-Ponty says, we cannot be "seeing" without being simultaneously "visible." "The body is caught in the fabric of the world, but the world is made of the cloth of my body." Now the impulse of the Artist, in Flaubert's sense, begins with de-situation. He constitutes himself as *panoramic consciousness*. He tears himself from the world *fictively* by leaving it his hide, and pretends explicitly to totalize the infinity of things and men without becoming integrated as subject in the totalization. This denial of all perspective, this move to the absolute gaze, can only be an imaginary attitude. Gustave unrealizes himself as omniscient subject. He dreams himself, gliding above creatures and enveloping them all in the unity of clairvoyance (double sight), but this phantasmagoria is not in fact accompanied by any *real* displacement. Indeed, considered objectively, it contributes to situate him more precisely; it is he, Gustave, the younger son of the Flauberts, who is bored in his room and whose fictive evasion is conditioned by his past, by his attachments, by the room itself, which imprisons him in its all too familiar landscape; *for us,* he becomes more himself by his way of willing himself a universal subject.

But if the subject is imaginary, the object of his contemplation must be as well. The world that delivers itself to this pseudo-gaze contains, to be sure, lands, seas, sky, animals and men, beings and events, but they are mirages, borrowed no doubt from memory but distorted by the new curve Gustave imposes on them and by the necessity of appearing only as parts of a whole that claims to be immediately visible.

Gustave had already attempted this panoramic totalization in his thirteenth year. We have seen him, clinging to Satan's coattails, fly above continents and conclude that "this world is Hell." Taken literally, his conclusion was neither true nor false. The world in which I am stuck is perhaps *my* hell or, what amounts to the same thing, it may be that *my* world is Hell; but these two judgments are acceptable only if they are applied exclusively to my objective surroundings and to my anchorage or, if you prefer, to a situation and a person. Even then they elude the categories of true and false: the word *hell,* when the verb "to be" links it to the word *world,* cannot refer us to a precise concept. In the system of Christian and medieval thought, "hell" designates a definite object that derives its meaning from the structured collection of religious myths and rites. No Evil without Good, no Devil without God, no Hell without Paradise, no eternal suffering or eternal bliss without a retributive justice which itself would make no sense without putting the defendant through the test of life. If divine justice, in which Flaubert cannot believe, must be eliminated in favor of the punishment of life, not *post mortem* but from the beginning of human development, in the time of innocence, conceptual knowledge becomes confused, its elements deteriorate or block each other: Evil is utterly disconcerted to reign over its colleague Good, survival is astonished at beginning with existence only to end with death, the supreme judge is horrified to punish without a reason. Thus the conclusion of Gustave's first panoramic view is, in the strict sense of the word, nonsignifying.

This conclusion, however, will serve as a start for the conscious efforts he makes from the age of fifteen to transform himself into an artist. In other words, this proposition will be the point of departure and the conclusion of his new panoramic views. It becomes the generating idea of the imaginary world that constitutes itself before the eyes of the unreal subject: it will be the matrix of the creative imagination that will produce this universe and provide it with its rules. In *Smarh*, Flaubert takes up the plot of *Faust*: there is a wager between God and Satan, the object of the wager is Smarh, the hermit; the Devil will tempt him. But God appears here only to be flouted: Good must exist so that Evil might continually triumph. Indeed, to follow it through, the guiding idea of his cosmogeny is the hypothesis of the Evil Genius. In Descartes, however, this hypothesis is a logical fiction: it is considered *possible* until it leads by a dialectical process to the *cogito*, which reveals its impossibility; limited, it is an unreal moment of a real thought, which eliminates itself when the truth appears which it has helped to produce. But Gustave never uses the cogito as a reducing agent: unrealized in a contemplative subject, he does not engage in the reflective act that would dissipate the nightmare; if he does produce reflections, they themselves will be imaginary and will fall under the law of the evil spirit. Thus the world remains a dream, but it is a bad dream from which one never awakens. *La Danse des morts* is a directed nightmare, and equally so are *Smarh* and the first *Tentation*. Thus, from the age of fifteen to twenty-seven, Gustave unceasingly recreates the same totality according to the same rules.

If we want to understand the essence of the "artist" for the young Flaubert, we must ask the crucial question: what connection does he establish between the panoramic imaginary world and the real universe that is crushing him? Let us observe, to begin with, that *this* question—formulated in *these* terms—concerns Gustave alone. There would be no reason to put it to writers of the following generations who, whether naturalists or symbolists, claim to be his disciples. The naturalistic novelist, indeed, although he might will himself a creating subject, claims not to leave the actual world but to reconstitute a social whole (events and structures) *from a certain perspective*. And this perspective translates, in spite of everything, the writer's *anchorage:* Zola speaks of courtisans, high bourgeoisie, peasants, workers, never of *Man*. He is *of his time;* he sees things from the perspective of *his milieu*. What he totalizes, for example, is the temporal fate of a family. The problem of naturalism—and equally of realism—is the problem of the veracity of fiction. "One lies the better to tell the truth: what does this mean?" Conversely, the symbolists—many of them, in any case—valorize the imaginary to the extent that it *is not* the real. The structure of pure unreality fascinates them: "nothing is beautiful but what is not." Their "world" is a nonworld, which they often call the "dream," and if one should ask them what connection they make between the imaginary and reality, most of them would answer none. The question to ask them is rather: what real elements are introduced, in fact, into the "dream" in order to condition it from outside and inside as a half-real event? But for Flaubert, the ambiguity of his position—which allowed Naturalists and Symbolists alike to find themselves in him—derives from the fact that he knows the unreality of the panoramic world perfectly well yet continues to affirm its identity with the real world in which he is rooted.

At any rate, he is certainly lucid. Never, when he creates, does he take himself for a philosopher in search of new truths: his letters and his *Souvenirs* show that he scorns philosophy at this time. No doubt the "artist" also produces *ideas* that manifest themselves in the work; but, as an imaginary subject, his ideas are merely the *appearance* of real ideas. Forged in imitation of mental conceptions, each one of them is merely the totalizing unity of a certain category of mirages, and consequently they themselves become mirages. To double Satan with Yuk, the god of the grotesque, is to create a fleeting idea that vanishes when anyone tries to ponder it. Let us not imagine that we are here concerned with metaphors in the strict sense of the term. A metaphor is a translation; it can therefore be retranslated. But when beautiful Truth perishes, suffocated in the arms of the grotesque God, what will you translate? We need not seek behind this archetypal *event* for one of those "axioms" Flaubert is so fond of. We have seen that allegory depends on a hermeneutics that reveals a plurality of independent meanings in it. Taken literally and logically, it does not *mean* anything: it refers merely to false concepts, to a thought-mirage. Take truth, for example: at times Gustave is tempted to declare it grotesque, but still more often he comes to think of it as excruciating and distressing. Doctor Mathurin dies laughing; but Flaubert does not find Mazza laughable when she kills herself. At other times, the true seems attractive to him (isn't he the son of a scientist, doesn't he boast of having "the surgical eye"?). And on other occasions he declares himself "antitruth," which sometimes means that he deliberately rejects it, preferring the shimmerings of error, and at other times means that it does not exist ("there are neither true ideas nor false ideas"). So that no plot would remain if one stripped it of its anthropomorphism and especially its *temporality*. Indeed, these various conceptions of the True—none of which is *intelligible*—have no common bond. Temporalization is the decisive factor: one or the other will be the form and will raise itself on the foundation constituted by phe interpenetration of them all, according to the variable but always motivated fashion in which the young man lives his contradictions. In consequence, the only possible unification of this multiplicity must be temporal: the function of Plato's myths was to reintroduce time into a static universe; similarly, the narrative Gustave forged reintroduces temporality as the only admissible synthesis. He simply objectifies it; he makes that interior duration, which slips away bearing twenty different conceptions of the true, into the objective time of a *story*. Is he aware of it? More or less: the anecdote appears as a metaphor. But it is a metaphor-mirage. Flaubert really needs to tell stories: the simple, logical union of the grotesque and the true would not satisfy him; in this invented universe where ideas are human creatures, each one of them must be allowed the time to *make a choice*, the time to fall from grace. For this very reason, however, temporality shatters concepts. The mobile unification of this meandering and heteroclite diversity can only be *artistic*. Flaubert is not unaware of this: the "artist" plays at having ideas. Yet when he rereads *Smarh* a year after finishing it, he writes an afterword: "Illusion is not slight; you must begin by having ideas, and your famous mystery is bereft of them." Are we to understand that he "deluded himself" when he was working on it? Yes and no. Let us observe first of all that Flaubert reproaches himself for a defect of method: you must *begin* by having ideas. Did he *not* begin this way? Well, no: let us recall that he presents his mystery play in December 1838 as a colossal work, "unintelligible to myself and to others." This means that he chose to begin with obscurity: he writes quite purposely in order to be surpassed by what he writes; in what comes from his pen he recognizes himself by a kind of sympathy, not by understanding. If he then complains of the difficulties he encounters, the issue is always artistic *expression* ("Oh, Art, Art, bitter disappointment") and not—as would be the case for a philosopher—the encumbrance of his thought. He speaks of a "standoff with the in-finite," which he immediately describes as an "upheaval of the soul": indeed, we have seen that it is a certain *attitude*—and not a signifying intuition—which leads him to this confrontation. And all of a sudden: "I stop short, I don't know how to express [this standoff]." True, sometime later, rereading what he has written (24 February 1839), he declares severely: "What I have done so far is absurd; not the smallest idea." But then what he reproaches himself for is characteristic: "My thoughts are confused, I can do no imaginative work." He is clearly assimilating the ideational function and the faculty of imagining. And certainly the imagination is a necessary moment of all heuristic thought, even that of the mathematician. But out of this transitory moment Flaubert does what is essential: he deliberately seeks the symbolic incarnation without concern for first establishing what must be incarnated; he counts on the density of the symbol to suggest, after the fact, to others and to himself, an unrealizable and distant meaning inseparable from the fictive events that express it, that is, impossible to translate by another discourse. He is conscious of producing great imaginary wholes, not the Idea but images of the Idea so that it might be caught in the trap of its reflection. From this point of view, this universe is not the copy of our own, and Flaubert knows it; moreover, the panoramic world is enchanted; specters, dead men who talk, gods hold sway there like men, and the relation that binds them together is one of interiority. In other words, Gustave intentionally produces a *sacred* universe which cannot be a "model"of that profane universe we inhabit.

Yet Gustave does not want to invent an *other* universe: the father of symbolism is in this respect very different from his spiritual sons. His concern is not to construct out of hatred of the real a Leibnitzian possible that would remain until then in the state of possibility and would, in his hands, take on its full consistency and modeling without leaving the realm of pure possibility. Indeed, when the fictive subject surveys, we know that a real subject is at the same time creating the imaginary contemplator and the object contemplated. He structures both of them as a function of his own determinations. The hypothesis of the Evil Genius corresponds to *domination by the Other*, to the paternal curse; if the cogito does not intervene, it is not because Flaubert is unable to carry it out at any moment; it is because his passivity prohibits him from using it methodically. At the very source of his imagination we find pessimism, misanthropy, misogyny, which are intentional determinations of his sensibility. And if mythic beings,

458

usually evildoers, people the fictive world he describes, it is because this creator intentionally projects into his creation his "religious instinct," his mysticism, his faith—flouted, crushed, continually reborn—his superstitions, his profound taste for fetishism and idols. As for the triumph of radical evil, the inevitable conclusion of his works, this is the very meaning and direction, for him, of lived experience, his real certainty that every man has a *fate* which is always unbearable and is the vow of his own meanness. This entire structured whole, joined to other impulses that we have described or shall describe—by serving as the matrix of the fabulous opera that is the panoramic world, that is, by producing, selecting, systematically distorting the images that constitute it—presents itself in sycretism as the generating principle of the imaginary object or, if you will, as the law of its nature. And, of course, these confused, muddled, sometimes contradictory tendencies cannot project themselves into this object as a system of coherent and hierarchical laws, as a body of intelligible connections, in a word, as articulated significations. How could understanding admit this nature in which everything is *analyzable*—reducible to invariable elements—and at the same time *sacred*—irreducible? How could a rational ethic accommodate itself to a system of negative values, to a radical Evil that *always* triumphs over Good? Radical evil, in Kant, is conceived at the level of intelligible choice only in connection with an absolute Good that we have freely denied by opting for sensibility, but which our development, after this life, permits us slowly to approach. Here, nothing of the sort: just the untenable affirmation that the Good is the privileged means of Evil. But beyond significations—there are none or they are incorrect, incomplete, imprecise, or mutually destructive—a *meaning* appears, the *poetic* structure of the imaginary, which surpasses Flaubert's words and images and which we would could not render in words. Indeed, it is the internalized totality of the poet externalizing itself as objective totalization. In other words, the *perspective* that his particular roots give him on his real surroundings (what the Germans call *Umwelt*) is extrapolated in its very ambiguity as the objective principle of imaginary totalization. Unrealization therefore does not take place on the level of *meaning*; but meaning is lived inside the real world by the real subject; it is Flaubert's being-in-the-world on the level of everyday reality; every perception, every event confirms and contradicts it simultaneously: everything is unbearable and nothing is *so terrible*; life is unlivable and goes on; contingency of fact makes neither wrong nor right his "presentiment" of radical evil insofar as this inflexible preconception refers to another order and postulates absolute necessity. Flaubert's being-in-the-world is thus situated in relation to the earthly horizon such that it is lived as the permanent surpassijg of an ambiguous experience. In short, the *meaning* of the world becomes the object of a corrosive postulation that remains in the realm of faith, for it could be verified only at the end of an infinite quest. This meaning is there, however; it casts a strange light on the facts, a light that plays over them but does not illumijate them. The moment of the imaginary is the shift to the infinite by which, assuming the quest completed, Flaubert takes this syncretic meaning as the organizing principle of his images: in other words, he does not imagine the meaning; he imagines that the meaning—instead of being the object of a premonition without confirmation or invalidation—is immediately given to intuition as the principle of totalizing unification. But this intuition can be merely *practical:* I know with certainty the inherent reason for a construction only if I am doing the constructing. Art consists, therefore, according to the young Flaubert, of objectifying his *Weltanschauung* by perceiving it as the guiding scheme of his construction of the world as image. Thus Gustave's experienced world and his imaginary world have *meaning* in common. But meaning does not play the same role in each world. In the first, it unifies a posteriori, as best it can, phenomena as an affective hypothesis. In the othar, ip *produces* them. The result is evident: imaginary facts will be less abundant and more rigorous than real facts. This is certainly not a matter of logical rigor: nonetheless, as each one is produced as part of a preexisting whole and delivers this whole in its own way, facts and beings—squeezed, condensed, bound by relations of interiority—will exchange contingency and ambiguity for an inflexible *aesthetic* necessity. But this is not yet the place to define the laws of this necessity: Flaubert between the ages of fifteen and eighteen was very far from articulating the rules of this art. Let us say simply, as he does then, that he "writes in order to *please himself.*"[70] This does not mean that he wants to give himself a pleasure that is contingent and bound to the charm of the recounted subject: indeed, the substance of the narrative he proposes for himself is his life at the *collège*, "a time of inconceivable boredom and stupid sadness mingled with spasms of clownishness."[71] Nothing seductive, as we see, except that pleasure inheres in the *form*. But this

70. Ibid., p. 103: "Everything I do is to give myself pleasure. If I write, it is for the purpose of reading myself," etc.
71. Ibid., p. 103.

form itself is nothing more than *meaning* taken as the principle of totalization. It is really a question of producing an unreal object whose every part, engendered by the syncretic unity of a meaning, proclaims the whole in itself and in its relation to all the other parts. Against analysis—which for him is Truth—Gustave conceives of Beauty as a quasi-dialectical synthesis. Now appears the organ of control, taste, which is nothing more than *meaning* itself grasped as critical demand and verifying that the part, in its singularity, presents itself as an expression of the whole, that it is neither more nor less than a view the whole has of itself synchronically or diachronically particularized by its relation to all the other views it can have of itself. As each part has a tendency to be posed for itself, constant vigilance must be exercised to avoid refinement, excess, exaggerated singularization: any complacence is necessarily a *lapse of taste*. Gustave fears such errors more than anything because he still writes at whim and spontaneously, at the sway of inspiration, not always concerned with connecting a page written one day to the page written the day before. There will be from the outset—that is, from his fifteenth year—a close struggle between *improvisation*, the source of broad rhetorical impulses that are isolated, cut off from the construction of the whole or repetitious, and critical control; between passive activity and the synthetic activity that the adolescent dreams of exercising in the imaginary and that is so contrary to the nature with which he has been endowed. Thus, taste has no rules other than those of its own making, for it is merely *meaning* itself; and these rules cannot be codified because then meaning would have to *be known* through concepts, whereas it is actually the negation of all conceptual and critical connections: it is a "multiplicity of interpenetration" that becomes a producing unity only by objectifying itself in an imaginary world.

At this level, then, what is the world created by Flaubert? It is ours as it would be if it really became what it tries to be without great success, in other words, if events and beings were content to be the consequences of principles and were determined, in their very substance, to demonstrate those principles. Since *meaning* is, roughly, radical evil—that is, the impossible positivity of the negative—for the world to be perfect, everything must be radicalized, every individual must bear witness in himself, by his meanness and his misfortunes and in his relations with others, who torture him and by whom he is tortured, to the triumph of the Evil Genius. In short, the world must continually denounce itself as an *other world*, or *counter world*. If the real universe were manifest thus in its austere rigor, it would

461

not be better for all that: it would be beautiful. This is the period when Flaubert observes in his notebook of *Souvenirs:* "the beautiful is of more use than the good." Apart from a slight weakness in the thought—which still retains the word "use" that Flaubert will soon reject—we might think we are reading one of Oscar Wilde's aphorisms. Indeed, we now more clearly distinguish the aesthatic commitment that the proposition conceals: the world is Hell. Since it is not good, the world will be ugly—chaotic, ambiguous, shifting, and black in its disorder—unless it is *absolutely* bad. But this aesthetic is in certain respects Platonic: indeed, for Flaubert the real is not consistent with his *eidos;* it participates in it, nothing more. The rigorous complementarity of evil and beauty exists only in Heaven, our universe is that of the *hule* in which spatio-temporal dispersion and dumb inertia vaguely reflect eidetic structures that they cannot entirely realize. This means that it has and does not have truth: *if it had,* it would be the magnificent place of evil. Thus the role of the artist, according to Flaubert, is to *institute* what the world should be and what it is not, not because it is *other* but simply *by default.* To *institute:* by producing the work out of meaning, he gives the world a *model* and calls upon it to recognize in the imaginary object the singular universal it ought to *be.* Beauty as rigorous totalization becomes an *ontological necessity:* by its exemplary structure it requires a tightening and an activation of earthly materiality; it demotes analysis and unmasks it: analysis is based merely on the essential inadequacy of reality; the elements exist only because nature is part of the impossibility of totalizing. At this period Gustave would not say, as Wilde does, that nature imitates art but that it *should* imitate it in order to become itself. Here we see clearly the satisfactions provided by resentment: as a product of a universe that is mediocre and certainly bad rather than good, the adolescent demands that it be still worse, bad to perfection. He denounces reality doubly—it is so tainted in principle that it does not even succeed in producing the radical evil to which it is sworn—and at the same time wishes exquisite suffering on the human race: the new stories rework the "malign" wishes of Mazza or Marguerite only to give them the structure of categorical imperatives. Beauty demands universal suffering. And these imperatives—unlike the Kantian imperatives—do not inspire respect but shame. Those of practical reason—even if never executed—are accompanied by a "You must, therefore you can," which at least establishes their possibility. The aesthetic imperative is the torment of matter and its impossible leavening: to real nature, the Other Nature declares: "You must, but you cannot." We are rediscovering, in all its profundity, the dialectical relation uniting beauty and malice in the artist."

Until December 1838, Flaubert still doubted that the artist could be the mean-spirited man par excellence. It can be said that he receives this revelation in full force when he decides to take exterior totalization as the object of art. Of course, discoveries of this kind are *prepared for*. The idea is simple: since one writes out of resentment, the purpose of literary activity can only be to do harm to the human race. This is a very early idea, but Gustave was not at first conscious of it, and his intention in his first stories was rather to express his pessimism than to infect the reader with it.

Nonetheless, he fairly soon begins to suspect the venom he distills in his works, for he often adds postscripts or introductions meant to discourage readers—generally out of scorn for the public but also, at moments, out of prudence. At fifteen he is still hesitating, for on 24 June 1837 he declares to Ernest that he prefers "pure poetry, the cries of the soul," etc., to knowledge of the heart. As he has written most of his *black* tales at this period, we can deduce that he does not entirely understand himself. The letter, full of rage, bears witness to that atrabilious humor and excessive irritability which would never leave him again. One year later, after the failure of the *Mémoires*, his decision is made: "I deeply admire only two men, Rabelais and Byron, the only two who have written with the intention of harming the human race and laughing in its face. What a tremendous position a man occupies who stands in this relation to the world!"[72] He does not say that he wants to take such a position: that would be showing too much pride and, besides, he mistrusts Ernest. But it is certainly Isambart's position in relation to Marguerite, and it will be the purpose of the desituated consciousness that in *Smarh* works a panoramic totalization. Five months later, on 24 February 1839, he writes these three lines *in the same letter:* "I have too much contempt for men to do them either good or ill . . ." "I will never plead cases in court except to defend some famous criminal or a vile cause . . ." and "If ever I take an active part in the world, it will be as thinker and demoralizer." The succession of these declarations admirably shows us his state of mind: on the surface it is quietism, the same attitude he affects in 1838. "I have now come to regard the world as a spectacle and to laugh at it. What is the world to me? I shall ask little of it." But this time he insists on its negative aspect. Indeed, his quietism would be more comprehensible

72. To Ernest, 13 September 1831, *Correspondance* 1:29.

if it were born of an arrogant indifference. And we must not under-
estimate the component of aggression that is contained in the word
contempt. Soon afterward, however, he informs us, that he will defend
famous criminals and these alone: in order "to do them good"? No,
surely not, but in order to *demoralize* the jury and the public by wrest-
ing an acquittal from them: that would be the supreme scandal. And
if there were even a chance of success, it would be splendid to save
the guilty man's head. Indeed, he wishes to defend evil against honest folk. He takes his revenge against those who want to force him to
do his law degree: he will do it, certainly, he will become an attorney,
but he will use his office to mystify the jury and "laugh in its face."
Upon which he confesses his deep desire: "To act as thinker and demoralizer." He adds: "I will act only to tell the truth, but it will be
dreadful, cruel, and naked." "As always Flaubert betrays himself
through words: the future tense he uses to designate truth shows that
he is hesitating between the real and the imaginary. He is no doubt
led on by the tense of the first verb, "I will act," which is itself perfectly justified since what is involved is a project. Still, the "will be" is
not inevitable. The truth Gustave is referring to must be dreadful *in
the present:* for our author, it is a matter of revealing the world, life,
death, man, etc., such as they have been, are, and always will be. The
present alone is suitable insofar as it also expresses the nontemporal.
He should therefore have written: "I will tell the truth as it *is:* dreadful, cruel and naked." Gustave uses the future tense because that
truth does not yet exist and because its dreadfulness, its cruelty, will
depend if not on pure invention, at least on a selection made by the
"thinker." And it is thus that he envisages it, for he is less interested—as this passage clearly shows—in knowledge and the *communication* it requires than in the fright it provokes in his reader. What is
at issue, we see, is tightening relations within the world and producing, at the end of this complex operation, an object of hideous beauty
that is none other than the world become Hell. But the emphasis, this
time, is on the demoralizing effect Gustave counts on producing in
the other.

The future tense has another meaning here as well. In February,
Gustave worked constantly on his "Mystery." He was extremely unhappy with what he was doing. Would he finish it? The following
letter (18 March) informs us that he had abandoned it for some time.[73]

___

73. To tell the truth, it slightly contradicts the preceding letter, which said: "I have
begun a mystery . . . I may stop there." And here we find: "I have taken up a work long

The previously cited line must therefore be read in the light of this particular uncertainty: if I manage to finish *Smarh,* and if I decide to make it public, I guarantee that this work will be cruel for the reader—that is, it will satisfy *my* cruelty.

This cruelty, moreover, manifests itself with greater clarity in a letter of July 1839 (by now, *Smarh* is finished):

> Lacenaire . . . dabbled in philosophy . . . in his fashion, and a droll, deep, bitter sort of philosophy. What a lesson he gave to morality! What a public spanking he gave that poor desiccated prude. What a beating she got! How he dragged her in the mud, in blood! I do so love to see men like that, like Nero, like the Marquis de Sade . . . Those monsters explain history for me . . . Believe me, they are great men, immortal as well. Nero will live as long as Vespasian, Satan as long as Jesus Christ.

Three names, three "Satanic" creatures for whom Flaubert has boundless admiration. Lacenaire was for some time a symbol of social demoralization: through him, crime fascinated honest folk. From the time of his adolescence, Gustave dreamed of *being* Nero. In *La Danse des morts,* Satan calls that emperor "the darling of my heart, the greatest poet the world has known." Here, poetry has nothing to do with language but resides in the destructive act: the greatest poet in the world is the arsonist of Rome. Listen to him speak to us, risen from his tomb:

> I want to die of love, of sensuous pleasure, of drunkenness! And while I shall eat dishes for myself alone, and there will be singing, and girls naked to the waist will serve me on plates of gold and bend over to look at me, someone will be slaughtered, for I love, and it is a Godlike pleasure to mingle the scents of blood with those of the betrothed, and the voices of death will lull me at the table.[74]

This emperor is the precursor of the "happening": thanks to him, poetry becomes a provocative and destructive event. And above all demoralizing, for the beauty of Rome burning is in the service of death; sensuous pleasure is more exquisite when it is accompanied by

since abandoned, a mystery play." If he was still working on it on 24 February, how can he have *long since abandoned* it on 18 March? True, on 26 December 1838 (within two week of its conception), he had declared: "I do not know whether to continue my work." Had he effectively stopped, then taken it up again? What is certain in any case is that from 26 December on he is constantly tempted to let it drop.

74. *La Danse des morts.*

murder. In a word, Sade: Gustave did not yet know him by his works, for he tried to obtain them through Ernest; but an article by Janin informed him of the life of the marquis. These three men mock the human race *by their acts*. What does it matter whether they make blood flow in rivers or in driblets? The chief thing is that their crimes make manifest the underlying identity of beauty and evil.

But Gustave can only dream of imitating them or, rather, can imitate them only as a dream. He claims to have too much contempt for men to do them good or ill. But, as we well know, it is not contempt that restrains him but impotence. He knows it, and yet he cannot help desiring supreme power. On this point, a passage from the *Souvenirs* is informative.[75] Gustave has finally found a work by de Sade; he reads it, it is a revelation. He is deeply affected by it and writes in his notebook: "When you have read the *Marquis de Sade* and have recovered from the dazzlement, you take to wondering if it might not all be true, if the truth were not all he teaches—and all that because you cannot resist the hypothesis in which he makes us dream of unlimited potency and magnificent powers." He has profoundly understood that the principal theme of the divine marquis is human relationships, and thinks he has understood that in the absence of all real communication, the fundamental relation between men is one of *power*, the right that some claim for themselves to treat others, *with their complicity*, simply means of gratification. A human being in himself is an absolute: absolute power will consist in making him a relative and dependent term. This is a kind of freedom too: absolute freedom will consist in leading him freely to deny himself. In a word, the only conceivable bond is that between the executioner and his victim.

The real meaning of de Sade's works is of scant importance here. Flaubert has merely rediscovered his own phantasms in them. Indeed, the "Pastiche"[76] is merely a reply of the orgiastic reminiscences he lends to Nero in *La Danse des morts*, written two years earlier. At issue is a *black* radicalization of the feudal bond. What matters is that beneath this violent illumination we grasp another meaning of Flaubertian art: the obtaining of de Sade's omnipotence, which intoxicates Gustave and is denied him, *by means of discourse*. We just as surely subject the freedom of the other if through words we inclined him to despair. Gustave needs the great "immortals" of vice as a guarantee: they are the saints and martyrs of his calendar; he will speak of

75. Previous to 1841, p. 70.
76. Probably inspired by *La Philosophie dans le boudoir.*

them and cite them as examples. But the work of the artist, although situated on another terrain, is equivalent to theirs and pursues the same end. "To harm the human race" is indeed what Gustave proposes to himself when he conceives *Smarh;* better still, he wants to incite the human race to harm *itself* in the person of his readers. Only recently, in *Agonies,* he purported fear lest "these lines burn and wither the hand that touches them, tire the eyes that read them, murder the soul that understands them." And he added: "No! If someone should discover this, let him beware of reading it!" But from December 1838, when he conceives *Smarh,* his fears are changed to hopes: may his work burn and wither the hand that turns its pages! may it lead the reader *to despair* and *degradation.*

I have chosen these two words to mark the ambiguity of the enterprise of demoralization. For if the issue were to push men to absolute despair, all Flaubert needs to do, according to the very principles of his dolorism, is to help them, at the price of a difficult ascesis. Does he not repeat, from adolescence on, that sorrow is proper to great souls? Will he not write in 1841, in his *Souvenirs:* "I believe that humanity has only one purpose, to suffer"? By infecting them with his own suffering, we might think, Flaubert brings his readers close to him; he makes them more lucid, more authentic, more courageous. But it isn't so; it would be true if Flaubert did not hate his public, his class, in advance. He does not believe that a book, however sublime, can tear the bourgeois away from the bourgeoisie. They will continue to do what they do because it is their lot. And if, through a piece of writing, one could reveal to them their secret stench and the fragility of the principles to which they cling, one would not help them for all that: their souls, to the contrary, would become uglier still, for they would become conscious of their baseness yet lack the power to escape it, and would preserve their principles without believing in them. To demoralize is not to demystify: surrounded, the bourgeois would defend themselves by seeking refuge in bad faith, by pretending not to see the new evidence. And the fact is that they *would not see* that evidence, but one still would have spoiled their life. This is exactly what Gustave wants to do: indeed, the word "demoralization" was not chosen at random; it means to corrupt morals *as well as* to effect a loss of morale. If he can, Flaubert will kill two birds with one stone: he will deprive men of the support of morality, and, while they cannot replace this cluster of prohibitions and commandments with anything else, they are too petty, unlike the author, to know how to suffer. So the first moment of the operation, good in itself—it is good to challenge false values and false imperatives—is expressly conceived to be followed by the second, meaning that this challenge, intolerable for the weak, must plunge them into abject despair. Good is done with a view to accomplishing evil. Does Gustave, then, never hope to find a reader worthy of him? Yes, *one*; Alfred. Yet he is afraid that Alfred is turning into a bourgeois. And it will be observed that *Smarh*, the most ambitious of Flaubert's works, is not dedicated to him. But even supposing there were many Alfreds in the world, Gustave does not imagine that his work can enlighten them: if they understand it, it is because they are *already* in despair. No: the "mystery play" is addressed to the bourgeois: it is the demoralizing narrative of an enterprise of demoralization. The reader is asked to identify with the pious hermit, who will end by turning in the void. And, of course, this exterior conclusion is the same as that found in the *Mémoires*, which is drawn from the point of view of interiority: "at the brink of the abyss I closed my eyes; I fell in." But the artist has bounced back after the fall: his panoramic consciousness glides above the world, and in order to infect other members of the species, he uses his own hide, the carcass he has left on earth. *Smarh* is the result of that rebound: it cannot even be conceived without the disappointed author of the *Mémoires* transforming himself from the inside, taking the *attitude* of pride, of contempt, and perching on the summits. And the exterior totalization must be made *by laughing* "in the face of the human race"; it is for this reason that the duo of Man and the Devil, which tends to be too dramatic, is changed into a trio by the addition of the God of the Grotesque. No pity for our species: were it to twist and turn in misery, its cries of suffering would only provoke the hilarity of the artist who had provoked them. It is really a matter of *perverting*, and curiously, this is the theme of *La Philosophie dans le boudoir*, a work unknown to Gustave in December 1838 but in which, in 1840, he will recognize, "dazzled," his own enterprise. By *making himself* the artist, Flaubert moves from dream to act: writing will be his "absolute power"; he tears language away from the bourgeois and turns it against them. By demoralizing, the little vassal, drunk with his own omnipotence, will be the black Lord of words.

But it is not merely a matter of insinuating doubt into other souls. In a curious passage, Flaubert affirms that beauty possesses the magic and direct power to *degrade* them. In the midst of his enterprise, he abandons Yuk and Satan for a moment and speaks in his own name:[77]

77. At the end of the fourth part.

One day in my imagination, when I have been thinking of Nero on the ruins of Rome and of dancing girls on the banks of the Ganges, I will insert the most beautiful page one could possibly write; but I warn you in advance that it will be extravagant, monstrous, apallingly brazen, that it will affect you like a mouthful of cantharis, and if you are a virgin, you will learn all sorts of things, and if you are old it will make you young again. It will be a page . . . which, posted on the walls, would send the walls themselves into heat and make whole populations run to the brothels, now overcrowded, and would force men and women to couple in the streets like dogs, like pigs, a race greatly inferior to the human race, I grant you, which is the gentlest and most inoffensive of all.

Gustave certainly does not think the pig inferior to man: he wrote in *Rêve d'enfer* that we are "a little less than dogs, a little more than trees." But he is assured that by reducing his fellow men to "human beasts" he is casting them to the lowest level of animality: they will couple like pigs but without innocence, obscenely. It will be observed that this time Flaubert no longer even pretends that debasement follows the revelation of a "cruel" truth: the "most beautiful page in the world" acts as an aphrodisiac; it changes man into what he *can be*, no doubt, but what he would never be without it. In a word, beauty *dehumanizes*. Certainly the author recognizes that he has not yet written those burning lines; but he does more than wish he will one day be capable of doing so: he promises himself that he will, in defiance of his readers. Here, then, the ambiguity disappears: by telling the truth of our condition, Flaubert could still give the illusion of pushing his brothers into a healthy revolt; but when he pushes men and women to couple like pigs, he reveals his hatred of man and his desire to degrade him. His art seeks to be the elixir of Circe. We see the path taken: first useful to the soul, then useless to men, art, along with exterior totalization, becomes harmful to them.[78]

We ought not believe, however, that Flaubert reduces art to injury. This is both a goal and a consequence. As we have observed, when Gustave conceives exterior totalization with *Smarh*, he tries to work a double demotion: that of the finite by the infinite, which is mysticism, and that of the real by the imaginary, which is artistic creation. What connection should be found between these two enterprises? I con-

---

78. He will never give up this idea. In November 1851, he writes to Louise: "It is a fine thing to be a great writer, to hold men in the pot and make them sizzle with your words and jump like chestnuts. There must be rapturous pride in feeling that one weighs on humanity with the entire weight of one's idea."

tend that they are inseparable and that they continually interpene-trate. And this interpenetration defines Flaubertian syncretism.

To begin with, the infinite can demote the finite by its presence only if it is incarnate in a finite reality. If not, it will become the object of a "recurrent" thought, or else it will appear to a situated being as his horizon. In religious mysticism, it is the mystic's interior-ity which, by a series of challenges and asceses, bursts his finitude. But when totalization is exterior, the infinite cannot introduce itself into the midst of the objects it totalizes except through the me-diation of the art that produces a finite center of unrealization in the midst of the real. Hence the beautiful object, for Flaubert, is *transfinite*, an imaginary totalization of the infinite by a finite and open object: this is what *Smarh* ought to be, thinks Gustave, if I hit my mark. But, conversely, in Flaubert the mystic attitude is imagi-nary: his quasi-religious consciousness of the infinite is structured like panoramic consciousness—principle and consequence of an ef-fort of de-situation. As we have seen, de-situation can be reached only through unrealization. But all imagining consciousness is self-conscious. Therefore the mystic option, here, implies the non-thetic consciousness of being a choice of the imaginary. When Gustave de-cides to write *Smarh* so as to mediate between the finite and the in-finite, he buries himself in the imaginary by pretending to de-situate himself; but as a result he becomes the real mediation between the imaginary and reality, for he produces by means of the work done by unrealizing objects. If mysticism is a *role*, [79] art is an activity that aims to inscribe this role in our world. It is a matter of constituting a real object with real tools, in short, of producing by work a determination of the world that can be a door opened onto nonbeing. Nonetheless, as this unreality is none other than the compressed unity of being and, ultimately, the full ontological development that is assigned to it and altogether forbidden, art is called upon by impossible Being to *give form* to the imaginary, to fix it in the world through something material (signs, colors, marble, etc.), and, while preserving its unreal character, to make it—as a beautiful work of art—a whole instituted by unrealizable prescriptions. In short, art manifests the completion of our world, or the deepest Being, as a having-to-be within the world. Hence its real mission: to make the real pass into the unreal by

---

79. This description is meant obviously for Flaubert alone and not the "real" mystics; Theresa of Avila or John of the Cross live their non-integration with a *religious* commu-nity. This means that faith exists *at the outset*, as a fundamental given.

producing the unreal in the heart of reality; to denounce, at the end of the *poesis*, totality in its plenitude as nothingness of being (or the pure streaming of disordered appearances) by establishing through the work of art (a *shapeless* macrocosm) a perpetual comparison between the real, which *by default* is not, and absolute being, which is not *by excess* (in the sense that we say something is too good to be true).

But if Gustave recognizes that the message of the infinite—which he must transmit to men to torment them all the more—is merely an imaginary one, what about predestination? Where will he find his mandate? If he sets the pure fictions of the artist against the difficult quest for truth, will he not be disqualified in advance? And in Gustave himself, isn't the average man likely to expose the unreality of his end?

Indeed, Gustave does hesitate: if he must enumerate all human "pettiness," why should art escape his irony? Already in the *Mémoires* he had written:

> Oh Art, Art! What a beautiful thing, this vanity! And what pettiness . . . If I have felt moments of enthusiasm, I owe them to Art, and yet what vanity art is! To want to portray man in a block of stone or the soul in words, feelings through sounds and nature on a varnished canvas . . . If there is on earth and among all nothingnesses a belief one adores, if there is something holy, pure, sublime, something that harks to that immoderate desire for the infinite and the vague that we call soul, it is art. And what pettiness! A stone, a word, a sound, the disposition of all that we call sublime . . . man with his genius and his art is but a miserable aping of something more elevated. I seek beauty in the infinite, and all I find there is doubt.[80]

In this complex passage, Flaubert reduces aesthetic creation to the mere "aping" of a Creation—beauty in the infinite—which does not even manifest itself and probably never happened. This aping is itself a failure: how can nature be portrayed on a varnished canvas? If it is captured there, it is by mutilation. The insubstantiality of art makes it a vain imitation of what should be but does not reveal itself. Without denying that this "vanity" stirs him, Flaubert makes no essential distinction between it and other products of human praxis. Genius exists, but its hands bring forth only nothingness. The accent is on the heterogeneity of the object of production or reproduction, and of the material employed. The inertia, the compact immobility, the inpene-

80. *Mémoires d'un fou*, chap. 18.

trability of stone disqualifies in advance any attempt to render in stone the life of the human organism. Similarly—we shall return to this— words are constitutionally unfit to embody the thing they designate. In these moments Flaubert, while recognizing the existence of "geniuses," doubts their *vocation*. It is their constitution that makes them such, in short, the accident of birth. There is resentment in this attitude: Gustave doubts the predestination of others when, comparing their writings to his, he thinks he will never be one of them. "Convinced of my impotence and my sterility, I was overcome by jealous hatred: I told myself it was nothing, that chance alone had dictated these words,"[81] and: "I would write a book, it would be on the turpitude of great men—I am glad that great men should have had any."[82] But whatever the motivation, he discovers that this attitude is untenable. Predestination, the essential characteristic of the artist, is revealed for what it is: an imaginary determination; even if he writes a masterpiece, Gustave will not change his being. Who knows if it is not that being itself, his bourgeois being (its income, its culture) that gives him the advantage to write. Later, in moments of discouragement, he will sometimes resign himself to considering art merely an *occupation*. He writes to Alfred, for example: "I swear I don't think about fame, and not much about Art. I seek to spend my time in the least boring way, and I have found it." And to Maxime: "I am a bourgeois who lives in retirement in the country, busying himself with literature."

But most of the time he stands fast, thanks to his syncretism: he does not want to let go either of truth or of unrealization; of the surgical eye or of lyric escape; of absolute power or of the dolorism of impotence. Even as he emphasizes the unreality of the image, he has two contradictory and often simultaneous ways of affirming the truthfulness of art and hence the authenticity of his mission.

The source of the first is the intention to beat men of science at their own game. Flaubert recognized in himself quite early the faculty of *imagining the true*. Now he gives it to the artist; provided it is engendered methodically, the image anticipates reality or resuscitates a past that has not been lived: "Sometimes historical revelations come to me, certain things appear to me clearly—metempsychosis may be true— sometimes I believe that I have lived at different periods; indeed, I have memories of them."[83] Of course, the underlying meaning of this

81. Ibid.
82. *Souvenirs*, p. 64.
83. Ibid., p. 51. This note is contemporaneous with the writing of *Smarh* or slightly later.

attitude is *sorcery:* we shall not deny that Gustave had a tendency to surpass the laws of the imaginary, to confer upon imaginative forces the power of enchantment, of indirect creation at a distance that would in part compensate for the unreality of the work. But there is more: for in his eyes, as we have seen, exterior totalization engenders a sur-truth. When he declares, later, that "his Bovary" suffers and weeps in twenty villages, he is not claiming that his Emma *as such* is to be found reproduced in twenty copies. Taken this way, the remark might have been made by Duranty; but let us not forget that Flaubert has repeatedly condemned "realism" in literature, and that the object of his totalizing ambition is not to describe correctly so particular a generality. If Emma were merely a déclassée provincial woman who had made a poor match, *Madame Bovary* would not be worth an hour's effort in the eyes of its author. Indeed, those weeping village women have a *lesser-being* than his conception, they are *less* Bovary than his Emma, they express more obscurely the bond of the microcosm to the macrocosm. Since the real world for Flaubert is partly totalized according to the scheme of radical evil, and since accidents and dispersion alone detotalize it, imaginary totalization alone is rigorous; as a consequence, it produces archetypal images, which—starting with the preconceived principle and archetypes—it engenders as singular manifestations of the All. As such, these images cover a sector of the quasi-creation, and certain existing things seem to manifest them to a greater or lesser extent as their being-in-exteriority (contingency, accidents) permits. Emma, a creation of art, is beautiful, that is, she expresses an imaginary macrocosm that has been the object of a free creation. But to the extent that nature should imitate art, real women can find in Bovary the supreme and unrealizable demand to become entirely what they are. There is in Flaubert a Platonism of the imagination: the real Bovarys *participate in the singular eidos* of "Emma" as the contingent objects of the perceptible world participate, for Plato, in intelligible Ideas.

The imperative of the unreal—Beauty as impossible necessity—addresses itself primitively to the real in its universality, but it is internalized by readers or spectators and becomes a personal imperative: always seek to perceive the world in yourself and outside yourself as if it had been made the object of a concerted creation. Through a beautiful work, Flaubert will give orders to those who have always given him orders; he will establish himself in them *as other* by imposing on them the duty to grasp *their* world through the vision of another. In short, he will pay them back. But what they see will not be error: it is

473

the sur-truth—cruel, dreadful, etc.—which is imaginary. Archetypal images derealize perception insofar as they take its "meaning" to the point of incandescence. In this conception, confused as it still may be, so false? To the extent that we use the creations of novelists as grids for deciphering real individuals, we unrealize these individuals by considering them as *creatures*. And when it will later be said of a woman that "she is a Bovary," no progress will have been made in the knowledge of her character, but she will be seen through the totalizing intuitions of a demiurge who is none other than Flaubert. This is the trap: we believe we *recognize* ourselves in a fictional character, whereas we merely internalize the impossible necessity of being the synthetic product of a divine totalization. But *is it merely a trap?* No; for this imperative leads us to shape and deepen ourselves.

Simultaneously, Flaubert continues to affirm that artistic creation is in essence imaginary, an "aping." One is the creator of images for lack of the power to create *being*. There is a curious and revealing passage in the *Mémoires;* after denouncing the vanity of art, Flaubert continues: "I would like something that required neither expression nor form, something pure like perfume, strong like stone, ineffable like a song, something at once all and none of these things." Here he abandons the ideas of sur-truth and of totalization: the created object would express nothing, it would not express the meaning of the world; it would simply *be,* unlike the image, which is nothingness. Curiously, he usually derives confirmation of his mandate from the "vanity of art." The existence in man of imagination, that nothingness of being, he sees as a *cipher* in Jaspers's sense of the word. From the sole fact that it detaches from being and fulfills our nonsatisfaction with nonbeing, it vaguely reveals *something* inarticulable and inconceivable. Or, if you will, because of this faculty the problem of the ontological Creation remains in a state of mystery. If the world were noncreated, there would be merely being, and we ourselves would be entirely conditioned by our facticity; but since, through the image, we are capable of putting the real to the service of nothingness, we are not limited to what we are, and the nothingness that we produce demands an explanation that cannot be given. The truth of scientists is mechanism: the universe has always existed, nothing is lost, and nothing is created. But imagination, as the imperative of nonbeing—the impossible absolute-being—presents the science of being with an enigma it cannot resolve: Being cannot produce nothingness. Yet *there is* nothingness, art bears witness to it. On this level, the artist himself is a cipher: why is this being devoured by images, why this determination to ape the Creation, which either never occurred or conceals itself, and to produce nonbeing? Where does he get the inclination for it? Where does he get the power for it? Flaubert suggests that the artist is called forth by the absence of God. Before the indifference of the invisible All-Powerful, he takes responsibility for the world's demand to be created, to be produced in the synthetic unity of a free activity; his determination to reproduce the creative act—though he knows it is merely a gesture and that he is a substitute for God only in the unreal—bears witness at once to the necessity and the impossibility of being a *creature* for himself and for others. But this futile passion—in which one makes oneself a fake creator for lack of being a real creature—is itself inexplicable without the strange solicitation of what is by what is not. At the core of utilitarianism—that passage from being to being which is effected in the middle of being—the mandate of the artist if revealed by the presence in him of nonbeing *as concern*. Later, Mallarmé—at once more aristocratic and, by his own choice, more plebeian—will judge himself mandated by *being from below*, by what Merleau-Ponty calls the "fabric of being in a rough state," in order to bear witness to a universal aspiration of the world to deliver itself from chance. The issue here is also one of an impossible necessity; but he will claim to express in his poem the savage need of all reality, a need he knows he is incapable of satisfying except through the total and conscious failure of the poet. Flaubert, however, still imbued with the theological idea, maintains that the call—if it existed—would come from above. Beauty is sur-truth: truth says what is, namely that the world is an uncreated non-sense; Beauty, a demand from above, reveals the sense of this non-sense; or, if you will, the Absolute becomes realized *by default*, in its very unreality, as the meaning of the relative, the infinite as the meaning of the finite, nothingness as the meaning of being. The artist is the man who abandons the world in order to bear witness that God *should be*, and—by this *inexplicable* occupation—he bears witness to himself, to the irreducible authenticity of his vocation.

Flaubert is not the only one to formulate the problem in these terms. His entire generation regrets the loss of faith; with God dead, these unbelievers become artists in spite of themselves for having understood—more or less obscurely—that the imagination is a fundamental and constitutive relation of the existing to the reality it surpasses. It is as if the imaginative function had become their proof of the greatness and weakness of man without God. His greatness is that he substitutes himself for eternal Being and creates the world in

475

its place, displaying the world as it would be were it based on an intentional freedom. Man's weakness is that his creation can be only imaginary, because at the same time he knows he is the derisory demiurge of a cosmos that *is not*. Be that as it may, the artist reverses the relation that the Christian of the preceding centuries established between being and nonbeing. For the Christian, God is Being par excellence, thus we attach ourselves to him insofar as we participate in Being; error and sin exist only to bear witness to the nonbeing that is in us. For the artist, the opposite is true: as God is not, we bear witness by the nothingness that is in us to our vain, inconsolable denial of his nonexistence; it is by making ourselves imaginary that we render ourselves most like him. Flaubert's originality resides in his sado-masochism: since beauty is evil, the demiurge he vainly calls to bear witness is the Evil Genius; the artist, in exterior totalization, makes himself unreally possessed and guided by Satan.

As we see, Gustave proves his mandate simultaneously by being and by nonbeing: imagination is prophetic; it captures truth, namely being, *before* science does and *more effectively;* imagination is the nothingness at the core of being, it is negation and failure as vain testimony to an unreachable Elsewhere. This contradiction is not unsurpassable: it is *true* that the image is nothingness but also that it is, as Merleau-Ponty says, "the reckoner of being." But we need not attempt this difficult synthesis here, for at the time *Smarh* is being written, Gustave has only gone so far as to hold thesis and antithesis together in a syncretism of interpenetration.

When Gustave discovers the general lines of *Smarh*, at the beginning of December 1838, his morose mood of the autumn gives way to an almost *dazzling* state of mind. The choice of subject is inseparable from the subjective metamorphosis of the attitude. He can begin this *other* work only by becoming *another* man. The *Mémoires* have run aground because of the truths they contain: their contradictions urge Gustave to practice self-analysis, which he is neither willing nor able to do; moreover, interior totalization, even if it were effected in the milieu of universal subjectivity, assumes a clearly masochistic character because of the author's pessimism. *Smarh* is the joyous denial of masochism and reflexive knowledge; it is the proud and authoritarian "rebound" into the imaginary, the deliberate choice of sadism, the substitution of laughter for dolorism; it is the antihumanism of the panoramic consciousness that tears Flaubert from his kind of compelling him to work against it; it is the unreal "standoff" with the infinite that specifies the very notion of the artist by making him a mediator between the imaginary and lived experience; it is by the same token the discovery of the Satanic mandate, that radioactive nonbeing which turns a bourgeois son against the aims of his class and replaces inspiration with the proud concern of nothingness; in short, it is the simultaneous choice of a theme and an attitude that reciprocally condition each other. In that winter of 1838–39, the vexed adolescent *takes himself in hand*; hope is born of taking a stand that radically denies that which had presided at the making of the *Mémoires:* the disdainful denial of subjectivity leads Gustave to define art as a total and unreal objectivity. He escapes from his family, from his milieu, from his kind; he escapes from himself and, cheerfully deciding to remain ignorant of himself, ensconces himself in the imaginary. At the same time he believes he has grasped the fundamental meaning of literature: it is *sacred;* sometimes it is a black magic produced by the artist's sorcery, and sometimes an even blacker religion, of which the artist becomes a priest. The *numen,* in its most primitive form, manifests itself in things as a collapsing of being which reveals a having-to-be; producing aesthetic necessity from the crumbling of verbal material, the artist participates in the numinous: from the dispersed elements of our experience, he produces unreally the worst of all possible worlds. In any case, this world is *created,* it symbolizes the great religious ceremony of the divine Creation, the course of things is disclosed in it as a providence in reverse, and to each creature a place is assigned by special intention. In order to release the sense of the nonsense of our world, Flaubert will make himself victim and high priest; he will always regard aesthetic work as a cult. This idea will recur throughout his correspondence, never better expressed than in 1876, in a letter to George Sand: "You accuse me of not letting myself go 'naturally.' All right, what about discipline, virtue? What are we going do with them? I admire Monsieur de Buffon for putting on clean cuffs to write. That luxury is a symbol." Yes. A symbol like the tonsure. From the age of fifteen, writing tends to become a priestly vocation: the "natural" and improvisation, still dominant in 1837, are gradually rejected; writing becomes a *spiritual exercise.* As the object of art challenges nature—that is, everyday reality—the creator must reject spontaneity: he tears himself away from it, *puts himself in the right frame of mind* to make contact with the imaginary. Solicited by the absolute end to anchor the impossible in the real by tearing himself away from the world, the very being of the mediator is a having-to-be. It is no accident that Gustave all his life will persist in confusing the artist with the saint, to the point of embodying himself in Smarh the her-

477

mit, in Saint Antoine, and compelling his friends to celebrate his birthday on Saint Polycarp's day. Beginning with *Smarh*, he almost feels a religious imperative in himself again ("Write! Subordinate everything in your life to this absolute end!")—the aesthetic imperative he wants to impose on others through his work. He is carrying sado-masochism to incandescence: "Make a martyr of yourself so you can make martyrs of others by compelling them to admire your work, namely the presentation of the uncreated world *as if it had been created by Satan.*"

Until the autumn of 1838 the young man was inconsolable at not being the object of a special decree from Providence. Engendered by an absolute Will, he might have been absolute in his turn. In more than one passage from the early works he cries out his rage at being a product of chance: "You were born fatally because your father, no doubt, returned one day from an orgy heated with wine and dirty talk, and your mother, taking advantage of it, employed all the feminine wiles, impelled by her instincts of flesh and bestiality . . ."[84] This description is scarcely suited to the reasonable and calculated embraces of the Flaubert parents. But it clearly marks Gustave's rancor against the couple who made him a younger son. Above all, we sense regret at not having been *summoned.* The passage, taken in its entirety, describes the human being as Achille-Cléophas sees him, that is, as a system in motion whose present position is rigorously defined by its immediately prior position. By his angry suppression of ends, Gustave strips all human meaning from the universe and from man. But as a result, he glimpses salvation: in the heart of darkness, he has a presentiment of the bouncing back of *Smarh.* And this is just what he discovers in December of the same year: even if we accord to mankind that there is a particular teleology belonging to our species, this finality, conditioned by the most elementary needs and by particular interest, is merely an effect of our natural disposition; man as being does not escape the laws of being, that is, the most rigorous determinism. What saves the artist is that his aim is a nonbeing; external to our race, his aim does not identify itself—quite the contrary—with the perpetuation of life, not even with the tendency of being to persevere in its being: from the outset, it tears its servant away from the world of possibles because it asks him to sacrifice his own existence to a pure and simple impossibility. The universe of "beings" has never been able to engender that end. It must have produced itself as pure de-

84. *Mémoires d'un fou,* chap. 20.

mand and must have made inhuman man emerge from earth, with the obligation and inability to meet that demand. Beginning with *Smarh*, Flaubert wants to see himself as such: he is the one who bears in his heart the demand of the impossible. It has summoned him, but he, through his torments, gives its presence to the world. From the depths of the future, of his always future nonbeing, it conditions him down to his least impulses. In this basic and sacred relationship, Flaubert sees, starting with *Smarh*, what might be called a daily predestination, a reversal of mechanistic time: his very needs—which he nonetheless continues to despise—become secondary ends; to write, one must live. Certainly the faculty of imagining belongs to everyone—although the grocer hardly makes use of it, according to Flaubert. But in the artist alone it appears as a categorical imperative: contrary to commonsense, Gustave does not consider it a gift but a lack; certainly the artist abounds with images, but spontaneity doesn't have much of a hand in it. Beauty, that bitterly resented absence, is his leavening. Starting here, this mediator of the impossible will tear men away from their human condition by forcing them to receive the imaginary message and to develop their imagination through his works.

This conception may be a kind of Catharism, a kind of utterly black Jansenism. For good reason. But we must see it not as a liberation but as a counteralienation. Determined, well before birth, by the pleasure of a father who wished him bourgeois and a younger son, constituted by the care of a mother as passive activity, Flaubert, as she made him, cannot effectively combat the father's curse. Never in his entire life will he feel free; never will his will escape heteronomy. He must save himself, however. But as revolt is forbidden him, he will escape alienation only by binding himself to another object. He can replace bourgeois-being only by being-for-art, and *profession*, that fatal future defined by the father, only by another fatality. Thus salvation seems to him *other*, that is, an *other* damnation: in order to oppose the father's will retroactively, from before Gustave's birth, art must be destiny and heteronomy, an *other* will. The forces that will do battle with each other are future demands—"Be a notary," "Be a writer"—and the fate of the young man will be determined by the victory of one over the other without playing any part himself. The artist is put into the world to create a masterpiece—a derisory image of the inconceivable Creation. If he succeeds, all the data of his protohistory are altered with a single stroke: the paternal intention is changed into illusion; believing he has engendered a bourgeois, this bourgeois has

479

fallen into a trap of history—he has produced exactly what a future imperative demanded of him. In short, the artist is the son of his masterpiece. He is put into the world in order to sacrifice himself to the object that must be constructed. This is binding the man to his product, no doubt: but Gustave had no other way out. In the Flaubert family, from father to son, one *works*. To remain a poet—in Gustave's sense—is to fall into a suspect quietism which the paterfamilias will accept only if he sees it as a symptom of illness and which, even tolerated, will be immediately disqualified by the incessant activity of the two Flaubert doctors. But if art is a practice, if the work of art demands of the artist that he carry on an uncertain combat from day to day, if it is to be realized through a labor still harder and more thankless than that of the physicians, Gustave will be able to reassure himself: he will apply in good conscience the familial norms, the morality of the class he denies without being able to contest its virtues, to his extrahuman activities; it is his work that must be objectified and crystalized in the chosen material.

At the same time, the aesthetic imperative valorizes him because it is addressed to his singularity: if one must become a notary, what matters is one's family background, one's parents' style of life and their ambitions; when these external conditions are brought together, individuals can be otherwise nondescript; they are merely required to have average intelligence, which is the commonest thing in the world. Thus, the experienced certainty of self is changed into pure illusion, at the very least into an epiphenomenon, and the truth of the person resides in the profession of notary. But when the exigency of art selects the future artist, it is the work of art that commands as singular universal, and not the generality of the profession: being singular, it demands the sacrifice of a definite singularity. Don Quixote claims Cervantes, and Richard II Shakespeare. Thus the laborer in art remains the means of the work of art; he is forbidden to prefer himself or to pose for himself; but his permanent sacrifice demands that he possess self-assurance and transmute it in the apodictic unity of the masterpiece. A unique means, the artist is chosen by the work-to-be as its *essential* instrument. This conception of art gives Gustave the chance if not to accept himself at least to recuperate the self by regarding his particular traits and even his bourgeois origins as tools to employ dispassionately, uncomplacently, and pitilessly in order to produce the irreplaceable disintegration of matter by means of the imaginary in a definite time and place. Everything in him becomes necessary, for the vampire-object will nourish itself from everything. Pride, envy, malice, rages, and fits of despair will serve; the anomaly of which he is ashamed and which separates him from men can be one of the signs of his election, for the masterpiece-to-be never chooses a *replaceable* worker.

We ought not, however, to confuse Flaubert with the individualists who preceded and followed him. His Self troubles him, and only half of it belongs to him, even in experienced certainty. Moreover, he doesn't see the work as a reflection of his person—ever. As an exterior totalizer, he cannot imagine really expressing himself. The work is nourished by the author's singularity, but it does not restore it, it transforms it into itself. It is not the face of the artist, the microcosm, that surfaces on every page read; it is the face of the macrocosm such as it would be if it had been created. The surveying subject alone can see a world surveyed: thus can it guide the real writer who chooses real signs in order to express what his imagined self discovers and produces all at once. This doubling of the subject as a fictive seer and a real worker is peculiar to Flaubert; and through the necessity of unrealizing himself he understands that he unrealizes his character. The panoramic subject, an abstract figure who at bottom expresses only the totalizing intention, is confused with the demoralizers of *Smarh*, now with Yuk and now with Satan; on the other hand, the author is at one with the surveyed world, for the *meaning* of the created macrocosm sums up Gustave's *Weltanschauung*. Thus the worker loses himself entirely in the work and remains unrecognizable in it. A little later, Flaubert will voluntarily insist on the objectivity of art. But the texts are clear: he deems it indispensable that the artist put himself into his object; he simply forbids him to *show* himself in it. The singular universal cannot be reduced to the singularity of its author; the imaginary is not made to reproduce the real, which would be impossible anyway. So Gustave is now disencumbered of himself: his anomaly is justified, for it makes him the essential means of the work, but at the same time it is alleviated: the absolute end consumes it, and it is no longer mentioned. Nonetheless, this austere conception still aims to sacrifice the man to the work. It could not be otherwise in the universe of absolute pessimism: alienation is total, for men are the products of their products, to the point that these products are the absolute ends for which they are born and lose themselves. The artist sacrifices his person to his work so that the work may hold sway over men and impose its aesthetic imperatives.

481

The Failure of *Smarh*

In December 1831 he is overwhelmed by this flash of enlightenment: I am the Artist, he thinks. As Jean Genet will say: I am the *Thief*. Does he entirely believe in it? Does he believe in his predestination? He changes his tune quickly enough, for two weeks later he cries: "Oh Art! Art! bitter disappointment, nameless phantom that glitters and dooms!!" Subsequent letters inform us that he has fallen back into heavy ennui. What does this mean? That he is renouncing his conception of artists? Or that he has retained it but has lost hope of being one?

He surely believes in predestination—which is at the foundation as well as the pinnacle of any edifice—*when it involves others*. Nothing is more specious than retrospective illusion. And one is all too inclined to conclude from the fact that Shakespeare wrote masterpieces that he was born to write them. In short, we read his life in reverse, which is easy enough since it is over and we alone decide the direction of the reading. Respect plays a role as well; it is easy to see that inert exigency which summons us when we listen to Shakespeare's plays as the same imperative that earlier required him to write them. There is no doubt that Flaubert was taken in by this illusion: he reads the great authors, admires them, and from childhood he believes they are mandated; what he affirms, in his enthusiasm at the beginning of December, is that he too has received a mandate to write. At the moment when he is fascinated by his subject—the totalization of the infinite—this affirmation is not too difficult. But can he sustain it for long? He would have to grasp in himself the summons of nonbeing as a singular categorical imperative. Is this possible? For others, certainly—whatever the value of what they will write. I have recounted elsewhere how a misunderstanding made me believe at the age of eight that my venerable grandfather was ordering me to write. That was enough to make me believe I was entrusted with a mission. Yet this was a particular situation, a family, a patriarch who showed me the way. No doubt it is the same for many writers. But Flaubert? Far from showing him the way, his parents discouraged him from following it. If not through words, at least through their absolute indifference. Let him make a career and take up a profession, that was the order; after that, no one prohibited him from tormenting the Muses, but in his eyes this tolerance sufficed to discredit his literary vocation. If he made himself an artist, it was in defiance of them. No doubt Alfred advised him to write, but casually, and without really believing that Art was either a salvation or a justification. Yet it is impossible to confuse a spontaneous decision with an imperative: the former reflects only our subjectivity, the latter is an alien voice, it is the Other in us, irreducible. We do not have to relate the commandment that inhabits us to a particular face: it can come from *everyone* or remain in us, abstract, undated and unconnected to the one who originally uttered it. Still, *Others* are necessary to justify the particular quality of the order that is *otherness*. Yet in this particular case they are missing, for it is against them that Flaubert has chosen this way out. He is remarkably alone and reduced, for once, to pure interiority. His decision is certainly marked by extreme gravity: he knows that if he does not win on this field, he loses on all. But his will involves only him: no one has asked anything of him or promised him anything. How can you find in yourself that "you must" whose harshness would permit the hope of a "you can"? Gustave undoubtedly comes to take his passion and the urgency of dangers for an order; but you cannot deceive yourself for long in this domain, not without extreme fatigue. All we can say is that the paternal curse comes to his aid in these sleights of hand: beyond any artistic vocation, Flaubert perceives he is predestined; he sees himself slide toward that "profession" which has always awaited him, the profession of barrister, of physician, of solicitor; he feels *in his being* a profound complicity with the having-to-be that his father imposes on him and which his *existence* denies. This subjectivity, haunted by imperatives, is hence qualified to take *for an imperative* the claimed summons that will deliver it from them. Occupied by the Other, Flaubert's consciousness is structured as otherness, and his own desires can appear to him as other. No doubt the young man, when he conceived *Smarh,* saw himself from the outside, like one of the artists he admired and believed mandated, because he had not yet taken up his pen or tried to internalize this external scheme.

But he begins to write. What happens? The *Souvenirs, Novembre,* and the correspondence tell us that he is enthusiastic at the moment of conception, gloomy and sober from the moment he begins the execution. This is because Flaubert's ego has a tripartite structure: the real activity of the writer is conditioned by two imaginary elements: the totalizing subject that surveys the universe and, from below, the predestined subject that gives the writing its meaning. The Artist is a role. At best, Flaubert succeeds for some time in really writing even while *playing at writing;* he gives his real practice an imaginary meaning: it is elevated by an *other* and future end; he lives spontaneity as an alienation. The real subject of a hazardous enterprise, he regards

483

himself, deeply but unreally, as the essential means of an inspired and certain end. Of course, he is not unaware that he is giving himself over to phantasms. But he believes in his role—as professional actors do, no more, no less—and his degree of belief is variable: it is considerable if the pen runs easily over the paper, and sinks toward zero every time it stumbles over a difficulty. At this moment, praxis reveals its true characteristics: heteronomy gives way to hesitant autonomy; destiny, the imperative, the promises vanish together, giving way to the dismal melody of lived experience and of chance, to ruminations, to fumbling and ever renewed inventions, to contestable and ever contested decisions. Then Gustave leaves his writing table and falls back into ennui; gratuitous, profane, and contingent, his activity cannot satisfy him: nothing grounds it, nothing demands it; so he judges it an *occupation*. A little later, when he *is no longer writing*, he resumes the role and manages to believe in it by referring to what he *will write*. Hence he can observe: "The future ravishes me, the present is nothing, the past leaves me in despair, and I gain nothing from experience. I love to think of the future, and never is a single thing accomplished that I had hoped for, awaited, feared."[85] The past is the abandoned work, his last failure; the present is disillusionment: the man who writes *is no writer*, and, in fact, he can write only by renouncing being; writing, even if one lies, is a moment of truth because it is *practice;* Buffon's cuffs will not transform it into ceremony, hence the *ennui of writing*. The future, on the other hand, is the work that awaits composition; when Gustave dreams, immobile, of the future end that governs him, complex relations become knotted in imagination between the panoramic subject and the Artist; though neither is entirely identified with the other, a veritable dialectical unity is established between them, and limits are abolished in a movement of reciprocal confirmation. Indeed, two negative and unreal moments are involved, but the projection of these negations into a real future (the Artist *will realize* the panoramic vision and will offer readers the world as a center of unrealization) tends to facilitate the confusion of being (as practico-inert and real determination of the present by the future) with nonbeing (as imaginary projection of the self and unreal determination of the future moment).

85. *Souvenirs*, pp. 103–4, written in 1840. Of course the text is not concerned solely with literature, though it has been introduced by some literary remarks. It must be observed that it contradicts numerous passages from his correspondence in which Gustave declares himself to be a *prophet*. Nothing surprising in that: the passage from *Souvenirs* was written in the midst of a depression.

Can we say that Gustave writes solely to *be a writer?* No; after all, he composed an entire book of narratives *before* discovering that he was imprisoned in his bourgeois-being. But there is no doubt that from the time of the *Mémoires,* and especially with the writing of *Smarh,* he wanted to turn his penchant for writing[86] to other ends, for his justification, his salvation, and his transubstantiation. This explains his growing anxiety: he tries in vain to combat a real being with a being of imagination. It is *true* that he *is* bourgeois, and this means only that society, through his family, has given him from birth a material status and inert imperative that define him in his generality. After this, he must *exist his being,* that is, he must produce himself from these coordinates as an existence subjugated to predeterminations and perfectly incommensurate with them. If there is thus a possibility of combating his original prefabrication, he will find his pure existence in it—or annihilation of being. To write will then become the praxis of someone existing, and the free production of a work of the mind—*which no one and nothing awaits*—will not refer to him as an ontological determination. Literature, in the best case, will have the capacity to excuse him from taking up a profession or, if he has already done so, allow him to quit it; literature will change nothing of his class-being. He will be a bourgeois who writes. If indeed we can call a man who makes literature his primary end a writer, and if we thereby recognize his being, it is to the extent that the sum of his works, the ideological interest they represent, the necessity of defending *his* aesthetic, philosophical, political, etc., positions increase the weight of the practico-inert in him and outline certain fixed demands in his future. The enormous weight of things done and said makes the past a future imperative and negatively underscores finitude: he is a writer when he can no longer do anything but write what he has gradually condemned himself to write. This is what Flaubert will be after *Madame Bovary:* the chips are down, he has defined and classified himself as member of a small "elite," all of whose members call themselves Artists. But in 1838 this is certainly not what he wants, nor can he obtain it; for such ontological dignity is generally acquired late in life: it is the victory of death, the social aspect of aging. Therefore he can only *playact,* but he is aware of it—insincerely, of course—and takes fright. Hence his mania for comparing his young life to those of the celebrated dead: when and how did they feel called? Late in life, perhaps, like Rousseau: then there is hope. But if it was before the age of fifteen, he is lost. As

---

86. For which we have offered motivations above.

I have said, he sought out the pettiness of great men: he confides to us that he does it out of jealousy, and he is surely right. But it is also to bring them closer to himself: by discovering their weaknesses he unmasks the contingency of their lives, which, like his, progress haphazardly. Some of them, perhaps, were unaware of the secret designs of Beauty—artists without knowing it. In any case, this exhausting game consumes him; always disappointed, he grasps at a phantom. This is the source of his anguish: transubstantiation is necessary and impossible. To succeed in what he desires, he would have to be entirely devoured by the imaginary, in short, go mad. Maybe that is what the future author of *La Spirale* is dreaming of.

Yet this impossibility is merely in principle: what is eroding is the very idea of vocation; when Gustave contests it in spite of himself, he is at his best; in other words he doubts the vocation and not himself. But when he is unhappy with what he writes—as happened the previous summer with *Mémoires d'un fou*—the situation is reversed: vocation exists, and predestination, only they are reserved for others: if Gustave has heard nothing, it may be because he was not called. We are reminded of Kierkegaard's *Am I Abraham?* Flaubert attaches prime importance to the answer; more than life is at stake, it is salvation and damnation. If the world is ruled by the Evil Genius, the young man's mad love for Beauty may have been given him merely to delude him more effectively. In Gustave's sadistic universe, virtue is always punished and misfortune is strictly proportionate to greatness of soul: since Gustave is dying to write, isn't it logical that he should lack the means? The *one* means, for there is only one in his eyes: genius. And how does one prove one has genius except by producing a masterpiece? At fourteen, Gustave wrote without much concern for the result. From sixteen on, he wants to attempt a great coup. If he doesn't have genius, he *deserves* the future his father has reserved for him. The masterpiece alone will *institute* another future. So, he must produce one. *On the double:* the cycle of secondary studies is approaching its end; in three years there is law school, Paris, and then the bar or the profession of notary. Beginning in 1838, the adolescent is fitted with the utmost ambition; when he conceives *Smarh*, he has *consciously* aspired to write a masterpiece. In it, he wants to say all there is to say about everything. To take the measure of his works, he will not hesitate to compare them to the *Confessions*, to *Faust:* his work will have to come up to snuff. If not, farewell Artist; what's left is a maladjusted petit-bourgeois, inferior indeed to Big Brother Achille. The proud austerity, the profound naïveté of this attitude will be appreciated; we should simply observe that it leads him astray by forcing him to choose a cosmic subject which he does not yet have the means to treat and which is glazed with insincerity: to write *in order* to create a masterpiece is to falsify the direction and meaning of writing. One writes *in order to write,* by doing one's best; and of course, one must— even to produce a mediocre work—have the certainty that one will succeed. It is even possible, without betraying literature, for a young man working on his book to think that it *will be* a masterpiece. This idea is thus merely a marginal element that accompanies the enterprise without governing it. In *Smarh,* however, we feel that Flaubert is impelled by the idea of genius, and that he demands of his sentences not only that they say what he means but that they say it with genius. We might reproach the author of *Smarh,* as Cocteau reproached Barrès, for "his sentences, immortal in advance," if we did not sense his anxious, almost desperate need to achieve his salvation.

Indeed, this autumn he has little concern for glory and never asks himself how a masterpiece achieves recognition. Time is pressing: if he must await the judgment of his grandnephews, it will be too late; moreover, since in his eyes the work of art is accomplished against men, their approbation is not required. All his life, Gustave regarded the public as inessential. Alfred's and Ernest's votes will be enough for him. Yet this will be merely a verification. He is really counting on the internal evidence of *Smarh*—in other words, on himself. This is because the masterpiece, just as it conjures a center of unrealization in the midst of the real, seems to him a metaphysical event: a reverse image of the divine Creation, it is, like the True of Spinoza, *index sui.* The same man produces the work of art and judges it. Gustave is convinced that through "taste" he will himself be able to discern the validity of his labor, and that if he wholeheartedly approves it, the operation will be completed. The result: beginning in 1838, he lives in perpetual anguish; with every word he writes he puts his *being* in question. He notes that year, in the *Souvenirs:* "I swing from hope to anxiety, from a mad hopefulness to a sad negation, it is rain and sun, but a sun of gold paper and a dirty, dull rain." He never stops *judging Smarh* as he is writing it. And the judgment is severe.

On 26 December, after the enthusiasm of conception, disillusionment sets in: the past fifteen days Flaubert has moved to the stage of execution. "I do not know if I should continue my work, which offers me nothing but insurmountable difficulties and failure as soon as I advance." Art is a "bitter disappointment." He feels "all the things that are weak in me, the heart as much as the mind." "There are places where I am brought up short," he writes. "Just recently I had serious difficulty in the composition of my morality play, in which I was always face to face with the infinite; I did not know how to express what overwhelmed my soul." In February 1839, he complains of his literary impotence: "In earlier times, I used to reflect . . . dash down on paper all the verve I had in my heart; now I no longer think, I no longer reflect, I write even less." He has lost the secret of those great mystic elevations that he used to call poetry: "Poetry may have grown bored and left me." Yet he writes—*Smarh* is ever in hand. But in killing the poet, the Artist in him fares scarcely better than his victim: "I cannot do any work requiring imagination, everything I produce is dry, labored, forced, painfully extracted . . . What I have done (of my morality play) is absurd, devoid of ideas. Perhaps I'll drop it." The lines that follow clearly mark the importance of his disappointment: "My existence, so beautiful in my dreams, so poetic, so vast, so full of love, will be like everyone else's, monotonous, sensible, stupid, *I will do my law degree, be admitted to the bar,* and end up as assistant district attorney or royal prosecutor in some small provincial town." In short, *Smarh* is no masterpiece, *therefore* Gustave is merely a petit-bourgeois. After this letter (or perhaps before), he abandons his work: why continue if he *knows* now that he is not a genius? In March, however, he once more takes heart and sets himself to the task. For he is fascinated by the idea he wanted to render at the moment of its conception; he describes the subject to Ernest and concludes: "There it is, a terrific plan and with only a few rough edges." The thing that revives his interest is also the "demoralizing" aspect of his work. He writes proudly: "I create works which will not receive the Montyon prize and *which a mother will not allow her daughter to read;* I will be sure to put this fine phrase in the epigraph."[87] But in April he demurs: "I have finished a morality play that takes three hours to read. There is hardly anything admirable in it but the subject. A mother will allow her daughter to read it." This means, first of all, that he is disappointed in his demoralizing ambition: he knows now that the work will shock no one. More important, we learn that he has never questioned the value of his *conception.* In the first letter (26 December) he declared he had ascended "to the highest reaches of heaven," had conceived something extraordinary, gigantic, absurd," and subsequently he proudly

---

87. *Correspondance* 1:45. Underlined by Flaubert. Claims have been made to the effect that this citation proves he already knew de Sade's work. But he could have taken it from Laclos, from whom de Sade borrowed it.

reveals to Ernest a "terrific plan with only a few rough edges"; finally, having taken up his work again and finished it, he concludes: "There is hardly anything admirable in it but the subject."

Did he read it to his two friends? I doubt it—they did not often come to Rouen. In any case, he put it in a drawer almost immediately and paid no more attention to it. He preserved an ambiguous memory of it, I imagine. Indeed, never—even in his bitter lucidity—had he been entirely sincere. Even when he abandoned his work, even when he treated it as "salmagundi," he remained confident, despite everything, of the obscure forces that guided his pen: he doubted, but at same time he played out the drama of doubt because genius must doubt itself, and the true artist must never be satisfied with his labor. Counting on the unintelligible, he tried to surprise himself, tossed off words at random, thinking they would create their own order on the paper and that he would discover the meaning of his sentences by re-reading them. He took his allegories, his symbols, his myths as they came, believing they had surged up from the "dreadful depths" and would preserve in broad daylight some sort of shadowy opacity; in short, when he sternly catalogued his "weaknesses," he was playing "Devil's advocate," counting on it to prove his predestination after the fact. In any event, success or failure, the work would be striking in its originality. It would be "extraordinary, gigantic, unintelligible," or at least it would remain the *disjecta membra* of a giant. The last page turned, the notebook closed, he preserved a little of this hope: maybe he had not proved himself the Artist; still, he seemed not to have demonstrated the contrary. At worst, everything would have to be done over again.

But his malaise grows during the summer and autumn of 1839. He no longer writes, except during the month of August when he produces *Rome et les Césars*, a short historical essay,[88] and *Les Funérailles du docteur Mathurin*. He seems to have thought then: I have said

88. Or, rather, a bit of eloquence in which the theme of totalization and death are developed together. Taken as a whole, this text is worthless. It is bombastic, the metaphors are precious, the meaning nonexistent. It must simply be noted how totalization is made the absolute power and leads to sadism and annihilation: "Power is thus so heightened that those who grasp it suffer increasing vertigo and are seized with an insane mania: the world belonging to one man alone, like a slave, he could torture it for his pleasure, and it was indeed tortured to its last fiber." Here we find the inevitable Nero: "He said to the executioners: 'Do it so that they feel they are dying,' and leaning over the open chests of the victims . . . he found unknown delights in those final groans of a being departing life, the height of sensual pleasure, as when a woman, quivering beneath the eye of the emperor, fell into his arms and expired in his embrace."

everything, so I cannot say *something else* but only the same thing *differently,* since I have said it badly. In other words, *Les Funérailles* has the same subject as *Smarh:* exterior totalization. But Flaubert, inspired by Rabelais or by what he believed he saw in this author, abandons Romantic eloquence for a sort of black humor: after all, shouldn't one "laugh in the face of the human race"? Perhaps the chief failing of *Smarh,* despite the presence of the god Yuk, is that it takes itself seriously. Irony may be the best way to demoralize. But although he had kept the manuscript of *Les Funérailles,* he seems not to have been satisfied with it: a little later, after rereading his "morality play," we shall see that he decides to give up the pen forever: Mathurin has not saved *Smarh.* In short, he is discontented, empty, uninspired, devoured by doubt. At the end of several months, he no longer cares about it and again asks himself: "What am I worth?" meaning, "What is my work worth?" On 28 February 1840, he writes in the *Souvenirs:* "I just reread this notebook, and I was sorry for myself." Will *Smarh* be any better? At this particular time, or a little later, he dares to reopen his manuscript. He crudely records for us in the afterword what he feels at the time: "It is permissible to do pitiful things, but not this sort." This time it is a *discovery,* and his sincerity is not in doubt: after these twelve months, his creation has closed itself, it lies before him: he no longer enters it, and can observe it, judge it as a foreign object; he can now see its weakness. Curiously, he claims that during the winter of 1839 he was perfectly satisfied with it. "What you admired a year ago is awfully bad today." On the other hand, we have just seen that Flaubert was very hard on his "morality play" while he was writing it. But what the young man of 1840 does not forgive in the young author of 1839 is that he *played at writing:*[89] "I had awarded you the name of future great man, and you regarded yourself as a little Goethe; the illusion is not negligible." Gustave deliberately deluded himself when he was playing the role of the Artist. In truth, he was not cut out for Art: "The best advice I can give you is to stop writing."

This sentence would express merely an impulse of ill humor if it were not preceded and followed by a long silence. Flaubert has just spent five or six months without taking up his pen, and—before writing out his travel notes—he will spend six months without writing anything but his notebook of *Souvenirs.* It is enough to open this

---

89. Indeed, he writes in the postface, apostrophizing: "What you admired a year ago . . ." But, as Flaubert began *Smarh* a year and four months earlier, we do not know to what moment—while he was writing it? the day it was finished?—this "a year ago" refers.

work, moreover, to understand the shock he suffered in rereading *Smarh*. Until 28 February 1840, his *Notes et pensées intimes* have a tranquil tone and, although he mentions it in the work itself, a kind of objectivity. His pessimism is not exempt from gaiety: this is because the entries go back, for the most part, to the end of 1838. Then suddenly, after the rereading, the tone changes:

> I am no longer writing—in the past I wrote, I was impassioned by my ideas, I knew what it was to be a poet . . . I would be laughed at if anyone knew how I admired myself . . . and now, though I may still have the conviction of my vocation or the fullness of an immense pride, I am more and more in doubt. If you knew the extent of this anguish! If you knew the extent of my vanity! What a savage vulture, how it tears my heart out! . . . Love, genius, that was the Heaven I glimpsed, I felt its emanations, had maddening visions of it, the Heaven that was closed forever, who will have me . . . I am conceited, they say—and why then this doubt I feel at each of my actions, this void that frightens me, all those illusions vanished? . . . Oh, the same man who is writing this might have had genius, borne a name in the future. Oh! I am so miserable . . . Oh, how pitiful, how pitiful to think of it, how even more pitiful to write to oneself about it, to tell oneself about it.— Yes, I am a great man *manqué*, a common enough type today. When I consider everything I have done, everything I might have done, I tell myself that this is nothing—and yet what power I have in me, if you knew all the flashes that illuminate me. Alas, alas! I tell myself that at twenty I could have already created masterpieces—I hissed at myself, humiliated myself, degraded myself, and I do not even know what I hope for, what I want, or what I have—I will never be more than a dishonored scribbler, a conceited wretch.

These undated laments are distributed between February and August 1840. Did he write any letters at this period? None has come down to us: it seems that he might have wanted to retreat, to avoid epistolary contacts with Ernest—who had long been a source of irritation to him—and even with Alfred. And as if all that were not enough to show us how deeply wounded he was, a later note, which was cited above, implies that he is physically affected to the point that his nervousness worries his father, who prescribes sedatives for him.[90] In December he gets himself dismissed from school, and the process of

90. On 2 January 1841: "How long ago that was written, my God! It was one Sunday afternoon . . . as harassed by remedies as by illness," etc.

sequestration has begun. To cut it short, Achille-Cléophas sends him to the Pyrenees, to Marseille, then to Corsica with Doctor Cloquet. Arriving in Paris, he immediately pays a visit to Gourgaud. We read in the *Souvenirs:* "Visit to Gourgaud . . . I communicate my doubts on my literary vocation, he comforts me." It is striking that he did not seek "comfort" from Alfred, to whom *Les Funérailles* is still dedicated: he is not sure of his older friend or of his confidence in his junior's vocation. Disconcerted, Gustave returns to his childhood, to the young professor who had given him a glimpse of a happy future. This shows in the author of *Smarh,* a loner who defies the world and rejects the judgment of the public, a sudden, surprising humility. He went for a stroll with Gourgaud, and told him: "I have done nothing that's any good, I am afraid to write, what's the point of going on?" Gourgaud was probably the one who advised him to give up overly ambitious subjects for the time being, and, since Gustave was starting off on a journey, to practice recounting his impressions. But if Flaubert accepts the advice, it is because he no longer has anything to say, as we have just seen, yet is still tormented by the desire to write. In short, he turns away from the imaginary for a time and forces himself simply to describe what he has actually seen and felt.[91] We might almost say that he is horrified by cosmic totalization right now, although he continues to regard it as the sole subject of his art. But Gourgaud's encouragements are not enough for him; he pushes humility to the point of reading his notes to his traveling companions: "At Pau, I am cold—I read my notes to Monsieur Cloquet and to Mademoiselle Lise, little approbation and little intelligence on their part; I am nettled, in the evenings I write to Maman, I am sad; at table, I can hardly keep back my tears." His disarray is such, at the time, that he would accept any kind of approval. But he is hardly fond of Doctor Cloquet, who, "though a man of intelligence," blabbers platitudes; Gustave later tells Alfred that the Doctor made him travel *like a bourgeois.* Be that as it may, he seeks his advice and, in the face of Cloquet's polite coldness, feels on the verge of tears—because his "vocation" is always in question. He will revise his notes in the autumn of 1840 and then fall silent until 1842.

A strange silence, formed of refusal and impotence. He is faithful to his decision of April 1840 to write nothing short of a masterpiece, but at the same time his hand is itching. Sometimes he jots down notes, a

91. Although, as Bruneau has shown (*Debuts littéraires de Gustave Flaubert*) the real voyage is doubled by an "Imaginary Voyage": "for us, a palm tree is all of India."

few lines, but impulsively, carelessly: sometimes, however, his need to write is stronger than his refusal. On 21 May 1941, for example, he writes: "A day of lethargy and anguish—a need to write and to discharge my feelings and I know neither what to write nor what to think. Yet it is always this way with vague instincts; I am a mute who wants to speak." Predestination is no more than a "vague instinct"; similarly, ambition has collapsed: "everything I do is to give myself pleasure—if I write, it is to read myself." Only this remains: a hedonistic principle too often affirmed, a relationship with instinct that no doubt conceals a ray of optimism but a very weak one. Above all, the void: what to write? In the same passage, Flaubert thinks to recount his school life—what a falling off from exterior totalization. Even so, he does not get down to work: he will write it "one day," he says, which is a way of giving up writing because it is today that the mute wants to speak. In other words, he is afraid of resuming—even on a more modest level—an enterprise doomed to failure. To recount the "history of his school life" would perhaps be a return to the *roman intime,* to interior totalization, to the temptation to know himself (he begins to experience it once again: he constantly wonders what he *is worth,* which obviously implies an influence on what he *is*). But he let himself be taken in by all that . . . at the time of the *Mémoires,* and finally he told everything, and everything ended on the rocks. The pen falls from his hands. This is what he calls "his intermittent moral sickness." He adds: "Yesterday I had some superb projects for work. Today, I cannot go on." All that is *suffered,* not *decided:* it is striking that Gustave does not dream of reproaching himself here—as he does elsewhere—for his laziness, a character defect that can be fought, but objectively denounces a sickness that is probably incurable. A little earlier, in the same notebook, he observed: "I have not worked this month of January [1841]; I don't know why—inconceivable laziness— I have no backbone, there are days when I will leap into the clouds, others when I haven't the strength to open a book." We shall again find this mood swing accentuated, in *Novembre;* it actually corresponds to two quite distinct views of his Ego. There is the moment when the old dream of *saying everything* comes back to him: he himself observes that it always begins with particular scenes that he invents, which amuse him and of which he believes he has grasped the totalizing meaning. And then, suddenly, he is face to face with himself: the totalization separates itself from the anecdote that expressed it, he should *know clearly* what he wants to say; he falls back into the deceptive schemes of *Smarh* or the *Mémoires.* He considers recounting a

493

story by itself, for example his school years; he is enthusiastic at the idea of at last having "something to say." And the next day he perceives the abyss that separates this singular anecdote from the earlier lofty ambitions of his pride. These alternating moods are not only, of course, the simple circularity of a sudden literary insight—he sees a "subject"—and of the pessimism that follows it—it is worthless or he will not be capable of treating it: everything is lived *physically*, to such an extent that *despondency* often precedes the author's simple disappointment or pessimistic lucidity. The *flesh* is sad. But what in turn conditions these organic manifestations is at bottom the struggle between his anomalous singularity and his class-being. This sums it all up: genius or petit-bourgeois. He moves from one to the other and, thinking of the failure of *Smarh*, becomes distrustful of his flights; the words "great man *manqué*" are chosen quite precisely to define the idea he then has of himself: neither a great man nor a bourgeois; he has moments of genius but impotence dominates; he will therefore have to resign himself to becoming an attorney or a notary, although even from that point of view he may be a failure, unable to adapt himself to his duties with an attitude of calm mediocrity. "There are days when I would like to shine in the salons, to hear my name pronounced with a flourish, and other times when I would like to degrade and debase myself, to be a notary in the depths of Brittany." To degrade himself, to debase himself: to clip the stumps of wings that he still has, *to lose himself, to fall:* let us note in passing this fascination with falling. When he believes he is merely a failure, he grows dizzy: in the depths of Brittany he might forget himself and find a bitter peace in resignation. This is really a dream of death; only death can resolve the contradictions of a soul too ambitious for its gifts.

This description will suffice, I think, to show the cruelty of the torments Gustave inflicts on himself: he suffers, his nerves leave him no peace. He experiences his unhappiness with an extreme seriousness and violence, as a Christian might have done in the gloomy fifteenth century when so many doubted their salvation. And, to make matters worse, as an imaginary adolescent he is in doubt about the authenticity of his sufferings: "I am always playing at comedy or tragedy." But as our aim for the moment has been merely to show how deeply the failure of *Smarh* perturbed him, let us return to *Smarh* itself the better to understand his distress, and let us try to determine the author's own reasons for his disappointment.

Not the slightest idea." "I ought to have begun by having ideas." As we have seen, this reproach is not aimed at the conception but at the execution. The word "idea" must be taken in the sense a screen-writer would use it, saying to his collaborators: "I have an idea: what if Françoise had a son?" Organizational plans on the level of artistic invention are at issue here, not philosophical concepts. Flaubert reproaches himself, within the totalization, for not conceiving of episodes and characters that would more effectively, and with greater variety of detail, have communicated what he regards as the generating *idea* of *Smarh*. When Gustave writes later, "Alfred had ideas, I hadn't any," he means determinations of thought; here, to the contrary, he is concerned with imagination.[92] We know from Flaubert himself that this concern is new: toward the age of fifteen, he tells us, his imagination has run dry. But what is especially striking is that the young author, at this time and especially in *Smarh*, wants to assign a new function to the "madwomen of the house" (as Malebranche called the imagination). Or, if you like, until that time the image was merely an end; now it becomes both end *and means*. What has happened is that the inadequacy of language had led the young author to see a work of art as the *indirect* expression of the idea.

He has experienced this inadequacy from childhood: in him, language is other, as we have seen; he sees it not as the supple instrument of his thought, but as a material system which he must hear and partially *observe*, for it is introduced in him from the outside and manipulated by others. It is at this point that Flaubert believes he thinks without words and then translates this silence by selecting words like flowers for a bouquet. As his first stupors, reworked, change into elevations, as he leaps into the infinite to escape his humiliations, he verifies the inadequacy of the Word and the Idea. What he really loves in this poetic escape is, as he himself says, the "vagueness," and discourse annoys him because it forces him to be more precise, to structure his ecstasies: they are unutterable or, as he says, "unsayable" because they do not resist the harsh treatment of *expression*. But in an early period, this incommensurability hardly bothers him: for the young boy, poetry is a mental attitude that is self-sufficient. The poet is one who surpasses himself toward the infinite, or, better yet, who surpasses the finitude of real phenomena toward the unreal infinity of the imaginary. In these conditions, the act of trans-ascendence is

92. In fact, there is not so much contradiction between those two meanings of the term: what Alfred offered as ideas—for example, his theory of metempsychosis—he only half believed, and was enchanted, rather, with the beauty of his theories. And Gustave himself, when he received them, took them less for philosophical speculations than for beautiful and terrifying conjectures.

sufficient to itself and suffices to mark the superiority of the soul. Then the poet is free to *express himself:* he will betray himself, but this compromise is unimportant. Moreover, at this period he was not writing *his* poem but philosophic tales, short stories; in short, prose works. On this level of abstraction, the schematic characters he imagined remain perfectly homogeneous with the restrained and abstract vocabulary he employs—and which, according to him, we all employ. From *Voyage en enfer* to *Passion et Vertu*, invention and expression are one: the thickness and opacity of Mazza, of Marguerite, come to them from discourse, and it makes no difference whether one attributes to Marguerite the real quality of ugliness or simply calls her ugly, or attributes to Mazza beauty or calls her beautiful. This is a period of improvisation, spontaneously eloquent discourse, flights, great rhetorical flourishes, metaphors.

With *Mémoires d'un fou,* however, the difficulties begin. True, he bemoans the inadequacy of the word to his sublime conceptions—"for speech is merely a distant and feeble echo of thought"—but this is done at the outset, in a melancholy, dispassionate tone, and with the general intention of exposing the nothingness in every enterprise. The new element in his rage, in one of the last chapters, at the impossibility of rendering *even the finite.* "Can you say a tear and paint its humid crystal . . . Can you say everything you feel in a day?" He is still concerned merely with *sentiments.* But he goes further. We have seen in the preceding chapter that he has experienced two kinds of stupors: in the earlier kind he escapes into "vagueness"; in the other, a bit more recent, he is fascinated by things in detail: "as a child, I loved *what is seen,*" so much so that he often felt his very identity fused with the invested thing. Transubstantiation is at issue here: he would like to implant the very matter of the thing in himself—and simultaneously merge with it. This relation of substance to substance, this recognition of our being in exterior being and of exterior being in our being, is much more radical than the "glancing acquaintance" of observation; yet the latter is always richer if it is based on the former: it seeks then to retain the seed of being, its basic structure still more than its superficial configuration. Flaubert is an observer because the impossible fusion of his inner reality with the materiality of things leads him to take his distance in relation to the object even while making a final effort to preserve its singular essence. And that can be done *only through words.* Words *should be able* to render the singularity of a thing, its shape, its basic structure, and its texture; for Flaubert, the verbal operation—in which subjective and objective are fused—

ought to be a substitute for the ontological operation that escapes. And this is what he means when he writes, at the end of chapter 21 of the *Mémoires:* "Poor human weakness! With your words, you speak and you stammer; you define God, Heaven and Earth, chemistry and philosophy, and with your tongue you cannot express all the joy a nude woman gives you . . . or a plum pudding." Let us make no mistake: although he speaks of our joy, Gustave has left the subjective world, it is no longer a question of Maria—whom he never saw nude—and the two examples are invented; what is certain, on the other hand, is that you cannot express your state of mind at the sight of a female body or, if you are a glutton, of a piece of pastry, without *providing the sight and the feeling* of that body or that cake. This will be understood still better after reading the following passage from the *Souvenirs*—written in 1840:

> When you write, you feel what must be, you understand that in such a place this must be, at another that, you compose pictures that are seen, you have in some sense the feeling that you are hatching something—you feel it in your heart as the distant echo of all the passions you will bring to light—and the powerlessness to render all this is the eternal despair of those who write the misery of the tongues that have hardly one word for every hundred thoughts, the weakness of man, who does not know how to find the approximate, and mine in particular, my eternal anguish.

This page obviously follows the rereading of *Smarh* and translates Gustave's disappointment. And it will be noted that the word is accused of inadequacy *in relation to visual pictures and sensations.* This, Flaubert tells us, is his eternal anguish. Eternal, no: it does not appear before 1838, and we know, to the contrary, that Flaubert, an inspired musician, was more anxious about the melody he carried in his head than about the instrument on which he played it.

The Poet has given way to the Artist. And for the artist, language is of central importance. Flaubert observed in 1838: "Between the artist and the poet there is a vast difference; the one feels, the other *speaks.*" The heart is the poet's alibi: speech is not essential to him. The artist, on the other hand, is a worker: he must act on a defined material to produce an object. That object may well be a center of unrealization; it only demands more imperiously to be constituted by rigorous techniques. If the work of art is the goal, language must, one way or another, be adequate. In short, the question of expression demands to be dealt with at all levels of the work. And we better understand

497

Flaubert's bitterness when he writes to Ernest, while working on *Smarh:* "There are places where I am brought up short; just recently I had serious difficulty in the composition of my morality play. I was always finding myself face to face with the infinite; I didn't know how to express the awe in my soul. The infinite has hardly changed: in *Smarh* it remained what it was in the time of the mystic flights that carried the schoolboy "to the limits of Creation." But the task is no longer the same: yesterday, all he had to do was "drown in it"; today, he must create, tell. Quasi-artistic creation—unlike divine creation—cannot be done *ex nihilo.* It begins with words, those ambiguous beings, already full of nonbeing, whose tenuous materiality is a very real opacity but which transcend that materiality by an empty intention aimed at an absence. The problem is to fabricate an unreal totality, a permanent derealization, by assembling words, to produce our world as a permanent absence by putting to use the nothingness that is in words, our world made beautiful by the tightening of its interior bonds. But the rule of the game, for Flaubert, is that words are not invented: they are chosen out of the great practico-inert mass that is constituted language, which is for him the language of *others.* Since he began by affirming that the thought of the poet is idiosyncratic, how can it be cast without breaking it into the socialized forms of a language? It becomes collective itself; we shall find it again, made banal, disqualified, in the form of a commonplace. Gustave takes a dislike to speech: "There is a rather stupid axiom that says that speech renders thought—it would be truer to say that it disfigures it. Do you ever articulate a sentence as you think it? Do you write a novel as you have conceived it?" On the one hand, there are ineffable and beautiful intuitions; on the other, the language of practitioners, of men of science, of philosophers, and of daily life. Between the two there is no common measure. Or, if you will, in relation to the "thought" of the Artist, language as a whole is *nonsignifying.* The task of the creator is therefore theoretically impossible since the materials provided are antithetical to his project. Flaubert does not at first see this clearly. Between 1840 and 1842, he accuses either language or himself. Sometimes it is the word that is lacking because of the essential poverty of a mass that is not made for Art but for utility. And sometimes, angry and envious, Gustave recognizes that there are great writers, geniuses: the words exist, but he cannot find them.

Throughout this desperate quest, however, we see an idea coming to birth, growing, and finally asserting itself. The notebook for the *Souvenirs* ends in this central discovery: "If sentences produced thoughts[93] . . . I would tell you all my reveries, and you know nothing of all that because there are no words to say it—art is nothing other than this strange translation of thought by form."[94]

The meaning is clear: it is not the *saying* that manifests the artist's thought but the *way of saying*. From direct expression we pass to *indirect* expression. Language, cut off from meaning, has fallen back on itself and is posed for its own sake. It is only then that he discovers its riches. Since we are no longer concerned with putting them to use, words are profound and beautiful objects we can admire for themselves; their visual and especially auditory materiality plunge Gustave into ecstasy; and what abundance: a multitude of meanings are entwined in every word, provided none is privileged for the practical ends of communication. The very contradictions of syntax itself reveal a minute structuring of the Word. How beautiful speech is when gratuitous, when we can consider it from an aesthetic point of view, when we steal it from the bourgeoisie. Would it not be possible to work these raw beauties to make them render Beauty? A "strange translation," says Gustave, astonished at his discovery. Indeed, the situation is paradoxically reversed: for all men, words *signify* provided they follow a verbal intention by ignoring the nonsignifying materiality that is its support; for the artist, words *are,* considered strictly as nonsignifying signs; they will render his thought only if he makes use of their nonsignifying materiality to render exhaustively the *meaning* he wants to transmit. No *statement* can render Flaubert's "reveries," but it is the business of *style* to communicate them to us. Style, a strange mixture of materials and intentions, does not neglect saying, but in order to fill those abstract significations which serve merely as guidelines, it evokes in each term, by means of all the others, the multitude of entwined meaning, and uses them all together—those that refer to the shadows of childhood and those that designate external objects—to capture in the targeted reality a little of its secret opacity. In short, style is the full use of language; everything serves, everything signifies, and direct signification is no more than one of the functions of a supersignifying object. At the same time, it is its unrealization: nonsignifying materiality can furnish meanings only in the imaginary. We see the path taken: before 1838, Gustave sees form merely as a *completion;* style, often confused with the beauty and

93. As the context suggests, this means: if my sentences *reproduced* my thoughts in the mind of the reader.
94. *Souvenirs,* p. 110.

strength of images, of metaphors, is the last treatment of a moving, pathetic story; form is posed for its own sake: the story must be told *and* must be beautiful. These are two inseparable but not inevitably connected ends. Toward 1840 we have, all told, two beauties: that of the subject (exterior totalization) and that of style; there is no work of art that does not combine them, but their dialectical bond is not yet perceived. The failure of *Smarh* has the effect of deeping Flaubert's thought: the beauty of writing becomes the *means* of absolute expression. Form is a language that could be called parasitic, for it constitutes itself at the expense of real language without ceasing to exploit it, forcing it to express what it is not made to tell us.

In this process, can the difference Gustave establishes between practical language and his thought be maintained? Thought not only is the guiding scheme of style, taken as its indirect expression, but constitutes itself in its richness *through* style. Style reveals thought to itself and creates it. By reestablishing, in the second step, adequacy of expression to the Idea, Flaubert rediscovers the thesis he denied in the first step: language *produces* thought and is indistinguishable from it. The superexploitation of language by tightening all the material ties between words can have no other effect than to create that supersignification, Beauty—the tightening of intramundane ties, or the radicalization of Evil. Flaubert glimpsed this in 1839 when he foresaw the demoralizing effect of *the most beautiful page:* it was style itself that degraded men by arousing violent sexual impulses in them. Now everything is clarified: a single theme, radical Evil, a single expression, style. Gustave will later take this idea so far as to say that the search for style, beyond any other previous intention, produces its own contents. The beauty of writing is an indirect sign and symbol— whatever the subject being treated, and even if there is no subject at all—of the unreal beauty of the world. We are familiar with the famous passage from his letter to Louise on 16 January 1852: "There are no noble or ignoble subjects, and from the point of view of pure Art, one might almost establish the axiom that there is no such thing as subject—*style in itself being an absolute way of seeing things."* [95] Style, an absolute way of seeing: seeing things from the point of view of the Absolute (panoramic consciousness) and as if they were produced by the Absolute (Creation in view of radical Evil). It is sentences which, by means of their construction, will testify allusively to that double *as if:* there is no need to consider the results of the panoramic view as

95. My italics.

direct signification, as Gustave was still doing in *Smarh,* to *say,* for example, the world is Hell; this idea, if it is the contents of the *lecton,* is not acceptable to reason, and its abstraction prevents it from having emotional resonance. On the level of the language of information, it is something *inarticulable.* Let one write as an artist, however, and there is the idea, a parasite of lexemes, haunting every statement, every word: there is its real dimension, there alone it finds its incarnation in the imaginary splendor of a style. Indeed, style is the very image of the Creation: it makes language visible, that practico-inert mass which imposes itself on man as if it were the product of some freedom. In the letter of January 1852, Flaubert expressly says: "Form, in gaining skills, becomes attenuated, it leaves behind all liturgy, rule, measure . . . there is no more orthodoxy, and form is as free as the will of its creator." The author of these lines is, as we know, the same man who endlessly repeats, "*I* do not feel free," and who declares that he writes merely by following the bent of his fatalities. But there is no contradiction here: the will of the creator is not free, here, except to the extent that it subjects language by means of technique and presents it to men on the basis of creative freedom. He tells us, in sum: steal language from men, derail it from its practical ends, force its matter itself to render inarticulable imaginary things, and you will have incarnated in your sentences the magnetic pole of all imagination, Beauty or radical Evil, by conveying with respect to language that the world is produced and sustained by a malign freedom. Style is the silence of discourse, the silence in discourse, the imaginary and secret purpose of written speech. Hence that other famous declaration in the same letter: "What seems beautiful to me, what I should like to write, is a book about nothing, a book dependent on nothing external, held together by the internal force of its style, just as the earth is suspended in air without external support; a book that had almost no subject, or, at least, a book in which the subject was almost invisible, if that were possible." [96]

All things considered, the context indicates that Flaubert is not entirely certain of his thought. It oscillates—as often happens—between two affirmations that seem opposed to each other. On the one hand he effectively shows us style producing thought (it is "in and of itself an absolute way of seeing things"); and, on the other hand, he writes

96. Let us not forget that he is in the process of writing that book—*Madame Bovary.* Louise just wrote to him that she loved the first *Tentation.* He answers that it was merely a trial run. We shall have to recall later on, when we come to *Madame Bovary,* that this is indeed the work whose subject would be almost invisible.

501

in the same breath: "the closer expression comes to thought, the more the word clings on and disappears, the more beautiful it is." This entirely banal affirmation seems to indicate that thought—as he formerly declared—precedes its expression. This sounds very much like Boileau:

> That which is well conceived is clearly stated
> And easily come the words to say it.

But we are dealing here with an aesthetic and nonconceptual thinking, a thinking that Flaubert never clearly conceives unless style reflects it to him. He is merely trying to say that the word must efface itself before the totalitarian order of the sentence or paragraph. In these twenty or so lines, thought sometimes appears to create its own sumptuous order, which supersignifies the thought, and at other times the order appears to be the thought itself, or to produce the thought within it as it composes itself. But even if he seems a bit muddled, Flaubert clearly sets the limits of his oscillation (as we know, and he admits it himself, each of his ideas is a pendulum); whether thought precedes style or whether style creates thought, aesthetic thought exists only in and through style. He repeats at ten years' distance what he observed on the last page of his notebook: form translates thought; in other words, information is in the domain of signs, but the *meaning* of a work of the mind is communicated to us indirectly through its formal beauty.

We shall return much later to this aesthetic. What matters here is that it was slowly constituted during the dark years, in doubt, in despair, and as a direct consequence of the failure of *Smarh*. For Flaubert, beginning in 1840, *Smarh* is a logical assemblage of significations, a sequence of accounts and demonstrations: what is lacking is invention in both plot and language. It should have "made us sizzle with the beauty of the words"; if it had, its anguish would have clutched at our hearts. In short, this artist discovers negatively the terrible exigencies of art. At eighteen, as at thirty, he would be able to write the insincere and deeply felt words, "Art terrifies me." A dreadful labor is entailed: to steal the tools, to use them according to invented and rigorous laws, to pour his thought into style, to learn his thought through style without ever being able to say it or even to say it *to himself*, always to search for the indirect effect, producing a logical assemblage of significations *so that* the vocables that claim to communicate them are in fact ordered in such a way as to fill us with an unutterable meaning; always to aim at two goals: the coherence of a directed discourse and the unrealization of this discourse through formal beauty, never to lose sight of the one or the other on pain of falling either into incoherence or into pure information; above all, to *compose:* to go from the whole to the detail and from the detail to the whole, so that the whole is present in each part and the succession of parts reproduces the whole; unceasingly to survey, to be all the more vigilant as "form has left behind all rule, all measure," and as one must invent the rules and continually judge the result oneself; in a word, to curb inspiration and submit it unceasingly to criticism—this is what is demanded of a young hyperbolic orator. Now we understand the reason for the abrupt appearance in Flaubert's notes of that unromantic notion, *taste.* At the end of 1839 he writes: "It is not enough to have taste. One must have the palate for it. Boileau certainly had taste, and a fine, urbane, delicate taste it was . . . But Racine had the palate: he understood its savor, the flowers of the aroma, the purest essence of whatever it is that charms, that titillates and makes us smile. That sense, for those who have it, is more infallible than two plus two makes four." Racine has more taste than Boileau not because he can better appreciate a work by La Fontaine but because he has *creative* taste. The immediately preceeding note explains the one just cited, which it surely engendered:[97] "There is . . . something that judges better than judgment, namely tact, which is none other than inspiration given for physical things, for the active life." Tact directs actions; taste directs the creative imagination. Flaubert returns to classicism, but he merely borrows an idea from it, which he transforms and modernizes. In the seventeenth century, certainly, taste is on the side of the "spirit of finesse," as Pascal describes it: it appreciates a work on the basis of a myriad of veiled principles that are never made explicit; but *in any case* these principles, numerous and subtle as they may be, are not intrinsic to the work judged: they belong to the culture of the gentleman and define the structures of the objective mind. Of course, the creator always goes *further* than these guiding schemes, and the work is by definition their surpassing. Thus, at the extreme point of taste—appreciation of what he does—the writer judges in solitude, he takes his chances. The guiding schemes sustain him or serve him as jumping-off points; at the same time he remains, even in the midst

97. We see the parallelism of the two movements: "There is something that judges better than judgment," "There is something finer than taste."

503

of invention, the society man, the courtier: he judges what will please; the other is present and consulted, author and reader surpass principles together and tell each other "where to draw the line."

But Gustave himself feels asocial: he has no complicity with his class or the ruling class; he would reject its aesthetic a priori if, by some impossibility, the bourgeoisie had one. So he cannot rely on objective determinations nor on the rules to be divined from past masterpieces: each writer creates his work in solitude, and if there is progress in form it is because form detaches itself from those assumptions in order to create according to its own law. As for the discipline of putting oneself in the reader's place, Flaubert does not even give it a thought: the reader must suffer as an inner confusion the unexpected, unforeseen beauty of a vrork that imposes itself by degrading the person who reads it. Every artist has *his* subject, *his* absolutely new manner of treating it—the two are merely one. Consequently, every artist is utterly abandoned—by everyone and particularly by God. In order to invent the rule, to engender the object from that rule and judge it at the same time in relation to the law and that singular law, subjective caprice, valid only once, as if it were a universal determination of objective nature, and to do all this vigorously, without words, without explanation, we would need at our disposal that "intelligible intuition" Kant spoke of, which, he said, is denied us on principle. In short, we ought to be able to confuse creation and knowledge in ourselves. To conceive a genetic law would be at once to create a being and to possess the key to it; conversely, creation would not distinguish itself from the translucent vision of oneself and from being in the process of becoming. What Flaubert anxiously feels is that there is no safety net: the author is at once the subject who invents and the only objective judge he can accept. But this judge refers to no code: it is the act that produces the law in the name of which it must be judged. How can we reconcile these opposites—a total objectivity that affirms itself *in the name of nothing*, a profound subjectivity that invents *in the name of the All?* After *Smarh,* the young man attempted to conceive that difficult activity of the modern artist as the exercise of a *gift.* This is, of course, coming down on the side of God and His gifts, poorly distributed as they are. But we must remember that at this period there are only two men—two very young men—who will conceive and forge modern literature: Baudelaire and Flaubert. They will say that one must rely on nothing; and, to say so, they will have to feel deeply that they have nothing to rely on. Relapse into materialism is fatal—at least in the early stages. It is fear that makes

Flaubert speak of taste as a *sense*. Comparing it with tact—the object of the preceding maxim—which he calls "inspiration given for the active life," we see the basis of his thought: taste is inspiration granted for poetic creation (in the sense of "poesis"). Inspiration, a divine gift, is denied on the level of spontaneous invention: God no longer whispers in his ear. But it is merely displaced: inspiration becomes the controlling faculty specifically destined to govern the uncontrollable, the unique. By an impulse we easily recognize, however, Gustave has no sooner reassured himself than he despairs: this "infallible sense exists," it's true, but *in others:* this gift has been forever denied him.

He does not limit himself to rereading his own works: he reads those of the great writers, and each day, he tells us, he finds new beauties in them that astound him. Gradually the multiplicity of relations that unite a part of a work to the whole and to all the other parts is revealed to him: he feels he is Boileau but not Racine; in the created work he perceives its singular law and its totalizing development, but as for writing himself, he has no *palate* for it. As a result, envy consumes him: "I am jealous of the life of great artists, joy of money, joy of art, joy of opulence, all these things." He is determined, he tells us, to strip them of all merit by reducing the finest effects of style to fortuitous encounters. In vain: he also tells us that he does not succeed. All that remains is the mediocre pleasure of collecting their accidental stupidities—which are not lacking. But this hardworking stupidity collector does not destroy the beauty of their works: he proves that every man is stupid on occasion, just as every man is mortal. Taste still seems to Gustave a power all the more real as he believes he has discovered it *in the object*. And we shall see him conclude, at the end of 1841 or the beginning of 1842, with these despairing lines:[98]

> What I lack above all is taste; I mean, everything. I grasp and I sense things as a whole, in synthesis, without perceiving any detail; net fabrics suit me, everything that is obvious suits me, otherwise nothing. The weave, the structure, elude me; I have clumsy hands, and it is hard for me to feel the softness of the fabric, but I am struck by its sheen—the halftones do not suit me—I love spicy things too . . . but the delicate not at all—color, especially image, I lack . . . and precision even more so—no unity, movement but no . . . of invention but not the least feeling for rhythm, there I am most lacking—and above all a long-winded style, stiff and pretentious.[99]

98. *Souvenirs*, p. 105.
99. Several words are missing, indicated here by ellipsis points.

I have cited the whole of this text because it is striking: taken simply as a set of criticisms Gustave addresses to himself, it clearly anticipates the judgment he brings to bear against *Smarh*. Considered on the other hand, as the negative definition of what a masterpiece should be in his view, it can be seen as a presentiment of what he will try to do—and will do—in *Madame Bovary*. Softness of fabric, halftones, delicacy, precision, rhythm, a compressed, unified style— aren't these the qualities universally recognized in this novel? And are we not aware that they are *mastered*, and that with every new book Flaubert will have to master them anew—with more or less success? This desolate page is like a hinge between two conceptions of art. This time improvisation and spontaneity seem quite dead. Unless *one has taste*, one cannot give oneself over to writing.

But let us leave the mature works for the moment. What matters to us is that Flaubert experiences his discovery as an additional frustration: he is lost if he does not write. And after an ambitious attempt, he concludes: what I lack is taste, I mean, everything. And it is true: he grasped and felt *Smarh* "as a whole, as a synthesis"—it was a happy time of "conception." And then, when the time for execution arrived, he could not perceive the details, he lacked rigorous inventions, ideas. He tries to "go after it," to "write exorbitantly," as he will say later: eloquence is the abuse of metaphors, the pretention that characterizes the writing of his "old morality play." Today he understands that supersignification cannot be born of a style that is labored, "strained," pushed to the point of protestation, but is constituted, on the contrary, by the judicious exploitation of halftones especially in the verbal "fabric," in the "soft texture" of sentences; in short, style appears when the mute part of language is made to speak. This is what a few days later he will call the "strange translation of thought by form."

Why, then, does he experience his discovery as a new damnation? Can't he condemn *Smarh* and rejoice in having understood its defects? The more so as these defects proceeded entirely from an erroneous conception of the work: *Smarh* sought supersignification through direct eloquence and the abuse of metaphors; now the young man must devote his efforts to honing a technique of indirect illumination. Why does he hesitate to throw himself into this enterprise? Isn't it exciting to strike out on a new path, one that is marked out solely for him?

The fact is, Gustave is desolate because his conception of form, born of a verification of failure, remains purely theoretical in 1842 and goes against his "character," against the *constituted-being* that he has gradually given himself through the personalizing movement by working on what others have made of him. In other words, he conceives of real art as a negative through the defects and shortcomings that he discovers not only in his past being but in the present. He denounces his incapacity to *compose*—to pass dialectically from the whole to the part and from the part to all other parts conceived both as a succession of moments and as the temporal realization of the whole. This denunciation does not suddenly give him the power he lacks: *Smarh* is laborious, disordered, abounding—as are the *Mémoires* or *Agonies*—in repetitions. But *Novembre*, written in 1842, will be battered by the same reproaches, the first *Education* will escape them only in part, and in the first *Tentation* we shall find Flaubert in full possession of his faults. As an even more serious charge, he brings judgment against his "long-winded, pretentious style"; but for all that he still *loves* oratorical flourishes, lyric flights, the profusion of images and metaphors: for this uncontrolled exuberance, this letting loose, this *cultivated spontaneity* is natural to him—in the sense that habit is second nature; it reflects his passive activity, constituted from his early history, as well as the character he has made of himself, that gigantesque interpreter of great telluric forces: when he wrote *Smarh*, it was an evil Gargantua—among other vampires—who held the pen. He will therefore have to write *against himself*, against everything that gives him pleasure; the "joy of art" is always forbidden him because it presupposes a certain complicity with the self that he cannot allow. And certainly no writer can be satisfied with spontaneity; the "first outpouring" must be corrected, even this correction will be corrected, and so on. But for the fortunate author, correction presents itself as a progressive improvement. One is wedded to the impulse and preserves the form: one simply changes words, cuts a sentence, reverses the order of phrases, accentuates, emphasizes one idea, interpolates another, which enhances the preceding one. All these modifications are produced in accord with the first draft and in conformity with certain schemes that have become habitual: although dialectical, literary work does not necessarily break the author's accord with himself. For Gustave, on the other hand, it is himself that is in question. What he writes spontaneously changes before his eyes into an example of what one must not write; every line demonstrates to him that he lacks taste, meaning talent. Sometimes he shamefully throws himself into improvisation, takes pleasure in the great impulses that carry him away, and lapses into disgust upon rereading his work; at other times, overcome at every word by the conviction that he is doing the opposite of what he should, he approaches the line yawning. Just as every kind of writing, every fledgling style has its models, we are well acquainted with Flaubert's: the discourse of the great revolutionaries, the lyricism of the Romantics. If he accepted them, he could bring to bear on his work differential judgments that would challange the detail in the name of certain ideals, without rejecting it in its entirety. But after the failure of *Smarh*, his models are challenged, one after the other; nevertheless, they continue to influence his writing, and the task imposed on Flaubert is to shatter them in the name of another model, which he conceives in theory and in the abstract but of which he hasn't the least practical intuition—quite understandably since this system of rules does not yet exist. He writes, therefore, with a bad conscience, out of *need*, but he spoils the pleasure of writing by condemning his prose from the point of view of a simple undefined aspiration that becomes the taste *he does not have*, the inspiration of others. Speaking like his master, Buffon, the style is the man: it is himself he condemns, not only because he *recognizes* that he lacks the gift, but because he is irritated at every sentence by his personal exis; no sooner does he write a line than it reflects back to him the loud, loutish provincial or the lyrical masochist he has chosen to be but is disgusted by. He catches himself playing at writing and is dismayed by his insincerity though unable, of course, to cure himself of it. If only he knew what he should do and be: he would have new models and would try to approach them. But he is still stammering, and the conception I have outlined appears to him only in its negative aspect. He knows precisely what he should not do: it is *what he does spontaneously;* he knows very well too what he should not be: it is *what he is*—not only the bourgeois but the insincere writer. His crowning unhappiness at this period is that he cannot make *himself* an artist without displeasing himself; but if he chooses to keep quiet, he falls back into the bourgeois-being that horrifies him even more.

What is left, in this case, of his vocation? Nothing. "A vague instinct." He adds: "It is a need to write and to pour out my heart, and I know neither what to write nor what to think." [100] Unceasingly tormented by the desire to take up the pen, he has no subject, for the aborted *Smarh* contained the absolute subject, the World; and besides, when impulse pushes him to write a line, he perceives that his language betrays him, diverts his primary intention—the outpouring becomes pure information. He tried to steal language, and now lan-

100. *Souvenirs*, p. 102.

guage robs him of his vague desires. Except that there is *this need*, a divine torment, this dream of a word not entirely our own yet not totally different from it. We shall be struck by the similarity of this observation and the frequently repeated remarks on the religious instinct. What does he say, in sum, about this instinct? That it is the greatness of man and his misery; whatever the dogmas and rites that aim to satisfy that naked demand, they will be merely myths and mummery, for our religious invention is not equal to our need for the infinite. All so-called "revelation" is, in Flaubert's eyes, amenable to a double evaluation: it is a lie, a *finite* image that fails to satisfy our hunger; but on the other hand it is *sacred* because it bears witness in us to that higher nature—dissatisfaction—which Nature will never be able to fulfill. The artistic instinct, at this period, is also an infinite, unassuageable demand; any attempt to satisfy it through a work is—at least for Flaubert—doomed to failure; it will not even be the crude caricature of what *might have been*, for the young artist hasn't the vaguest notion of what he would like to do; it will be *something else:* a determination of current language, one signification among others. Nonetheless, these despicable literary attempts, secretly, have a sacred character to the extent that they bear witness to a "vague instinct" unceasingly reborn from its ashes. A mute *cannot* speak, but surely his grotesque efforts and the monstrous sounds he produces bear witness in him to a presentiment of language. At this period, if Gustave wants to preserve some metaphysical hope, he must invest it in an inarticulable dissatisfaction (once articulated, it becomes foolishness), and if he is still strong enough to believe in his dignity as artist, he will find it in the incommensurability of his need to write and the miserable products he has botched in order to satisfy that need. In both cases, Absence is a cipher: with no God, nor any of his works able a priori to satisfy Flaubert, what remains is to emphasize an unsayable and unassuageable desire. This parallelism, more than anything else, marks the deep kinship in him of art and faith.

Between 1840 and 1842, failure is the sole mark of a *possible* election. If he must die without having done anything, where does his invincible obstinacy come from? It makes him more distinguished, perhaps, than a facile talent would do: was he not born to live out in his flesh the impossibility of art? Might he not have purposely been denied a feeling for nuance, halftones, soft textures? We should observe, indeed, the ambiguity of the words Flaubert uses to define himself in the greatest depths of his despair: "I am a great man *manqué*." For if one insists on introducing hierarchy among men, one must in all logic say that there are very great men, rather great men, and little men.[101] And a little man could not be a great man *manqué:* he is what he is, nothing more, nothing less. Unless, someone will say, he had tried to join the great men's club and had not succeeded. No doubt; but the frog who wants to make himself as big as the ox is not an ox *manqué,* he is a crazy frog. And certainly Gustave takes his formula also in this sense: I made myself, he says, a promise that I could not keep; I am not equal to my ambition. But very soon that same ambition becomes his singular essence: where does it come from? Was the frog crazy to want to raise itself to the dignity of the mammals? Other frogs are not considered to be. And through this shift, the other meaning of this ambiguous sentence is introduced: to desire to be a great man, one must have some intuition of greatness; but can that be possible if one hasn't received, even imperfectly and to one's misfortune, some means of becoming so? The mediocre are usually perfectly comfortable: they judge everything from a mediocre perspective and see nothing beyond mediocrity. To conceive of greatness is to bear witness to an openness of mind, a fullness of imagination that puts us two steps away from realizing it. Two steps: certain indispensable qualities—taste, for example—can be lacking. But if we perceive their absence into the bargain, have we not defined in a stroke the gaping space that work—who knows?—can fill?

A great man *manqué,* for Gustave, is not a little man. He is a man *already great* whom Destiny condemns to unfulfillment. There we have Flaubert's only hope, at this time. It is awfully slim: vocation is not a gift, a plenitude, it is a lack, an inextinguishable torment; it is thankless and ugly, it is a form of particular damnation. Unlike other animals, as Merleau-Ponty suggests, man is born without equipment. So, according to Flaubert, is the genius: he is not equipped as other men are who have the necessary tools to be doctors or prosecutors. A single but extremely hazardous chance—"We have been promised nothing"[102]—to forge one's own tools through work, starting, in the literal sense of the word, from *nothing.*

Dating from *Smarh,* Gustave's idea of genius is going to suffer a radical reversal: it was a divine gift, now it is a dubious battle waged confusedly against one's own fatalities. The time is not far off when he will write to Louise: "Buffon's maxim is the greatest blasphemy:

101. Obviously these conceptions are utterly alien to me.
102. The saying is Alain's.

genius is not a long patience. But there is some truth in it and more than is generally believed, especially nowadays."[103] And a little later: "Buffon's maxim is blasphemous, but it is too hotly denied; modern works are there to say so." At this period—the end of his twenty-fifth year—he preserves his former conception and juxtaposes it with the new one: by reducing inspiration to work, Buffon *blasphemes;* this means that he attacks the sacred conception of genius as a divine gift. This blasphemy contains a portion of truth, however. What is it? Is it merely a simple assertion: it is never enough to be gifted, one must still work? Certainly truisms never alarmed Flaubert; yet it is hard to believe that his insistent repetition of Buffon's maxim does not mean *something else.* What *does* Buffon mean? He is not concerned with the subjective qualities of the scientist or the artist: he turns toward the object, toward the *invention* (a new hypothesis, the invention of a comic or sublime "maxim," of a well-turned phrase) which will indirectly allow the attribution of genius to the inventor—and contests the idea that this invention can be the fruit of chance or divine inspiration. It has, like Hegelian truth, *become:* that which runs easily from the pen can be merely a platitude; one can be lucky at the end of a series of negations, or rather one will *never* be lucky; the first conception is born to exercise the negative freedom that is set against it, in discomfort and irritation, so as to preserve *almost* nothing of it; thus it is with what follows; spontaneity is therefore a stupid faculty, it never stops laying despicable eggs that are broken on the spot. Work, as Buffon understands it, is *criticism:* this means that it *is exercised against lived experience,* it denounces the immediate, the stuff we're made of, in the name of what does not yet exist; the artist or the scientist is in a reflexive situation, and the quality of this reflection must be discontentment. At first Gustave is delighted by this characteristic: is he not the perpetual malcontent? Certainly, it is not a condition sufficient to make him the great man he wants to be; but if we are to believe Buffon, contentment is nonetheless necessary. Besides, from the necessary to the sufficient is merely a step, quickly taken by bad faith. Insofar as Buffon's saying can be taken in a highly optimistic way, it is enough to wait, to examine and reject; after a hundred false combinations, inspiration, gradually becoming oriented, will bring forth the true idea. Buffon is not saying, of course, that *every* long patience is genius, but he is not far from thinking it. In any case, this is how Flaubert understands it, as we can tell when he writes: "Would that

103. *Correspondance* 1:255, 15 August 1846.

Buffon's impious maxim were true! I would be sure of being one of the first!"[104] A sentence repeated *in the same terms* two years later: "Would that Buffon's impious maxim were true! For I believe that no one has the patience I have."[105] He said it more clearly elsewhere: "When genius is lacking, will to some extent replaces it . . . After this characteristic modesty (on my part), I bid you adieu."[106] Does will really replace genius? The example he gives is surprising: "Napoleon III is no less an emperor, just like his uncle." Yet at that time he saw Napoleon III as a mere caricature, a Satanic and empty reflection, of the first Napoleon; not long before, he had admired him merely as a demoralizer. A mediocre but forcible demoralizer, who "crushed France under his boots." The means are unimportant, provided one achieves omnipotence and radical Evil.

This conception, however, seems blasphemous to him, impious. It risks putting art within everyone's reach, destroying its sacred quality. In this case, even if Gustave succeeds by means of incessant work in creating a masterpiece, his vocation will be done for. "One succeeds in making beautiful things by dint of patience and sustained energy." Who is *one*? It's all there. Gustave seems to vacillate between two conceptions, both of them desperate: either patience suffices, there is no *call*, art is one activity among others and does not *save;* or else it succeeds merely in producing second-class works that are to real masterpieces what Napoleon III is to Napoleon I. In this case, there are those who are called, but Flaubert is not among them: "All I ask is to continue to be able to admire the masters . . . But as for becoming one of them, never; I am sure of it. I am enormously lacking: first in the innate gift and then in perseverance in work." In this second hypothesis, salvation is possible, but only for others: Gustave's damnation is all the more atrocious because the elect exist. A letter from 1846 informs us that he is leaning toward the second idea: after *Smarh,* he took his measure and verified his mediocrity:

The greatest, the rare, the true masters mirror humanity . . . ;
they reproduce the universe, which is reflected in their works . . .
Then there are others whose every creation is harmonious . . .
who need merely speak of themselves to be eternal. They might
have been incapable of going farther in another field; but in place
of breadth, they have ardor and verve . . . Byron was of this class;
Shakespeare of the other . . . I see myself as neither great enough

104. *Correspondance* 2:373, 20–21 March 1852.
105. *Correspondance* 4:49, 1 March 1859.
106. *Correspondance* 3:180.

to produce real works of art nor original enough to fill them with myself alone . . . I am condemned to write solely for myself, as one smokes or rides horseback.[107]

These lines clearly summarize Flaubert's position after *Smarh:* the supreme goal remains exterior totalization: "Who will tell me . . . what Shakespeare loved, what he hated, what he felt? He is a terrifying colossus." The failure of the *Old Morality Play* has convinced Gustave that he is incapable of capturing the universe and presenting it to men. He still has interior totalization. But neither the *Mémoires* nor *Novembre* satisfies him: he has to be "original." He has understood that the universal subject who was to suffer the World is merely an abstraction; on the contrary, one must particularize. The conclusion is inevitable: "The first man to come along knowing how to write correctly would produce a superb book by writing his memoirs, if he wrote them sincerely, completely." Therefore, originality is found *in depth:* why, then, doesn't he try to write his own? He does not say, but we know why: he refuses to know himself *on this level* and remains on a superficial plane where he encounters only banality. Everything has collapsed: for him, in any case, art is merely an occupation.

Is he entirely sincere? Probably not. When he writes this letter, he has already seen Brueghel's painting and conceived *Saint Antoine,* which will be his new attempt at exterior totalization. But it is also true that he scarcely writes anything: from January 1845 to May 1848, he merely reads or rereads the "Masters." There is no doubt that his moroseness of 1842 persists—we shall see, however, how the crisis of 1844 has radically transformed it. Above all, two considerations shed a singular light on the meaning he gives to Buffon's saying. For more than three years he remains inactive; then, in eighteen months, he writes *La Tentation,* with "lyricism, movement, excesses . . . reckless turns of style." "I merely had to let myself go," he would say later. Where is the long patience? He loiters, then bolts—nothing could be more contrary to the *labor improbus* he so strongly vaunts. It is at this period, however, that he repeats the "blasphemy" of his master. Doesn't he take it to mean the reverse of what it says? Instead of replacing genius, isn't patience the *sign* of genius? It is an anticipation, therefore a faith. It manifests itself especially in work, of course. But, patience, in itself, is the effective grace that in its absurdity bears witness to the artist of his election.

107. To Louise Colet, 23 October 1846.

513

B. Taking Up a Profession

As I observed above, the theme of literary failure and that of taking up a profession are inseparably bound together, and we have made a somewhat arbitrary distinction between two periods in the great movement that carries Flaubert toward the crisis of January 1844. As early as 30 November 1838—he is not yet seventeen years old—he first speaks of joining Ernest and Alfred in Paris after he has taken his baccalaureat exam. Inversely, in 1842, after his first failure in law school, he completes his last attempt at interior totalization, *Novembre*, which he will not disavow. Beginning in 1840, however, the emphasis shifts: he takes the baccalaureat exam on 23 August 1840; this means he is finished with his general studies; nothing now separates him from higher, specialized studies, from the necessity of choosing a career; on the other hand, during the same period he writes little, doubts his vocation, and ponders the "failure" of *Smarh*. Yet it is not only a matter of dismissing his dreams of glory: his destined profession is in itself mediocre. When he writes in 1840, "Oh, my God, my God, why did You cause me to be born with such ambition;" he is no doubt thinking explicitly of genius. But shortly afterward[1] he dares to acknowledge: "There are some days when I would like to shine in the salons, to hear my name announced with pomp." We are a long way from the purely solitary joys that art must procure for a writer who desires no other confirmation than his own and, perhaps, that of one or two intimate friends. "To shine in the salons": there is no sillier ambition, and we know this thanks to Gustave, who has been frank enough to reveal it to us. He will shine, moreover, or will later believe he shines, in the salons of Princess Mathilde. But will the law alone allow him this possibility? He knows very well it will not, and he adds: "at other times . . . I would really like to degrade and debase myself and be a notary somewhere in the depths of Brittany." However, he is going "to do" law; why?

According to Caroline Comanville, it was Achille-Cléophas who made this decision—and very late.

> The happy period of leaving the *collège* arrived, but the terrible question of choosing a profession, of embracing a career, poisoned his joy . . . My grandfather would have liked his son to be a man of science and a practitioner . . . A man with an eminently strong character, of active habits, he had difficulty understanding

1. *Souvenirs*, p. 100, note of 8 February 1841.

the nervous and slightly feminine side that characterizes all artistic organizations. My uncle might have found more encouragement from his mother, but she maintained that he should obey his father, and it was resolved that Gustave would do his law degree in Paris. He departed, sad to leave his family, especially his sister.[2]

This interpretation in particular is given the lie by the correspondence. Certainly, in the letter of 30 November Flaubert does not specify which professional school has been chosen, but it is hardly in doubt: "When I am finally with you, my dear friends, what a fine threesome we shall make! How I yearn for the moment when I shall come and join you! We shall have a great time philosophizing and pantagruelizing." The threesome evoked seems to be too closely united for its members to be devoting themselves to different courses of study. Three months later, in any case, the choice is made, for he writes on 24 February 1839: "Do not believe, however, that I am undecided about the choice of a profession. I have quite decided to make none. For I despise men too much to do them good or ill. In any case, I will do my legal studies, I will receive my law degree, even a doctorate to idle away another year. It is highly probable that I will never plead a case." And he is far from having completed his secondary studies, for he will sit for his baccalaureat only eighteen months later.

But must we conclude, with Dumesnil, that the paterfamilias had *always* destined his younger son for a judicial career? That would be too hasty. There is no apparent reason why this "eminently strong" man, enamored of scientific exactitude, would have engendered a second son expressly in order to make him a barrister or a prosecutor. It is clear that Achille-Cléophas hardly admired the law; he saw it as neither the best method for educating a rigorous mind nor the most direct way to gain access to the respectable professions. Can he have wanted to provide the bar with still another prattler? As a physician, he surely wanted to found a family of physicians.

It must be observed, moreover, that Gustave twice *informs* Ernest, during the year 1839, of the decision he claims to have made. "In any case, I will do my law degree," he says in February. And on 23 July:

Here I am, on the verge of *choosing a profession* . . . I will therefore be a stopgap in Society, I will fill my place in it, I will be a dutiful man and all the rest, if you like; I will be like any other man, proper, like everyone, a barrister, a physician, a subprefect, a notary, an attorney, a *judge*, just that, a man of the world or the office . . .

2. *Souvenirs intimes* (*Correspondance* 1:xxii, xxiii).

515

For I shall have to be one of those things, and there is no middle ground. Well, then, I have chosen, I have decided: I will do my law degree, which instead of leading to everything, leads to nothing.

If Flaubert had known from early childhood that he was destined for the bar or the magistrature, why did he wait until 1839 to inform his friend? And why write to him about it *twice* in six months? Wasn't it because in February he hoped that the option was not definitive? Wasn't it because he was locked in a silent struggle with his family— the struggle that was echoed in Caroline's commentary? The July letter is still more peremptory than that of February: "Well, then, I have chosen, I have decided . . ." Obviously he has decided nothing at all: at most he is battle-weary and accepts the profession imposed on him. After all, he adds parenthetically: "the Law, which instead of leading to everything, leads to nothing." This critique, slyly introduced, cannot be aimed at *him* but at an alien will: the decision is absurd, it goes against its maker's intentions, but I resign myself to it. And there is something even more curious: *all* the professions he examines—including that of subprefect—require previous legal studies. All *except* one: that of physician. Why include it if it is understood that he will not enter medical school? The line is ambiguous; we *might* read it: "I will be a man like others, like those who are barristers, physicians," etc. "We *might* do so, and this is in part what Flaubert wanted. But neither is it what he has written: taken literally, it is *he himself*, having decided to enter the law school to which Ernest and Alfred have preceded him, who will perhaps be a physician nonetheless. Whence this affirmation, nullified by the paragraph's development? We could say that, in face of everything to the contrary, he wants to maintain an old certainty—"My father produced me to be a physician"—and to discredit the medical profession by mentioning it in his inventory of ridiculous careers. There is no doubt that the two intentions are present simultaneously. He must have said to Ernest a hundred times that he wanted to become an actor or a writer but that his father had destined him for medicine: a *noble* conflict, for he admired Achille-Cléophas. What he did not say is that the chief surgeon had always preferred his eldest son, so that Gustave would be a second-class practitioner. In a word, he was presenting the paternal decision in a flattering light: you, Ernest, you will be a prosecutor; as for me, I shall become a man of science, I will have the surgical eye. He slips the word *physician* into the enumeration because he cannot resign himself to confirm the new paternal will as definitive: you will *never* be a physician. At the same time he avenges himself by degrading the "profession" from which he has been banished.

Moreover, despite his peremptory declarations, he still thinks that everything has not yet been determined; Ernest must be of this opinion, for he asks Gustave in January '41 about his future projects. Gustave answers on 14 January:

> You tell me to tell you what dreams I have? None. My future projects? Aren't any. What I want to be? Nothing . . . But as the most piebald, flayed donkey still has some hairs on his hide . . . I shall tell you therefore, my good friend, that next year I shall study the noble discipline that you will soon practice: I shall do my law degree, adding a fourth year to shine with the title of Doctor.

How shall we interpret these texts and Flaubert's attitude? For want of certainty, we shall have made a few assumptions if we recall that the first letter follows shortly after the moment when Achille-Cléophas withdrew him as a boarding student at the *collège*. A decision whose motives we do not know but which—if we are at all acquainted with the good doctor—can only be explained by his worries on the subject of Gustave's health. This would allow an interpretation of the previously cited passage from Caroline's *Souvenirs*. Looked at more closely, its obscurities conceal a secret meaning. What is she saying? That the paterfamilias wanted his son to make a "career" and become, like him, a man of science, a practitioner rewarded for his social services, in short, a physician. The occupation of engineer would also have been a success, but, as I have shown above, the liberal bougeoisie had not yet understood the importance of industry. Commanville observes that the chief surgeon, in making his plans, does not take into account the nervous and feminine nature that is proper to artists. She shows us that her grandmother refused to intervene in favor of her uncle. The conclusion should be: "It was resolved that Gustave would study medicine in Paris." Not at all: he will study law there. Since Madame Flaubert declines the role of intermediary, and since Achille-Cléophas does not take Gustave's wishes into consideration or—who knows?—does not even know what they are, why did the choice change? Why is the future man of science going to become a future attorney? Everything is there in the text, provided we know how to read it: the younger son's "nervous side" is the underlying reason for the change; but Achille-Cléophas does not see its real meaning, since "to devote oneself to the unique and exclusive search for beauty . . . seems to him almost madness." For him, Gustave's nervousness is

517

not the result of a frustrated vocation; quite to the contrary, he sees it as merely a *natural* inferiority, purely physiological, that proscribes much continuous effort. If the chief surgeon decides to register his son at the law faculty, it is not to work a compromise between his desires and Gustave's, for, in any case, he denied his son's "literary vocation"; it is just that he is struck by Gustave's *fragility*. The younger son does not resemble the elder, who isn't in the least nervous; in his early years, Gustave was a backward child whose stupors seem premonitory in the light of what followed. For Achille-Cléophas, his second son was a mediocre student; he must have been informed of the little schoolboy's bouts of apathy, his extreme nervousness, perhaps even his nightmares. The teachers and tutors told Achille-Cléophas: the boarding situation is not good for him. Hence this dual decision: in 1838–39, the paterfamilias took his son home, making him a day student in order to oversee his health more effectively; around the same time he abandoned the idea of a medical career for Gustave and looked for a less arduous profession: the law would do, Gustave would be a prosecutor or a barrister. This about-face occurs at the end of the summer of 1838. Achille-Cléophas has not failed to observe Gustave's somber mood ("No, the spectacle of the sea is not in the least a cheerful prospect"[3]) and the extreme nervousness that accompanies it. But he is unaware that the deepest reasons for these troubles are the young man's family situation and the failure of *Mémoires d'un fou*. In Achille-Cléophas's eyes it is a matter of constitution. His decision, moreover, comes too late, for an unknown malady seizes little Flaubert in the second half of October and forces him to take to his bed.[4] The father had undoubtedly been worried for a long time: there is nothing unexpected in his new decision; rather, it is a *conclusion* that events have only hastened.

Flaubert appears not to have been immediately hostile to the paternal will. In modern terms, he was told, in effect, "You are not a scientific type, you are a literary one," and it was proposed that he put to the best possible use the capacities he was known to have. Besides, legal studies seemed easy to him: Alfred and Ernest were succeeding without great effort. And the paterfamilias must have told him more than once, around this time: "The law leads to everything." To everything: to high administrative posts and even, perhaps, to a seat in parliament, or to the peerage. On 30 November 1838, the young man

3. *Correspondance* 1:29, Thursday, 13 September 1838.
4. Ibid., p. 32, 28 October 1838.

is still looking forward to meeting Ernest and Alfred in Paris soon: "How I yearn for the moment when I shall come and join you!" Everything seems clear to him: he is in his year of rhetoric at the *collège*, two years separate him from that happy moment. Subsequently, he would often deride the young provincial who leaves his native town in such enthusiasm to complete his studies in the capital. Surely because he was himself so vulnerable to this mystification: disgusted with Rouen, exasperated by family life, he sees his departure as a liberation. Again in February 1839,[5] in an ambiguous letter (the process of demystification has begun), he congratulates Ernest on leading a "good and joyous existence." And he adds: ". . . to live from day to day without a care for tomorrow, without anxiety for the future, without fears, without hope, without dreams; to live a life of wanton loves and glasses of Kirchenwasser, a profligate, fantastic, artistic life that jumps, that leaps, a burning and intoxicated life . . . You will live this way for three years, and they will undoubtedly be your best years, the ones we are nostalgic for, even when we have grown old and staid." To tell the truth, he is already asserting his superiority over Ernest: for him, at least, concern for the future is consuming. But if he judges the *carpe diem* unsatisfying, he is nonetheless certain that his friend is leading a joyous life. And then, from the autumn of 1838 to the winter of 1839, his dominant concern is a *literary* one: there is the pondered failure of the *Mémoires*, the fall, and the rebound, the conception of *Smarh*.

Yet during the same period, an unpleasant job is accomplished in him: Gustave gradually comes to understand that by assigning him this new "profession," his father has merely confirmed his inferiority. Actually it is Gustave himself who has pushed his father into it by his unsuccessful behavior; he did not want to be a lesser Achille, a second-rate physician. But the result surpasses his hopes: the father concludes that his younger son *will not even be a physician.*

The situation, however, is not so simple, and here we find Gustave thrust into one of his usual vicious circles. He has not stopped feeling jealous of Achille, the triumphant older brother, the father's favorite, the privileged son. But a lengthy process, whose stages remain unknown to us, have led him from hateful admiration to contempt. In *La Peste à Florence*, he furiously humiliated himself before his brother and grudgingly acknowledged all his qualities, "since he was the eldest." Several lines from his correspondence of 1839 show that he

5. Ibid., p. 40, 24 Feburary 1839.

has quite changed: "Achille is in Paris, he is doing his thesis and settling in. He will become a dutiful man, like a polyp sticking to the
rocks."[6] And on 31 May:[7] "They are getting married tomorrow . . . I am
in a whirl of dinners. Last Wednesday, Achille gave us his farewell
dinner at Jay's . . . And with all that I am bored, I am fucking bored!"
The result is curious: in his older brother, dutiful, married—qualities
he detests most in the world—who will soon have "the finest medical
position in Normandy,"[8] he discovers the mediocrity of the profession that still fascinates him when Achille-Cléophas is the one to practice it. But he is so "invested" in this business that he still suffers
extremely from the "usurpation": hence, this disqualified profession
disqualifies all others. A physician is worthless, nothing is equal to a
physician. Let us not imagine that Gustave is comforted by this—
quite the contrary. When he imagines that his father has *condemned*
him to the law, he is convinced that Achille-Cléophas has pushed
malice to the limit by publicly acknowledging the lesser-being with
which he had afflicted his younger son from the outset. So he suffers,
he is Garcia. But from the time Achille lost his prestige, merely thinking of him was enough for Flaubert to cast contempt on all professions: "I will be a barrister, a physician . . . meaning: a stopgap in
society."[9] He is now in a strange and scarcely tolerable situation: without ceasing to feel anguished resentment at his frustration—and quite
contrarywise, since he knows now that he will not even be a neighborhood doctor—he grasps the vanity of all professions, including
the one his father practices. At any event, it is a matter of *settling
down,* of being useful, of defining himself within his class by his function. In order to obey his father he must let himself be absorbed by
the "social service" to which he is destined and must find his own
essential truth in that: he is reminded of his essence as average man,
as mean of means.

This rediscovery would be less painful to him if he had the certainty
of being above all the Artist, the privileged means of an absolute and
transhuman end. But he writes *Smarh* in haste, to give himself proof
of his genius, and, indeed, the proof is lacking. At the same time his
horror of a "profession," whatever it might be, is affirmed with such

6. Ibid., p. 46, 15 April 1839.
7. The "they" who are getting married is Achille. Several lines are skipped. The two
texts were no doubt followed by crude and violent comments which the chaste Ernest
has unfortunately suppressed (*Correspondance* 1:47, 31 May).
8. Ibid., p. 180.
9. Ibid.

violence because,—as the letters to Ernest demonstrate—it is directly linked to his literary anxiety. On this point the letter of 23 July 1839 is perfectly instructive: Gustave rebels against the necessity of taking up a profession, not because he dreads seeing his genius spoiled or destroyed by his future professional activities but, quite to the contrary, because he *lacks genius* and the profession appears to him as his ineluctable *truth:*

> I have ravaged my heart with a heap of artificial things and endless foolishness: it will all come to nothing! So much the better! As for writing, I have totally given it up, and I am sure that my name will never be seen in print; I have no more strength for it, I no longer feel capable of it, that is unhappily or happily the truth. I shall have made myself unhappy, I shall have pained all my friends. In wishing to climb so high, I shall have torn my feet on the pebbles along the way. What is still left are the great highways, *the ways already forged,*[10] the holes, the thousand holes stopped up by imbeciles. I will therefore be a stopgap in Society . . . I will be very proper, like everyone else, a barrister, a physician . . . etc.

In short: since I cannot be the unique means of a supreme end, I will be, like all members of the middle class, a mean in the circle of means.

Does this suggest that he would take his law degree without repugnance if he had a firm consciousness of his talent? Of course not: the frustration would remain, and let us not forget that his haste to affirm himself as Artist has its source in his denial of the bourgeois within him and outside him. But he might have said to himself that one must render unto Ceasar that which is Ceasar's, give some hours to Society to pay for the prerogative to write. At this period, the study of law— about which he knows nothing—seems an easy thing to him. Easy, too, the profession of barrister: he has long arms for waving about and a strong voice. He might have resigned himself to considering his practical activities his appearance, his work as artist his reality. All the same, that invincible repugnance would remain: as he says in *Novembre,* money is not made to be earned; one must *have it.* This is a dream he has long embraced and which he shares with us in his *Souvenirs:* to have money so as no longer to think about it.[11] Underneath, as we know, he is haunted by the desire to be an heir, to hold his wealth from the father as a gift to compensate for the inexplicable res-

10. My italics.
11. *Souvenirs,* p. 53. The text, undated, seems to have been written at the latest in 1839.

521

urrection of the right of primogeniture in the Flaubert family. But at the same time he would agree, *at this period,* to acquire money by the exercise of what is in his eyes a secondary art. He writes: "I am jealous of the life of great artists, the joy of money, the joy of art, the joy of opulence, it all belongs to them. I would have liked only to be a beautiful dancer or a violinist." [12] It will be observed that he envies them *first* their financial success. Framed by the joy of money and that of opulence—which only money can buy—the joy of art seems secondary. But what Flaubert really envies them is the possibility of giving themselves over to their artistic activities and that wealth should come to them as well, the sign and recompense of a frivolous talent. [13] Gustave's horror of the liberal professions comes primarily from the fact that he sees in their mediocrity a reflection of his own. To become a barrister, after the failure of *Smarh,* is to abandon the imaginary in order to coincide with himself, with his class individuality, the accidental individual being merely the poor, inadequately gifted child who, lacking genius, hasn't even the brilliant and contemptible abilities of his older brother.

The Future

Between 1838 and 1844, Flaubert's relation to the future is crucial: *he fears it.* In the last pages of *Mémoires d'un fou,* he writes: "I shall be thrown into the maelstrom of the world, I may die there, trampled by the crowd, torn to pieces. Where am I going? What will I be? I wish I were old, and had white hair; no, I wish I were handsome, and had genius . . . and I have none of those things."

This passage is quite clear: in the present, Gustave is nothing, or rather he is an irresponsible child whose "life is reproduced"; he wishes he were satisfied with this as yet indeterminate subjectivity, which takes on in his eyes, at times, the appearances of universality. But the Father has decided: his son must take up a profession. The profession is future *being,* subjectivity reabsorbed by an objective reality. A notary, for Flaubert, is an object defined, first of all, as a set of practico-inert requirements. But this object immediately begins to govern the subject that must fulfill these requirements: Gustave's subjectivity is no more than the means to be a notary. The future, for

12. Ibid., p. 69, written in 1840.
13. The artist makes Art *for Art,* and nonetheless gets paid for it. This absence of visible connection between activity and gain makes him the equal of aristocrats.

the Flaubert younger son, has always been a prefabricated itinerary. The "complete presentiment of life" appears only to a consciousness concerned with grasping existence in its totality and deciphering it in retrospect, from the final wreckage. In every life, Gustave might say—parodying Auguste Compte—"progress is the development of order." And order is the internalization of an alien plan. The fear of the future is now *determined* since the latter now appears in the guise of a *singular* trust, the fatal outcome of legal studies: it becomes the truth of the present, the light that illuminates it and the force that molds it. A single hope: to draw out his time and retire; delivered from his activities at the price of certain physical and mental degradations, the pensioner can at last live off his property, like an adolescent supported by his family. Indeed, the difference between a schoolboy of sixteen and an old man is the desert of active life, Gustave's real terror, which he would like to have already crossed over so as to find himself once again irresponsible and calm at last, a child with white hair.

There is doubtless another future: the one he would give himself by devoting himself to his work. But after *Smarh*, Gustave wonders if this is not a deadly trap. He still wants to believe in his genius, for he writes, during the winter of 1840: "I recall that before the age of ten I had already composed—I dreamed of the splendors of genius, a brightened hall, applause, crowns—and now, although I still have the conviction of my vocation, or the plenitude of an immense pride, I am increasingly in doubt." [14] This conviction is consumed by doubt, however, and the vocation may be merely the vain demand of pride. In short, genius may be only imaginary. The real future, which is the "wound of the present," is covered by a dreamed future which masks it. But is this "always future" phantasm merely an innocent chimera? As early as 26 December 1838 he was writing: [15] "Oh, Art, nameless phantom that glitters and *dooms you*." He would develop his thought in January 1840: [16]

Oh future, rosy horizon of exquisite shapes, of golden clouds, where your thought caresses you, where the heart leaps in ecstasy and which, as you go forward, indeed like the horizon, for the comparison is correct, recedes, recedes, and disappears! There are moments when you believe it touches the sky and you can grasp it

14. *Souvenirs*, p. 57.
15. *Correspondance* 1:38.
16. Ibid., p. 65.

with your hand—poof, a plain, a descending valley, and you keep running, carried along by your own momentum, only to break your nose on a stone, to get your feet stuck in shit, or to fall into a ditch.

The dreamed future, Destiny's ruse, is in the service of the real future; as we flee from the latter into the former, we give up trying to change it and give it every chance to become our truth. Rebellion, suicide would be acts. But by running after glory, Gustave does literally *nothing:* he loses all chance of actually escaping from the *other-will* of the paterfamilias; "carried along by his own momentum," he runs *only to . . . fall into a ditch."* The false writer is in complicity with the average man he is in the process of becoming: he plays the ostrich and as a result loses any chance of escaping his fate. The importance of this passage must be emphasized: Flaubert, the imaginary adolescent, turns against his attempt at unrealization precisely because it is unreal. We read between the lines a contradictory demand that will serve as guiding scheme to his future evolution: he must *give himself an unreal status through an act,* and as this cannot be writing, he must find a radical means of making *his unreality instituted by everyone.*

He hasn't gotten this far: when he doubts himself for the moment, he sees only one solution: to suppress both futures *at once,* the one that deceives him and the one that consumes him. In a word, to stop time; write no more and resist as much as he can the real flow of duration. We feel this almost physical resistance, experienced even in his muscles, when we see him, 18 December 1839, make this wish: "If only my years could fall softly, like the feathers of the dove flying calmly in the winds, without being broken, softly, softly!" [17] Still, this is merely a matter of *slowing down.* In the other letters, the negation is radical. It is manifest in two very different if not contradictory ways, the first of which remains on the surface and the other in the depths.

1. There is no doubt that the first has literary origins; it is a *cultural* attitude. Its aim is to retrieve through analysis the hedonism that is at the basis of utilitarianism and is both its source and its contestation. It is the *carpe diem* opposed to anxiety. Flaubert is inspired also by Rousseau, whose *Confessions* he read during the summer of 1838: this

---

17. We shall observe the discrepancy between the terms of comparison: Flaubert wants to "*fall*" (we shall see the importance of the scheme of the fall) from day to day like feathers that "*fly away.*" There is no contradiction: the wind—like a rising whirlwind—must somehow make the feathers rise so that gravity can then make them fall. These are but two different instants of the same movement. Beneath the asymmetry there is a hidden equivalence of flight and fall. We shall return to this.

author reproaches men for not knowing how to live the present in all its fullness; devoured by ambition or fear, they are always ahead of themselves, in the future, and neglect the pantheistic fusion with Nature that demands nothing less than the suppression of time. In a word, Gustave's first reaction is not *original;* he borrows his first defense from others. On 15 April 1839, for instance, he writes to Ernest:

> The circumstances surrounding me are rather more favorable than injurious. And for all that, I am not content; we make endless lamentations, we create imaginary ills (alas, those are the worst kind); we construct illusions that are swept away; we ourselves plant the brambles in our path, and then the days pass by, real ills arrive, and we die without having had a single ray of pure sunshine in our soul, a single calm day, a cloudless sky. No, I am happy. And why not? What is there to afflict me? The future will be black, perhaps? Let us drink before the storm; never mind if the tempest breaks us, the sea is calm now.

Here the two futures are confounded: we construct illusions (the unreal, glorious future); we create imaginary ills (fear of the real future, of a profession). It will be observed that Gustave insists on the unreality of his future condition while elsewhere he contrasts it to his dreams, as truth is contrasted to phantasms. Here again, his reaction is *cultural:* for numerous authors—and particularly in the eighteenth century—the future *does not exist.* Reality is defined a priori by the present, by the vivid and powerful impressions that are imposed on us moment by moment and—at least for certain writers—by the material realities that act on us through our body. It is not difficult to see this conception as a result of analytic thought: one "dissects" duration in order to reduce it to a pure succession of temporal invariants; the external time of the mechanical is substituted for the *internal* temporality of psychic processes. In this case, one does not dream of denouncing the contents of future moments as unreal; quite the contrary. Condillac, Hume, Berkeley, each according to his own system, tried to base scientific conjecture on reason and to establish, for any given conjecture its degree of probability. But they insist that the future is merely a future present, and that it will have concrete reality only at the moment of its appearance. Thus, for Gustave there are "real ills," meaning the ills that will be realized as concrete determinations of a lived moment; but though one might foresee them correctly, the conjecture is *imaginary* because it concerns something *that does not exist.* If the present is the basic condition of existence, the future profession (barrister, solicitor, notary) is in the actual moment a nothingness of being, and Gustave torments himself *for nothing,* which means that his malaise is imaginary, a void in the midst of present plenitude. The conclusion is obvious: let us enjoy the moment. "Let the cork pop, the pipe be filled, let the whore strip, hang it!" Anxious anticipation of the future is the malady of the "younger generation." "In former times, they had more spunk, they were busy with women, duels, orgies."

This attitude of Gustave's is merely an artificial and willed reaction against his own intuition of temporality. We have seen him, two months earlier, assure Ernest of the fundamental priority of the future in temporal ek-stases: "What will you do? What do you imagine becoming? Where is the future? Do you sometimes ask yourself these questions? No, what does it matter to you? And you are right. The future is what is worst in the present. The question *What are you going to be?* fired at a man is a gulf opening up in front of him, continually advancing as he goes along." The condescending tone will not escape us: Ernest's heedlessness, his "wanton loves," and the little glasses of kirschenwasser protect him and provisionally deter him from discovering that the future is a structure of the present. And we know Gustave well enough to detect the scorn in the "No, what does it matter to you? And you are right." Gustave is not unaware, moreover, that Ernest indulges in moderate debauchery, and that the future prosecutor prefers grisettes to whores. He reproaches his friend not so much for forgetting his own future as for consenting to it and being content with it. Indeed, Ernest is a plodder; he works easily and comfortably: in short, he takes his future "profession" seriously and prepares himself zealously for the magistrature. As a result, his career, accepted, even *desired,* scarcely preoccupies him: the future is not his concern, and precisely for that reason he can drink and amuse himself after a day of studying. Gustave's superiority, in his own eyes, lies in the fact that he rejects the destiny that Ernest finds good enough for him; the Flaubert younger son does not coincide with his future, he knows it is inevitable, but nothing prevents him from condemning in silence the fatality that leads him to it. Hence he is not in a position to enjoy the present. Where would he have the appetite for such an enjoyment when the "gulf" of the future is opening up in front of him? He knows it so well that he declares, as we have seen, in a note written at the same period:[18] "To be happy, you must already

18. *Souvenirs,* p. 54.

be happy." You don't fight worry with pleasures, for it is the nature of worry to spoil pleasure.

After two months, however, he is claiming his own the attitude he attributes to Ernest. Why is this? We can easily discern the circumstantial causes: "You pity me, my dear Ernest, and yet should I be pitied? . . . And you, too? I believed you had more good sense than I, dear friend. You weep and wail too?" Chevalier has *dared* to pity him—Gustave cannot put up with that. And what pretension: the future prosecutor has the gall to compare his own weeping and wailing to his comrade's noble anguish! Flaubert quickly puts him in place: "Let us put our sadness into Art . . . But let us put gaiety into life." The Lord, exasperated, rejects this promiscuity: in order to put the Vassal in his place, he overturns his theories. But from the time he makes his thought specific, the difficulties begin: how to fill the moment? It is as if he were hesitating between two contents: "the extravagant orgy" with duels, whores, and the very opposite, *calmness*, "a cloudless sky," "family, friends, affections." On closer reading, we perceive that he exhorts Ernest to shed all sense of shame,[19] and demands for him merely a better use of the good fortune he enjoys; for the same reason he will reproach himself in his *Souvenirs* for turning away from his family without a worthy motive when he should cling to them. Yet the pivotal line is, "Let us drink before the storm." It is as if, unable to enjoy his objective happiness, he dreamed of drowning his pain with alcohol, with a futile agitation. Besides, he invokes the whores especially to shock Ernest. A little later, on 19 November 1839, he reveals his true feeling: "Going to Paris all alone . . . and no doubt you will offer me the diversion of a cup of coffee at the Golden Colonnades, or some dirty whore from the Chaumière. Thanks! Vice bores me quite as much as virtue." What does matter to him—as we shall see more clearly in *Novembre*—is drinking. However, what he seeks in wine is not gaiety but stupefaction: when he is drunk, the future rankles less cruelly.

To conclude, we must see in this passage the sign of a desperate effort to *kill time*. Against himself, against his deepest intuition, against his presentiments, against the bitter taste of fatality that pushes him to totalize his life in advance, Gustave begins by inspiring himself

19. After having harshly rebuked his friend—"You, too, weep and wail"—he introduces the theme of "gaiety in life." In short, he advises Chevalier to make his stay in Paris more profitable.

with analytic realism and complete bad faith to confuse the future and the imaginary. But he does not succeed in convincing himself and seeks some better means to destroy in himself what Husserl calls the "internal consciousness of temporality." He knows full well that what will be is a necessary determination of what is. The adolescent cannot ignore the fact that he is gripped by fear of becoming an adult, or that—whatever he does—his condition as irresponsible schoolboy is by definition precarious. What he must annihilate definitively is his very lucidity. Not the objective future—which does not depend on him—but his subjective intuition; and he can do this only at the price of mutilation. The stupor, when it comes spontaneously, can provide him some respite. But it is not enough, and above all it cannot be reproduced at will. Alcohol, on the other hand, will have the advantage of plunging him into a provoked stupor. In 1839, of course, the young man—at the *collège* and in his family—hardly has the means to get systematically drunk: but he dreams of it. In 1842, as we shall see, alone in his Paris digs, he will remain chaste but will deliberately indulge in solitary drinking. In short, beneath the analytic hedonism— which is borrowed—we shall discover, beginning in 1839, the will to fall below the human condition, to reduce as much as possible the scope of his consciousness in order to escape from temporal ek-stases; he knows that the moment is nothing, and in order to coincide with this nothing he tries to annihilate himself, or at least to plunge himself artificially into the torpor of vegetative life. He will not avoid his destiny—no one can, according to him—but he will not see what happens to him, he will not feel the hours go by, the event will jump him without his having tasted its bitterness in advance. But at a still deeper level, isn't there a more radical intention? Isn't Gustave acting like the peasant who cuts off his finger to escape conscription? If he stupefies himself to the point of becoming subhuman, he becomes incapable of fulfilling the human future that awaits him. Drunk, stupefied, he *can no longer* "do his law degree"; he truly becomes the family idiot, the backward child kept at home by his parents. Of course, this is still a nightmarish choice. Yet Gustave senses that there is a unique way of exploding time and reducing himself to the sluggish brutishness of a mechanical system. There is no question of revolt or of choosing another end: one allows oneself to be carried along, inanimate, but abolishes the future by the annhilation of the man. All or nothing.

2. These remarks can serve as introduction to the second negation. This, although still ineffective, is more precise, more spontaneous,

personal: it does not depend on a bookish knowledge; it does not at first appear to be a meditation on temporality but a concrete decision made as a function of the family situation and of Gustave's knowledge of his own character. We earlier saw it emerge in the form of a resigned wish; Gustave said in the *Mémoires:* "I wish I were old." Old, we know, means a property owner. Between 1839 and 1840, the wish becomes a decision and is consequently transformed. On 24 February 1839, he writes to Ernest: "I will do my law degree, I will pass the bar, and then, to end things suitably, I will go and live in a little provincial town like Yvetot or Dieppe with a job as assistant royal prosecutor." On 23 September of the same year: "Well! I have chosen, I have decided: I shall do my law degree, which, far from leading to everything, leads to nothing. I will stay three years in Paris, catch syphilis, and then? I desire but one thing: to go and spend my whole life in a ruined old château overlooking the sea." On 14 January 1841: "I will do my law degree, adding a fourth year . . . After which it may well be that I shall become a Turk in Turkey or a mule driver in Spain, or a camel driver in Egypt." On 22 January 1842: "I am not yet a barrister, I have neither the robe nor the patter. We can think of better things than that for our old age: screw it all and simply go off with an income of four thousand pounds to Sicily or Naples, where I shall live as I would in Paris for twenty."

"To end things suitably in Yvetot . . .": this vow finds an echo in the *Souvenirs* (January 1841): "There are days . . . when I would really like to degrade and debase myself, to be a notary in the depths of Brittany." This is *losing himself* in obscurity. Similarly, after his studies, he chooses to be nothing: rags in the sun, a tramp's life; or again, solitude and oblivion: he will live without writing in an old château overlooking the sea—like Almaroës. Another time, more self-indulgent, he sees himself in Naples, living on his income. In the light of his confidences, Alfred's question, later on, is more understandable:[20] "I would like to see how the thing will end, and how *the father* will take your announced resolution to conclude your active life with the diploma." The issue for Flaubert is one of a constant determination. Naturally, this is just one of the factors in a complex process leading to the "attack" at Pont-l'Evêque. But we find the same tendency from 1839 to 1844. It sometimes happens that Gustave gives it a more positive turn: he has taken heart again and once more hopes to write a worthy work. On 22 January 1842, for example, the very day that he

20. On 25 July 1843.

declares to Ernest his intention to "screw it all and simply go off with an income of four thousand pounds to Sicily or Naples," he writes to Gourgaud-Dugazon:

> I have arrived at a decisive moment: I must go forward or withdraw, everything is there for me. It is a question of life and death. When I have made my decision, nothing will stop me, should I be hissed and hooted at by everyone. You are familiar enough with my stubbornness and my stoicism to be convinced of that. I will become licensed as barrister, but I hardly believe I will ever plead a case for a common property division or an unfortunate householder . . . I do not feel made for this materialistic and trivial life. Therefore, this is what I have resolved: I have in mind three novels . . . That is enough to prove to myself if I have talent or not . . . In the month of April I count on showing you something. It is that sentimental and amorous ragout I spoke to you about.

Novembre is the work in question—Flaubert has begun it. He will abandon it and will not take it up again until August 1842, after his first failure in law school. He is in doubt, but the very fact that he is writing proves that he has recovered some confidence in his vocation as artist. It is striking that he does not breathe a word of it to Ernest, although he spoke to him at length, three years earlier, about *Smarh*. Now he conceals himself in order to write, a secret that he confides to Gourgaud alone. For Ernest, he will live off his income in Naples, which—in the light of the preceding letters—means that he will do nothing there, not even write a book. To his former teacher he implies that if he has talent, he will withdraw from active life (when I have made my decision, nothing will stop me). But the positive and the negative formulation have in common that *primarily* he wants to do nothing and to be nothing.

Has he already clearly understood that he must be nothing *in order* to write? No. The will to annihilation is first of all for its own sake, and its most apparent meaning is to express resentment and passivity. Not for an instant, in the passage cited above, does he imagine interrupting his studies: quite the contrary, he declares he has *decided* to pursue them as far as the doctorate. Therefore, he accepts the *Fatum* that pulls him along, inwardly protesting all the while against the *alien Will* that has decided his fate. But since the law "leads to nothing," meaning since the paternal curse remains inexorable and chooses annihilation for him, Gustave will push his rancorous zeal to the end: the last exam over, he will annihilate himself, and the chief surgeon will discover, with remorse, the truth of his malign intention.

On the nature of this annihilation, the young man hesitates. One fact is certain: *he will never plead a case*. But what will become of him? In his masochistic resentment, he wants to push debasement to the limit: he will hide in the depths of Brittany—which is not reputed, at the time, to be one of the places "where the spirit breathes"; he will no longer see either his family or his compatriots, he will be forgotten; overburdened with sordid labors, he hopes to forget himself and become a robot, a notary. He would do better, surely, to dream of being a great barrister, as Frédéric will do. To tell the truth, Gustave is sometimes tempted. Why shouldn't this adolescent, who wants to "shine in the salons," cherish the ambition of "shining at the bar" once in a while? But no—it's all or nothing. In the Flaubert family, the most distinguished orator is just a chatterer, innately inferior to the lowest scientist or practitioner. Unable to be chief surgeon or genius, Gustave wants to go all the way to the bottom, to drop to the lowest rung of the social ladder. Notary in Brittany: the lowest of the bourgeois professions. Or else—why not?—he will drop *beneath* his class, he will be a mule driver, a camel driver: sunshine, an empty head, the lumpenproletariat. This presupposes that he should flee, stealing the money for his trip, and realize the paternal curse by bringing shame upon his family. At other times his nihilism is more self-indulgent— here he is, living off his income in Naples. He doesn't write at all; he lives, ignored, amid strangers whose language he doesn't know, and spends his days fascinated by his own inner emptiness. Where do the four thousand pounds come from? From the Flaubert inheritance, no doubt. This detail is instructive: more or less lucidly, Gustave has convinced himself that he will realize his project of "concluding his active life" only with his father's death; this is the reason he "so often foresaw" that death in his adolescence. Foresaw and *dreaded* it, to be sure: but the fear conceals a kind of impatience. Everything is ambiguous, moreover; and Flaubert also wants the paterfamilias to survive his younger son's decline so as to taste the bitter fruits of dishonor he has prepared for him. But—and this is his contradiction—he is not unaware that his father, while alive, will oppose his son's radical decisions: Achille-Cléophas does not intend him to play at "all or nothing"; he has condemned him to mediocrity—which is worse than nothing— and will be on the watch that he remain mediocre. Moreover, income from properties is not obligatory: he can live out his life in a ruined old château. The essential thing is to be empty—or filled with a base, material task—and to be conscious of it. Base tasks or no tasks all. A living death. Earlier, Gustave dreamed of arriving as quickly as possible at old age, which *naturally* "concludes active life"—in short, he wanted to obey to the end. To the extent that the threat is more specific, the tone changes: he will obey, but after the doctorate we shall see what we shall see.

To be nothing is to deny time, to dissolve the future. A while ago he was reducing duration to the nontemporal moment; now he substitutes for fatality—that orientation toward becoming—an eternity of repetition. Nothing will change, nothing will happen: everything will begin again each day. The will to decline will have shattered Gustave's ambition and his jealous passions. Both solutions are suicidal: since the future is an integral part of his constitution, the young man must kill himself in order to kill time. Dead drunk or a notary in Yvetot—or perhaps a dead drunk notary—after his law degree Flaubert will be no more than one of the living-dead: the future is nothing because he will figure in it as a nothing.

The Third Denial of Time

Beneath these declarations of Gustave's, which are simultaneously wishes, theoretical considerations, and abstract decisions with no impact, a silent and real battle is being waged: against the father and against the clock. For him, to lose his time is *to gain time.* Just as he is dreaming of the sullen decline that must follow the end of his studies, the young man contrives to delay it. Troubles, the nature of which we are at present ignorant—but which we shall attempt to describe when we study *Novembre*—ravage him, plunging the paterfamilias into anxiety. Gustave reveals to Doctor Flaubert (or allows him to discover) his "nervous organization." Achille-Cléophas is cunningly led to keep his younger son in the family setting for some time yet. The facts speak for themselves: in October 1838 the young man is authorized to take his teachers' courses as a day student; in December '39 he gets himself dismissed and prepares for the baccalaureat exam *at home.* At this period, he still counts on rejoining Ernest and Alfred in Paris as soon as the vacation is over, hence in October 1840. "But what shall I do after leaving the *collège*? Go to Paris all alone?" Then, nothing more. The chief surgeon, in order to calm his nerves, entrusts him to Dr. Cloquet, who is leaving for the Pyrenees, bound for Marseille and Corsica. Gustave returns to Rouen, happy with his trip but all the more miserable at finding himself once again in Normandy. One would expect his subsequent departure for the capital. But it doesn't happen. No explanation is given, and it is not until 14 January 1841 that he says in a letter to Ernest: "Next year, I will do my law degree." Next year means the autumn of '41 until the summer of '42.

These silences seem to indicate that it had been decided long before, and probably in the summer of 1840, that Gustave would stay home with his family *in any case*.[21] By the end of 1840, a perceptible improvement in his condition must have allowed his parents to hope that he would not lose more than one academic year. But almost immediately this hope seems to have been dashed. At least we are led to think so by the abrupt resolution he imparts to Ernest. Ernest must return to Andelys for the Easter vacation, he invites Gustave to spend the time with him, Gustave is overjoyed by this and on 29 March writes to his friend: "You will find me still the same . . . transcendent at seasoning pipes." He adds, on 6 April: "I shall arrive [at Andelys] . . . with many tips, cigars, matches . . . for smoking purposes; I shall bring jokes and pipes of various sizes to beguile you." And two days later he announces his arrival for the following Saturday, and adds: "I may bring you a lady's cigarette; as for me, I no longer smoke, having given up all my bad habits. Perhaps a pipe or two from time to time, but still?" He would have made this decision on the 7th and announced it to Ernest without comment. This is hardly his way: it's really he who decides, he comments abundantly on his resolutions. Here, on the contrary, he seems embarrassed and in too much of a hurry. We might think he communicates the news so that Ernest will know it before their meeting and no further question will be asked. So? Are we to believe that he fell ill again on 7 April? This is hardly credible. But rereading the preceding letter, we observe that it is highly ambiguous: who are the cigars for? Gustave does not say. As for the pipes, the text is clear: "to beguile you," in other words, for Ernest alone. We might say that Gustave is embarrassed, fearing mockery or, still worse, pity, and therefore boasts again of his "bad habits" when he has already given them up. The letter of 29 March,

21. It must be observed that the text of *Souvenirs*, "as harassed as much by the remedies as by the illness," written 2 January 1841, refers to a period *at least six to seven months* earlier: "How I have lived since, and how many things have intervened between the line finished then and the one begun here! The labors for my exam, my passing at last. I want to try to summarize that life of *five months*." And he begins his narrative: "I received my degree on a Monday morning." In short, there was the "illness," the "labors for the exam," then in August success and the departure on his "dear journey." We can therefore consider that the troubles to which he alludes took place *at the latest* in July (if "labors for the exam" designates the final period of preparation, in which one "reviews" one's courses) and perhaps much earlier (if we take "labors" in a larger sense).

on the other hand, seems sincere: ". . . transcendent at the seasoning of pipes . . ." In other words, unless we accept the utterly improbable hypothesis that Gustave decided on the 7th to give up tobacco—which he would never do again except by constraint and forced by his "attack" in 1844, and then only temporarily—and informs his friend of this decision without even adding "I will explain my reasons at Andelys," we are likely to have recourse to the simpler and more probable hypothesis: Achille-Cléophas fears that nicotine has ill effects on his younger son's already shattered nervous system. He has often begged him to smoke less. Between 29 March and 6 April, Gustave collapses, the reappearance of worrisome symptoms forces the philosopher-physician simply to proscribe his use of tobacco. Irritated, Flaubert takes an expedient to announce it to his friend (might as well tell him, since at Andelys he will perforce see it for himself).[22]

What is certain, in any case—and this is the only thing that matters to us—is that in April 1841, the chief physician is far from considering his son cured: troubles persist, he must be kept under observation. Indeed, when October '41 arrives, instead of leaving for Paris, Flaubert stays home. He writes from Rouen to Gourgaud-Dugazon, in January 1842: "So I am doing my law degree, meaning, I have bought law books and registered." And the same day, to Ernest: "I have not yet opened my law books. That will come toward the month of April or May." In fact, beginning in February, anxiety impels him to open his books, but he immediately closes them, then takes them up again toward the middle of March "with extreme distaste." He will not go to settle in Paris until July 1842, in order to take his first exam in the month of August. In short, from December '39 to July '42, he *steals* two and a half years (the first six months at the *collège* and the other twenty-four at his law studies) to spend them in the bosom of his family. Yet in more than thirty months he works only one full year: from December '39 to August '40, he prepares for his baccalaureat; from March or, more likely, April to August '42, he studies "the Code and the *Institutes*." Eighteen entire months remain (August '40–March/April '42), during which he does nothing but Greek and Latin, in a very relaxed fashion at that, beneath the tolerant eye of the fearsome philosophical practitioner.

22. We recognize Gustave's methods. In December '39, he does not write to Ernest: "I was expelled" or "I got myself expelled," but simply, "I am no longer at the *collège*," adding that he is tired of telling this story and that he "sends him to Alfred for the narration."

Is this to say that he is cheating? Cheating himself? Playing at being ill? Evidently not. The point is not whether this passive resistance is conscious but whether it does or does not bear an intentional structure. In order to decide, we must return to his correspondence and his *Souvenirs* of 1840 to 1842. On 14 Novembre he writes: "I have a dry and tired mind . . . I have nothing but vast and insatiable desires, an atrocious boredom, and continuous yawning." On 14 January '41: "I am fatigued by dreams, bored by projects, saturated by thinking of the future, and as for being *something*, I will be the least possible." On 29 March '41: "I am doing Greek and Latin, as you know, nothing more, nothing less; I am rather a sad fellow." On 7 July '41: "As for me, I am becoming colossal, monumental, I am an ox, a sphinx, a dolt, an elephant, a whale, everything that is hugest, thickest, heaviest, morally as well as physically. If I had shoes with laces, I would be incapable of tying them. All I can do is breathe, pant, sweat, and drool; I am a digesting machine, an apparatus that manufactures blood that pounds and whips my face." On 21 September: "I am bored, bored, bored . . . I am stupid, idiotic, inert . . . I haven't the strength needed to fill three sheets of paper. For the month I've been at Trouville, I've done absolutely nothing but eat, drink, sleep, and smoke." On 31 December '41: "I go nowhere, see no one, and am seen by no one . . . As the old wiseman says: 'Hide your life and abstain,'" On 23 February '42: "For six weeks it has been impossible for me to construct anything whatever." The *Souvenirs* are still more explicit; in January '41 we read: "What am I doing, what will I ever do— what is my future? Nothing else really matters—I would truly have liked to work this year, but I haven't the heart, and that bothers me a lot; I might have known Latin, Greek, English, a thousand things pull the book out of my hands and I am lost in reveries longer than the longest twilight evenings." And at the end of the same month: "I have not worked this January; I do not know why—an inconceivable laziness—I have no [moral] backbone, there are days when I could leap into the clouds, others when I haven't the strength to move a book." He adds, on 8 February:

> I have an intermittent moral malady, yesterday I had superb plans for work. Today I cannot continue. I have read five pages of English without understanding a word; that is nearly all I have done, and I have written a love letter in order to write and not because I love . . . For several days I was firmly resolved to make sure that at the end of six months, around July, I should know English, Latin,

535

and be able to read Greek at the end of this week. I ought to have known Canto IV of the *Aeneid* by heart. I do not read much.

After reading the preceding passages, we are certain of at least one thing: Gustave's apathy is really experienced, suffered. It appears, moreover, as the intensification and generalization of a trait that he observed at the end of childhood: let us recall Djalioh, incapable of *sticking with* a project or a feeling, and whose exultations collapse the moment they verge on paroxysm. It is as if behind this increasing loss of willpower there were a constant of lived experience; we know this constant: it is passive activity, constituted from Gustave's proto-history. But constituted though it may be, it must also be lived and made temporal; in short, it constitutes *itself* in the very movement of life. Suffered, it is charged with intentions; intentionalized, it becomes a *means* to live, it is transformed into active passivity: it does not hold its ends before it, it absorbs them, making them into its immanent meaning. This meaning is obvious: to let passivity unfold in the self as the result of an *alien force,* doing nothing, here and now, *in order* to be nothing. The impossible plenitude of the present—which it opposed in theory to the unreality of the future—is replaced in fact by the void of total inactivity. The vain negation of what he must be becomes the *existed* denial of every pro-ject: the future, which he sees at the time as a present future, will be nothing if the actual present is nothing. One denies the ek-static structure of time by rejecting all *activity,* meaning that Gustave exploits his original passivity and attempts to make it into something invalid, a negation suffered and denuded of all praxis. It is an expelling of man from the self. He works at it, bringing about what a highly directed thought today calls the "decentering of the subject." And Flaubert presents this decentering, as is his way, now as the fundamental characteristic of his idiosyncrasy and now as a permanent trait of the species. On 2 January 1841, he observes in the *Souvenirs:* "Even in my calm state, my physical and moral temperament is an eclecticism led briskly along by fantasy and by the fantasy of things." And in a passage from the first *Education sentimentale,* written during the summer or autumn of 1843, he declares: "Man seems made to be ruled by chance; every event that depends on his will astonishes him, troubles him as a task too difficult for him; he hails its arrival with ardent desires, and suddenly he conjures it away, like a summoned phantom that scares him." The reference here is to Henry, who both wishes and fears to leave for America with Madame Emilie. But Flaubert—who, as we know, never really wanted to leave his milieu—transposes his experience: what he desires and dreads, all at the same time, is the decision he must make *after* his law degree: "a question of life and death." While waiting, he abandons himself to chance—in other words, he *is lived*—or to imagination, a sudden tear in the monotonous texture of reality. If it is true that the subject constitutes and discovers itself through praxis, Flaubert regards himself at this period as a subjectivity without subject: "meaning befalls him" through circumstances and undoubtedly through those layers of subterranean being he calls his "dreadful and boring depths" (dreadful because he regards them as his own without recognizing them, boring because they manifest themselves by monotonous repetitions which do not issue in any enterprise). In short, he absents himself. The mature man will never entirely renounce this attitude of the young man he was.[23]

Art, no doubt, requires a certain form of activity, a labor that adapts the means to the end, that renders thought "indirectly," through form. But—he will often return to this later on—"one does not do what one wants." In other words, the underlying themes *impose themselves*, artistic activity is exercised in the direction defined by passivity haunted by lived experience, by intentions that one *learns about* rather than constitutes. In any event, from *Smarh* to *Novembre* the problem of labor in art hardly troubles him, for he has decided not to write and

23. In the letters to Louise and later, he puts himself *above* the action out of contempt: according to him, he would be perfectly capable of acting, he would have proved his mettle, would have shown himself more effective even than the so-called "men of action," but renounced such pointless agitation in order to devote himself to Art. It must be observed, however, that these declarations—at the time they took place—referred to well-defined situations. For example, after his father's death, Gustave is persuaded that Achille owes his post at the Hôtel-Dieu even more to him than to the paterfamilias (*Correspondance* 3:110, 4:98). Indeed, we know that the elder brother did not manage to be his father's successor without some difficulty. Did Gustave take steps to intervene? It is likely. But the young recluse had no real power: things were arranged elsewhere and through other transactions. For the younger son, however, the intervention he attempted was his recuperation of the paternal will. By pushing resentful obedience to the end, as always, he recuperated his destiny: death having reduced the father to impotence, I alone, with my own hands, have put Achille the usurper on the throne that should have been mine. I have "made" my brother, and I am the sole and proud artisan of my unhappiness. Which does not prevent him from asserting in other passages that Achille owes *everything* to the chief surgeon: the point is to make his older brother look like a dwarf perched on the shoulders of a giant. Gustave's attitude toward action rests, then, on a more general attitude toward his family and his past: he cheats himself in order to suffer less, to escape the jaws of envy. But later on, after more than twenty years of monastic life, he abandons his defensive tactic on this point and makes significant confessions: I was a coward in my youth, he says to George Sand. And he must be seen at work when it is a question, for example, of performing *Aïsse* (cf. *Correspondance* 6:327, 343, 349, 353, 363). What *acknowledged* impotence, what disgust!

remains almost faithful to this commitment. At this period, as we see, the "all or nothing" of pride is integrated with a more complex proceeding; not writing, of course, is choosing nothingness rather than mediocrity; it is a literary suicide that engages him alone. But this refusal to be a passable writer, without genius—in short, to devote himself in vain to the superhuman and antihuman end which is beauty—must also be read as the justification of a more hidden enterprise: the realization through illness of a social annihilation *in the immediate*. He lives both refusals without distinction: since, for lack of genius, I want to realize nothingness in myself by forbidding myself to write despite the abiding desire to do so, I can escape the other term of the alternative, the "profession," only by suffering *in the present* the impossibility of preparing myself for it. The illness is nothing more than this impossibility *lived out*. And, certainly, the writer's terrible disappointment is one of the chief reasons for his nervous troubles; it provokes them and at the same time leads from a quasi-exteriority into interiority (failure is *internalized* as troubles, but these troubles in themselves and on the level of interpretation *do not signify* failure). However, they receive an intentional signification from the fact that they realize *in daily life* the impossibility of preparing for the law exams. The present has henceforth the double function of producing *in the moment*—through nervous agitation, instability, a crushing and apparently gratuitous fatigue—an internal emptiness which is the very symbol and anticipation of future nothingness, and on the other hand of preparing in the long term the desired annihilation (the denial of *Fatum* and the future) by stripping Gustave of the powers necessary to pursue his studies. The illness is a result that is suffered but intentionally structured as means. As soon as we have grasped this orientation of lived experience, it is easy to fathom its meaning.

1. The battle against the clock necessarily implies the negation of change. When Flaubert writes to Ernest, not without a certain smugness, "I feel . . . confusedly, something stirring in me, I am now in a transitional period and I am curious to see what will come of it," he is still working on *Smarh*, and what he believes he feels is the slow maturation of his genius. But after his smarting failure, what dominates in his letters is the theme of *immutability*. Transformation of the self is, then, becoming reconciled to the "profession." Actually, this motif is initiated in the autumn of 1838: "I am still the same, more clownish than jolly, more inflated than great," [24] but this is because he is dissat-

24. To Ernest, 30 November 1838, *Correspondance* 1:36.

isfied with *Mémoires d'un fou*. He will be more explicit on 29 March 1841: "You will find me again still the same, troubling myself very little with the future of humanity, transcendent in the seasoning of pipes." That day he adds, for the benefit of Ernest, who irritates him: "As for you, it seems to me that you are changing, something I cannot congratulate you for . . . [I am afraid] that in a short time you will become a sensible man, admired by respectable householders, reasonable, moral, a booby, well off, very silly." Immobility is his defense against this evolution—foreseen very early *in others*: we recall the preface to *Agonies*. He describes himself, in July '41, as "colossal, monumental . . . an ox . . . everything that is hugest, thickest, heaviest, morally as well as physically." To fight movement he fills himself with the viscous heaviness of fatty substances; for directed temporality he substitutes the time of organic repetition: "I am a digesting machine, an apparatus that manufactures blood." But the image does not entirely satisfy him: he intends to escape from lived experience itself, from physiological duration; what he desires is unorganized materiality, pure and inert, faceless being-there. Already in the following letter he identifies *laziness* with *inertia*.[25] The idea becomes more specific, and in a passage from *Novembre* written three or four months later we learn that he has begun to envy "those long stone statues sleeping on tombs . . . one could say . . . that they savor their death." He wants, then, "for death to delight in itself and admire itself; just enough life to feel that one no longer is."[26] Nothingness is identified, here, not so much with death as with an inert, self-conscious minerality. He knows, however, that he is changing, but the change terrifies him: he feels on the threshold of "that nameless thing, the life of a man of twenty [which is not] especially in my nature, neither youth nor middle age nor decrepitude; it is all that at once, it grabs hold by every protuberance, every projection."[27] In other words, the denial of time is confused with the pure and simple horror of becoming adult. To persevere in his being, for him, is to cling to adolescence. To be filled with inert matter, to be empty: two contrary images which express the same intention; for emptiness is immobility, naked passivity, and matter receives its movement only from the exterior. In any case, he musn't raise a finger: the least spontaneous movement reconciles him to the moment when he will have to earn his living, take

25. Trouville, 21 September 1841, *Correspondance* 1:85: "You must curse my crass laziness . . . I am foolish, stupid, inert."
26. *Novembre*.
27. *Souvenirs intimes*, pp. 77–78, written 2 January 1841.

on responsibilities. Does he cling so violently to his youth? No. Certainly, if he needed merely to mature in order to become a great artist, he wouldn't hestiate to shed it. Moreover, he *does not feel young*—he has said so repeatedly. But since he is disabused, since he knows the fate that awaits him, since he sees in Ernest's changes a prefiguring of his own metamorphosis, which he dreads, he clings to his adolescence. Let it remain eternally or let it be stopped by death or issue immediately in senility! Time has already run out: he knows that the "life of a man of twenty" is merely a transitional period. Be that as it may, he will eternalize the transition by absolute inactivity: anything rather than become a grown man. He shrivels up; contracted, knotted, his muscles grow tired fighting against time, producing an image of inertia through an exhausting effort. Even immobile, however, he feels the implacable sliding that carries him, passive, toward the denied destiny. What resistance should he summon? The tension within him, which can have no outcome, ends only by provoking psychic headaches, which he certainly complains about to Doctor Flaubert:[28] one more symptom suffered and exploited.

2. Immobilism, experienced in shame, implies the radical negation of social bonds. From 1840 to 1842, Gustave is ill, it is not a family secret; his "anomaly," although he plays at it, embarrasses him by its increasing virulence. He no longer wants to show himself to the people of Rouen. He does nothing, *therefore* sees no one, in order to escape social status (ill, ill adapted, the second son of Flauberts does no honor to his father, etc.). In other words, he wants to recognize his attempt at annihilation only in its subjective reality: as he lives it and not as it makes him for *others* a certain real and radically different object from what he tries to be through his internal enterprise. This tendency is manifest in his letter to Ernest of 31 December 1841:

> Tomorrow I shall be alone, and as I do not want to begin the New Year by admiring the neighbors' new toys, making New Year's resolutions and visits, I shall get up as usual at four o'clock, I shall

---

28. He makes mention of them beginning on 20 October 1839 (during the period of depression following *Mémoires d'un fou:* "I had a headache when your letter came a quarter of an hour ago, and the headache went away; I am delighted, enchanted, charmed." Nothing could be clearer: he suffers because he puts his whole self into the negation of duration, and this interior negation does not prevent the flow of social time. Ernest gives him a bit of good news: in two weeks, they will see each other (at this time their friendship is still lively); this is a reason to relax, to accept a future in the short term, to make social time coincide with interior duration as much as possible. With the passing days, he will no longer see an intolerable violence leading him toward a cursed destiny, but for a time he will count the days impatiently because he wants to

do Horace and smoke at my window . . . and I shall not go out all day!!! And I shall not pay a *single* visit. Too bad if people get angry! I go nowhere, see no one, and am seen by no one. The Chief of Police is unaware of my existence; I should like it even more so. As the ancient sage says: "Hide your life and abstain." So they think I'm wrong, I'm an original type, a bear, a young man like few others; I surely have squalid habits and I haunt cafés, taverns , etc.—such is the opinion the bourgeois have of me.[29]

This is *surely not* the opinion of the bourgeois—the Flaubert family's acquaintances. We know that the young man has not begun his higher education, that he is felled like a wounded beast: this is enough to stimulate talk of fragile health, mental troubles, or laziness. In the eyes of these practical men the Flaubert son is a misfit, a backward child; happily, his father can be proud of Achille: there's a fellow with a future who does honor to the family. Gustave prefers to *imagine* that he is seen as a denizen of the brothels, a monster, but to support this illusion he must keep to his room and carefully avoid the gaze of others ("*I am not seen* by anyone) and their pitying benevolence. To scandalize, fine! To be pitied, never! But the sequestration is not voluntary—although it may be intentional. It is shame, suffered in horror, that prompts it. Toward the same time, Flaubert dreams again of "shining in the salons." And that is precisely what he cannot do: no one can shine with verve, wit, and superior ideas alone; one must have a social status that puts one's interlocutors at ease, that confers the right to dazzle. A chief surgeon, a popular barrister, or the fellow who completes his medical education without any trouble are the people who shine; their least word draws profundity from their objective importance. The statements of a sickly youngster who has no future will be regarded a priori as pointless paradoxes.

Quite often, recluses adore the "world"; their sociability is not at issue. They shut themselves up because they cannot keep up the role they have assigned themselves and because they are originally bound by the opinion of others. Gustave's is such a case:[30] he is actually

---

see them merely as a regulated sequence that brings him closer to Ernest. Immediately, the psychic headaches disappear.

29. To Ernest, *Correspondance* 1:89.

30. However, we must not exaggerate his desire for solitude: he sometimes goes to the dance hall—for example on 2 January 1841, three days after the letter I have just cited. But he feels ill at ease there: "How sad are worldly joys, and they are even more stupid than sad . . . a bunch of people emptier than the sound of a boot on the pavement surrounded me, and I was forced to be their equal, with the same words in my mouth, the same outfit; they surrounded me with foolish questions, to which I made

afraid that his peers regard him a priori as an inferior, take his stoic "abstention" as proof of his incapacities. The Other has already triumphed in him: after the failure of the Artist, he is tempted to believe that his father is right to see in him a mediocre nature destined to become a "stopgap" in society.

3. The result of seclusion is clear, however: it incorporates him even more into the family setting. From the autumn of 1839, as a day student dismissed from school, then ill, what does he do, indeed, but make himself each day a bit more dependent on the paterfamilias? Not only because he condemns himself to remain in what he curiously calls in the *Mémoires* "my father's house," but also because he palms off all responsibilities on the chief surgeon, and primarily the responsibility for sustaining him. Had he left for Paris in the autumn of 1840, he would still have lived for several more years on paternal subsidies: at least he would have given proof that he was accepting them *provisionally* as the only means that would one day allow him to become self-sufficient. If his passive resistance becomes ingrained, he must croak or live on the money of others. Can this prolonged minority be described as the simple *consequence* of his directed apathy? No; as with all our behavior, understanding must be *circular*. If he rejects the idea of earning his living, he must of course take money from the father. But conversely and more profoundly, he continually delays the moment of taking up a profession *in order to put the father in the position of having to support him.* Against Achille, the usurper who will soon have clients, income, "the most attractive medical position in Normandy," he has only one means of defense: to remain at any price the little vassal who benefits from his Lord's gift. From the time he earns his own living, Achille leaves the family, or rather he alone becomes the Flaubert family *on the outside;* his marriage, on the first of June 1839, serves only to accentuate this "distancing." Gustave, on the other hand, thanks to his illness, remains in the family warmth, supported, cared for, nurtured by his parents: in a certain way, he assumes the advantage over his older brother. Achille's superiorities, seen from a distance, are abstract; moreover they no longer have much meaning: Achille is merely a "reasonable man," a "bourgeois"; if he is still the object of paternal preference, this infuriating senti-

---

analogous answers. They wanted to make me dance! The poor children! The nice young people! How I wish I could enjoy myself as they do." Spite, scorn, the compensatory leap of negative pride, shame and arrogance at being a "young man unlike the others"—it is all there.

ment is less and less in evidence; certainly there is the "medical position"—which the father will deliberately bequeath him—but that is in
the future. In that future which Gustave is determined to deny. In the
present, on the other hand, the overprotection he solicits and is accorded, the anxiety of his parents, manifested by severities but also as
a constant valorization—all this rediscovered family life, in a word,
offers him a hundred concrete privileges, experienced superiorities,
revenge on Achille. From this point of view, it is as if this ill-born
child, unable to be reborn through art, were attempting to live the
coddled childhood he never had and so cruelly missed. And because
in Flaubert's view money must not be earned, because it must be the
object of a gift or transmitted through inheritance, the younger son of
the chief surgeon, by affirming his incapacity to work, makes himself
heir and property owner in anticipation (pending the "four thousand
pounds a year" we know he dreams of). In short, family life is found
to be the best means of doing nothing and—insofar as it provides
affective compensation—an end sought for itself.

By this means he realizes the bourgeois-being he wants to flee.
Even beyond his chief concern, see how he imagines the daily life he
will have to lead in Paris. In 1838, when Ernest and Alfred have just
left, he looks forward—sure that long years at the *collège* still separate
him from his friends—to sharing their Parisian existence one day:
this is sheer imagination. But when the end of his secondary studies
approaches, the tone changes: "Go to Paris, *all alone*, lost among
ruffians and ladies of pleasure?" [31] What is he afraid of? In the first
place, poverty: the students live on allowance from their families,
he knows that. But he thinks he knows, too, that they are supported
parsimoniously. Whores are the only women he will be able to afford.
We are far from his old dreams and from the "philosophical love" he
claimed to have for whores when there was no question of having
anything to do with them. [32] He is now a few months away from his
baccalaureat. And why ruffians? In 1839, such people were unlikely to
keep company with a well-off student. But Gustave makes everything

31. Written 19 November 1839; he will leave the *collège* at the end of the academic year.
32. To Ernest, 18 March 1839, *Correspondance* 1:43. "As to your horror of *those
ladies* . . . I am entrusting Alfred with the task of changing it logically into a philosophical love . . . Yes, and a hundred times yes, I prefer a whore to a grisette . . . I much
prefer the ignoble for its own sake . . . With all my heart I would love a beautiful, ardent woman who was a whore in her soul." Let us observe that he is sincere, and that
he will later preserve his preferences, with the proviso that the whores he loves must be
expensive.

543

look as black as possible: sluts and scoundrels, he will see no one else. We understand this to be an economic issue: he will frequent the same public places as the petite bourgeoisie. Indeed, he adds: "And you will offer me, no doubt, for amusement a cup of coffee at the Golden Colonnades, or some dirty whore from the Chaumière. Thanks a lot! Vice bores me quite as much as virtue." Vice? Going into a hotel with a prostitute, hastily and miserably satisfying a need—is this succumbing to vice? It is the need that horrifies him; on the other hand, he would not despise seeking a costly satisfaction for a really luxurious vice. And is it so depraved to drink coffee at the Golden Colonnades? Isn't it the modest price that repels Flaubert, the long evening spent over empty cups without refills, while at Tortoni's privileged youth pour out torrents of Tokay? Besides, independence is solitude. He has the choice between two kinds of destitution: alone, yawning in his room, or alone in the midst of the crowd. He fears the crowd to the marrow of his bones: it passes judgment, it lynches, it was the crowd that compelled Marguerite to throw herself into the Seine; the thousand eyes of this hydra will scrutinize the poor young man and discover his anomaly—then he will be lost. As for the room, he will rent it in a furnished apartment house—and his repugnance is revealing. In the summer of 1842, at the end of *Novembre*, he explains: "He went to stay in a furnished room, where the furnishings had been bought for others, used by others than himself; he felt as if he were living among ruins." Bought for others, used, dirtied by others, the furniture—wretched in any case—does not designate him as an owner but as another among others, a transient; he feels digested, he lives in the belly of a stranger. This promiscuity disgusts him to the point that he manages in November 1842, with Hamard's help, to find an empty lodging and to buy furnishings. But this time it is the impersonality of his room that horrifies him. The bed, the table are of course not the property of others but neither are they his; this is impersonality itself, and therefore it depersonalizes him: time is needed for possession. He writes, characteristically, to Caroline: "I like my old room at Rouen better, where I spent such sweet and peaceful hours . . . To be comfortable somewhere, you have to live there for a long time. You cannot make your nest in a day and feel good in it." In the family, the act of appropriation involves a transfer: the furnishings of the Hôtel-Dieu are Gustave's because primarily they belong to Achille-Cléophas, who gives them to him every day, or at least allows him to use them. The furniture therefore designates him the Flaubert son; mute and benevolent presences surround him that symbolize the paternal gift, the continued reproduction of his life by his lord. The pleasure has a double meaning: he need merely open the armoire to constitute himself as vassal by his gesture and to regroup around himself the *reified* family in a practical synthesis. A family in wood surrounds him, twenty inert arms designate him, every object by its transitive virtues qualifies him in his *Flaubert-being*. In 1840, especially in a semipatriarchal family, *real* property preserves feudal qualities. The relation is no longer one of man to man, but goods are human things. What alarms Gustave when he is in new digs is precisely the *real* or bourgeois relation of man to the animate thing. It confers on him, of course, a kind of independence: behind the merchandise there is nothing but human work—which he mocks—and the price that he had paid. But it is this very independence that alarms him: he is designated in the universal as the ordinary subject of basic activities, sitting, getting dressed, lying down. An individualist would be pleased by this, perhaps; no prejudices, no mortgages on his person. But Gustave feels too light, lost; he is afraid of going up in smoke. In short, while he dreams of the "key to the fields," he shuts himself up in his room, which stabilizes him with the whole familial weight. This young servant knows that he must *depend* on a master. The inner life is not acquired by freedom but by the experienced, surmounted, endlessly reborn repugnance of a slave adoring and detesting the hand that chains him, whips him, and feeds him. Look at the anguish that grips him when a journey is suggested: "I am in the greatest distress over whether I should make this journey to the Pyrenees. Reason and my interest commit me to it, but not my instinct." *Reason and interest:* he must get well; and besides, travel is educational for young people. Sad reasons for an adolescent infatuated with freedom. Instinct, on the other hand—which ought to push him to profit from the opportunity with enthusiasm—what exactly does it tell him? There is the risk that Doctor Cloquet may not be a good companion. Does one hesitate for such flimsy reasons at the age of eighteen? His worry is merely a pretext: instinct, here, is fear; his passive nature dreads leaving Rouen, is already terrorized by the semblance of activity expected of it; and then, if Doctor Cloquet, "of excellent character and disposition," is not up to it, Gustave will find himself once again, alone and inept, faced with nature and monuments; he will be without the mediation of his parents to make them his own. And of course at Genoa and Milan, in 1845, when such mediation will be offered to him, he will take exception to it: it is both necessary and insufficient.

But if the truth of his sequestration is nothing but a prolongation of the family tutelage, against which his imprecations—at this very period—recall Gide's famous cry, "Families, I hate you," and if he reproaches Achille for being a "polyp stuck among the rocks," is he not disposed to lead an even more sedentary life? In the autumn of 1840, he returns from his travels. At Marseille, in Corsica, he seemed to be cured. But the return is immediately followed by a serious relapse: "When I go back in imagination to my dear journey and then find myself here, I really wonder if I am the same man—is it the same man who walked along the beach at the gulf of Sagone and who is writing here at this table during a mild, drizzly winter night, full of damp mists?"[33] He will long after recall his disappointment of the autumn of 1840, for he writes to Ernest on 21 October '42:[34] "You are quite right to anticipate the tedium of the return . . . I myself experienced that love of the sun during the long twilights of winter. I hope they will be slighter for you than for me; Western spleen is no fun." Indeed, the academic year 1840–41 will be worse than those preceding. Five years later, he remembers it with horror: "I have not felt upon return [from traveling in Italy] the sadness I had five years ago. You recall the state I was in for a whole winter . . . I truly had a bitter youth, which I would not like to relive."[35]

Yet at the basis of this horror there is the lucid consciousness of his contradiction. At the end of January 1841 he observes: "I love the celibacy of priests—although I am no worse than another, family seems to me something rather narrow and miserable—the poetry of the fireside corner belongs to shopkeepers; frankly, despite the poets who make such fools of us, there is nothing much in it."[36] But on 8 February he reproaches himself for his contempt: the reason he does nothing, the reason he suffers from an "intermittent moral malady," is that he is not sufficiently part of his milieu: "I would need to be more deeply attached than I am to everything that surrounds me, to the family, to the study of the world, everything that I swerve away from and do not know why, that I would like to force myself not to love (the world is superfluous in this sentence). I take them and leave them in my heart only." The study of the world: frequenting of people, the surgical eye, psychology. One year later he will say:[37] "We must simply get used to seeing the people around us as books. The sensible man

33. *Souvenirs*, 2 January 1841, p. 78.
34. *Correspondance* 1:117. Ernest was traveling in the south of France.
35. To Alfred, June–July 1845, *Correspondance* 1:185.
36. *Souvenirs*, pp. 94–95.
37. To Ernest, 23 February 1842.

studies them, compares them, and makes a synthesis of it all for his own use. For the true artist, the world is merely an instrument." In short, to know people, the artist must be resolved to visit them. In other words, he denounces his seclusion, which deprives him of the experience necessary to artists, and then, decisively, comes back to it: "the world is superfluous in this sentence." The family remains. He indicates the ambivalence of his feelings for the family, but he does not put the negative and the positive on the same plane. He swerves away from his relatives *without knowing why:* the source of this behavior escapes him, but he judges it to be *forced* and not very effective either: "I *would like* to force myself . . ." He *would like* to, so he can't? And finally, this attempt runs counter to his *need.* When is he right, then? When he condemns the family or when he avows that he must— the word must be taken at full strength, it is spoken by a lost adolescent—*attach himself* to it? As far as he is concerned, both comments are true: the real and intentionally realized dependence is constantly opposed by a dreamed independence or, better, a dreamed-of wish to be independent; these attitudes exist on different levels, but they are reciprocally conditioned and are like two complementary faces of the horrible labor he has undertaken. To the extent that he cunningly manipulates himself in order to stick "like a polyp" to the familial rocks, he must mask *from himself* his underlying intention by an imaginary de-situation. He admits this quite lucidly to Louise one day in a spell of sincerity: he is merely a plant; the more deeply it takes root, the more violent are the winds that toss its petals—read: his desires to be *elsewhere.* Taking root is a slow undertaking, passive but obstinate, the orientation of vegetative life: the thickness of lived experience conceals an inflexible intention; this intention *must* remain obscure, or it could no longer subsist—do we see Gustave admitting to himself that his physical troubles themselves serve a concerted effort to be supported by his father? He would then have to explain his behavior: first of all, if the headaches or the "intermittent moral malady" are not *suffered;* if they *are not constituted as such,* they will have no basis for existence and will be instantly transformed into playacting: Gustave will play a role and *will feel* nothing—like those soldiers who pretend to be mad during a war in order *to be removed from the front.*[38] This is just what is impossible for him: such an attitude would imply an ag-

38. Curiously, many of these simulators are in fact neurotics. Here we have the inverse: they tell the truth about themselves by believing they are lying; Gustave finds himself lying while certain he is telling the truth.

gressiveness incompatible with passive submission, the characteristic common to all his inner impulses. But above all, the aim of "taking root" cannot be admitted without his going to pieces; can he propose for himself the conscious purpose of justifying his father's contempt? He wished to be nothing. Can he recognize unambiguously that the reality of his annihilation is simply to *diminish* it, and that *something* of him will remain, in any case—a mediocrity who has not left the realm of average men but who accedes to becoming a marginal end, an ex-future means that the family supported in order to give him the effectiveness demanded of all the members of the middle class, and continues to support, not as a luxury (unlike Alfred's parents) but as a duty and as a rebuke? Can he, in full consciousness, want his anomaly to be a pure and simple case of inferiority? More directly, can he propose for himself the unique objective of sequestration in the gloomy Hôtel-Dieu, which repels him? In a sense, of course, he is bitterly attached to the place to the very extent that the right of primogeniture has made Achille its lord: he "clings" to it because he knows that sooner or later he will be booted out. But this attitude is itself *inarticulable;* what he would like is to walk in with his head high, as successor to the chief surgeon. How could he bear the truth, the certainty that he is booted out *already,* that he ought to be in Paris *already* studying law, and that since the autumn of 1840 he owes it strictly to his physical misfortunes that he is *tolerated?* How could he admit to *wanting* those precarious hours, gained one by one against the will of a progenitor who is growing impatient? Each hour, stolen or grudgingly conceded, contains in itself a repetition of the primal scene, namely his frustration; each signifies for him that he should be elsewhere, and that he is dragging out his stay, like an indiscreet guest.

In order to take root, Gustave must, in other words, act—or rather let himself act—unwittingly; the firmness of his intention comes from its obscurity: a fish of the depths, it would burst if exposed to open air, to the light of day. But the dreams of the imaginary adolescent function not only to distract him from his intention: they preserve its cohesion by giving an unreal solution to the very real disgust and the contradictions it arouses. Gustave will be able to keep on burying himself inflexibly in the horror of his illness, of the family mediocrity, of the sad hospital where other patients reflect his own painful condition, if, when the repugnance is too extreme, he throws himself into condemning family life, extolling the celibacy of priests, dreaming of fabulous travels. These agitations are precious to him because they

FROM POET TO ARTIST

are at once highly motivated and perfectly futile. He is anxious and bitter, and "avenges himself through monologue"; but the very monologue is a derivative, an outlet; let him cry, let him curse, let him rave—the roots take hold. The fact is that this subterranean effort disgusts him, that he scarcely loves his father any more, rancor having killed love, that he is dying of boredom in his room, and that the *aurea mediocritas* of the Flauberts often makes him sick. If he were a real child, he would doubtless abandon his sickening effort: he would have to look his repugnance in the face. As imaginary child, when he feels reluctant he leaps into the unreal, to Italy, to the Orient: it is on this level that he detests his dependence. Let us return to his "dear journey." It gave him undeniable pleasure. But what anguish at the outset; he is not impelled by the great Romantic desire to be *elsewhere* but rather by "reason" and calculation: it is in his *interest* to leave Rouen and the pathogenic family setting in order to cure his illness. In short, if he departs, it will be out of utilitarianism. On the other side is *instinct*, which uses Cloquet's defects as a pretext for a violent refusal of this "detachment." He departs in anguish (as he will do later when Maxime will tear him from his mother's arms to lead him, half-dead, to the Orient.) Here is the return: "Was this the same man who went along the beach at the gulf of Sagone . . . Oh Italy, Spain, Turkey. Today is Saturday . . . It was also a Saturday, a certain day . . . in a room like mine, low-ceilinged and paved with red paving stones, at the same time, for I just heard it strike half past two. They say that time flees like a shadow. It is more like a phantom slipping from our hands, or a specter weighing heavily on one's chest." The past challenges the present: the present flees like a shadow, and lived experience becomes memory "weighing heavily on one's chest." The regret, no doubt, is sincere, but the underlying intention is to destroy the future by letting himself be dragged backward, his gaze directed toward the past, toward a painful and fixed absence. What is important to us here is not this attitude, so familiar in Gustave, but rather the fact that the shift from one memory (the gulf of Sagone, the man he was then) to another (Eulalie's room) is effected by the mediation of the purely imaginary. He cries out, indeed, all at once: "Oh Italy, Spain, Turkey!" Starting with places he has visited, he dreams of those he has never seen.

Why hasn't memory led directly to memory? Because the journey, partially imaginary while it took place—every Mediterranean landscape being grasped as symbolic of other more romantic landscapes, Sierra Madre, Abruzza, Atlas, etc.—is entirely unrealized, through

549

deliberate idealization, now that it is over. On many points, indeed, Gustave has not been satisfied. A note, dated after his return, tells us that he did not change his mind about Doctor Cloquet, "who, while a man of intelligence, utters many platitudes." At Sagone, the young man *felt free*, but unreally: how could he have truly been free when the head of the expedition was a mentor chosen by his father and represented the Flaubert family? Moreover, several lines indicate to us that he reconstructed his travels from the time of his return. Indeed, he writes that time "is a phantom slipping from our hands or a specter weighing heavily on one's chest." Doesn't this imply that his night of love with Eulalie took on its fullness only by slipping into the past? When he was living it, he could not *fix* its richness: he would have had to stop time, to tear himself from the "claws of the future." Slipped away, distant, it congeals, contracts, eliminates its poisons, its risks; but it has become a lacuna, absence in the heart of the present. We find here once more the move to the imaginary that we observed apropos of the "phantom of Trouville" or, if you will, the unrealization of memory. He has deleted everything that had jolted him from day to day. For this reason we can understand how his "dear journey" will change, beginning in 1845, into the "travels of a grocer": after the attack, his objective is attained; he has no more need of an alibi. In 1840, when he again takes up his work of becoming rooted, he needs one: there, at Sagone, with Eulalie, I was able to be free, "whole, complete"; what wouldn't I have done if I were not riveted here, to my family. Even as he is burying himself again in illness, he must persuade himself that at Marseille, in Corsica, under the southern sun, he left *another* man, the *real* Gustave. For what horrifies him is not only the mists of Rouen, the urgency of capitulation (his father judges him cured: he will register for his courses in the autumn, says Doctor Flaubert), the bourgeois connections of his family, but also the anguish of foreseeing—without being able to formulate it—that his psychosomatic difficulties will begin again, of sensing his underlying intention, of understanding that the solution to his family problem can be found only in the bosom of his family.

Indeed, headaches, nightmares, apathy mixed with feverish agitation, anguish, the resistance of his whole person to the time that runs on and drags him in its wake: everything resumes as in 1839—and the obsession with dying without being affirmed has chased away the suicidal impulses. The trip to Corsica, reconstructed, provides material rich enough for the dreams of escape. But for him whom care tears away from every present joy, what are these dreams but the mad, unreal desire to receive the grace of *pleasure?* Thus he secretly follows his way by dissimulating his efforts through a directed oneirism, through the unreal desire to be *another,* a man of the moment and of nowhere, a being "from elsewhere."

The refuge in illness can be only *provisional.* Not in itself—there are such illnesses that last a lifetime—but because it is expressly lived *as such.* His troubles, although intentionalized, are not assumed. They are disturbing, of course, but in this diffuse nervousness that is released in disconnected disturbances, Achille-Cléophas cannot see symptoms; Gustave himself could not yet envisage them as corporeal symbols: nothing gives them a *meaning,* and this indicates that Flaubert himself does not live them as a means of definitively escaping the necessity of taking on a profession. He limits himself to delaying the moment when he will leave his family and go to Paris to do his apprenticeship. In the face of this constant but superficial nervous irritation, the father's inflexible decision raises itself up like a barrier: Gustave will remain *one more year* in Rouen, to calm down, to rest, to retrieve a compromised equilibrium. After that, he will begin his specialized studies.

The school year 1841–42 shows clearly that the father was not easily deterred from his intentions: the troubles persisted in vain. Gustave merely obtained a compromise: he will spend many months at the house, will go to Paris only *at the last possible moment,* but he will register for courses, will work alone at Rouen (he proved, after his dismissal from the *collège,* that he was capable of doing this, which convinced Achille-Cléophas), and will commit himself more or less seriously to taking his first law exam during the summer of 1842. To put an end to paternal obstinacy, the young man would have had to give his troubles a *radical* meaning; he would have to think, not merely "I am ill," but "I am *an* invalid"; in short, on the psychosomatic level his passivity would have become a vow, a mortgage on the future. Is Gustave tempted to transform this operation of deferral into a definitive incapacity for work? Not yet. The Flaubert pride would balk: an invalid is a family taint equivalent to a failure. He is a subman; and of course submen have long fascinated him: since his adolescence he has *recognized himself in them,* but what he seeks in them is *animality.* He does not yet intend to lower himself to the level of idiots. We shall see this temptation emerge in 1842. For the moment, Gustave, submissive, does not imagine even in his deepest self that he might escape from the "profession" through disobedience. As we have seen, his most explicit self-affirmation—often repeated but of a purely unreal sort—situates the conquest of independence *after* the "law." He will be a mule driver, a camel driver, live on his income in Naples, but *first* he will do four years at the university, as his father requires. In short, he puts off his revolt—if it is one—till doomsday and does not for a moment imagine opposing his father *in the present*. Quite the contrary, his illness translates the impossibility of refusal. To the extent that an underlying intention structures lived experience, it is merely a matter of *gaining time*. And why gain time? What will he achieve apart from becoming an *over-age student?*

In a sense, indeed, these provisional troubles lead to nothing, and for that very reason the intention that animates them cannot be clear to him: otherwise Gustave would perceive that time is working against him. On the contrary, the intention is obscure; being absorbed in present reality, it masks the future and at the same time defers its appearance. Gustave seeks no solution; he wants a respite, nothing more, because he lacks the means to confront his destiny now and does not feel strong enough to submit *right away* to the father's will, to the requirements of milieu and class. If his nerves dominate him, irrascible or prostrate, Gustave *can* feel the succession of present disorders as an impenetrable thickness. It is the psychosomatic illness—and not champagne, whores, and orgies—that makes every moment a consolidated present. And then, who knows? If he gains time, genius may suddenly appear. Not writing, at this period, is also *waiting*.

Is this all? No. He will later declare to Louise [39] that he had "witnessed his father's burial" long before he died. "And," he will add, "when the event occurred, I was familiar with it. There may also be bourgeois who could have said that I seemed very little moved or that I was not moved at all." He presents the return of these funereal presentiments and the train of images that accompany them as a spiritual exercise: "I accustomed myself to drinking wine in the evenings . . . As for feeling, it happened to me the same way." In other words: he was not suffering at his father's death, but the bourgeois would have been wrong to reproach him for it: he trained himself by often invoking this imagery; in short, he suffered in detail, ahead of time and in his imagination, so that his mourning did not take him by surprise. These lines leave us wondering: must we really believe in a voluntary ascesis? But in this case, why does Gustave write, "It happened to me," which implies that he *suffered* the return of these un-

39. *Correspondance* 1:384, 21 October 1846.

pleasant evocations? Wasn't it rather an irrepressible desire, one of those "secret, base impulses that rise up in you and later subside, leaving you utterly astonished"? Twenty times, I suppose, Gustave surprised himself *imagining the scene*. But rancor does not suffice to explain the "base" desire that takes him by surprise. A stronger motive is heeded, and I see only one: for Gustave, Achille-Cléophas represents the perfect identity of the symbolic father and the real, concrete father. While he lives, his will cannot be opposed; the illness is merely a futile procrastination. But *if he should die?* In this case, *gaining time* would be a profitable operation. Yet the philosophical practitioner is in quite good health; chance alone can put a premature end to his days. Most probably he will live another twenty years and leave Gustave, in his forties, an attorney in Brittany or Yvetot. Thus his decease is merely a frequent fantasy that gives his son's troubles an imaginary efficacy. If Moses were no longer, Gustave would abandon the law before having begun. Such is the meaning of his desire "to live in Naples with an income of four thousand pounds." We can be sure that he took the trouble to estimate his inheritance. He must *hang on* until then.

At once he perceives the other consequences of this event: the triumph of the usurper;[40] booted out of the Hôtel-Dieu, he will have to bury himself in Naples, in Sicily, and live modestly. That is the desired annihilation, of course: but this "become-nothing" serves merely to realize prefabricated Destiny through an unjust paternal preference. The desire is rotten: the father's death has contradictory consequences; Gustave would accede to independence, but he would be expelled from the warm intimacy of the family; no more roots; he would be in direct contact with a hostile and cold world, without the indispensable mediation of the original group. This malign desire horrifies him; when it comes to his family, the angry younger son is a conformist: your father and mother . . . Moreover, Alfred and Achille-Cléophas are the only men he has loved: resentment can kill love, but a dead love does not change so quickly into indifference. If it does not veer toward hatred, which is not the case, it leaves in its wake some-

40. It will be noted that the scene frequently evoked by Gustave is not the deathbed of father Flaubert but his burial. He jumps over the biological fact in order to settle himself in the social fact. Here is the hearse, the family follows, in mourning. What are the idlers saying? What does the Rouen bourgeoisie have to say? And the colleagues of the chief surgeon? There they are, glancing sideways at Achille, thinking: "There's the successor." Death, properly speaking, which has a sickbed as its theater, is accompanied by the sorrow of the living. But burial—or the recuperation of the departed by Society—is a step toward that other socialization of death: inheritance.

thing uncomfortable and jarring that has no name, refuses the ex-
tremes, and is lived in a sickening unease. In short, the young man is
in dread of himself. Self-censoring: the ambiguous phantasm vanishes, the illness becomes once again what it was: the real consequence of a disillusionment transformed into a *provisional expedient*, a
battle against time lost in advance, a final and futile effort to cling to
the family and the irresponsibility of adolescence.

Let us not believe, however, that this "criminal" desire remains ineffective. First of all, while it exists, or while the memory of it remains, it has the double effect of transforming Gustave's pathological
behavior into imaginary and teleological behavior; in short, he must
forget it or become conscious that one unrealizes oneself in order to
await an unreal deliverance by an external event that is not in the least
foreseeable except in its abstract generality (one day the father will
die). From time to time, therefore, Gustave's attachment ceases to be
suffered and appears to him in the imaginary as a malicious enterprise.
He *does not believe in it* (rightly), since the interpretation presents itself
as fictive. It is actually the illness which, in his confusion, gives itself
a rigorous and invented end. Be that as it may, from time to time this
forged optative suffices to unrealize the whole in his own eyes; what
is truly suffered (and quite simply exploited) seems to him playacted.
Everything is directly buried in oblivion, except an uncertainty regarding the entire process. This uncertainty is not even the beginning
of a *piece of knowledge,* since it rests on the assignation (frequent but
often forgotten) of a fictive purpose that wrongly transforms the process into praxis. Moreover, the process *is also* passive action, and it is
directed toward inarticulable ends whose unreal objective can seem a
total rationalization and radicalization: psychosomatic troubles would
be a rational praxis only *if they were organized to delay Flaubert's departure until his father's death made it pointless.* From there to envisaging
them as very likely organized is merely a step. Which means that the
young man remains ambivalent in relation to his illness: he does not
cease either to suffer it or to perceive *for the wrong reasons* that it is
intentional. From the fact that it is sometimes explained—falsely—by
the expectation of a death, it *reeks of the devil,* and Gustave, uncertain,
considers himself both its victim and diabolical organizer. And everything is not unreal in his interpretation: it is certainly not the parricidal
wish that gives rise to the illness, but the illness that exploits the wish
in order to rationalize itself. On the one hand, this rationalization can
take place only in the moments when Gustave suspects that an obscure intention unifies and perpetuates his agitation; it is, if you will,

another way of masking his true end, which is "unsayable." And, on the other hand, the father's death, although an imaginary optative, is born of a *real anger*. It is known that all rage destructures an unlivable situation: it is a simplification of the problem by the suppression of certain givens. When the adolescent feels caught between untenable alternatives (professional mediocrity or the subhumanity experienced in the family), his anger, induced by a real resentment, aims at destroying both possibilities by a devastating explosion. Either he desires the annihilation of the universe: "Oh please God that lightening crush Rouen and all the idiots who inhabit it, myself included,"[41] Or else his rage, less rhetorical, limits itself to suppressing secretly the chief difficulty through an optative parricide. Thus the wish, in both cases, although perfectly unreal, has *real* motivations (the explosion tinged with rancor that aims at suppressing the actually experienced malaise), and as a result, it becomes "a fugitive lightning flash that reveals everything but in return . . . blinds you for a long time."[42] This text—already cited—will be better understood in this new perspective. The lightning flash—here the explosion of fury—reveals everything and is blinding because it is simultaneously false and true. Gustave's imprecations—because they unrealize real lived experience—reveal to him the *stress* which sometime later will have to be called neurosis and which, as we shall see, he will finally *understand;* but at the same time, these imprecations reveal nothing because they do not correspond to an actual murderous intention. He thought he saw, he saw nothing—and yet something must have been there. He turns back on himself, tries to observe himself, to reconstitute the procedure so brutally illuminated, but he merely finds his illness, a suffered event whose teleological meaning escapes him. Yet he no longer doubts that it is intentional. But it will be more than half a century before a new method permits the deciphering of the real through the products of unrealization.

By presenting itself as unreal, the parricidal imagery exposes the whole enterprise as lacking an "articulable" end. It is as though Gustave were saying two things: "I am awaiting my father's death" and "Unless some unforeseen accident delivers me from him, I am selling myself without sufficient purpose, for nothing." Hence, he spills over into a new unrealization: for his passive activity to take on

41. *Correspondance* 1:90, 31 December 1841. This is the first appearance of a theme that we shall soon meet again.
42. *Correspondance*, Supplement, pp. 49–50.

a meaning, for his underlying intention of making others reproduce his life to become a veritable right which he might peacefully enjoy in exchange for the acceptance of his dependence, he would need another status. Deeply rooted in him is the desire to *change sex*. At the source of this demand lie multiple motivations, the deepest of which are sexual. But if acquired passivity makes him dream of swooning in someone's caressing arms, it also encourages him, in the 1840s, to realize his irresponsibility as a family-supported adolescent not as a phase of life but as a permanent status. As a young man, he is nurtured provisionally so as to do his apprenticeship in a professional field; as a woman, he would be *forever* at the heart of domestic life, in the family, with no responsibilities other than the "house." He envies his sister Caroline, who does nothing during the day but wait for a husband and cultivate a few social graces: "You have a less vulgar life than mine, and one which smacks more of gentility," he will write to her from Paris in 1842. In the meantime, he enjoys sociable behavior, which transforms him into a young lady. He will tell her of the things he misses: "I much prefer the old room at Rouen, where I spent such sweet and peaceful hours . . . when you used to come at four o'clock to do history and English, and instead of history and English you chatted with me until dinner." Two young girls gossiping together: he has dropped his role of lord, of educator, to put himself within reach of the adolescent girl so that in these conversations she can reflect his own feminized image back to him (or, if you will, so that he might discover in her his imaginary feminity). The feminine condition, here, is quite simply the permanence of youth dreamed through passivity. It does not suppress the ambiguity of familial relationships: in the projects for novels that he sketched out much later, these preoccupations are rediscovered: that ill-married woman who despises her husband but stays with him out of cowardice and love of luxury, while "avenging herself through monologue," is himself; he has transposed the problem of his youth. Something slightly grating translates his presence: this hussy has too many scruples; a bourgeois wife can love jewels and have no love for the husband who gives them to her, but *at this period*, accustomed from childhood to the destiny of her sex, she thinks it perfectly *normal* to be kept. This acceptance of the female condition—conceived as nature and fatality—is lacking in Flaubert's creature: she feels cowardly, *as if* she could act otherwise. Yet that is clearly impossible for her, whereas it has *always* been possible for Gustave—in 1840, he *could have* laft for Paris, worked, earned his living, etc. This retrospective scenario in which he depicts himself without really knowing it shows us that his second fantasy, continually destroyed, continually resurrected, is no more qualified than the first to give meaning to the intentional troubles with which he is afflicted: as a girl, he would have the right to remain in the family, at least until marriage; as a boy, he is obliged to challenge that right at the very moment he dreams of possessing it—"I was cowardly in my youth . . ."

The death of the father and feminity are two unreal and continually evoked means of perpetuating and legitimating the precarious inactivity he owes to his illness. Gustave's terrors arise from the fact that the demise of Achille-Cléophas and the sex change are imaginary. The one is the object of an energetically censored wish, metamorphosed into anguish, and in any case seems improbable; the father is quite well. The other is merely a role, played "between flesh and blood," and cannot even be named. He is, then, woman and parricide in imagination, an imaginary traveler who challenges the family in the name of an independence he does not want, a real polyp clinging to his rock but feeling that a mere wave will detach him from it. The illness is worthless: he *feels* it, but the father has had enough. Registration is made, books are bought. Gustave is *forced to live*. What will he do?

The Conduct of Failure (January 1842 to December 1843)

To better understand Flaubert's conduct, let us compare him to Ernest Chevalier. At the *collège,* Ernest's advantage in age of sixteen months is transformed into two academic years. Ordinarily, Flaubert would have taken his first law exam two years after his friend. In fact, Ernest did his first year from November 1838 to August 1839. After four years without a hitch, he would receive his Doctor of Law degree in June '42, before Flaubert was settled in Paris. The two-year advantage has become four. His thesis is accepted in '43, when Gustave fails his second-year exam. The four years become five. In the spring of '45, finally, Ernest "enters his profession": he is named assistant to the prosecutor at Calvi; this is the beginning of a "brilliant" career that will end with his election to the Senate. In this period, Gustave is barely recovering from his crisis of January 1844; he finally passes the first-year exam by taking it twice. Still, Ernest *wanted* to succeed. But Alfred, nonchalant as he is, having left for Paris in 1838, returns in '41 with a bachelor of law degree obtained without great effort. The example of his two friends must have convinced Gustave—rightly—

that the study of law was easy. Indeed, during his "illness" he speaks of it with arrogance, not even conceiving of failure where the other two so easily succeeded. "I will go and do my law degree . . . I will stay three years in Paris, catch syphilis, and then?" "I will do my law degree, adding a fourth year to shine with the title of Doctor." In this period it seems obvious that he will do the work with the utmost ease—a marginal occupation, one might say. His two chief concerns are of another kind: how to live in Paris, alone and shabbily, *during* his studies; what to do *afterward*. He is not wrong: at the *collège*, without excelling he stayed clearly above the average; he can expect to become a fairly good law student; even if he endures one or two failures through mischance, four years should amply suffice to make him a Doctor. Yet what actually happens? Against every expectation, he hardly manages to pass a *single* exam between October '41 and January '44. He cannot consider this normal, nor can we; we must therefore seek the reasons for his failure. We shall try to reconstruct the history of these three years and then interpret them.

From Autumn 1841 to Autumn 1842—the Facts

At the beginning of the new academic year, Gustave registers for courses, buys the Civil Code and the *Institutes*. But he has not yet set to work by the end of November '41. Ernest has already returned to Paris, and Gustave mocks his zeal: "You are slogging away? That's rather humiliating—work is what diminishes man," and in the same letter, he adds: "How I wish I could exchange my law school registration cards for menus! How I wish I could light ten-cent cigars with a page from the Code! etc. I am not yet even working at the noble science in which you are nimbly scrambling up the ladder with such solid hams." In all likelihood, he has begun or resumed writing *Novembre*. It is difficult to provide exact dates: the episode of Maria is a transposition of his adventure with Eulalie Foucault. He could therefore have thought of recounting this brief love affair any time after the autumn of 1840. But during the winter of 1840–41, he complains of "knowing neither what to write nor what to think." And he adds: "I am a mute trying to talk." In March '41 he does "Greek and Latin," "nothing more, nothing less." In July, he "merely breathes, pants, sweats, and drools." On 21 September: "For the month since I've been in Trouville, I've done absolutely nothing but eat, drink, and sleep and smoke." However, *he has spoken* to Gourgaud-Dugazon of a "sentimental and amorous ragout." When? Certainly not in 1840, when he saw his old teacher, since he had not yet met Eulalie. It must have been at the beginning of the autumn, when he made a short journey to Paris to register at the law faculty. In any event, even if the conception dates from a much earlier period, the composition begins in November, as the title indicates. Perhaps there were several previous drafts, but in November '41 Gustave made the decision to undertake a new interior totalization—or, if you will, to begin once again the *roman intime* he had unsuccessfully attempted at the time of the *Mémoires*. It is as if he had lacked the audacity until then: the memory of his failures still sickened him; he dared not break his vow not to write. The course registrations, the Code, and the *Institutes* were like direct challenges: the threat defines itself, he is inexorably *awaited* by a career. Against that, he decides to give himself a chance to prove his literary vocation just one more time, and the law books remain closed. When he writes to Ernest on 22 January, he has not yet opened them. "That will come," he says, "around the month of April or May." And the same day he says to Gourgaud-Dugazon: "In the month of April I count on showing you something. It is that sentimental ragout . . ." We must therefore conclude that he is deeply into his literary work, that he counts on having finished his work in April, and that he has resolved not to begin the study of the law before that work is done.

A month later, however, on 23 February 1842, discouragement has set in again: "I do nothing, make nothing, read nothing, write nothing, am good for nothing." *Novembre* is abandoned: he worked on it no more than three months. Bruneau has rightly observed that the work bears the trace of successive bouts of disgust (like *Mémoires d'un fou*), and that it was frequently cast aside and taken up again. At what point did he stop? We know nothing about it, but his correspondence until the month of August—we shall return to this—is marked by the consciousness of his impotence and by despair. It is inconceivable that he would have worked on his project during this period except in brief spurts followed by torpor. I would be inclined, therefore, to believe that he wrote what might be called the two first parts (until the break with Maria) in a single burst, and that only the last part was composed in September 1842, after he failed his exam. Later I will support this conjecture with further evidence. The letter to Ernest of 22 January shows that Gustave clearly sees the horns of the dilemma on which he is caught: "[Either] I shall be denied and shall then deal with my blockhead examiners, or else I shall pass . . . the bourgeois will regard me as a strong man and destined to shed glory on the Rouen bar and to defend perforce the party stalwarts, the people who shake their rugs out their windows," etc. Failure or success: the first is merely ridicule and resolves nothing, he must begin again; the second leads to ignominy, to the "profession." There is no escape but the possession of genius: this is what he says, the same day, to Gourgaud-Dugazon:

> The matter of my morale is critical; you understood this when we last saw each other . . . I am therefore doing my law degree . . . I will apply myself to it for a time and count on taking my exam in July . . . But what surges up inside me every minute, what snatches the pen from my hands if I am taking notes, what steals the book I am reading,[43] is my old love, the same obsession: to write! . . . I have arrived at a decisive moment: I must retreat or go forward, it's all there for me. It is a matter of life and death. When I have come to a decision, nothing will stop me . . . I will make myself get the law degree, but I hardly think I will ever plead a case . . . I do not feel made for that materialistic and trivial life . . . Therefore, this is what I have resolved: I have in mind three novels, three tales of quite different genres and each demanding a very particular style of writing. This should be proof enough for myself of my talent, yes or no. I will put everything I can into it—style, passion, wit, and afterward we shall see . . .

Once more he throws himself into literature to give himself proof that he is the means designated by an absolute End; he writes against the bourgeois-being that threatens him, in order to raise himself to the aristocracy of geniuses. In short—an attitude which is most unfortunate and disillusioning—he does not regard his work as his product pure and simple: to the degree that it progresses, he seeks in it the sign of his election. Such an over solicited proof escapes him: *Novembre* remains mute; Gustave merely rediscovers himself and abandons it. We can easily imagine his state of mind. "I do nothing, I read nothing, write nothing, for six weeks it has been impossible for me to construct anything."[44] As a result, he is seized by anguish: What if he fails the exam? He opens his law books sooner than he had foreseen, in the middle of February: "I have begun the Civil Code, read the preliminary chapter, which I haven't understood, and the *Institutes*, in which I have read the first three articles, which I no longer remember; what a

43. The context indicates clearly that he is speaking not of the Code but of literary works (Greek and Latin).
44. *Correspondance* 1:96, 23 February 1842. So when he writes to Gourgaud-Dugazon, 22 January, he has *already* abandoned *Novembre*, or is continuing it apathetically and with distaste.

farce! In several days, perhaps, an urge will seize me again and I will set to work at three in the morning." The urge does not return. On 18 March he set to work again, but with repugnance: "I see nothing more stupid than the law, except the study of the law; I work at it with extreme distaste, and that robs me of all heart and mind for the rest. My exam is even beginning to worry me a little, a little but not more than a little, and I will take it even easier for that." He studies but neither understands nor retains anything: this begins to worry him— much more than he admits to Ernest. And here is the rub: in order to scorn the law, you have to have succeeded effortlessly, to have found yourself a Doctor by surprise; *only then* can you refuse to plead, be *nothing* or become the Artist; but in these difficult days when Gustave doubts his talent, success at the exams is already a concession; it threatens to lead him to that cursed moment when the will of the father will compel him to take up a profession. In April he spends two weeks in Paris without working. He returns to Rouen, finds his books again and his distaste: "I am in a state of prodigious boredom . . . I am at chapter XIV of Book II of the *Institutes,* and I still have all of the Civil Code, not one article of which I know. Holy God of shit . . . I am three-fourths done in. Happy the people who find this curious, inter-esting, instructive, who sees its connections with philosophy and history and other things! All I see in it is an excessive dose of bore-dom . . . Axiom on the study and profession of barrister: the study is boring and the profession ignoble." The denial is clear: in Flaubert's eyes, the law is of *no interest,* it relates in no way to the great problems of history and of life; it is meaningless nonsense and must be learned by rote. Denying it any meaning, Flaubert makes the study of the law even more tiresome, and it is not surprising that he should write a month later:[45] "The Law is killing me, stupefying me, aggravating me, it is impossible for me to work at it. When I have spent three hours on the Code, during which I have understood nothing, it is impossible for me to go on: I could commit suicide . . . the following day I have to start over what I did the day before, and this way you scarcely make any progress." Memory itself refuses to register. The result: "I believe I would do well to give up the idea of taking my exam in August: I know almost nothing—nothing, in fact. I still need at least two weeks for Roman law, and as for French law, I am at article 100; but I would be perfectly stumped if they asked me a single one of those hun-dred." He leaves for Paris, however, on Thursday, 30 June 1842, and

45. *Correspondance* 1:106, 23 June 1842.

settles into Ernest's apartment, Ernest now relaxing at Andelys after taking his exam. Gustave writes to his sister:[46] "I spend two and half hours every morning at the Law School, and I use the afternoon to study *the fine works* these gentlemen have wrought on what they preach in the morning." He gives evidence of a little more confidence: "I believe I will now be able to report at the end of August, with some luck; my situation is beginning to clear a little. But it is still terribly obscure." Let us not forget, however, that the letter addressed to Caroline is meant to be read by the family. Indeed, beginning on 21 July, he loses control:

> It may well be that I will see you again within a few days. Here's how: we have until the 28th to be admitted, and you can be admitted only on the presentation of a certificate of attendance delivered by the idiot whose courses you've supposedly followed. Monsieur Oudot, my professor of Civil Code, delivers them to you only if you have presented him with the sheaf of notes taken at his lectures . . . Until now I've knocked myself out trying to get some. But it is rather difficult, though I will offer him something. If he then perceives that they are not mine, or that I can't produce good ones, my exam is going to be pushed back to the month of November or December, which would annoy me awfully, for I would much rather finish right away. I went to observe some exams the other day, and I would have given very good answers to all the questions asked.

On 22 July he writes to Ernest: "The other night I dreamed of the law, and I was humiliated for the honor of dreams. I am sweating blood and tears, and if I cannot succeed in finding notes for Oudot's class, I'm screwed, I am put off until next year." He is still working, however. To Caroline, 26 July: "The study of law sours my character to an extreme; I am always grumbling, muttering, fretting, growling, I mutter even against myself and all alone." And to Ernest on the first of August: "The law puts me in a state of moral castration strange to imagine." On 5 August, the matter is not settled: "I would be quite comfortable if my exam were over with, good or bad, whichever, but if only I were rid of it." A curious wish: if he is "put off until November," indeed, it is true that he will not be free. But he will not be any freer if the exam "goes badly," that is, if he flunked. Moreover, as we have seen, he should have registered for admission to the exam on 28 July. And another passage of the same letter seems to indicate that

46. To Caroline, 9 July 1842, *Correspondance*, Supplement, 1:10.

his candidacy has been approved: "Next Saturday they will give me a definite day to take my exam. I will let you know immediately." According to these lines he is not waiting for them to tell him *if* but *when* he is permitted to report to his examiners. Whatever the case, Gustave returns to Trouville at the end of August 1842 without having passed the exam. Did he flunk, or, as Dumesnil would have it, did he decide not to take the exam because he was unable to procure the "course notes"? It is impossible to determine. But the two hypotheses translate the same malaise. Let us imagine the second: whether he had given up the idea of taking the exam, or whether his candidacy was not accepted—what was the hitch? That he discovered Oudot's requirements, of which he was previously ignorant. But this ignorance is suspect. How is it that Ernest and Alfred did not inform him? How is it that when Alfred was in Rouen and Gustave saw him quite often, he did not mention those attendance certificates? And even allowing—which is highly unlikely—that Le Poittevin's nonchalance made him perfectly indifferent to the risks his friend was running, can we imagine that Ernest, the grind, the "serious" student, would not have warned him? He saw Gustave in Paris at the beginning of April: if he had apprised him of this custom, the notes for Oudot's courses might have been less difficult to find. Gustave, in any case, could have warned his father and settled immediately in Paris to take the courses in civil law. Gustave certainly did not breathe a word of it to the paterfamilias. His letter of 21 July is addressed to Caroline, but it is understood that the father and mother will know about it: and Gustave *informs* his correspondents of the reasons for his possible postponement: "It may well be that I will see *you* [plural] again . . . *Here's how* . . . ," etc. He may have believed that one could easily—perhaps for a certain sum—procure someone else's notes. Maybe Alfred, whose attendance must have left something to be desired, reassured him. In any case, he would have let himself be persuaded quickly enough. He did not want, I imagine, to warn Achille-Cléophas for fear of being sent off to Paris on the spot. A good deal of lightness, therefore, a somewhat suspect insouciance, a lie of omission; and then, those famous notebooks, was it so difficult to procure them? He says he "knocked himself out" to find them. Is this true? We have read that odd sentence, "I would be quite happy if my exam were over with, good or bad," etc. And we have observed its internal contradiction. Isn't it written expressly to convince the parents that Gustave is really put out by this new misadventure? And isn't it *from the moment he fears seeing his candidacy postponed* that he goes about observing the exams of others and claims that he is suddenly reassured ("I would have given very good answers to all the questions asked")? This is what he tells the family. With Ernest, he is more sober: "I went yesterday to watch exams being given; that, I think, is what I had best be doing." Nothing more. Let us read: I am giving up reviewing the material (or I am devoting less time to it), and I am going to watch others take their exam because I am no longer sure of reporting for mine. In short, the story of the certificate of attendance—whatever the outcome—without having been *contrived*, was experienced complacently. I would not say that Gustave, convinced he would flunk, *saw* in it the possibility of a further solution; he simply let a door open, but we know him from way back, and we know what his "glidings" mean: he never chooses the current that carries him; but when it comes along, he doesn't see any of the other possible choices.[47]

By the end of July, his intentional heedlessness has put him at the mercy of a chance occurrence. If he found that notebook at the last moment, it was because he was looking for it (or someone was looking for it for him) after all, but I did not say he *did not want* to find it: the lived intention simply aimed to render the quest more difficult. In other words, if he had the authorization to report for the exam, it was merely by chance that favorable circumstances emerged in spite of himself, which *he could not fail to exploit*. Or, if you will, he was unable to avoid the moment of truth.

Whatever the case, he must begin again in November. From Trouville, on 6 September, he writes an awkward letter to Ernest. One feels that his failure has very much exasperated him. Not a single direct allusion to what happened in August. However, he has certainly not seen Chevalier since the exam, for he returned directly to Trouville and remained there without doing anything: "This is my life: I smoke, I lie in the sun, I dine, I smoke again, and I lie down again, just to eat again, smoke again, lunch again." He has not yet resumed work on *Novembre:* "It's been a long time since I have taken up a pen, and my hand is shaking. The joints in my fingers are stiff; you'd think I was

47. What seems dubious too, as we have seen, is the contradiction in dates. He should have registered on the 28th. On the 5th, he is waiting for the following Saturday for them to set the date of his exam. Ordinarily, we should expect more precise information. Let him write, for example, "I have finally found a notebook," "I have registered." Or, on the other hand, "The registration date is postponed to Saturday: on that day they will tell me if and when I report." Nothing. Perhaps we do not have all the letters. In any event, this is rather his style. He might very well, without lying, have sustained his parents' hope, knowing quite well that his fate is fixed. Of the "ifs" and "whens," he need only present the "when" without the "if."

an old man." He reads—but "little and rarely"—"some Ronsard, some Rabelais, some Horace." and then, at the end of the letter, the obsession with the law suddenly resurfaces: "Oh usufruct! Oh servitude! I am certainly screwing you now! But how you will soon be screwing me again."

Indeed, he returns to Paris around 10 November (thus, between 6 September and 10 November he resumed and completed his manuscript), and the complaints begin again almost immediately. However, he has spared some leisure time for himself: gets up at eight o'clock, goes to class, returns, lunches works until five o'clock, dines "at a wretched neighborhood eatery." By six o'clock he has returned to his room, "where I amuse myself until midnight or one in the morning." What does he do? He reads, no doubt, or he writes. But he soon grows nervous: the exam is approaching, he must really work. Luckily, a toothache comes along to torment him.[48] He writes: "while I am suffering, I am vexed by the time it makes me lose; the pain grips me while I am in the midst of study and compels me to stop work. With this, I make no progress, I go backward, I have everything to learn. I do not know how to begin. I want to send the Law School packing once and for all and never set foot there again. Sometimes I could die of the cold sweats." The same refrain as in December: "I will end by falling into a state of idiocy or craziness. This evening, for example, I feel in two states of mind simultaneously. I am so enraged, I am so impatient to finish with my exam I could cry. I think I would even be content if I were rejected, so heavily does the life I have led for six weeks weigh on me." The same theme as at the beginning of the summer: to finish with it, even through a failure. No doubt he will have to report for the exam again, but he will have gained time. Toward the middle of the month, he seems more sure of himself, but the exasperation remains: "I regard my affair as almost botched . . . for example, I am always irritable and ready to greet the first man that comes along with a punch on the jaw and a couple of sharp kicks for no reason at all." He passes his exam on 28 December and immediately leaves for Rouen, stays a month with his family, returns to Paris at the end of January, and again lets himself go, doing nothing: "Since the month of January I have been living rather peacefully,

48. *In any case* he exaggerates his sufferings and the risks he is running. To his father: "I ought to have three or four teeth pulled." To Caroline, sometime later: "Yesterday morning I went to the dentist. He put silver nitrate on a tooth." Gustave adds: "I shall go and see him again if the pain continues." But this single visit must have sufficed: the subject of teeth no longer appears in the following letters.

seeming to do Greek, pulling out a few lines of Latin here and there so as not to read French, saying that I am going to the Law School and not setting foot there."

These are the facts. What are we to conclude? That Gustave was not working? That is surely what his parents thought: his mother wondered if she should have his relatives intervene; at the end of July 1843, his father, sending him funds to settle his debts, rebukes him sharply and urges him to work, though without many illusions. But nothing is so simple: it is true that Gustave goes for many months without opening his books, that he lies a little in his letters to Caroline, that his letters to Ernest have quite another tone; but it is also true that he has never become "dissipated," that he lives—we shall return to this—chastely, that apart from brief "worldly" periods he goes out scarcely more than once a week and leads a relatively austere life; and it is true as well that when he stops musing, he spends hours at his writing table in front of the Code, the *Institutes*, or works of procedure. It is impossible to understand anything of this attitude if one sees it merely as idleness; by looking more closely at it, on the other hand, we shall discern a quasi-pathological aspect which, as the study of *Novembre* will show us, did not escape Gustave himself.

Attempt at Interpretation of the Facts.

No sooner has he stuck his nose in the Code than his anguish surfaces. He thought a good effort would carry him through, and suddenly he perceives that his mind refuses to function: a blocking of intelligence and memory. He understands nothing and retains nothing. Or, rather, he retains nothing because he understands nothing. His head grows foggy; his old habits have returned in full force and undisguised: no mystic elevations or Satanic panorama, the simple stupor occurs as it once did when he was confronted with the alphabet. In nearly every one of his letters, the same words recur: the study of the law is stupid, it makes one stupid, I "am growing stupid"; I am making no progress, I am regressing; I will end by falling into a state of idiocy. He thought he would work fifteen hours a day, and I admit he exaggerated his capacities; but what he worriedly discovers is that he can study no more than two or three hours at a time without the Code's falling from his hands. We shall share his surprise. It is permissible to dislike legal studies, to be insensitive to the odd combination of empiricism and the a priori found in legal arguments; it is true that at a certain level of exigency the law is not intelligible unless it is studied simultaneously as structure and history. But for the first two years a little flexibility—and Gustave is not lacking in this—and goodwill are enough to succeed. Of course, certain characters have been specially formed to take delight in the *Institutes;* but the Law School has long swarmed with semi-dunces, there because they could not find a place elsewhere, and who take their exams with a minimum of work and attendance. But Gustave is, precisely, not one of them: he hardly likes to *reason,* as we know, but this is not what is required of him; it is enough that he understand the texts superficially, that he know the meaning of certain words, and especially that he learn by heart a certain number of articles. At nineteen years old, the memory is excellent; Gustave's, in certain respects, seems exceptional. How can we imagine that he should so pitifully miscarry?

Shall we say that he does it on purpose? Surely not. Otherwise, would he be so afraid? If he did not force himself to read, to take notes, would he so loudly protest his disgust and his "stupefaction?" Would he *hate* his professors? He sounds like a convict speaking of his wardens: he dreams, in one of his letters, of having the omnipotence to inflict on them the ills they make *him* endure and to condemn Monsieur Oudot to *forced labor. Forced Labor:* that's what it is, that's what they are imposing on him. But however forced it may be, he must take responsibility for the labor himself; and what is he doing in Paris, relatively chaste and alone, if not working? On the face of it the quantity of work is sufficient, it's the quality that is inferior—and the yield practically nil. But he is distressed by it, he is continually distressed. He *must* take his exam. First of all, it is a dilatory means: if he imitated Ernest and "scrambled nimbly up the rungs of the noble Science," he would delay until the doctorate—at least until his law degree—the moment of his impossible and necessary revolt; to obey for three or four years and then turn back to his father and tell him: no!—that is his dream. But in order to communicate to his family "his decision to conclude his active life," it must have begun. What a strong position he would be in if he could say to them: there; I have brilliantly succeeded, as you had wished; now, on the threshold of a dazzling career, I declare that I refuse to enter it. And then, the "comparison" persists: in this inferior branch of knowledge to which Achille-Cléophas's caprice has relegated him, he must triumph effortlessly in order to punish the paterfamilias by demonstrating that the younger son is the elder's equal, or would have been had the unjust decision not deterred him from medicine. Finally, there are his comrades, his friends: he must equal them. He was making fun of Ernest

when he saw him "slogging away." Chevalier's success had then persuaded him that he would earn his degrees without ceasing to "idle
away his time." Now, he must keep his word or lose face. And from
the very beginning he encounters insurmountable difficulties. How
can we imagine that his exasperated pride should not suffer? Is he not
compelled to set himself to the task? He sets himself to it, indeed, and
certain passages from his letters imply that he feels the resistance of
the Code as a physical force that opposes itself to his efforts: "Like
swimmers in strong currents, I do one stroke in vain, the swiftness of
the current carries me back two." In a word, he has every reason to
"slog away." To the extent that the failures only prolong his torture,
he loses these months in vain, he must report for the exam all over
again.

Unfortunately for him, he also has—from the outset—every reason
to fail. To open the Code is to get caught up in the machine; one finds
oneself exercising the "ignoble" profession of barrister without knowing how one got there. Of course, at the end of his studies he must
stand up to his father and finally rebel against the other Will: but he
begins by obeying. When he declares and predicts his future revolt, he
is living in obedience; that is his sole future, it refers merely to itself,
and the "no" he will say four years hence itself exposes his derisory
inconsistency: it will have to be born out of nothing, for in the present
and in the near future nothing is paving the way for it. The worst
thing is that everyone congratulates him for having the means requi-
site for his future condition; he has large shoulders, his arm movements are ample; his voice is strong, it carries. Alfred's father repeats
complacently that "this morning" Gustave has what it takes to become
the darling of the bar. Gustave is inhabited by these images: for him,
Truth is always the discourse of the Other. Sometimes, he dreams
complacently: he is a good actor, might he not, with his "big mouth"—
oh, very rarely, in a few atrocious cases—convince the jury to acquit a
monster? Flaubert has known this temptation, as we have seen from
his letters; and in *L'Education sentimentale*, Frédéric, his insipid double,
will wish, with more banality, to become a great barrister. But these
dreams no sooner surface than Flaubert is horrified by them: this
would be to *consent*. When he wishes, master of eloquence, "to shine
in the salons," he knows that he is stooping from his highest ambition
and betraying it. Isn't this the best proof that he is no longer worthy of
it? Immediately, by a movement of a perfect logical rigor, he tramples
his vanity, compels himself to desire mediocrity: he will be a notary in
Brittany. And this would again be to consent: one comes to the pro-

fession of notary through the law. Threats, insidious temptations—
Gustave rejects everything: I will be *nothing*. But then, he would have
to quit it all, and right away. Impossible—that would be disobedience. So, he opens the Code, and it is the future that is opened, his
future, fixed and legible until death. This book *speaks to him of himself*:
through the barbaric words, he glimpses a destiny that is repugnant
to him.

He has known this destiny for quite a while; he has complained of
it in a thousand ways. And yet it seems new to him. What has
changed? In order to find out, we must return to the notion of passive
activity. We shall no longer consider it, this time, as it is constituted
but as Gustave has taken it in hand and assumed it by a new spiral of
his personalization. Let us recall that others, and language as other,
installed in him, direct the flow of lived experience, and that he feels
it. This does not mean that it is pure inertia or exteriority: internalization is as necessary in his case as in that of a practical agent. But it
works differently: his spontaneity unifies the succession of experiences by giving them the character of imposed realities. And of course
these passive syntheses are penetrated by intentions that come from
Gustave himself, though these intentions can modify the course of
lived experience only on the condition that they are not *acknowledged*,
that their real end and their meaning are veiled. They are enveloped
in the density of lived experience and appear to the consciousness to
be produced by it, although they produce themselves in relation to it;
far from clearly posing their objective—as in the case of practical intentions—they never make it explicit or else they present it as fatality.
And certainly, if one defines action by its results, Gustave's passivity
is action: he engages, as I have said above, in gliding; he uses the currents of interiority, and when he believes he is letting go, he governs
himself. But this type of activity is in another sense the opposite of
methodical praxis, which holds its ends at a distance, defines them,
and thereby determines a field of possibilities among which it must
choose the most economical means. There is a double decision, since
the objective is *assumed* and the tools are chosen that will further its
attainment. Passive activity attains its ends only for having hidden
them from itself, for having lived them in obscurity as the internal
structures of passivity; if by some misfortune these ends were to deviate from that passivity and establish themselves on their own—an
operation necessary to assume them ("What exactly do I want?")—the
passive agent would first have to *admit them to himself*. But they are
inadmissable to the extent that he is directing himself by claiming to

569

be carried away. Or, rather, he *is* carried away, but for that very reason he must adapt to exterior movement and make it his unique truth. To state his ends openly is to affirm his autonomy, whereas his patient labor only makes sense *through* the proclaimed and consciously lived heteronomy of his will. No sooner would his ends be stated, however, than they would have to be adopted as the meaning of an enterprise: such a decision is impossible for passive activity, which discovers that the Other has affected it with irresponsibility. Passivity would have to deny itself, which is inconceivable when it is *constituted*. For this reason, we cannot even imagine that it might define a field of possibles and throw itself into an enterprise characterized by a series of successive options. The passive agent, though bound, remains nonetheless free: he preserves the initiative for changing direction, but he can guide the processes of internalization and reexternalization only by staying in the shadows. If it happens, however, that his own ends reveal themselves to him, it is because they present themselves as *imaginary*. And they are, indeed, since he cannot *desire* them but only dream them. Let us recall Gustave's embarrassment when in *La Peste à Florence* he finds himself compelled to describe a *premeditated* crime: Garcia's vengeance must be an enterprise; he would have had to draw up plans. Computations, calculations of opportunities, invention, decision: everything would have had to be done in full consciousness, like setting up a budget. But Gustave hides from us this moment of truth and the *fiat* that follows it: manipulated passivities are anything but cynical; if they have to commit the crime, they must arrange it so that passion pushes them to it, which implies that they allow themselves to be led to it with a premeditated innocence. Gustave is made such that the *practical attitude* is alien to him. An attempt is being made to force him to manifest the sovereignty of man over things, but he should not first have been put in bonds; sovereignty escapes him, he has no experience of it, but, quite to the contrary, he does know constraint. His way of acting is to fool himself in order to influence the course of things through the will of the Other; he has just succeeded in doing this for two years by *afflicting himself* with a nervous illness which he can experience only by *suffering* it. What they ask of him is the opposite of these difficult maneuvers; he is incapable of determining himself in terms of a transcendent end—even when it is a matter of passing a law exam—simply because his ends are immanent and he has neither the habit of praxis nor the mental tools that would permit him to invent it.

Here we have the movement of recuperation and personalization: in 1842, Gustave was twenty years old; he knew himself. His distaste for action is not simply the lived expression of his incapacity to act: it is the object of a complicit reflection which assumes it, supports it, and justifies it by basing it on an ethic. He *condemns* action in the name of quietism. Moreover, this is not new with him: he has had normative intuition from the time he was fifteen years old—and perhaps well before. Now he systematizes. But if we reread *Quidquid volueris,* we shall see that he gave Djalioh the most exquisite and vibrant sensibility and yet denied him any possibility of acting, denying him in particular the entirely intellectual capacity for decomposing a whole and recomposing it—which expressed his humiliations as a "backward" child but can seem prophetic in relation to his twenty years. He identified unreservedly with his incarnation and, in a leap of wounded pride, assumed the values of Romanticism: what good is it to know how to read when you have passions? Certainly, passion is explosive, it leads the poor ape to a rape followed by a murder and a suicide. But these heinous crimes are not acts: Djalioh hasn't in the least pondered them. Undoubtedly they have come from him, and producing pain and death they have engraved on the external world their author's unbridled violence. That was the externalization of interiority. Yet, Djalioh cannot recognize himself in it, for the murder of Adèle leads him to suicide (it is not that he wants to punish himself by killing himself but rather that an equal fury, unassuaged by the murder, *reflects* and suppresses itself by suppressing him). We can hardly say that he is conscious of what he is doing. He is a virgin, and the rape is born of his instinct, not of knowledge; the murder is at once necessary and accidental, etc. This objectification does not define a *subject:* it is the externalization of a subjectivity that has constituted itself without the ego or against it. Man, for the young Flaubert, is a powderkeg: sometimes a little heat is enough to make him explode; the explosion expresses him entirely, adequately, but *only insofar as* the will does not come into play. For this same reason, the *pathetic,* unless it is an accumulation of sufferings and disgusts, often has no "efficacy": poor Djalioh's emotions dominate him, make him tremble from head to foot, but often disappear as quickly as they have come. They depend on the universe: he does not "hold" them enough to appropriate them for himself, to capitalize on them, and by viewing them in the light of the future to transmute them into the motivations of an elaborated act.

571

Did Gustave remember the monster fabricated by Science, his former incarnation, when he wrote—this time about himself—in January 1841: "Even in my calm state, my physical and moral temperament is an eclecticism led briskly along by fantasy and by the fantasy of things"? There is no better definition of *passion* as both the classical and Romantic writers describe it. Objective causes maintain a precarious equilibrium between the individual and the external world; so futile desire manifests and translates itself through reverie—this is the reign of fantasy; a change in the universe causes this equilibrium to break: hence the disordered movements of the individual (organic and psychic), who blindly attempts to restore the lost stability—and of course merely aggravates his case. But Gustave, unlike the classical writers, *valorizes* passion and, unlike the Romantics, holds as his fundamental value passivity rather than violence.

Three years later, in any case, in an important passage from the first *Education*, he clearly expresses his ethic of affectivity. Henry and Madame Emilie have often dreamed, between embraces, of escaping the constraints of their milieu, of living openly together, alone and free. At first this does not go beyond the realm of fantasy; words, however, gradually make their daydream more specific: they will leave for America. It is still a game; they begin preparations, but they are merely making gestures. It is the "fantasy of things" that carries them along: "everything easily accomplishes itself, without encumbrance, without obstacle—they say there is a god of rogues, what happens, then, when love lends him its assistance? . . . They were astonished themselves by how few obstacles they found, and they regarded this as a good omen."[49] In short, they do not know whether they are playing at traveling, or whether some memorable and future journey chose to realize itself through them. Love is propitious to those ambiguities. Comes the day of departure, everything is ready, their place is reserved in the coach under a false name. Nothing is easier than leaving. Nothing easier than staying, either: no one is informed of their intentions; if they were taken by the desire to renounce their escapade or to defer it, their life would continue as before, Emilie's husband would preserve his blind confidence, the two lovers would see each other each evening without much risk. This is the unstable moment of the equilibrium: on one side, a passionate dream of freedom, of an unshackled love on virgin ground,

49. We recognize here the suspect complicity of the world that we observed in *La Peste à Florence*.

572

on the other the force of habit, the fear of the new joined with the certainty that their liaison, even if they remain in Paris, will continue unencumbered. Therefore they must *decide*, they must *cold-bloodedly* give birth to irreversible events. All at once, circumstances endow the two lovers with a power they neither suspected nor asked for. What has happened? Nothing except that the "fantasy of things," which led them briskly along without letting them up for air, is suddenly blocked. When opposing forces thus find an equilibrium outside of us and in us, nothing will produce itself unless we give the signal that will tip the balance to one side or the other. Freedom of indifference? No, let us say that in these dead times the whole negative and the whole positive are given to us at once, our passions have not disappeared but they are awestruck, the possibility of an explosion is excluded. At this moment, the objective and subjective situation demands of us a *fiat* that can no longer derive its force from a divided emotion. For Flaubert, this decision-making capacity would be the will. But the will is just what he does not believe in: reading him, we might say rather that things inscribe the will on our subjectivity. Indeed, how can we have that capacity when chance alone governs our options? Chance: the course of the world internalized as passion. In ordinary times, I do not choose; slipping toward the future, I feel in terror or delight that I am chosen; I do not think, I am thought; meaning comes to me, as anyone would say, whims and obstinacies come to me as well. And suddenly it is *up to me* to forge ahead. Me? But what am I? A phantom, created for the sake of the cause and who makes his appearance for the sole purpose of charging himself with unbearable responsibilities: following my whim, I was against, then I was for; now, in the silence of passions, in this stability that is merely another face of chance, I must weigh the for and against, calculate, choose the end, select the means for the intended objective. Can anything but anguish be born, then, in my all too tranquil heart? And what does this anguish mean but that subjectivity, haunted by a phantom ego, feels at once the objective reality of the demand and its incapacity to fulfill it? One fine morning, Henry wakes up; it is the day of departure: "Increasingly as evening approached, he would have liked it to retreat indefinitely or to arrive right away, unexpectedly, so true is it that man seems made to be ruled by chance . . . Every event that depends on his will surprises and troubles him, like a task too great for him." It is clear that Henry wishes the world would decide in his place: if the sun did not set, he would remain on this side of the irreparable; if suddenly it were night, he would find

573

himself already in the diligence, the moment of decision would have already passed, his will would seem to him like an *alien will*, and the consequences of that *previous* choice (Emilie's flight already discovered, etc.) would force him to continue the enterprise. Indeed, anguish will grip him until the boat's departure, as long as there is the slightest chance of pulling back, as long as he *is making* the event and can *unmake* it. Then they lift anchor, and suddenly "in Henry's soul [there is] an impulse of immense hope, when *alone* on the boat that carries all his heart and all his love, *he feels on the way* to a new land." [50] I have italicized the verb: hope, joy, and even—some lines lower— pride return swiftly as soon as the "fantasy of things" takes over again and the young man rediscovers through the gentle rocking of the sea the impossibility of annulling his decision, the liberating effects of passivity, the obligation to live the consequences of a *fiat* already fixed as a destiny, the reaffirmed power of chance, the inflexible course of the world that carries him toward a new and already formed future.

"Man seems made to be ruled by chance." Again, an abusive generalization: we have already seen that for Flaubert the shift to the universal is defensive and is equivalent to a refusal to know oneself. If, however, he extended to the human race the characteristics that his reflexive experience here reveals to him, he would be knowingly telling a lie: the man of his life, his adorable Lord and executioner, whom he has constantly in mind, is obviously made of other stuff. If the chief surgeon sinned, he did so out of voluntarism, and Gustave knows it; having suffered from it, he is intimately acquainted with the paternal activism. Should we imagine he suspected his father of secretly resembling Henry? No. And the universalization takes a particular turn here; this is indicated by the use of the verb *to seem*, which at first sight appears displaced, as it suggests a hesitation that is very far from Flaubert's view. Here, as everywhere in his work, the example is conceived to introduce the "axiom" that begins with "Man is . . ." But he really does not want to show us an uncertainty he does not feel, and the part of the sentence "seems made to be" discloses his true intention: the generalization does not bear on facts but on values. "Seems" merely indicates the author's agnosticism: if there is

50. Let us note in passing this curious formula: Henry and Emilie are on the bridge, side by side. Hence one would expect "on the boat that carried them." But that isn't said; the "them" would again charge him with too much responsibility. He is *alone* on a boat that carries his love. Emilie becomes a precious object, and Henry gives the ship the burden of bringing her safely to port.

a God—which I'm uncertain of—he has made man *in order* to be ruled by chance. And if there is no God, if the Creation is merely a lie, we shall still identify ourselves all the more by our essence, we shall let ourselves be guided more constantly by the course of things. In other words, action is to be condemned because it deprives us of *authenticity*. Indeed, in Gustave's novels we find *active* men in considerable numbers. But these people—presented sometimes as the "monstrous products of civilization"—are seriously deficient because they live on the surface of themselves, never at one with the slow and somber flow of their lives. Nothing could be drier, in Flaubert's eyes, than the ego that affirms itself in the silence of passions: if it appears only at rare moments, when opposing impulses balance each other and disappear when that equilibrium is broken, the harm is not very great. But if that ego persists for an entire existence, it is because the passions do not exist in their owner or because he has denied them, perhaps stifled them. To calculate, arrange, decide—even if the final purpose is a subjective satisfaction—is to take one's distance from subjectivity and even, in a way, to eliminate it, at the very least to strip it of its own efficacy, to be no more than an abstract and cold mediator between the cost and the profit of an enterprise. Differently put, the ego of praxis is in his eyes the unity of calculated movements as a function of the *objective* situation, and of it alone.

Here at a glance we grasp a constellation whose terms—action, utilitarianism, bourgeoisie, profession, the reign of means, civilization—mutually condition each other without ever becoming integrated in an ideative synthesis. Practical life, he thinks, is gauged by nothing: it establishes itself autonomously on the negation of the inner life. For inner depth and richness *befall* us: this is lived experience itself as it is *suffered*. To *suffer*, to undergo, that is the fundamental value, the real human greatness: for Gustave, frustrated child, victim of the paternal curse, it is at once to receive the immediate as a gift—meaning: to live his own spontaneity as other—and to justify himself for what he is by *suffering* it as an imposed reality. He howls when he "feels he is going off" toward his destiny. But even in his terror at becoming a notary, we sense a kind of complacency: he feels the irresistible power of the sliding that leads him toward the profession of notary, but the very fact of "being led off" makes *Fatum* less unbearable. In this light, Flaubert's famous dolorism takes on a singular meaning: lived anguish is the futile denial conscious of its perfect futility; indeed, even though it knows itself to be ineffective, this felt, playacted, proclaimed denial encloses a secret acceptance. He

575

must cry no: that is doing what he must to hedge his bet; incapable of revolt and of armed negation, the young man bears witness before a hidden God: one of the functions of his masochism is to give himself the bitter pleasure of showing that he is not responsible for his ills. But at the moment he declines all responsibility; he is clinging to himself as other—as impotence—by this very denial. We can say that anguish, for him, is the ideal way of savoring his inertia. The destiny arranged for him, so atrocious in his eyes, conceals another destiny that is not at all displeasing to him: mocked, reviled, dismissed by everyone, led systematically to his doom by the force of things and the paternal will, he will be a *martyr*, such is his deepest vocation.[51] Great unsatisfied desire is merely a means: through it, lived experience takes on its true value, Gustave delights in his own nobility through and by means of his frustration, which designates him as one of the elect. Certainly he would have preferred to end in a Roman circus, between a lion's teeth, surrounded by angels, but this is not so bad, the calvary of a great mutilated, tormented soul whose cries bear witness that God *should* exist. He never says it to himself, yet the anguished and comfortable acceptance of powerlessness is the very taste of lived experience for him, the fundamental structure of his existence. He experiences his passivity not as the simple being-there of a thing but as the powerlessness of a prisoner being carried, bound hand and foot, toward the place of his final execution, and this miserable fate signifies much more for him than simple inertia, a material determination unrelated to human activity: he lives it as the destruction in him, by the other and by the world, of his practical capacities. He is a man fettered; just for that reason he is suffused with his innocence: he isn't even responsible for his quietism—since it is imposed on him—nor for the shame of being a paralytic, a mental cripple. Hence, his passive activity recognizes and condones itself by experiencing itself as nobly suffered injustice. It is not only the acceptance of a prefabricated future that conceals itself in his anguish, it is a humble acceptance of himself.

On other levels he is enraged to be what he is, cries that he hates himself, and indeed he hardly loves himself. But on the level of the unreflected, of the immediate, his constituted passivity *adapts* and justifies itself. Translated into words, Gustave's "unsayable" sentiment could be expressed as follows: "In this universe of active and responsible people, I have been stripped of all powers and all respon-

51. Cf. *Souvenirs*, pp. 60–61: "I would have liked to die a martyr."

sibilities, including those that others have toward themselves. My total and absolute freedom is to be in no wise guilty of what they made me. I *should not* because I *cannot*." This strange pleasuring of the self, which realizes itself through the terrible searing burns of pride, most people would not want; nor can they experience it. In order to seek and obtain it, you must be *already* passive and constitute yourself every moment, in the heteronomy of spontaneity, as a flow directed by passive syntheses. *Pathos* is both a *deed* and a *right:* thus, every mental structure can live itself only as an ethical option. Passive, Flaubert continually produces an ethic of passivity: he *makes himself* passive, there is no other way of *being* so, even if some primary situation had constituted us thus. He has not clearly explicated this system of values, yet we find it everywhere, in his letters and in his works: dolorism, man's vocation for martyrdom, the ethical predominance of the affective over the will, instinct over intelligence, the recognized superiority of the idea that imposes itself and torments us over the ideas that we invent, obscurity over transparency, the contemptuous refusal to *conclude,* to decide—this suffices to define a moral attitude. The words are still lacking, but what he extols, alone in his time, is the decentering of the subject, the refusal of conscious meditation, the giving over to spontaneity conceived and experienced as *other,* namely as unconscious. Thus, as long as Gustave, ill and sullen, finds himself pushed toward the law by the father's hand, he is merely a martyr: his unhappiness is at once total and bearable. He is responsible neither for the career that is imposed on him nor for this illness which, deferring the paternal decisions, gains him a miraculous respite. The young victim accommodates himself rather well to the situation, *provided he suffers because of it.*

In this framework and from this perspective, he *acts* without even being aware of it: he washes and shaves, he dresses, eats and drinks, studies at the *collège,* does his baccalaureat, chooses the intinerary of his strolls during his "dear journey," enters into a liaison with Eulalie Foucault. To give himself short-term objectives, he needs to feel that the long-term objective escapes him; the feeling of constraint is the necessary basis for his spontaneous choices. For this reason the style of his "acts" is quite particular to him: in themselves and in the way they develop, they contain a fundamental passivity. With what disgust he dresses and shaves: he cannot become conscious of his behavior without bursting into bitter laughter: the repetition proves his impotence; here he is every morning, trying to rid himself of a vegetation determined to grow again; what is he doing with his razor but mechanically obeying social constraints? Certainly he comes and goes, he chooses the destination of his strolls or his visits: but this is in the framework assigned to him by the *alien will*—the father's or Doctor Cloquet's, no matter. Of course, when he opts for the path to the left or the one to the right the choice is *insignificant* except in the immediate present; it will change neither the near future, the general course of the journey, which is defined by Cloquet's plans, nor the distant future, the law, which refers to paternal options. Moreover, he can enjoy the beauties of Corsica only if he begins by protesting, by condemning each day's plans, by persuading himself *that he is being forced* to "travel like a grocer." Thanks to this precaution, to this carefully sustained irritation, he will have for a morning, for an afternoon, while waiting for the coach to arrive, the feeling of going where he likes. But *does he desire?* Isn't he borne along by passion? In the final reckoning, isn't his route determined by chance? Every traveler experiences the "fantasy of things": nothing is known in advance, therefore choices are fortuitous or made blindly. Gustave is led by the beauty of the site; the course of the journey is conditioned by the contemplative passivity of the gaze; and besides, what he is seeking—and finds, as Bruneau has shown—is pantheistic ecstasy, the moment the landscape enters him and becomes a state of the soul, while he forgets himself and loses himself in the landscape. And what anguish, as we have seen, when he had to leave the sedentary life for the regulated nomadic existence of the tourist. He had no need, however, to *decide:* everything was orchestrated by his father. But simple change—to the limited degree that he was required to be, *relatively* speaking, its agent, climbing into coaches, entering inns, etc.—horrified him. Eulalie? But he did not seduce that experienced woman at all, his elder by seventeen years. He openly admits it to the Goncourts, who observe in their Journal: "He threw her one of those kisses into which one throws one's soul. The woman comes in the evening to his room and begins by . . ." The kiss is torn from him by emotion—he threw his soul into it. The decision comes from Madame Foucault: she comes that evening to join him, and shows herself to be highly active from the start. This is what Gustave himself testifies in an astonishing passage from *Novembre* in which he recounts their first night of love: "All at once she broke away from me and leaped onto the bed with the swiftness of a cat . . . she abruptly threw back the curtains and lay down, she stretched out her arms to me, *she took me.*" [52] Which is

52. My italics.

echoed, a little further on, in these revealing lines: "All at once I heard [Maria], who was saying this: 'If ever you forgot yourself, what if you became a mother,' and then I no longer remember what followed." We have read it correctly: Maria does not mean, "What if, in your emotion, you put me in a family way?"—which would be translated, in short, by the usual phrase: "Be careful"—but really means, "What if your amorous rapture led to metamorphosis, what if you became a woman and I, active as a man, were going to make you pregnant!" In other words, *everything happens to him*, and his minor decisions are conditioned by the fantasy of others and the emotion of the moment.

He has finished his studies, but if he worked at the *collège*—much less than he could have done and erratically, taking refuge a hundred times in stupor or in the imaginary—it was because a young student is carried along: the courses recur with the immutable necessity of the seasons, the programs are fixed, homework consists of obligations that reveal themselves one after the other; for this reason, many passable secondary students are bewildered when they approach higher education, where they fail to find that objective will imposed on them by a fixed and quasi-natural future. Lecture courses are rare, the professor soliloquizes and then leaves: the program exists, but one must invent the order of subjects; abruptly granted freedom transforms itself into anguish, the responsibility for options falls to the student. Moreover, while he had before him the masters who *decided in his stead*, and behind him the terrible paternal will, Gustave did not stop hating the semblance of activity that the *collège* demanded of him. And just before leaving his province, when he is consumed with vexation by rereading *Smarh*, he reveals to us the reason for his literary failure: to move from lived poetry to composition, one must tear oneself away from rumination, find a style, decide, act. The discovery that terrified him around 1840 is that the artist is, in his way, a man of action.

And one day in February 1842, he opens the Code. He is still obeying. But in this paradoxical moment, obedience is transformed into praxis; to attain the height of submission, passive activity and its train of minor acts must transform themselves into an enterprise; he must tear himself away from the effeminate intimacy of futile denial and live on the surface of the self, uncomplacently, in the arid desert of the objective world. However, the incapacity to act remains: the young man rediscovers his passive habits with a new clarity: they were merely his style of life, his way of existing his martyrdom; to the extent that he is induced to want to pass his exams brilliantly, his passive habits becomes obstacles to surmount. He must tear himself away from quietism or suffer it in shame as an infirmity. But even as he condemns these resistances of fact, his practical attempts are condemned by his ethic of passivity. Indeed, the highest values of praxis are decision and responsibility, which base themselves on other norms: a clear perception of ends, a methodical inventory of the means, a repression of the vain desire for the impossible, a firm determination to base options on given possibilities, etc. This set of requirements presents itself to Flaubert as a system of anti-values. For him, action is not only the supreme difficulty, it is Evil. This denial of pathos and of all abandon, this utilitarian dryness, this calculation of interests, this systematic rejection of all poetry, this silly pretense of governing the world when actually it is the world that governs us, this abrupt appearance of an abstract ego above the dark tides of lived experience, of an "I want" that dares to appease the tempests of instinct—is this really what characterizes the new Gustave he is in the process of becoming? In this case, it is radical decline. He could excuse the worst strayings when they were dictated by "fantasy, or that of things": he delighted in giving himself up to it and not being responsible for it. But at issue here is something quite different, for in order to make himself into "a grocer," he must *take on responsibilities* by deciding to decide. But in fact, does he *desire* or *is he desired?* Who, therefore, has decided that he will decide? This is beyond his understanding.

His submission to the paternal will was in conformity with the norms of his moral code. By pushing it to the extreme, he finds himself thrust into action. To continue to suffer, to undergo, he must act, but action pulls him out of passivity and forces him to combat it; in other words, he was fashioned by other hands, innocent of his essence; this innocence changes, unprompted, into guilt. Indeed, from the moment when Gustave, alone and entrusted to himself, opens the Code or the *Institutes,* the end he pursues reveals itself to him: he is learning in order *to be* a judge or *to judge, to be* a barrister or *to plead.* He cannot read one line and understand it, retain one article in his memory without deliberately bringing himself closer to his future "profession": he is laboriously *making himself* bourgeois, with premeditation, without the slightest attenuating circumstance. As a result, his ethic explodes into contradictions: how can this *active obedience* be judged, how can voluntary submission be evaluated? What is there to say when heteronomy, without losing its content, becomes metamorphosed into autonomy? And how is it conceivable that this autonomy, so abruptly manifested, should freely possess the laws of heteronomy? Indeed, what strikes Gustave is that the same destiny radically changes meaning according to whether it is imposed on him or whether he consciously fabricates it. The end that sketches itself on the horizon is still a decline, the "ignoble, trivial" profession that will imprison him forever in middle-class mediocrity. But when he was carried to the torture chamber, at least he could quietly enjoy his martyrdom: now, he makes himself the executor of the paternal sentence. Powerless, he used to cry out: see my sufferings, I am innocent of the Evil they are doing me. His bonds are broken, his guardians have scattered, he walks to the torture chamber unfettered. Martyr, no. But accomplice to his executioners. Therefore guilty. But of what? In his heart he knows but will not admit it to himself: his fault is to have pushed passivity too far; in order to escape his prearranged destiny, a negative act was needed, revolt; unable to risk it, he took on himself the decisions of the Other and found himself *assuming* alien responsibilities. In other words, the manipulated inertia was merely provisional; to make it permanent, Gustave first had to deny it. And if he did not deny it, that provisional state—which was merely adolescence—had to find its normal extension in an enterprise. In short, he discovers with horror that he has replaced martyrdom by a systematic attempt to become bourgeois. He feels it irremediably and silently in the activity of his gaze running across the printed pages, in that of his hand taking notes, even in the efforts of his understanding. The worst pains are those you inflict on yourself: you can endure the worst headaches but nothing is more intolerable, in purulent pleurisy, than tearing apart your bronchia with every breath; you must breathe, however—and this automatic behavior transforms itself into an enterprise: you want to avoid both extreme suffering and asphyxiation, and you are thereby led to inflict on *yourself* a little of each. So it is with Gustave: every minute of his day becomes a means deliberately chosen to deal himself the worst ills, to realize an enterprise that continues to repel him. Every minute an abstract ego must surmount this disgust, deny his veritable subjectivity. His life remains a directed process, but he is the one at the helm. Thus the alien will has become his will. But this will, born of nothingness, disquiets him doubly. *First of all, because it is will;* Gustave did not know he had one; now, he still wonders if it is not a fake. *Then because it is his:* indeed, although his decisions depend only on him, this will nonetheless pursues an *other* end, since it puts everything in operation to realize the paternal curse. Thus, the alien will is extended as his will to the precise degree that this will of his preserves in the midst of transparency an inexplicable alterity. A strange condition of this obscure and tormented soul: when the demands of the situation tear it away from its passivity, it takes the autonomy and translucidity of its practical consciousness for a dangerous decoy or an alien offshoot.

At the end of the autumn of 1841 he registers at the law faculty, buys books, and makes his first decision, which is to delay action until later. Until the month of April or, better yet, May. "Then I shall work fifteen hours." Read: fifteen hours a day; he will be the Gargantua of work. At this time he still envisages praxis as a gigantic and violent but short-lived effort. In order to accept the mere idea of it, he must compare it to the passions, and he imagines it to be, like them, brutal, explosive, ephemeral: it absorbs its man entirely, shakes him from head to foot, and passes away. Above all, nothing methodical or concerted: one can hardly speak of enterprise: praxis is a frenzy of unhappiness, an irrepressible itching in which Gustave will exhaust himself for two months and then collapse on his bed, a conqueror, and annihilate himself in sleep.

But shortly afterward anxiety erupts. Curiously, it comes from a literary failure—and an entirely provisional one. He is discontent with *Novembre* and casts it aside. He had begun it *against* the bourgeois fatalities that lie in wait for him, and as always, his vocation unproven, he is sent back in despair to the necessity of taking up a profession. But this time, doubt has made some inroads: as if, having recognized his incapacity to compose, *to act as artist*, he were also questioning his capacity to *study*, which until then he did not doubt. He opens the Code two months earlier than he has foreseen, not so much actually to begin work as to prove to himself that he can work. The book falls from his hands. He picks it up again a bit later: not worth the trouble—he understands nothing, retains nothing. Why? Because action, at the outset, reveals itself in its truth. It designates *him* as agent, designates *itself* as enterprise, and designates its end, which is none other than the liquidation of the accidental individual to the profit of the class individual. Impossible to lend himself to it. Impossible, however, to deny it. We know what follows: the act, for lack of being denied, transforms itself into a gesture. In other words, Gustave makes the necessary movements: he turns the pages, his glance runs down the lines one after the other, he will go so far as to take notes, that is, his pen will copy articles of the Code. In short, he *will play the role of student*, will sit a certain number of hours at his desk, and, looking at him, no one would suspect that the agent is merely an actor. But why this drama? In order to persuade others? Certainly not: Gustave gives himself over to it *faute de mieux;* it is like an echo of the Pascalian aphorism "Go down on your knees and you will believe." Make the gestures of action, and activity will give them a practical meaning: he waits for it to come. What is "it"? Well, the abstract ego that will take charge of his enterprise. He invokes this ego through a pantomime. It should be added that this pantomime itself costs him something. Indeed, what he likes is comic exaggeration (the Garçon) or surrender: in the first case he appeases his rancors; in the second he reproduces his own style of life by amplification through imaginary passions. Playing the role of practical agent is repugnant to Flaubert: he "is not in character"; he must make a great effort, it is a composition. In this sense, activity unrealizes itself as gestures, but the gestures—by the effort they cost him as much as by the purpose they propose (to invoke the practical ego and trap it) are like the dawn of an act. He hates his little drama and flushes with anger every time he must start it again—indeed, every day. He forces himself minute by minute to pursue it, fixes in advance the duration—three hours, for example— and cannot help looking at the clock a hundred times. In this sense, imaginary action is based on a real but passive activity: he must *endure*, force himself to remain seated, not raise his head, let the time flow, abandon himself to that broad, muddy stream that must carry him slowly toward this new stage—three hours gone. As *gestures* imitating praxis and products of passive activity, his behavior is not only an attempt to capture the practical ego, it is meant to convince Gustave that he is working and, in a sense, that he will have done his best, that he will therefore not be responsible for his failure. He is the mad actor who wants to interpret Hamlet so magisterially that he will breach the wall of the imaginary and really become Hamlet; but when the book is open, the proposed tasks reveal to him the vanity of his attempt, so he hangs on in order to persuade himself that work is none other than this blind presence at his desk.

The object designates him and dictates his task. His *primary* reproach against the texts he must learn is not, whatever he says, that they are "gibberish" but that they present themselves as *tools* waiting to be *utilized*, requiring a praxis of the understanding. An initial synthesis must make an approximate meaning emerge; a methodical decomposition on the basis of the totality—the entire book or the paragraph—must allow a specification of meaning, an exposure of its nerves and articulations; a recomposition must follow with the purpose of allowing the studied ensemble to *engender itself freely* as a whole that produces itself by producing its parts. And not only does Gustave feel repelled by doing this, he is authentically incapable of doing it. We have seen that he places himself—in his letters, which are the very expression of his thought—sometimes on the level of ready-made analysis (which amounts to affirming the general principle that everything can be analyzed), sometimes on the level of syncretism (a synthesis that remains dreamed and, as it has not been preceded by analysis or phenomenological description, is merely a nonstructured multiplicity of interpenetration). These operations, inscribed in objectivity, demand an effort he neither wants nor is able to make. He *reads*, but there are many levels of reading, and he places himself at the lowest, that of the proofreader who, in order to discover typographical errors more effectively, refuses to clarify the sentence in terms of the paragraph or the argument in process and limits himself to verifying the syntax and orthography. This verification, despite everything, presupposes a synthesis—that is, a certain intellection—but it remains quasipassive. The proofreader reduces exploration to a minimum, he *anticipates* almost nothing, just the end of the sentence as a function of its beginning; his unifying power is limited to letting words accumulate between them, that is, invoking the forces of unification that are contained in written language. In other words, statements structure themselves before his eyes—one would hardly dare say through his eyes. If he let himself try, if he were interested in the content, the morphemes would disappear to the advantage of meaning; he would no longer be able to see them or survey their elementary connections. Gustave studies the Code like a proofreader. He is only too inclined to isolate words, to consider them for themselves as external objects, admiring their beauty or being sickened by their ugliness. We are familiar with the reasons for this attitude. But this original relation to language does not prevent him, quite the contrary, from being a reader when he is in the presence of Montaigne, Rabelais, or Shakespeare. In those moments he knows how to exploit passive activity in depth and, even while letting the discourse recompose itself inside him in its sumptuous materiality, to penetrate it with an intention that surpasses it and refers us precisely to its meaning.[53] The reading of a literary work, for Flaubert, is never *aggressive*, it does not reduce itself to abstract meanings: these come to him through the activity of his passivity, not on the collapse of the verbal material but as the problematic beyond of that materiality. In short, through a ten-

53. We shall see what it is in a later chapter.

sion all his own, he knows how to maintain himself on two levels of reading at once, at the risk of snapping—which often happens to him—and falling into a sort of daze, which he experiences as an admiring stupor. But in this case we are speaking of moments of fatigue due to the constant effort to divine an *other* activity beyond the passive syntheses of the material reading. This material reading is the only kind he practices when it comes to the Code.[54] As soon as he opens it, unable to seek a poetic or artistic *sense*, which does not exist, he maintains himself on the lowest level, rejecting the aggressiveness which goes beyond the sentence toward its strict meaning. We have seen with what violence he protests when someone claims to give depth to the law by seeing it from a historical or philosophical perspective. No: the law is the law, namely the *letter*. He applies himself to discover the ugliness of its terms and signs: "One need not be condemned by the Criminal Court to create a similar literature and say the words *usucapion, agnate, cognate!*"[55] During the principal courses he will take the same attitude: a show of work, actual passivity: "I am indeed attending courses, but I no longer listen, it is a waste of time. I'm fed up with it, I'm sick of it. I admire the people patiently taking notes, who don't feel bubblings of rage and boredom rise to their heads."[56] In sum, positive motivations lead him to play a role, all the while hoping that he will catch himself at the game: the negative motivations have the effect of making these attempts perfectly futile.

Must we see the behavior that translates this contradiction as the "conduct of failure"? Not entirely. Certainly, deep down he refuses success, both because he cannot attain it without transforming himself into a practical agent and because, if he does, it will proceed with the metamorphosis, making him slip toward becoming bourgeois. We cannot say that the self-styled end of this passive resistance, engendered and combated, both together, by the conscious project of passing the law exams—if possible, brilliantly—is failure *as such*: to feel repelled by practical success is one thing, to turn oneself into a "human failure" is something else. An intention to miscarry exists, however: if we have not found it, it is because it postdates the two others and is aroused by them. Certain passages of his correspondence suggest that while he claims to combat his repugnances by

54. The *Institutes* are written in Latin, which does require additional effort. He translates. But this almost automatic activity (he knows the language) does not necessarily imply intellection.
55. To Ernest, 21 May 1842.
56. To Ernest, 1843.

ceremonies and gestures, he invests some complacency in surrendering himself to them: he attends courses but no longer listens; rage, entirely absorbs him. To read his *excessively* violent diatribe, one is struck by doubt: and what if he were attending *in order* not to listen? *In order* to absorb himself in a silent and vengeful fury? *In order* to renew and reinforce daily his defeatist conviction and prove to himself—by his growing horror—that he *cannot* pass his exam?

The letters he writes to Ernest in the course of these two years have, in a more general way, an unusual tone, which we must interpret. That he should complain to his sister, that he should want to demonstrate to his family his futile obedience and his father's implacable meanness, is only normal. But why is he determined to prophecy his failure when he is addressing himself to a former friend whom he now regards as a fool and who brilliantly passed the same exams four years earlier? This is not his way: has he lost his pride? Apparently not: two letters to Chevalier constitute exceptions to the rule: those of 6 September 1842 and of 2 September 1843—each written after a failed exam. They bear a curious resemblance to each other—again we find his bristling pride. In both letters, Gustave is silent about the misfortune so often predicted, or refers to it merely allusively; yet we are sure, at least in the first case, that he has not seen his friend for a long time. Therefore he is counting on others to announce his bad news: his pen refuses to do it; he strikes grand attitudes, displays his arrogance, or claims that Attila is coming at the head of four hundred thousand horsemen to torch France, starting with Rouen. This is the real Flaubert: humiliated, displaying wounded pride, unable to resolve himself to convey his reaction to what is happening to him, although he knows his friend knows about it, and masking his silence by noisy imprecations. Is he really the same fellow who frankly admits: I am not progressing, I am regressing, I retain nothing, I understand nothing? Yes, he is the same. And looking more closely, we contend that these admissions show no trace of humility. Quite the contrary: if Gustave does not take to the "noble Science," he is not at fault, it is the law. He will miscarry *through superiority*. At issue is the sly devalorization of Ernest's success: "I see nothing more stupid than the law." We understand: if the study of the law is stupid, to excel at it you need only be a fool. And as Chevalier counts on making a career in the standing magistrature, this line is leveled at him: "Human justice is . . . the most clownish thing in the world; one man judging another is a spectacle that would make me die laughing . . . if I were not now forced to study the series of absurdities by virtue of which he judges him." These words indicate rather well the line of defense Gustave has chosen: he understands nothing of the Code because, in fact, *there is nothing to understand:* man has neither the right nor the means to judge his neighbor—it being understood that judge and accused are both scoundrels, and that no one can fathom the depths of the human heart (which is why, in a note from *Souvenirs,* written in 1841, he condemns *criticism,* which pronounces sentence on works without concern for intentions).[57]

This is actually an a posteriori justification of his incapacity. However, as we shall see a little further on, it corresponds to sincere convictions. But what matters here is that it allows us to grasp Flaubert's *third intention.* The intelligibility of the law escapes him. Not that it is a discipline—as would be the case for "higher mathematics"—that is beyond his understanding, but simply that it requires of him a *total praxis* culminating in the career of barrister. For his pride's sake, then, the law must be unintelligible. And how should he prove it but by outdoing his incomprehension, by heaping scorn and anger on the law, which effectively allows his incomprehension to be characterized as the denial and condemnation of the Code, as negative activity? But is the law, in fact, so *stupid?* Let us acknowledge, with Flaubert, that one "man sitting in judgment of another" is idiotic or odious. But this is in a historical context: there is a class justice, which will disappear if classes disappear. The Code is neither foolish nor intelligent: it clearly translates the interests and ideology of the dominant class by a normative system that regulates human relations—*from the point of view of this class.* The Civil Code, in particular, attempts to define and protect the right of real property, which Flaubert, as we have seen, would not dream of challenging. The only possible challenge would therefore be *social* and would target the law as the superstructure of civil society. But Flaubert, bourgeois in spite of himself, cannot even conceive of such a critique: deep down, he accepts the judicial norms of his class. How can he present a challenge, then? By one means, soon adopted: to render the law stupid, he will render himself stupid in the face of the law. It is much easier for his passive resistance to prevent him from understanding a word of what he reads. Now it is a question of consolidating it and reading it as the normal reaction of a superior man to an absurd task. Let him open his books, let him attend a course, he puts his mind on hold, slyly producing the daze, the mental void, he

---

57. Later, instead of rejecting it whole cloth, he will accept it when it is *comprehensive* and when it evaluates the result only as a function of what the author meant to do.

becomes once more the inert martyr, borne by time toward his destiny. The operation is not cynical of course, since its self-appointed end is to prove to Flaubert himself that *it is the law that is stupefying.* If he has difficulty studying, it is because he is above this "series of absurdities." In short, it is a matter of objectifying his own stupidity, of projecting it onto the Code. A formula, caught in one of his letters, indicates rather well the meaning of this enterprise: "Nothing is more stupid than the study of the law." Here the judicial object is no longer the direct target;[58] it is the enterprise itself—methodical and objective—of studying it: whoever is doing it is plunging head first into the abyss of human foolishness; that *collective* reality submerges and penetrates him. It is not his own stupidity that Gustave experiences in the face of the *Institutes:* it is that of others. It is as if, indeed, his behavior were *words,* as if he were saying (to his father, to God, to himself): I obey, I am going to the limit of my powers, but I will not succeed, because in order to succeed in these foolish matters, you have to be a fool.

Is there a conduct of failure? Without any doubt. With two qualifications: the intention is intermittent and superficial; and it is not radical.

1. As we have seen, it is a reaction of pride to a deeper contradiction, which it claims to surpass and which conditions it; in this sense it is more explicit than the two preceding intentions and thus erupts on the surface. This explains its intermittence. In the course of the year, when he is yawning over his books or "living rather peacefully . . . saying that he is going to the Law School and not setting foot there," the intention of failure is not in doubt. When the examination is near, he struggles with himself, angered and anguished, to do what is necessary to pass: his great furies burst out in July–August '42 and July–August '43. It should be noted that he was distraught after his first failure, worked from 10 November to 28 December, and, continually grousing and groaning, ended by passing. Which proves that, at least in the beginning, the resistance—on both levels—was not so strong that he could not break it. This mediocre success, however, far from soothing his pride, serves as clarification. Everything begins again *as at the collège;* he was a poor student, he will be a bad student; better a great disaster than a wretched little success after repeated failures. Between January and March '43, he consciously sought the worst.

2. Can we say, however, that his intention to *fall short* had been

58. It will be in the second proposition, have no fear.

radical? No, since from April to August he is repossessed by the anguish and rage of "slogging away." The scenario of the preceding year is reproduced this year without the slightest change.[59] We should, therefore, be more precise about his intention and set out its limits. Let us say that he must miscarry from day to day, minute by minute, here and now, in the sickening enterprise of *studying* the law. This permanent wreckage must be that of the whole man: "The law is killing me!" The "moral" castration he speaks of to Ernest translates the sullen refusal he sets against the fleeting pleasures his student life might bring, even directed oneirism. He creates a void in himself, deprives himself of the joy of writing and even of reading, tolerates in his vacant and frustrated soul only the obsession with the Code (he even dreams about it at night) accompanied by a dismal "boredom," which is punctuated by rages and homicidal impulses otherwise carefully controlled. All this *in vain*, of course, since an alien force paralyzes him as soon as he tries to work. In short, he is sinking slowly *in the present; in the present* his enterprise is suicidal: he would be only too happy if the law killed him for good. But does the intention of failure extend to the end-of-year exams? At certain moments, perhaps, when, sickened, sure of having done what he could, he throws down his books and works no more. At other moments, not—this much is clear. To translate into words his contradictory and unavowed desire, we would have to make him say: I wish to prove undeniably from October to July that I am *incapable* of comprehending the nonsense I am being taught—not for lack of intelligence but for too much—and that at the end of the academic year, by a brilliant achievement, I can make up for the lost time and in a flash of genius give meaning to what has none, comprehend the incomprehensible, and force my memory to regurgitate the articles it refused to ingest.

Behind this inconsistency, we shall find two opposing "axioms." One comes from the Flaubert family and from received wisdom: he who can do most can do least. If you want to show yourself superior to the assigned task, begin by excelling in it: in order to have contempt for the law, you must first raise yourself in one jump, without a hitch, to the doctorate. We have seen this *positive* principle guiding Gustave's thoughts in 1840–41, when he thought it "a little humiliating" for Ernest to "slog away" and, certain of his own superiority, reckoned on "loafing" for four years. The other axiom, the negative

59. Rather, it would be if Gustave were to take his exam during the winter of 1843–44.

one, comes to him from Romanticism; as a solitary and wounded child, he adopted it enthusiastically: he who can do most *cannot do* least. A noble soul has ideals too pure, ambitions too high, a view too penetrating to enter into the Lilliputian concerns of jurists. The theme of the magnificent misfit—which was of great solace to him at the *collège*—again offers its services: failure is the sign of election. Gustave is torn between the two principles. In the course of the year it is the second that prevails, but the first remains virulent, if masked, as is proved by the young man's increasing anguish; in the final months everything is reversed: the chief surgeon will never be convinced that his younger son failed out of superiority; so Gustave starts to work like mad, too late. And the second axiom does not cease for all that to distill its poison: if you succeed, it is because you are a man of action, practical, utilitarian, reasonable, serious, you deserve to be the bourgeois that you will be. Thus, in the course of the year the intention of failure remains strictly limited, not only because it does not extend itself to the end of the enterprise, but also because its aim is above all to save face: Gustave outdoes his incomprehension in order to persuade himself that it is a sign of the nobility of his soul.

As in the general movement of a society we must take account of a certain circularity, since superstructures turn back on the infrastructures from which they dialectically emanate, so in a particular subjectivity the surface intentions, evoked by underlying intentions, exert real influence on these. The tailormade failure that Gustave has agreed to corresponds, as we have seen, to a partial assumption of his passive resistances and of the norms of his constituted passivity. *Partial* and, to a certain extent, *playacted*, this assumption nonetheless determines, in the depths, a new intentionality: we might say that this phenomenon of circularity is interpreted by the abysses as the index of a totalizing reconciliation of the deep waters with the surface, or, still better, that the abysses discover in the determination from above the vectoral meaning of their agitation and assume that meaning by pushing it to the extreme. In other words, the limited failure that Gustave assigns himself as a restricted objective is lived subterraneanly as an extremist vertigo: in some part of him, the conduct described above gives birth to the temptation to lose himself through radical failure.

Shall we say that he *knows* it, or simply that he senses it? No. He may sometimes be struck by a singular and illuminating idea: the chief surgeon will remain unshaken as long as his younger son has not demonstrated to him that he is *not up to* the imposed task. But instantly Gustave takes fright: his pride will not accept that he owes his salvation to *real* inferiority—both physical and mental. In those moments, we can be sure, he clings to the good family principles and swears to beat the fools at their own game so as later to scorn them. Beginning in 1841, however, he is worried: until then, without really knowing himself, he understood himself well enough. Now he is outflanked. It is not so much his hesitations that worry him, nor his passivity when faced with the Code. *Deep down*, however, a still obscure meaning comes to his experience, prepares a certain future, still masked, which Flaubert can neither look in the face nor, above all, assume. He discloses none of this to Ernest or Alfred, or to Caroline. If we want to glimpse this *fundamental* as it is lived in 1842 by the son of Achille-Cléophas, and grasp from the inside his efforts to comprehend and control the troubles that are beginning to unsettle him, we must abandon the correspondence—which is a *discourse to others*—and reread the discourse he addresses to himself, *Novembre*.

Gustave and His Double

Conceived during the winter of 1840–41, *Novembre* is several times abandoned and taken up again. In January '42, Gustave is still working on it. In February, he is disgusted with it, the pen falls from his hands. This time the interruption will be a long one. A letter dated 15 March informs us that he is studying the Code, "and that robs me of any heart and mind for the rest." On 25 June, the same story. It is almost certain that he did not touch his "sentimental ragout" between the month of February and the end of August. He applies himself to it again *after his failure*, and finishes it on 25 October 1842. Where does this break occur in the text? One thing is clear: the initial project was to write an autobiographical novel in the first person that would evoke the author's adventure with Eulalie Foucault. The words "sentimental and amorous" are sufficient evidence of this, although the adjective "sentimental," chosen later to qualify both *Educations*, indicates that from the outset Gustave meant to show the general development of his sensibility; he was returning to interior totalization. He remains faithful to this project for the first eighty pages;[60] he turns away from it completely in the last ten. Maria is no longer present, the autobiography is interrupted, a stranger appears, who declares, "The manuscript breaks off here, but I knew its author," and substitutes

60. Charpentier edition.

591

himself for that "author" in order to recount, with deliberate dryness, the sequel and end of this life. Yet it is not credible that Gustave had begun to write in the first person with the specific intention of ending in the third. Of course, the passage from one to the other—and vice versa—appears commonly in the nineteenth century as a novelistic procedure: witness, for example, *Le Roi des montagnes*. The procedure was employed by certain authors from the beginning of the eighteenth century. Defoe, in the preface to *Moll Flanders*, declares that he has merely polished and perfected "a manuscript . . . written in Newgate prison and . . . which came into my hands." [61] But here the question is not one of rhetorical artifice: Daniel Defoe, a journalist, intended to pass off his fictions as faithful accounts of lived events. In fact, it was the success of *Werther* that later transformed what could first have been a precautionary measure into a kind of literary genre. We can see in this work—in which Werther's friend publishes the journal and letters of the unhappy young man, then stands in for him in order to recount his final days and his death—a kind of transitional point between the epistolary novel and the so-called confessional novel found or received by another. We can easily understand why this strategy was a favored technique among the Romantics: people are always killing themselves in their narratives, and if you want to recount the hero's final moments, the pen must be given to someone who has witnessed the hero's life. This mode of narration tends to become a substitute for the "epistolary" genre, because it preserves both the latter's subjectivism and "distancing." In the eighteenth century, authors would say: here is an entire correspondence; I am publishing it, but I am not the author; the correspondents depict themselves, they are subjectivities the reader will do well to observe. In the following century they would say: I am publishing an eyewitness account that I did not write myself; here are the objective data I have been able to gather concerning the man who put it in my hands; readers will compare them to the subjective certainties expressed in his narrative. Hence that efflorescence of confessions found abandoned in an attic or in a hat, discovered among someone's papers after his death, handed over to a professional writer by a madman who saves his skin by running away.

But in every case the technique requires that premeditation shall be formally established: "I was alone, that evening . . . Someone came to my door . . . I saw a strange person holding a manuscript under his

61. Hamilton himself claims to write under the dictation of the Count de Gramont.

592

arm," etc. etc. These statements are made in the opening lines by the writer, who sometimes reappears at the end to conclude the story. It is a law of the genre: the confession must be *introduced*. In order that every line of the pseudomanuscript should seem to us *at once* distant and more spontaneous, we must be separated from the text by that pane of glass, that transparent separation, the author who publishes the text and claims not to have written it. And Flaubert is twenty-one years old; he is lacking neither in culture nor in experience; some time ago he read *The Sorrows of Young Werther* with enthusiasm and did his apprenticeship in this "fashionable" technique: when he conceived *Novembre,* if he had wanted to provoke in us that recoil and that solidarity, we would expect him to have taken his distance from the first word on. The second character is necessary, so be it; he represents the posthumous. All the more reason for introducing him from the beginning. Yet he breaks in and disconcerts us by his incongruity. Although the orientation of the lyric manuscript is very distinct, the author expresses himself with such freedom and, frequently, disorder, and there are so many repetitions, that we find in it the internal rigor of a quasi-organic sliding, starting with the first experiences and ending in death, but not the rigor of a plan, an aesthetic construction imposing its clarity on the reader. Flaubert seems to throw himself on his desk and write what passes through his head without worrying about repeating himself.[62] The idea of suppressing his hero ripens from one page to the next, true; it is equally true that this ripening is conscious, but we cannot confuse it with a deliberate enterprise. When Flaubert has begun *Novembre,* he is overwhelmed for a time by the temptation to totalize himself through interiority: first of all, there are those notes he jots down from time to time in a notebook, which demonstrate his sporadic desire to adopt the introspective attitude once more, both as a means of knowing himself and as an effort of *self-presentation;* and then there was the adventure in Marseille which, he tells us, took on its importance several months after it happened. Finally, Gustave is still suffering from the failure of *Smarh:* the swing of the pendulum is accentuated; he must come back to the *roman intime,* to the history of a martyr. In fact, the structure of *Novembre* is related to that of the *Mémoires.* Here, as there, a transparent veil of fiction cautiously covers real confessions; in both cases, the central episode is furnished by a romantic experience: the *Mémoires* tell us of

62. For this reason, the lyric manuscript often resembles a private journal. Moreover, he borrows passages from the *Souvenirs, notes et pensées intimes,* written between 1838 and 1841.

Flaubert's first love; *Novembre* gives us an account not of his sexual education but of the revelation of pleasure as *total* reality (carnal and affective). The remainder of both narratives have the same plan: child-hood and school life, then the amorous encounter, finally the separa-tion (in the *Mémoires* the woman does not return to Trouville; in *Novembre* it is Gustave who leaves), and in the last chapters the au-thor returns to lyric effusion. The difference: much more than the *Mémoires*, *Novembre* is a treatise on futile desire and the techniques of unrealization. The result, without any doubt, is that the author puts himself in this second *roman intime* still more than in the first; both because he has gone more deeply into himself and because he is more complacently at one with himself. But even this is instructive: Gustave's initial project was to begin the *Mémoires* again, and this time to succeed. He must have thought an unhappy and solitary love, like the one he described there, could not be of interest—everything happened in one person's head. The Eulalie episode—beyond his resolution to render his dazzlement in words—provided him with the occasion to interact verbally with *another* (another whom he could not prevent himself, moreover, from transforming into himself). And the *Mémoires* ended with the disappearance of Madame Schlésinger. The death of the hero was envisaged only in its aspect as totalization: here was an old man who told the story of an existence soon settled by death, that's all. Still, we have seen that Gustave is not always faithful to his purpose, and that the old man often becomes an adoles-cent again. Thus, in the very interior of the "I" there is a sort of doub-ling: without abandoning the point of view of the interested party, Gustave professes to be both himself and another. In *Novembre*, on the other hand, the idea of death is omnipresent: "I was born with the desire to die"; this is not, properly speaking, a discovery, but the fail-ure of 1839, the abortive attempts that followed, the growing urgency of choosing a profession, passive resistance experienced as an ill-ness—all conspire together to accentuate this desire. In the same pe-riod, he wishes to be nothing. To be *nothing*, in a sense, is to be dead. Consequently, however, this black sun illuminates and highlights the singularity of the subject; not that Gustave reveals to us the deeper aspect of his "anomaly" but because a life that wants to be lived in its "being-for-death" manifests itself through the very annihilation that awaits it, like something that will never reproduce itself twice. No doubt Gustave, a mortal subject desiring death, had wanted to expose himself in his singular universality. The first words he wrote are de-cisive, "I love autumn," as are those that begin the second paragraph,

"I just returned from my stroll on the empty plains," a personal taste—a dated, irreversible event, an individual moment of his history. From this moment, the chips are down: the young writer will render through words the taste of his daily life. Not the slightest "distancing" in the relation of lived to reflexive experience; every sentence is a grazing of the self against the self. Total concurrence: the author *justifies himself*, that is, he accepts himself and wants himself to be as he feels. To the extent—always slight for Gustave—that he writes for a reader, the reader plays the role of a loving father who has the tender understanding of a mother; there is a virtual eclipse of the verbal aggression still found in *Smarh*—and of the demoralizing intention as well.

At the same time, in these eighty pages the author, far from dreaming of dying, believes the totalization is *already accomplished:* his sentimental education is complete; he survives himself, he is at the end of the adventure while remaining in accord with his defunct sentiments: "I savored my lost life at great length." This sentence is proof that he began the work naively. He speaks of death, he dreams of it, but it is still a way of living: the desire for death is a character trait. Why should his hero die? He is already *everyman*, a complete martyr. Certainly we sense an increasing malaise, but the reason is purely literary: he feels he is treading water and repeating himself. If he sometimes thought of suppressing his character—by suicide or accident—this liquidation was suggested to him by his concern with concluding the narrative. For the autobiographical section stops clumsily and abruptly, just as the hero resumes his imaginary gymnastic exercises. Nothing prepares him to become an *object*, to designate himself to us as that Other he is for Others. Quite the contrary: just as he becomes disgusted with writing—in February 1842—he finds to his surprise that he is no longer telling about himself but complacently espousing his dreams, "creating a little style," as he says. His situation has hardly changed since the *Mémoires*. So he asks himself—more pompously but in the same fashion: "Where shall I go? . . . If only I were a mule driver in Andalusia . . . Would that I were a gondolier in Venice." We know what is concealed by these desires: the regret for his "dear journey," the vain desire to be nothing, the greedy wish to know everything, and his growing fear of student life, Paris, and the law. Why did he stop? Both because he was not finding the fall at all desirable—how could he end by exposing those vast appetites in a work begun by the celebrated confidence "I was born with the desire to die"?—and because for nearly a year he had been condemning

595

eloquence: those grand rhetorical flourishes are the opposite of the new aesthetic he glimpses, which seeks indirectly to translate idea through form.

Gustave's models during the winter of 1842 remained Rousseau and Musset: he was reading them. At the end of the summer of '39, just after finishing the *Mémoires d'un fou*, he shares with Ernest his enthusiasm for the *Confessions:* this means that he has bitterly measured the distance between his sketch and Rousseau's masterpiece, but also that he has not entirely lost hope of equaling Jean-Jacques. In starting *Novembre*, he gave himself a purpose: to approach his model by forcing himself to be sincere, by really speaking *of himself*. Unfortunately, Gustave's *ego* is a fictional being: unless he is going to pry into his shadows, he has nothing to tell us but his dreams. And these are scarcely distinguishable from a form of writing that is profoundly his own and is now repugnant to him. The pen falls from his hand in February 1842 because he is disgusted at once with the rhetoric, with his character, and with himself. In short, he interrupts himself at the very moment the first narrator disappears. This break corresponds in no way to the death of the hero—who survives for a long time—but to the decision that the latter made to *keep quiet* (as the second narrator informs us)—a decision that corresponds precisely to Flaubert's in this month of February, as we can ascertain by reading this passage in the light of the afterword to *Smarh*. There he promised himself to write no more. In starting *Novembre*, he had hope. Now he despairs and returns to silence. From this moment he "suffers even more," that is, he begins the fastidious study of the law. Once again he is convinced that he is a "great man *manqué*"; when he decides to open the *Institutes*, it is with the feeling of a radical failure: not only fear but an urge for resignation compels him to forestall his scheme.

After his failure of August 1842, Flaubert returns to his manuscript. But he makes a peculiar resolve: to change the narrator. Without any concern for concluding the unfinished paragraph, he goes on to the next line, and it is *another* he makes speak, a friend of the first narrator. Aesthetically, this mutation is so unexpected that it is disturbing: a brutal rupture, the discomfort into which it plunges us is reminiscent of the sensation provoked in the theater by obvious "cutting." But this is precisely its value: this failure of the narration is all the more striking, underneath, because it seems less willed on the surface. Something comes to life before our eyes: a real event that happened to the author, which we read between the lines. If asked to be more specific, we shall say that Flaubert took up his manuscript again with the intention of finishing it when he perceived that he *could no longer* speak of himself in the first person. This is the rupture of concurrence with lived experience, that abrupt distancing which arises in the intimate relation of the self to itself, which helps us to understand how Flaubert, in his depths, lived his experience of the preceding eight months. But we must examine it more closely for fear of interpreting it incorrectly.

What is striking, first of all, is that Flaubert *foreswears without foreswearing* the two first parts of *Novembre*. He does foreswear them: the first words of narrator no. 2 are a condemnation of the literary effort of no. 1: "If someone, to arrive at this page, having passed through all the metaphors, hyperboles, and other figures that take the place of the preceding pages . . ." He will add a little later, speaking of his deceased friend: "He was a man given to falsity, ludicrousness, and great abuse of epithets." Elsewhere he reproaches the dead young man for his poor literary models, as could be seen, he says, in his style. Discreet but peevish criticism, condescension: this is Flaubert, if you will, judging Gustave. In April 1840, a year had elapsed since he had finished *Smarh;* he no longer entered into what he had written, hence the afterword and the use of the intimate *tu* that doubled him in it. In September '42, only eight months had elapsed since the abandonment of *Novembre.* However, the passage to the third person separates Gustave from himself much more radically than the intimate *tu.* The furor of 1840 was a sign of life; the peevish despair that pushed him frankly to detest what he had loved, to double himself in order to insult himself, was still a sign of hope. At the end of the summer of '42, when he returns to *Novembre,* he is not angry, never raises his voice: he simply no longer enters into his work, and the first narrator appears to him a stranger; he speaks of him—that is, of himself—as *another,* as an acquaintance rather than a friend, without warmth, without complicity, with evident concern not to fall into "ludicrousness." The style is compressed, hard, often striking but cold: for the first time, Gustave produces a work that might belong to what he will call "impersonalism," and—which says a good deal about this literary doctrine—he himself is the object of this impersonal narrative. Besides, more than a narrative it is a statement, a report of proceedings: one man reports the acts and deeds of another with a curious mixture of application and indifference; the sole affective determination revealed by this discourse is a sense of aggrieved superiority. This condescension accounts for all the ambiguity—hence the aesthetic density—of these pages: Gustave gives us an anatomy lesson, and we are tempted to share his feelings about death. Should we do so, he would be falling into a trap that he sets us almost unconsciously: if the new narrator is superior to the dead man, he is at the same time convinced that this dead man is superior to everyone else. One legitimately wonders, therefore, what gives the second narrator—who is still living, and who commits the enormous stupidity of writing—the right to claim superiority over the first, who killed himself and realized, in the end, that marvelous suicide "of dying by thought." We shall come back to this. Let us simply observe that the circular movement manages to give these pages a new dimension precisely because it derails the reader and puts him in an untenable position. It all happens, from this point of view, as if the second narrative of *Novembre* represented Flaubert's first attempt to realize "that strange translation of thought by form" which he had first conceived at the end of 1841. For form is not primarily a "beautiful" sentence; it is the construction of a trap using the elements of discourse. This is what Gustave seems to suggest when he makes the second narrator say: "It must be that feelings have few words to deploy, otherwise the book would have been completed in the first person." We recognize the theme, of course: for several years this writer has continually condemned language. But there is more: feelings will be expressed by words only if one falsifies the discourse by transforming it, for example, into a discourse on a discourse.

Flaubert, however, *does not foreswear* the beginning of *Novembre*. The last part is so different from the first two in tone, intention, and content that a few trivial changes would seem to suffice to make it entirely separate. But the author did not for a moment consider such a thing: discontented as he was with his former work, he introduced the second narrator expressly *to complete it*. Better: having managed to conclude it, he seems to imagine that by a peculiar retroactive effect this sending transforms the beginning without touching it, changes defects into delights, and in some way redeems the pages written prior to February. Indeed, as we know, Flaubert, who never sinned by an excess of self-complacency, will always hold this "last work of his youth" in high esteem. He will get Maxime, Louise, and later the Goncourts to read it. And the addition of the second narrator does transfigure the whole novel. In other words, although the brutality of the rupture astonishes us, it is apparent that the conclusion cannot be isolated or stand on its own without diminishment, and derives its richness precisely from what precedes it. Or, if you will, the young man that the second narrator speaks of appears as the realized truth of the first: the events of the period February–September can only offer us, in the setting of objectivity, the meaning of what Flaubert lived as a simple subjective certainty. And, conversely, through this second part, subjective experience and the undistanced oneness with the self become constituted retrospectively as *summoning* a reflexive and distanced unveiling of their objective dimension. He who says complacently that he is born with the desire to die is the same man that a neutral but pitiless gaze will reveal as a ludicrous author. And this does not cast doubt on his spontaneous sincerity: it is rather a deliberate attempt to show its other face. Here the passage from *Novembre* cited above takes on its full weight: "the book would have been completed in the first person" if the discourse, without being falsified, could have rendered the "feeling" as it appeared to the one who lives it: which means that pathos contains in its very fiber— which is the subjective accord with the self—a summons to objectivization or, if you will, that affect is at once lived as itself and as other, as it appears to the eyes of others. Discourse requires a choice of *one* of the two simultaneously existing points of view: if anger *speaks itself*, it must, in Gustave's view, pass itself off as utterly justified or describe itself coldly as an impulsive and singular reaction. Art will therefore break speech in order to arouse in the reader the perception of these two faces of lived reality. Manipulated from his early childhood by others, Gustave, in the midst of the infinite accord of self with self, always felt himself to be a finite object for others. The successive employment of the "I" and the "he" seemed to him the best way of designating himself as concrete object—as singular universal. Indeed, the theme of the double appears from his first works: it is the opposition of Almaroës and Satan, and it is also the peevish resolution to participate only halfway in the joys and suffering of Marguerite, of Djalioh, of Garcia; it is the very meaning of his sadistic masochism and of the contradiction he discovers early on in the artist, universal genius soaring above everyone and simple particular determination of the human race. The flight into the imaginary is conscious of being rigorously defined by a real anomaly that prescribes its limits by compelling it to repeat itself endlessly in the same forms. The genius of *Novembre* is to make the doubling explicit.

The appearance of the double is an event in novelistic temporalization, preceded by that other event, the death of the first narrator. Whatever the explanation, the newcomer is posthumous: he is someone who *comes after*. Hence the paradox that the theme of doubling, prompted by a crisis, is discovered and exploited literarily before the crisis and the break have actually taken place. In effect, after 1844 Gustave will feel *the same* and *other*. The attack at Pont-l'Evêque will have liquidated a certain individual, and another, born on the spot, will live in the skin of the first; between the deceased and the survivor there is only one point of difference, mental age: the second is an old man without passions, the first, who wept and wailed so, was a young man; his embalmed corpse is at the mercy of a memory that is growing torpid. When Flaubert tries to transmit this barely communicable experience to Louise, he writes: I am two. If we push aside the rhetorical foliage, we are struck by what remains. Indeed, the theme of the double is familiar in certain neuroses; some worthy authors have concluded that Gustave resorted to it *after the crisis* in order to signify his difficulties for himself, then for the Muse. They are right, except for one point: the dichotomy—pathological as it may be—preceded the attack by fourteen months. The strangest thing is that Flaubert himself does not seem to perceive it; when he writes to Louise, "My active, affective, passional life . . . came to an end at twenty-two years old," he is referring explicitly to his nervous illness, that is, to the period following the crisis of January 1844. Yet *beginning in 1842* he described the death of the passions in his burned-out heart and the appearance of the *other* Gustave. Has he forgotten? Certainly not: he read this same Louise the "last work of [his] youth"; moreover, he alludes to this ultimate autobiographical attempt, to the "unsayable" it suggests, even in the letters that seem to contradict it and push back the date of the *event*. He is quite comfortable placing the appearance of the other-in-the-same in the winter of '42, in Paris, and at times placing it—even simultaneously, in my opinion—in January '44 at Pont-l'Evêque. These affirmations are perfectly coherent in his eyes. Gustave is lucid, he is *truthfully* trying to explain himself to his mistress (even if this frankness is secretly designed to keep her at a distance), he knows that she has the facts in hand. He is at his best, neurotic, certainly—who isn't?—but on the way to recovery, delivered from the Father, having arrived (as we shall see in the next part) at a surprising understanding of his malady, animated by a real desire to communicate his experience. If the contradictions we have just revealed do not exist for him, it is because they do not exist at all. For him, the break in *Novembre* is the prefiguration of the one that will actually take place in January '44: two men for a single life, the abrupt silence and death of the first give rise to the discourse of the second, emerged from nothingness to publish and comment on the incomplete work. The newcomer *possesses* the dead young man through memory, as two years later Gustave-the-Old will make himself possessor and guardian of Gustave-the-Young. We understand that the lyric and passionate "I," this confiding of a wretched soul in his subjective intimacy, has fallen apart: the time for distrust has come. A somber and reticent character is going to recount, analyze, explain. Of the two subjectivities, the first closes itself up and becomes an *object*; the other—for occasionally the unknown witness must say "I" or "me"—Flaubert intends us to know nothing about. It *passes over itself in silence* and is absorbed in retracing the last years of the deceased. The biographer, however, depicts himself through his enterprise: his laconic statements betray a constant concern with denying pathos. But beneath the affectation of impartiality, beneath the condescending irony, one discovers violence, a strange, jarring, precipitate rhythm. This man is not detached: we sense he is ill-fated, anguished. We cannot take him simply for the passive product of the hero's death: he has been called in, one might say, in a case of extreme urgency to make a diagnosis. This is in part the source of his formal attitude: he is a doctor or a cop. The reason he behaves impartially and blocks his feelings is that he is conducting an inquiry: seeking to understand the motives of the accused or the patient, he first of all forbids himself to share in them. But to what is he seeking clues or symptoms? To a murder, an illness? It amounts to the same thing. As to what event—internal or external—is at the source of the rupture and the inquiry, I contend that the answer may be found in the third part of *Novembre*: at the end of August or the beginning of September, Gustave wanted to kill himself. It is true that, as author, he places the episode in winter, but this is deliberately misleading; when he decided to get rid of his hero and make him die for good in a certain month of December,[63] the month of October 1842 is not yet over, and he has firmly decided to pass his exam—which he knows will take place the following December. As we have seen, this is certainly not the first time he flirts with suicide. Narrator no. 1 tells us, "I have always loved death"; he approached "the attic window in order to throw [himself] out." And then, at the last moment, some force held him back. The scenario will be replayed without variation in August–September 1842: one day he wants to revisit a seaside village "before dying."[64] He arrives, leans over the edge of the cliff, and "ponders for a moment whether he shouldn't end it

---

63. Therefore at least one year after the failed suicide.

64. The question is not one of a voluntary death; Flaubert's hero has entered into moral death throes which, as we shall see, will merge with physical death throes: he will die "by thought."

all; no one would see him, no hope of help, in three minutes he would be dead." No: "Directly, by an antithetical movement common at such moments, existence came to him smiling, his life in Paris seemed charming and full of the future . . . But the voices of the abyss called to him, the waves opened like a tomb . . . He was afraid, he turned back home, all night he listened in terror to the wind." Gustave is probably describing an actual experience. What is convincing is the "terror" that grips the young man in the face of the opening waves, and this is what prompted Gustave to relate his failed attempt: he approached the edge of the cliff as he previously did the attic window. He leaned into the void and delighted in *imagining* his fall—as before. But there the similarities end: as a child, his suicidal behavior remained ludic, he was unrealizing himself as a suicide. Not without terror, I agree, but that was part of the ritual: he played at making himself afraid. In 1842 there is no more playacting. Yet there is: at the outset he has begun his exercises, once again, he has imagined everything, even the "plop" he would hear while sinking into the sea. But this time the unreal has another consistency: Gustave *feels* that he has every actual reason to kill himself. Consequently, the image of the plunge is transformed into vertigo: a force attracts him, the waves open *for him*, he is convincing himself that he *is going* to throw himself into the water. This is enough to awaken his powerful will-to-live, which manifests itself by a memorable fright: he flees. But during the night, anguish mingles with retrospective terror: he has just learned both that suicide is the only solution to his problems and that his instinct for life prohibits him from killing himself. This is summed up extremely well in a sentence spoken by the second narrator, which occurs before the account of this temptation: "There are kinds of suffering . . . from the heights of which one is reduced to nothing . . . When they do not kill you, suicide alone delivers you from them; he did not kill himself." No comment: a statement of failure, that's all.

There he is, then, in this Idumaean night, enclosed in his room, where he "makes an enormous fire that roasts his legs." This last detail—Gustave placed the scene in winter—takes the place of another that we shall never know.[65] He reflects; he wonders at once: what to do, what to become if I can neither live nor die? And: *why* did I *want* to kill myself? The two questions receive a single answer: I must first of all know myself; I have both the need and the means to do it since I *do*

---

65. There may have been two attempts, the more serious being unquestionably the second. Gustave would then have amalgamated them.

not recognize myself. In this moment of my life, when I seem *other* to myself, I must observe and judge myself *as another.*

He very nearly threw himself into the sea. Could he have been pushed to it by the shame of having failed his exam? He doubts it. Even the loathsome experiences endured in the recent past do not seem to him to explain his sudden violence. And what if it was *to avoid the worst?* What "worst"? It's all there. During this night and in the days to follow, Gustave has made two decisions: he will pull himself out of the torpors of passivity and will take his exam; he will make an inquiry into the self, because a danger threatens him that does not come from the outside but *from himself.* He must see clearly, "analyze himself," recompose himself, or else *something is going to happen to him.*" As the humiliating, absurd, and logical conclusion of his efforts, this *failed* suicide suddenly makes him see the two previous years in another light: he turns back and discovers what he forced himself not to see: his *psychic* malady of '41, his insurmountable resistances, the suspect calm of his senses. This is the end of the period in which he began *Novembre.* The two first parts were written *before* his departure for Paris; therefore they reflect his troubled discomfort: he will make use of them, he will attempt to interpret them and say *today* who the young man was who wrote them. These will be the documents relevant to his self-appointed trial. He will take up his novel and finish it. If he could tell the truth about himself, show both the subject Gustave in the spontaneity of his inner life and the object Flaubert through his behavior and his conditionings, if he succeeded in showing his meaning and direction—which he was unaware of until now—would he not approach the masterpiece he was so desperate to write? In this "paradoxical" moment, full of fears and hopes—and not when he was leaning over the water—his life seems to him "full of the future." The break in *Novembre* is not simply the literary prefiguration of the later crisis: it is the beginning of a systematic investigation, born of a presentiment. In the last pages of the novel we shall see Gustave's final effort—his most vigorous—to know himself. When he begins the inquiry, he has fallen into the most profound *estrangement.* We know that he has had crises of estrangement since childhood. Never so acute. For the reason that he discovers himself *other twice over* and yet the same.

1. The unhappy candidate of August 1842, stiff, dismal, anxious, humiliated, who refuses all surrender, who prudently takes himself in hand, regards the young writer from the time before February *as another:* too much passion, too much magnificence in his desires, too

much enthusiasm in his suffering. Flaubert is astonished at having been this naive flaunter of despair. He knows that he was not lying then, that he really felt and thought what he was writing; therefore, this is a valuable document on his youth, *provided* he denounces the mirage of subjectivity and shows the objective reality of the first narrator, his particularity. The "I," as we have seen, is of itself universalizing: all young men should be able to recognize themselves in the hero's violent impulses. But *who* is this hero? Flaubert wonders: "Who was I?" For the universal of February seems to him in September a *particular* and dated disposition. Was he not writing then: "I was what you all are, a certain man . . .," etc.? It was an aggressive denial of the anomaly or, in any case, a claim that all men are equally affected by it, each in his own way. In September the anomaly becomes *his* property. The two failures make him finally admit to himself: "I am not like the others." Not different from everyone the way everyone is different from everyone else, but *absolutely different*. To be sure, the "great man *manqué*" is a species he calls "common" in his *Notes et souvenirs;* be that as it may, this species represents the extreme minority of the genus; and of course the species is created only from "cases" that lend themselves to careful study rather than to generalization. In short, in September the daydreamer of February must be designated by his idiosyncrasy *as it appears to others' eyes:* the Flaubert son, an imaginary child with infinite aspirations, is *in reality* a failure. The appearance of the witness marks the distance that separates the student of September from the young author of the preceding winter: it consecrates if not the triumph of the *alien-gaze* at least the angry and bitter decision to privilege it. For Gustave, to know himself is to begin by *not justifying himself.* The subject of infinite desire becomes this object: an original from the provinces whose means are not up to his ambitions. The two first parts of *Novembre* might be called "The Story of my Dreams," for reality appears there only to be devoured by imagination. In the third, the process of derealization is stopped: in between, Gustave encountered reality in the form of a socialized negation of his own person (his Parisian solitude, the failure of the month of August); the purpose of the third part is to encompass the imaginary and define it by its unbreachable limits, as a practical agent defines the real field of his possibilities: *this* man, in his objective reality, is conditioned by his character and his history to push evasion *to this point*, no further. The actor wonders: what lies behind my roles? What makes me play those roles—always the same—rather than others? To question the imaginary is to seek beneath permanent derealization the real that motivates and directs it. Behind the "flight of the eagle," Flaubert, disabused, looks for the "telling little fact."

Who am I? On this level of the inquiry, this means "What can I do?" In the third part, Gustave undertakes to discover and fix precisely the relation between his ambitions and his capabilities:

> His great regret was not to be a painter; he used to say he had such beautiful pictures in his imagination. He was equally dismayed not to be a musician . . . Endless symphonies played in his head. Moreover, he knew nothing about painting or music, I saw him admire really terrible paintings and have a migraine leaving the Opera. With a little more time, patience, and work, and above all with a more delicate taste for the plastic arts, he could have written mediocre verse . . . In his early youth, he nourished himself on very bad writers, as one could see from his style; growing older, he lost his taste for them, but excellent authors no longer evoked in him the same enthusiasm . . . He had the vanity to believe that men did not like him: men did not know him . . . He had . . . too much taste to fling himself into criticism; he was too much a poet, perhaps, to succeed in letters . . . When it was sunny, he went strolling in the Luxembourg, he walked on the fallen leaves, recalling that he did the same thing at the _collège;_ but he would not have suspected that ten years hence he would come to this . . . As he hadn't the energy for anything, he began to drink . . . He no longer read, or else only books he found inferior and which, nevertheless, gave him a certain pleasure by their very mediocrity . . . It is easy to imagine that he had no purpose, and that was his misfortune. What might have animated him, moved him? (Neither love nor ambition.) For money, his greed was very great, but his laziness had the upper hand . . . His pride was such that he would not have wanted a throne . . . He was a man who gave himself over to the false, the ludicrous, and a great abuse of epithets.

This portrait takes on its full weight when we bear in mind that it describes the first narrator; he is clearly presented to us for what he is: wild with pride, of mediocre talent—he is a contradiction. He dreams of symphonies, he has pictures in his head but understands nothing of the arts. Even if he had taste, genius would be sorely lacking in him. Moreover, he lacks energy and has no purpose. Not even writing? No: after February '42, not even that. His defects—which are going to lead him to his death—are perhaps the reverse of secret qualities: he is too much a poet to become an artist. Ultimately, poetry is imagination, and what is the imaginary in a mediocre soul who does not even succeed in imprinting it on the real? Emptiness. Here, then, are the flights of the lyrical young man reduced to their bitter truth. The proof of it, narrator no. 2 tells us, is that they will soon leave him. What will remain? Nothing, except the impossibility of living.

We recognize the portrait: it is the one that is sketched in the Notebooks, beginning in 1840. Everything is there, but the lighting differs: in the *Notes et pensées*, Gustave is desolate. Here, nothing but a statement of failure made by an officer of the courts. The subject of *Novembre* is transformed: the "story of my imagination" becomes the "novel of a failure." The reader falls into a trap: that undefined young man who takes himself for the infinite was reliving his youth, and now he finds himself caught in the matrix of his pitiful and only too real individuality. He must throw away the book or detest what he was first compelled to love.

2. It is not only the dreamer of the 1840s that Gustave no longer recognizes; it is also the young man who comes *afterward*, the restive student of Rouen, of Paris, the candidate in spite of himself, who desires and does not desire failure and suffers it, finally, simply as an accident and the profound image of his destiny. He has gone astray in himself, loves blindly, understands himself too much and not enough. *Not enough:* he has, as we have seen, sudden illuminations that dazzle without enlightening; *too much:* his bewilderment would be nothing if it were merely a question of a moment to live, flowing from day to day; but he discerns in it a prophecy. Not surprising: all of life prophesies at every moment since it unfolds in a spiral; thus premonition—which is irrational—is based on reason in its pure, unusable guise, on the very structures of existence in which every new and irreversible change is at the same time repetition. And Flaubert, as we already know, is more inclined than others to consult lived experience as a permanent oracle. But in this particular case, there is more: the young man is afraid of discerning in premonition a secret intention, at once his and other; in short, he is two steps away from understanding that a man's destiny is merely *himself* coming to the self as an alien future. This intention creates the urgency of the inquiry: he must discover it in order to suppress it or accept it in full consciousness, just as we seek to disclose an enemy's plans in order to thwart them or turn them against him. A single means: to put a cop onto the case. And it just happens that the cop is right at hand: he is the young flunk-out who has rejoined his family at Trouville; he is on vacation there, his passions are still. Paris is far away, *he no longer knows what is going on.*

But we should not confuse this precarious silence of the heart with happiness: at the very most, it is the suspicious absence of unhappiness; he is hardened, sullen, he has conceived a horror for the flights of the soul and the pen, his vexations in Paris have made him mistrustful and cynical: he looks unsympathetically at the future notary, who for six months has fruitlessly toiled over the Code. He borrows the Flaubert father's surgical eye and with cold curiosity undertakes to dissect. In order to adopt this new tone, this somber objectivism, he has no need to force himself: quite the contrary, it is enough for him to yield to his anxious sullenness and make that the chief tool of the investigation. Before, he did not like himself; now he fears himself: these are necessary and sufficient conditions to effect the doubling. The narrative of the second narrator derives its force from a breathless, confused, universal terror that barely disguises the sustained effort to remain objective. The certainty of the worst has remained until now a metaphysical imaginary; it has served as the operative scheme for his confused rumination, for his literary creations. Now, it is actually lived: the metaphysical universal has gone under; what remains is a young man's anxiety at his singular adventure. He says to himself, simultaneously: "What am I preparing for myself?" and "It had to end like that." As for the results of the inquiry, we shall discover their multiple meanings if we attempt to analyze the record.

Appearance of the Preneurosis

At the end of the lyric manuscript, there is a striking dissonance: "In former times, before Maria, my boredom had something beautiful, grand about it; but now it is stupid, it is the boredom of a man full of bad brandy, the dead drunk's sleep." Several lines further on, there is the new flight: "Oh, to feel myself sitting on the backs of camels . . ." Be that as it may, Gustave is worried—a recent development, no doubt. What he called dissatisfaction is now sheer stupefaction. Alcohol? He drinks, of course; he gets drunk now and then in imitation of Alfred; but let us not imagine enormous excess: this adolescent has all the faults and all the virtues that protect against alcoholism, and, besides, he is being supervised at home. What he reveals to us here is not his experience as a drunkard; he is illuminating by a comparison the dense stupidity that is crushing him *even when sober*. The essential information indeed concerns his *degradation*. Lacking the strength to claim a "beyond," an "elsewhere," his dissatisfaction, emptied of all demand, is changed into stupor, pure suffered maladaptation; the vain Desire for All, an imaginary determination, is effaced, and what remains is this truth, that he has no interest in anything. No more evasion: his nonpresence in the world becomes an obtuse presence; inert, tossed about by the course of things, he dozes with his eyes open. This collapse is expressly dated: "Before Maria . . . now . . ." Gustave refers back to the years 1840–41, and what he means to describe is that "malady" which allowed him to sequester himself. What is the source of this metamorphosis? The author is surprised by it but does not explain it, and we are hardly tempted to attribute it to poor Eulalie Foucault. However, the comparison of his condition with drunkenness is very meaningful: for brandy does not really pour itself into glasses, one must get drunk; from this time on, then, Gustave is to some extent tempted to emphasize the intentional aspect of the whole process.

Indeed, seven months later, the second narrator describes the same behavior from the outside by insisting on the intention: "He began drinking brandy and smoking opium, he spent his days lying around and half drunk, in a state suspended between apathy and nightmare." Flaubert was in Paris, he must have gotten drunk frequently with his comrades, or all alone.[66] Drunkenness is explicitly given as the cause of his collapse: if he spends his days "lying around" and in a state of apathy, it is because he has been "half drunk" since morning. He means to place an activity at the origin of his condition. Let us observe, however, that it is a passive activity. It is true that for every glass drunk a certain choice is required; but it is also true that one *addicts oneself* to drink, one abandons oneself to it. And this is neatly summed up in the expression "to start drinking." Gustave is so conscious of it that he goes so far as to give us the imperious though negative motivation that drives him to drink. Indeed, the whole sentence is: "As he had no energy for anything, and time, contrary to the opinion of the philosophers, seemed to him the least generous thing in the world, he started drinking." Three paragraphs further on, we read: "It is easy to imagine that he had no purpose." Flaubert, in effect, even in his very earliest narratives, always presented his quietism as a vicious circle: he has no energy because, through pride, he has placed himself above human ends; he has no precise objectives because he lacks energy, above all for ideas. As a result, he *suffers* the

66. I do not believe he took opium. This was the literary piety of the period. Who would have obtained it for him?

passage of time. In 1839, Gustave tried to escape it by practicing hedonism. That was a pipe dream: in order to believe in it, one had to imagine that a whole person, with all his resources and all his passions, could resume himself in the pleasure of a moment. Impossible: man is future. In order to tear oneself away from temporalization, one must cut oneself off from the species, and alcohol will accomplish this goal. By plunging us into stupor, an imitation of the pure being-there of things, it will amputate us from our future. Gustave knows it, accepts it. If man is to come, let us be submen and vegetate in an eternal present.

These texts are clear: they present the collapse as intentional. The result is not brilliant: he spends his days "in a state suspended between nightmare and apathy." Let us understand that his apathy disarms the nightmare by suppressing the anguish, and is itself nightmarish because he lives it in horror as the systematic and, moreover, futile degradation of his existence. And no doubt he has moments of pure anxiety as well, and others in which the stupor is total, in which he casts the same indifferent eye upon life, death, genius, glory, failure, and the process of becoming bourgeois. In any event, what remains is the more or less obscure consciousness of having *drunk to the point of collapse.* The objective of this operation is not simply the clouding of consciousness but its permanent mutilation. Or, if you will, drunkenness has a double function for Gustave: superficially he gets drunk, one evening, in order to forget his bourgeois future; underneath, he realizes a collapse which, if it were permanent, would make him incapable of becoming bourgeois.

Here, a suspicion comes to mind: in order truly to degrade yourself, you must get drunk *every day.* One isolated drunk can, strictly speaking, *symbolize* irreparable destruction; in fact, it destroys nothing at all. And neither Gustave's letters nor the testimonies of those who were then his classmates make it thinkable that he had *actually* undertaken to destroy himself with drink. From this point of view, the affirmation "he started drinking" is false. However, as the author is trying here to tell the truth about himself, it must be true from another point of view. In short, it is a *manner of speaking* that attempts to signify the "unsayable." Even in the first text, alcohol was merely a term of comparison. In the one we are studying, the comparison is condensed, syncopated, veiled by an imaginary act: what Gustave means is that he has the feeling that without wine or drugs, without any external instrument, solely with the means at hand, he has undertaken his self-destruction. He feels he is capable of producing all alone, without external aids, the results of an inveterate alcoholism—mental decay or *delirium tremens*—and he is terrified at discerning his effecive intention to doom himself. Witness the fact that his alcoholism is not mentioned again. On the other hand, immediately after the passage we have just cited, seeking another code to deliver the same message, he insists on his increasing complacency with his torpors: "Worn out by boredom, a terrible habit, and even finding a certain pleasure in the stupefaction that is its sequel, he was like those people who watch themselves dying, he no longer opened his window to breathe the air, he no longer washed his hands, he lived in the filth of poverty , the same shirt served him for a week, he no longer shaved or combed his hair," etc. Two passages are striking in this text:

1. The pleasure Gustave takes in the collapse is accompanied by an attempt at *deculturation*. Far from trying to combat his apathy by social activities, he protects it by rejecting society as a whole insofar as it is "culture" in contrast to simple "nature." He no longer holds to basic roles, those he was taught from childhood that seem to him to define the basis of what is *human*, meaning bourgeois: what good is it to wash, to shave, or to air out his room? He will abstain from these things henceforth, even if he himself must put up with the inconvenience of this negativism: "However chilly, if he had gone out in the morning and got his feet wet, he went without changing his shoes and without making a fire." We note that these abstentions are presented as conscious and deliberate: they seem neither the effect nor the direct expression of apathy. We might say rather that he profits from this experienced inertia to devastate large socialized areas in himself and to return to the time when men did not know the use of fire. Even his displeasures no longer seem to him sufficient reasons for undertaking a human action: he must *suffer* damp clothes, the icy room, out of a stoic skepticism that challenges all ends of the species and, *at the same time*, out of an applied sluggishness that makes him incapable of attaining them. Just now we saw him reading "books that he finds inferior" with a kind of *Schadenfreude* and the bitter pleasure of surprising literature in the process of being ridiculous. Now he goes further: he destroys in himself what seems to him the essence of man, thought. Not, of course, with drink but by sustaining in himself a state of permanent distraction with "auxiliary fascination": "He threw himself fully dressed onto his bed and tried to sleep; he watched the flies crawling on the ceiling, he smoked, he followed the little blue spirals rising from his lips." He needs to sustain "his void" through a strange ascesis, to constitute his mind, purged of its ideas and its

words, as an inert lacuna. In order to become wholly matter, he allows only material facts to penetrate; still, they must be insignificant: the spots on the ceiling, that's enough. Perception, in Gustave—especially around this time—is a *thing-becoming* of the perceiving subject: no more ego, deliverance.

This ascesis—return to total void, figure of nothingness, to the total plenitude of matter, to the absolute impotence of the first man, to vegetative life, to inhuman nature through the systematic destruction of cultural equipment—is conscious and quasi-deliberate. It must be seen as the *imitation* of apathy, a conjuring in order to provoke its return and, when it finally exists, an effort to radicalize it. In any event, these are secondary "counteractivities" that can be developed only on a prepared terrain. The primary and fundamental reality is "stupefaction": to the extent that *it makes itself lived* without being explicitly desired, to the extent that its appearances are suffered, stupefaction gives meaning to the negative behavior that Gustave has recorded. Why does he no longer wash, no longer open his windows? Because he is "like those people who watch themselves dying." Dying is an *endured* process. For Flaubert, the end of this involution—which is the most fundamental thing—is foreseen; rather, it constitutes the near and concrete future of the lived present, that is, a counter-future; it qualifies every moment in its irreversibility as the certainty of having no more future. Whatever the proposed act, even pulling off his rain-drenched boots, Gustave no longer even needs to refuse it, no longer feels the least injunction to accomplish such an act: the bond between him and the most urgent ends is broken. The sensation of cold, the fear of catching cold, are no longer surpassed in an act that would aim at suppressing them—they endure and, if I may say so, *vegetate;* this is the experienced break with the most immediate future, it is the spontaneously felt equivalent of all sensations, pleasant or unpleasant, of all sentiments, of the thought of emptiness and of the emptiness of thought. When at last this attitude is *suffered,* Gustave takes fright. "I am exhausted," he thinks. "Exhausted": the word indicates well enough that *dying* is merely a term of comparison: he should have said "collapse." In the passage I have cited, collapse is envisaged as an irreversible process and as a counterfuture, as the possibility of having no more *human* future. I say "possibility" because the "like" has two functions here: on the one hand it introduces the image ("like people who watch themselves dying"), on the other hand it indicates that the two terms of the comparison are not strictly equivalent, it introduces the idea of *nearly.* There is prophecy, that is certain. But it is the body that prophesies: people who watch themselves dying have the certainty of their approaching death; Gustave himself has merely an intermittent belief varying in intensity. He "sees himself" slip toward mental decay, toward senility, but *not all the time*. Be that as it may, the counterfuture is the meaning of his stupors: they come, more and more frequently, of increasing duration, increasingly profound, and then they disappear, but one day they will become his permanent state. And it is this conviction which allows him to *playact* apathy in empty moments or to reinforce it when it appears again. *What good is it* to behave like a man who possesses a human future since my real future is a return to the brutish state, to the state of the brute, to that senility which is merely the resurrection of earliest infancy? You wash yourself if you are destined to become a notary; if it is early senility that awaits you, what good are hygiene and cleanliness?

In short, he is a mystic of stupefaction: he is visited by stupors whose future meaning is the definitive fall into subhumanity. But it will be remarked that he has had these dazed ecstasies since early childhood. Precisely: it is their meaning that has changed. They were escapes; later he saw them as proof of his genius. Now, they are premonitions: they *signify* his future madness. And this is just what worries him: why does he *delight in them?* Don't we do *with* pleasure what we do *out of* pleasure? In Flaubert's case, the sign of hedonism is disturbing: his apathetic ecstasies have no *external* conditioning. Certainly he suffers them, but no one imposes them on him except, of course, his body. Gustave says it clearly: "At night, he did not sleep, insomnia caused him to toss about on his bed, he would dream and wake, so that in the morning he was more tired than he was the evening before." Why should we be surprised, after this, that during the day he had no more strength to do anything? Behind him, that obscure mass, the fantasmagorias of nightly insomnia; before him, a future of obscurely prophesied madness. In the present moment, a weariness with living of which he is innocent. Innocent? That's where the shoe pinches. Of course, we are speaking of nervous troubles. But the characteristic of nervous illnesses is that they have a double meaning: they are both suffered and created; the nerves often impose on us merely what we have first imposed on them. After all, don't insomnia and nightmares contain on a certain level the *intention* of prolonging themselves through the apathy of the following day? Indeed, in the second narrator's description, day and night seem to be blurred during the first narrator's final months. Stupefaction, waking nightmares, sleep in the afternoon; sleep, stupefaction, nightmares from dusk to dawn. Hypnosis has little effect on certain kinds of insomnia: the in-somniac, even if his superficial behavior seems to deny it, is deeply bound by the *intention of not sleeping*. In short, if apathy is a pleasure, it is Flaubert who reproduces it; it has become—on a certain level—an end in itself. Can we say that he knows it? Yes and no: for ultimately this pleasure horrifies him. He dreads his collapse. He evokes it or maintains it through imitative behavior, but at the same time he is ter-rified by the suspicion that it might one day be definitive. *Novembre* does not clearly say this, but the "pleasure" in question will better reveal its nature if we compare these imitative counteractivities with other imitations Gustave enjoyed doing at the same period, which he will mention four years later to Louise: "My father, in the end, for-bade me to imitate certain people (persuaded that I must have been suffering greatly from doing it, which was true, although I denied it), among others an epileptic beggar I had encountered one day at the seaside. He had told me his story; he had first been a journalist, etc., it was superb. It is certain that when I rendered this odd character, I was inside his skin. Nothing was more hideous than I was at that mo-ment. Do you comprehend the satisfaction I experienced in doing it? I am sure you don't." [67] The letters of 1842–43 inform us that this "odd character" came from Nevers and that Flaubert had made him the fa-vorite role in his repetoire. Why? We already know the answer: what attracts him in this unfortunate is his idiocy. We know the story: idiots, children, and animals fascinated him: he fascinated animals, children, and idiots. In the latter, raw nature reveals itself as the vio-lent and radical negation of man; better still, it ridicules and cari-catures him: the idiot is man satirized.

Furthermore, "it was superb." What is superb in the stories of this unfortunate? That he claims to have been a journalist. Is it true? Is it a lie or simply a fabrication? Flaubert doesn't care. What matters to him is that these statements bear witness to a bruised dignity, whether the illness had made him incapable of exercising his profession or whether he invented for himself a brilliant past in order to compen-sate for the horror of his present. Fallen below what is human, the poor man is determined to respect bourgeois values, to boast of titles that he doesn't have or hasn't any longer. What is "superb" is this cir-cularity: men are contemptible, but we debase ourselves still further by falling below them, especially if—as never fails to happen—we feel humiliated, yet still value the sordid activities that we can no longer

67. To Louise, 8 October 1846, *Correspondance* 1:362.

even scorn since we are incapable of engaging in them. Gustave speaks of this "odd character" in a tone that is patronizing and unindulgent: he reproaches him for still worshiping bourgeois idols. But at the same time he recognizes himself in the man from Nevers or, rather, he recognizes *his own vicious circle:* in order not to do his law degree, he would have to become afflicted with some sort of mental misery, but as a result he would lose the resource of despising his good friends and would suffer, with impotent rage, the weight of their righteous pity.

So he throws himself into imitating the "journalist." He mimics his gestures in order to awaken the feelings and know the taste of abjection: his aim is to exhaustively assuage, in the imaginary, the obscure desire to lose his dignity that he divines deep down in himself; degradation must be *savored.* Until 1844, however, it will remain unreal. Does Gustave seek it out despite its unreality or because of it? Both. In a sense, he never loses the consciousness of *playing a role,* and this is not displeasing to him: the danger remains limited; by this false collapse he can unmask his forbidden desire, see it in the light of day, assume it or free himself from it. He is playing not so much the man from Nevers as himself, but he plays *himself* as the man from Nevers. The pleasure exists on this level: he abandons himself to the imitation, passivity does the rest; he enjoys satirizing, acting stupefied, throwing himself on his back, writhing in spasms. For a moment he is below the human, delivered from the future by his abjection; for a moment his implacable masochism finds a radical outlet: before the eyes of his family, Gustave sinks into ignominy, he wants to *make people laugh* at his misfortune. He makes his getaway, he takes a break. He makes himself utterly contemptible *for others,* and if he mimics abjection it is *also* to force his father to curse him one more time: in this sense, the collapse is a repetition of the primal scene. But Gustave, drooling and delirious, quickly becomes disturbing and knows it; he knows that he worries his father and rejoices in it: "This is what you have made of me." Thus, as always happens with him, masochism turns into sadism. The imaginary child, agitated by fictive convulsions, is in these moments *intact.*

Yet his father says to him: "You are suffering from it." "This was true," Gustave admits at the end of four years. This suffering I shall rather call anguish. To the same degree that the imitated crisis harbored a cathartic intention, it disturbs him—is it not prophetic? What if the fictive collapse were merely an anticipation of what he is preparing for himself on the sly? What terrifies him is precisely his "satisfaction": this excessive pleasure can only signify his compliance with the maneuvers of a hidden ego. Could this really be true? Somewhere inside him, could there be a vow to lose his dignity? If there is, surely a day will come when it will find expression. He playacts this intention, in a certain way, in order to reveal it. But he finds it nowhere; there is this awful pleasure, that is all. Perhaps I am thoroughly mistaken, he thinks; instead of being the conscious and voluntary author of my behavior, I am being led by it; when I roll around on the floor, I am animated by a deeper self that escapes me. In this case, the imaginary would come dangerously close to the real: after all, true madness is the imagination. "I mimic madness" would mean "I am on the way to becoming mad." It is all the more disturbing that when he plays his favorite role, the imaginary takes on an unaccustomed consistency. It no longer has anything in common with that tenuous, fleeting imaginary external reveries: it is an *occupying force,* Gustave is no longer entirely master of it; he feels increasing difficulty in leaving the role, which tends to prolong itself beyond the limits fixed by conscious decision. What has changed? Something about the *belief:* his gestures *persuade* him; it is not that he *believes he is* the journalist from Nevers, but he believes he could theoretically believe it permanently. In short, he discovers for the first time in its full force that autosuggestibility of which we shall speak at length in the third part of this work. Moreover, the "aping" must have strongly resembled "possession" for Dr. Flaubert to have finally forbidden it. This honest practitioner knew our mental fragility: "[He] kept repeating that he would not have wanted to be a doctor in a mental hospital, because if you work conscientiously with madness, you may well end by catching it." This is what he used to say to his son, we can be sure. "Bah," answered the other, "it's a laugh." But Achille-Cléophas, comparing these dubious farces with the nervous troubles that affected Gustave, wondered if he should not see them as symptoms of some mental illness. Despite his denials, Flaubert wondered about it as well. He admits as much to Louise. What the father and son have in common, in any case, is the idea that madness "is catching"; whether studying epilepsy or imitating an epileptic, one knows a similar dizziness, one enters the skin of the patient and risks finding no escape. When he aped the man from Nevers, Gustave persuaded himself that *he was doing what he had to do* to become mad, that every repetition of the aping brought him closer to that fatal end: if ever this became *habitual,* he would be lost.

2. "Worn out by boredom, a terrible habit . . ." These six words begin the paragraph and are offered as an explanation: unlike the sen-

tences that follow, they do not aim at describing behavior but at illuminating it. On other points we have seen Flaubert more doubtful, but here he shows himself to be categorical. He shares with us a certainty acquired at least six months earlier: *boredom is a habit*. A habit begins by being taken up: originally it is an intentional behavior which, frequently repeated, ends by reproducing itself spontaneously and, when defied, becomes a need. Gustave takes the word in the strong sense since he adds "terrible," which makes one think of the "fatal," "pernicious" habits that Monsieur Prudhomme attributes to dissolute young men. Is boredom, then, *first of all* a behavior?

Gustave is really not sure of anything. For a constituted passivity, boredom is above all primary matter: it exists first, it is the taste of lived experience. Yet in order to radicalize it, behaviors must *animate* it: "the boredom that two men have brought to the *boil*," he writes later to Bouilhet. He fully recognizes that they have forced primitive boredom to its limit since he immediately adds: "Beware, when you are amused at being bored, it's a slippery slope." A line that cannot help evoking the six words from *Novembre*.

Thus, Gustave considers that from age fifteen to twenty he sinned through complacency. In the same letter, the metaphor is multiplied: that stagnant liquid which he used to "bring to the boil" and of which he used to "feel the weight" has now become a "slippery slope." But these transformations are quite instructive: the three images, used simultaneously, can render what one might call the three dimensions of boredom. The weight defines it, in effect, in its original inertia, in its being-there; the provoked boilings manifest Gustave's activity, the grand gestures he makes in order to stir up the liquid, but the comparison preserves a ludic and gratuitous character for these enterprises; we are merely at the moment when one *is amused* at being bored. The more banal image of the "slippery slope" has the advantage of indicating the underlying attraction Flaubert feels for the bottom of the precipice where, dizzying as it is, radical boredom awaits him. At the outset, the exercise of boredom seemed merely a means of keeping the world at a distance: one was perched above it all. Now, quite to the contrary, he rolls down to the bottom; the world closes over him, swallowing him up. The amusement was merely an enticement disguising a dangerous fascination, a distant magic charm or perhaps a summons: in any case, this broken metaphor serves to introduce the relation to the Other—even if this Other were merely an alter ego. Some otherness has slipped into the relation of self to self— the boredom that is suffered and is suddenly conjured up as a demand from the depths, as something *to realize*. It has become a habit, and Gustave has lost control of it; invaded, he suffers it. But he suffers it as he made it: this foreign body inside him carries his label; he must recognize it as *his* (as the result of his exercises), as *other* (as the present heteronomy of his spontaneity), as *his own as other:* you wanted it, Gustave Flaubert. This, at least, is what the author of *Novembre* says to himself *in order to reassure himself:* the *other* intention would be merely *his* intention, but in the past. Does he fully believe it? What if it were—like the stupefaction that precedes and provokes it—the forewarning or symbol of a deeper and wholly alien intention? Passive activity is no doubt in itself the setting of surrender; like the original boredom, it is what makes the crisis of boredom possible. But if there were nothing to reinforce it, Gustave could combat it and win provisional victories over it. What is the source of its present power? It is as if someone in Flaubert were making use of it in order to attain a monstrous end. We are familiar with this end: we have seen Flaubert imitate the epileptic of Nevers in order to create *in the imaginary* the experience of subhumanity. Unreal as it was and remained from beginning to end, that experience terrorized him. He wonders now if the underlying intention of an unknown ego which he shelters in his depths would not be to make him fall *really* and *permanently* into the state of human rubbish. He tried to fight the bourgeoisie by perching above it: well and good, but that would have taken genius. Lacking genius, didn't he persuade himself that one leaves the bourgeois environment only by falling below it? The only way out was to become the family idiot—hadn't he already chosen that way? In this case, the failure of August '42 would manifest his underlying intention: to lose everything and constitute himself truly, by means of a slow internal effort, as failed-man. From this moment, Flaubert is afraid. He feels as though he has a suspect and hidden accomplice who executes promptly but *badly* the sentence he has brought against himself, who gives an effective reality to what remained until then on the border between the imaginary and the real.

And what, then, is this Other inside him whose poisoned compliance risks realizing the unreal? A little later, in Paris, a strange experience enables him to discover it—it is his body. In *Novembre* he goes on at length and repeatedly about his abstinence. He *wills* it. And in the most radical way. An impecunious student goes to bed with grisettes—as Ernest does—or with whores. Gustave means to pass up both. And abstinence is not enough for him, there must be a total absence of desires in him. Making love hastily for four sous is

617

relieving a need—and needs, as we know, horrify him. Early on, plagued by sex, he dreams of cutting off his balls: "[Louis Lambert] wants to castrate himself. At nineteen, in the midst of my Paris boredom, I had this wish as well (I will show you, in the rue Vivienne, a shop where I once stopped, seized by this idea with an imperious intensity)."[68] And then the desire disappears: Flaubert says at the time that the law killed it: "The law puts me in a state of moral castration strange to conceive." *Moral*, certainly: literary impotence, indifference toward everything that formerly moved him, in particular toward books. But the *physical* soon gets into the act. We read in the Goncourts' *Journal:* "Yesterday, Flaubert told me: I did no fucking from the age of twenty to twenty-two because I had promised myself not to fuck."[69] Which is explained and confirmed by a letter to Louise: "I loved a woman . . . until the age of twenty without telling her, without touching [her]; and I was almost three more years without feeling my sex. For a moment I thought that I would die this way."[70] This last text, still quite close to the period in question, insists on the experienced, suffered aspect of this anorexia—Flaubert says clearly to Louise: I thought I had no more desire, you are the one who awakened me. His confidence to the Goncourts emphasizes—a bit too heavy-handedly—the *voluntary* aspect of this abstinence: "I had promised myself not to fuck." Gustave in 1863 is playing a role: he wants to prove that he can control his needs. Be that as it may, when we compare these three citations it seems that his impotence is *intentional:* it corresponds on the sexual level to the stupefaction Gustave intentionally affects when he opens his Code. Furthermore, there is only one intention which—in two different domains—is replayed by the body with similar docility: as passive activity, if Flaubert can't rebel, he wants to *swoon;* through the provoked stupor he refuses the "trivial" condition imposed on him, and through frigidity he refuses the "mean" life he would lead if desire were no more than a need. No more needs, no more intelligence: to be nothing. His body realizes in 1842 what he wished for after the failure of *Smarh.* Indeed, considered on the level of sexuality, the negative enterprise has immediate results, complete and lasting. It is as if the organism, with a slight delay, were penetrated by these castrating intentions, had assumed and realized them spontaneously. Gustave explicitly acknowledges these in-

68. To Louise, 27 December 1852.
69. *Journal,* 2 November 1863.
70. To Louise, 8 August 1846.

tentions as his own: yet this docility disturbs him. In 1863, he tries to rationalize the event: he speaks to the Goncourts of voluntary chastity and not of anorexia. But his confidences to Louise still bear traces of his disarray. A surgeon's son, he is—we can believe—highly informed about the anatomy and physiology of sex; he knows how one gets an erection and how one ejaculates, that is, he *also* knows these phenomena *in exteriority,* as the *inhuman, of which man is made.* These are chain reactions, nothing more; excessive chastity is an accumulation of energy; once beyond the alarming level, this energy will dispense itself in a violent discharge: here we have the need, the nocturnal emissions, and, with a little luck, coitus. And in front of Gustave's eyes this rigorous and nonsignifying process is transformed into discourse. The silence of "that brave genital organ" is a *speech,* the flesh signifies. But the signification, here, is not separable from a real work: in his interior monologue, in his letters, Gustave speaks of castrating himself; he speaks of it *in order not to do it,* disarming the future act by describing it as a *possible.* And the body *does not know possibility:* castration can become a corporal discourse only by realizing itself as a fatality. For this reason it is an oracular language, effective but maliciously indeterminate. The death of sex is a signifying fact; it is said to Gustave: you desired it, here it is. As a result, Gustave thinks that he did not entirely desire it, or not this way. First of all, who will say whether it is provisional or definitive? Limited to a few years, it might have turned out all right. But, he says, "I thought for a moment that I would die this way." To lose his virility forever is to become an invalid, a subman. Besides, he doesn't like the way *they* took him at his word. What should he believe? he asks himself. Must we see in the body an obscure, confused thought which overflows and harms us because it takes our conscious desires literally and, for lack of understanding them, caricatures them? Or, on the contrary, is it from organic materiality that we learn our true options in their radical form? If the first hypothesis disturbs him, the second terrifies him: if I must read my intentions in the spontaneous comportments of my organism, Gustave says to himself, I must be inhabited by a self-destructive frenzy; when I dreamed of castration in front of the shop in the rue Vivienne, I saw it merely as a gesture appropriate to soothe my rage. Now I perceive that thought is not the mere representation of possibilities but that, through the play of corporal mediations, it is permanently an act. In other words, the body has no imagination, and my little dramas become real in it; my own truth, the flight into the imaginary, is forbidden me, or rather it is an appearance, for sooner or later I am organically conditioned by what I imagined. *I have emasculated myself:* in order to avoid debasing myself with random whores, I have chosen *against myself* to fall still lower through a curse that puts me beneath men. At any event, for Flaubert *corporal speech* bears witness to the existence of a black radicalism that torments him: the process is exactly the one we described just now with regard to boredom: it is the politics of the worst. One tries to escape from desire by rising above it, and one removes oneself from it only by falling below the level of man. One tries to be *nothing,* and precisely because of that one makes oneself into *something:* a failed man, a hominid, a child of man made to accede to the human condition and which a monstrous anomaly retains in a state of quasi-animality. In both cases, Flaubert has recourse to Reason to protect himself from the horror: the chastity, he says to the Goncourts, was voluntary; boredom, he writes in *Novembre,* is the result of a reasoned asceticism. But at the same time that he claims through his interpretations to maintain himself in *normality;* he senses that he has lost in advance, that he is not simply anomalous but is becoming truly abnormal. His experience of 1841–42 leaves a clearly pathological aftertaste: he was playacting brutishness, that's for sure. But it was not only habit that abruptly provoked boredom and "the resulting" apathy: the body produced it spontaneously, like a certain state of being savored, that settled in unexpectedly and disappeared without any explanation. Suddenly, arms, legs, and head *were putting themselves spontaneously* out of commission. And this happened at the very moment he had decided to "slog away" seriously. Similarly, in certain novels we encounter a loyal servant who seems to do nothing but obey. But gently, imperceptibly, out of hatred or perversity, by his way of fulfilling his master's commands with a little too much alacrity, just a little too quickly, or sometimes with a slight lag, carrying out the previous day's orders the moment they have just been repealed—but he has all the excuses, he *cannot* be conscious of his abrupt about-face—this valet leads the young son of the family to ruin, to vice, to irreparable degradation. The procedure is as simple as can be: *signifying* to the master his *ill will* as his truest nature, bringing him a glass of alcohol just as he has given up drinking. Gustave's body has chosen the same procedure. And he is certain that something is not right, for out of intermittent apathy and permanent anorexia it is the *soma* that signifies and the mind that becomes the signified.

Such is the underlying motive of the inquiry undertaken in the third part of *Novembre:* behind his superficial conduct of failure, which often becomes the will—equally superficial—to succeed, Gustave understands that a still obscure meaning has come to his experience: he is in danger, and dangerous to himself. For silent corporal speech signifies the mind itself (or the total person) insofar as an unexpected and certain future threatens it or, which amounts to the same thing, structures it. What frightens him, in any case, is the plasticity of his body. We shall see more clearly in the third part how passive activity, constituted by the first relations with the Other, is always supported by the organism's *active passivity*. It is at the point where the two meet that the phenomena of autosuggestion arise in certain persons—and Gustave is one of them. He is not unaware of his pithiatism: he will give Louise a rather good description of it: "You told me that I seriously loved that woman [Eulalie]. It is not true. Still, when I wrote to her, with my ability to move myself through the pen, I took my subject seriously. But *only while I was writing.* Many things that leave me cold, either when I see them or when others speak of them, arouse my enthusiasm, irritate me, wound me if I speak of them or especially if I write. This is one of the effects of my mountebank nature." [71] What follows is the anecdote about the journalist of Nevers. Of course, this confession dates from October 1846, and Flaubert at this date had all the time to reflect on the "nervous illness" that became manifest at Pont-l'Evêque in 1844. But a note from the *Souvenirs*, dated from 8 February 1841, confirms what he says about his relations with Eulalie Foucault: "I wrote a love letter in order to write, and not because I love. I certainly wish, however, that I could make myself believe in it; I love, I believe, by writing." In the light of this text we can better understand the quality of quasi-pathological autosuggestion in the *Erlebnis* of Trouville when, a year after Madame Schlésinger's departure, Flaubert evokes her at his side and conceives an *imaginary* love for her that he will call, in *Mémoires d'un fou*, a *finally true* love. No doubt; at the time of the *Mémoires* he was already conscious of manipulating himself. Only he is not at all afraid of himself: it is a simple game played by a child actor. No risks, he thinks. This is the practical affirmation of the predominance of the imaginary over the real, that's all. In 1842, everything changes: what fascinates him now, and doubles him, is that the unknown enemy, whose aggression he dreads and which manipulates him through his materiality, *can only be himself.* The course of lived experience is *directed*, he feels it. But it is guided neither by others nor by external events; he fears this already revealed

71. Letter to Louise already cited, *Correspondance* 1:362.

fury of his, which will one day be capable of hurling him down to the lowest rung. Has he vowed it? And what is the ego that is sworn to fall? The worst is that from time to time this foreshadowed collapse consciously fascinates him; he cannot then prevent himself from acting it out (systematic deculturation, imitation of idiots, of epileptics). This ludic conduct, he feels, functions as restitution and invocation. He is literally *tempted;* the body, manipulated by stupors and impotence, does not stop at revealing a manipulator; it designates in lucid will itself an obscure core of ill will. The heteronomy of the enslaved will may be merely superficial; perhaps its only function is to mask from him a patient and monstrous freedom that surrounds itself with a murky core in order to mask precise and rigorous operations; in this case, his disgust and his fear would merely be little dramas, or even epiphenomena destined to mask his underlying accord with the self. At other times, it is the opposite: he is led to his fall, he shrieks, he feels he is drowning. Gustave no longer has any means of distinguishing the mirage from the reality in this revolving ego that occupies him, since the horror of becoming a monster and the dizzying consent to the fall are by turns reflections and truth. To say, "I am two," is to make one more urgent attempt at reasoning. In this sense, the appearance of the second narrator corresponds to a healthy reflex: Gustave feels he is *going mad,* a sudden pause: he will go no further; the narrator breaks in two—above all, no compromises; "I" stands up above the groveling "he" by a flight of pride. With a gigantic effort he tears himself away from pithiatism to *choose* his Self. He is helped by the fact that in this month of September the failure so painful to his vanity has torn his concurrence to pieces: before his retrospective reflection Gustave conjures up a past in which he no longer believes. His purpose is less to understand himself than to know himself objectively in order to recuperate himself. For this reason, we see the second narrator do a clinical analysis of the neurotic troubles of the first. The doubling is a *fiat:* now, that's enough! Gustave decrees that he is a man of experience, at the end of a process which he describes with some severity. He preserves the same principles and the same passions, but he is quite committed to distancing himself from them, to thinking about them without living them: when he takes up his manuscript again, the will to cure himself and the will to succeed in December are one and the same. Thus the invention of the second storyteller is less a procedure than the preliminary to a therapeutic technique. After his failed suicide, Flaubert—belief and decision—thinks he will find himself *on the other side* of the proof; dry and sullen, under the protection of his family, entirely occupied with drawing up the balance sheet, having opted—at least provisionally—for one of the two contradictory futures that tear him apart (he will do his law degree efficaciously), denying the enchantments of passive complicity and considering them from the point of view of a rational and disenchanted activity, he enjoys a period of certain remission. Narrator no. 2 remains gloomy, but he is healthy. No doubt in his time he was familiar with the strayings of no. 1, but he is now surpassing them: we are not told toward what, nor is it known. All he has to do is rid himself of no. 1: if Gustave succeeds in liquidating him *in the work*, this fellow, he thinks, will no longer return to haunt him in life. It will be enough to choose a radical and literarily worthy means of eliminating him. But the choice is not that simple: the author hesitates, and his final option proves that, despite his firm resolution to be cured, he is convinced deep down that the illness is inexorably following its course.

The healthiest solution would be to shut him up in Charenton: this will be the fate reserved for the painter of *La Spirale*. Gustave will adopt it after the attack at Pont-l'Evêque, that is, at the time of *consensual* neurosis. But the third part of *Novembre* is denied neurosis. The doubling is a jump. In every detail of the inquiry, Flaubert has made the most of the neurotic aspect of his experience, but every time, as he is about to conclude, he does an about-face and, for example, translates what is psychosomatic in terms of pure *soma*. He no longer washes or opens the windows, stays prostrate all day long, empty, playing and suffering with dubious pleasure a growing brutishness that degrades him: these are the symptoms, and it is the author who gives them to us. But at the crucial moment of diagnosis he does an about-face and distracts our attention by a casually inserted comparison: "Like those people who watch themelves dying." Of course, we are not told that the hero is one of those people. No: he is simply like them. What is the difference? It is that—as the author says further on—"the organs are healthy." Curiously, about the same time, he contrived to reassure Caroline—who was not worried—by affirming to her that he was enjoying excellent health.[72] As if he wanted to dissipate his own anxieties. But what are they? If the organism is healthy, can one have the experience of dying? Of course, he wants to use a

---

72. Let us recall *Mémoires d'un fou*: "*Although in excellent health,* [I was suffering from] a nervous irritation . . ." And his way, later on, of boasting of "his vigors." He always tried to dissimulate his mental troubles by means of his *physical* health.

metaphor to render the increasing *lack of interest* he was feeling in 1841. But the one chosen shows that what is at issue is a process directed toward an end. In other words, death is invoked here as a screen image, it comes in the nick of time to mask the inexorable sliding toward mental decay or madness. It is a noble end: Gustave consents to desire it, to explain his behavior by his desire for it, but in the process of his inquiry he refuses to reveal the base aim of his project of collapse. Or, rather, he has revealed it but wants to keep his conclusions outside the discourse, in the obscure realm of the *unsayable*. Like those ladies who report to you in detail the inexplicable behavior that one of your friends is supposed to have adopted toward them—he never stops looking at them, he pays them little attentions, etc., etc.—and when you conclude, out of goodwill: "Well, he is in love with you," they reply, dumbfounded: "But you are mad! Not a chance! I am giving you the facts, that's all." The real message he addresses to himself is thus blocked by another. But as always happens in such cases, the words of the second message lose their original meaning and are replaced by the words of the first. In context, "death" signifies "neurosis," as we shall see.

Flaubert's hero is "born with the desire to die." He adds: "Nothing seemed more foolish to me than life and more shameful than to cling to it." Here we have death raised to the rank of fundamental end. And right away, through tactical and defensive generalization, he declares: "Man loves death with a devouring love." We know that for him, this love situates itself at the level of religious impulses; must we conclude that had Freud read *Novembre*, he would have found in it the prefiguration of his "death wish"? Let us allow Flaubert to speak: "Almost all children act the same way and seek to kill themselves in their games." A rather arbitrary affirmation if intended as universal (although the young man had seen, profoundly, that such death games exist the world over), but a penetrating remark if applied to Gustave alone: from childhood he played at dying, but death was merely the imaginary purpose of a game. Besides, he adds: "As a child, I desired [death] only to know it." Which indeed sheds light on the ludic side of his suicidal behavior, for death is the unknowable. In order to know it, one would have to survive it. And this is just what he is seeking.

The young hero tells us very clearly that he is awaiting his decease—the cessation of his sufferings. Its entirely negative function is therefore to suppress the evil that birth has created:

It is so sweet to imagine that one no longer exists! There is such calm in all cemeteries! There, stretched out and wrapped in a shroud . . . the centuries pass without . . . waking you . . . How many times in the chapels of cathedrals have I contemplated those long statues of stone lying on the tombs! . . . One would say they are sleeping, savoring their death. To have no more need to weep, to feel no more those swoons in which it seems that everything is broken, like rotted scaffolding, that is the ultimate happiness . . . And then perhaps one enters a more beautiful world . . . Oh no, I prefer to believe that one is quite dead, that nothing leaves the coffin: and that if one must still feel something it would be one's own nothingness, that death feeds on itself and admires itself; just enough life to feel that one no longer exists.

No more suffering, but also the consciousness of no more suffering. The evocation of eternal life is touched upon only to be vigorously swept aside. Death must be savored: this is ataraxia. But above all it is the suppression of the primary temporal ek-stasis, the relation to the future. Passive activity bespeaks its deep desire to be pure passivity. One preserves in memory "just enough life to feel that one no longer exists." This is maintaining the relation to the past, recrimination, but the become-nothingness remembers its previous sufferings merely to rejoice at no longer being affected by them. No one can act on him: reclining, he is matter triumphant and conscious of itself in its inflexible inertia. So narrator no. 1 is seeking not to realize a total abolition of his person but to change himself into a pure and empty present that has its future behind it. Under these conditions, are we not forcibly reminded of the cry of the *Mémoires:* "I wish I were old, and had white hair"? Death, here, is synonymous with old age; Gustave asks two things of it: superannuation (he has *obeyed*, he is freed of all obligation) and ataraxia (no more desires, therefore no more suffering). But this onset of premature old age is itself highly suspect. The old man of twenty, incapable of feeling, decrepit, utterly passive, who does nothing but meditate on his past, strongly resembles the idiot Flaubert fears he wants to become. In the letters to Louise, written after the attack at Pont-l'Evêque, Gustave uses both metaphors interchangeably in order to communicate his suffering: "You did not want to believe me when I told you that I was old. Alas, yes! . . . if you knew all the internal forces that have drained me." And: "It is a phantom and not a man you were addressing." "He who is living now and is me does nothing but contemplate the other, who is dead." Is it death or senility he is describing? Calm, without passions, without regrets, hasn't this "peaceful pool" "just enough life to feel that it no longer exists," like the reclining statues he envied in 1842? And when he speaks of his emptiness, of the passion he devotes to contemplating it, isn't he defining the landowner who, after forty years of labor, lives in ataraxia and idleness? In truth, neither state is the point: the two images—which are interchangeable—aim to *signify* the neurosis.

More striking still is the kind of end Flaubert invents for his character. He has given up the idea of assigning him a voluntary death—out of honesty, after the failed suicide of September. However, since he denies him madness, he will not be rid of him without killing him off. And it is time to wrap up the story. It hardly matters: "Finally, last December, he died, but slowly, little by little, solely by the power of thought, without any organic illness, the way people die of sadness." It is a dream rather than an affirmation, for he acknowledges in the following line that this end will seem "marvelous," especially to people who have greatly suffered. Indeed, several years later he will explain to Louise that our passions are too mediocre for us to die of sorrow. Be that as it may, at the time he is tracing these words on the last page of the manuscript, he still believes that the thing is possible. At least for certain men who have lived out the human condition to the end. At least for him. And the "thought" in question, here, is the very thing Gustave spoke about in the *Mémoires* when he declared: "My life is a thought." It refers not simply to an idea but to a totalitarian synthesis of ideative processes and of affectivity: it is lived experience itself at the end of a grueling and despairing experience insofar as it comprises at once the ancient desire for death and the progressively acquired certainty that man is impossible; let us add a certain lassitude of the imagination ("What to do? what to dream?"). What is new, however, is that this thought is given an explicitly *physical* force. In fact, it easily replaces a pistol or a knife. Better still, it takes the protagonist in complete health and kills him without damaging any organ: the heart ceases to beat, that is all. This passage is elliptical—and rich in proportion to its obscurity. Is this strange power an external characteristic of thought—a permanent action of thought on the organism, a usury that thought produces from birth and that leads to biological death? Or must the "force," in order to manifest itself, wait for the interior totalization to be nearly concluded? And, in this case, what is the precise role of the subject? This last question will seem legitimate if we recall that "thought" for Gustave, greatly overflowing the realm of concepts and judgments, is identified with lived experience. One can therefore ask oneself whether totalization is achieved by the annihilation of itself and without the hero having really intended to die, or, on the other hand, whether the hero concentrates his reflection on the impossibility of living with the express intention of compelling his body to draw from itself the inevitable consequence.

Gustave offers no answer. Indeed, he has willed this ambiguity. The comparison he makes is not enlightening, quite the contrary: "The way people die of sadness," he says. And we recall the death of Madame de Rênal.[73] She, at least, was truly sad: she suffered the death of her lover like an external act of violence, it broke her heart. The hero of *Novembre*, however, is not even affected: so that we might understand his suspect demise, his death is *compared* to those deaths that are provoked by sorrow. What is involved is the realization, rigorous but painless (after such unhappiness), of the impossibility of living. "He wrote no longer and thought more," we are told. Which would presuppose a strong intentional concentration, a mental exercise. It is true that the narrator adds: "He judged it proper to stop complaining, proof perhaps that he truly began to suffer." But the troubles he subsequently describes can arouse neither physical pain nor moral suffering in the one who experiences them. Anguish, certainly, and disgust with living, nothing more.

The richness and obscurity of this paragraph have been willed by Flaubert himself. And they serve merely to translate his own hesitations in the face of a new experience. Indeed, what could have prompted him to invent this "death by thought," which he himself says will be "difficult" to believe in "for people who have greatly suffered"? There can be only one motive: he is trying less to imagine a fictive end to an autobiographical work than to express through words and images a disturbing intuition. We are struck, when we re-read this passage, by the body's incredible docility. What? No organ is affected and yet, when the hero is convinced of the impossibility of living, the entire organism *realizes* his conviction by suspending its functions? When Gustave writes, "which will seem difficult . . . but must be tolerated in a novel, for love of the marvelous," he is making fun of us—the marvelous hardly attracts him and would be singularly jarring at the end of a realistic *roman intime*, a thinly disguised autobiography. If he pretends to have been seduced by the strangeness of this directed dying, we can be sure that he wants to lead us astray and give what is *true* the color of falsehood. He is not dead, that is a fact,

---

73. Flaubert will not read *Le Rouge et le Noir* until 1845.

but he *believes* people can die this way—something he could not even imagine at the time of the *Mémoires d'un fou* (or it would have served as an elegant and economical ending). This flexibility of the body is something he is very familiar with; he knows that the organism, assuming the negative idea, turns it into an inert, material negation. By pushing this docility to the limit, why wouldn't the organism materialize the radicalized negation simply by resigning from *all* its functions? Hence we can understand the intentional ambiguity of this conclusion. "The power of thought" is not, cannot be, the power of the thinker. He would have commanded his organism in vain, it would have obeyed only in the areas where the central nervous system commands the striated muscles. But strictly organic and vegetative life would not be modified for all that. On the other hand, Flaubert believed he understood in these last months that if one is penetrated by a thought, if, without ever abandoning it or trying to realize it through a sovereign fiat, one continues to ponder it, it descends into the body *unknown to us* and becomes, muddled but recognizable, a law of organic life. And that is true for him, for a passive agent. In this case, indeed, meditation is already *suffered*, it installs itself, it occupies, and this persistence is quickly sustained by the active passivity of the organism. Or, if you will, in cases of autosuggestion, "thought" has two faces: it is consciously lived as passive activity because it is realized as active passivity in the very functions of life; and, conversely, the conscious effort to *believe in it*, to make it a vital determination of the person, accelerates its organic realization. I have said that it all happens *unbeknownst* to the pithiatic subject; but it must be understood that this unknowingness is not unaware, it is an intentional unknowningness that is *playacted* as the necessary condition of the process. In the depths of this reflexive intimacy, meditative thought *conceals itself* and by the same token *senses* that it is *suffered*, that without the body's docility it would remain imaginary, that it finds its *seriousness* and its reality in the way the organism receives it and, by comforming to it, gives it a dimension of *nonthought*. These remarks allow us to understand why Gustave chose a "marvelous" end for his hero.

Not much is known about the end he was imagining before February 1842. For the young "madman" of the *Mémoires* had survived. I suspect that at the moment of conception, Gustave wanted to leave us guessing: after all, the author, like his character, aspired to die and lived on. His work was supposed to be read like a manuscript slipped into a bottle and thrown into the sea. In any case, the first narrator of *Novembre* is initially conceived to signal the *impossibility of living*. Gustave quite effectively describes the contradiction between Great Desire and passive activity; he declares to us at once: "Have I loved? Have I hated? Have I searched for something? I doubt it still: I have lived outside of all movement, all action, without bestirring myself either for glory or for pleasure, for knowledge or for money," and "I would have liked to be emperor, to have absolute power." Which leads him to conclude, "I found nothing that was worthy of me, I found myself equally suitable for nothing"—an admirable definition of that perpetual rending that is negative pride. Flaubert's resolution is simple: a great man *manqué* can create a masterpiece, he says to himself, if he frankly exposes the reasons for his failure. This will be *Novembre:* "I was neither pure enough nor strong enough for anything." Someone has thought *this,* and no one knows what has become of him. The most likely thing is that we were hearing a voice from the dead, but it is not impossible that he is lost in the crowd, that he is still living and is, for example, a notary in Lower Brittany. In any case, Gustave expressly saw *Novembre* as *his* swan song: the unique testimony of a man torn between the infinite grandeur of his desires and the paltriness of his means—torn as we all are, or *ought to be*. At the outset, he thought to draw talent from his misfortune and write an extraordinary but buried book: the narrative of a total failure written brilliantly by the failed man himself. The great man *manqué* was becoming a true great man, time to take an inventory of what he had lacked. By a common reversal of thought, he thought to draw something positive from the negative itself. But this, of course, was a literary testament: the last page written, he applied himself to his studies and became a barrister or judge. Swallowed up, lost in the provincial crowd, incapable of rising above it except through imagination, he would continue to live, retrospectively justified by a masterpiece that would prevent him, whatever he did, from letting himself be entirely defined by his profession. A genius affirms himself and disappears, saying: "I am too small for myself."

Six months later, everything changes: *first of all,* he persuades himself that his new work is lacking, he perceives *subsequently* that his illness is *mental:* in the third part of *Novembre* he carefully describes the progress of his neurosis, but he presents it as the symptoms of actual dying. For death is a noble end. This falsification is all the easier for him as the second narrator is basically in agreement with the first, convinced that he has neither the desire nor the capacity to live, and although he wants to define himself in his objective particularity, he persists in thinking that the world has made him unviable, that he is living in Hell. In this sense, his troubles appear to him sometimes as the effects of his own intentions and sometimes as the only justifiable way of existing in a wicked universe. *Objectively*—this is the point of view of no. 2—his anomaly is the neurotic way he lives the disproportion between his desires and his capacities; it threatens to structure itself as neurosis, and the neurotic intention is to bring the process to a close with insanity. But *subjectively* (retrospective reflection remains, despite appearances, a complicit reflection), the ends are not rejected: the second narrator, as we have seen, must have them in order to comprehend the first. From this point of view, the Romantic "all or nothing," the refusal to be *something* or *someone*, must be lived as the progressive realization of death. Thus, *subjectively*, apathy is an imitation of death, an ascesis, and a real moment of dying; *objectively*, it is the real moment of a neurosis that is quite particular and structured as an enterprise by the intention to flee from unbearable tasks into insanity. *Subjectively*, ataraxia simply manifests the disappearance of desire in the face of the mediocrity of the desirable (this was already one of the two possible interpretations of Almaroës), and as desire defines man, it barely precedes burial. Besides, the presentiment of death is merely the present ataraxia dreaming of itself, like an external consciousness of nothingness; *objectively*, on the other hand, ataraxia is merely anorexia, and this apathetic anorexia is a certain psychosomatic state which reproduces itself spontaneously and intentionally *in a certain man*. *Subjectively*, the journey toward death is merely the necessary relation of microcosm to macrocosm, the abolition of the first being the totalization of and solution to the contradictions of the second; at issue is a metaphysical attitude. *Objectively*, the foreseen and sought-after insanity expresses nothing about the relation of the individual to the world; it is the way that one individual, characterized by a certain anomaly, tries to resolve the contradictions that tear him apart. We shall find again later, in January 1844, this double aspect of lived experience. Let us observe here that subjectivity and its objectification are indissolubly linked in the person of Gustave, and that each one is penetrated by the other. His subjectivity slips into his attempt to objectify himself and replaces the ignoble end with the most aristocratic one. Conversely, the objectifying tendency ensures that the noble end, in its strangeness, can pass itself off as merely a futile disguise of the vile world.

There was a time when he found glory in being "a madman"; his anomaly, at that time, remained insufficiently determined: madness, genius, who could say? From the first pages of the *Mémoires*, remonstrating that the microcosm is at once the product of the macrocosm and its image, he secretly made his delirium the expression of his genius. In February 1842, he lost his illusions; others found the means to tell the world. If he were sinking into madness, he would not bear witness beneath an empty sky to the human hell but only to his own contradictions. It would no longer be a question of a specific event, indicating to the human race that man is impossible, but of a singular shipwreck, a nonsignifying accident. This could pass if it were due to external causes—a case of meningitis, a bad fall—but what is unbearable is the dizzying idea that a sly intention sustains the entire process. Mental decay is a fall; death too, but it is the common destiny and, further, it is consecrated—all the more aristocratic if it appears as the logical conclusion of the refusal to live, a categorical imperative that must impose itself on everyone. He feels himself slipping toward an ignoble mutation, inquires, understands, and at the last moment substitutes necrosis for neurosis. By rationalizing, the intention will appear clearly: in 1842 he grasps the teleological structure of the troubles that are leading him slowly but surely to imbecility, but he wants to see it as merely a provisional moment; he must pass through this stagnation in order to realize "death by thought," the become-truth and radicalization of his neurosis. Conversely, however, he cannot prevent it from appearing to him as his near and real objective, relegating the dying to the attic of comparisons. By hiding from himself the true nature of the troubles he detects, by regarding that imaginary construct, "death by thought," as a borderline case of autosuggestion, he ingenuously admits to himself that the fundamental structure of his neurosis is pithiatism, and to cure himself of it he outdoes his suggestibility by aspiring *to die of hysteria* and thus favoring his slide toward idiocy.

Let us recall Kafka's *Metamorphosis*. Gregor Samsa, transformed into an insect, runs across the ceiling: this vile being, without ever attaining the natural perfection of a cockroach, no longer has anything but a muddled memory in common with the bureaucracy whose last avatar he is, a memory less legible each day. Shame and unhappiness are all that's left. I have not chosen the example at random: Kafka loved Flaubert and cites him often; both writers suffered from an abusive father. In Kafka's narrative, remorse and resentment are inseparable. And, ultimately, what does he describe? The *crisis*. What

Kafka dreads but will never fall victim to—immunized against it by the tuberculosis that killed him—is precisely what Flaubert manages for himself. We divine Gustave's intention when we reread *The Metamorphosis:* that horrid beast who dies of shame and plunges his family into disgrace, guilty, punished, innocent victim of his family, that utterly repulsive beast is an excellent symbol of the dreadful unknown person he is preparing to become *by means of the crisis.* Something is going to happen to him, something terrible—death, old age, it doesn't matter what it is called. The main thing is that he will be *other.* Other and degraded. The muddy flow of his life rolls toward this inevitable fall: he is awaited by a being that he must become, that will not be him and that will say: myself. Other and born of an Other, otherness will destroy his new existence. Horrified, Gustave sees the moment and place of his metamorphosis into an insect approaching. He is all the more certain of his final tumble since the fall has already begun. *Novembre:* a life tragically illuminated by the evident necessity of an early death; a death inexorably woven into *estrangement* by life itself; an already foreseen survivor, this phantom: nothingness become subject by the annihilation of subjectivity; nonbeing deliberately confused with the lucid consciousness of no longer being—a train hurtling toward that ultimate confusion, the crisis, where the irreversible metamorphosis of one form of life into another—imbecility—proffers itself in advance as the abolition of the living. Here we have the unbearable truth: the young man will not escape the demands of his family without rendering himself forever incapable of fulfilling them; in other words, the way out is not into Heaven but into Hell; he must plunge, he will plunge. He knows it, but he tries for the last time to give a funereal luster to his fall by styling it a passing on. From 1842 on, Gustave has the subjective certainty that he is hastening toward the worst unhappiness, and that he when he gets there he will lose if not his skin at least the integrity of his being: the ultimate metamorphosis haunts him, invisible but inevitable, he is as good as changed already. Above all, it already presents itself as a direct relation of the subject to himself, of the psyche to the soma without foreign intervention; this relation is totalizing and conclusive: a complete experience is realized in it and burns itself out. In short, the neurosis is actual and the crisis potential. Still, after the incubation period, the crisis must be actualized in its turn. This will be Pont-l'Evêque. Of course, the man will not die: the impossibility of living did not kill Gustave. Nonetheless, his life leads him toward public collapse, his unique and strict duty toward himself, his unbearable destiny.

1842–1843: Remission

The manuscript is completed; Gustave seems liberated, as after a course of psychotherapy. What has he learned about himself? Nothing very definite, but in general a confused truth: I have neither the desire to live nor the desire to kill myself; my cunning efforts to reduce myself to *nothing* will only result in my diminishment. It is enough for him to glimpse this eventuality to reject it. The liquidation of his hero *on paper* seems to him a symbolic liberation: he has gone, through writing and in imagination, to the very end of himself, to senility in the guise of a death "by thought." This oneiric satiation is accompanied by a voluntarist reaction: enough morose complacency, I shall take my exam, do my four years of law school, and *only then* will I renounce the active life.

In the beginning, everything goes splendidly. Of course, he does not cease to rage against the law: "I want to tell the Law School to go to hell, once and for all, and I never want to set foot in it again. Sometimes I have such cold sweats I could die. My God, what a good time I am having in Paris and what an agreeable student life I am leading."[74] Curiously, a short time before the exam he assimilates his angers and his stupors: "It cannot go on much longer like this. I will end by falling into a state of idiocy and fury. This evening, for example, I am experiencing both of those pleasant states of mind simultaneously."[75]

Be that as it may, his very rages and anxieties are proof that he takes it upon himself and succeeds, with perhaps excessive zeal,[76] to do violence to his "nature"; superficial pride triumphs, passive activity surpasses itself and produces a fury of activism. The results are excellent; shortly before the exam, he writes to Caroline: "I am breathing a little easier now, and I regard my affair as almost concluded. I am joyful, jocular . . . I see myself arriving in Rouen on Tuesday morning . . . If I don't pass, no one can boast of passing, for I believe I know my first year of law as well as anyone."[77] He does pass, not brilliantly but without difficulty, and rejoins his family. As his first "attack" will take place in January 1844, we can say that from his anguish in September

74. To Caroline, November 1842, *Correspondance* 1:122.
75. To Caroline, December 1842, *Correspondance* 1:123.
76. "Last Wednesday, I forced myself not to go to bed." It is characteristic of passive constitutions that, in extreme cases, they conceive of activity only in the form of "forcing."
77. To Caroline, December 1842, *Correspondance* 1:126.

until the "mathematical result" of his neurosis, he will enjoy *an apparent* respite of fourteen months.

Fear, we know, has dammed the torrent that was leading him toward collapse. But it is not the only barrier: there is also, and especially, the fact that for the first time in five years he is not dissatisfied with a work coming from his pen. It is true that it will not be published[78] in his lifetime, but he has decided that an author must never speak of himself. As I have said, it still pleased him as a man in his forties to have his friends read it. If the middle-aged man still thought so highly of this disguised autobiography, one can imagine the enthusiasm of the adolescent who, in October 1842, had just completed it. The wager was kept: the great man *manqué* had made his failure the source and subject of a masterpiece. And there is no doubt that *Novembre* manifests a great advance over the previous writings; for the first time we encounter Flaubert's major theme in all its complexity. In the *Mémoires,* the accent was on the inadequacy of the real; a great soul was defined in terms of the depth of its dissatisfaction. In 1841 Gustave is discontented with himself: he wanted to be the *Artist* and thinks that he has fallen short; henceforth it seems to him that passion is not enough, one must also have capability. Consequently, his character gains in complexity: he is both big and small. This mediocrity is not saved by the force of his desires: quite to the contrary, it kills him, making him feel all the more his incapacity to satisfy those desires. Or, if you will, the flight into the imaginary is exposed as a strategy: he has symphonies in his head but understands nothing about music; in short, he plays at being a man with symphonies his head. In a sense, the unreal remains the supreme value, but by the same token it denounces the impotence of the real man who is incapable of engraving it on reality. Lacking the artistic act, the imaginary is merely insubstantial. Who will judge the unhappy hero of this adventure? No one, since he is simultaneously all and nothing. And this is just what Flaubert wants: to conduct his trial and let the jury of his peers, when the time comes to issue a verdict, acknowledge his incompetence. Alone, perhaps, the great artists of past times, Shakespeare, Rabelais . . . In short, Gustave is enchanted: by taking up his "sentimental ragout," by inventing the second narrator and thereby restoring the first narrator's infinite desire as an objective and determined character trait, he has saved his work *in extremis.* He has

78. He writes in 1853: "Ah, how far-seeing I was in my youth not to publish it. How it would make me blush now!"

even given it *a form:* the passage from no. 1 to no. 2 and the abrupt transformation of subject into object, the formal structure of the novel, *"indirectly express"* the author's thought, make us see the contradiction of this unhappy consciousness without saying it.

This success has the effect of prolonging the crisis. From February to August, the consent to take up a profession was an acknowledgment that, apart from his dreams, he was made of the same stuff as the bourgeoisie and had no other mandate than to be useful to society, to become one of the means society requires to perpetuate itself as it is. Against this perfectly deserved destiny, against the rigorous adaptation of his future duties to his merits, he was passively trying to protect himself by becoming *nothing,* and it was on this level that the organization of neurosis began. Now, he is the *artist,* he has proved it to himself: he escapes his fatalities *from the inside;* this means that he has ceased to deserve his "trivial" future because of his inadequacies. Certainly his father has not repealed his decisions; but since these are no longer justified by an original taint, they merely indicate the regrettable obstinacy of a respected adult. The idiosyncratic determination by Achille-Cléophas, ceases to be something dreaded when Gustave no longer combines it with the paternal curse, in other words, when he no longer feels that curse as the very essence of lived experience. Consequently, his neurotic resistances decrease: he must first succeed and then speak to the Father; it goes without saying that the Code remains a deadly bore, but it is no longer unintelligible, and Gustave's memory no longer refuses to register the articles.

Buried, however, the neurosis persists: sexual anorexia is reinforced. And then, toward the end of November 1842, we see the appearance of a suspect toothache, the same one that will recur, opportunely, in July of '43: "This is nothing but tooth trouble, and the tears that come to my eyes in the worst bouts of pain are not comparable to the atrocious spasms I get from the charming science I am studying."[79] A very significant passage: this strict comparison of physical pain with psychological malaise inclines us to think that the dental "neuralgia" would be categorized with what we call today "psychic pains." It torments him, moreover, only in the uncertain period when he has forced himself to work blindly and without being certain of the result. As soon as the future becomes clear, it disappears.

After the exam, the future is doubly assured: he has *Novembre* behind him, and he has proved to all the Ernests of the Law School, to

79. *Correspondance* 1:122.

his parents, and to himself that in the "active life" he could be as successful as the others if he wanted to take the trouble. So he returns to Greek and Latin, "cuts" his classes, and undertakes a new novel: the first *Education*. For Gustave, this is a moment of equilibrium— one of the few he has ever known. Wild as he was in 1842, he even goes so far as to "dine in town," visits the Colliers, the Schlésingers, Pradier, Vasse, Doctor Cloquet, etc. It is around this time, also, that his friendship with Maxime begins. But this apparent stability is slightly disquieting. "Since the month of January I have been living rather peacefully, inclined to do Greek, tracing out here and there a few lines of Latin so as not to read French, saying that I am going to the Law School and not setting foot in it." His experience of the preceding year seems to have taught him nothing. Doesn't he know that he needs *a lot of time* and *persistence* to succeed in his studies just because they are repugnant to him? In the same letter, however, he says: "In one month, it will be time to think about another exam." But he is quite determined not to prepare for it before the beginning of April and describes himself "doing literature and art every hour of the day and night, yawning, doubting, dawdling and fantasticating." On Saturday, 8 April, he leaves for Rouen; it is Easter vacation. On his return, he once more finds his room in the rue de l'Est, and "on [his] table the law books [he] had left there." But not until 11 May does he announce to his sister that he has set to work. In a word, from December to May he has taken four months to "toughen up." Unconsciousness? No: the fear does not leave him, it poisons his "*dolce farniente.*" In February, in the midst of his peaceful little life, he complains of carrying "the Law School on his shoulders." And in March: "another exam. It's like hammers on an anvil; when one stops, the other starts up. And I'm the anvil." The future is always there, threatening: it is as if he were refusing to profit from his experience and were repeating, at a year's distance, the ploy of passive resistance.

During this calm, moreover, he does not cease to rage; but his anger has found another object; he complains bitterly of his poverty: "the joyful student feeds himself for thirty-five sous at Barilhaut's . . . This joker of a student *loves* grisettes with chilblains on their hands . . . When he has paid his tailor, his shoemaker, his bookseller, the Law School, his janitor, his café, his restaurant . . . he has nothing left, he has a head full of worry."[80] According to Du Camp, Flaubert senior forked over a decent allowance to his son. But "alone in his room,

80. To Ernest, 10 February, *Correspondance* 1:129.

with Ducaurroy, Lagrange and Boileux," Gustave is racked by his usual tormenter, envy: "On the other side of the tracks, there is a youth with thirty thousand francs who goes about in a carriage, *his carriage*"; he is ashamed of his "greasy frockcoat," his "three-year-old black suit." Between the mediocrity of his life and the vulgarity of his studies he establishes a reciprocity of perspective.

Novembre gave him a respite but not the cure. If Gustave can now regard his work as a masterpiece, he is also compelled by the subject itself to see it as his testament. As we have said, it is the story of a failure. It draws its power from its radicalism: the unsuccessful man dies of failure, a martyr to the impossibility of living. And although Gustave survives, in a way he has killed himself since he will later say to Louise that *Novembre* is the *last work* of his youth. Something is just finished: through this new interior totalization he has said everything he was trying to say since *Agonies;* in a word, he is emptied out. It is true that he is sketching out the first *Education:* he worked on it more than a month during the winter of 1843, and it was surely the under-lying reason for his "calmness." But what does he put into it? Ini-tially—at this very time—Henry was the hero: "At first I only had the idea [for the character] of Henry. The need for a contrast led me to conceive that of Jules." Had he already projected his protagonist's final transformation into a bourgeois? I am inclined to believe it, though there is nothing to suggest it in the first two-thirds of the novel, and the author embodies himself in each character by turns. Henry's fate was sealed by February 1843 because Flaubert wanted to illustrate this "axiom": whoever you are, whatever your initial ap-titudes, success will kill your soul, you will become bourgeois. Henry is not antipathetic at the outset; moreover, in his way he tries to es-cape the future that has been set out for him. Naive, intelligent, ca-pable of passion, this boy has the sole defect of being attractive to women: he wins the heart of Madame Emilie (E as in Elisa, LIE as in Eulalie); lives a fine love story; has the luck to travel and then, back in Paris, to find a job and money. There he is, doomed: this, Gustave sometimes thinks, is the future that awaits me; this is how romantic adolescents are processed and turned into "worldly people" with fine, cold, and skeptical minds.

Jules—a "great man *manqué*"—becomes important only in the sum-mer of '44, after the crisis, when Gustave has opened his manuscript again. In February '43 he was of no account, and the reason is clear: it had been scarcely three months since Gustave completed *Novembre;* he had said *everything* there was to say about the big-hearted failure.

In order to go further—as he will do in the admirable chapters that conclude the first *Education*—his neurosis will have to transform him by radicalizing itself. *Novembre* put the accent on failure; at the time of its conception, *L'Education sentimentale* is intended to be its counterpart: this time the anomaly is suppressed, we are given an *adapted* man whose very adaptation is the original taint and becomes his destiny. I believe we can discern in Gustave at the outset a proud and aggressive reaction to his own admissions: "I said in *Novembre* that I was good for nothing but to die. But hang on, you lottery winners, don't go believing you are better than me; whatever your intentions, you will end up as grocers." The choice between "succeeding and debasing oneself" or "miscarrying and losing face" forever torments him. When he begins *L'Education*, he knows quite well that he is not doing anything new, that he is going to treat the same theme but by approaching it from the other side. Of course, the second narrator's stern inquiry developed Flaubert's taste for the "telling little fact"; the time for lyricism is past, now comes the time for detail: through Henry's impressions he will detail his own experience of Parisian life, he will minutely describe the birth and progress of his love for Madame Emilie. This new concern, this new writing, gives him some pleasure. Let us not forget, however, his groaning later on, at the time of *Madame Bovary*, over the base triviality of his protagonists. Is it credible that he can be interested in this son of a bourgeois, the lover of a bourgeois woman, who after a lark becomes bourgeois in his turn? It must be admitted that Henry is extremely mediocre; we hardly notice his faults, but he is lacking in the *negative*: rage, hatred, envy, unhappiness, the frantic dramatizing, the pithiatism, everything that makes up the author's powerful personality—and will be retrieved in Emma. When Henry embodies Flaubert, Flaubert has chosen to resemble everyone, to have the reactions of all young provincials who study in Paris, all amorous youths. Reading this life is rather boring, and it must have been boring to write. In fact, Gustave took little pleasure in it, as we see well enough from the objective judgments that he subsequently levied with cold severity on his work. During the winter of '43, somewhat reassured by the quality of *Novembre* but tormented by the fear of having nothing more to say, he writes by sheer momentum, just to continue writing, waiting for inspiration to be reborn, without enthusiasm and without much confidence in what he is doing. *L'Education* is something more than an exercise, but he certainly does not see it as his justification. And when he returns to the worries, the urgency, the imminence of the second exam, the work in progress—provisionally abandoned—remains too thin, too slight to compensate for his anguish. He has said everything the previous year, he feels empty and finds himself facing the same dangers as in 1842.

No sooner has he put himself back in harness than everything begins again. First, the jeremiads: "I am so irritated, so annoyed so furious that I often have to whip myself up so as not to let myself fall into discouragement." The stupors follow: "Montaigne said: 'We must grow stupid in order to grow wise.' I am always so stupefied that this can pass for wisdom and even for virtue." Time is inexorably running out; Gustave has the feeling he is losing it: "Sometimes, I have the desire to pound my fist on my writing table and send everything flying; then, when the fit has passed, I perceive by my timepiece that I have lost half an hour in jeremiads, and I set myself once more to blackening the paper and turning pages more quickly than ever."[81] In June he returns to the charge:

> I am still going to class, but I no longer listen; it is *time lost*. I have too much of it, I am drunk on it . . . The hatred I bear for the science flows, I believe, over those who teach it, unless it is the other way around. While waiting, I am working like a desperado to take my exam as early and as well as possible. But anyone who could see me when I am alone, injecting all the French of the civil Code into my brain and savoring the poetry of the procedural Code, could boast of having seen something lamentably grotesque.[82]

Rejecting all synthesizing activity, as he did the previous year, he scatters himself and drowns in details: "I have begun to study for my exam with too many details, so that now I am burdened by them." To such an extent that his toothache "returns, even more resplendent," and compels him to measure time's "coefficient of adversity, during the day by preventing me from working, at night by preventing me from sleeping."[83] However, "Toirac does not think that my rotten teeth are the only cause. According to him, it's neuralgia; in effect, I have perfectly sound teeth which cause me horrible pains."[84] The

81. To Caroline, 11 May 1843, *Correspondance* 1:137.
82. To Caroline, June 1843, *Correspondance* 1:141.
83. "Imagine the mug I have when I am tormented by a good attack and must continue to work." Another function of these troubles is to show more clearly that he is a victim: he suffers, a resistance for which he is not responsible makes work almost impossible for him. And yet—it is the Father's command—he *must* work.
84. *Correspondance*, Supplement, 1:33–34. There will be no more mention of these

toothache is the *suffered* resistance of temporality and his own incapacity, lived *painfully,* to instrumentalize duration. And here again, almost in the same terms, we have the confession of '42: "Ah, it is high time to finish with all this business! I believe that even if I should fail my exam, I would be content, for at least I would be rid of it."[85]

But while he panics, claims the task is killing him, says he is swollen with an excessive, overdetailed mass of knowledge, his old desire for immutability returns in a new form. Certainly he has a reflex of pride when his mother proposes to introduce him to his examiners: "I would be extremely humiliated by it, and all those fawnings are not my sort of thing . . . Besides, *men like me* are not made to fail in examinations." But he soon admits that he is striving to "keep a stiff upper lip" and that he is still "a bit shaky." And in the following letter, he writes that he is at the end of his resources. "If my exam were not this week but were only two months away, I believe I would say to hell with it. I am just about done in. If by some misfortune I were to fail, I swear to you on my word as a man that I would not do more the second time around, and that I would continue to present myself with what I know [now] until I passed." In short, he wants to make his examiners sick and tired of him. Above all I see in this determination a return to passive activity: he becomes frozen, blocked, a stone, or an old man before his time; he will not change: he will be, as he has been fond of repeating since 1838, "always the same," the immutable Gustave pushed by time from the outside toward death.

We find this intention again on the psychosomatic level in the periods of deep sleep—perhaps alternating with the insomnia due to his "neuralgia"—from which he emerges so weary, so "stupefied," that he later has no hesitation, as we know, in considering them pathological.[86] This lethargic behavior denies the passing of time and, for lack of "dying by thought," reconciles it with the condition of the reclining statues he so envies, denying tomorrow and the tasks of the everyday world. This is running headlong into failure. And the words, the images gathered here and there from his letters show that the binary structure of verticality (ascension-tumble) tends to modify itself to the advantage of the second term, which becomes concrete as a motivat-

---

troubles until January 1844. They will recur *after the crisis* and will end with the pulling of three teeth.

85. To Caroline, July 1842, *Correspondance* 1:142.

86. "Two or three times a week I sleep fourteen to sixteen hours at a stretch, so weary am I, to the point that I am fatigued when I wake up."

ing scheme: the *fall*, in the physical sense of the term. Already in February he was writing these suggestive lines: "I am a famous mule . . . carrying a load I'm not proud of . . . It is the Law School that I have on my shoulders. You will perhaps find the metaphor ambitious; it is true that if I were carrying it on my shoulders, I would quickly roll over on the ground to break my burden." Could he say it any better? Hè will fall down in order to crush the bourgeois imperatives that bind him. And we have seen him "whip himself up" so as not to *let himself fall into* discouragement. And in June 1843: "rather than inject the civil Code into my brain . . . dammit, I would rather do 'the journalist of Nevers.'" When an epileptic fit is coming on, the journalist of Nevers begins by falling to the floor; he rolls around, writhing, like the ass carrying the Law School on its back. Later, after the attack, Gustave liked to compare himself to a pool, a calm, flat surface close to the ground, that wants to remain unaware of its muddy depths: this is the absolute horizontal.

"Monday, 21 August, at one o'clock in the afternoon," he ran aground: it was foreseen, and his father foresaw it. The Flaubert family, then in Paris, immediately takes him to Nogent. We know of the unhappy candidate's mood from his letter to Ernest of 2 September 1843. Of his failure, not a word—as in the previous year. What does he say? Literally nothing. That he is smoking—a long discourse on the subject of smoking. That he goes bathing. That he will get back to Rouen in about a week. But in each paragraph a few words betray him. One feels him bristling with anger and humiliation. "There is nothing that seems to me as comic as a serious man"—that is for Ernest. And then, apropos of Ronsard, he gives it to his compatriots: "Oh taste, oh pigs, pigs in full dress, pigs on two feet in an overcoat!" The final tirade is especially reserved for his native town:

> It has beautiful churches and stupid inhabitants. I detest it, I hate it, I call down on it all the curses of heaven because it saw my birth. Misfortune to the walls that sheltered me, to the bourgeois who knew me as a brat, and to the paving stones on which I began to sharpen my claws! Oh Attila, when will you return, good humanitarian . . . to put this "belle France" to the torch . . . ? Begin, I beg of you, with Paris first and, at the same time, Rouen.

Even taking into account his taste for hyperbole and for the hateful desire to shock Ernest, the serious man, the imbecile who succeeded in his exams, Gustave's imprecations are disturbing: he wants to annihilate Rouen and the bourgeois who knew him as a brat because he is dying of shame at the idea of returning, vanquished, to his home ground.[87] What he dreads above all is the pity or the irony he will imagine behind the very silence of his family's friends. His angry dream: to suppress the memories, efface the traces of his existence. To die? Perhaps, but not alone: he wants to bring down with him the milieu that produced him and knew him; it is no longer a matter of putting an end to his existence but of having never existed. For lack of having redeemed his birth by a true masterpiece, Gustave wants never to have been born. And as the human adventure is irreversible, he sees only one way: to expunge himself from history by abolishing all those who witnessed his life. Attila's horsemen will be the new men who will begin a new world on the anonymous ruins of the world destroyed. For none of them will the name of Gustave, younger son of Doctor Flaubert, have any meaning. This horror of the Other and his judgment is manifestly pathological: the defeat of 21 August is too much for the young man's pride, and it is not enough: his imprecations tell us that behind this defeat he has divined the forgotten presence of his vow to fail.

He is thus thrown into confusion. But what does he do, on returning to the Hôtel-Dieu? Not much. He works on *L'Education* in September and October, but without much zeal since he abandons his manuscript *even before* leaving again for Paris. This occupation, however, seems to have calmed him a little. What is striking, when he resumes his "hard-up" student's life in the rue de l'Est, is that he *keeps his word;* he had said: "I will do nothing more, I will keep presenting myself with my baggage until they pass me," and he is determined to loaf. The law books remain on the shelves; he might at least take up *L'Education*, but he doesn't. He goes out a great deal, to Pradier's, to the Colliers', dines on Wednesday evenings at the Schlésingers'. In the previous autumn, at least, he was preparing for the final examination in December, which he had not been able to take in August. In 1843, nothing of the sort. He seems to have thought of sitting for the exam in February, for he writes to Caroline: "I will not stay long with you, a dozen days at the most. On the other hand, I count on spending the whole of March in Rouen."[88] Counting on leaving Paris on 1 January 1844, however, he gave himself scarcely thirty days— perhaps less—to revise his notes. This surely means that he was blocked: to revise, refresh his knowledge, okay; to learn, change his

87. He is still at Nogent when he writes.
88. *Correspondance,* Supplement, 1:37.

methods, no. "They will take me as I am." This blockage seems to me midway between an active revolt against the studies imposed on him and the *suffered* fall into subhumanity. After the "illness" of 1840–41, the failures of '42 and '43, for the people of Rouen Gustave has already become the Flaubert younger son who-does-not-do-honor-to-his-father, a poor boy who is hidden or sequesters himself, who "has turned out badly." Perhaps the surgeon hopes to have a second son like Ernest, that brilliant fellow who crowned his parents with joy. The young man *says all that to himself*, as witness his imprecations against Rouen. Better still, he ponders it, it is the perpetual subject of his monologue. In any case, he does nothing to prevent a new failure; this autumn, he doesn't even try to affirm himself through art; he gads about, visits people here and there, writes his sister jolly letters, but something in him is stuck, dry, and hardened; we might say that he lets time work against him, as if he were asking it to give gradual proof of his collapse by indefinitely repeated failures. On the surface he feels nothing except a slight, joyous excitement. He hardly speaks of Paris in his letters, but seems extremely curious about the Rouen gossip: "I impatiently await Achille and what he has to say about Bourlet; so tell him to write to me, tell him he had promised me he would."[89] This is incontestably an attempt to tear himself away from the capital and retrieve his Rouen attachments. Doctor Flaubert had bought a plot of land in Deauville and planned to build a chalet there. In the last days of December, Gustave is obsessed by this project: "I do nothing but think of the chalet, which prevents me from working." Working, no: nothing prevents him from doing that but himself, since he has done nothing for four months. But these evasions, multiplied by the approach of the vacation, evoke familiar objects, faces, destinations, or compel him to claim the paternal projects as his own again—and passionately—and thus function to persuade him that his presence in the rue de l'Est is perhaps accidental and unreal, that his reality is only at the Hôtel-Dieu, under the family roof. But he hates Rouen, it will be pointed out. Rouen, certainly, but not familial sequestration and dependence, nor "the old room where [he] spent such sweet and peaceful hours, when [he] heard the whole house stirring around [him]." By an unhappy paradox, he finds in his native

89. The three signatories to the edition of the *Supplément à la Correspondance* note that this refers to a friend of Achille's who was smitten at the age of thirty-five with his young cousin. In one of her letters to Gustave, Caroline had told how, in her presence, Bourlet had spoken to Monsieur and Madame Flaubert of his emotional troubles. See *Correspondance*, Supplement, 1:36.

town simultaneously a tribunal and a refuge. He will take refuge there *in* "his father's house," *in* his bitter and yet fascinating adolescence, because he lived it in a state of irresponsibility, *in* sweet gossipings with Caroline, that sister to whom he is, despite his joyful brutalities, more of an older sister than a brother. In short, *in* his secret femininity, *in* his relative being. In those last days of 1843, he prepares himself *to rediscover his truth:* the fatalities of passive activity. It is a matter of convincing himself that he is not "playing the anvil," that an inflexible imperative does not await him in February, in Paris, that he is forever escaping the necessity of *acting.*

He does not succeed in this: "I already hate the thought of returning, for I shall not stay long with you." It is not the prospect of a new separation that saddens him, but he knows from experience, having plunged into it three times, the hell that awaits him. In the spring of '42, he thought he was capable of enduring it. Now he knows how things stand; he has not forgotten the nightmare of the summer: at the end of January he will have to drink the all too familiar drought one more time. To the dregs, perhaps, to a third failure. Everything is settled: he knows what he must learn since he has already learned it; he imagines his torments, his stupors, his lethargic slumbers, his despair, he can imagine the final interrogation and even the list where he will look for his name posted. When he leaves for Rouen—he will be there the 1st of January, after spending 31 December at Vernon— he knows that he *can no longer* bear this trial a fourth time, and he knows too that he *will bear* it, that he will leave again docilely around the 12th and set to work once more. He wanted to escape the future. Now he meets it again, horribly predictable, in all its details, *already lived* and *to be lived* again. He tears himself away from it by traveling toward the Hôtel-Dieu, and every turn of the wheel brings him closer to it. No sooner has he arrived than he wants to cling to every minute, but they collapse: the truth of this journey *is the return.* From the first hours he understands it, he understands that he can no longer obey nor can he rebel. Two strict and contradictory impossibilities—and yet it is urgent. There is no choice, and yet a choice *must* be made. Then, "something rather tragic happens in [his] brain case."